Paralegal Studies:
An Introduction

The West Legal Studies Series

Your options keep growing with West Legal Studies
Each year our list continues to offer you more options for every area of the law to meet your course or on-the-job reference requirements. We now have over 140 titles from which to choose in the following areas:

Administrative Law	Family Law
Alternative Dispute Resolution	Federal Taxation
Bankruptcy	Intellectual Property
Business Organizations/Corporations	Introduction to Law
Civil Litigation and Procedure	Introduction to Paralegalism
CLA Exam Preparation	Law Office Management
Client Accounting	Law Office Procedures
Computer in the Law Office	Legal Research, Writing, and Analysis
Constitutional Law	Legal Terminology
Contract Law	Paralegal Employment
Criminal Law and Procedure	Real Estate Law
Document Preparation	Reference Materials
Environmental Law	Torts and Personal Injury Law
Ethics	Will, Trusts, and Estate Administration

You will find unparalleled, practical support
Each book is augmented by instructor and student supplements to ensure the best learning experience possible. We also offer custom publishing and other benefits such as West's Student Achievement Award. In addition, our sales representatives are ready to provide you with dependable service.

We want to hear from you
Our best contributions for improving the quality of our books and instructional materials is feedback from the people who use them. If you have a question, concern, or observation about any of our materials, or you have a product proposal or manuscript, we want to hear from you. Please contact your local representative or write us at the following address:

West Legal Studies, 3 Columbia Circle, P.O. Box 15015, Albany, NY 12212-5015

For additional information point your browser at
www.westlegalstudies.com

PARALEGAL STUDIES:
AN INTRODUCTION

Paul D. Jordan

**WEST
THOMSON LEARNING**

Australia Canada Mexico Singapore Spain United Kingdom United States

WEST LEGAL STUDIES

Paralegal Studies: An Introduction
by Paul D. Jordan

Business Unit Director:
Susan L. Simpfenderfer

Executive Editor:
Marlene McHugh Pratt

Senior Acquisitions Editor:
Joan M. Gill

Developmental Editor:
Rhonda Dearborn

Editorial Assistant:
Lisa Flatley

Executive Production Manager:
Wendy A. Troeger

Technology Project Manager:
James Considine

Production Manager :
Carolyn Miller

Production Coordinator:
Matthew J. Williams

Executive Marketing Manager:
Donna J. Lewis

Channel Manager:
Nigar Hale

Cover Design:
john walker design

COPYRIGHT © 2001 Delmar. West Legal Studies is an imprint of Delmar, a division of Thomson Learning, Inc. Thomson Learning™ is a trademark used herein under license

Printed in the United States
2 3 4 5 XXX 05 04

For more information contact Delmar,
3 Columbia Circle, PO Box 15015,
Albany, NY 12212-5015.

Or find us on the World Wide Web at
www.thomsonlearning.com or
www.westlegalstudies.com

ALL RIGHTS RESERVED. No part of this work covered by the copyright hereon may be reproduced or used in any form or by any means—graphic, electronic, or mechanical, including photocopying, recording, taping, Web distribution or information storage and retrieval systems—without written permission of the publisher.

For permission to use material from this text or product, contact us by
Tel   (800) 730-2214
Fax (800) 730-2215
www.thomsonrights.com

Library of Congress Cataloging-in-Publication Data
Jordan, Paul D.
  Paralegal studies : an introduction / by Paul D. Jordan.
     p. cm.
  Includes bibliographical references and index.
  ISBN 0-314-12723-2
  1. Legal assistants—United States. 2. Law—Vocational guidance—United States. I. Title.
KF320.L4 J67 2001
340'.023'73—dc21   2001017791

NOTICE TO THE READER

Publisher does not warrant or guarantee any of the products described herein or perform any independent analysis in connection with any of the product information contained herein. Publisher does not assume, and expressly disclaims, any obligation to obtain and include information other than that provided to it by the manufacturer.

The reader is notified that this text is an educational tool, not a practice book. Since the law is in constant change, no rule or statement of law in this book should be relied upon for any service to any client. The reader should always refer to standard legal sources for the current rule or law. If legal advice or other expert assistance is required, the services of the appropriate professional should be sought.

The Publisher makes no representation or warranties of any kind, including but not limited to, the warranties of fitness for particular purpose or merchantability, nor are any such representations implied with respect to the material set forth herein, and the publisher takes no responsibility with respect to such material. The publisher shall not be liable for any special, consequential, or exemplary damages resulting, in whole or part, from the readers' use of, or reliance upon, this material.

Dedication

This book is dedicated to the fine legal assistants who have been my mentors, colleagues, friends, and occasional saviours—Pam, Deborah, Susan, Lois, and Kasey.

CONTENTS

PREFACE xi

PART I

A PROFESSION EVOLVES 1

CHAPTER 1

PARALEGALS AND LEGAL ASSISTANTS 3

SECTION 1. THE PARALEGAL PROFESSION 5
- Two Terms for the Same Role 5
- How Paralegals Came to Be 8
- Legal Assistants as Professionals 9
- Where Paralegals Work 9
- Career Satisfaction Among Legal Assistants 10

SECTION 2. THE PARALEGAL PROFESSIONAL 10
- Distinguishing the Roles of Attorneys and Paralegals 11
- The Paralegal as the "Accessible" Legal Professional 11
- The Crisis in Affordable Legal Service 12
- The Legal Assistant's Role in Reducing Client Fees 14

A CASE IN POINT 14
- A Rapidly Growing Career Field 17

SECTION 3. CHOOSING A PARALEGAL CAREER 17
- The Attraction of a Paralegal Career 17
- The Characteristics of a Successful Paralegal 19
- Compensation for Legal Assistants 22
- Qualifying for a Paralegal Career 23

A QUESTION OF ETHICS 25
CHAPTER SUMMARY 26
ACTIVITIES AND ASSIGNMENTS 27

CHAPTER 2

CAREERS IN LAW FIRMS AND BEYOND 29

SECTION 1. WORKING IN LAW FIRMS 31
- How Law Firms Are Organized 31
- First, There Were Lawyers and Apprentices 32
- "Who's Who" in Today's Law Firm 33
- Small Firms and Large Firms 35
- Realizing the Legal Assistant's Full Potential 36

- Freelance Paralegals 43
- Nonparalegal Careers for Paralegals 46
- Legal Technicians—Providing Legal Services to the Public 49

A CASE IN POINT 50

SECTION 2. FINDING THE RIGHT JOB 52
- The Open and Hidden Job Markets 52
- Using the Legal Press 53
- Placement Offices and Employment Agencies 54
- Job Searches on the Internet 55
- Using Directories of Attorneys 57
- Evaluating Yourself as a Job-Market Prospect 58
- When "Experienced Only Need Apply" 60
- Developing an Effective Marketing Plan 63
- Sources for Further Guidance 65

A QUESTION OF ETHICS 65
CHAPTER SUMMARY 66
ACTIVITIES AND ASSIGNMENTS 67

CHAPTER 3

LEGAL ETHICS AND OTHER PROFESSIONAL ISSUES 69

SECTION 1. THE ROLE OF ETHICS IN THE PRACTICE OF LAW 71
- Motivating and Enforcing Ethical Conduct 71

A CASE IN POINT 73
- Ethical Standards for Attorneys and Legal Assistants 75
- The ABA's *Model Rules of Professional Conduct* for Attorneys 76

A CASE IN POINT 78
A CASE IN POINT 81
A CASE IN POINT 87

SECTION 2. ETHICAL ISSUES OF SPECIAL IMPORTANCE TO LEGAL ASSISTANTS 93
- Disclosing One's Status as a Legal Assistant 93
- Concerns about Representing a "Guilty" Client 94
- Concerns about the Client's Ethics 95
- Concerns about an Attorney's Conduct 95
- When Nonlawyers Provide Legal Services to the Public 96

CONTENTS

The Seasoned Paralegal as a Perceived Legal "Expert" 98
The Dangers of Casual Advice 98
Talking and Teaching *about* the Law 100
SECTION 3. VERIFYING PARALEGAL COMPETENCE 100
Protecting the Titles "Paralegal" and "Legal Assistant" 101
State Licensure for "Legal Technicians" 102
Licensure for Attorney-Supervised Legal Assistants 103
Professional Certification: Not a Simple Issue 103
NALA and NFPA: Two Visions for the Future 105
A CASE IN POINT 106
The American Bar Association as *de facto* Arbiter of Paralegal Education 108
A QUESTION OF ETHICS 109
CHAPTER SUMMARY 110
ACTIVITIES AND ASSIGNMENTS 111

PART II

INTRODUCTION TO THE LEGAL SYSTEM 113

CHAPTER 4

THE LAW AND THE COURTS 115

SECTION 1. THE NATURE OF LAW 116
The Impossible Task: Knowing the Law 117
Distinguishing Civil and Criminal Law 118
The Hierarchy of Legal Authority 119
A CASE IN POINT 121
The Authority for State and Federal Legislation 124
SECTION 2. LAWS OF THE STATE GOVERNMENTS 125
The Uniform Acts 126
The Common Law and its Application 126
Enforcing the Laws and Official Acts of Other States 128
State Regulation of Interstate Commerce 130
SECTION 3. THE STATE AND FEDERAL COURTS 130
Jurisdiction: The Authority of a Court to Hear and Decide a Case 131
Questions of Venue and Forum 134
State Court Systems 134
When a Court Decision Is Appealed 136
The Federal Court System 138
Judicial Immunity from Lawsuits 142
A CASE IN POINT 142
Public Opinion, Partisan Politics, and the Courts 145
A QUESTION OF ETHICS 145
CHAPTER SUMMARY 146
ACTIVITIES AND ASSIGNMENTS 148

CHAPTER 5

ADMINISTRATIVE LAW 149

SECTION 1. THE NATURE OF ADMINISTRATIVE LAW 151
Agencies that Create Administrative Law 152
Creating Administrative Law 153
Policies, Rules, and Regulations 153
Legal Authority for Administrative Rule Making 154
A CASE IN POINT 154
Public Participation in Agency Rule Making 156
Administrative Orders 157
Mandatory Record Keeping and the Subpoena of Records 157
SECTION 2. ACCESS TO PUBLIC RECORDS 157
Using the *Freedom of Information Act* 158
Privacy Restrictions Under the *Freedom of Information Act* 159
A CASE IN POINT 159
SECTION 3. ADJUDICATING ADMINISTRATIVE LAW DISPUTES 160
Due Process in Administrative Law 160
A CASE IN POINT 160
Administrative Agency Hearings and Public Access 162
A CASE IN POINT 162
Administrative Law Penalties 163
Judicial Review of Administrative Actions 163
The Role of Legal Assistants in Administrative Law 166
A QUESTION OF ETHICS 168
CHAPTER SUMMARY 169
ACTIVITIES AND ASSIGNMENTS 170

CHAPTER 6

CIVIL LITIGATION AND ALTERNATIVE DISPUTE RESOLUTION 171

SECTION 1. THE NATURE OF CIVIL LITIGATION 172
Why People Sue 173
Court Proceedings Other than Litigation 174
The Adversary System of Justice 174
Standing to Sue 174
The Statute of Limitations for Asserting a Claim 175
The Doctrine of Laches 176
Monetary and Equitable Remedies 176
SECTION 2. THE RULES OF EVIDENCE AND THE SEARCH FOR JUSTICE 177
Balancing Probative Value against Prejudicial Effect 178
Other Reasons for Excluding Evidence 178
The "Best Evidence" Rule 179
Why Hearsay Evidence Is Excluded 180

Section 3. Pretrial Procedures   180
- The Plaintiff Initiates the Lawsuit   180
- The Defendant Responds   181
- Motions for Judgment on the Pleadings   185
- Discovery and Preparation for Trial   186

A Case in Point   187
- Videotaping Dispositions   194
- Pretrial Motions   198
- Pretrial Briefs and Stipulations   199

Section 4. Trial Procedures   200
- Jury Selection   200
- Opening Statements   201
- The Plaintiff's Case in Chief   201
- The Motion for Nonsuit or Directed Verdict   203
- Presenting the Defendant's Case   203
- The Plaintiff's Rebuttal Evidence   204
- Closing Statements   204

Section 5. Verdicts and Judgments   205
- The Standard of Proof for Civil Lawsuits   205
- The Difference between a Verdict and a Judgment   205
- The Motion for Judgment NOV   208
- The Case before the Appellate Court   208
- Enforcing Court Judgments   210

Section 6. Paralegal Responsibilities in Litigation   211
- Information: The Indispensable Foundation of Litigation   212
- Typical Assignments for New Legal Assistants   212
- Cooperation between Opposing Counsel   213
- Complying with Deadlines   214
- Drafting Discovery Requests and Responses   214
- Notices to Appear for Deposition   215
- Summarizing Depositions and Other Discovery Information   215
- Preparing Trial Exhibits   216
- Obtaining Government and Business Records   216
- Cite Checking   216
- Locating Case Law on a Particular Issue   217
- Preparing the Trial Notebook   217
- Working with Witnesses   218
- Legal Assistants in the Courtroom   219

Section 7. Alternative Dispute Resolution   220
- Advantages of Alternative Dispute Resolution   221
- Mediation   221
- Arbitration   222

A Question of Ethics   225
Chapter Summary   225
Activities and Assignments   227

Chapter 7

Criminal Law and Procedure   230

Section 1. The Nature of Criminal Law   231
- At Least Two Victims for Most Crimes   231
- The Criminal Act and Criminal Intent   232
- Common Law Crimes and Statutory Crimes   235

A Case in Point   236
- Defenses to Criminal Charges   238
- The Three Categories of Criminal Offenses   240
- Civil and Criminal Offenses   241
- Grand Juries and Trial Juries   241
- The Presumption of Innocence   242
- Rights of the Victims and Rights of the Accused   243

Section 2. Due Process in Criminal Procedure   244
- The Miranda Warning   246

A Case in Point   248
- Double Jeopardy   250
- A Speedy Trial   252
- A Public Trial   252
- Impartial Jury   253
- Self-Incrimination   253
- Confronting and Cross-Examining Adverse Witnesses   254
- The Right to Legal Counsel   255

A Case in Point   255
- The Right to Self-Representation   258
- The Exclusionary Rule   259

A Case in Point   261

Section 3. Criminal Law Procedures   263
- Inquiry, Detention, and Arrest   263

A Case in Point   264
- Bail Hearing   268
- Indictment or Prosecutor's Information   270
- Arraignment   272
- Plea Bargaining   273
- The Preliminary Hearings for Felony Complaints   274
- Pretrial Discovery   274

A Case in Point   275
- Pretrial Motions   276
- Trial   276
- Appeals   277
- Writ of *Habeas Corpus*   278

A Question of Ethics   278
Chapter Summary   279
Activities and Assignments   280

CONTENTS

PART III

PARALEGAL SKILLS AND PROCEDURES 281

CHAPTER 8

LEGAL ANALYSIS, RESEARCH, AND WRITING 283

SECTION 1. LEGAL ANALYSIS 284
- The Purposes of Legal Research 285
- Understanding the Assignment 285
- Defining the Issues 286
- Understanding Legal Sources and Legal Authority 286
- Analyzing a Legal Question 288
- Applying a Statute to Specific Facts 289
- When a Court Opinion Is "On Point" 290
- Using Analogy in Legal Analysis 290
- Concurring and Dissenting Opinions 291

A CASE IN POINT 292
- Avoiding Irrelevant Tangents 294
- Knowing When to Stop 294

SECTION 2. LEGAL RESEARCH 296
- Finding a Starting Point 296
- Identifying Key Terms 296
- Using Statutory Codes 297
- Using Case Reporters 301
- Using Digests to Locate Case Law 305
- Understanding the Parts of a Court Opinion 307
- Following the Paper Chase 312
- Using Treatises 314
- Evaluating Large Numbers of Potentially Useful Cases 314
- Using Case Citators 314
- A Closer Look at a Case that has been Reversed or Overruled 322

SECTION 3. LEGAL WRITING 323
- Clear Legal Writing: *Not* an Oxymoron 324
- Writing "Like a Lawyer" 327
- Editing and Revision 328
- Legal Correspondence 328
- Pleadings: "May It Please the Court . . . " 331
- Briefing a Court Opinion 332
- The Memorandum of Law 333
- The Memorandum of Points and Authorities 334
- Citing Legal Authorities 336

A QUESTION OF ETHICS 336
CHAPTER SUMMARY 337
ACTIVITIES AND ASSIGNMENTS 338

CHAPTER 9

COMPUTERS IN THE LAW OFFICE 340

SECTION 1. THE IMPACT OF COMPUTERS ON THE PRACTICE OF LAW 342
- Computer Use in Law Firms 342
- Computers in the Courtroom 343
- Paralegals Bearing Notebooks 345
- Computer Literacy for Entry-Level Paralegals 345
- The E-Mail Challenge 346

A CASE IN POINT 350
- The Power of Word Processing Software 351
- Using Database Systems for Information Management 354
- Using Spreadsheets for Numerical Data 355
- Office Suites: Integrated Software Packages 358
- Software Designed for the Practice of Law 358

SECTION 2. COMPUTER-ASSISTED LEGAL RESEARCH 361
- The Internet and the World Wide Web 362
- Online Legal Research with Westlaw and LEXIS-NEXIS 362
- KeyCite: Westlaw's Citator Service 373
- Evaluating the Authorities That a Case Relies Upon 375
- Using *Shepard's Citation Service* On-line 376
- Using CD-ROMs for Legal Research 380

SECTION 3. THE INTERNET AS A RESEARCH TOOL 380
- The Internet: Not a Single Entity 381
- Using Internet Service Providers 381
- The World Wide Web: Only One Part of the Internet 381
- Using Westlaw and LEXIS-NEXIS on the Internet 386
- Uncle Sam's Web Site for Primary Source Legal Authority 386
- Internet Sites for Federal Court Opinions 387
- Internet Sources for Statistical Information 388
- On-line Discussion Groups 389
- Internet Sources for Legal Ethics 390

A QUESTION OF ETHICS 390
CHAPTER SUMMARY 391
ACTIVITIES AND ASSIGNMENTS 392

CHAPTER 10

INTERVIEWS AND INVESTIGATION 394

SECTION 1. THE PARALEGAL ROLE IN INVESTIGATION 396
- Investigations that Paralegals Often Perform 397
- The Objectives of a Legal Investigation 398

Planning the Investigation 399
Eight Stages of an Investigation 400
The Paralegal's Notes as Attorney Work Product 406
A CASE IN POINT 407
Learning about Potential Jurors 408
SECTION 2. OBTAINING INFORMATION ON-LINE 409
Locating Individuals 409
Searching Public Records 410
Information about Businesses 411
Evaluating On-line Information 412
SECTION 3. CONDUCTING INTERVIEWS 413
The Psychology of the Witness 413
Seven Steps for Successful Interviews 414
Using Questions Effectively 418
Handling an Unfriendly or a Hostile Witness 420
Verifying Information from an Interview 421
Witnesses Who Fabricate Information 423
Recording Interviews 425
Signed Witness Statements 426
Interviewing the Client 426
A QUESTION OF ETHICS 428
CHAPTER SUMMARY 428
ACTIVITIES AND ASSIGNMENTS 429

CHAPTER 11
LAW OFFICE MANAGEMENT AND PROCEDURES 431

SECTION 1. THE SUCCESSFUL LAW PRACTICE 433
Success in a Private Practice 433
Success in Corporate and Public Agency Legal Departments 434
Keys to an Effective Law Practice 434
Dedicated and Qualified Professionals 434
Effective Law Office Organization 438
Members of the Legal Team 445
Establishing a Sound Attorney-Client Relationship 449
Meeting Billable Quotas 453
Timekeeping and Billing 454
Client Trust Accounts 456
A CASE IN POINT 457
When a Client's Attorney Leaves the Firm 458

SECTION 2. EFFECTIVE LAW OFFICE PROCEDURES 459
The Client Conflict Check 459
Docket Control and Tickler System 460
Law Office Files 463
Authorization to Release Documents or Information 466
Archiving Inactive Client Files 466
Law Office Communications 467
A QUESTION OF ETHICS 468
CHAPTER SUMMARY 468
ACTIVITIES AND ASSIGNMENTS 470

APPENDIX A
DEPOSITION TRANSCRIPTS AND SUMMARIES 472

APPENDIX B
SAMPLE BRIEF OF COURT OPINION 479

APPENDIX C
MEMORANDUM OF LAW 481

APPENDIX D
THE NALA CODE OF ETHICS AND PROFESSIONAL RESPONSIBILITY 485

APPENDIX E
THE NFPA MODEL CODE OF ETHICS AND PROFESSIONAL RESPONSIBILITY 487

APPENDIX F
THE ABA MODEL GUIDELINES FOR THE UTILIZATION OF LEGAL ASSISTANT SERVICES 497

APPENDIX G
THE U.S. CONSTITUTION 499

GLOSSARY 517

PREFACE

This is an exciting age in the practice of law. In recent decades, we have seen non-attorney legal assistants become essential members of the legal team, assuming many responsibilities once thought to be the exclusive province of attorneys. Several states appear on the verge of some form of licensure for legal assistants. And now, new technology is challenging paralegals and attorneys alike to adapt to new ways of working—even changing some of the ways we communicate with our clients. The Internet, on-line research, electronic court filings, e-mail, and digital signatures—all are signs of the impact technology is having upon the practice of law.

A STUDENT-CENTERED APPROACH

The idea for *Paralegal Studies* grew out of two concurrent personal experiences: working as a paralegal in a law firm with high professional and ethical standards, and teaching an introductory paralegal course—the very same course in which the author was himself a student in 1987. The law firm is committed to developing the full potential for paralegal practice. The paralegal program at the University of California, Irvine, is committed to preparing students to achieve that potential. The author's perspective has been influenced also by two decades of teaching college-bound high school seniors.

Paralegal Studies: An Introduction will inform, stimulate, and guide your students as they contemplate entering upon this exciting and challenging career. There are four key themes throughout the text:

1. understanding the paralegal's role
2. facing ethical issues
3. understanding legal concepts and terminology
4. using new technology

An introductory paralegal course should provide an overview of the career and a general understanding of the nature of paralegal work. *Paralegal Studies* does this through a combination of its content, practical tips in each chapter, and activities and assignments that call upon the student to perform typical paralegal tasks. Students will develop a good understanding of the paralegal's role in the practice of law and an appreciation for the high ethical standards that guide the professional legal assistant.

Many students come to us with little background in the law. This can be a source of apprehension for any student who might fear that he cannot compete with his better-prepared peers. Throughout the text, there is a strong emphasis upon building a broad legal vocabulary that will help the student to succeed in his later paralegal courses.

Paralegal Studies introduces essential topics that will prepare your students for success in their paralegal curriculum:

- careers
- ethics
- the law and the courts

- administrative law
- civil litigation and alternative dispute resolution
- criminal law practice
- legal analysis and research
- legal writing
- computers in law
- computer-assisted research
- investigation and interviewing
- law office organization and management

For more comprehensive courses, or as supplemental reading, four additional chapters on substantive law are available on the West Legal Studies Web site, at **www.westlegalstudies.com.** These on-line chapters introduce the law of torts, real property, contracts, family law, and probate law.

Fundamentally, a textbook must serve the needs of the student. And to meet those needs, a textbook should offer students at least four key attributes:

1. solid content
2. accessibility
3. stimulating challenge
4. opportunity for skill development

The success of paralegal programs is truly measured when the graduates are on the job, working as legal assistants. So, a sound program must also prepare the student for the real world of paralegal practice. *Paralegal Studies* has been written to achieve dual goals: meeting the student's need for intellectual growth in law, and providing an introduction to her future role as a legal assistant.

ABOUT THE CONTENT

Paralegal Studies is composed of four parts. Parts I through III are in this print edition of the textbook. As mentioned above, Part IV, "Introduction to Substantive Law," is available on the West Legal Studies Web site, at **www.westlegalstudies.com.** The book's organization follows a logical progression, with a separate part for each of the following: the paralegal profession and career, the legal system and litigation, paralegal skills, and substantive law.

Part I, "A Profession Evolves," introduces the paralegal profession and role, followed by career opportunities, strategies and choices. An extensive chapter on legal ethics, licensure, and regulation completes this first part. Part II, "Introduction to the Legal System," begins with an explanation of legal authorities (constitutional, statutory, common law, etc.) and the relationship between state and federal law. This is followed by administrative law, access to public records, and adjudication of administrative law disputes. Next comes a thorough introduction to civil litigation from pretrial preparation through entry of judgment, followed by alternative dispute resolution. Part II concludes with criminal law, due process, and criminal procedure. Part III, "Paralegal Skills and Procedures," begins with a chapter on legal analysis, legal research, and legal writing. The chapter on computers in law describes the role of specialized legal software programs, computer-assisted legal research, and the Internet as a research tool. This is followed by paralegal skills in investigation and interviewing. Part III concludes with law office organization and management, and the paralegal's contribution to a successful practice.

Part IV, which appears on the West Legal Studies Web site, is titled "Introduction to Substantive Law." Each chapter includes a discussion of the substantive law and the paralegal's role in that field of practice. Part IV begins with a discussion of the law of torts, intentional and negligent, and strict liability. Next is a chapter on legal persons and real property. This is followed by the law of contracts, rights and responsibilities, and remedies for breach. The final chapter begins with the law of marriage, marital dissolution, and parent and child. This is followed by probate law and procedures.

SPECIAL FEATURES

There are a number of special features that appear throughout *Paralegal Studies*. These are designed to highlight special issues, illustrate real-life situations, provide practical guidance for new legal assistants, and add interest for the student.

DEALING WITH REAL-LIFE SITUATIONS

The goal of every paralegal student is to become a capable legal assistant, ready to deal with real-life situations on the job. Several features in *Paralegal Studies* contribute to that goal:

Practice Tip. These boxed-in features provide real-life guidance for career planning, office relationships, procedural short-cuts, and professional development.

Ethics Watch. This feature alerts the student to a wide variety of ethical issues, providing sound guidance on avoiding ethical lapses.

A Question of Ethics. This feature appears at the end of each chapter, presenting a hypothetical ethical problem for the student to resolve.

BUILDING A LEGAL VOCABULARY

A strong legal vocabulary is an indispensable tool for the successful legal assistant. In addition, legal terms of art (e.g., "constructive fraud" and "real party in interest") provide an identifying "label" for complex concepts that paralegal students must learn. As a student progresses through the paralegal curriculum, legal terminology becomes a prerequisite to understanding the course content.

Throughout *Paralegal Studies,* key terms appear in **bold** and are accompanied by margin definitions. In addition, all key terms appear in the Glossary—which contains more than 600 definitions for legal and technical terms. In some cases, the margin definition differs slightly from the Glossary definition for the same term. But that is done so that the student can compare the two definitions and determine their common meaning—a useful exercise in logical analysis. A special effort has been made to provide the greatest possible clarity in defining even the most complex terms.

DEVELOPING SKILLS

An introductory course should expose students to some typical tasks that legal assistants perform. This achieves two objectives:

1. It develops in the student a realistic awareness of the work that legal assistants actually do.
2. It begins the development of skills that students will need in their later paralegal courses and, ultimately, on the job.

Each chapter includes "Activities and Assignments," many of which provide a "hands-on" example of a typical paralegal task—everything from drafting a simple letter to locating factual information on the Internet. If assigned by the instructor, several of these tasks would require the student to spend substantial time and effort doing such things as the following:

- summarizing an excerpt from a deposition transcript
- briefing a court opinion
- drafting a short memorandum of law

Each of these more extensive assignments is supported by an exemplar document in the appendices to *Paralegal Studies*.

INTERNET ACCESS

Throughout *Paralegal Studies,* the Uniform Resource Locators (URLs) are provided for Internet sites (almost all of them on the World Wide Web) that are useful resources for on-line research. Although some students might not have Internet access at home, virtually all of them can obtain access from a computer in a public or school library.

READING THE LAW-A CASE IN POINT

For those students who have no legal background, "reading the law" can be an intimidating prospect. But, if anything sets the legal assistant apart from other non-attorneys, it is the ability to understand and work with the *substance* of the law. One of the most effective ways to develop that ability is to read and analyze court opinions.

Case law provides much more than an intellectual explanation of the court's legal reasoning in a particular case. It provides a model for applying abstract legal principles to concrete facts. It demonstrates the crucial role of *stare decisis*. It illustrates the practice of citing legal authorities to support one's legal reasoning. In appellate decisions, it reveals how well-qualified jurists can reach opposite conclusions about the identical case.

Although a few statutes are quoted *verbatim* in the text, court opinions are the primary focus for "reading the law." Each chapter includes at least one "Case in Point" feature. These are either *verbatim* excerpts from published court opinions or paraphrased summaries of selected opinions. In the earlier chapters, most of these court opinions are paraphrased to make them less obscure—in other words, less intimidating for the student. In later chapters, however, *extensive verbatim excerpts* from court opinions are used so that the student can become accustomed to reading actual judicial decisions. This incremental introduction to reading the law will enable the student to embark upon subsequent courses in both legal research and writing with greater confidence and success. The Study Guide (on CD-ROM) accompanying this textbook includes the complete text—including summary and headnotes—of eleven cases that are excerpted in Parts I–III of the text.

ADDING HUMAN INTEREST

Paralegal instructors know that legal assisting can be exciting, stimulating work. But how is the *student* to know? Our students might wish that we would tell them endless "war stories" and humorous anecdotes in class—and those can be highly motivating—but we know that ethical pitfalls and ruined lesson plans *can* be the result. *Paralegal Studies* offers an alternative in the form of chapter-opening scenes and hypothetical paralegal "Scenarios." With the exception of Chapter 9, the opening scenes are entirely fictional, although *most* are not unlike what happens in real life. A few of the opening scenes are obvious parodies. The mid-chapter Scenarios are fictional, but realistic narratives that illustrate professional experiences and career opportunities for legal assistants.

NEW ROLES FOR PARALEGAL SKILLS

From an ethical perspective, the paralegal's role is most often defined by her professional relationship with a supervising attorney. Yet, the skills and knowledge of a paralegal have wide application in other career fields. *Paralegal Studies* recognizes these possibilities and encourages the student to view the paralegal career as one that can open many doors of opportunity—including opportunities outside of the practice of law.

A COMPLETE STUDENT AND INSTRUCTOR PACKAGE

Paralegal Studies: An Introduction comes with a complete package of supporting materials for the instructor and the student. The components of this package include:

- *Instructor's Manual*
- Test Bank on CD-ROM
- *Study Guide* on CD-ROM
- Web page

The *Instructor's Manual* is a separate publication. The *Manual* and the Test Bank are available free of charge to instructors who adopt *Paralegal Studies* for their classes.

The *Study Guide* is on a CD-ROM packaged with each copy of *Paralegal Studies* and is included in the price of the textbook.

The *Instructor's Manual* and the *Study Guide* are each organized to be used with the textbook, chapter by chapter. In addition, each includes supplementary materials that support and correlate with the content of the textbook. The *Instructor's Manual* also contains general information and suggestions that will help the instructor to plan and present the entire course. The manual also provides an extensive discussion of considerations and suggestions for the less experienced instructor.

INSTRUCTOR'S MANUAL

Written by the author of the text, the *Instructor's Manual* includes:

- Sample course syllabus
- Lecture outlines for each chapter
- Teaching suggestions
- Analysis of end-of-chapter "Question of Ethics" issues
- Discussion topics and questions for each chapter
- Answer key for test bank questions
- Overhead masters
- Supplemental assignments

STUDY GUIDE ON CD-ROM

Written by the author of the text, the *Study Guide* includes:

- Chapter outlines
- Chapter review quizzes
- Answer key for review quizzes
- Key term lists with space for student notes
- Hypothetical ethical scenarios
- Analysis of ethical scenarios
- Supplemental reading materials on key topics
- Sample documents (forms, letters, resumes, etc.)
- On-line Exercises
- Complete text of eleven court opinions

ONLINE RESOURCES WEB SITE

A downloadable study guide is available online at **www.westlegalstudies.com**.

You will find the direct URL, user ID and password information on the CD-ROM in the back of the textbook in the 'readme.txt' file.

THE WEB PAGE FOR *PARALEGAL STUDIES*

The Web page is located on the West Legal Studies Web site at **www.westlegalstudies.com.** That site will include a page devoted exclusively to *Paralegal Studies,* and includes:

- Sample chapter, preface & T.O.C.
- Updated information
- Hot links to other useful Web sites
- Part IV, "Introduction to Substantive Law," and supporting materials

ABOUT THE AUTHOR

Paul D. Jordan received a *Certificate in Legal Assistantship, With Honors*, from the University Extension program in Legal Assistantship at the University of California, Irvine. He earned a bachelor degree in international relations and a secondary school teaching credential at the University of California, Los Angeles. Since 1992, Mr. Jordan has been an adjunct instructor in the Legal Assistantship Program at the University of California, Irvine. Prior to becoming a paralegal, Mr. Jordan taught high school civics, history, and economics. He currently is the executive director of a union that represents community college faculty members in Orange County, California.

In his present position, Mr. Jordan coordinates the union's needs for legal services with outside legal counsel. He also negotiates collective bargaining agreements, represents faculty members in college grievance hearings, prepares grievance cases for hearings before neutral arbitrators, and researches issues in employment and collective bargaining law.

Mr. Jordan is the author of a monograph, *Worlds Apart: A Special Guide for Firms Serving Japanese Clients*, Estrin Publishing; Los Angeles (1992).

ACKNOWLEDGMENTS

Bernadette Agresti
Gannon University, PA

Linda Anderson
Woodbury College, VT

Laura Barnard
Lakeland Community College, OH

Beverly Broman
Duff's Business Institute, PA

Audrey Casey
Andover College, ME

Mark Ciccarelli, Esq.
Kent State University, OH

Carl Cone
South College, GA

Linda S. Corvallis
Sanford-Brown College, IL

Susan De Matteo, Esq.
Boston University, MA

Bob Diotalevi, Esq.
The College of WV, WV

Christine S. DeBoer
Rancho Santiago College, CA

Lisa Morris Duncan
Coastal Carolina Community College, NC

Katherine Duren
WI

Dora Dye
City College of San Francisco, CA

Wendy Edson
Hilbert College, NY

Ellen Erzen
Cuyahoga Community College, OH

Nancy Hart
Midland College, TX

Paul Guymon
William Rainey Harper College, IL

Deborah Howard
University of Evansville, IN

Susan Howery
Yavapai College, AZ

Ann Hooper Hudson
Durham Technical College, NC

Joseph J. Mallini, Jr.
Midlands Technical College, South Carolina

Ted Maloney
Skagit Valley College, WA

Leslie D. McKesson
Western Piedmont Community College, NC

Mary Ming
Capital University Law School, OH

Dr. Pamela Moore
Phillips College, Inc., CA

Lee Edwards
Draughons Junior College, TN

Gerald A. Loy
Broome Community College, NY

Vitonio San Juan
University of La Verne, CA

Bryan Sanders
Evangel College, MO

Anita Tebbe
Johnson County Community College, KS

Janet E. Sellers
Santa Barbara Business College, CA

Cynthia Weishapple
Chippewa Valley Technical College, WI

Mary Whiting, Esq.
New York

PART I

A PROFESSION EVOLVES

CHAPTER 1

Paralegals and Legal Assistants

A legal assistant or paralegal is a person, qualified by education, training or work experience who is employed or retained by a lawyer, law office, corporation, government agency, or other entity and who performs specifically delegated substantive legal work for which a lawyer is responsible.

Adopted at the 1997 Annual Meeting of the American Bar Association (ABA).[1]
www.abanet.org/legalassts/def98.html

Chapter 1 introduces the paralegal profession and describes the qualities needed to be successful in this stimulating occupation. This chapter also introduces career options for paralegals, and describes the paralegal's role in law firms, corporations, and other settings.

The student who has *carefully* read this chapter should be prepared to answer these questions:

- What is a paralegal or legal assistant?
- Why do attorneys use paralegals?
- What do paralegals do?
- How does the use of paralegals reduce a client's legal fees?
- What attracts people to this profession?
- What range of career opportunities are available for paralegals?
- How much can a paralegal earn?
- What types of non-salary compensation do paralegals receive?
- What qualifications are necessary to become a paralegal?

SCENARIO

"I See Here that You Spent Three Years in the Air Force..."

Jennie Rabine straightened her skirt as the law firm's managing partner studied her resume.

She seems to be spending a lot of time reviewing my resume—I wonder why. They called me for the interview, so surely she has seen it before. Maybe she's just refreshing her memory. As they say, "too many resumes, so many interviews." Yeah, that must be it. But she isn't revealing a clue about what she really thinks of me. Oh, oh—here comes the first question.

"Why do you believe you are qualified for this position, Ms. Rabine?"

"Well, as you can see from my resume, I recently completed a paralegal certificate program, and for the past three years I have been the administrative assistant to the CEO of a real estate mortgage firm. Although this would be my first position in a law firm, I believe that my training and experience will be very useful to your firm."

Without looking up: "We usually insist on a four-year college degree."

I know, I have only three years of college—so why did they even call me for this interview? I'm not going to apologize for something they already knew about me. "As you see, I do have three years of college, and I am taking classes in the evenings and hope to finish my degree within the next two years."

"Yes, but this is a litigation firm—we handle lawsuits, mostly. How can you help us with that?"

Jennie hesitated, searching for an appropriate response. "What kind of support do you expect from your litigation paralegals?" *Geez. All I know about litigation is what I learned in that Civil Lit course.*

Without responding to Jennie's question, the managing partner continued, "I see here that you spent three years in the Air Force. What did you do in the service?"

"I was an avionics technician—that means I repaired electronic equipment, mainly radios and radar, but sometimes other kinds of electronics, also."

"In that work, did you have to interpret schematic diagrams of the electronic systems?"

"Oh, yes. That was part of my work." *Why is she asking about the Air Force? I included it on the resume just so they wouldn't wonder if I was unemployed those three years.*

The managing partner appeared interested. "Are you familiar with the quality control standards that Defense Department contractors must meet?"

"Well, that was always an issue with the tech reps ... that is, with the manufacturers' technical representatives, who support the equipment used by the military. If the equipment failed to meet the specs, we would charge the manufacturer for necessary modifications."

The attorney glanced again at the resume. "But, none of that detail is reflected in your resume, Ms. Rabine."

"I'm sorry, I didn't realize it could have anything to do with working in your law firm. Perhaps I should have included it."

The managing partner smiled warmly. "Well, we are interested in your technical background because we handle a lot of product liability cases, including some that involve federal government specifications. And we often need someone who can understand technical material in various fields of engineering. Why don't you come back next Wednesday, and we'll explore this a bit further."

Yes! "Well, thank you. I can be available anytime in the afternoon on Wednesday." *Who would have guessed? My Air Force experience, of all things!* ■

SECTION 1. THE PARALEGAL PROFESSION

So, why was there so much interest in Jennie Rabine's Air Force experience? Apparently, this law firm has a **litigation*** practice that can benefit from her technical expertise, especially her knowledge of federal government standards. That might seem to be a bit esoteric, but the fact is that a wide range of past experience and education can lend itself—one way or another—to the work of paralegals, and thus help to qualify the candidate for an entry-level position.

> **Litigation** is the legal profession's term for lawsuits. An attorney with a practice in litigation represents clients who are suing, or being sued by, other persons.

The work of paralegals can involve a wide variety of legal specialties: from litigation to real estate transactions; from corporate mergers to patents and copyrights (to name but a few). A solid general education (generally, at least one or two years of college) combined with completion of a paralegal program can qualify one for an entry-level paralegal position. Prior experience in other occupations—such as Jennie Rabine's Air Force service—is simply a plus.

One exciting feature of paralegal work is the opportunity it provides to take on increasingly challenging assignments. As will be explained in this and later chapters, the potential for paralegals to do sophisticated legal work is still being explored. Highly qualified, experienced paralegals often perform the same type of work that new attorneys typically do in large law firms. Although there are legal and ethical parameters that limit what paralegals can do, those parameters still permit paralegals to take on a remarkable range and complexity of tasks.

In addition to their typical roles in law firms, corporations, and government agencies, trained and experienced paralegals can find new and interesting challenges in "nontraditional" roles outside of the field of law. These opportunities exist because paralegals possess legal skills and knowledge that have great value in other occupations. This text will identify examples of such alternative career fields and will identify the unique qualities that paralegals bring to those career fields.

TWO TERMS FOR THE SAME ROLE

A **paralegal** is a professional trained both in the substance of the law and in legal procedures, who uses that knowledge and those skills to provide limited legal

> **A paralegal** is a professional trained both in the substance of the law and in legal procedures who uses that knowledge and those skills to provide limited legal services under the supervision and direction of an attorney.

---

*Terms printed in **bold type** can be found in the Glossary of this textbook. Generally, those terms will appear in **bold** *only once,* when they first appear. Although a term in bold might appear in its plural form, in the Glossary it will be found in the singular form. From this point forward, all notes will appear as endnotes at the end of each chapter—no more footnotes will appear.

services under the supervision and direction of an attorney. Paralegals *assist* attorneys in the practice of law, but do not *practice* law. Paralegals may not:

- give legal advice,
- represent clients in court,
- establish the attorney-client relationship, or
- set fees for legal services.

That might sound pretty straightforward, but in real life there are occasional "gray areas" between the practice of law by attorneys and the functions of paralegals who have direct contact with clients and others. The appropriate role for paralegals will be discussed at some length in later chapters.

Because paralegals *assist* in the practice of law, they are also known as **legal assistants**. "Paralegal" and "legal assistant" identify the same profession in most regions of the nation and often are used interchangeably—as they will be in this textbook. One can compare their interchangeable use to the similar usage of both "attorney" and "lawyer."

Various organizations have adopted formal definitions of the paralegal/legal assistant profession. The American Bar Association's definition appears at the top of the first page of this chapter. The National Association of Legal Assistants (NALA) and the National Federation of Paralegal Associations (NFPA) are the nation's largest membership organizations for professional paralegals (and legal assistants). Their definitions of paralegal/legal assistant appear in the accompanying sidebars.

> **Legal assistant** is a another term used to describe or identify a legal paraprofessional (or "paralegal") who works under the direction and supervision of an attorney.

Internet Access
The American Bar Association:	http://www.abanet.org
National Association of Legal Assistants:	http://www.nala.org
National Federation of Paralegal Associations:	http://www.paralegals.org

The Paralegal Role

The paralegal profession is a career field that has drawn upon the job descriptions of both legal secretaries and attorneys. Consequently, the role of paralegals (or legal assistants) overlaps somewhat those of attorneys and legal secretaries. Like attorneys, paralegals do legal research and draft court documents. And legal assistants also coordinate with court officials and with attorneys representing other parties regarding court hearings and other calendar matters—a responsibility that legal secretaries often have.

Paralegals generally have more formal training in law than do legal secretaries, but much less than attorneys. Most who enter this profession today have completed an academic paralegal program, including the study of both substantive law and legal procedures. **Substantive law** is the *essence* of the law: one's rights, responsibilities, and duties under the law. *Legal procedures* are the actions taken to carry out the intent of the law and to enforce those respective rights, responsibilities, and duties. In a specialized paralegal practice (e.g., litigation, bankruptcy, corporate law, family law, or probate) the paralegal's duties usually require a general understanding of the substantive law of that specialty, together with a thorough understanding of the related legal procedures. *In fact, the paralegal's job description often is distinguished from the legal secretary's by the requirement that the paralegal know and apply substantive law.* In contrast, the responsibilities of legal secretaries usually emphasize court procedures and rules, word processing, calendar coordination, and document organization.

> **Substantive law** defines one's legal rights and obligations, and also the power and limitations of government authority.

CHAPTER 1 ⚖ Paralegals and Legal Assistants 7

Although legal assistants spend the great majority of their time in the law firm office, they do "get out of the office"—for example, to the county law library or a client's office—more than do most legal secretaries. Finally, paralegals and attorneys bill clients for their time, but legal secretaries rarely do so. Although legal secretaries continue to work in firms that also employ paralegals, the paralegal profession has become a distinct career field.

Typical Duties for Legal Assistants

Typical paralegal tasks include:

- filling out legal forms;
- preparing legal documents for filing with the courts;
- coordinating formal delivery of legal documents to affected persons;
- organizing a client's records and other documents;
- drafting letters and simple court documents;
- drafting uncomplicated contracts and simple wills;
- preparing financial summaries for a debtor in bankruptcy;
- locating a debtor's assets;
- coordinating calendar dates with the courts and with attorneys for other parties;
- preparing maps, charts, and other exhibits for use in trial;
- using computers for word processing, legal research, and document management;
- organizing and maintaining files for each legal matter; and,
- summarizing the testimony of witnesses.

Tasks for experienced paralegals might also include:

- conducting field investigations;
- reviewing and summarizing court files and other public records;
- coordinating with appraisers, accountants, real estate brokers, and other professionals;
- coordinating foreclosure proceedings;
- preparing and filing applications for patents, trademarks, and copyrights;
- maintaining corporation minutes;
- drafting corporate bylaws;
- preparing and filing tax documents;
- reviewing pending legislation;
- attending court proceedings as an observer and assistant;
- assisting at closings for real estate transactions or corporate mergers;
- coordinating business affairs for a debtor in bankruptcy;
- researching complex legal issues; and,
- drafting motions and other complex court documents.

Paralegal Duties: Small Firms and Large Firms

All of the tasks listed above are performed, at times, by legal assistants working in law offices of every size. But there are some general differences in the legal assistant's role that tend to relate to the size of the office and the numbers of legal assistants and attorneys employed there. Because small firms tend to have less

---

Definition of "Legal Assistant"

National Association of Legal Assistants

Legal assistants, also known as paralegals, are a distinguishable group of persons who assist attorneys in the delivery of legal services. Through formal education, training and experience, legal assistants have knowledge and expertise regarding the legal system and substantive and procedural law which qualify them to do work of a legal nature under the supervision of an attorney.
www.nala.org/whatis.html

Definition of "Paralegal"

National Federation of Paralegal Associations

A paralegal/legal assistant is a person qualified through education, training or work experience to perform substantive legal work that requires knowledge of legal concepts and is customarily, but not exclusively, performed by a lawyer. This person may be retained or employed by a lawyer, law office, governmental agency or other entity or may be authorized by administrative, statutory or court authority to perform this work.
www.paralegals.org/Choice/whatis.html

support staff (secretaries, file clerks, word processors, etc.), legal assistants must sometimes provide that support for themselves—and for the attorneys who employ them. Other "large firm-small firm" differences that affect legal assistants are discussed later in this text.

HOW PARALEGALS CAME TO BE

During President Lyndon Johnson's "War on Poverty" in the 1960s, non-attorney assistants were used by lawyers in federally funded programs to reduce the cost of providing legal services to the poor. Some say this was the origin of paralegals, but others say that the legal secretary is the true precursor of the paralegal. Before it was common for trade schools, colleges, and universities to offer paralegal degrees or certificates, most paralegals were legal secretaries who had acquired substantial legal knowledge and intimate familiarity with court procedures. Although prohibited from practicing law, they began to perform tasks (under attorney supervision) that required knowledge and legal skills beyond those usually expected of a secretary. Eventually, they became "paralegals" by virtue of being so designated by their own law firms.

Paralegals were rare at first. But their legal knowledge and skills made it possible for the attorney to justify billing clients for their time, and that led to the beginning of a dramatic growth in their numbers. The legal assistant became not only a source of professional support for attorneys in their law practices, but a new source of profit as well. Billing privileges and a new job title carried prestige for the legal assistant.

SCENARIO

Jewell Nelson had been a secretary in a large real estate brokerage firm for seven years before she went to work in a small law firm in 1974. The law firm specialized in real estate law, and found Jewell's expertise in real estate law, documentation, and procedures to be invaluable. In fact, the firm's attorneys soon found that Jewell could do much of the document analysis that they had been doing while preparing for lawsuits that involved real estate transactions. Meanwhile, the attorneys and other legal secretaries in the firm were teaching Jewell about court procedures, an area in which she had no background.

Within less than a year, Jewell's role became more like an "attorney-assistant" than a legal secretary. And Jewell found that she loved the increased responsibility and the greater sophistication of her tasks. She found one source of frustration, however: She really lacked the skills needed to do serious legal research. So, one of the attorneys suggested that she take a research course in a new paralegal program at the local community college. The firm even offered to reimburse her for the cost of tuition and books. That was an offer too good to forgo, and Jewell enrolled.

"I found I enjoyed the legal research class so much that I decided to complete the whole program and get my paralegal certificate," Jewell reports. After about two years of evening classes, Jewell completed the program. "It was a struggle, at times, but it gave me so much satisfaction to finish—and I learned much more about the substance of the law than I had expected." Jewell is proud of the fact that her work now includes what she calls "serious" legal research—and that clients are now billed by the hour for her work as a legal assistant. "The raise I received when I officially became a legal assistant was very nice, as well," Jewell says. ■

The paralegal's role in the practice of law is still being defined, and the coming decade almost certainly will bring remarkable changes. Although the **American Bar Association** and some state bars have professional guidelines for the *use* of paralegals, those rules actually govern the conduct of the supervising attorneys, not of paralegals. At the time of this writing, not a single state requires a license for paralegals. Although this lack of licensure creates a somewhat uncertain situation, it also offers the opportunity for paralegals to contribute to the definition of their role and to influence the development of professional standards, whether prescribed by state law, by paralegal associations, or by the bar associations.

The **American Bar Association (ABA)** is the nation's largest organization of licensed attorneys. Membership is voluntary.

LEGAL ASSISTANTS AS PROFESSIONALS

The term "paralegal" is derived from "paraprofessional." The *Random House Webster's College Dictionary* defines the latter as: "a person trained to assist a doctor, lawyer, teacher, or other professional."[2] The same dictionary defines "profession" as: "a vocation requiring extensive education in science or the liberal arts and often specialized training." Are paralegals truly "professionals"?

Clearly, paralegal duties do not require the level of education and training that attorneys or doctors must have. But paralegal responsibilities do require specialized skills and knowledge. And, as the profession matures, it is possible that entry requirements will become more formalized and demanding. Even today, a degree or certificate from a recognized paralegal program is required for many entry-level paralegal positions, especially in metropolitan areas. Some law firms insist upon a paralegal degree, or a four-year degree *plus* a paralegal certificate—a combination that brings the level of education close to that required of public school teachers.

Professional status is important for several reasons. It can have a significant impact on the assignments given by attorneys. It can influence the attitudes of clients, the public-at-large, court officials, and the attorneys in other law firms. And it can influence the perquisites and even the salary that a paralegal receives. Paralegals who are regarded *and treated* as professionals will be more highly motivated and will be given assignments that make them more valuable to the attorneys and to the clients.

In practice, a paralegal's professional standing is determined primarily by his employer. But, the paralegal can improve that standing by convincing the employer that he merits recognition as a professional. Persuading the attorney of that fact, however, will require excellent educational credentials, as well as strong legal skills, intelligence, social poise, and maturity.

Practice Tip

When interviewing for a paralegal position, it is a good idea to observe any indications of the professional standing of legal assistants in that firm. In a final interview when considering an actual job offer, the candidate might ask some specific questions: Do legal assistants receive secretarial support? Do they have their own offices? What type of assignments do experienced paralegals in that office receive? An opportunity for an informal, private conversation with one of the legal assistants currently employed in that office can provide valuable insight on this issue.

WHERE PARALEGALS WORK

Legal assistants are not limited to working for law firms, nor are they limited to working in **civil litigation** (e.g., lawsuits)—although that is the most common paralegal field of practice. Within law firms, legal assistants also work in real estate, bankruptcy, family law, immigration, criminal defense, estate planning, probate, and many other specialties. Outside of law firms, many paralegals work within a corporate legal department, in banks and other financial institutions, in real estate companies, and in a variety of government agencies.

Some paralegals ultimately apply their knowledge and skills in positions that do not carry the title "paralegal" or "legal assistant." Depending upon the degree of attorney supervision of their work, they may no longer refer to themselves as paralegals. These nontraditional "paralegals" may, for example, be contract negotiators or equal employment opportunity administrators, legal librarians or law firm marketing specialists, insurance claims adjusters, or labor relations

Civil litigation is the use of a lawsuit—as opposed to a criminal prosecution—to establish the rights and obligations of opposing parties in a matter of controversy, and to determine any remedies that the court might grant under the law.

> **Practice Tip**
>
> In some states, non-attorneys are authorized to represent clients before worker compensation boards, motor vehicle departments, and other nonjudicial state agencies. The same opportunity exists in some federal agencies, most notably the Social Security Administration.
>
> Depending upon state law, a non-attorney employee may be able to represent a company, an association, or a partnership in **small claims court**.

A **small claims court** hears minor lawsuits that might not justify the expense of hiring an attorney. In most states, neither party can be represented by an attorney in small claims court. There is a dollar limit (e.g., $5,000) on the amount a small claims court may award to the winning party.

representatives. The potential for applying paralegal skills and knowledge in other professions is extraordinary and is still being explored by innovative and ambitious paralegals.

CAREER SATISFACTION AMONG LEGAL ASSISTANTS

Although nonscientific in their design, surveys by paralegal periodicals and associations generally reflect a high level of job satisfaction among paralegals. Many legal assistants find their particular specialty (e.g., real estate or bankruptcy) to be interesting. Satisfaction in helping clients to resolve their problems is rewarding to many, especially those with heavy client contact. Those who are *most* content with their work usually report that they find an opportunity for advancement and enjoy being treated as professionals. Yet, those paralegals reporting *dis*satisfaction—a much smaller group—generally state that their abilities are *not* challenged, and they do *not* see much opportunity for advancement.

Without the benefit of a scientifically designed study, it is difficult to evaluate these apparently contradictory experiences. It might be that the two groups are having very different experiences even though both are working in the same career field. However, a question arises: If the dissatisfied group sees little opportunity for challenging work and advancement, is that a reflection of their employers' attitudes or does it reflect the paralegals' failure to demonstrate their own abilities and to seek more challenge?

SCENARIO

Robert Mulder works in a mid-sized Chicago law firm. "This is my second job as a paralegal. I got my first job right out of paralegal training, and I didn't have any legal *experience*, at all. In fact, I got that first job by interning in a small law office that then hired me at the end of the internship. I wasn't really excited about taking that job, because it didn't appear that there was much opportunity for advancement. But, of course, I wasn't *ready* for challenging assignments at that point—I was just beginning to learn the ropes. I figured that a year or so wouldn't be too bad. Actually, I stayed almost two years before a paralegal friend in my present firm tipped me to a really good opportunity here. By then, I had the experience to feel confident in seeking a new job and taking on more challenging work. And, that's exactly what happened. I feel really pleased with the move and plan to stay with this firm indefinitely." ■

SECTION 2. THE PARALEGAL PROFESSIONAL

Because this profession is relatively new, a continuing issue has been the definition of an appropriate role for paralegals within the practice of law. The most obvious question is how to differentiate the paralegal's role from that of the supervising attorney, without unnecessarily limiting what paralegals can do. A related issue is the public's need for affordable legal services and proposals by some that non-attorneys be authorized to provide limited legal services directly to the public. These issues will be explored here and will occasionally recur in later chapters, as well.

DISTINGUISHING THE ROLES OF ATTORNEYS AND PARALEGALS

Where is the dividing line between the responsibilities of attorneys and paralegals? It varies with each law firm and each attorney. The attorney ultimately governs that division of responsibility, although a capable and assertive legal assistant certainly can influence the line of demarcation.

With *very* few exceptions—which will be discussed in later chapters—only attorneys may give legal advice to clients and appear in court on their behalf. Legal assistants are generally prohibited from doing either, although they may communicate the attorney's advice to a client *upon specific instructions from the attorney*. Paralegals are involved primarily in the process of providing legal representation: doing the things that move a case along. Legal assistants usually support attorneys in the *functions that an attorney must assume:* giving legal advice; preparing contracts, wills, and other legal documents; and appearing in court. During trials, legal assistants sometimes assist with jury selection (as an additional observer of the attitudes and reactions of prospective jurors) and also manage the numerous exhibits and documents in complex litigation. In an important case, a senior legal assistant might sit with the attorney at the counsel table for the entire trial and participate in the daily out-of-court strategy sessions.

Legal assistants and attorneys sometimes share the support services of the same secretary, although legal assistants in some offices—especially small law offices—receive no secretarial support and might have to perform secretarial functions as well. In some firms, legal assistants might be expected to decide for themselves when to be in the county clerk's office, the law library, or the law firm office, based on their workload and previously established priorities.

THE PARALEGAL AS THE "ACCESSIBLE" LEGAL PROFESSIONAL

Busy attorneys can be difficult to reach: Often they are with another client, in court, in conference, "on the other line," or "out of the office" *whenever* the client calls—or so it can seem to an anxious client. This situation is especially frustrating to the client when she experiences an emergency—or *perceives* something to be an emergency.

Paralegals, in contrast, can be more responsive to clients because they usually spend much less time in conference or out of the office. On balance, it often is far easier for the client to reach the legal assistant working on the client's case. A legal assistant who is familiar with that client's legal matters, and who has excellent communication skills and a professional (but friendly) manner, can be a valued asset to any law firm. Of course, the extent to which the legal assistant should discuss the substance of a legal matter with a client depends upon the attorney's instructions and the law firm's policy. (Chapter 3 will discuss professional ethics and the legal assistant's role in client contacts.)

But in many instances, the client simply needs to "tell her story" to someone who is familiar with her case and who can relay the gist of her story to the attorney. Sometimes, clients need to vent their frustrations (about their own circumstances, not the law firm), and it's certainly less expensive to vent on the legal assistant's billable hour than on the attorney's. In those situations, the legal assistant does not need to respond much beyond the assurance that he will brief the attorney. Leaving a message with the receptionist cannot meet the needs of these clients as effectively as can a conversation with the legal assistant.

THE CRISIS IN AFFORDABLE LEGAL SERVICE

The rising cost of legal services and the ever-increasing number of lawyers have put great pressure on attorneys to control costs. Many corporate clients carefully scrutinize the bills submitted by their outside legal counsel and sometimes dispute them in detail. Small businesses and individual clients are less likely to dispute a bill, but they are not reluctant to shop around for law firms that control costs and charge lower rates. The result is unprecedented competition among law firms—so much so that some predict that profits and the traditional high salaries of attorneys might be in jeopardy. Clearly, attorneys are eager to find ways of controlling costs without sacrificing the quality of their services, or their income.

In addition to intense competition among attorneys, there is competition from other sources. Self-help legal guides are abundant. Many "do-it-yourselfers" are purchasing computer software programs that guide the consumer through the steps of drafting a will or living trust, a lease, an employment agreement, and other legal documents. Some unsupervised, but self-styled "paralegals" are pushing the limits of the law by providing assistance directly to individuals who are preparing to represent themselves in court appearances. Of course, these unsupervised *non*paralegals are pushing the limits of the law because all states prohibit non-attorneys from giving legal advice or practicing law in other ways.

Conventional wisdom suggests that competition among the thousands of new attorneys who enter practice each year will eventually drive legal fees down until their services are reasonably affordable to all but the poor. Unfortunately, that expectation might never be realized. For one thing, such low fees might not justify the exorbitant expense and grueling effort necessary to complete three years of law school and pass the bar exam. And before legal fees fall that low, the image of law as a financially rewarding career might disappear, and law school enrollments might shrink. People with the ability to complete law school and pass the bar exam might seek other, more lucrative careers, rather than practice law for cut-rate fees.

The "Legal Technician" Proposal and Affordable Legal Services

Unlawful detainer is the illegal possession or occupancy of land or buildings that belong to another person; an *unlawful detainer action* is a lawsuit to evict a tenant who has breached the rental agreement or lease.

A **legal technician** is a non-attorney who is licensed (or otherwise authorized by law) to provide legal services directly to the public without supervision by an attorney.

The high cost of legal services has actually sparked a movement to authorize "qualified non-attorneys" to provide legal services in relatively simple matters such as an uncontested divorce, an uncomplicated will, or an **unlawful detainer** action (i.e., a lawsuit to evict a tenant), *without the requirement that they be supervised by an attorney.* If such **legal technicians** were to be licensed to provide limited legal services directly to the public, they might be roughly comparable to optometrists, who may prescribe corrective lenses, but are also trained to recognize possible symptoms of pathology so that the client can be referred to a medical ophthalmologist. In other words, the legal technician could be trained to recognize factual situations that raise legal issues requiring the expertise and guidance of an attorney. Obviously, the prospect of licensed, unsupervised legal technicians raises serious questions about competence and consumer protection. The issue of legal technicians will be discussed further in a later chapter.

Affordable access to legal services has become an important political issue, as well. Several state legislatures have debated the legal technician issue, and it appears possible that licensed *non*-attorneys who provide legal services *directly* to the public might soon become a reality in some states. There is a national organization of legal consumers, HALT, Inc.—An Organization of Americans for Legal Reform that is pushing for legislation to increase competition among the providers of legal services—that is, to "break the attorney monopoly" (as HALT

CHAPTER 1 — Paralegals and Legal Assistants

sees it) over legal services and to ensure affordable access, including the licensure of non-attorney legal technicians. The organization's shortened name, HALT, is an acronym for "Help Arrest Legal Tyranny."

Internet Access

HALT, Inc.: http://www.halt.org

One State Challenges a Legal "Self-Help" Computer Program

In Texas, the state's Unauthorized Practice of Law Committee filed suit against Parsons Technology, Inc., the publisher of *Quicken Family Lawyer (QFL)*, alleging that the software program violated the Texas statute prohibiting the **unauthorized practice of law (UPL)**. The committee sought a court order that would deprive Parsons of some $500,000 in sales and over $100,000 in profits. Although not a party to the lawsuit, HALT, on behalf of some 2,800 of its members in Texas, submitted its views on the case as a "friend of the court," and argued that *QFL* did not violate Texas law, and in any case should be protected under the First Amendment rights to publish and read without government censorship.

> **Ethics Watch**
>
> State laws generally prohibit the practice of law by non-attorneys (known as the "unauthorized practice of law", or UPL). Legal assistants must always be on guard against the danger of crossing the line between *properly supervised* practice as a paralegal and the unauthorized practice of law. The unauthorized practice of law carries civil—and in some circumstances, criminal—penalties.

Sidebar: The **unauthorized practice of law (UPL)** is the illegal practice of law. What constitutes the practice of law varies with the laws of each state, but generally includes giving others legal advice, drawing up legal documents for another, or representing others in court. In some states, these activities are forbidden to nonlawyers even if no fee is charged.

The Texas unauthorized practice statute states, in part:

(a) [T]he "practice of law" means the preparation of a pleading or other document incident to an action or special proceeding . . . on behalf of a client before a judge in court as well as a service rendered out of court, including the giving of advice or the rendering of any service requiring the use of legal skill or knowledge, such as preparing a will, contract, or other instrument, the legal effect of which under the facts and conclusions involved must be carefully determined. (b) The definition in this section is not exclusive and does not deprive the judicial branch of the power and authority under both this chapter and the adjudicated cases to determine whether other services and acts not enumerated may constitute the practice of law.

Texas Government Code, Section 81.101

In fact, *QFL* does offer more than 100 legal forms for purposes as diverse as real estate leases, wills, and employment contracts. And when a consumer uses *QFL*, the program guides her through an interactive interview process to aid her in selecting and filling out the appropriate legal form.

Because Parsons Technology was incorporated in another state (California), it was able to have the case transferred from the Texas state courts to the U.S. District Court in Texas. In the following "Case in Point," the federal court applies Texas law and finds in favor of the Unauthorized Practice of Law Committee (UPLC). Ultimately, however, the Texas state legislature made this court decision moot by enacting a statute exempting software programs such as Parson's from the Texas unauthorized practice statute. This new state legislation made moot the court's finding because the federal court was applying *state law* in this case, not federal law. However, the district court's opinion merits consideration because it addresses some important issues regarding self-help programs and the unlicensed practice of law. In the excerpts from the U.S. District Court's opinion, below, the court refers to the committee as "UPLC" and to the software program as "QFL." (Footnotes in the court's opinion have been omitted below.)

A Case in Point

Unauthorized Practice of Law Committee v. Parsons Technology, Inc.

1999 WL 47235 (N.D.Tex.)

* * * *

On the initial use of QFL, or anytime a new user name is created, QFL asks for the user's name and state of residence. It then inquires whether the user would like QFL to suggest documents to the user. If the user answers "Yes," QFL's "Document Advisor" asks the user a few short questions concerning the user's marital status, number of children, and familiarity with living trusts. QFL then displays the entire list of available documents, but marks a few of them as especially appropriate for the user based on her responses.

When the user accesses a document, QFL asks a series of questions relevant to filling in the legal form. With certain questions, a separate text box explaining the relevant legal considerations the user may want to take into account in filling out the form also appears on the screen. As the user proceeds through the questions relevant to the specific form, QFL either fills in the appropriate blanks or adds or deletes entire clauses from the form. . . .

* * * *

QFL goes beyond merely instructing someone how to fill in a blank form. While no single one of QFL's acts, in and of itself, may constitute the practice of law, taken as a whole Parsons, through QFL, has gone beyond publishing a sample form book with instructions, and has ventured into the unauthorized practice of law.

* * * *

Parsons' arguments to the contrary notwithstanding, QFL is far more than a static form with instructions on how to fill in the blanks. For instance QFL adapts the content of the form to the responses given by the user. QFL purports to select the appropriate health care document for an individual based upon the state in which she lives. The packaging of QFL makes various representations as to the accuracy and specificity of the forms. In sum, Parsons has violated the unauthorized practice of law statute.

The district court also rejected Parson's contention that the Texas statute violated First Amendment rights. It permanently barred Parsons from selling *QFL* within the state of Texas. Parsons appealed the court's decision to the U.S. Court of Appeals. Before the appellate court could rule, the Texas legislature had enacted the new legislation discussed above.

THE LEGAL ASSISTANT'S ROLE IN REDUCING CLIENT FEES

With all of these economic and political pressures, it clearly is in the legal profession's self-interest to control the cost of legal services. *Now comes the para-*

legal as a cost-effective assistant who reduces the client's cost for legal services. The following discussion explains why paralegals offer a solution that is so financially attractive to both clients and attorneys.

Paralegals make economic sense for two reasons: lower bills for clients and increased profits for law firms. At first thought, these two benefits might appear to be contradictory, but they are not. In fact, this financial benefit to both clients and attorneys has fueled the dramatic growth in the paralegal career field. A large portion of an attorney's typical workload requires the training and knowledge of a lawyer and cannot be delegated to non-attorneys, but the remainder of that workload *can* be delegated to a trained legal assistant working under the attorney's supervision.

For example, an attorney might spend four hours drafting a legal document for submission to the court. A less experienced paralegal might do the same job in *six* hours (taking more time because he is not as knowledgeable about the law). If that task is delegated to the paralegal, the attorney might spend twenty minutes giving instructions and another forty minutes revising the paralegal's draft. Even so, the client saves money, as shown by the calculations in Figure 1.1.

In this example, the client saves $90, or 15%. In other situations, the client would save more because an experienced legal assistant often can complete less complex tasks just as rapidly as the attorney could. In this example, if an experienced legal assistant had completed his draft in four hours, the client would have saved $210, or about 35%. It is easy to see why clients appreciate paralegals.

FIGURE 1.1 Savings from Delegating Task to Paralegal

Preparation by attorney *only*		
	4 hours @ $150 per hour	$600
	TOTAL COST	$600
Preparation by supervised paralegal		
Attorney:	20 minutes to give instructions to the paralegal	
	40 minutes to revise the paralegal's draft	
	1 hour @ $150 per hour	$150
Paralegal:	6 hours to draft the document	
	6 hours @ $60 per hour	$360
	TOTAL COST	$510

Legal Assistants Facilitate Adding New Clients

But what about the attorney's income? Has not the attorney given up three hours' worth of income ($450, at a billing rate of $150/hour) by letting the paralegal prepare the draft? Actually, that possibility does exist. But, by having paralegals do some of the less sophisticated legal work, the attorney will be free to take on *additional client matters* so that the law firm's total business expands. And, while taking on additional client matters, the law firm will also make a *profit* on the paralegals' work for both the "old" and the "new" client matters. Conceptually, Figure 1.2 shows how *one week's* workload might be redistributed.

If this rearrangement occurs, the attorney is serving two new clients and billing just as much time as she did before hiring a paralegal. And the paralegal is billing time also—although at a much lower hourly rate than the attorney. If one adds the attorney and paralegal fees for each client, she will see again that each client's total bill has declined as a result of using paralegals. Client A's bill dropped from $1,800 to $1,560; Client B's from $1,050 to $930—and so forth.

FIGURE 1.2   Redistribution of Workload by Delegating Tasks to Paralegal

BEFORE: Attorney *only*
Client A   12 hours @ $150 = $1,800
Client B   7 hours @ 150 = 1,050
Client C   6 hours @ 150 =   900
Client D   5 hours @ 150 =   750
       TOTAL: 30 hours $4,500

AFTER: Attorney *plus* legal assistant

	ATTORNEY	LEGAL ASSISTANT
Client A	8 hours @ $150 = $1,200	6 hours @ $60= $360
Client B	5 hours @ 150 = 750	3 hours @ 60 = 180
Client C	4 hours @ 150 = 600	2 hours @ 60 = 120
Client D	3 hours @ 150 = 450	3 hours @ 60 = 180
New Client E	6 hours @ 150 = 900	2 hours @ 60 = 180
New Client F	4 hours @ 150 = 600	2 hours @ 60 = 120
TOTALS:	30 hours $4,500	19 hours $1,140

Paralegals as Profit Generators

The paralegal even becomes a source of profit because the time he bills will cover more than the cost of his compensation and his share of the office overhead. Assuming an annual salary of $30,000, plus $20,000 for fringe benefits and his share of the office overhead (rent, support staff salaries, equipment, library, supplies, etc.), the paralegal must bill a total of $50,000 in a year for the firm to break even. If the paralegal works 20 days per month for 11 months, he can meet the breakeven point if he bills an average of only 3.8 hours per day. Figure 1.3 demonstrates the billable hours needed to financially support a paralegal position.

But most legal assistants work more than 220 days per year and bill much more than four hours per day. Figure 1.4 demonstrates how the paralegal would create a profit of $29,200 per year for the firm—or $132.70 per day—if she bills 6 hours each day (still assuming only 220 working days).

It is not difficult to see why attorneys appreciate the profit potential of paralegals. As the hardworking and productive paralegal gains experience, his billing rate should be increased to reflect the rising value of his work—and to support salary increases. The important thing to remember is that the client, the law firm, *and* the paralegal all receive a share of the economic benefits of using paralegals. Financially, no one loses.

FIGURE 1.3   Billable Hours Needed to Support a Paralegal Position

220 days × 3.8 hours = 836 hours
836 hours × $60   = $50,160

FIGURE 1.4   Profit Generated by a Paralegal

220 days × 6 hours = 1320
1320 hours × $60 = $79,200

$79,200
−50,000   (Salary + overhead)
PROFIT $29,200

The American Bar Association's Position on Paralegals

The good news for paralegals is that the American Bar Association (ABA) strongly supports the use of non-attorney legal assistants, so long as they are adequately supervised by an attorney who follows the ABA's professional guidelines.

In 1968 the ABA established the Special Committee on Lay Assistants for Lawyers to study the use of non-attorneys as legal assistants and to determine the standards for paralegal education. In 1975 this special committee became a permanent standing committee—The Standing Committee on Legal Assistants—and continues to grant ABA approval to paralegal programs that meet specified standards and pass an on-site review process. Practicing paralegals serve on the ABA's visitation teams that review programs seeking ABA approval. As of this writing, more than 250 educational institutions have received ABA approval for their programs.[3]

A RAPIDLY GROWING CAREER FIELD

Citing statistics from the U.S. Department of Labor and other sources, the news media have trumpeted the rapid growth of the paralegal career field. Although there are no dramatic statistics about the rate of growth in legal secretary positions, if one counts the number of newspaper ads for legal secretaries and for paralegals, he will find that the former outnumber the latter by a wide margin. In other words, the ads suggest that there are far more job opportunities for legal secretaries than for paralegals. This can be misleading, however, because most paralegal positions are never advertised; they are filled by word-of-mouth, paralegal placement agencies, and other avenues.

The fact is, although there are more currently employed legal secretaries than currently employed paralegals, *newly created* paralegal positions outnumber new positions for legal secretaries. The U.S. Department of Labor's Bureau of Labor Statistics estimates that in 1998 there were 136,000 employed paralegals. The bureau estimates that in the year 2008 there will be 220,000 paralegals, an increase of 84,000 positions (or 62%) in 10 years. During the same period, legal secretary positions are predicted to increase by 13%, from 285,000 to 322,000, an increase of only 37,000 positions.[4] If those respective rates of growth were to continue, the total number of paralegal positions would exceed that for legal secretaries by the year 2020.

Internet Access

U.S. Dept. of Labor, Bureau of Labor Statistics: http://stats.bls.gov

---

SECTION 3. CHOOSING A PARALEGAL CAREER

People are entering the paralegal career for more than the relative job security that tends to follow a rapid growth in demand. One inducement is the opportunity to work in the field of law. Many are searching for a new career after leaving other fields of employment. Also, a significant minority are exploring paralegal work as a prelude to becoming a lawyer.

THE ATTRACTION OF A PARALEGAL CAREER

Most paralegals find the law and the American system of justice to be intriguing. They find it especially interesting to see the way legal principles apply to the facts of a particular client's legal matter. They are challenged by the analysis of those basic legal principles in order to discover their logical implications (e.g., "If both *A* and *B* are true, then *X* must be true as well."). And, they receive professional satisfaction from the opportunity to see justice realized and to play some part in that process. Many legal assistants enjoy the challenge of litigation. Certainly all paralegals are aware of the power of the courts—even though they know that real-life court proceedings bear little resemblance to the old *Perry Mason* films.

One of the benefits of being a legal assistant is the opportunity to work on *the kinds of tasks that lawyers perform*, without spending three years and untold tuition dollars for law school, *and* without assuming the enormous responsibility of an attorney. How close can a paralegal really get to "practicing law"? Actually, without violating state laws or professional ethics, an attorney can permit his legal assistants to perform a very broad range of sophisticated legal tasks so long as he directs and supervises their work. In some nontraditional "paralegal" roles, there is even greater latitude.

Career Changers Drawn to the Field of Law

Many students have already established themselves in another career field but are considering a change into paralegal work. For example, engineers, schoolteachers, real estate agents, and registered nurses are often found in paralegal classes. Those potential career changers have been attracted by the opportunity to work in the legal field and by the job security of a rapidly growing career field. Some career changers recognize the potential synergy of skills and knowledge between their present occupations and paralegal work, but a remarkable number do not—until that potential is pointed out to them.

Some examples of this synergy are obvious. Real estate agents can apply their knowledge in real estate procedures and law without having to sell. Registered nurses are in demand for personal injury, medical malpractice, and worker compensation practices. Somewhat less obvious, perhaps, is the engineer's opportunity to apply technical expertise to litigation involving such things as motor vehicles, machinery, and construction. Teachers are valued for their skills in research, communication, and organization.

Paralegal students, regardless of age, can develop the potential for synergy between their legal training and other fields by pursuing self-improvement in one of those fields: refreshing unused foreign language skills, taking course work in anatomy and medical terminology, becoming expert with computer software, obtaining a real estate license, or studying accounting, for example. It is not essential that the self-improvement course be completed prior to landing that first paralegal position—the very fact that one is pursuing it will set him apart from the crowd of applicants. Of course, it might be necessary to assure potential employers that the objective is to develop skills and knowledge that will be useful in paralegal work, not as a step toward leaving the field of law. In addition, it would be wise to focus the job search on those law firms or companies that can benefit from the nonlegal expertise the candidate is developing, as well as his paralegal skills.

From Legal Assistant to Attorney

Some individuals see paralegal work as a logical prelude to law school. That view has merit in several respects. The obvious advantage is that most *new* lawyers have received precious little law school instruction about actually *practicing* law. In particular, they usually know very little about court rules and procedures, client relations, or law firm management. Although some law school students work in law firms as "summer associates," following their first and second years of law school, these **summer associates** usually spend most of their time on legal research and drafting legal memoranda. Paralegals, on the other hand, typi-

---

Practice Tip

Career changers often have an unsuspected advantage: their age. Many attorneys appreciate the maturity of older paralegals with a varied life experience, because they often bring sound judgment, a broad perspective, and polished interpersonal skills to their practice as legal assistants.

A **summer associate** is a first- or second-year law school student who is employed by a law firm during the summer. The summer associate experience provides both the firm and the law student with an opportunity to evaluate the possibility of future employment in that law firm.

cally participate in the "nuts and bolts" of practicing law—under attorney supervision, of course.

SCENARIO

María Estrada is a Los Angeles paralegal working her way through law school. Because she works full-time at her day job, she anticipates it will take at least five years to complete her law degree at night.

"This really is a difficult way to go to law school, but going through a regular, three-year day program was not an option. That would be far too intensive to do while I hold down a full-time job. So, I consider the night class option as a blessing, even though it will take several more years to finish. The law school I'm attending isn't famous, but you'd be amazed at how many of its graduates are deputy district attorneys or public defenders—and a few are even serving as judges here in Los Angeles County. So I figure, if I work really hard, I'll get a good legal education and have a good shot at passing the bar exam."

María's law firm has been very supportive of her ambition and efforts. "The firm has allowed me to schedule my vacation time just before final exams, so that I can study. And, although they haven't made any promises, I think there's a good chance they will hire me when I pass the bar. And it would be great to start practicing with so many people I already know and respect. I actually decided to become a legal assistant *after* I decided to go to law school. So, first I got my certificate and this job. That was a great decision, because when I pass the bar I'll know how to really *practice* law, not just talk or write about the law!"

> ### Practice Tip
> Just one year as a practicing legal assistant can provide a law school student with an insight that can never be gained in the classroom or during a stint as a summer associate.
>
> In addition, paralegal employment can provide contacts and references that will be invaluable when the time comes to seek a position in a law office. Small law firms that cannot easily train new attorneys might be especially receptive to a law school graduate who already knows something about the actual hands-on practice of law.

THE CHARACTERISTICS OF A SUCCESSFUL PARALEGAL

A paralegal's job can be demanding, requiring specific skills and favoring certain personality traits. Anyone considering a paralegal career should assess his own aptitudes and traits, because he would not want to spend a great deal of time and money on paralegal courses only to discover that this career is not for him. Although responsibilities and working environments vary, there are some fundamental skills and traits needed for the great majority of legal assistant positions.

Skills for Success

Expressed in broad terms, the *key skills* for a paralegal are:

- communicating effectively and with correct English usage, both orally and in writing;
- interacting effectively with other people;
- working independently and without constant guidance;
- managing multiple, unrelated assignments;
- thinking logically and critically, and understanding legal principles;
- analyzing facts, issues, and arguments, and drawing conclusions;
- using the resources of a law library;
- using computers for word processing and legal research;
- organizing files, information, and tasks; and,
- comprehending and summarizing a large quantity of data.

Special attention should be given to writing skills. The ability to write clearly, succinctly, and correctly is absolutely essential if a paralegal is to progress beyond

> **Practice Tip**
>
> Every student should take full advantage of the courses in legal research and writing. Of course, paralegal programs usually do not try to teach the writing skills that one should acquire before entering college-level courses. Those without strong writing skills might pursue additional course work in English composition, even if they must find those courses outside the paralegal program.

routine assignments. Poor writing skills can create a genuine barrier to advancement as a legal assistant. Another skill deserving emphasis is the ability to use a law library. Even if legal research is not one's favorite assignment, at the minimum a paralegal must be able to locate an elusive state court opinion or federal regulation, find out if a lower court decision has been overturned by a higher court, and locate a helpful article in a legal encyclopedia.

Of course, one must add any special skills needed for a particular practice or position. For example, some paralegal positions might require the use of particular computer programs, and paralegals in a personal injury or worker compensation practice are expected to know common medical terms. Some law firms even require bilingual skills to serve their clientele.

Personal Traits for Success

But skills provide only one part of the equation for success as a paralegal. *Key personality traits* for paralegals include:

- personal integrity and the ability to keep confidences;
- attention to accuracy and detail;
- flexibility;
- the readiness to ask for clarification, and also to question instructions or documents that appear to be incorrect;
- the willingness to do clerical tasks along with more challenging and interesting duties; and
- the temperament of an effective team member.

Integrity and Confidentiality

Personal integrity and scrupulous regard for confidentiality are absolutely essential in legal work, and anyone inclined to "fudge" the truth or to share juicy secrets with friends and family should stay out of the legal field. Beyond the obvious moral reasons for adhering to ethical conduct, there are serious practical consequences when attorneys or paralegals violate professional standards. Paralegals who violate client confidences can be fired by their employer and can be sued by the client. Underlying all of this are several *principles of duty* that cause the law to judge legal professionals more harshly than other persons for transgressions that harm clients or interfere with the proper administration of the justice system. Although these duties apply primarily to the attorney, the attorney is responsible for the actions of her employees and agents—which include her paralegals and support staff.

The first principle is called **fiduciary duty** and is one that attorneys share with trustees, bankers, stockbrokers, and others in a position of special trust and responsibility. Although a fiduciary duty is owed only to the client, it carries a very heavy responsibility. Its most important element is *loyalty* to that client. Fiduciary loyalty means that an attorney must always act in the best interests of the client, even when the attorney would rather do otherwise. The duty of loyalty forbids conflicts of interest, such as representing two clients with opposing interests, or buying the client's real estate in a foreclosure sale.

Maintaining the confidentiality of a client's legal, business, and personal matters is part of an attorney's fiduciary duty. If the client cannot rely upon that confidence, he might be reluctant to share vital information with the attorney. If his confidence is violated, the client might be harmed legally, financially, or socially.

Fiduciary duty is the special duty of loyalty and diligence owed by a trustee (or anyone in a comparable position, such as an attorney) to the person whose property or legal interests he manages or controls.

Accuracy and Attention to Detail

No matter what their legal specialty, paralegals must be very detail-oriented and must strive for accuracy. Missing a court deadline or failing to include important information in legal documents can result in such things as:

- the client losing her lawsuit,
- beneficiaries being omitted from a will or trust,
- increased tax liability for the client,
- lack of adequate remedies when someone breaches a contract, or
- the client suing the attorney for professional negligence.

Although the above list is incomplete, it makes the point.

> **Ethics Watch**
>
> A paralegal's carelessness could cause the client to sue the attorney for legal **malpractice**—*and* the paralegal for negligence. (The possible personal liability of a paralegal for her own "malpractice" is discussed in Chapter 3.)

Malpractice is the negligent, incompetent, or unethical performance of professional duties. Examples are medical malpractice and legal malpractice.

Assertiveness in Obtaining Clear Instructions

Because attorneys are so intimately familiar with client matters, they sometimes give assignments with brief, almost cryptic instructions: "Prepare the file for the Yeltsin deposition tomorrow." If the paralegal has been involved in the case only occasionally, he might not have sufficient background to know how to approach the task. Or he might assume he understands the task, when in fact he does not. In situations like that, a legal assistant must ask for clarification, and if he is working with a busy, impatient attorney, that can be difficult. If intimidation prevents him from seeking help and the result is a botched job, things will only become worse. There are occasions when a paralegal needs to say firmly and calmly, "I cannot do this job properly unless you give me more information"—and the paralegal should be specific about the information needed.

The self-assertiveness suggested here should not be confused with offensively aggressive behavior. One can be polite, respectful, and professional when insisting on adequate instructions or explanations. Paralegals need to be *appropriately* assertive in all aspects of their work—even when interviewing for their first paralegal position.

Working as a Team Member

An essential part of being an effective team member is establishing and maintaining positive, professional relationships. As a "junior" member of the legal team, the new paralegal will need to exercise tact and diplomacy in offering suggestions and disagreeing with the views of others. Good listening skills are important, because without them one cannot understand and appreciate differing viewpoints.

The team member mentality can be important, but it also can be the source of misunderstanding and frustration, even for the most dedicated legal assistants. Law firms as employers and paralegals as employees sometimes have different roles in mind when they speak of "team members" or "team players." The law firm might be thinking in terms of dedication and sacrifice, whereas the legal assistant is thinking in terms of full participation and recognition.

Practice Tip

If a legal assistant has a strong desire to work as part of a legal service team, that topic should be explored in the final interview before accepting a position.

COMPENSATION FOR LEGAL ASSISTANTS

The majority of paralegals are full-time employees of law firms or corporations. They are on a straight salary with prepaid health insurance, and many receive annual or semiannual bonuses.[5] In the late 1990s, starting salaries for paralegals without prior *legal* experience were generally in the range of $24,000 to $30,000, although this varied significantly from region to region. Salaries tended to rise significantly during the first five years of paralegal employment, then more slowly thereafter. Those with ten years of *paralegal* experience generally received salaries in the range of $32,000 to $40,000. *Exceptionally well-qualified* paralegals with 10 to 20 years of experience could command salaries in the $50,000 to $70,000 range, but relatively few legal assistants were in that elite rank.

Some Factors That Influence Salaries

A number of factors influence the salaries of all paralegals, from beginner to seasoned professional. Among the most important are the demonstrated abilities of the paralegal and the paralegal's skill in salary negotiations. Perhaps equally important is the setting in which the paralegal is employed. A paralegal in a firm where attorneys bill hourly rates of $250 to $350 per hour has better earning potential than one in a firm where the attorneys charge between $100 and $250 per hour. In the "high-rate" firm, more of the overhead costs can be supported by attorneys. That can be true despite the more expensive offices the firm maintains and in spite of the larger incomes received by those attorneys. Consequently, in a "low-rate" firm, the paralegal's salary might be limited because a larger share of her billing rate goes to support office overhead.

Equally important, the paralegal's billing rate in a low-rate firm is restricted by the lower billing rates for attorneys in that firm. It is much easier for a high-rate firm to justify billing a paralegal's time at $90 an hour if the firm's *least expensive attorney* bills her time at $200 per hour, rather than $120.

Although a four-year degree is helpful in obtaining an entry-level paralegal position, the amount of general education appears to have only a modest influence upon the individual paralegal's total compensation (i.e., salary plus bonus). Years of experience, firm size (i.e., numbers of attorneys and paralegals), and city size appear to have much more influence upon compensation. In addition, there were remarkable differences among compensation levels in various regions of the nation.[6]

Salaries Vary by Region and Specialty

In November 1999, the National Federation of Paralegal Associations (NFPA) reported an average paralegal base salary nationwide of $38,085. But average salaries for legal assistants working in San Francisco and New York City were reported to be $47,239 and $48,277, respectively. The nationwide average salary had increased by 29% since the NFPA 1991 survey.[7] In February 2000, the National Association of Legal Assistants (NALA) reported average salaries (for all legal assistants) to range from a high of $51,075 in the far west, to $31,413 in the Rocky Mountains region. Salaries vary also according to the specialty in which the legal assistant practices. The NALA survey reported that the highest average salaries were found in the following fields: securities law, environmental law, intellectual property law, and banking and finance.

Bonuses and Overtime Pay

It is very common for law firms to pay annual or semiannual bonuses. These bonuses average about $2,000 per year. The bonus might be tied to the number of hours billed by the paralegal during the preceding six or twelve months; if the paralegal has met or exceeded his annual **billable quota**, he will be rewarded ac-

---

Because most law firms are paid only for the hours billed to clients, many firms impose a **billable quota** on all attorneys and paralegals in the firm. The quota is the minimum monthly or annual hours each professional is expected to bill to clients.

cordingly. (Billable hours and quotas are discussed in Chapter 11.) Other firms use entirely different criteria, so a new employee needs to ask about the bonus system when he joins a firm.

The question of overtime pay for paralegals is still unresolved. Although the federal *Fair Labor Standards Act* exempts professional and administrative employees (usually termed "**exempt employees**") from mandatory overtime pay, the position of the U.S. Department of Labor has been that paralegals do not qualify as "professionals" or "administrative employees." In large measure, this is because the department does not consider the duties of legal assistants to require knowledge of an advanced type acquired by a prolonged course of specialized intellectual study and because the legal assistant must work under the supervision and direction of an attorney and cannot exercise independent professional judgment. If paralegals are *not* exempt from the *Fair Labor Standards Act*, they must be paid for any overtime.

In spite of the position of the Department of Labor, however, many law firms do not pay overtime for legal assistants, usually because they disagree with the Labor Department's interpretation and application of the statutory criteria. In some firms compensatory time off is given, or the quantity of uncompensated overtime is figured into the calculation of bonuses. Other law firms simply regard overtime work as "part of being a professional" and offer no compensation at all.

> The *Fair Labor Standards Act* is a federal law setting minimum standards for the working conditions of employees.
>
> An **exempt employee** is one in an executive, administrative, or professional position who is, for that reason, exempt from the overtime pay requirement of the *Fair Labor Standards Act.*

Compensation for Corporate Paralegals

With the exception of banks and other financial institutions, paralegal salaries tend to be somewhat higher in corporations than in law firms. This might be because corporations are not limited by a client's reluctance to pay as generously for paraprofessional legal services. Also, unlike law firms, corporations do not look to their legal departments to generate profits.

Legal assistants working in corporations generally receive a straight salary and possibly an annual bonus. Because the corporation is "the client," there is no need to bill the client for each discrete task the paralegal performs, and thus there is no issue of billable quotas. Bonuses are likely to be based upon the *quality* of the paralegal's work, as much as upon the quantity (i.e., productivity).

Fringe Benefits

Except in very small firms, paralegals generally have fringe benefits including health care, paid sick leave, and two or three weeks per year of paid vacation. Some firms add disability insurance, life insurance, and some type of retirement benefit, usually a **401(k) plan**. Because the cost of these benefits is generally tax-free or tax-deferred, such benefits can have substantial value for the employee. For that reason, some legal assistants negotiate a lesser salary in exchange for some type of tax-free or tax-deferred benefit. Legal assistants without employer-paid health, life, or disability insurance can sometimes purchase insurance at group rates through their local paralegal association.

> A **401(k) plan** is a pension plan, sponsored by the employer, to which the employee makes tax-deferred contributions from her salary. In some plans, the employer also makes matching contributions for the benefit of the employee.

QUALIFYING FOR A PARALEGAL CAREER

There are several paths commonly followed by those who want to become paralegals. The most time-honored is on-the-job training in a law office. Countless thousands of paralegals employed today entered the career in that way, and it remains a viable path for many. Over the past two decades, however, increasing numbers of new paralegals have brought formal education in law or paralegal studies to their first paralegal position. Paralegal programs are offered by two-year colleges, four-year colleges and universities, university extension programs, and commercial trade and business schools. There are even correspondence programs leading to a paralegal certificate.

Although some colleges offer two-year and/or four-year degrees with majors in paralegal studies, other paralegal programs award a certificate in paralegal studies upon completion of a specified number of required and elective courses related to the practice of law. A few universities offer master's degrees in paralegal studies. According to the American Association for Paralegal Education (AAfPE), about 63% of their member institutions offer an associate degree in paralegal studies.[8] The paralegal degree or certificate is often a minimum, entry-level qualification for many employers. In some metropolitan areas, many law firms insist upon a degree or certificate from a program approved by the ABA. However, many fine paralegal programs exist that have not sought ABA approval because of the time and expense involved in the approval process. Some programs have such well-established reputations in the legal community that prospective employers regard them as equal in quality to ABA-approved programs.

Selecting the right program is an important decision, because the quality and reputation of the school can have a significant effect upon one's chances for entry-level employment and upon the salary offered. As paralegals gain some years of legal experience, however, their opportunities and salaries are influenced more by the quality of their work than by the nature or amount of their formal education.

The Advantages of College Education

The U.S. Department of Labor has identified the paralegal career field among those that require some post–high school education, but not necessarily a college degree. The amount of education expected beyond a high school diploma varies by region and by law firm. Certainly, a two-year associate degree would be an advantage, if only to set one apart from applicants having only a high school education and a paralegal certificate. Some two-year colleges offer an associate degree in paralegal studies, or an associate degree *plus* paralegal certificate. Both options offer desirable entry-level qualifications.

Several paralegal organizations—such as the National Federation of Paralegal Associations (NFPA) and the Legal Assistant Management Association (LAMA)—have taken the position that a four-year college degree is becoming a common minimum qualification for entry into the paralegal career field. Beginning in 2001, the four-year degree has become a minimum requirement to take NFPA's Paralegal Advanced Competency Exam (PACE). On its Web site, LAMA has published the following statement regarding the degree:

> The requirement of a four-year degree is strengthening among employers. Due to the complex nature of work performed by legal assistants and because of the need for advanced writing and research skills, many employers will only consider candidates who have baccalaureate degrees. However, many employers will consider non-degreed candidates who have expertise or relevant experience in certain areas.[9]

In the same document, LAMA states that employers wanting a four-year degree do not usually accept a paralegal certificate as a substitute for that requirement.

Internet Access

Legal Assistant Management Association   http://www.lamanet.org

---

There are several reasons for this increasing emphasis upon college degrees. There is a common presumption that college graduates have superior skills in communication—especially writing skills—and in library research.

Many people believe also that college graduates develop greater poise and self-confidence and are more likely to interact comfortably and appropriately with college-educated clients and other legal professionals. There also is a perception that clients are more receptive to paying higher rates for work billed by a paralegal with a four-year degree. Finally, law firms might have more confidence in hiring a professional who has devoted the time, money, and effort required to complete the degree.

The college major usually is not of overriding importance. Any four-year liberal arts degree is likely to be favored, and technical degrees are highly valued. Degrees in business administration, accounting, and criminology can find direct application in business law, bankruptcy, and criminal law practices, respectively. Even a degree in drama, astronomy, or archeology will usually give a neophyte paralegal a significant advantage over novices without a four-year degree.

On-the-Job Training for a Paralegal Career

On-the-job training remains a viable option for some candidates, particularly those with four-year degrees. In fact, with fully trained paralegals already in the law firm, most of the essential instruction can be provided by them rather than by attorneys, which makes the training process more flexible and economical. The advantages of this method are that a law firm can train the new paralegal "its way," and the trainee might be a candidate who has already proved herself to the firm in some other capacity, such as legal secretary or word processor. On-the-job training can be supplemented by a few evening courses in a paralegal education program, without taking the entire curriculum required for graduation or a certificate. In reality, a large portion of paralegals who have trained primarily on-the-job choose to take paralegal courses, and many decide to obtain a degree or certificate. They do this to broaden their knowledge of substantive law, sharpen their skills, increase their employment options, and improve their bargaining leverage. Law firms sometimes pay a valued employee's tuition for paralegal courses.

> **Practice Tip**
>
> *Every paralegal student should consider joining a local paralegal association to establish contacts with working legal assistants—all of whom will be potential sources for job information.*

Finding That First Paralegal Position

According to paralegal association surveys from around the nation, the members responding usually found their *first* paralegal position through school placement offices, newspaper ads, or by "broadcasting" their resume and cover letter.

There has been a remarkable growth in the number of paralegal programs offered by universities, colleges, and trade schools, and a corresponding growth in the enrollment of paralegal students. More than 600 programs have been identified by the ABA. One result is that significant competition exists in some areas for the entry-level paralegal positions, especially during periods of slow economic growth.

A QUESTION OF ETHICS

Lynnette Blackwelder is a new legal assistant with less than six months of experience. Her supervising attorney has a somewhat brusque manner that Lynette finds rather intimidating. Being very busy, he tends to give rapid instructions and appears impatient with any questions Lynette poses.

Lynette has been working most of the day drafting a memorandum summarizing a court opinion, when a chance comment by another paralegal causes her to realize she has misunderstood the attorney's instructions. Most of what she has written will have to be redone. Realizing that the client is being billed by the hour for her time, should she:

- Delete the unproductive time from her time sheet, so that the client will not be charged?
- Inform the attorney about her mistake and get instructions about the unproductive time she has recorded?
- Leave the time sheet unchanged, but not record any time required for her to redo the memorandum?
- Leave the time sheet unchanged, and record also the time required for revisions?

Chapter Summary

- Paralegals (or legal assistants) are nonlawyers trained to perform some legal tasks under the supervision of an attorney, but who are not licensed to practice law.
- The responsibilities of paralegals overlap the job descriptions of legal secretaries and attorneys.
- The rising cost of legal services, public demand for access to affordable legal services, the extraordinary numbers of attorneys, and the intense competition for clients have caused the legal profession to look for ways to cut the cost of legal services.
- Legal assistants provide a way to reduce legal fees and, at the same time, provide a new source of profits for law firms.
- Legal assistants relieve attorneys of the more routine tasks in the practice of law, while making it possible for the attorney to take on additional client matters.
- The American Bar Association (ABA) encourages the use of legal assistants, provided they are properly supervised by lawyers, who are responsible for their conduct.
- Although most legal assistants work in law firms—and the majority of those practice in litigation—there is a broad range of career opportunities for paralegals in other legal specialties.
- Some government agencies permit non-attorneys to represent clients before quasi-judicial boards or commissions.
- Career changers bring special knowledge and skills, as well as maturity, to their role as paralegals—a distinct advantage in landing their first job as a legal assistant.
- Although the U.S. Labor Department considers paralegals to be "non-exempt" employees entitled to overtime pay, it is a controversial issue and many law firms do not pay overtime to paralegals.
- Key skills for paralegals include communication, critical thinking, research, interpersonal relations, computer operations, organization, and summarization.
- Key traits for paralegals include integrity, attention to detail, flexibility, assertiveness, and cooperation.
- Although on-the-job training can qualify one to be a legal assistant, the great majority of new paralegals are graduates of formal legal assistant training programs.

KEY TERMS

(See the Glossary for definitions.)

401(k) plan	fiduciary duty	small claims court
American Bar Association	legal assistant	substantive law
billable quota	legal technician	summer associate
civil litigation	litigation	unauthorized practice of law
exempt employee	malpractice	unlawful detainer
Fair Labor Standard Act	paralegal	

ACTIVITIES AND ASSIGNMENTS

1. Conduct brief interviews with five individuals who are employed (or are students) *outside the field of law*. Try to interview people from a variety of career fields and educational levels. Ask the following questions:
   - What is a "paralegal"?
   - What do paralegals do?
   - Where do paralegals work?

   When appropriate, at the end of the interview explain to the interviewee what a paralegal is.

   After you have completed all five interviews, prepare a summary showing the ability of the interview subjects to provide reasonably accurate answers for each question. Also, identify any misconceptions discovered during your interviews.

2. Chapter 1 presents various definitions for "paralegal" or "legal assistant," adopted by three different organizations in the legal field: the American Bar Association, the National Association of Legal Assistants, and the National Federation of Paralegal Associations. (The ABA definition appears on the very first page of the chapter.)

   Compare the three definitions in the areas of:
   - how one becomes qualified to be a paralegal (or legal assistant);
   - the duties or functions of a legal assistant;
   - the matter of supervision by an attorney; and,
   - where paralegals are employed.

3. Review the "help wanted" ads from the Sunday or Monday edition of the largest general circulation newspaper serving your community, or from a major city such as Seattle or Atlanta. As an alternative, review the job listings at state employment development offices (sometimes called "unemployment offices").

   Check under "paralegal," "legal," and "law." Prepare a tally comparing the *number* of paralegal positions with the number of legal secretary positions advertised. Then do the same for positions advertised in a legal newspaper serving your state or community. (Such a paper should be available in a law library, university library, or large public library.)

   Identify how many positions appear to be entry-level, and how many require at least one year of legal experience. Among the ads requiring *at least two years* of legal experience, what is the *average* amount of experience required?

4. Review at least twenty advertisements for paralegal positions that are found in a newspaper serving your community or region. (If possible, use a newspaper published for the legal community. You might have to continue your survey for a month or more, to find twenty different positions advertised.)
   - Prepare a distribution showing how many ads require no prior experience, how many require one year, etc.
   - Determine the percentage that require a four-year degree.
   - Determine the percentage that require a paralegal certificate.
   - Of those that require a certificate, determine the percentage that mention an "ABA-approved" certificate.

5. Using the sources described in Exercise 3, above, look for ads and job announcements for *non*legal positions *in which paralegal skills and knowledge would be valued*.

   Prepare a two-column chart with the ad or announcement summarized in the left column, and with corresponding skills or knowledge in the right column.

6. Prepare a chart with three columns. In the left column, list skills and personal characteristics that are important for success as a legal assistant.

(Your instructor might supplement those found in this text.) As you list those traits, leave some vertical space so that only three or four traits can fit on a single page.

In the middle column, make notations about your own strengths and weaknesses regarding those traits. Then, in the right column, identify ways that you can (1) improve upon your weaknesses, and (2) use to advantage your strengths (e.g., in job hunting or in choosing a paralegal specialty). If you are concerned that one or more deficiencies would be difficult to remedy and might prevent you from being successful as a paralegal, you might want to discuss that privately with your instructor.

7. Review your life experience, including education, employment, travel, family responsibilities, and so on. Identify several aspects that, although not directly related to the practice of law, might enhance your appeal to a prospective employer in the legal field. If you did not read the chapter's opening scenario about Jennie Rabine, do so before completing this exercise.

8. Review the discussion and "Case in Point" under the section, "One State Challenges Legal Self-Help Computer Program." The district court distinguished *Quicken Family Lawyer* from "a sample form book with instructions...," *possibly* implying that such a form book would not violate Texas's law on unlicensed practice of law. Call a bookstore or library to find a self-help legal publication by NOLO Press. If you locate one, compare its presentation in print to the interactive process the court attributes to *Quicken Family Lawyer*. Does the book appear to cross the line into the practice of law as the court said the software program did?

END NOTES

[1] http://www.abanet.org/legalassts/def98.html

[2] _____, *Random House Webster's College Dictionary* (New York, N.Y.: Random House, 1991).

[3] _____, *AAfPE 2000 Directory* (Atlanta, Ga.: American Association for Paralegal Education, 2000) p. A-2.

[4] U.S. Department of Labor, Bureau of Labor Statistics, *Occupational Outlook Quarterly,* Vol. 43, No. 4 (Winter 1999-2000).

[5] The generalizations in this paragraph are based upon a variety of recent surveys taken by paralegal periodicals and associations. In particular, see the *1999 Paralegal Compensation and Benefits Report* by the National Federation of Paralegal Associations, and the National Association of Legal Assistants' *2000 National Utilization and Compensation Survey Report.* The NALA report appears on that organization's Web site (http://www.nala.org). Instructions for obtaining the NFPA report can be found on its Web site (http://www.paralegals.org).

[6] _____, *2000 National Utilization and Compensation Survey Report* (National Association of Legal Assistants, 2000).

[7] _____, *1999 NFPA Paralegal Compensation and Benefits Report* (National Federation of Paralegal Associations, 1999).

[8] _____, *AAfPE 2000 Directory* (Atlanta, Ga.: American Association for Paralegal Education, 2000), p. A-2.

[9] _____, *How to Find a Job as a Legal Assistant* (Legal Assistant Management Association [undated]), http://lamanet.org.

CHAPTER 2

Careers in Law Firms and Beyond

Every calling is great when greatly pursued.

Oliver Wendell Holmes, Associate Justice of the U.S. Supreme Court (1902–1932)

This chapter introduces career options for legal assistants. Practice specialties are discussed, as well as the advantages of being a paralegal "generalist." In addition to traditional paralegal roles—in law firms and the legal departments of government agencies, corporations, and financial institutions—this chapter also discusses occupations outside of the legal field that offer interesting opportunities for paralegals.

After studying this chapter, the student should be able to answer these questions:

- How are law firms organized?
- How do legal assistants relate to other legal professionals?
- How do paralegals account for their time?
- What is a paralegal "specialist"?
- What is the special importance of litigation for *all* paralegals?
- Why are the talents and knowledge of paralegals so highly valued outside of the legal field?
- Where can paralegals apply their special skills in non-paralegal positions?
- Why is the "hidden" job market so important for legal assistants?
- How does the inexperienced paralegal tap into the hidden job market?
- How can the applicant obtain information about prospective employers?
- How can the applicant evaluate herself as a job-market "product"?
- How can the new legal assistant overcome the "*experienced only need apply*" barrier?

Scenario

Monday Morning at the Firm

It was a typical Monday morning at the firm. By nine o'clock, John, the office manager, was already an hour late—he probably had a late gig at the Coach House last night. Barbara, the receptionist, was fielding about three calls a minute from clients who had spent all weekend thinking about their legal matters and wondering what their attorney was going to do to make their problems go away.

I was trying to locate my "Things to Do List," which I *always* leave on my desk every Friday afternoon. That was serious, because "The List" is my indispensable link between the chaotic conclusion of one week and the opening turmoil of the next.

As I rustled through the papers on my desk, I could hear Barbara answering yet another phone call: "Smith Down Torres & Balthor, this is Barbara." She always said the firm name like that, without comma pauses.

Within thirty seconds, flat, I knew that a client wanted to speak to Laura... *now*. But Laura was not in the office that morning. So Barbara did the logical thing: she passed the call to Laura's secretary, Stephanie.

Stephanie's voice is always *so-o-o* smooth, yet completely professional. "I'm sorry, sir, but Ms. Nothom is due in court at 9:30, so she will not be in the office until noon, at the earliest." A long silence followed. Not a true silence, you understand, because Barbara and I could easily hear the client's muffled frustration—though not his words. And maybe just as well we couldn't. His tone didn't sound too happy.

There was something in Stephanie's expression and the way she held the receiver—about 6 inches from her ear—that suggested this wasn't her favorite way to start the day.

But then, Stephanie also did the logical thing: She politely put the client on hold, explaining that she would find someone who could help. O.K. so far, but that's when she turned toward me.

Now, I knew *exactly* what she had in mind. "No way, Stephanie—there's *no way* I'm taking that call. I can't even find The List."

"Forget your list, Paul, you've got to take this call. It's the chairman of the IBM Special Committee, and he's out of his mind about the article in today's *Wall Street Journal*... something about IBM accepting a buyout offer from a consortium of Japanese companies. Is that *possible?* Anyway, he says we've *got* to get a denial out immediately. You know I've been too busy with the Watergate thing to keep up with IBM, and you're the only one here, right now, who's up to speed on IBM."

That was true, of course. But I was *not* prepared for the chairman of the IBM Special Committee—especially so early on a Monday morning. I hadn't even found The List yet!

"*You* handle him, Stephanie. I'm just too busy getting ready for the Yeltsin deposition, and I have about a thousand cases to Shepardize this morning." That latter statement might have been a slight stretch on the truth, but then....

Stephanie smiled, but the look in her eyes was positively homicidal. It occurred to me that she wasn't very happy with me, at the moment. "*Oh, she'll get over it,*" I was thinking. But it was *at that very moment* that I recalled what was on

The List for Monday, and I realized *instantly* that I would desperately need Stephanie's help in updating the service list for the Notice of Hearing to 7,573 creditors in the ROXON bankruptcy. That mailing *had* to be out the door by the end of the day, or I'd be duck soup.

Calling upon all of my experience as a paralegal, I quickly reconsidered my situation. "Wait a minute, Stephanie, you're absolutely right. I'll take the chairman's call." After all, it *was* IBM.

"Too late, Paul. I told the chairman you were busy. And, boy, was *he* upset! Sorry." I noticed that Stephanie wasn't smiling, anymore. "By the way, I hope you're not expecting me to help with the ROXON mailing today. I'm *totally swamped*, and Jack will have my head if I don't get this deposition summarized. Sorry about that."

The migraine began as a tightening at the base of my skull.

* * * *

The bright flash penetrated my eyelids, rousing me from slumber. And as the thunder instantly exploded outside the window, I opened my eyes. The clock-radio showed 6:17 a.m.

"Thirteen minutes before the alarm. No need to rush things. Oh, yeah . . . there's a huge mailing to go out today. I'd better be in by 8:00, or I'll never get it done. Thank heavens for Stephanie, though—always the lifesaver."

"Now, what was that about . . . I was dreaming, wasn't I? Something about IBM and a Japanese buyout? And Watergate? What nonsense. Ohhh . . . feels like the start of a migraine . . . right at the base of my skull. What a way to start Monday morning. . . ." ■

SECTION 1. WORKING IN LAW FIRMS

Paul's little nightmare raises several questions: Where do legal assistants "fit" in a law firm, and how do they relate with the attorneys, office manager, legal secretaries, and support staff? Because their own success often depends upon the efforts and goodwill of so many others, how can legal assistants be sure of receiving that support?

Because every law office is unique, it is difficult to generalize about these relationships and the working environment of all paralegals. There is a world of difference, for example, between small firms and the very large firms in which there might be more than one hundred attorneys in a single branch office. And paralegals should keep in mind that their role is still being defined as law firms and paralegals continue to explore the range of responsibilities that can be assumed by non-attorneys.

HOW LAW FIRMS ARE ORGANIZED

Most law firms are either sole practitioners, partnerships, or professional corporations. A **sole practitioner** is one attorney who practices law alone and owns her entire practice. A **partnership** is an unincorporated law firm owned by two or more persons, each of whom shares in the profits and liabilities of that business. Although **partners** are not necessarily equal shareholders (e.g., three attorneys could own a firm in a 40/40/20 split), each partner is individually responsible for the *entire* liabilities of the partnership. The partners must agree on

An attorney who practices law alone and owns his entire law practice is called a **sole practitioner**.

A law **partnership** is a law practice owned jointly by two or more attorneys, each of whom shares in the firm's liabilities and net profits.

A **partner** owns a share of the law firm. Although the partner receives a proportionate share of the firm profits, each partner is responsible for the partnership's entire liabilities.

how the ownership interest is divided among themselves. Their respective shares might be determined by the capital they have invested in the firm, by the amount of client fees each has generated, by seniority in the firm, or any other criteria they agree upon. In the hypothetical 40/40/20 partnership, the division of any profits would be determined by those ownership shares. Thus, one partner would receive 20% of any profits, and the other two partners, 40% each.

Professional corporations are a special type of corporation established under state laws that permit medical doctors, accountants, attorneys, and some other professionals to practice as corporations. Professional corporations have tax advantages in some states, but their main advantage is to limit the individual liability of the attorneys or other professionals who own the professional corporation. Although creditors of a partnership or of a sole practitioner can go after the personal assets of the attorneys, creditors of a professional corporation cannot reach those personal assets and are limited to the assets of the corporation itself. In most states, even a single attorney/shareholder may incorporate her individual practice as a professional corporation.

> A law firm organized as a **professional corporation** under state law is owned by attorney shareholders.

However, the structure of law firms can be much more complex than this brief summary suggests. For example, in some law partnerships all of the partners are individual attorneys—perhaps former sole practitioners who formed a partnership without first creating any professional corporations. But other law firms are partnerships in which *some* partners are individuals, while *other* partners are individuals as professional corporations. And some professional corporations are.... Well, suffice it to say that a law firm's structure can be quite complicated. (More about this in Chapter 11.)

FIRST, THERE WERE LAWYERS AND APPRENTICES

Long ago, before the modern law firm and corporate legal office, all lawyers were sole practitioners—although the earlier ones probably weren't familiar with that term. People *became* lawyers by "reading the law." That is, they read the few published decisions of courts and the writings of legal scholars on the common legal problems of the day (e.g., inheritance rights, land disputes, and oral contracts). The word "lawyer" meant one who made a living by the law, much as "sawyer" meant someone who made a living by sawing wood.

The most articulate person in a community—who also could read and write—was a likely prospect to become a lawyer. Lawyers helped folks write their wills, draft contracts, and settle disputes. A few became judges, and other lawyers would argue their clients' cases before them. Young men aspiring to become lawyers first became apprentices, reading the law in the office of a practicing lawyer. Abraham Lincoln became a lawyer in that way.

The Organized Bar and State Regulation of Lawyers

Eventually, it became apparent that some kind of formal qualification was needed to ensure the competency of lawyers. Ethical standards were needed, also, to protect the public and preserve the integrity of the justice system. The development of professional and ethical standards varied from region to region, but key players included the courts, bar associations, and state legislatures.

> A **bar association** is an organized group of lawyers. The only bar associations with official legal standing are the state bar associations. In most states, an attorney must be a dues-paying member of the state bar in order to practice law.

Judges regulated lawyers by controlling the proceedings in court and disciplining those appearing before them; court rules continue to be an important form of regulation of the practice of law today. Lawyers organized themselves into **bar associations** that established ethical standards and lobbied the state legislatures for laws regulating the qualifications of lawyers. The legislatures enacted laws that established minimum qualifications and often authorized the courts and/or bar associations to establish ethical standards and disciplinary procedures for lawyers practicing in that state. Today's ethical standards and the disciplinary procedures used to enforce them are discussed in Chapter 3.

Becoming a Lawyer Today

To become an attorney today, one must be "admitted to the bar." The word "bar" originally referred to the low railing that separates the spectators' section from the front of the courtroom where the judge, court clerk, and attorneys participate in court proceedings. Today, it is used to mean the bar association and/or the lawful practice of law.

Admission to the bar requires that a qualified candidate pass the state bar examination. The written examinations generally last one to three days. Each state determines who will be permitted to sit for the bar examination in that state. Most states require graduation from a post-graduate law school, usually equivalent to three years of full-time study. Other common qualifications include legal residency, a minimum age, and no convictions for serious crimes.

Upon passing the bar examination and taking an oath of office, the successful candidate is admitted to the bar of that state. Admission to the bar usually entitles one to practice before any court of that state. It is not unusual for an attorney to be admitted to the bar in more than one state. To appear in federal courts, however, the attorney must be admitted to the federal court in which he desires to practice. Admission to the federal bar does not involve an examination process; generally, the applicant simply needs to be a member in good standing of the bar in his own state.

"WHO'S WHO" IN TODAY'S LAW FIRM

Unless a law firm is a sole practitioner, lawyers in a firm generally fall into two basic categories: (1) partners and (2) associates. (Even in a professional law corporation, the attorney/shareholders often are informally referred to as "partners.") Unlike partners, **associate attorneys** do not have an ownership interest in the firm. Instead, an associate attorney is essentially an employee of the firm, just as paralegals are, and receives a straight salary. In large firms, associate attorneys are often assigned to work under the supervision of a particular partner, often doing the "grunt work" on the partner's cases.

Some law firms have an attorney who is "of counsel" to the firm. This term has several usages, but generally an attorney **of counsel** is a part-time consultant to the firm. Senior partners sometimes assume this status in semiretirement. It is not unusual for retired judges to join a prestigious law firm on an "of counsel" basis. The attorney of counsel might take on some legal matters as the primary attorney on the case, but more often assists the responsible attorneys on questions of legal analysis and strategy.

In most law partnerships, one senior partner is designated the "managing partner." Depending upon the firm, the **managing partner** might have virtual *carte blanche* in the management of the firm: establishing client priorities, setting employment policies, and determining which associate attorneys will be promoted to partnership status. Unless the other partners mount a small rebellion, the managing partner's wishes govern that firm. More frequently, however, the managing partner has only limited authority: For example, she may hire and fire support staff and otherwise manage the firm's routine business operations (as opposed to its practice of law). In the latter case, there often is a management committee composed of senior partners that sets firm policy, hires new associate attorneys, and promotes associates to partnership status.

An **associate attorney** is an employee of the law firm and does not have any ownership interest in the practice. An associate receives a salary, and possibly an annual bonus, but does not receive a share of the firm's profits.

An attorney who is **of counsel** to a law firm usually serves as a part-time consultant on legal analysis and strategy, although she might also be the primary attorney on some client matters. Semiretired partners of the firm and retired judges often have this status.

A law firm's **managing partner** coordinates the day-to-day operations of the firm and often has authority to hire and fire support staff and (possibly) associate attorneys.

Positive Working Relationships in the Law Firm

The paralegal's relationship with attorneys and the firm's support staff is key to her professional success and personal job satisfaction. If she cannot gain the confidence and respect of attorneys, she will suffer on both counts. The following paragraphs offer suggestions for establishing a professional reputation with attorneys.

Mistakes and missed deadlines can be devastating in the practice of law. The opportunities for legal malpractice abound. That is why attorneys are sometimes cautious when using new legal assistants. When a legal assistant conducts a field investigation, the attorney cannot be absolutely certain that it is has been thoroughly completed unless the attorney tags along. When a paralegal researches some legal issue, the attorney is relying on that paralegal's thoroughness and her ability to understand both the issue and the legal sources she studies. It is only natural that paralegals will not be given the more sophisticated assignments until they have earned the confidence of the attorneys with whom they work.

The legal assistant who demonstrates consistent punctuality, reliability, and accuracy will earn the respect and trust of attorneys. The legal assistant who asks for clarification demonstrates that she will not attempt to muddle through an important assignment that she does not really understand.

Unless one has total recall *and* a fail-safe system to prevent errors, in all probability he eventually will make a significant mistake affecting the interests of a client. That is a devastating experience for a conscientious legal assistant. The value of *acknowledging* the error promptly is illustrated by a common method for repairing the damage: As a professional courtesy, many attorneys will forgive a minor deadline missed by the opposing party and then expect similar professional courtesy in return. Equally important, taking the initiative to report one's own mistakes actually increases one's credibility with the supervising attorneys. Attorneys will place more confidence in a paralegal who demonstrates loyalty by informing the attorney of his own errors and who shows maturity by accepting responsibility for his mistakes. Keeping guilty secrets is a sure way to lose credibility.

> ### *Practice Tip*
> *When a serious mistake is made, the wise paralegal promptly informs the attorney responsible for that client's legal matter. It might be possible to rectify the mistake. But if it is not, being forewarned, the attorney can avoid being caught unaware later (perhaps even in court—the ultimate embarrassment). By reporting the problem promptly, the paralegal lessens the likelihood of a malpractice suit. It might also save the paralegal's own job.*

> ### Ethics Watch
> If a legal assistant tries to conceal a significant mistake affecting the interests of a client, the attorney's fiduciary duty of loyalty to that client has been compromised. Although the legal assistant has no direct fiduciary duty to the client, he does have a fiduciary duty to his own employer, the attorney. A breach of the latter duty is grounds for dismissal.

Working Effectively with Secretaries and Support Staff

Although it is important to have good working relations with all firm employees, legal secretaries deserve special mention. With a bit of exaggeration, it can be said that legal secretaries are to law firms as first sergeants are to military units. Simply put, they make the organization function as it should. The attorneys and military officers are *officially* in charge, but the legal secretaries and first sergeants are those who really make things run smoothly. Woe to the new associate attorney or brash second lieutenant who gets started on the wrong foot!

What does this suggest for new paralegals? Well, they might have crisp new paralegal certificates or degrees, but that is not likely to impress a legal secretary with ten or fifteen years of experience who knows far more about the hands-on practice of law than any new attorney right out of law school. The bottom line is this: Paralegals—especially new paralegals—should treat legal secretaries with the utmost respect. Any legal assistant who goes into a law firm and tries to impress the secretaries with his profound legal knowledge is headed for trouble. Neophyte legal assistants should accept their own inexperience and not hesitate to ask legal secretaries for guidance. A talented legal secretary can be an invaluable colleague.

Of course, a paralegal should also receive the respect of legal secretaries. Completing a paralegal program requires a great deal of work, expense, and intellectual skill, and that accomplishment deserves recognition. If the law firm provides secretarial support for legal assistants, there should be no reluctance on the part of the secretaries to provide that support. The best safeguard against any problems is an attitude of *mutual* respect and an *appropriate* level of self-confidence.

The dividing line between paralegals and legal secretaries often is one of title and duties. But that line can be rather fuzzy. In theory, paralegals do not address envelopes and legal secretaries do not do legal research. In practice, sometimes both do both. It all depends on the law firm and the priorities on a given day.

SMALL FIRMS AND LARGE FIRMS

The subheading above would imply that all law offices fall into only two categories, with regard to size. But, of course, that would be an artificial and not-very-useful perspective. For the legal assistant, the significance of firm size lies in such qualities as the following:

- opportunities for challenging and varied assignments
- opportunities to become a specialist or generalist
- opportunities for advancement
- support staff services available to the legal assistant

Of course, the smallest firm is a sole practitioner. But the "small firm" label is sometimes applied to any office with fewer than fifteen attorneys. "Mid-sized firms" might have between fifteen and, perhaps, fifty attorneys. Everything else is usually described as a "large firm." The *very* largest firms number their attorneys in the hundreds—perhaps even a thousand or more. But these numbers are rather arbitrary, really, because there is no magically defining difference between firms with fifteen or twenty attorneys or those with between fifty and eighty.

In smaller firms, legal assistants are usually responsible directly to attorneys, and the support staff—the legal secretaries, word processors, receptionists, and so on—are supervised by the office manager. Larger firms with many legal assistants usually designate one of them to act as "paralegal coordinator," or "legal assistant manager." Legal assistant managers assist in the hiring of new legal assistants, coordinate assignments and work loads, and serve as mentors for those with less experience.

The paralegal role tends to be more clearly defined (some might say more restricted) in many larger law offices. Another way of stating that might be to say that small firms expect paralegals to take on a wider range of responsibilities—including clerical tasks, at times—than do large offices. And although it is the exception for a large-firm paralegal to do extensive legal research, smaller firms are sometimes more inclined to give legal research assignments to paralegals. Large-firm paralegals have greater opportunities to specialize in a particular practice area (e.g., real estate transactions) than do paralegals in small firms that practice in many different areas of the law.

Another significant difference between larger and smaller firms is the amount of support staff services that the legal assistant can call upon. The larger the firm, the greater the support services available to the legal assistant. Larger firms are more likely to have the latest equipment and technology, as well. Legal assistants in smaller firms might have to do more things "the old-fashioned way," simply because the firm cannot afford the latest technology.

Finally, large firms sometimes provide more perquisites: tuition for continuing legal education courses, 401(k) savings plans, and in-house training. Paralegals in smaller firms, however, may prefer the more personal working environment, variety of assignments, and greater responsibility. For the paralegal, the preference regarding firm size is a personal and professional one.

REALIZING THE LEGAL ASSISTANT'S FULL POTENTIAL

Working as a legal assistant is especially challenging and rewarding when one receives assignments that go beyond those traditionally given to non-attorney assistants. It also makes economic sense for clients, because it reduces the cost of those services, and in the long run it will allow law firms to bill paralegal time at higher rates. As more clients—especially corporate clients—learn about paralegals and appreciate their value, they look for firms that "keep a lid" on legal fees by increasing their use of legal assistants. The assignment of sophisticated tasks to paralegals simply multiplies the advantages already discussed in Chapter 1, including the ability of attorneys to take on additional client matters. The goal, then, is to find ways to make even better use of the talents of paralegals.

When an attorney is busy, a paralegal can volunteer to draft a piece of correspondence or a memorandum. If an attorney gives the paralegal a modest research assignment (e.g., "Find me some cases about 'excusable delay'. . ."), the paralegal can work late that evening and draft an outline of the case law he has found on the subject. The paralegal can demonstrate analytical ability by becoming thoroughly familiar with the facts and legal issues in a case, and then asking how the attorney intends to handle a difficult legal problem.

As suggested in the preceding paragraph, initiative can go a long way toward gaining more challenging assignments. But initiative in seeking better assignments might not be enough. Paralegals need to gradually gain the trust and confidence of attorneys, so that the latter appreciate the similarities paralegals share as legal professionals, rather than focusing on their differences as non-attorneys. If paralegals appear to "walk, talk, and think" somewhat as attorneys—demonstrating analytical ability and knowledge of the law—*without any air of false self-importance*, attorneys will be more accepting of them as professionals. The importance of tact in these efforts cannot be overemphasized.

Part of the solution is professional dress, grooming, speech, and manners. Reading and listening with care will help legal assistants to participate intelligently in office discussions or lunch time sessions about current legal issues. Paralegal periodicals, such as *Legal Assistant Today* and the publications of the NALA and the NFPA, can keep a legal assistant current on developments in the profession. Reading the weekly newspaper *National Law Journal* and the local legal press can broaden the legal assistant's knowledge of the law and of developing trends in the practice of law. None of these efforts will earn one professional respect, however, unless the legal assistant consistently produces top quality work.

Avoiding Glass Ceilings

In law firms, glass ceilings—if they occur at all—usually operate in this fashion: The firm fails to recognize a paralegal's ability to take on sophisticated assign-

> **Practice Tip**
>
> *As part of a self-improvement program, one can arrange with an attorney to borrow each issue of the* American Bar Association Journal *when she has finished reading it. The periodicals of state bar associations are often equally informative. The legal assistant can photocopy for his own files those articles that will be helpful in honing his abilities or advancing his career. He must be sure to return all issues promptly!*

ments, either based upon the firm's perception of *that individual's capabilities* or upon the firm's view of *the paralegal role*. Most glass ceilings can be avoided (or their effects diminished) by careful career planning. The diamond glass-cutters will be the paralegal's credentials, his demonstrated abilities, and careful evaluation of potential employers.

Persuading an employer of the legal assistant's full capabilities starts even before she is hired. Because first impressions can be so lasting, she wants the law firm to believe *from the beginning* that she can grow into the most challenging assignments possible. Her resume, cover letter, and interview must create a strong impression of maturity, intelligence, resourcefulness, and thorough preparation for the job. If the new legal assistant lacks extensive professional work experience, her degrees and certificates become doubly important.

Paralegals must make sure that they have made the most of their opportunities to get a solid paralegal education. Advanced courses in writing, legal research, litigation, and any appropriate practice specialties (e.g., probate or bankruptcy) can be very helpful. By enrolling in continuing education courses for paralegals, the paralegal sends a message to his employer that he is ready for professional growth.

Once hired, the quality of work obviously is a critical factor. But the early assignments might not provide the legal assistant opportunity to really show her talents. After all, the new legal assistant will always go through a proving period before the attorneys become confident of her abilities. But after a reasonable period the legal assistant might need to suggest that she could take on more challenging tasks: "I've noticed that you've been unusually busy recently, why don't you let me draft the responses to those interrogatories?" Of course, if she has been drafting interrogatory responses already, she might need to suggest researching a pending legal question, or some other task. Knowing when to become more assertive can require a delicate sense of judgment.

Paralegal Specialties

Just as some attorneys and medical doctors are generalists while others specialize, some paralegals work in a "general" practice and others in a specialty practice. The general practice of law usually encompasses civil litigation, business law, and real estate law. In smaller communities, family law, criminal law, probate, and bankruptcy might also be part of a general law practice. A legal assistant can specialize in any one of those components of a general practice, provided that sufficient work is available. But some paralegals specialize in other areas of law rarely seen in a general practice (e.g., patents and copyrights). The many legal specialties span a broad spectrum, from criminal law to entertainment law, and from labor law to corporate mergers and acquisitions. But, those latter four specialties employ only a small fraction of all paralegals.

By the very nature of his practice, a generalist has more variety in his work. On the other hand, a specialist might have the opportunity to learn more of the substantive law of her specialty, and more quickly becomes an expert in the procedures of a single field. Although a few specialties such as personal injury and worker's compensation offer many job opportunities, a generalist usually finds more job openings for which he can apply. Naturally, a legal assistant working for a nonspecialist sole practitioner cannot practice as a specialist herself. In fact, a legal assistant in a sole practitioner's office might be a *receptionist secretary file clerk paralegal* combination.

If non-attorney legal technicians are eventually licensed to offer legal services directly to the public, the paralegal specialist might be in an excellent position to qualify. The most promising specialties for legal technicians are those that are most frequently needed by the general public and that do not require *in every case* the full expertise of an attorney: family law, bankruptcy, unlawful detainer, wills and probate, collections, worker compensation, patents and copyrights, and so on. But some specialties have virtually no chance for legal technician authorization because their complexity will require the training of an attorney in almost every case: antitrust law, environmental law, corporate mergers and acquisitions, product liability, and so forth.

Litigation: The Predominate Specialty

Litigation predominates as a specialty because American society is so remarkably litigious, and because legal assistants are able to do so much of the preparation for trial. Although paralegals sometimes assist in court—taking notes, managing exhibits, and offering feedback on the progress of the trial—courtroom assistance is a very small fraction of the work most litigation paralegals do. The vast majority of the work is done in the law firm or law library, and occasionally in the offices of clients.

Although *insurance defense* cases can become large-scale, complex litigation (as in the asbestos cases), the less complex insurance cases are far more numerous. Some paralegals are employed in the legal departments of insurance companies, but most insurance litigation paralegals work in law firms that represent insurance companies. Insurance litigation involves such issues as personal injury, wrongful death, construction defects, professional malpractice, product liability, and environmental pollution.

Legal assistants with a medical background are especially valued in insurance defense and personal injury plaintiff firms. The *personal injury* plaintiff firms (sometimes termed "PI firms") represent the injured person and usually work under contingency fee arrangements. Personal injury paralegals interview clients and witnesses, and some eventually specialize in field investigations. Many personal injury law firms handle a very high volume of uncomplicated matters, such as "slip-and-fall" cases. Because very few of those cases actually go to trial, personal injury law firms occasionally have more paralegals than attorneys, and the paralegals might do the great majority of the legal work on an uncomplicated case. Some firms even train senior paralegals to negotiate out-of-court settlements under attorney supervision, where that is not prohibited by state law or bar association rules. In some states, paralegals also represent injured employees before worker compensation hearing officers.

Opportunities in Paralegal Management

As noted earlier, larger law firms often have a paralegal manager or coordinator who is responsible for recruiting, training, and supervising other paralegals. She might coordinate the paralegal work assignments, especially in firms where individual legal assistants are not regularly assigned to work directly with specific attorneys. Mid-sized firms might not need a full-time paralegal manager, in which case she will spend part of her time on regular paralegal assignments or in supervising the non-paralegal support staff.

The paralegal manager might prepare job descriptions, screen resumes, and interview paralegal applicants. She will train inexperienced legal assistants who have recently graduated from a paralegal program, orient experienced legal assistants to the firm, and coordinate on-the-job training for legal secretaries upgrading to legal assistant status. She might be responsible for training attorneys and paralegals in the techniques of computer-based legal research. In some firms, the paralegal manager is responsible for the performance evaluations of

---

Practice Tip

Although a practice in personal injury can place enormous responsibility on the shoulders of the legal assistant, it is an excellent way to learn the nuts and bolts of civil litigation. That is particularly true when the law firm handles a large volume of relatively simple cases, because the legal assistant will usually work on virtually every aspect of the case from the client's intake interview to collection of the judgment.

paralegals, in which case she might make recommendations for salaries and bonuses. Because of the responsibilities of her position, the paralegal manager's salary is usually higher than that received by senior legal assistants in the firm.

The Legal Assistant Management Association was organized in 1984 to support the role of legal assistant managers in law firms, corporate legal departments, and government agencies. It includes affiliated associations in various regions of the nation, sponsors conferences, and maintains a Web site.

Internet Access

Legal Assistant Management Association   http://www.lamanet.org

---

Teaching in Paralegal Education

Experienced legal assistants are needed to teach in paralegal education programs, because the perspective, responsibilities, and skills of a legal assistant are somewhat different from those of an attorney. Some paralegal programs have attorneys teach courses on substantive law (e.g., contract law and real estate law), and paralegals or attorney/paralegal teams teach paralegal procedures (e.g., in litigation or bankruptcy). Well-qualified legal assistants can teach legal research and writing, *for the needs of paralegal students*, just as well as can attorneys. As with any subject, teaching ability can be equally as important as subject matter knowledge. Most paralegal instructors teach courses on a part-time basis, but some institutions employ full-time instructors. One source of information about paralegal teaching is the Internet Web site for the American Association for Paralegal Education (AAfPE).

Internet Access

American Association for Paralegal Education   http://www.aafpe.org

---

Nonparalegal Positions in Law Firms

It never occurs to some paralegals that alternative careers (and perhaps higher salaries) can be found within law firms. But the knowledge and perspective of experienced legal assistants gives them a great advantage when applying for "nonlegal" positions within law firms. Two of the fastest-growing of these positions are computer systems manager and marketing director. Positions such as law firm librarian and legal administrator have been around much longer, and they too offer opportunities for the experienced paralegal to move into related, but nonparalegal, work.

Computer Systems Manager

Because of their inherent conservatism, law firms were among the last of all business enterprises to recognize and exploit the potential of personal computers. Initially, computers were used almost exclusively for word processing and accounting. Then came computerized legal research. But in the past decade, there has been dramatic growth in the application of computers to other aspects of the practice of law, particularly in litigation. Most of the new legal applications

A **systems manager** is a computer specialist who establishes and maintains the hardware and software needed for a computer system, usually including multiple computers connected by a local area network.

A **local area network (LAN)** is a combination of hardware and software that permits computers in the same office to share application software (e.g., word processing and accounting software) and to read and/or revise the same documents.

use computers to store and manipulate great quantities of text and data. A recent innovation has been computer simulation, used to demonstrate visually a sequence of events (e.g., an auto accident) before a jury.

This growth in computer applications has created a demand for **systems managers** who can set up, maintain, and troubleshoot various computer software and hardware systems. **Local area networks (LANs)**, which interconnect all computers within a firm and allow attorneys, paralegals, and other staff members to share the same software and work on the same documents, require a systems manager experienced with LAN software.

Paralegals with the requisite computer expertise make excellent candidates for law firm systems managers. They understand the requirements of law firms and will have experience with software that has been created specifically for the needs of law firms. Equally important, paralegals understand the law firm subculture (i.e., the values, traditions, jargon, and politics of the firm) and can work effectively with attorneys and other paralegals.

Marketing Director

Another law firm position that might be attractive to some paralegals is that of marketing director, which might carry a title such as "director of client relations." Just as law firms were slow to accept computers, so too were they reluctant to market their services. For many generations, attorneys believed that word-of-mouth publicity and an occasional game of golf or tennis with a prospective client were all that a "good firm" needed to attract business. Any marketing efforts beyond that were generally regarded as "unprofessional." In fact, until the U.S. Supreme Court decision in *Bates v. State of Arizona*, 433 U.S. 350 (1977), most states prohibited any form of advertising by attorneys. But the Supreme Court held in *Bates* that such laws violate the First Amendment rights of attorneys.

Media advertising by sole practitioners and small law partnerships is no longer unusual, but law firms that wish to be regarded as "prestigious" still shun most media advertising. Increasingly, however, even highly regarded firms are using more sophisticated efforts to gain new clients. Instead of paid media advertising, these firms use carefully designed brochures, client newsletters, free informative seminars, high-profile charitable works, and press releases to publicize their firm's expertise and gain wider recognition.

Because marketing can be so foreign to and discomforting for conservative attorneys in prestigious law firms—and because it detracts from their time to practice law—large firms usually rely upon the guidance of a marketing specialist. Many firms retain outside public relations firms to provide that guidance, but those relationships are sometimes unworkable. The values of the legal subculture are so different from those of the broader world of commerce that few public relations firms are able to adapt well to the special needs and desires of law firms. Increasingly, larger law firms are bringing specialists on board as full-time marketing directors. That arrangement provides them greater control of the marketing program and also facilitates communication between the firm's management and the marketing specialist.

Here again, paralegals with marketing expertise can have a great advantage over other candidates for the position. The reasons include easier communication and a better understanding of the practice of law and the legal subculture. Law firms that hire former paralegals to serve as marketing directors might experience less turnover, which has been a major problem with marketing specialists who have not come from a legal background.

Law Firm Librarian

Any law firm with fifty attorneys or more needs a librarian, or at least a part-time librarian. In the latter case, a legal assistant is an ideal candidate because she can handle regular paralegal assignments when her librarian duties permit. The librarian might train attorneys and paralegals in the use of computer services for legal research. A paralegal will have a much better understanding of the materials a law firm needs, and of how attorneys and paralegals use those materials, than would a librarian without legal experience.

Most large law firms require librarians to have a degree in library science, but an exception might be made for a paralegal wishing to make a lateral transfer within the firm. If the firm is large enough to support two full-time positions, a paralegal might have an excellent chance of obtaining the position of assistant librarian.

Legal Administrator

Under the supervision of the firm's managing partner, a legal administrator is generally responsible for the business side of a legal practice. Depending upon the firm and its size, the administrator will supervise non-attorney employees (perhaps including paralegals) and might be responsible for the accounting department. She might be the immediate supervisor of the systems manager, marketing director, and firm librarian, as well. Usually, the administrator is responsible for recruiting and training the personnel she supervises.

An experienced paralegal might become a legal administrator in a mid-sized firm. But large firms generally require an administrator with strong qualifications in personnel management, accounting and finance, computers, and business development. Of course, some paralegals have worked in one or more of those fields before becoming paralegals.

The Association of Legal Administrators was founded in 1971 to promote the professionalism and competence of legal administrators. The association has numerous local affiliate associations and a membership in excess of 9,000 as of this writing. It sponsors conferences and also maintains a Web site.

Internet Access
Association of Legal Administrators   http://www.alanet.org

Paralegals Working Outside of Law Firms

Although the vast majority of legal assistants work in law firms, there are attractive paralegal positions in corporate legal departments, financial institutions, real estate companies, and government agencies. These positions account for about 15% of all employed legal assistants.

Legal Assistants in Corporate Legal Departments

Legal assistants employed in corporations generally work in either litigation, corporate law, or contract law. Some corporate legal assistants also work in human resources, research and development, compliance with government regulations (including environmental law), and corporate taxation. Insurance companies and corporations that are at risk for **product liability** litigation (e.g, manufacturers of consumer power tools or motor vehicles) employ a substantial number of legal assistants. Usually, those legal assistants will work under the supervision of in-house legal counsel, although a few companies employ in-house paralegals to coordinate litigation matters with outside legal counsel. In the latter situation, the paralegal has less direct supervision by the corporation's outside attorney and might have more responsibility and independence than in a typical law firm or corporate legal department. Outside of law firms,

Product liability is the doctrine that the manufacturer and retailers of a product should be liable for any injuries that result from defects in the product.

A **billable hour** is 60 minutes of professional services for which clients are billed at a fixed hourly rate.

paralegals never have to worry about **billable hours** because their own employer is the only client. There is opportunity for specialization, and there might be opportunity to transfer laterally or vertically to nonparalegal positions.

SCENARIO

Eric Mizutani has worked for nine years in the legal department of a fast-food restaurant chain. From the beginning, a large part of his work involved leases for restaurant locations.

"When I started, I was working mostly with boilerplate language for a lease, inserting names, addresses, rental amounts, and so on. As I became more experienced, I began to draft different or additional lease clauses to meet the needs of our company or the landlord. Eventually, I began to accompany our in-house attorney when she negotiated the more difficult lease arrangements. That made it easier for me to draft the lease provisions, because I was part of the give-and-take that arrived at the terms of the deal."

Several years ago, Eric's company opened a regional office in the Midwest, and Eric was transferred to that office. There is no staff attorney in that office, so Eric handles all of the face-to-face negotiations with prospective landlords. "I discuss the situation with Margaret in advance—she's the in-house attorney I've always worked with—and consult with her as needed during negotiations. I always make clear to the landlord that the terms are subject to final review by our in-house counsel, although I have broad authority to reach a tentative agreement. After Margaret has given the O.K. for the terms, I draft the lease documents and e-mail them to her. When she and the landlord have both approved the documents, I sign them on behalf of the company. My title now is Regional Coordinator for Facilities. This transfer has given me a major promotion and a generous salary increase. I really enjoy having the increased responsibility and recognition. And it was my qualifications as a paralegal that opened this opportunity for me." ■

Some legal assistants find that corporate legal departments draw less rigid boundaries between the status and functions of attorneys and legal assistants. They report a tendency for legal assistants and attorneys to work as a team, sharing many of the same duties and responsibilities. This might occur because the attorney is not dealing with outside clients who need reassurance that their legal matters receive the constant attention of the most highly skilled legal professional. In a corporate setting, results are what counts, and the company's top management might be comfortable with a legal team in which the attorney plays the role of team leader without excluding the legal assistants from substantive roles. The structure and operation of a corporate legal department is discussed in Chapter 11.

Legal Assistants in Public Agencies

A wide range of public agencies employ paralegals. Some of these agencies serve as *law firms* for government. Examples include the following:

- U.S. Department of Justice
- state attorneys general
- state and county prosecutors
- state and county public defenders

- county counsels
- city attorneys

Working in these agencies is much like working in a law firm, except that the client is always a government entity. A county counsel's office, for example, would provide legal advice and representation to the county board of supervisors (i.e., the county's governing body), the health department, social services department, and other county government agencies—and possibly to school districts, water districts, and the like—that operate within the county.

Some government agencies have legal departments, but the practice of law is not the primary function of the agency. Representative examples include the following:

- U.S. Department of State
- U.S. Department of Labor
- U.S. Department of Defense
- Federal Aviation Administration
- Federal Communications Commission
- Federal Trade Commission
- state departments of education
- state motor vehicle departments
- state insurance commissioners
- county transportation departments
- county social welfare departments
- county education departments

In these agencies, the legal department serves functions similar to those of a corporation's own legal department. For example, the in-house counsel for the state motor vehicle department would advise and represent the department in most legal matters, coordinate with state legislators on pending legislation affecting that department, and review department publications that summarize or explain state motor vehicle laws.

Each of the military services has legal assistants—some civilian and some uniformed service personnel. In addition to the enforcement of military criminal law and discipline, military legal offices advise and represent military units in their dealings with private vendors. They also assist service members with a variety of personal legal matters, including wills, residential leases, registration of births in foreign nations, and other simple matters that relate to their military service.

FREELANCE PARALEGALS

Working as self-employed **independent contractors**, some legal assistants sell their services to law firms that do not need (or want) to employ full-time legal assistants. Because they work under the supervision of attorneys and do not provide legal services directly to the public, **freelance paralegals** never cross the line into the unauthorized practice of law. In fact, because most freelance paralegals have much less client contact than do in-house paralegals, there are fewer opportunities to inadvertently give legal advice.

In some regions, freelance paralegals are also known as "independent" paralegals. However, the latter term has different meanings in other regions. In some areas it has been used to describe self-styled "paralegals" who may lack any professional qualification but deliver legal services directly to the public without

An **independent contractor** is not an employee, but provides services to others on specific projects or assignments, and for a limited duration of time.

A self-employed **freelance paralegal** works as an independent contractor providing paralegal services, usually to a number of different attorneys.

any attorney supervision. On the other hand, NFPA uses the term to describe a *qualified professional paralegal* who provides legal services to the public. NFPA defines "independent paralegal (legal technician)" to mean: "[A] paralegal who provides services to clients in regard to a process in which the law is involved and for whose work no lawyer is accountable." To avoid confusion, this text does *not* use the term "independent paralegal." Instead, it uses the terms "non-attorney provider" to identify the unsupervised non-attorney providing legal services to the public and "legal technician" for the non-attorney that, in the future, might be authorized by law to provide services to the public and "freelance paralegal" for the paralegal who works as an independent contractor under attorney supervision.

Opportunities for freelance work are found wherever attorneys are willing to use freelance paralegals and where enough law firms exist to generate sufficient business. The first requirement is mentioned because attorneys in some smaller communities have not had the experience of using paralegals and might be apprehensive about doing so. Sole practitioner attorneys, for example, seldom need a full-time paralegal. Consequently, they often work with a secretary-receptionist, doing all the substantive legal work themselves. Although a freelance paralegal could offer a sole practitioner the same economic benefits that larger law firms derive from full-time paralegals, the attorney might be hesitant to depart from her usual way of practicing law.

Freelance paralegals control their own daily schedules and can adjust their workload by pursuing or turning down additional work. That very independence is one of the great attractions of freelance work. Other attractions of freelance work are the opportunity to work out of a home office and the income potential. A busy freelance paralegal billing at $40 per hour can easily gross in excess of $45,000 per year—and possibly much more. That is also a good value for her law firm "clients," because they are not paying for office space, equipment, or health benefits. And, because many law firms bill paralegal time at $75 or higher, there is plenty of room for a freelancer to bill at rates higher than $40 per hour.

On the negative side, there is no guarantee of steady work, and freelancers receive no employer-paid health insurance, vacation pay, or other benefits. Some regional paralegal associations, however, do offer medical, disability, and life insurance at group rates to their members. Most freelancers must also provide their own office space and equipment, and they must either work without secretarial help or employ a part-time secretary.

There also is a middle ground between the typical "8-to-5" law firm paralegal and the freelance paralegal. Some firms will accommodate a flexible schedule that allows a legal assistant to perform some tasks in the law firm and other tasks at home. This really is not a "freelance" arrangement, because the paralegal remains a full-time employee of a single law firm that allows her to telecommute part-time. Of course, this option is more often available to the paralegal who has demonstrated solid competency in the traditional office setting and now desires to have more flexibility. That experienced paralegal can draft documents and use **Westlaw** or **LEXIS-NEXIS** to perform legal research from her home computer just as effectively as she could in the office.

The Importance of Qualifying Experience

For obvious reasons, an attorney is usually unwilling to delegate important legal work to a freelance paralegal who has not established a strong reputation for his ability and professionalism. Consequently, *this is not a field that an inexperienced legal assistant can enter fresh out of paralegal school.* The typical freelance paralegal has worked for five or more years in law firms *before* attempting to "go freelance." Usually, he starts by doing additional part-time work (on a contract ba-

---

Practice Tip

Five or six small firms (i.e., having between one and ten attorneys each) in a community should be enough to keep a freelance legal assistant busy, even if one or two of the larger firms already employ full-time paralegals. But because so many law firms in small communities have had limited experience with paralegals, it often is easier to market freelance services to law firms in larger communities.

Westlaw and **LEXIS-NEXIS** are competing computerized information retrieval systems, from which attorneys and paralegals can locate and read statutes, court decisions, and a broad range of other materials that are useful in legal research. The two remote database systems are among the primary tools for computerized legal research.

sis) for the firm where he is currently employed, and perhaps for other firms where he is known. Through networking and marketing efforts, he gradually expands his circle of clients to include additional law firms. At some point, he leaves his regular paralegal employment so that he can build his freelance work into a full-time occupation. Some freelancers eventually employ additional legal assistants to help with the workload, and that can generate additional profits for the paralegal entrepreneur.

> **Ethics Watch**
>
> It is a conflict of interest for one law firm to represent opposing parties—even in unrelated legal matters. This conflict can arise from the mere fact that an attorney or paralegal once did legal work for one of the parties *while employed in a different law firm*. Law firms use systematic conflict checks to prevent this from happening. (Chapter 3 explains this problem more fully.)
>
> But the use of freelance paralegals can introduce new risks that a conflict will not be discovered until it is too late. Consequently, freelance paralegals must work very closely with their client firms to ensure that the system for checking conflicts is effective.

The Well-Equipped Home Office

The freelance paralegal's work can be electronically transmitted to the client law firm via facsimile or modem, and the attorney can then review the work and give instructions by telephone or facsimile for any necessary modifications. The minimum equipment needed for a freelance paralegal's home office would include a computer, laser printer, modem, scanner, facsimile machine, photocopy machine, and voice mail or a telephone answering service. Word processing software is an absolute essential for every paralegal practice. Depending upon the type of practice, other special computer software might be needed. The freelance paralegal will require a small legal library, principally for reference books, practice guides, and selected statutes.

Freelance Practice Specialties

The most promising fields for a freelance paralegal are those in which a substantial amount of work can be done by a paralegal without *direct* attorney supervision—especially those in which a careful review of the paralegal's *final product* will be adequate protection for the law firm's client. Such practice specialties include those listed earlier in the discussion of future legal technicians who might be licensed to provide services to the public: family law, bankruptcy, unlawful detainer, wills and probate, collections, worker compensation, patents, and copyrights. But because the freelance paralegal still works under the supervision of an attorney, he can also practice in additional, more complex areas that would be beyond the abilities of an unsupervised legal technician.

> *Practice Tip*
>
> *Like any new businessperson, the freelance paralegal needs a generous capital base to survive the first year or so. A freelance paralegal can minimize her start-up expenses if she can arrange to work in the offices of her clients, using their space, telephones, computers, and so forth. Under that arrangement, however, her billing rates would have to be lower than would be the case if she provided her own equipment and office space. Some freelancers operate out of their homes. This allows them to deduct business expenses for tax purposes, although IRS regulations on this point are quite strict.*

Scenario

Brenda Morrie has been working as a freelance paralegal since 1982. She specializes in creditors' claims in bankruptcy.

"What really got me to thinking about freelance work was the approaching birth of my first child. I wanted to stay home until she was ready for first grade.

However, my husband and I also wanted some source of additional income to save for her college education. So we agreed that I would give freelance work a twelve-month trial period. I sold the idea to the law firm where I worked, which wasn't too hard because it really wanted to keep me on.

"The firm hired an experienced bankruptcy temp for two months—the month before and the month after my due date. I spent the six months *before* my daughter's birth learning all I could about freelancing, and acquiring the hardware and software that I would need. Five weeks after my daughter's birth, I began working about four hours a day. The rest of my usual workload was absorbed by three other paralegals in the office. I worked on the assignments that were most suited to being done at home, and the others took the things that were most suited to being done at the office. Much of my initial work involved creditors' claims, and now I do that exclusively. My second child arrived in 1984, and that reduced the amount of work I could handle for awhile. But now both kids are in school, and I'm working around thirty hours per week.

"Reviewing creditor claims involves large quantities of documents. At first, my husband stopped by the law firm every afternoon on his way home from work, to pick up and drop off documents. But within a month we decided it was worth the expense to have UPS deliver both ways. I now work for five different law firms, which provides me with as much work as I want. I bill the firms at $50 an hour, which generates about $70,000 in gross income.

"My husband and I have incorporated the business, and I am paid a salary out of the corporation. The corporation also pays us rent for the den and the spare room that I turned into my offices, and it also pays for electricity and heating. After paying for supplies, equipment, deliveries, and so on, there is enough remaining to pay me a salary of $50,000, and the corporation is accumulating an annual surplus. We are thinking of using the surplus to rent office space and hire a part-time secretary and another paralegal or two, to expand our business. Whether we do, or not, will depend on the economy and the prospect of a growing clientele of bankruptcy attorneys. By the way, out of my salary I pay for a weekly housekeeper and a good deal of baby-sitting time, but I think the potential is there to make this a very lucrative living. And, I enjoy the independence and love being home when the kids are out of school." ■

NONPARALEGAL CAREERS FOR PARALEGALS

The above heading might appear to be an oxymoron, but in reality it is not. An extraordinary thing about legal expertise is that it has so many potential applications outside the field of law itself. Because every aspect of life involves legal issues in some way, many nonparalegal career opportunities exist for experienced paralegals. But please note that word, "experienced." It is the particular knowledge, skills, judgment, and sophistication that paralegals accumulate that provides them with such a unique and multitalented background. A better criticism of the above heading is that it implies that "paralegal" and "nonparalegal" careers are easily distinguished from each other. The fact is, however, that the paralegal profession is still evolving.

Without intending to take a position on the nature of the paralegal identity, this text has approached the topic from the perspective of the business community at large—those who might employ experienced paralegals in positions that do not carry the label of "paralegal" or "legal assistant."

An important caveat is in order: A paralegal certificate or degree *alone* is unlikely to open doors to the nonparalegal careers discussed in this chapter. But three to five years of paralegal experience, or other experience related to the field of interest, can be the key to those doors.

Alternative Career Fields for Paralegals

The following list is just a small sampling of the many occupations in which an experienced legal assistant can apply her legal knowledge and skills:

- contract negotiator and administrator
- legal nurse consultant
- insurance claims adjuster
- real estate property manager
- real property title insurance representative
- political campaign assistant
- legislative staff assistant
- lobbyist
- human resources and personnel manager
- labor-management relations representative
- corporate ombudsman
- mediator and arbitrator
- journalist

The Legal Assistant Management Association's Web site offers a guide entitled, *How to Find a Job as a Legal Assistant.* It comments upon the opportunities for paralegals to be found outside of the traditional paralegal role:

> As you conduct your job search, be creative! Look beyond the traditional law firm paralegal role. Many administrative positions in business and government involve the interpretation and application of legal principles, as well as the ability to write and perform research. This is where the real job growth in the profession is occurring. While these jobs may not be listed under "paralegal" in the want ads, their job functions and responsibilities clearly require a knowledge of the law, and the administrative and organizational skills paralegals are trained for. Today, almost every business is affected by some form of government regulator or policy. Survey the businesses in your area and target positions likely to benefit from your legal experience, interest in the law and abilities.[1]

Special Attributes Paralegals Bring to Other Occupations

Experienced legal assistants have a number of desirable attributes. Because of the demands of their work, experienced legal assistants tend to be exceptionally capable in these areas:

- attention to detail
- organization
- multiple, concurrent assignments
- summarization
- complex procedures
- research and planning

Although these strengths are found in other occupations, the paralegal combines them with her legal background—and perhaps with knowledge and skills from other education and professional backgrounds, as well. As important as the above attributes are, it is the legal perspective that really sets the experienced paralegal apart from others who have no legal background.

For one thing, paralegals know a good deal about working with attorneys, and because most businesses must retain outside legal counsel, that knowledge has useful application in a multitude of occupations in the world of commerce. Paralegals are in a better position than most people to understand an attorney's way of thinking, to appreciate her advice, and to anticipate questions that a client should be asking.

Although legal assistants are not competent to evaluate an attorney's legal advice, they will be among the first to realize that a second opinion should be obtained. Legal assistants can often spot "red flags"—indications that something is not right in an attorney-client relationship or can often notice that the attorney has misunderstood a question. Legal assistants more easily recognize subtle clues that are indicators of an attorney with exceptional professional integrity—and other clues that *might* suggest a lack of that integrity.

Paralegals often recognize legal implications that are not apparent to many people. For example, paralegals know that ordinary business correspondence—and even personal correspondence—can have enormous importance if a lawsuit ever occurs. When paralegals read outgoing correspondence, they often ask themselves: "How would this letter appear—and what difference might it make in the outcome—if we were involved in a lawsuit over this matter?"

From their experience with lawsuits, paralegals know—as few others do—the importance of a paper trail for establishing a history of events. They recognize the *type* of documents that typically begin to appear when someone is consciously building a paper trail in preparation for a lawsuit.

Legal assistants tend to be far more sensitive to the specific requirements of law. They know that it is not enough to have a "perfectly good reason" to discipline an employee for using too much sick leave, for example, if the law protects an employee's right to sick leave. They also know that selling something "as-is and without warranty" will not protect the seller if he has failed to disclose a defect he already knew about.

Legal assistants are familiar with legal vocabulary and know that many common words like "avoid" and "constructive" have special legal meanings that are very different from their ordinary meanings. They have learned the *importance* of words. Legal assistants read important documents—not just "legal" documents—*critically*, looking for hidden consequences.

Paralegals know the importance of logical analysis. They have been disciplined by the legal process to question their own view of things and to anticipate the opposing side's analysis. They also know that logical analysis does not help much if the facts of the case do not support their cause.

Every large business enterprise, nonprofit organization, and government agency needs people with the knowledge, skills, and *perspective* described in the preceding paragraphs. Of course, someone with a paralegal background is no substitute for an attorney, and that is a point that should be made crystal clear with any employer who is hiring an experienced paralegal because of his legal background. A legal assistant doesn't offer legal counsel "on the cheap"—but he *is* someone who might say, "We need to talk to our attorney about this," when others have not yet recognized that a significant legal question might exist.

Carving Out a Personal Job Niche

Some people set out to become paralegals, only to end up creating their own job opportunity outside the legal field. For example, a former high school teacher with a paralegal certificate might find employment in the county law library, where his teaching and legal research skills can be combined. Some county law libraries are crowded in the evenings and on weekends with paralegal students working on assignments. It might not occur to the chief librarian to hire a paralegal to answer their many questions, but the resourceful former teacher might be able to sell the chief librarian on the value of instituting that position.

Similarly, a paralegal with personnel experience might be able to persuade an employment agency to hire her as an account executive specializing in the needs of law firms. Paralegals with other professional experience will think of additional possibilities for using their paralegal training to carve their own niches.

A rapidly growing career field is that of the **legal nurse consultant.** These are registered nurses who also have legal training, a combination in great demand for medical malpractice, personal injury, and wrongful death practices. Some legal nurse consultants work as independent contractors, much like freelance paralegals. Others work full- or part-time for a single law firm.

Legal nurse consultants obtain their legal training in a variety of ways. Some pursue a formal course of studies and obtain a paralegal degree or certificate. Others take selected paralegal courses that will be most helpful in their consulting work. Some are hired by law firms based upon their medical training and then acquire legal skills and knowledge through on-the-job training. There is a national organization, the American Association of Legal Nurse Consultants, that offers an examination for certification as a Legal Nurse Consultant Certified (LNCC).

> A **legal nurse consultant** is a registered nurse who, after obtaining education or training in the law, serves as a medical consultant to attorneys.

Internet Access

American Association of Legal Nurse Consultants   http://www.aalnc.org

---

LEGAL TECHNICIANS—PROVIDING LEGAL SERVICES TO THE PUBLIC

As already discussed, some expect that a number of state legislatures might soon authorize the provision of limited legal services directly to the public by legal technicians working *without attorney supervision.* This is a very controversial issue within the paralegal profession. Some see it as the trend of the future, and others see it as a professional anathema. Regardless of what the state legislatures might do in the future, *at the present time* a paralegal would be treading upon very hazardous legal ground if she were to set herself up in business as a legal technician, without attorney supervision.

The great risk, of course, is that of civil and/or criminal penalties for the unauthorized practice of law. (The latter topic is discussed further in Chapter 3.) The practice of law is governed by state law, and the federal courts recognize and apply the standards and restrictions of the state in which they are situated, or of the state in which someone purportedly "practices" law. In the following "Case in Point," a federal bankruptcy court applies both federal and Idaho law to a situation in which a non-attorney has assisted a married couple in filing a bankruptcy petition. As it turned out, the bankruptcy petition was defective in its preparation, and the debtors ultimately retained legal counsel who then filed a satisfactory petition.

In this case, the United States Trustee (an officer of the U.S. Government) has filed a motion in the bankruptcy court, asking the court to review, and possibly deny, the fees that the unlicensed petition-preparer charged the debtors. For some unknown reason, the trustee did not petition the court to order the petition preparer to abandon his occupation (i.e., preparing bankruptcy petitions for future debtors)—as the court could have done under federal bankruptcy laws. The only remedy sought by the U.S. Trustee was surrender of the fees that the debtors had paid to the unlicensed petition preparer.

All statutory references (e.g., "§ 110(a)(1))" and "chapter 13") in the court's opinion are to the *U.S. Bankruptcy Code* (Title 11, U.S.C.). The *Bankruptcy Code* defines a "bankruptcy petition preparer" as one (other than an attorney or his employee) who, for a fee, prepares a document for submission to the bankruptcy court (11 U.S.C. § 110(a)(1)). In the following excerpts from the court's opinion, all footnotes have been omitted.

A Case in Point

In re Herbert and Nita Farness, Debtors

244 B.R. 464 (2000)

* * * *

Herbert and Nita Farness ("Debtors") contracted with L.D. Wees ("Wees") to prepare their chapter 13 petition, schedules, statement of financial affairs, and proposed chapter 13 plan which were filed on July 29, 1999. Wees is a "bankruptcy petition preparer" as defined by § 110(a)(1).

On August 27, 1999, the first meeting of creditors was held in the Debtors' case. Subsequently, on September 2, the United States Trustee ("UST") filed a motion to review the fees paid to Wees alleging that he had violated several provisions of § 110. Specifically, the UST contends that Wees provided incorrect information in the Debtors' statement of affairs . . . and engaged in the unauthorized practice of law. The UST's motion requests that, based on these violations, the Court should review the fees Wees charged for reasonableness or sanction him by denying them entirely.

On September 3, 1999, attorney Jake W. Peterson entered an appearance on the Debtors' behalf, and with his assistance, the Debtors proposed an amended chapter 13 plan, which was ultimately confirmed on October 21, 1999.

In 1994, Congress enacted § 110 of the Bankruptcy Code which sets standards for bankruptcy petition preparers, and provides penalties for the failure to meet such standards. [Citation omitted.] The House Report explained the rationale for § 110:

> Bankruptcy petition preparers not employed or supervised by any attorney have proliferated across the country. While it is permissible for a petition preparer to provide services solely limited to typing, far too many of them also attempt to provide legal advice and legal service to debtors. These preparers often lack the necessary legal training and ethics regulation to provide such services in an adequate and appropriate manner. These services may take unfair advantage of persons who are ignorant of their rights both inside and outside the bankruptcy system.

H.R. Rep. 103–384, 103rd Cong., 2nd Sess. at 40–41 (1994). [Additional citations omitted.] Thus, the statute's main purpose is to protect consumers from abuses by non-lawyer petition preparers. [Citation omitted.] The key to § 110 is that a petition preparer may provide typing services, but may not in the guise thereof advise debtors of their rights and options or otherwise engage in the practice of law. This Court in Mitchell [a prior case] recognized the distinction:

> Document preparers are not attorneys . . . The task to organize information and type it, is something that a trained legal secretary can do, no more and no less. A document preparer may not give legal advice . . . Consequently, a document preparer should be compensated in the same fashion, and in the same amount as a legal secretary.

[Citation omitted.]

By virtue of the express provisions of § 110, and case law construing and applying those provisions . . . petition preparers such as Wees are on notice of the limits of their authority, and the potential consequences should they transgress those limits.

* * * *

The UST contends that Wees is engaged in the unauthorized practice of law, as reflected by his conduct herein. Thus, the UST asserts that § 110 is violated. See § 110(i) & (j).

Section 110 does not specifically prohibit the unauthorized practice of law. But neither does it excuse what would otherwise be unauthorized practice. Section 110(k) provides:

> Nothing in this section shall be construed to permit activities that are otherwise prohibited by law, including rules and laws that prohibit the unauthorized practice of law.

* * * *

The Idaho Supreme Court has defined the practice of law as:

> [T]he doing or performing services in a court of justice, in any matter depending [sic] therein, throughout its various stages, and in conformity with the adopted rules of procedure. But in a larger sense, it includes legal advice and counsel, and the preparation of instruments and contracts by which legal rights are secured, although such matter may or may not be depending [sic] in a court.

[Citation omitted.]

The UST alleges that Wees engaged in the unauthorized practice of law by assisting the Debtors in making determinations concerning what should be set forth in the filing, specifically in determining and claiming exemptions and deciding how the plan would treat certain creditors. Wees denies these allegations.

At hearing Wees testified that he met with the Debtors twice and prepared their forms with their assistance. Wees contends that, at these meetings, he read the actual forms to the Debtors question by question, and recorded their responses in his computer. This information would then, through use of software, be entered automatically into all appropriate places on the schedules. Wees also provided the Debtors with a list of available exemptions and their applicable Idaho Code sections based on publications in his possession. He further assisted the Debtors in completing this District's model chapter 13 plan.

* * * *

Wees . . . engaged in the unauthorized practice of law. He is not saved by his use of preprinted bankruptcy forms or bankruptcy software which automatically placed the information he solicited from the Debtors into the appropriate schedule. Wees' approach requires debtors to rely on his judgment as to the forms required to successfully file and prosecute a bankruptcy case, his use of computer software to ensure that information is correctly disclosed, and his resources as to what exemptions were available and the legal authorities supporting those claims. . . .

* * * *

Additionally and importantly, the completion of the model chapter 13 plan requires a significant amount of legal judgment as to the proper classification and treatment of creditors. [Citation omitted.] There is essentially no way the plan can be prepared without providing legal advice. And, there is no evidence that here the Debtors made all relevant decisions about plan treatment of creditors on their own.

These services which Wees provided the Debtors clearly went beyond merely typing the Debtors' forms. Wees has performed tasks which necessitated the exercise of legal judgment. The Court finds that Wees has engaged in the unauthorized practice of law. . . .

* * * *

The Court . . . finds and concludes that the fee paid to Wees by the Debtors, under all the circumstances, is unreasonable and in excess of the value of services rendered, and the UST's motion in this regard GRANTED. The Court ORDERS that Wees pay $165.00 to the chapter 13 Trustee. § 110(h)(2).

* * * *

The Court finds and concludes that, in this case, Wees' conduct constitutes the unauthorized practice of law. However, inasmuch as the UST sought no relief under § 110(i) or § 110(j), the Court will not enter an injunction, nor refer the matter to the District Court.

In the preceding "Case in Point," the Bankruptcy Court also considered another, related issue. Wees, the unlicensed petition preparer, had advertised his services in the "yellow pages" as "Self-Help Legal Alternatives of Idaho." Section 110(f)(1) prohibits a bankruptcy petition preparer to use the word "legal" in any advertisement of his services. The bankruptcy court imposed a $500 statutory fine on Wees for this violation. In remarkable irony, Wees appeared without legal counsel and represented himself in the bankruptcy court's hearing.

SECTION 2. FINDING THE RIGHT JOB

Presumably, most paralegal students aspire to find jobs in this career field—although some might be developing legal knowledge and skills that they can apply in their present, nonparalegal occupations. Both aspirations are admirable and valid. This section, however, addresses primarily the first and larger group comprising those who soon will become job seekers in the field of law.

THE OPEN AND HIDDEN JOB MARKETS

It has become a cliché that the best jobs in many professional fields are found in the hidden, unadvertised job market. Paralegal associations across the country have surveyed their members regarding employment, salaries, responsibilities, benefits, and other perquisites. When asked how they learned about their current positions, about half of those responding usually said that they heard of the job opportunity through personal contacts. Because so many well-qualified paralegals respond to word-of-mouth news, law firms often feel no need to spend money for newspaper ads or employment agency fees.

With so few positions advertised, and with the clear preference for experienced paralegals, candidates without legal experience can face a daunting task. In some communities, the general circulation newspapers carry so few "position available" ads for paralegals that some neophytes begin to wonder where in the world the U.S. Labor Department got its data for the "dramatic growth" occurring in this career field. And most of the advertised positions require one to four years of experience. The reality is that both new and experienced paralegals must look beyond the "open" job market if they are to get a job quickly, or if they wish to have a choice among several desirable opportunities.

It is important to understand, however, that job turnover is rather high among paralegals. The Bureau of Labor Statistics estimates that an average of 24,000 existing paralegal positions (about 15% of the total) will become vacant *each year* between 1998 and 2008—not counting the new positions resulting from growth in this career field.[2] Although some legal assistants stay with one employer for ten years or more, it is common for others to change jobs every three or four years.

There are several reasons for this relatively high turnover rate. Large numbers of paralegals are entering the job market with new certificates or degrees, but without any legal experience. Although law firms generally prefer to hire an experienced paralegal who will need minimal training, the rapid growth of the paralegal field has kept the pool of unemployed *experienced* paralegals rather small at any given time. Law firms often must recruit paralegals currently employed in other firms if they are to find candidates with experience. That usually means a significant salary increase for the experienced paralegal. Thus, for many paralegals, job changes have become a common path to higher salaries.

Uncovering the Hidden Job Market

So, how does the paralegal student tap into that hidden job market? The answer is: through a lot of effort. This chapter will not reinvent the well-publicized techniques of networking, but that is not to denigrate them. Networking is not only valuable—in this career field it is essential. If a local paralegal association exists, the student should join it immediately. She should not wait until she has received her degree or certificate—*and she should attend meetings.* This will often open the door to the hidden, word-of-mouth job market.

Most paralegal associations offer a reduced rate for student memberships. Many associations publish job announcements in their monthly newsletters, and the authors of newsletter articles can be contacted to expand one's personal network. Paralegal students can obtain information about local associations by contacting these national organizations:

National Federation of Paralegal Associations
P.O. Box 33108
Kansas City, MO 64114
(816) 941-4000

National Association of Legal Assistants
1516 S. Boston, Suite 200
Tulsa, OK 74119
(918) 587-6828

Internet Access

National Federation of Paralegal Associations	http://www.paralegals.org
National Association of Legal Assistants	http://www.nala.org

Paralegal classmates can also begin getting together each month for lunch or dinner. If this habit is established while in school, it will be much easier to do this after graduation. Paralegals should view a commitment to networking as an essential, long-term investment in their careers.

USING THE LEGAL PRESS

Most large cities have a daily or weekly newspaper published for the legal community. There also is a national weekly newspaper, the *National Law Journal*, that carries ads for attorneys but only rarely does it include ads for paralegal positions. Knowing which firms are hiring attorneys, however, can be helpful to the paralegal's own job search. In most large cities, far more paralegal positions will be advertised in the legal newspaper than in all of the general circulation papers combined. Law firms know that the legal press is read by currently employed attorneys and paralegals, so that is where they usually put their advertising dollars.

In southern California, for example, there is only one regional general circulation newspaper, *The Los Angeles Times* (with a daily circulation in excess of one million). Yet, the far smaller *Los Angeles Daily Journal*—southern California's leading newspaper for the legal profession—carries more help-wanted ads for attorneys, legal secretaries, and paralegals *in one day's issue*, than does *The Los Angeles Times* in one month. For that reason, the *Daily Journal* is a prime source for advertised paralegal positions in all of southern California. *Figure 2–1* displays typical ads from one issue of the *Daily Journal.*

If a student is not familiar with the legal paper for her community, she should check with any large public library, the county law library, or the library of any law school. If the paper offers short-term subscriptions, she might want to pay for home delivery while she is actively job hunting. Law libraries, university libraries, and large public libraries usually subscribe to one or more legal newspapers. A review of advertised paralegal positions can provide the job hunter with a feel for the paralegal job market: employers' expectations, practice specialties in demand, and so on.

In checking the advertised positions, the job seeker should not necessarily limit himself to the "paralegal" or "legal assistant" categories. Firms advertising for new associate attorneys might need additional paralegals as well. But because of the extensive networking among paralegals, they might not believe it necessary to advertise those paralegal positions.

Reading the legal press is an excellent way to learn about law firms in the community. If the writer can mention something he has read about a prospective employer when writing to that firm, his letter will stand out. For this reason, it can be useful to keep a file of news clippings about law firm activities.

PLACEMENT OFFICES AND EMPLOYMENT AGENCIES

Some paralegal programs operate placement services, and a significant number of paralegals obtain their first jobs through those placement offices. Usually, one must be a student or graduate of that school in order to use its placement service. Placement offices sometimes charge a moderate fee to establish a placement file, which then is used to match one's qualifications with position announcements from employers.

Private employment agencies are used by many law firms. Some agencies specialize in serving law firms and might be able to direct an inexperienced paralegal to nonparalegal positions that can remedy any lack of law firm experience. However, it is important that the job candidate remember that her needs and the agency's needs might differ. A few, less professional, agencies might place job seekers in unsuitable positions just to collect their fees. By networking with other active legal assistants, the job seeker can learn which agencies are most professional and ethical.

One advantage of working with an agency is that the applicant often can obtain valuable information about the prospective employer prior to an interview. That can alert one to things to listen for, and it can be helpful in preparing questions to be asked at the appropriate time. An agency will also provide an objective evaluation of a candidate's resume and often will assist in making the resume more effective. The agency's placement fees are normally paid by the employer, *not* by the applicant.

FIGURE 2.1 Los Angeles Daily Journal

FRIDAY, FEBRUARY 26, 1999 • PAGE 17

Daily Journal Classifieds 213/229-5520 FAX 213/680-3682

RECEPTIONIST
Rapidly expanding Plaintiff's Litigation Firm seeks energetic receptionist, experience preferred. Bilingual strongly preferred. Computer and typing skills very helpful. Salary commensurate with experience. Fax resume and salary requirements to: **Mancini & Gallagher (818) 710-7193**

Employment Offered · Paralegal

Interim.
LEGAL PROFESSIONALS
Corporate Paralegals - 3-5 yrs. + experience
Litigation Paralegals - All levels of experience
Real Estate Paralegals - 5+ yrs. experience
Interested candidates - please fax resumes ASAP to **Denise Padden (213) 688-8723** or mail them to **700 S. Flower St., Suite 1050, Los Angeles, CA 90017.**

IMMIGRATION PARALEGAL
Busy immig. atty. needs paralegal for business related cases. Heavy contact w/corp., individual clients & gov't agencies. Req. degree, xlnt writing & computer skills. Near OC airport. Comp. sal. Fax resume/writing sample: 949-851-8954

LEGAL POSITION OFFERED
Estab. Estate Planning law firm seeks individual w/transactional exp.: preparation, review/editing of estate planning docs; WP 8.0 req. w/emphasis on application's merge feature (data/form transition). Non-lit. pos. Team atmosphere w/room for advancement. **Fax resumes: (818) 591-2718**

LITIGATION PARALEGALS
San Fernando Valley firm seeks top-flight, experienced Paralegals for major and challenging litigation. WP.8 and database experience required. **Please fax resume to (818) 345-0162**

LITIGATION PARALEGAL
Sherman Oaks firm seeks experienced business litigation paralegal. Knowledge of WP5.1, Windows and paralegal certificate are required. Fax resume and salary history to:
Barbara at (818) 501-0328

PARALEGAL
Litigation paralegal sought to manage large cases for West Los Angeles law firm. Prior environmental coverage experience a plus. Must have prior experience with large cases and sufficient computer knowledge including familiarity with databases and imaged documents. Send resume and salary history to: *P.O. Box #11213333*, Daily Journal, 915 E. First St., Los Angeles, CA 90012.

PARALEGAL
Redondo Beach firm seeks paralegal exp. in tort law. Xlnt. writing communication & organizational skills. Calendar exp helpful. Salary neg.
Fax resume & salary history to (310) 372-7715

PARALEGAL
Santa Monica firm w/6 atty. seeks paralegal with 3 years recent experience. WordPerfect 8.0 and Windows 95 a plus.
Fax resume to Christina: (310) 998-9109

PARALEGAL
Westside firm seeks experience (minimum 3 years) litigation paralegal. Experienced in construction litigation a plus.
Fax resume (310) 821-7828

PARALEGALS (2)
For 2 year period to complete data entry and corrections of estate managment system. Requires 5+ years experience, paralegal certificate, strong background in trust and California probate, proficient in MSWord/Excel. To 37K with benefits including paid vacation, medical, 10.5 holidays. Mail/Fax resume to: **The Salvation Army, 30840 Hawthorne Blvd., Rancho Palos Verdes, CA 90275: FAX (310)** *265-6533. EOE M/F/V.*

Copyright 1999, *Daily Journal Corp.* Reprinted with permission.

JOB SEARCHES ON THE INTERNET

As of this writing, there probably are not many legal assistants who have located their current positions by perusing job listings on the Internet. But, as technology advances and both employers and job seekers grow more sophisticated in using the Internet, that is likely to change. The number of Internet postings for attorney and paralegal positions is growing rapidly. The paralegal job seeker can use the Internet to locate openings, post his resume for potential employers to review, and locate information about (and often the Web sites of) potential employers.

The National Federation of Paralegal Associations offers a "Career Center" on its Web site that leads the viewer to job listings organized by state. The job postings provide basic information about the position and an address or a phone number for the employer. There is also a "Directory of Recruiters," and an "NFPA Referral Service" for those wanting to send information about themselves to paralegal recruiters. In addition, there is a "Paralegal Directory" of NFPA members, which potential employers can access.

The National Association of Legal Assistants' Web site provides its members with a link to *Lawmatch*, a resume bank and job posting site on the Internet. By accessing the site through NALA's own Web site, NALA members receive some free services and substantial discounts on other services. *Lawmatch* also incorporates job listings and resumes from numerous Web sites in the legal community, including the New York and Ohio state bar associations.

The Legal Assistant Management Association maintains a job bank on its Web site, with postings for legal assistants, as well as legal assistant managers. There is no charge for anyone to review the position announcements. The announcements typically provide information about the law office, position, desired qualifications, and the person to contact. This site does not provide an opportunity to post resumes or "position wanted" notices.

The Association of Legal Administrators also provides a free job bank on its Web site. All postings are for administrative positions (e.g., office manager, controller, and network administrator). Members of ALA may post a "position wanted" notice, but no provision is made for resumes.

American Lawyer Media is the publisher of newspapers and journals serving the legal community. It operates a national *Law Jobs* Web site designed primarily for attorneys seeking jobs and employers seeking to employ attorneys. However, the site provides a "Legal Support Positions" link that takes the viewer to ten of its regional Web sites. These sites include listings for paralegal and other support positions, along with openings for attorneys.

Two very large commercial Web sites that are not limited to jobs in the legal field, deserve consideration. CareerPath.com permits the viewer to search for positions among the employment ads in nearly ninety prominent newspapers across the nation. In addition, CareerPath maintains its own online listings placed directly by employers and recruiting agencies. A search for "paralegal" turned up job postings for "legal assistant," as well as some for "legal secretary." Results are displayed by job title, location, and employer (or recruiting agency). When the viewer clicks on a particular listing, the full job announcement is displayed. Although the newspaper listings are updated weekly, and the online listings daily, at the date of this writing the CareerPath Web site did not display a date for any listing.

The other commercial Web site that might be useful is TMP Worldwide's Monster.com. This site carries online listings only, but the number of listings is staggering. A recent query for "paralegal" resulted in more than 870 listings (nationwide) dated within the preceding thirty days. Here, too, a search for "paralegal" turned up "legal assistant" positions. All of the listings are displayed with a date and in chronological order, with the most recent postings listed first. Job titles and employers are displayed, as well. Clicking on the listing brings the full job announcement to the screen.

Both the CareerPath and Monster Web sites permit the job seeker to post her resume and receive e-mail alerts about positions that fit her prescribed criteria. Both sites are easy to navigate and use. It appears that the two sites duplicate many of the same job postings, as large numbers of the listings were placed by well-known recruiting agencies. There is no charge to the job seeker—employers pay all of the costs.

Internet Access

National Federation of Paralegal Associations	http://www.paralegals.org
National Association of Legal Assistants	http://www.nala.org
Legal Assistant Management Association	http://www.lamanet.org
Association of Legal Administrators	http://www.alanet.org
American Lawyer Media	http://www.lawjobs.com
CareerPath	http://www.careerpath.com
TMP Worldwide	http://www.monster.com

USING DIRECTORIES OF ATTORNEYS

Directories allow the job seeker to identify attorneys in specific practice specialities, identify law firms of various sizes, and learn more about a prospective employing attorney or law firm. There are several national and numerous state or regional directories listing attorneys, along with information about their professional qualifications and practice specialties. Two of the better known national directories are *West's Legal Directory* and the *Martindale-Hubbell Law Directory*. Both of these directories are available on the Internet, and *Martindale-Hubbell* is available in a print version, as well.

Internet Access

West's Legal Directory	http://www.lawoffice.com
Martindale-Hubbell Law Directory	http://www.martindale.com

Using the Print Version of the *Martindale-Hubbell Law Directory*

The *Martindale-Hubbell Law Directory*, available in large libraries and most law libraries, is a multivolume guide to attorneys and law firms nationwide. Organized by state and city, it provides information about a law firm's practice and includes information about each attorney in the firm, as well.

At the front of each volume, there are blue pages with very brief entries for each attorney and firm. The blue-page entries include the firm's "rating," which is based upon peer evaluations by other attorneys in the same community. The rating has two components: one for legal expertise, and one for professional and ethical standards. The highest possible combined rating is "av," and many law firms identify themselves as being "av-rated" when advertising positions for attorneys and paralegals. A detailed explanation of the rating system appears at the very front of each volume of the *Martindale-Hubbell Law Directory*.

The blue pages constitute a very small portion of each volume, however. The remainder of the guide is printed on white pages, and that is where one finds detailed information about the law firm's practice and the attorneys in the firm. If a firm has offices in other cities or foreign countries, that information will appear at the top of the firm's entry. Many firms also list representative corporate clients. The information about the firm's practice can be used in a cover letter and during an interview to set the applicant apart from less-informed applicants.

The biographical and professional data for individual attorneys will reveal the firm's gender and age makeup, the number of attorneys in that office, the

FIGURE 2.2 "Blue Pages" Entry in *Martindale-Hubbell*

Individual listing for name partner in Espinosa * Sitterly & Associates, P.C.

Code reflecting peer evaluation by other attorneys and judges in the community

NEW MEXICO—ALBUQUERQUE

Erickson, Craig T., (BV) ....'55 '85 C.508 B.A. L.629 J.D. [Sheehan, S. & S.]
  *PRACTICE AREAS: Personal Injury; Products Liability; Insurance Bad Faith Litigation.
Espinosa, Leonard G., (AV) ....'45 '71 C&L.560 B.A., J.D. [Espinosa *.S.&Assoc.]
  *PRACTICE AREAS: Real Estate Law; Business Law; Commercial Litigation.
Espinosa * Sitterly & Associates, P.C., (AV)
  P.O. Box 7790, 87194-7790
  Telephone: 505-242-5656 Fax: 505-242-9869
  Leonard G. Espinosa; Rebecca Sitterly;—Wendy L. Basgal1; Charles W. Brown.
  General Civil and Trial Practice. Commercial Litigation, Business Planning, Real Estate, Corporate Law, Title Insurance, Employment Law, Estate Planning and Probate, Personal Injury, Elder Law, Criminal Law, and Arbitration/Mediation.
    See Professional Biographies, ALBUQUERQUE, NEW MEXICO
Esquibel, Thomas C. .... '50 '75 C&L.560 B.S., J.D. [ⒶT.M.Padilla&Assoc.]
Esquivel, Martin R. ....'63 '89 C&L.560 B.A., J.D. [Dines, W.G.&E.]
  *PRACTICE AREAS: Media Law; Employment Law; Civil Litigation; Products Liability.
Estes, Charles N., Jr. ....'45 '72 C&L.309 A.B., J.D. Coun., Univ. of N. Mex.
Estrada, Michele U. ....'— '95 C&L.560 B.S., J.D. [ⒶMadison, H.M.&B.]
  *PRACTICE AREAS: Medical Malpractice; Insurance Defense; Employment Litigation.
Everage, Barbara C., (BV) ....'43 '76 C.1012 B.A. L.560 J.D. [Kanter&E.]
Everett, Peter, IV, (CV) .... '43 '71 C&L.861 J.D. 2301 San Pedro Dr., N.E.
Ewing, Steven C., (BV) ....'52 '77 C.560 B.A. L.862 J.D. [Marron,M.&E.]
Fairfield, Steven R., (BV) ....'44 '75 C&L.560 B.A., J.D. [ⒸFairfield, F.F.P.&S.]
  *PRACTICE AREAS: Real Estate; Alcoholic Beverages; Liquor Licensing; Business Law; Buying and Selling.

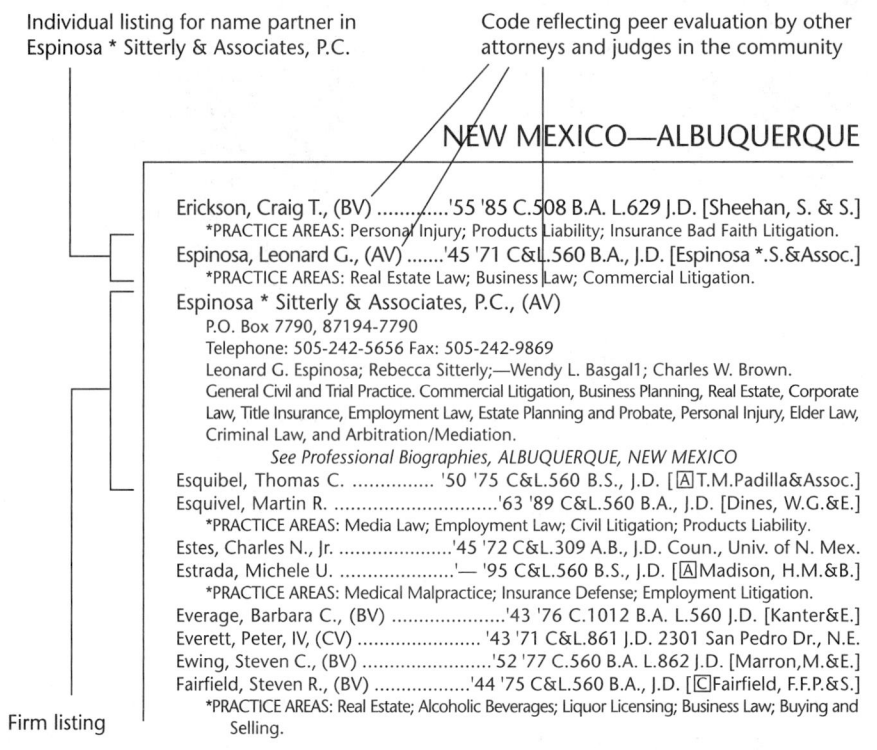

Firm listing

From *Martindale-Hubbell Law Directory*, 1998. Reprinted by permission of Reed Elsevier, Inc.

universities and law schools from which the attorneys were graduated, and publications that they have authored. An applicant who is a graduate of the same university that several firm attorneys attended might find that she is given special consideration. In recent years, Martindale-Hubbell has published the names of paralegals employed in a firm. The inclusion of paralegals in the firm's entry might be an indication of the importance which that firm places upon the paralegal's role. Sample pages from the *Martindale-Hubbell Law Directory* appear in *Figures 2–2* and *2–3*.

Using the Online Attorney Directories

The West and Martindale-Hubbell online attorney directories are used in a similar fashion. The researcher can either search the directory by practice specialty and community name, and receive a group of attorney listings that match the request or search by attorney or law firm name. Both services provide information on the attorneys' professional backgrounds. Because attorneys and law firms pay the publishers to have their listings included, some listings are more extensive than others. For example, some listings provide a link to the law firm's own Web site on the Internet.

EVALUATING YOURSELF AS A JOB-MARKET PROSPECT

When applying for a job, the applicant is selling himself to the prospective employer. If he has no legal experience, *everything else* about him becomes doubly important. An employer's first (and possibly final) decision will be based upon the letter and resume. These two or three pages must present the applicant in the best possible light as a job-market product—a "product" because he is a faceless unknown to the person making that first critical decision.

FIGURE 2–3 "White Pages" Entry in *Martindale-Hubbell*

NEW MEXICO—ALBUQUERQUE

Associations; The Missouri Bar; State Bar of New Mexico, **PRACTICE AREAS:** Commercial Litigation; Antitrust Law; White Collar Criminal Defense.

ESPINOSA *SITTERLY & ASSOCIATES, P.C.

P.O. BOX 7790
ALBUQUERQUE, NEW MEXICO 87194-7790
Telephone: 505-242-5656
Fax: 505-242-9869

General Civil and Trial Practice, Commercial Litigation, Business Planning, Real Estate, Corporate Law, Title Insurance, Employment Law, Estate Planning and Probate, Personal Injury, Elder Law, Criminal Law, and Arbitration/Mediation.
FIRM PROFILE: *Espinosa *Sitterly & Associates, P.C. was founded in January 1994 by Leonard G. Espinosa and Rebecca Sitterly, both attorneys were previously shareholders and directors with Moses, Dunn, Espinosa, Farmer & Tuthill, P.C. Mr. Espinosa has broad based experience in business planning, real estate law, corporate law, estate planning, probate, title insurance law and commercial litigation. Ms. Sitterly was previously a District Court Judge from 1983 to 1990, having served as the Chief Judge of the Civil Division in 1989 and 1990. She specializes in neurolaw and also practices in the areas of commercial litigation, civil trials, arbitration and mediation. Assisted by contract attorneys, paralegals and investigators, the breadth of expertise offered at Espinosa *Sitterly & Associates, P.C. allows the Firm to enjoy a diverse clientele throughout New Mexico.*

    LEONARD G. ESPINOSA, born Monte Vista, Colorado, December 23, 1945; admitted to bar, 1971, New Mexico and U.S. District Court, District of New Mexico; 1974, U.S. Supreme Court and U.S. Court of Appeals, Tenth Circuit. *Education:* University of New Mexico (B.A., 1968; J.D., 1971). Editor, Natural Resources Journal, 1970–1971. Member, IOLTA Grant Committee, 1990–1992; Chairman, 1991–1992. Member: New Mexico Public Defender Board, 1973–1979; New Mexico Supreme Court Disciplinary Board, 1984—. *Member:* Albuquerque and American Bar Associations; State Bar of New Mexico. Fellow, New Mexico Bar Foundation. **PRACTICE AREAS:** Real Estate Law; Business Law; Commercial Litigation.

    REBECCA SITTERLY, born New Mexico, August 13, 1950; admitted to bar, 1975, Florida (Inactive); 1976, Kentucky (Inactive); 1978, Arizona; 1980, New Mexico; U.S. District Court, District of New Mexico. *Education:* University of Kansas (B.A., 1971); University of Kentucky (J.D., 1975). Member, Adjunct Faculty, University of New Mexico School of Law, Evidence and Trial Practice, 1984—and Saturday Morning in Court (Full Civil Case Review), 1985–1990. District Judge, Second Judicial District, 1983–1990. Chief Judge, Civil Division, 1989–1990. Jury Instructions Editor, New Mexico Trial Lawyers Association, 1982–1983. Member: Commission on Professionalism, 1988–1992; Civil Trial Specialization Rules Committee of the Supreme Court, 1989—. Member, 1986–1993 and Chairperson, 1993–1994, Uniform Jury Instructions Committee of the Supreme Court. Chairperson, Roundtable Committee to Promote Professionalism, 1989–1991. President, 1988–1989 and Vice President, 1987–1988, New Mexico District Judges Association. *Member:* State Bar of New Mexico; New Mexico Women's Bar Association; The Association of Trial Lawyers of America; National Head Injury Foundation. **PRACTICE AREAS:** Neurolaw; Commercial Litigation; Arbitration; Mediation; Civil Trials.

From *Martindale-Hubbell Law Directory*, 1998. Reprinted by permission of Reed Elsevier, Inc.

    Somehow, the applicant must communicate clearly the qualities and experience that will attract the interest of the employer. The key, then, is that the applicant must evaluate himself carefully and objectively, keeping in mind the perspective of an employer who knows nothing about him.

    In *The Complete Job-Search Handbook*, Howard Figler identifies "The Ten Hottest Transferable Skills."[3] These are skills to which every employer responds, because they are important in virtually all professional positions. Among those ten, the following have particular application to the paralegal field:

- public relations
- coping with deadline pressure
- speaking

- writing
- organizing/managing/coordinating
- interviewing

The remaining four skills—supervising, budget management, negotiating/arbitrating, and teaching/instructing—apply to some paralegal positions, although not all.

The Legal Assistant Management Association has identified the following characteristics as ones that most employers expect as minimum qualifications:

- initiative and follow-through
- good research skills
- attention to detail
- excellent oral and written communication skills
- excellent interpersonal skills
- willingness to learn and continue updating one's skills[4]

From the beginning of her paralegal education, a student should consider the perspective of a future employer. Is she taking the electives that will best prepare her for the available jobs? Is she demonstrating a track record of academic excellence? Remember that most law firms are conservative institutions—they value maturity, integrity, and reliability. Attorneys also tend to be credential-conscious. Four-year degrees in both liberal arts and technical fields are valued. If the applicant has published nonfiction in any field at all, that also should appear on her resume.

WHEN "EXPERIENCED ONLY NEED APPLY"

The enthusiastic paralegal graduate with his brand-new degree or certificate and an up-to-date resume can run into a frustrating, seemingly unsolvable problem: Virtually every job advertised requires prior paralegal experience—often two years or more. The first-time job hunter is in a classic bind of the type made famous by Joseph Heller's novel, *Catch 22:* If the employers hire only experienced paralegals, how does anyone ever get the required experience?

One thing is certain: Responding to an announcement or ad that specifies experience (that the applicant does not have) will never *deprive* her of a job she otherwise would obtain, and she might gain useful experience and confidence—even if none of the interviews obtained thus produce job offers. So, the only things at risk are the applicant's tender ego, and the time and expense of sending a letter and resume. There are four possible results:

1. The firm offers an interview despite the applicant's inexperience.
2. The firm considers the applicant for a different position with the firm.
3. The firm gives the applicant job leads or other suggestions for her search.
4. The firm takes none of the actions listed above, and the applicant continues her job search.

None of these possibilities is disastrous. Out of ordinary courtesy, the applicant should not apply for a position for which she is hopelessly unqualified; however, if experience is the only thing she lacks, her other qualifications might compensate or even excite the firm's interest. She might turn out to be the most desirable candidate it has.

Fortunately, lack of experience is a temporary problem. Once a candidate gets that first job, the necessary experience comes automatically. It is possible that the reader's paralegal program receives job announcements or has a placement service. Understandably, attorneys do not expect many currently enrolled paralegal students to already have extensive legal experience.

Overcoming the "Experienced Only" Barrier

When the job seeker lacks a specific qualification, it is best not to *start* her cover letter by making that confession. Instead, she can point out a quality that makes her an appealing candidate. She can always conclude her letter with a statement such as the following: "My extensive experience in *[fill in the blank]* might compensate for my lack of paralegal experience," or "Please contact me so that we can discuss how my background would meet your needs, and also compensate for the experience that you have requested." It is important to *acknowledge* the issue of the missing qualification in some way. Otherwise, the employer might think that she has read the job announcement carelessly or that she lacks the sophistication to recognize an issue of obvious importance.

One's chances of overcoming the "experience handicap" are greatest when other professional experience or education has obvious application to the position. For example, a registered nurse might be able to substitute that qualification for three years as a paralegal in personal injury or medical malpractice. Entry-level paralegals, especially, might want to concentrate on job opportunities related to their prior experience or education. New paralegals with unusually valuable experience in a different career (e.g., law enforcement, engineering, or business) can sometimes make this tactic work when applying to a firm with a related practice (e.g., criminal defense, product liability, or bankruptcy, respectively).

Capitalizing on Unique Skills or Experience

Because the great majority of paralegal jobs are in civil litigation, every paralegal student should consider how her own background can find application in litigation. Technical fields such as medicine and engineering have obvious application to the paralegal field. A contractor's license and construction experience would be sought after by firms specializing in construction litigation. Accountants can apply their knowledge to business litigation and bankruptcy work. Similar possibilities exist for many other career fields.

Fluency in languages can be an important asset. The languages of large immigrant communities (e.g., Spanish, Vietnamese, Cambodian, and Farsi) are useful not only in immigration law, but in every practice where recent immigrants are clients. Large firms active in an international practice will be interested in paralegals fluent in French, German, Spanish, Mandarin, Cantonese, Japanese, and Arabic—especially the non-European languages just listed. Russian and East European languages have also become important in recent years.

Internship Programs

If a paralegal program offers an internship program as part of the paralegal curriculum, a student without legal experience should make every effort to participate. Typically, the internship occurs near the end of the paralegal program, so that the student enters it with some knowledge of substantive law and legal procedures. Interns are placed in law firms and corporate legal departments, where they work (usually part-time) for a period of four to eight weeks. During that time, the intern receives no pay, but usually is reimbursed for any out-of-pocket expenses (e.g., mileage, parking, phone calls, photocopies) incurred while on assignments. In most programs, the intern receives academic credit toward the paralegal certificate or degree.

The internship experience familiarizes the student with the operations of a law office and can increase the self-confidence with which he approaches job interviews. His resume can list the internship experience and identify the types of assignments he performed. If the internship goes well, he will have a useful reference to give to prospective employers. Occasionally, internships turn into job offers to work in the same office upon graduation from the paralegal program. Similar benefits can follow from doing volunteer work for the Legal Aid Society or other nonprofit legal services.

Using Contacts

Throughout the reader's paralegal education, she should be establishing as many contacts as possible. The student, in addition to networking with instructors and fellow students, can try to establish contacts in law firms. Some paralegal programs will provide the names and firms of their paralegal graduates. The student can call a graduate and ask for a twenty-minute informational interview. At the conclusion of that interview, she can ask for introductions to other paralegals in different firms. When she approaches completion of her certificate, she should give each contact a telephone call to remind them of her interest in an entry-level position.

When the student learns of a job opening, she can inquire among her entire network of contacts to find someone who knows something about that firm—and, hopefully, one who knows someone *employed* in that firm. The more information she can gain about the firm and the available position, the better she can tailor her resume and prepare herself for an interview.

Making Legal Experience Seem Less Essential

This is the toughest approach of all, simply because the experience requirement is often used to reduce the number of resumes received, as well as to find paralegals with valuable experience. Also, it is entirely possible that the employer *does believe* that the stated experience is necessary to succeed in the advertised position. The latter situation would make the experience barrier much more difficult to overcome, of course. An applicant without any connections in that firm, however, might be unable to evaluate how important the experience really is to that employer. In either event, to succeed in this approach, the resume and cover letter will have to "knock their socks off," and the applicant will need some significant qualification to substitute for the experience he lacks.

Starting in a Nonparalegal Position

If the job seeker has absolutely no legal experience at all, he might need to consider a nonparalegal position in a law firm, just to get his foot in the door. Positions for word processors, legal secretaries, assistant librarians, and receptionists are advertised in the legal press. Many firms would consider training an inexperienced paralegal if he has first proved his abilities and professional attitude as a word processor or an assistant librarian. To guard against the possibility that *other* potential employers might "type-cast" him in that nonparalegal support staff role—in spite of his paralegal credentials—he can volunteer his paralegal services to the local Legal Aid Society, or any other **pro bono** legal service, as evidence of his legal skills and professional commitment. As an added benefit, those volunteer activities will help him to retain—and even to improve upon—those skills.

Pro bono is a Latin term meaning "for the good [of others]." *Pro bono* legal services are offered free of charge to those unable to afford them, and *pro bono publico* services are provided without charge as a benefit to society at large.

Mass Mailing of Resumes

Unadvertised opportunities are sometimes found by sending unsolicited "cold" resumes. The resume and cover letter must be brief, articulate, and impressively presented. Law firms constantly receive such resumes, and most have a designated attorney, paralegal, or office administrator who reviews them. However, there are several disadvantages with a mass mailing:

- It is difficult to individualize the cover letters so that the prospective employer can see that the applicant knows something about that firm.
- It is impossible to target the letter and resume for a particular position, because the applicant has no information about an actual vacancy—otherwise, he would not send out a cold resume.
- It is difficult to make the letter and resume stand out from the crowd, so that they will be given serious consideration.
- It can be expensive.

Of course, the applicant should use a good guide to resume preparation. (See the Recommended Reading list at the end of this chapter.)

Even so, many paralegals have obtained jobs in just this manner. For them, it usually was a combination of lucky timing, strong credentials, and an outstanding letter and resume that did the trick. Anyone contemplating the cold resume approach should consider investing in professional assistance. There are many special techniques in resume preparation, and there are a multitude of pitfalls awaiting the unsophisticated job applicant. A hundred dollars or so invested up front can pay important dividends during the job search.

Targeting Specific Firms with Tailored Resumes

A variation on the cold resume approach is the *targeted* cold resume. Instead of blanketing the entire legal community, the applicant establishes a set of criteria for selecting the firms to receive the resume. Legal specialties, firm size, *Martindale-Hubbell* rating, and other criteria can be used. The resume and cover letter are then tailored to a hypothetical firm meeting the chosen criteria.

Because fewer letters are being prepared than is the case for a nontargeted cold mailing, more time can be invested in personalizing them to show some knowledge of each firm. By following the legal news and exploring other sources of information, the applicant can often identify a law firm or corporation that looks interesting. By citing a news story about that firm or company in the opening sentence of the cover letter, she will set herself apart from the vast majority of unsolicited applications. A follow-up "cold call" to the law firm can be helpful.

DEVELOPING AN EFFECTIVE MARKETING PLAN

Paralegal students should begin to develop a marketing plan. That plan should include the following:

- a thorough self-evaluation
- thoughtful selection of the elective courses in the paralegal program
- networking with instructors, fellow students, and working legal assistants
- resume preparation
- follow-up for every contact made with a prospective employer

The entire plan should be focused on the applicant's own strengths and the probable needs of prospective employers. A new paralegal graduate with a well-conceived marketing plan will have a great advantage over the majority of applicants who approach their job search in a haphazard fashion. The Activities and Assignments at the end of this chapter provide opportunities to practice self-evaluation and other aspects of a personal marketing plan.

SCENARIO

Noriko Kawamura is a legal assistant in an international law firm with offices in New York, Chicago, Los Angeles, and San Francisco. Among its international offices are two in Japan: Tokyo and Osaka. Noriko works in the San Francisco office, where many of the clients are Japanese business firms or western companies with business ties to Japan. Although she does some litigation work, most of her assignments involve international business transactions.

Getting to this point has been a long but intriguing journey for Noriko. She is a *Nisei*—born in the United States to Japanese immigrants. She grew up speaking primarily Japanese at home, but she spoke English in the neighborhood and at school. She attended public school during the week and a small, private Japanese school on Saturdays, where she studied Japanese culture and language.

"When I was very young, I never questioned why I was going to school six days a week, whereas my friends went only five days. The Saturday Japanese lessons were hard and the teachers demanding. My parents told me that it would be a great tragedy if I lost my cultural and linguistic heritage. But when I reached the teenage years, my interests changed, of course, and I lost interest in preserving that heritage. Pretty soon, I stopped going to school on Saturdays.

"The amazing thing is that a few years later I decided on impulse to take a course in *kanji*—the written Japanese language—when I was a student at UCLA. And I loved it! Of course, we had studied *kanji* in Saturday school when I was a kid, but we kids just thought it was a major bore. So, anyway, that class in college turned my attitude around, and I began a period of voracious interest in all things Japanese. My parents were *gratefully* incredulous! I took every course in Japanese language that UCLA offers, and then began to study with a private tutor. It was also while I was at UCLA that I took courses in international business and international law. The big decision became: Do I go to law school, or do I pursue my interest in Japan?

"I resolved that question by deciding that my interest in Japan came first, but that it could be combined with working in the field of law. My college roommate signed up for UCLA's University Extension program in paralegal studies, so I did, too. It was a full-time, six-month program that we both entered right after graduating from college. I now had a B.A. in political science and was about to get a highly regarded paralegal certificate from the same institution.

"But, how was I ever going to get a job that combined my two main interests: the law and Japan? I decided that I should find a paralegal position in a law firm that had Japanese clients or western clients with business in Japan. First, I contacted the Japanese Consulate in Los Angeles and requested a list of American law firms with offices in Japan. Second, I contacted the Japanese Chamber of Commerce in southern California and requested a list of their members and any law firms used by their members. After many hours delving into *Martindale-Hubbell*—and with lots of telephone legwork—I identified about six American law firms that appeared to be serious about establishing a presence in Japan and building a clientele in the States with Japanese firms doing business here. I prepared a resume in English and then had a translation service prepare its equivalent in correct, formal Japanese. Because of the extraordinary cultural and linguistic differences between Japan and America—perhaps this is what my parents were trying to teach me—I wasn't about to risk botching the translation!

"Anyway, I did get several interviews. Two of the firms said that my Japanese language skills are not truly bilingual—which is true. But the third firm offered me a job, with the possibility of a six-month assignment in Osaka in the near future. It's clear to me that this firm is thinking long-term and is interested in my potential. And I'm excited about the prospects. That possible assignment in Osaka is a great motivator! Meanwhile, this is a wonderful job. I guess I should say 'thanks' to Mom and Dad."

Noriko's work includes translation of Japanese documents into English, and she serves as an interpreter for visiting Japanese who are not confident of their English abilities. Her long-term goal is to participate in contract negotiations on behalf of western and Japanese business clients. ∎

SOURCES FOR FURTHER GUIDANCE

The Recommended Reading list at the end of this chapter includes several titles that will help the entry-level paralegal in her job search. Particularly useful for the neophyte paralegal is *How to Land Your First Paralegal Job*, by Andrea Wagner.[5] A former recruiter and placement director for legal assistants, Wagner treats the entire job-hunting process from the paralegal's point of view, with constant attention to the expectations of attorneys as employers. As the title suggests, Wagner's book focuses upon getting that *first* paralegal job, which can seem to be so elusive.

The Complete Job-Search Handbook, by Howard Figler,[6] provides a consistently thought-provoking analysis of the job search process, including a great many tools for self-evaluation and job selection. For example, one section entitled "Put Your Worst Foot Forward" identifies ten personality traits commonly perceived as negative—from "compulsive" to "slow"—and matches each characteristic with corresponding behavior that is an asset to an employer. Thus, the compulsive employee is described as one who "keeps perfect and orderly records of all calls, correspondence, visitors, and intrusions (birds flying in the window, etc.) in his department," and the slow employee as one who "takes care of difficult mechanical tasks that carry risks of overload or mechanical error; he's patient enough to work a task to death just so it will be done correctly." Humor aside, Figler's book offers an abundance of practical tips and techniques for finding the job that is right for the job seeker.

The reader might wish to subscribe to *Legal Assistant Today* magazine,[7] a popular and very informative magazine for paralegals, that frequently carries articles on paralegal career opportunities and job search techniques.

Membership in the NALA includes a subscription to *Facts & Findings*, NALA's quarterly magazine. Membership in the NFPA includes *National Paralegal Reporter*, NFPA's magazine. Occasional articles on rapidly growing paralegal specialties and the job search appear in both magazines.

A QUESTION OF ETHICS

Jesson, Arands, Warron and Fell, P.C., is a prestigious law firm in Albuquerque, New Mexico. Venicia Milton is a legal assistant in the firm's real estate section. She has been in that position for three years. Previously she worked as a litigation paralegal in another mid-sized law firm. It appears to Venicia that she is reaching a plateau in the assignments she receives, no longer experiencing the challenge that used to come from being offered progressively more responsibility.

A young associate attorney fresh out of law school has recently joined the firm's real estate section. It seems to Venicia that he is receiving assignments well over his head, although she could handle those same research and drafting assignments, if only she were given a chance. In fact, Mark, the new associate, regularly comes to Venicia for assistance in handling the tasks, and she regularly ends up "saving the day."

Venicia is thinking of telling the partner who supervises both Venicia and Mark that it really is her mentoring that makes Mark look so good. She feels it is grossly unfair that Mark receives assignments that he can't handle without her guidance—and even receives credit for results he couldn't achieve on his own—while the partner gives Venicia the less interesting "grunt" work.

Venicia is beginning to think that either the situation must change, or she will start searching for a new law firm. Under these circumstances, what is the ethical thing for Venicia to do?

Chapter Summary

- Most law firms are either sole practitioners, partnerships, or professional corporations.
- Most law firms designate one attorney to be "managing partner."
- If paralegals are to realize their full potential, they must demonstrate initiative and professionalism.
- Mistakes and missed deadlines can be devastating in the practice of law, and attorneys sometimes are cautious in their reliance on a new paralegal.
- Legal assistants must treat legal secretaries and support staff with respect, and will regret their error if they fail to do so.
- Experienced legal assistants can move into nonparalegal positions within law firms, including systems manager, marketing director, librarian, or law firm administrator.
- Approximately 15% of all paralegals work in corporate legal departments, financial institutions, real estate companies, and government.
- Freelance paralegals enjoy independence, flexible scheduling, higher incomes, and the ability to work out of their homes.
- Paralegals have skills, knowledge, and a unique perspective that makes them valuable in a wide range of occupations outside of the practice of law.
- About half of all legal assistants learned of their jobs through personal contacts.
- Internships and volunteer work with nonprofit organizations are excellent ways to obtain legal experience and references.
- The *Martindale-Hubbell Law Directory* is an important source of information about law firms and individual attorneys.

KEY TERMS

(See the Glossary for definitions.)

associate attorney	local area network (LAN)	pro bono
bar association	managing partner	product liability
billable hour	of counsel	professional corporation
freelance paralegal	partner	sole practitioner
independent contractor	partnership	systems manager
legal nurse consultant		

RECOMMENDED READING

_____, *How to Find a Job as a Legal Assistant* (Legal Assistant Management Association [undated]), http://www.lamanet.org.

Chere B. Estrin, *Paralegal Career Guide,* Second Edition (John Wiley & Sons, 1996).

Howard Figler, *The Complete Job-Search Handbook,* Third Edition (Henry Holt and Company, 1999).

Andrea Wagner, *How to Land Your First Paralegal Job* (Estrin Publishing, 1992).

ACTIVITIES AND ASSIGNMENTS

1. In small groups, discuss effective ways for breaking bad news to the boss—specifically, a mistake you have made that could harm a client. Anticipate an employer's possible responses to the bad news. What can an employee do to prevent the boss from "shooting the bearer of bad news," so that the problem is dealt with in a positive way?

2. Identify five things that a newly hired inexperienced legal assistant can do to establish good working relationships with a law firm's support staff. Be prepared to discuss this question: Are there "hidden pitfalls" for male legal assistants entering an office populated predominately by male attorneys and female non-attorneys?

3. Select a paralegal specialty (e.g., litigation, bankruptcy, corporate, criminal, or intellectual property) in which you have some interest. Prepare a tentative career plan for yourself in the specialty you have selected. In your plan, identify the course work you must complete and the entry-level and intermediate jobs you will seek. Then, prepare a rough timeline for progressing toward your final career objective.

4. Make a list of the skills and knowledge discussed under "Special Attributes Paralegals Bring to Other Occupations," in this chapter. Interview someone in a management position in a nonlegal field of business or government. Ask them about those skills and knowledge, and about the perspective that experienced paralegals can bring to other positions. Then, answer these questions:
    - What is the manager's reaction to the prospect of hiring a paralegal for a nonparalegal position?
    - Does it appear difficult for the manager to recognize possible application of paralegal talents to other positions?
    - How has this interview affected your view of paralegals entering other professions?

5. Identify, realistically, the characteristics of your next (first?) paralegal job. For this assignment, assume the employer will be a law firm. Divide

those characteristics into two categories: (1) the nature and professional standing of the law firm and (2) all other considerations.

Make a list of all sources you can draw upon to evaluate a law firm as a prospective employer. Select a firm from a legal directory for your community, or from the yellow pages; then, photocopy its listing in the *Martindale-Hubbell Law Directory*. Be sure to check the law firm's rating in the blue pages (found at the front of each volume).

Prepare a brief report on the selected law firm, including any advantages and disadvantages of employment with that firm.

6. Gather information about a large corporation (e.g., an airline or a manufacturer of consumer products) that is likely to be involved in litigation—increasing the likelihood that the company would employ paralegals. Using an on-line information service, or the indexes of the *New York Times* and the *Wall Street Journal* (available in public libraries), locate news stories that have been published about that corporation. Read relevant articles (either the full text or in abstract form) that would inform you as a job applicant about the business and legal matters of that company. If the public library has books that evaluate companies as potential employers (titles such as *The Best Companies to Work For*), review the comments on the corporation you are researching. Find the most recent issue of *Fortune* magazine featuring an article on the 100 best employers, and see if "your" corporation is listed.

Prepare a summary of information that would be useful in preparing your resume and cover letter, and in preparing for a job interview with that corporation.

7. Use the information you have developed in exercise 6, above, to prepare a resume and cover letter for a legal assistant position in that company.

8. Assume that you have no prior legal experience (which, of course, might be true). Select an advertisement for a paralegal position that specifies between one and three years of legal experience. Evaluate any of your education, employment and volunteer experiences, skills and traits, and so forth, that might compensate for lack of the requested experience. Describe how you would persuade the prospective employer to consider you for the job.

9. If you had experienced the nightmare that Paul had in the opening scenario to this chapter, what lessons would you derive from it? How would you change your behavior or attitudes to avoid a real-life "nightmare" of this kind?

ENDNOTES

[1] _____, *How to Find a Job as a Legal Assistant* (Legal Assistant Management Association [undated]), http://www.lamanet.org.

[2] U.S. Department of Labor, Bureau of Labor Statistics, *Occupational Outlook Quarterly,* Vol. 43, No. 4 (Winter 1999–2000).

[3] Howard Figler, *The Complete Job-Search Handbook,* Third Edition (New York, N.Y.: Henry Holt and Company, 1988).

[4] _____, *How to Find a Job as a Legal Assistant* (Legal Assistant Management Association [undated]), http://www.lamanet.org.

[5] Andrea Wagner, *How to Land Your First Paralegal Job,* Second Edition (Santa Monica, Calif.: Estrin Publishing, 1996).

[6] U.S. Department of Labor, Bureau of Labor Statistics, *Occupational Outlook Quarterly,* Vol. 43, No. 4 (Winter 1999–2000).

[7] *Legal Assistant Today* is published by James Publishing, Inc., 3520 Cadillac Avenue, Costa Mesa, Calif. 92626, http://www.paralegals.org/membership/parapartner.html.

CHAPTER 3

Legal Ethics and Other Professional Issues

There are . . . many forms of professional misconduct that do not amount to crimes.

Benjamin N. Cardozo, Associate Justice of the U.S. Supreme Court, 1932–1938.

Chapter 3 considers the great importance of legal ethics for paralegals and the controversy over establishing professional qualifications and standards through state licensure or professional certification. After completing this chapter, the student should have answers for these questions:

- What are the ethical standards that lawyers must uphold?
- What are the ethical standards for legal assistants?
- What are the consequences of ethical violations by attorneys or paralegals?
- What is the "unauthorized practice of law"?
- What are "attorney-client privilege" and the "attorney work product rule"?
- How can the paralegal deal with concerns that the client or the employing attorney might be acting unethically?
- Is regulation or certification the solution to high legal fees and unqualified legal practitioners?
- How does the American Bar Association influence paralegal education and the profession?

SCENARIO

A Lazy Summer Afternoon

Standing in the checkout line, Patricia gave a final glance at her shopping list. Thank goodness she remembered that Ed had said the Takadas are vegetarians. Fresh eggplant, corn, and sweet potatoes were there in her basket—along with the chicken and the salmon steaks. It had been a bit of a trial to find a recipe for barbecued eggplant, but she finally came across several on the Internet. *Let's see . . . did I get enough charcoal and eggplant. . . .?*

A familiar voice interrupted her thoughts: "Hi, Pat. Isn't this weather gorgeous?"

"Oh, hi, Louise! Yeah, the weather's great, perfect for the barbecue we're throwing for Ed's office."

"Say, how's that case you've been working on . . . Wasn't it a malpractice suit against some dentist?"

Glancing around, Patricia lowered her voice. "That case's gotta be a real loser, for sure. I don't know why the firm ever took it—we're getting creamed in court."

Louise smiled at the checker who was listening with obvious interest. "So, why's it such a loser, Pat?"

"*Louise*, not so loud!" Patricia continued in muted tones. "The dentist is such a lousy witness—his own worst enemy. Yesterday, on the stand, he couldn't keep anything straight . . . had his whole story all messed up. I think we're going to settle before it goes to the jury."

"Is plastic O.K., Ma'am?"

With lingering thoughts of dental malpractice and barbecued eggplant, Patricia turned toward the teenager's voice. "Oh, sure . . . Plastic's fine."

* * * *

Two hours later, hungry guests surrounded Patricia, savoring the aromas as she turned the food on the grill. She didn't know most of the guests, but they seemed to be a nice group. Ed's new office mate, Alex Takada, seemed especially nice. Too bad he was having problems with his landlord—a story that was already quite long, despite his opening promise to "make a long story short."

"Now, *you* know something about the law, Pat. Can my landlord refuse to repair the air-conditioning system when it's totally inop? Doesn't he have to keep the place in decent repair? Jill says I should . . . Jill's my wife, you know . . . you met her earlier? Anyway, Jill says we should go ahead and fix it and just deduct it from the rent. Whaddya think?"

Patricia brushed more sauce on the chicken. "Gee, Alex, I can't give you legal advice. I'm just a paralegal, not an attorney."

"Sure, sure. I understand. But what would you do if you were in my place? Seems to me that Jill's probably right, and I should just repair the darn thing and subtract it from my rent check."

"You know, Alex, I wouldn't do that. I don't think our state law allows you to do that. But, really, why don't you talk to a lawyer? Maybe I can get Margaret to talk to you. She's pretty new, but she's one of the best new associates in the firm."

"Hey, that'd be great. Say, that chicken *really* smells good. Jill and I are pretty much vegetarians at home, but we indulge a little bit when we're out."

Patricia bit her tongue as she turned the eggplant. "Well . . . sure, Alex. Would you like white meat or dark?" ■

Unfortunately, Patricia's conversations with Louise and Alex might be disturbing, but not beyond belief. Paralegals frequently find friends and family expressing interest in their work—and interest in their opinions on legal matters. If a legal assistant is not careful, she can slip across the line into unethical conduct—just as Patricia did on that lazy summer afternoon.

SECTION 1. THE ROLE OF ETHICS IN THE PRACTICE OF LAW

Ethical questions *routinely* occur in the practice of law, and paralegals are intimately involved with the law practice of the attorneys for whom they work. Paralegals can be sued personally—as individuals—for violating client confidences, for concealing evidence, for practicing law without a license, or for fraudulent billing. And that list is by no means exhaustive. Some ethical lapses could subject a paralegal to criminal prosecution—falsifying the date on a court document or insider trading in the stock market, for example.

For the legal profession, ethics have a special importance arising from the responsibility that attorneys and paralegals have to their clients and to society. As mentioned in Chapter 1, attorneys owe a special duty of loyalty—a fiduciary duty—to their clients. And legal assistants assume a responsibility to ensure that the attorney's fiduciary duty is not compromised by their own misconduct.

Attorneys are also **officers of the court**, which means that they have taken an oath to uphold the law, to respect the judicial process, and to seek justice in all matters. In that role, all lawyers bear a duty to society. It is impossible to fulfill their duties to both client and society without upholding ethical standards in the practice of law. Because an attorney's specific duty to a client might appear to conflict with her general duty to society at large, a difficult analysis of those competing ethical demands often becomes the only resolution.

Officers of the court (including judges and all attorneys) are those persons who have taken an oath to respect the judicial process, to uphold the law, and to seek justice in all matters.

MOTIVATING AND ENFORCING ETHICAL CONDUCT

High ethical standards have their own inherent value, of course. Otherwise, there would be no significance to our concepts of right and wrong. Ethical standards also bring their own reward for those who abide by them: They make it possible for the legal assistant to have self-respect, pride in his work, and the satisfaction of doing the right thing. Ideally, all legal professionals would have a single, deeply held value system, making formal rules of conduct unnecessary. But, of course, none of us lives in that ideal world. American society is such a melting pot of value systems drawn from every continent of the world that sincere, well-intentioned people do not always hold identical values. And, like other professions that provide access to power and money, some unethical people are inevitably attracted to the legal profession by the opportunity to gain power and wealth in unscrupulous ways.

Consequently, there must be safeguards to ensure that the client and the public are protected and well-served. The first necessity is clearly defined standards of professional responsibility. These standards might be determined by statute, by the rules of court, or by state bar rules. However they are determined, these standards reflect a broadly based social value system that must be followed, regardless of the personal viewpoint of any individual attorney or paralegal.

The American Bar Association (ABA) has taken steps to more clearly define the profession's ethical responsibilities and to ensure that both lawyers and paralegals are prepared to assume those responsibilities. And that is a task that must continue indefinitely, as changes in technology, the law, and social values present new ethical challenges to each generation. All law schools accredited by the ABA and all paralegal programs approved by the ABA must include legal ethics within their curriculum. State bar associations are progressively tightening their rules and procedures for attorney discipline, and in recent years the continuing legal education programs sponsored by the state bars have increased their emphasis on legal ethics.

Of course, the great majority of clients expect ethical representation by their legal counsel. Meeting that expectation requires that paralegals and other firm employees support the ethical standards set for attorneys. Consequently, law firms are increasingly sensitive to the importance of *paralegal ethics* and demand that their legal assistants perform their duties honestly, accurately, and with loyalty to the interests of the client. A legal assistant with lax ethical practices is likely soon to be without a job.

State Regulation of Attorney Conduct

The mandatory rules of professional ethics are *state rules*, and they are enforced primarily by the state bar associations and state courts. Federal courts play an enforcement role, but their role is limited to the conduct of attorneys in federal court proceedings. Even then, the federal courts look to state law and state rules of professional responsibility whenever ethical questions about the practice of law come before them. The authority of courts to discipline attorneys is provided by statute in some jurisdictions, but the courts already possess disciplinary powers as an exercise of their control over judicial proceedings, and because attorneys are officers of the courts in which they practice.

Discipline imposed by state bars or state courts might range from private or public reprimands (known as **censure**) to temporary suspension from the practice of law, or even permanent **disbarment**. Disbarment is the revocation of an attorney's license to practice law. Disbarment can be imposed only by the state's highest appellate court or by a special tribunal of the state bar.

When a lower appellate court or trial court enforces professional ethics, it is usually for misconduct in a matter before that court, and the enforcement is either through **sanctions** or a finding that the lawyer is in **contempt of court**. A sanction can be an order to forfeit a specified sum of money to the court or to the opposing party, or it can be a procedural penalty in the trial—for example, the exclusion of particular evidence. An extreme sanction would be the dismissal of some claim or motion presented to the court by the offending attorney. Because dismissal of a claim punishes the client as well as the attorney, it is rarely used, unless the client has participated personally in the misconduct.

A number of ethical violations are criminal, as well: **suborning of perjury**, embezzlement of client funds, **obstruction of justice**, and so forth. In the famous Watergate scandal during the administration of President Richard Nixon, a number of attorneys went to prison, including John Mitchell, who had been the U.S. Attorney General under Nixon. The savings and loan failures of the 1980s and 1990s saw a number of attorneys convicted for their involvement in fraudulent practices.

Censure is a formal reprimand imposed by a court or legislature.

Disbarment is the revocation of one's license to practice law.

A **sanction** is a penalty imposed by the court for misconduct in judicial proceedings.

Contempt of court is disobedience of a court order, or it may be any act that obstructs the operation of the court or offends the dignity of the court.

Suborning of perjury is the solicitation of a false statement under oath.

Perjury is the making of a false statement under oath.

Obstruction of justice is interfering with the normal judicial process so as to prevent or impede its progress.

Ethical Accountability for Paralegal Conduct

Although there is no statutory provision for a paralegal to be disciplined by the state bar or the courts, paralegals are subject to ordinary civil and criminal liability for their acts and omissions. Because paralegals are either employees or independent contractors working under the supervision of an attorney, that supervising attorney is *ethically responsible* for the paralegal's conduct and can be disciplined for the legal assistant's misconduct. The attorney also has civil liability for the wrongful acts of his legal assistant, *if* the legal assistant has acted within the scope of his employment. **Scope of employment** is a very complex issue, but the term generally refers to those activities that reasonably are part of the paralegal's normal functions and duties.

In the following "Case in Point," the State Bar of Maryland is seeking a disciplinary action against an attorney, Ronald S. Goldberg, for professional misconduct. The state bar's petition alleged neglect of professional matters. The Maryland Court of Appeals initially referred the matter to the Circuit Court for Montgomery County for a hearing on the allegations. Excerpts from the Court of Appeals' decision follow.

Scope of employment is the range of activities within which the employee is reasonably serving the purpose for which she is employed; thus, such activities are therefore presumed to be foreseeable by the employer.

A CASE IN POINT

Attorney Grievance Commission of Maryland v. Goldberg

441 A.2d 338 (1982)

The circuit court judge made the following findings:

The Respondent, Ronald S. Goldberg, has been in the practice of law since his admission to the Bar of this Court on October 20, 1961 . . . Sometime in 1978, upon the recommendation of one of his clients, he hired Sandra H. Ofterdinger . . . as a secretary. Subsequent to her hiring, Mrs. Ofterdinger was given increasing responsibilities, resulting in her position in the nature of an office manager. She had the responsibility to see that the pleadings were prepared from Mr. Goldberg's dictation, the cases properly filed, dates appropriately calendared, the keeping of the financial books and records, and authority to sign checks for disbursements from the office account and clients' trust account.

There came a time while in the employment of Mr. Goldberg that Mrs. Ofterdinger failed to prepare the necessary pleadings, documents or papers required to be done. As she got increasingly behind, she would remove the files and not calendar them, preventing the lack of progress on those files from coming to the attention of Mr. Goldberg. In order to cover her inactivity on those files, Mrs. Ofterdinger then started going through all of the office mail, removing any letters that had reference to the work that had not been done. She also removed any phone messages and intercepted calls to Mr. Goldberg. She made excuses or misrepresentations as to why the work had not been done in some instances and falsely represented that the work had been done in others. Checks received from clients were not deposited in the appropriate account, and from the exhibits it would appear that unauthorized checks were drawn by Mrs. Ofterdinger for improper purposes. She further intercepted the letters from the Attorney Grievance Commission.

From the testimony presented, there is no evidence that Respondent, Ronald S. Goldberg, was aware of any of the activity of Mrs. Ofterdinger until the time of her termination. None of the misrepresentations to clients were authorized by Mr. Goldberg. As soon as he became aware of what had occurred, Mr. Goldberg attempted to locate all of the removed or hidden files, contact the clients, and rectify the situation where possible. One might question whether an attorney can give effective representation to all of his clients with the volume that Mr. Goldberg has undertaken. There is, however, no indication that volume or improper delegation was a contributing factor in any of the incidents the subject of this complaint.

For the aforegoing reasons, this Court finds that there was no knowing violation of the Code of Professional Responsibility by Respondent, Ronald S. Goldberg. (At pages 339–340.)

Because the circuit court heard the matter by referral, in the role of a **master** assisting the court of appeals, the court of appeals was not bound by the circuit judge's findings. Consequently, the court of appeals reviewed the evidence *de novo.*

The Maryland Court of Appeals ordered that Attorney Goldberg be suspended from the practice of law for a period of 30 days. In reaching its decision, the court of appeals found the following:

- There were "instances in which deeds were not recorded and pleadings were not timely filed." (At p. 340.)
- The monthly gross income of Goldberg exceeded $12,000 from legal fees.
- "Goldberg never examined monthly bank statements." (At page 340.)
- At the time she was hired by Goldberg, Mrs. Ofterdinger was on probation in the District of Columbia for embezzlement from a title company.
- Previously, Mrs. Ofterdinger had misappropriated funds from another company that failed to bring criminal charges in order to avoid the publicity.
- Goldberg accepted a retainer of $350 for a lawsuit that was never filed.
- Goldberg failed to file an answer in a divorce action for which he was retained, resulting in a default decree against his client.
- There had been no previous complaints against Goldberg.

The court of appeals commented, "Goldberg asserts that no sanction should be imposed because the problem stemmed from the activities of his employee. Bar Counsel on the other hand suggests a reprimand. We are of the view that we cannot discharge our responsibility to protect the public by merely giving a reprimand." (At page 342.)

Although the non-attorney in the preceding "Case in Point" apparently was not a trained paralegal, many of her duties as described by the circuit judge commonly are performed by paralegals. The essence of this decision is that a responsible supervising attorney cannot escape discipline by pleading ignorance of the misconduct or omissions of his employee. He has a duty to supervise the non-attorney employee's activities and job performance, and to correct them when they are inadequate or unethical.

A **master** is an individual, usually a retired judge, appointed by the court to assist with judicial duties in a particular case (e.g., to receive evidence and recommend disposition of the matter).

To hear a case, or to review evidence, ***de novo*** is to hear the case (or review the evidence) as though no prior decision had been made regarding that case or evidence.

Ethics Watch

Both the attorney and the legal assistant can be sued as individuals for the legal assistant's misconduct that has harmed someone else. A prudent paralegal will make every effort to act ethically and responsibly on client matters; by doing so, the legal assistant also protects her employing attorney and herself from legal liability.

As mentioned earlier, a paralegal can be prosecuted for any criminal act committed in the course of his employment. In some states, for example, it is a crime for non-attorneys—including legal assistants—to solicit clients on behalf of an attorney. And a paralegal who has destroyed documents that might be damaging to a client could be charged with criminal destruction of evidence, or obstruction of justice. During a trial, speaking to members of a jury could lead to charges of **jury tampering**—that is, attempting to influence a jury in a pending matter.

Although professional standards of competence and diligence are not as clearly established for legal assistants as they are for attorneys, it is probable that there will be lawsuits in the future naming legal assistants as co-defendants for legal malpractice. In those lawsuits, the plaintiffs would try to establish that there are *generally recognized standards* for the professional skill and ethics that paralegals have a duty to apply to their work. The fact that legal assistants practice under the supervision of attorneys might not shield a given legal assistant from liability, because it might impute to the legal assistant substantial knowledge of the ethical standards that the attorneys must follow. The fact that the client has been billed for the paralegal's time might establish a presumption that the paralegal is a professional with specialized legal knowledge and skills, even though they are not equivalent to those of an attorney.

The *Code of Ethics and Professional Responsibility* adopted by the National Association of Legal Assistants (NALA) and the *Model Code of Ethics and Professional Responsibility* adopted by the National Federation of Paralegal Associations (NFPA) could be cited as evidence of generally accepted standards. (See Appendices D and E.) The fact that a paralegal is a member of either organization might actually strengthen the plaintiff's contention that the paralegal was aware of the ethical standards for legal assistants and had undertaken a duty to uphold those standards that had been adopted by the organization to which she belongs.

> **Jury tampering** is the attempt to influence a jury by means of unauthorized communication.

ETHICAL STANDARDS FOR ATTORNEYS AND LEGAL ASSISTANTS

The state bar association, state legislature, or highest court of each state has established rules of professional conduct that govern the practice of law in that state. The rules of most states follow rather closely either the ABA's *Model Code of Professional Responsibility* (adopted by the ABA in 1970) or its more recent *Model Rules of Professional Conduct* (adopted in 1983). Because licensure of attorneys and mandatory codes of ethical conduct are state responsibilities, the ABA standards are what their titles state: simply advisory models that the states are free to adopt or disregard.

On its Web site, the ABA offers a wealth of resources on legal ethics. The ABA's Center for Professional Responsibility is the focal point for these resources. Just a few of the resources featured on the Web site are listed below:

- the annotated Model Rules of Professional Conduct
- recent ABA formal opinions on ethical issues
- recent articles in *The Professional Lawyer* on ethical issues
- publications on ethical issues that can be ordered from the ABA

State bar associations offer their state codes for professional conduct on the Internet. Many of these bar association Web sites are easily accessed from the "links" page of the NALA Web site.

Internet Access

ABA Center for Professional Responsibility	http://www.abanet.org/cpr/ethicsearch/
NALA Links page	http://www.nala.org/links.htm

An attorney has an ethical duty (and, in most states, a statutory duty) to comply with the rules adopted by his state, so that any violation of those rules is an unethical practice and might also be illegal. Attorneys are also responsible for ensuring that their legal assistants comply with the ethical rules for that jurisdiction. So, indirectly, the standards for attorney conduct become *de facto* rules for legal assistants, as well.

Some rules can be difficult to comply with in every detail. In a few states, for example, it is an ethical violation for an attorney to *appear* to have acted unethically, even though her *actual conduct* is beyond reproach. In other words, those particular states impose a duty to avoid even so much as the *appearance of impropriety*. Because "appearance" is in the eye of the beholder, this is a severe standard for attorneys to meet.

The state bar associations often issue advisory opinions on those ethical issues that are not clearly determined under the established rules of professional conduct. Such a bar opinion might be requested by a law firm that is uncertain about some contemplated conduct (e.g., a particular form of marketing activity) or it might be requested by a committee within the bar association that is concerned about some conduct that is becoming common within the profession. Generally, these opinions are advisory only, but they might indicate a probable ruling if some particular conduct were to be challenged under the rules.

THE ABA'S *MODEL RULES OF PROFESSIONAL CONDUCT* FOR ATTORNEYS

The following is not a complete listing of the ABA's *Model Rules;* however, it highlights some that should be of special concern to legal assistants. It should be remembered that the specific rules of each state will differ somewhat from the ABA's *Model Rules.* The enumeration below conforms to that of the 1983 *Model Rules.*

Model Rule 1.1 Competent Representation

A client is entitled to the benefit of the special skills and knowledge that an attorney is presumed to have. Carelessly drafted legal documents and inadequate legal research are violations of this responsibility. Delegating tasks to a paralegal does not violate this responsibility if the paralegal is competent to perform those tasks under attorney supervision.

Paralegal Corollary to Rule 1.1

A paralegal must apply his best skills to every task undertaken for the client. He also should be aware of his own limitations so that the client is not receiving inferior legal services on work that really requires the abilities of a paralegal with better skills, or of an attorney.

Model Rule 1.3 Diligence in Representing the Client

Diligence is attention to one's responsibilities and the timely performance of one's duties to another person.

The attorney has a responsibility to use reasonable **diligence** working on client matters. "Diligence" means the application of sufficient effort and attention so that a legal matter does not languish, perhaps to be compromised by unnecessary delay. This can be critical, because success in lawsuits and other legal matters often depends upon meeting deadlines established by statute or court rules.

Paralegal Corollary to Rule 1.3

Legal assistants play a key role in monitoring timelines and ensuring that important matters do not "fall through the cracks." Law firms generally use a computer program that alerts attorneys and legal assistants in advance of each filing deadline, court appearance, deposition date, and so forth. A legal assistant who neglects to use such a system is jeopardizing the client's welfare.

Model Rule 1.4 Communication with the Client

One of the most common complaints among clients is the attorney's failure to keep them informed about the progress of their case. Although they see monthly bills, they are unaware of what is going on and might wonder what they are actually paying for. Clients must be kept reasonably informed of the progress of a legal matter, and the attorney must provide sufficient information so that the client can make an informed decision about her own legal representation. The lawyer may *never* withhold information for his own benefit.

Paralegal Corollary to Rule 1.4

Legal assistants can be a source of reliable progress reports to clients, and many clients quickly learn that the legal assistant is more accessible than the attorney. Obviously, the paralegal cannot pass on information that he himself does not have, and matters are made worse if he gives the client inaccurate information.

> **Ethics Watch**
>
> Generally, the legal assistant may give *procedural* status reports—the date of the next court hearing, for example—without seeking specific authorization from the responsible attorney. However, a legal assistant should seek authorization before giving any *substantive* information—the court's ruling on a motion, for example. The reason is that the attorney might need to provide further information or advice to the client *at the time the client learns of the court's ruling.* Information of that nature cannot be given by a legal assistant without specific direction from the attorney.

Practice Tip

If the paralegal is unaware or uncertain about the status of the case, he can nonetheless take the client's call and promise to provide that information within a day or so. The paralegal's access to the attorney is far greater than the client's, so that he can choose an opportune moment to ask the attorney the client's question with minimal disruption of the attorney's work. Keeping clients informed about their cases is a major contribution to the firm's client relations. Minimizing inopportune interruptions contributes to the attorney's effectiveness and productivity.

Model Rule 1.5(a) Reasonable Fees

The fees charged to clients should be reasonable, taking into account the value of the services to the client, the difficulty of the legal matters involved, and the amount of attorney and paralegal time required. Generally speaking, fees must also conform to the customary fees charged in that community by other attorneys of similar ability and experience for similar legal services.

Whatever fee system is used—flat rate or hourly rate—must be disclosed by the attorney upon being retained by a client. At that time, attorneys ask the client to sign a retainer agreement, which spells out the services to be provided and the fees to be charged, and the client then pays a **retainer**. A retainer is an amount of money deposited with the attorney and against which fees will be charged. When the retainer is exhausted, the client is usually billed monthly for any outstanding balance.

The **retainer** is a deposit that the client pays up front and against which the attorney then charges legal fees.

Paralegal Corollary to Rule 1.5(a)

A paralegal's time may be billed to the client, providing that it is for services requiring the knowledge, expertise, or skills of a paralegal. In small firms, a paralegal sometimes is required to do clerical or secretarial work on client matters, but those tasks should not be billed to clients unless they are an incidental part of the paraprofessional functions.

For example, a common paralegal task is to **Bates stamp** a large quantity of documents. A Bates stamp is a hand-operated numerical stamping device that advances one number each time it is used. Thus, the first document is Bates stamped with the number 0001, the second document becomes 0002 and so forth. Documents are Bates stamped for identification and indexing purposes. If

A **Bates stamp** is a hand-operated device for stamping documents with sequential numbers for the purposes of identification and indexing; used as a verb, to sequentially number documents using a Bates stamp.

700 documents in a single stack are to be stamped sequentially from 0001 to 0700 regardless of content, the stamping process is a clerical task that should not be billed to the client. But if each document must be reviewed, and only correspondence relevant to a particular legal issue is to be stamped, then the stamping process becomes incidental to the reviewing and sorting task that may properly be billed to the client.

The following "Case in Point," *Missouri v. Jenkins*, arose from litigation over school desegregation in Missouri. The plaintiffs—Jenkins, Agyei, and others—were awarded attorney's fees against the State of Missouri, one of the defendants. The *Civil Rights Attorney's Fees Awards Act of 1976* (42 U.S.C. § 1988) permitted the court to award the prevailing party, in its discretion, "a reasonable attorney's fee as part of the costs."

The State of Missouri contended that the U.S. District Court should have compensated the plaintiffs for the work of law clerks and paralegals at their *actual cost* to the employing attorney, rather than at the *market rates* that clients are regularly charged for these services. Missouri proposed an hourly rate of $15, based upon the employees' salaries, benefits, and overhead costs, whereas the market rates authorized by the district court ranged between $35 and $50 per hour. In the following excerpts from the U.S. Supreme Court's opinion, footnote 10 has been included. All other footnotes have been omitted.

A Case in Point

Missouri et al. v. Jenkins, by her friend, Agyei, et al.

491 U.S. 274 (1989)

Clearly, a "reasonable attorney's fee" cannot have been meant to compensate only work performed personally by members of the bar. Rather, the term must refer to a reasonable fee for the work product of the attorney. Thus, the fee must take into account the work not only of attorneys, but also of secretaries, messengers, librarians, janitors, and others whose labor contributes to the work product for which an attorney bills her client; and it must also take account of other expenses and profit. The parties have suggested no reason why the work of paralegals should not be similarly compensated, nor can we think of any. We thus take as our starting point the self-evident proposition that the "reasonable attorney's fee" provided for by statute should compensate the work of paralegals, as well as that of attorneys. The more difficult question is how the work of paralegals is to be valuated in calculating the overall attorney's fee.

* * * *

We reject the argument that compensation for paralegals at rates above "cost" would yield a "windfall" for the prevailing attorney. Neither petitioners nor anyone else, to our knowledge, has ever suggested that the hourly rate applied to the work of an associate attorney in a law firm creates a windfall for the firm's partners or is otherwise improper under § 1988, merely because it exceeds the cost of the attorney's services. If the fees are consistent with market rates and practices, the "windfall" argument has no more force with regard to paralegals than it does for associates.

* * * *

[In footnote 10, at page 288, the Supreme Court noted:]

It has frequently been recognized in the lower courts that paralegals are capable of carrying out many tasks, under the supervision of an attorney, that might otherwise be performed by a lawyer and billed at a higher rate. Such work might include, for example, factual investigation, including locating and interviewing witnesses; assistance with depositions, interrogatories, and document production; compilation of statistical and financial data; checking legal citations; and drafting correspondence. Much such work lies in a gray area of tasks that might appropriately be performed either by an attorney or a paralegal. To the extent that fee applicants under §1988 are not permitted to bill for the work of paralegals at market rates, it would not be surprising to see a greater amount of such work performed by attorneys themselves, *thus increasing the overall cost of litigation.*

[Emphasis added here.]

The Supreme Court affirmed the holding of the district court that the State of Missouri must compensate the prevailing plaintiffs for paralegal work at the market rates that clients normally pay.

Ethics Watch
Every paralegal has a responsibility to ensure that his time sheets are accurate and reasonably complete. If a client questions a bill, the paralegal should be able to reconstruct from his time sheet the nature of the work done for any time billed by him to that client.

Although attorneys are permitted to split fees between them (with the knowledge and consent of the client) in proportion to the work each has done, attorneys may not split fees with paralegals. Paralegals must be compensated by salary, or by some other method not contingent upon the collection of fees for particular client matters. Bonuses *in addition* to such compensation, however, are permitted. Paralegals must *not* be paid "referral fees" for bringing new clients to the firm.

Quotas for Billable Hours

As mentioned earlier, many law firms require attorneys and legal assistants to bill clients a minimum number of hours each year (the "billable quota"). There appears to be a range of about 1,400 to 1,800 hours per year for paralegal quotas. (Billing procedures and practices are discussed further in Chapter 11.) At first thought, it might appear that billable quotas should not present an ethical problem. After all, whether it is called exaggeration, padding, or invention, dishonest billing practices are ethically forbidden and probably fraudulent. All ethical law firms prohibit padding time sheets, and most would immediately terminate a legal assistant found to be doing so.

On careful examination, however, one discovers shades of gray between the absolutes of right and wrong. In the example of Bates stamping, discussed earlier, at what point does that clerical task cease to be an "incidental" activity that can reasonably and ethically be included within the much greater time that the legal assistant is performing professional paralegal tasks? If a legal assistant reviews twenty documents in an hour, during which time she spends two minutes Bates stamping those documents as they are categorized, it is clear that the clerical task is incidental. But if she reviews one hundred documents in one hour and spends ten minutes Bates stamping them as she goes, should she reduce the total time billed to the client by ten minutes? Other situations can be much more problematical than this simple example.

> **Ethics Watch**
>
> If a legal assistant is uncertain about billing time that includes a mixture of clerical and paralegal tasks, she should ask the law firm for guidance. It is the firm's responsibility to establish ethical billing practices and policies. However, it is the legal assistant's responsibility to bring uncertainties to the attention of the firm.

Model Rule 1.6 Confidentiality

The attorney must preserve the confidentiality of all client information. *That confidentiality extends even to the fact that the attorney is representing a particular client in a given legal matter.* The extraordinary strictness of this rule is modified, however, by the client's explicit or implied consent to disclosure. An attorney cannot obtain a client's release from jail without revealing that representation, nor can an attorney respond to a lawsuit on behalf of an anonymous client. By implication, the client consents to such disclosure when he retains the attorney for such purpose.

Under **subpoena**, an attorney is still obligated to protect most client confidences until ordered by a court to reveal them—and even such a court order might be appealed to the higher courts. However, most decisions on this issue have held that the *identity* of the client, *fee arrangements*, and the *client's location* (if known to the attorney) must be disclosed under subpoena.

> **Practice Tip**
>
> Under special circumstances, usually involving minors, courts will seal the true identity of a party and permit the party to proceed in the case under a pseudonym. Thus, a case regarding custody of an infant might be publicly known as "In re Baby M." or "In re Robert M.," for example. The famous Supreme Court decision recognizing a woman's right to an abortion used the pseudonym "Roe" for the plaintiff who brought that case. [Roe v. Wade, 410 U.S. 113 (1973)].

A **subpoena** is a court order to appear and give testimony.

> **Ethics Watch**
>
> As a practical matter, attorneys routinely disclose substantial client information even to opposing attorneys, but this is done as an essential part of effective representation of the client. Most such disclosures are made under the implied consent exception. In her contacts with persons outside of the law firm, a paralegal must use care not to disclose more than is necessary. Except for the most routine type of information, the responsible attorney's authorization should be obtained.

Paralegal Corollary to Rule 1.6

The law firm must protect client information regardless of the method of communication that is used, whether it be oral, on paper, or by electronic transmission (e.g., facsimile or e-mail). There is substantial concern about the use of facsimile and e-mail transmissions that contain confidential client information. Unlike the case of telephone conversations, a facsimile or e-mail transmission may easily be completed without the sender's realizing that she has transmitted it to the wrong telephone number or e-mail address.

> **Ethics Watch**
>
> What should the legal assistant do when she *receives* a privileged attorney-client communication *by error?* Technically, the privilege might have been waived by exposing the communication to a third party (i.e., anyone other than the client and his attorney). But if the recipient recognizes the error before reading the entire communication, she can decline to read further—just as she should do if her next door neighbor's mail ends up in her own mailbox at home.
>
> Most law firms now use facsimile cover sheets with statements (usually in rather small print) warning unintended recipients that it might be a privileged document and should not be read by anyone other than the addressee, in any case.

The following "Case in Point" concerns the removal—by a paralegal—of confidential client documents from a law firm's files. The client was one of the nation's largest tobacco companies. After leaving that firm, the paralegal provided copies of those documents to an attorney-adversary of the tobacco company, who then delivered them to a member of Congress. Ultimately, all of the documents became publicly known—even appearing on the Internet. Some might consider the paralegal a hero of sorts—an after-the-fact "whistle-blower," perhaps. Others might see him as an unethical opportunist. The reader will note that the following is not excerpted from a court opinion.

A Case in Point

The Tobacco Papers

In 1988, Merrell Williams was hired as a paralegal by a large Kentucky law firm. During his employment, he became involved in the review of thousands of documents from the files of a client, Brown and Williamson (B&W), the nation's third-largest tobacco company. At some point during that process, he decided to make *unauthorized copies* of some B&W documents. By the time he was laid off in 1992, the paralegal had copied well over 1,000 pages of client documents—by some reports, as many as 4,000 pages.

Among the documents Williams copied was a July 17, 1963, memorandum written by Brown and Williamson's general counsel, Addison Yeaman. The memorandum included this statement: "We are, then, in the business of selling nicotine, an addictive drug effective in the release of stress mechanisms."

More than thirty years later, in April of 1994, the CEOs of seven tobacco companies—including Thomas Sandefur of Brown and Williamson—raised their right hands before a committee of the House of Representatives and swore to tell the truth. In their testimony they stated that they did not believe nicotine to be addictive. They also testified that their companies had not manipulated the levels of nicotine in cigarettes.

Several months earlier, the former paralegal had begun talking to a plaintiffs' attorney who represented smokers (or their surviving families) in litigation against tobacco companies. Eventually, Williams delivered his copies of the Brown and Williamson documents to that attorney, Richard Scruggs. Attorney Scruggs then flew to Washington, D.C., and turned those documents over to Congressman Henry Waxman, chair of the committee that had heard the tobacco CEOs' sworn testimony. Shortly thereafter, copies were delivered to the Justice Department, the Food and Drug Administration, and the *New York Times*. The Yeaman memo became front page news, and a public furor ensued.

Actually, Brown and Williamson had known for ten months that unauthorized copies of their documents had been made by an employee of their attorneys. In July 1993, Attorney J. Fox DeMoisey sent a letter to B&W's law firm where Merrell Williams had made his copies. In the letter, DeMoisey said that his client, an unnamed former employee of the law firm, had a smoking-related claim against Brown and Williamson, and had made copies of B&W documents because he was "shocked at the fraud and hoax being perpetrated upon the government and the American people." DeMoisey wrote that he had advised his client to return those documents to B&W's law firm, but if his client's claim was not settled, he would file suit and demand production of those very documents in discovery.

The law firm and B&W then sued DeMoisey's client as an "unknown defendant" and obtained a court order for the return of the documents. Williams then

---

Practice Tip

Facsimile transmissions to the wrong party are more likely to occur when a legal assistant uses a single list *containing the facsimile numbers of all attorneys and parties in the case, regardless of their status as allied or opposing parties or their counsel. The mistake occurs when a busy legal assistant glances at the list while she enters the phone number for the receiving facsimile machine—and picks the wrong number.*

It is far safer to maintain at least three lists:

1. *one for the client, any co-counsel, retained experts, and so on*
2. *one for attorneys representing any allied parties (e.g., codefendants)*
3. *one for opposing counsel.*

If the lists are on paper of different colors—red is an effective choice for opposing counsel—it is easy to select the correct list. And with the correct list in hand, the legal assistant will never inadvertently send a memo meant for the client to an opposing counsel!

turned over to the law firm two boxes of documents and his personal computer. The *Los Angeles Times* reported:

> The tobacco company and the law firm for which Williams used to work have sued him, alleging theft and fraud in connection with the secret papers. Among them is a 30-year-old memo in which a top Brown & Williamson executive stated that nicotine is addictive, a conclusion industry officials publicly deny to this day.
>
> Other documents they accuse Williams of stealing concern plans to defeat smokers' lawsuits by hiding industry health research from plaintiffs' lawyers. Still others show Brown & Williamson hard at work on a safer cigarette it never marketed—apparently to avoid liability in the sale of conventional smokes.
>
> "Tobacco Firm Lawyers Try to Smoke Out Possible Mole," *Los Angeles Times*, May 17, 1994.

The "Tobacco Papers'" revelations also added fuel to an on-going criminal investigation by the U.S. Justice Department. In early 1992, the U.S. Attorney's office for the Eastern District of New York had begun an investigation of possible fraud by the tobacco companies. In 1998, PBS Frontline Online reported:

> . . . [T]he industry had claimed a reported $500 million in charitable contributions to its Council on Tobacco Research. Those contributions were tax deductible, and so the theory became that if it could be shown that the contributions were not for real research, but in essence public relations material designed to defeat lawsuits and regulation, then there might be tax fraud.
>
> "Inside the Tobacco Deal: The Government's Criminal Case Against the Tobacco Industry," *PBS Frontline Online*, June 11, 1998.

That investigation never produced major headlines, but the 1994 "Tobacco Papers," following upon the heels of the tobacco CEOs' testimony before Congress, re-lit some fires in the Justice Department. Initially, this new investigation focused on possible perjury by the tobacco CEOs during their testimony before Congress. Eventually, that angle was dropped, however, because of the difficulty of proving that someone had lied about his own "belief."

But the Tobacco Papers also provided evidence that might support charges of fraud. Finally, in 1998, the Justice Department's Task Force on Tobacco sent "target letters" to the attorneys representing Brown and Williamson, and to some of the company's senior executives. A target letter informs the addressee that a grand jury indictment is likely and invites the target to provide any **exculpatory evidence**. The PBS Frontline Online report continued:

> The Task Force is now focusing on allegations of conspiracy to defraud; violations of "1001"—false statements to the U.S. Government; tax violations related to the Council on Tobacco Research; and the degree to which the industry's lawyers conspired to deceive trial courts and the U.S. Government when it came to revealing what it knew about the health effects of tobacco.
>
> "Inside the Tobacco Deal: The Government's Criminal Case Against the Tobacco Industry," *PBS Frontline Online*, June 11, 1998.

According to news reports, Merrell Williams spent the latter part of the 1990s as a paralegal employed by the attorney who delivered the Tobacco Papers to Congressman Henry Waxman in 1994. As part of a tobacco litigation settlement with the State of Mississippi in 1997, William's former law firm dropped its civil suit against him.

Attorney-Client Privilege

All communications between attorney and client are considered privileged, which means that neither the client nor the attorney can be required to reveal their contents. The basis for **attorney-client privilege** is the need for free and

---

Exculpatory evidence is information that tends to establish the innocence of a person suspected of wrongdoing.

The **attorney-client privilege** protects communications (written or oral) between an attorney and his client from compelled disclosure in any judicial proceeding.

frank communication between the two. The U.S. Supreme Court has recognized a strong public policy interest in this privilege:

> Its purpose is to encourage full and frank communication between attorneys and their clients and thereby promote broader public interests in the observance of law and administration of justice. The privilege recognizes that sound legal advice or advocacy serves public ends and that such advice or advocacy depends upon the lawyer's being fully informed by the client.
>
> *Upjohn Co. v. United States*, 449 U.S. 383, 389 (1981)

The "client" must be either an actual client or a prospective one who is consulting with an attorney about possible representation.

Other similar privileges exist, and they also are based upon the need for open and unfettered communication: for example, the doctor-patient, clergy-penitent, and spousal privileges. The term "privilege" refers to the protection against compelled disclosure.

The attorney-client privilege applies also to information communicated between the client and any member of the attorney's staff or her agents: paralegals, secretaries, investigators, consultants, and so forth. Consequently, those staff members and agents cannot be compelled to reveal client confidences.

But the attorney-client privilege is not absolute. It applies only to those communications made with the purpose of informing the attorney, and for providing legal counsel and representation to the client. To be privileged, the communication must relate to a matter for which the client is seeking counsel and/or representation. Although the *fact of communication to the attorney* is privileged, the client might be required to disclose documents that she normally possesses or controls, even though those documents (or copies of them) have been sent to her attorney. For example, calculations prepared by the client or some other person for the purpose of income tax evasion do not become privileged by delivering them to the client's attorney. Attorney-client privilege is not a bottomless pit for concealment of wrongdoing.

Exceptions to the Attorney-Client Privilege

There are some important exceptions to the attorney-client privilege. If the attorney discovers that the client intends to commit a serious crime *endangering other people*, she has an **affirmative duty** to prevent that crime. Because it is an affirmative duty, the attorney must take some positive action, such as reporting the client's intent to the authorities. This obligation regarding crimes arises from the attorney's role as an officer of the court.

There also is a **crime-fraud exception** to the privilege. If the client seeks legal advice to *facilitate* an on-going or future crime or fraud, there no longer exists any public policy interest to be served by keeping those attorney-client communications privileged. If the attorney participates in furthering such a crime or fraud, that also invalidates the privilege. The exception does not apply if the client simply discloses past wrongdoing, unless the purpose in consulting legal counsel is to cover up and perpetuate the past crime or fraud.

If a client sues an attorney for malpractice, the attorney may reveal that client's confidences *to the extent necessary to show that malpractice was not committed*. This exception exists because the client has chosen to make the attorney's representation an issue in the lawsuit. The client may not have it both ways, by attempting to prove malpractice against an attorney who is prevented by the attorney-client privilege from defending himself.

Asserting the Attorney-Client Privilege

Both the attorney and the client may claim the attorney-client privilege and refuse to disclose what was communicated between them—as may both the doctor and the patient, the clergy and the penitent, and the two spouses. But the

---

Practice Tip

Every paralegal should have at hand rubber stamps to be used with confidential documents. Some firms use separate stamps for "PRIVILEGED" and "ATTORNEY-CLIENT COMMUNICATION," whereas other firms combine these statements on a single stamp. Those stamps are best used on the documents themselves, not on the envelopes containing them. For envelopes, "CONFIDENTIAL" or "PERSONAL AND CONFIDENTIAL" should be used.

An **affirmative duty** is a legal obligation to act on one's own initiative, even in the absence of any request or directive from another person or authority.

The **crime-fraud exception** to the attorney-client privilege requires the attorney to report any statement by the client that he intends to commit fraud or a serious crime at a future time.

> **Practice Tip**
>
> Attorneys representing allied parties in the same lawsuit often share confidential information for the mutual benefit of their clients, and there have been court decisions that have held that those communications do not constitute a waiver of privileged attorney-client communications or attorney work product.

> **Practice Tip**
>
> A less obvious form of inadvertent disclosure occurs when a client or other visitor happens to see confidential documents lying on the legal assistant's desk. This can be prevented by keeping client documents and other confidential materials in manila folders whenever the legal assistant is not actually working with them or by putting them out of sight in a desk drawer or returning them to a file cabinet.

Attorney work product includes any notes, memoranda, reports, analysis, legal theory, or data that an attorney—or those working for her on a client matter—create for the benefit of a client. Materials produced by legal assistants, retained experts, consultants, or investigators are considered to be attorney work product.

attorney-client privilege belongs to the client, and he alone may decide to waive that privilege. With the exceptions already mentioned, the attorney may not otherwise disclose privileged communications without the client's consent.

Even so, as the client's agent, the attorney, without client authorization, might create a legally effective waiver of the privilege if she improperly or inadvertently discloses the client's confidential communication to another person. Of course, such a disclosure might expose the attorney to liability for malpractice—but that liability wouldn't change the fact that a waiver had occurred. Consequently, attorneys must always exercise cautious judgment when they share any client information with other parties.

Inadvertent Breaches of Client Confidentiality

Although a legal assistant could never act on behalf of a client with the authority that an attorney has, an inadvertent disclosure of a client confidence could aid opposing counsel, embarrass the client, and damage the firm's ethical reputation. So, legal assistants must discipline themselves to protect client confidentiality. Although no research has been published on this issue, common sense would suggest that the *inadvertent breach* of client confidentiality is one of the most frequent ethical violations committed by legal assistants.

In the opening scenario for this chapter, the supermarket conversation involving Patricia and Louise illustrates one form of this ethical breach. Other breaches of confidence might be less obvious: for example, listing client matters on a resume or providing details about client matters during an interview for a position with a different law firm. Obvious or not, such actions can be breaches of confidentiality. Of course, if a paralegal accepts a new position, he might have to reveal the name of a former firm's client in order to explain why he should be disqualified from working on matters where a conflict of interest might occur. (See the discussion of *Model Rules 1.7–1.9*, below.)

Whenever paralegals are outside of the firm, someplace where others can overhear their conversation, it is particularly easy for them to breach a confidence. It is likely that the most common inadvertent breaches of confidentiality committed by paralegals occur in elevators, during meals in restaurants, and at parties or "happy hour" gatherings. It can be very tempting to entertain colleagues, friends, or relatives with intriguing tidbits about a client matter. Omitting the identities of the parties involved is *not* adequate protection, because someone listening might be sufficiently familiar with the facts being discussed to correctly guess the identities of the parties involved. Furthermore, the friends or relatives might later share those same tidbits with others who are able to recognize the parties. The only safe and ethical course is a strict code of silence about client matters.

> **Ethics Watch**
>
> A serious dilemma can be the talkative colleague. What should a legal assistant do if a colleague discusses confidential matters within the hearing of others? It is a difficult situation, but the legal assistant's ethical obligation to the client's interests must come first. If a private conversation with the offending colleague does not put an end to the loose talk, the legal assistant will have to inform a responsible person in the firm. Anything less probably breaches the firm's fiduciary duty to the client.

The Attorney Work Product Rule

Although the **attorney work product** rule does not fall within the scope of attorney-client privilege, it is discussed here because it shares a similar protection, and because attorney work product often is permeated with client confidences—in a memorandum analyzing the facts and legal issues of a case, for example. Consequently, the attorney-client privilege and the **work product rule** might both apply to some documents within the attorney's case file. Inadvertent disclosure of work product might result in a disclosure of client confidences, as well.

The privilege for attorney-client communications is based upon a special relationship between those individuals. The work product rule, however, is based upon a *balancing of interests* during **pretrial discovery:** That is, the right of the opposition to avoid court-room surprises is balanced against the right of the attorney to prepare an effective representation without fear that he will be compelled to surrender his entire files to the opposing side. Because unlimited discovery would have such a chilling effect upon the attorney's preparation for trial, the courts have held that his work product should be shielded from pretrial discovery. Unlike the attorney-client communication privilege, *the work product protection belongs to the attorney*, and only the attorney can waive its protection under the rule.

The work product rule does *not* apply to information, analysis, and theories held by experts retained to testify in court. Consequently, attorneys usually prohibit communication between expert consultants who will *not* testify and other experts who are retained for the very purpose of testifying. The crime-fraud exception, discussed above, applies to attorney work product as well as to attorney-client communications.

> The **work product rule** is a rule of evidence that states that neither side in a lawsuit can force another party's attorney to reveal the work that attorney has done in preparation for the lawsuit.
>
> **Pretrial discovery** is a process, established by statute or court rules, during which all parties in a lawsuit exchange the nonprivileged information that they have about the facts and issues in controversy.

Model Rules 1.7–1.9 Avoiding Conflicts of Interest

Attorneys must avoid all situations in which their loyalty to a client might be compromised by conflicting loyalties to others. The attorney's self-interest, above all, must not be permitted to influence her representation of the client: That is the clearest conflict of all. Attorneys are fiduciaries to their clients. As explained in Chapter 1, a fiduciary is a person in the position of a *trustee*—one who is entrusted with the property interest of another and owes that person the highest duty of loyalty. For that reason, an attorney is generally forbidden to have business dealings with clients outside of their relationship as attorney and client.

Attorneys must not represent two clients who are adversaries to each other. The reason is that the attorney's duty of loyalty might be divided between the adversarial clients—a violation of his fiduciary duty. It is not necessary that the two clients be direct adversaries in the matter for which the attorney is now retained—it is sufficient to create a **conflict of interest** if:

- there is a substantial relationship between the matters for which the two clients retained the attorney; or
- the attorney possesses prior client confidences that could relate to the new legal matter presented for his representation.

Some courts have held that it is a conflict if the clients are adversaries in *any* legal proceeding, past or present. Whenever a new client is obtained, law firms do a **conflict check** against a list of all past and current clients and opposing parties to ensure that the new client has no adverse interests to a prior or present client of the firm.

Law firms should disqualify themselves from acting as legal counsel whenever a conflict of interest arises. Even if the conflict exists for only a single attorney within the firm, the entire law firm might have to disqualify itself. However, an exception is permitted where the adversarial relationship is only a potential one, and the parties have consented to mutual representation by the same law firm. This can occur when several persons consult an attorney to draw up a partnership agreement. At the formation of the partnership, they have

> A **conflict of interest** is the existence of competing loyalties.
>
> A **conflict check** is the process used by law firms to detect possible conflicts of interest in the representation of a new client.

common interests. If later there is a falling out among partners, they will have adverse interests. Before giving advice and drawing up the partnership agreement, the attorney will have the partners-to-be sign a consent form for mutual representation. The consent form will alert the clients to the possibility of future conflicts that would prevent the attorney from continuing their mutual representation.

Conflicts Arising When Attorneys Change Firms

When an attorney moves to a new firm, the new firm is sometimes forced to consequently disqualify itself from representing current or new clients who are adverse to clients of the law firm the new attorney has just left. Depending upon circumstances, this can actually force a firm to withdraw from a case in progress, as well as to refuse new clients or new client matters that present a potential conflict. The only absolute protection against this problem is for the attorney's new law firm to obtain *the informed, written consent* of the attorney's former client.

In recent decades, the courts have become a little less Draconian in their response to potential conflicts arising from the movement of attorneys to a new law firm. Although the courts are far from unanimous in their approach, several general principles appear to be evolving:

- A law firm should not be disqualified from representing a client unless that representation would actually harm an attorney's former client or interfere with the proper conduct of court proceedings.
- In weighing factors that favor disqualification, the court should keep in mind that disqualification will deprive the law firm's current client of her right to choice of counsel.
- The mere appearance of impropriety does not require disqualification.
- The arriving attorney is *presumed* to have been privy to the confidences of clients of his former law firm—it is not necessary that he actually received such confidences.

Many courts have declined to disqualify a law firm from representation if it took *prompt and adequate measures* to isolate the new attorney from the client matter that presents a conflict. Known as "screening," this process requires the firm to erect an "ethical wall" (sometimes termed a "Chinese Wall," after the impregnable Great Wall of China) of internal rules and procedures that preclude even inadvertent contact between the new attorney and information about the sensitive client matter.

In those law firms facing potential conflicts raised by bringing aboard a new attorney or legal assistant (whose prior clients' interests might be adverse to those of his new firm's clients), court decisions appear to favor the following characteristics for an effective ethical wall:

- physical separation of the offices used by the new attorney and the attorneys and staff working on the shielded client matter
- separate support staff for the new attorney and the attorneys working on the shielded matter
- locked file cabinets for all files in the shielded matter, with strict limitations on access to keys
- special passwords for access to computer files involving the shielded matter
- a written statement (identifying the client matter to be shielded and setting out the procedures to be followed) that is read and then signed by each attorney and non-attorney in the law firm.

Paralegal Corollary to Rules 1.7–1.9

When paralegals change firms, an almost identical dilemma arises. But, in general, the courts have been somewhat more lenient in those cases, less often requiring the new law firm to disqualify itself based upon an **imputed conflict of interest**. The presumption that confidential information was acquired in the paralegal's previous law firm is more easily rebutted for a paralegal than for an attorney. Furthermore, if the paralegal was not privy to client confidences, then shielding becomes unnecessary in the new law firm. Of course, if the paralegal *does* know confidential client information from the old firm, she must be shielded by her new employer in the same manner as a new attorney in that circumstance.

What should a court do when an employee of the *defendant's* attorney—only 60 days prior to the start of trial—leaves that firm and accepts employment in the *plaintiff's* law firm? That was the issue before the Arizona Court of Appeals in the following "Case in Point." Important issues in this case were the "transient" employee's knowledge of client confidences (i.e., those of the defendant) and her subsequent level of involvement in the plaintiff's lawsuit against her prior firm's client. This is a summary of the court's opinion, with verbatim quotation of selected passages.

> An **imputed conflict of interest** is a conflict ascribed to an attorney because another professional in his office (e.g., an attorney or paralegal) has an apparent conflict of interest in the matter at hand.

A CASE IN POINT

Smart Industries Corp. v. Superior Court

179 Ariz. 141 (1994), 876 P.2d 1176

The defendant in this personal injury case moved to disqualify the law firm representing the plaintiff. Approximately sixty days before the case was to go to trial, Janet Gregston, a legal secretary/paralegal working in the law firm representing the defendant, suddenly left that firm. Ten days later she began working as a legal secretary in the plaintiff's law firm.

Constance Miller, defendant's counsel and Gregston's former employer, stated in an affidavit that Gregston "was privy to exhaustive client conferences, correspondences between counsel and clients, strategic planning, litigation preparation and documentation, pretrial conferences with clients, lay and expert witnesses."(At p. 1178.)

Mr. Engler, plaintiff's counsel in the case and Ms. Gregston's new employer, assured the court that she did not have "a broad spectrum of 'paralegal' tasks" in her new position. The court summarized: "Mr. Engler also avowed that he had given 'specific and segregated authority' to a separate paralegal with her own secretary" for discovery, client conferences, trial exhibits, and so forth. (At p. 1178) Ms. Gregston's affidavit stated that she had been assured by her new employer that she would not be asked to reveal client confidences from her prior employment.

The Arizona Court of Appeals observed: "However, Ms. Gregston's initials and signature appear on several pleadings in this case, both in the underlying litigation and in [this matter now before] this court. Thus, it is apparent that she is presently performing secretarial work on this case." (At page 1179.)

The trial court had ruled as follows:

"Plaintiff's counsel has contended that he has studiously insulated himself from any possible knowledge his employee might have, and the court accepts this as true.

"Were this an attorney there would be absolutely no doubt in the court's mind that disqualification would be proper. This is not an attorney.

"Not being an attorney, two thoughts are raised.

"The first is that the court really has no method of protecting the privilege of confidentiality which Ms. Miller's client is entitled to enjoy.

"The second is that there is no code of conduct in place which would guide a lawyer. The code of conduct is that of the employer.

"The upshot of all of this is that the continued representation of the plaintiff by her attorney and a defendant attorney's former employee looks bad. It cannot but be perceived by the public that something fishy is going on. Thus, it smells bad, too.

"However bad it might appear, mere appearance of evil is not a sufficient basis for the court to disqualify an attorney. While it might be that he should, ethically, withdraw, the court is not in a position to force the issue.

"ORDERED that the motion to disqualify plaintiff's counsel is overruled. (At page 1179.)"

The Arizona Court of Appeals then considered the trial court's rationale and conclusion. In reaching its holding, the court of appeals made the following points:

- "... Arizona does not recognize the 'cone of silence' or other screening mechanisms as an exception to a lawyer's imputed disqualification of the new firm...." (At page 1182.)
- Such a strict rule need not apply to nonlawyer assistants, who "have neither a financial interest in the outcome of a particular litigation, nor the choice of which clients they serve." (At page 1184.)
- An appropriate screening mechanism for non-attorneys would satisfy a lawyer's duty to supervise a nonlawyer employee under the rules of professional conduct, and thus prevent disqualification.

Nonetheless, the court of appeals held that the plaintiff's counsel must be disqualified, based on the facts before it. That holding was based upon the following:

- Ms. Gregston acquired client confidences during her work on behalf of the defendants at her prior law firm.
- Those client confidences are substantially related to the case at hand, which is about to go to trial.
- The defendant did not consent to Ms. Gregston's employment by opposing counsel.
- Ms. Gregston was not shielded by her new employer from participating in the case she worked on in her former firm.
- "Furthermore, we observe that counsel's refusal ... to even offer to screen this employee from working on the very matter which gave rise to the problem shows an apparent insensitivity by counsel to the valid concerns of the adverse client...." (At page 1185.) [Footnote omitted.]

"Under the facts of this case, we conclude that the trial court should have granted the motion to disqualify plaintiff's counsel, and abused its discretion in failing to do so. No screening mechanism was utilized to assure Smart that its confidences were preserved, and, at this stage of the litigation, given Mrs. Gregston's participation on behalf of the St. Germaines, we cannot fashion any remedial action that counsel could employ to mitigate Smart's perception that its confidences could be compromised, or to satisfy the duties imposed by [the ethical standards under the Rules of the Arizona Supreme Court].

"CONCLUSION

"For the foregoing reasons, we hold that the trial court abused its discretion in denying Smart's motion to disqualify. We remand this matter to the trial court for entry of an order consistent with this opinion. (At p. 1185.)"

In the preceding "Case in Point," the Arizona Court of Appeals *remanded* the case (i.e., sent it back to the trial court) with a very specific instruction: to enter a judgment disqualifying the plaintiff's counsel in the underlying lawsuit. In explaining its decision, the appellate court noted the proximity to trial and the difficulty in belatedly fashioning some satisfactory remedial measures that would protect the interests of the defendant. If the trial were six months away, however, the court might have reached a different resolution, short of disqualification.

Model Rule 1.15 Safeguarding Client Funds

Attorneys are forbidden to put law firm monies and client monies in the same account. Whether received as retainers, in escrow, or in settlements, all client funds must be deposited into special bank accounts, known as **trust accounts**. Occasionally, attorneys are disciplined for **commingling** client funds and law firm funds in the same account.

Paralegal Corollary to Rule 1.15

Although it is unusual for paralegals to handle client funds, a paralegal must have no part in mishandling client funds, even as a passive observer.

Model Rule 3.1 Avoiding Frivolous Claims or Contentions

The ABA's *Model Rule 3.1* forbids an attorney to assert a **frivolous claim** or defense for his client. A claim or defense would be frivolous if it were completely lacking in any possible merit under the law. But what appears frivolous to one attorney—or judge—might appear to be cutting-edge and justifiable to another, and an attorney has an affirmative ethical duty to raise any valid argument available for his client. It appears that *Model Rule 3.1* sets up a potential conflict between the attorney's ethical duty to vigorously represent the interests of his client and his duty under the rule to avoid frivolous claims or contentions. Of course, the basis for the rule is to protect the judicial process from the confusion and delays caused by whimsical and dilatory arguments perpetrated by irresponsible attorneys. The only resolution of this potential conflict is to convince the court of the attorney's own good faith.

Paralegal Corollary to Rule 3.1

While analyzing and researching legal issues, a legal assistant should not automatically disregard novel theories of the law. Today's novel theory could become the accepted legal standard for the future. For example, the nine justices on the U.S. Supreme Court seldom reach a unanimous decision—usually there is a minority opinion written by one or more of the justices on the losing side of the court's deliberations. Decades later, that minority opinion might be adopted by a different Supreme Court and become the law of the land. A more prolific source of novel legal theories are the numerous law review journals published by the nation's many schools of law.

The point here is that compliance with *Rule 3.1* is the responsibility of the attorney, and the legal assistant should not preempt that responsibility by keeping unusual legal theories to himself. It is better to report the novel idea to the attorney and permit her to determine whether it might be frivolous to argue it.

Model Rule 3.3 Candor before the Court

Not only is an attorney forbidden to deceive the court, he has an affirmative duty to inform the court of all material facts and relevant law, *including those unfavorable*

> **Practice Tip**
>
> A paralegal can prepare for future job changes by keeping a list of all clients on whose cases he has done work. Because this list is itself confidential, it is preferable that the paralegal applicant participate in the screening process and that the screening be done only when a final decision has been made to hire the paralegal.

An attorney must deposit client funds, which the attorney holds in trust, in a **trust account**, separate from other funds.

Commingling is the mixing together of funds belonging to different persons.

A **frivolous claim** is one completely without merit, lacking any reasonable basis under the facts and the law.

The **candor rule** requires an attorney to disclose to the court all evidence and law relevant to the proceeding, including evidence or law unfavorable to the attorney's client.

to his own client. The **candor rule** is intended to ensure that the court has before it all of the facts and law that are needed to arrive at a just determination. As an officer of the court, the attorney may not withhold that essential information—his first duty is to the court. Although the candor rule applies to both civil and criminal cases, a breach of this rule is most severely punished in criminal cases when the prosecution has withheld exculpatory evidence from the defense.

One obvious difficulty with the candor rule is balancing the attorney's two (potentially conflicting) duties: his duty to the court and his duty to the client. Although the rule requires the attorney to put his duty to the court first, in actual practice it can be exceedingly difficult to evaluate the *importance* of the facts or the law that is not yet before the court. Carried to its ultimate extreme, the rule would appear to require an attorney to compensate for his adversary's every ineptitude and oversight, no matter how minor, in presenting a case to the court. Judges understand this difficulty and generally use great discretion in enforcing the candor rule.

Of course, the candor rule also forbids active deception: misstating the law, distorting facts, and so forth. If the attorney discovers that his client has lied to the court, the attorney has an affirmative duty to report that perjury to the court. The latter example is an exception to the general rule that knowledge of past crimes shall remain in confidence with the attorney. Active deception is far less common than failure to be forthcoming and is more universally condemned in the legal profession. If a paralegal were to observe active deception, she might want to explore the options discussed under "Concerns about the Attorney's Conduct," later in this chapter.

Paralegal Corollary to Rule 3.3

If an attorney does not inform the court of an important but unfavorable case, the paralegal should probably discuss the issue with the attorney. It is quite possible that the paralegal does not understand the law of the case that appears to be unfavorable. The case might actually be irrelevant. Another possibility is that the attorney has simply overlooked relevant facts or law.

Ethics Watch

Legal assistants sometimes forget that an attorney needs all the news—the good and the bad. In legal research, this lapse can result in reporting to the attorney only those cases that are favorable to the client's position. But the rule of candor requires the attorney to divulge unfavorable cases that the opposing party fails to bring to the attention of the court. When the attorney relies upon the legal assistant for research, he expects to learn of *all relevant law,* not just the favorable law. In addition to the ethical question, the attorney must not be caught unaware when the opposing counsel cites an unfavorable case. A legal assistant's failure to report unfavorable cases might even expose the attorney to malpractice liability.

Model Rule 5.3 Utilizing Nonlawyer Assistants

Attorneys are required to ensure that their non-attorney assistants comply with the ethical standards for attorneys. That means that the attorney must ensure that the legal assistant acts with diligence, keeps client confidences, avoids conflicts of interest, applies her professional skills, and so on. A lawyer is personally responsible for the unethical conduct of a paralegal if the attorney:

- orders or ratifies the unethical conduct or
- has supervisory authority over the paralegal and knows (or should have known) of the unethical conduct and fails to take reasonable remedial action.

Paralegal Corollary to Rule 5.3

A legal assistant should approach his duties with the same sense of ethical responsibility that an attorney should apply. Clients expect their attorney to be diligent, prompt, honest, competent, and responsive to the client's needs and inquiries. They expect her to seek more expert counsel—or refer the client to expert counsel—whenever the client's attorney is not confident of her own expertise or skills. Because the attorneys who employ legal assistants are held to such high standards, the legal paraprofessional has an obligation to meet those same standards.

Although many law firms provide formal training in legal ethics for paralegals, some do not. Perhaps the latter firms believe that the training received in paralegal programs is adequate and that ethical issues can be addressed in the office as they arise. Understandably, malpractice insurance carriers are concerned about paralegal ethics and could require periodic formal training as a condition of coverage. If a legal assistant is uncertain about ethical issues, he should take the initiative to obtain further education either in the firm or elsewhere.

Model Rule 7.3 Soliciting Clients

Attorneys are generally prohibited from making a direct solicitation to a prospective client "with whom the lawyer has no family or prior professional relationship." This includes any solicitation by telephone, letter, or other means. Model Rule 7.3 does not prohibit, however, advertisements to the general public nor mass mailings to people not known to have a specific need for legal services. One concern has been the protection of victims and their families when a major disaster might trigger unethical solicitation for clients. The ABA has published a guide for local bar associations, *Bar Response to a Mass Disaster: Protecting the Victims from Unethical Lawyer Conduct.*

Paralegal Corollary to Rule 7.3

As the employee and agent of an attorney, a paralegal must not do what the attorney is not permitted to do. This is a rule that easily can be forgotten when friends are talking about a legal situation with which the employing attorney could assist them. Although the paralegal might have a pre-existing relationship with the prospective client, the employing attorney does not. In some states, it is a crime for a non-attorney to act as a "runner" who solicits clients at locations such as hospitals and courthouses.

Ethical Rules, Discrimination, and Sexual Harassment

The *Model Rules* do not address issues of discrimination. Nor do they address directly office romances or sexual relationships with clients, although the rule against conflicts of interest should apply to the latter. Some state bars are moving to update their rules to cover these topics, and future revision of the ABA's *Model Rules* might address them as well.

These issues raise ethical questions for legal assistants who could be potential victims *or defendants* in situations where improper conduct either occurs or is alleged. There are federal and state statutes and regulations that address discrimination. The federal *Civil Rights Acts* prohibit discrimination on the basis of race, color, age, creed, national origin and sex. In many states, the *Civil Rights Acts* are mirrored or augmented by state laws that often cover the smaller companies that are exempt under federal law. The federal acts and most state laws permit a private lawsuit for discrimination prohibited under those laws.

> **Practice Tip**
>
> *Attorneys often attend legal seminars for continuing legal education. Many of these are sponsored by state and local bar associations. Many seminars on legal ethics would be just as suitable for paralegals as they would be for attorneys. Some firms will pay the expenses of paralegals who attend such seminars. It is worthwhile to check with the local bar association to see if special rates are available for paralegals.*

An act of discrimination can be overt and obvious, as in an openly acknowledged firm policy that prohibits Muslim employees from working on matters in which the client is a Hindu—or Hindus from working on the client matters of Muslims—or it can be subtle, as in a silent practice of denying promotions to any employees over 50 years of age. Paralegals need to ensure that their personal prejudices (which presumably *everyone* has) do not cause them to deprive any client of their best professional efforts and do not cause harm to colleagues or anyone whom they supervise.

In the past decade or so, society at large has "discovered" what most women and some men have known for a very long time: A *power differential* between two individuals—for example, employer and employee, teacher and student, professional and client—can be the catalyst for sexual exploitation of the individual in the less-powerful position. Although the federal *Civil Rights Acts* do not mention sexual harassment, federal regulations implementing those laws have treated sexual harassment as a form of sexual discrimination, and that interpretation has been approved by the courts.

Quid pro quo is the exchange of something of value ("this for that") between two persons.

Originally, sexual harassment was defined narrowly as a **quid pro quo** demand (i.e., a demand of "this for that")—in this context, a demand for sexual favors in exchange for some advantage, or as the price of being *otherwise* left alone. More recently, a "sexually hostile environment" has been recognized as a distinct form of sexual harassment.

A **sexually hostile environment** exists when the conduct is unwanted comments or actions of a romantic, sexual, or suggestive nature, which are more than a reasonable person would tolerate.

Although the area of law dealing with various forms of sexual harassment is constantly evolving, a **sexually hostile environment** in the workplace is considered to be characterized by such things as:

- unwanted touching of a sexual or suggestive nature;
- unwanted advances, including repeated requests for dates after it is clear that the romantic target is not interested in a dating relationship;
- unwanted romantic, sexual, or suggestive comments directed by the harasser at the victim;
- unwanted comments or compliments upon the victim's appearance or sexuality; and
- unwanted communications (e.g., e-mail) or displays (including "pinups") of a suggestive nature.

Notice that each example includes the word "unwanted," because that is at the heart of sexual harassment. There is no legal bar to mutually acceptable flirting or touching, so long as there is no hint of coercion or duress.

SCENARIO

Eduardo Peña is a legal assistant in a small partnership of four attorneys. The firm specializes in professional malpractice defense, representing mostly doctors, lawyers, and accountants. Eduardo was recruited by the firm because he had worked for six years as a registered nurse, and he is knowledgeable about medical issues and hospital procedures.

"I decided to get my paralegal certificate because I was tired of working all kinds of shifts in the hospital, plus the stress was really getting to me. So many hospitals have been taken over by large corporations interested mainly in the 'bottom line.' And this whole 'managed care' thing has pressured even the independent hospitals to cut back on nursing staff. The patient load has really gotten out of hand as a result. Of course, all of this makes for more malpractice suits against hospitals and doctors, so now I'm helping doctors to put the blame on the understaffed hospitals when something goes wrong. I really love it when we nail one of those biggies for negligent understaffing."

Although Eduardo specializes in the medical malpractice cases, he also does some work in legal malpractice. "We have two paralegals: Joanna and I. Joanna is a CPA who got interested in litigation when she was sued by one of her own clients. She handles the accounting malpractice, and both of us share the lawyer cases. Joanna's going to law school at night and has this secret hope that the firm will take her on as an associate if she passes the bar. Personally, I think they'll jump at the chance."

What kinds of things get lawyers in trouble? "Things such as commingling client funds; failing to disclose a conflict of interest; self-dealing [trading for the attorney's personal benefit in client assets held by the attorney as a fiduciary]; failing to raise an important defense in a lawsuit; doing sloppy legal research. All kinds of things. Every once in a while some guy even lets the statute of limitations run out. Isn't that incredible?"

"My work is pretty much like any civil litigation. I do a lot of discovery work, especially in the medical cases. I coordinate trial preparation with the doctors and pharmacists that serve as our experts. If it's a medical case, I'm usually in court during trial. I do a lot of the legal research on medical malpractice—and sometimes in the lawyer cases, too. I'm really interested in ethical issues, so this is a great job for me. It has even motivated me to take some philosophy courses at the community college. Who knows? Maybe I'll get a master's in philosophy and start on a *third* career, in teaching. No, I'm just kidding. I like my job." ■

SECTION 2. ETHICAL ISSUES OF SPECIAL IMPORTANCE TO LEGAL ASSISTANTS

Although legal assistants and attorneys share many ethical concerns and responsibilities, there are some issues of particular importance to legal assistants. These issues involve interaction with clients and other non-attorneys, concerns about the ethical standards of clients and attorneys, and the unauthorized practice of law.

DISCLOSING ONE'S STATUS AS A LEGAL ASSISTANT

Paralegals often have extensive contact with clients. Until the client is clearly familiar with the paralegal's name and status, the paralegal must make her status clear each time she communicates with the client. The same rule applies to contacts with other attorneys and their staff. When contacting attorneys who represent other parties, the paralegal should identify the party her firm is representing in the matter. This latter disclosure is important, because some parties might be allied and cooperating with each other, whereas other parties might be adversaries.

Paralegals routinely contact witnesses, experts, librarians, police officers, and so forth, as part of their duties. Unless instructed otherwise by the attorney, the paralegal should identify her status and the law firm's name when making such contacts. In some circumstances, a paralegal might need to make inquiries of people who are neither potential parties nor potential witnesses, and who

> **Ethics Watch**
>
> If someone is represented by legal counsel, it is unethical for another attorney—*or her paralegal*—to have direct contact with that client. This applies to all clients, including corporations. Instead of contacting that person directly, the paralegal must contact that party's attorney. Occasionally, someone's attorney might authorize direct contact for some limited purpose, but that is not common. Even attorneys representing allied parties (e.g., joint plaintiffs in the same lawsuit) customarily make all contacts with the other parties through their legal counsel.
>
> If direct contact with another party has been authorized by legal counsel, it is essential that the paralegal identify his status, the name of the attorney with whom he is working, and the party that his firm represents. That disclosure gives the other party an opportunity to check with counsel before continuing with any further communication.

have no legal interest at stake in the case. For that type of inquiry, the attorney might suggest that the paralegal not disclose her affiliation with a law firm. But nondisclosure is never justified if the legal interests of the person spoken to could be affected in any way. Unless directed otherwise by the responsible attorney, the legal assistant should make the disclosure described above.

> **Ethics Watch**
>
> Paralegals can easily be mistaken for attorneys. For obvious reasons, the paralegal has an ethical responsibility to disclose her status when communicating with clients, attorneys, court clerks, and the public, and so on. And when an innocent assumption misleads someone, the paralegal has an affirmative duty to correct that impression by stating that she is *not* an attorney.

CONCERNS ABOUT REPRESENTING A "GUILTY" CLIENT

"*Even the bad guy is entitled to legal counsel.*" That statement summarizes a fundamental, but often troubling, principle of the American legal system. Some persons might prefer that attorneys appoint themselves as unofficial "judges" and withhold legal representation from anyone they recognize to be "undeserving" of a legal defense. Unfortunately, one's definition of "undeserving" can be influenced by political, socioeconomic, ethnic, and other perspectives—and also by misleading circumstances.

Every few months we read of wrongly convicted individuals being released after spending years in prison—some of them on death row. It is an increasingly frequent event now that DNA testing can be applied to human tissue or fluid evidence that has been held in storage since the time of trials that occurred years or even decades ago. Virtually all of these released prisoners were prosecuted, convicted, and sentenced *in good faith* by honest prosecutors, jurors, and judges trying to do the right thing—some were convicted based upon *multiple* "eye witness" identifications by victims and others. The problem was that those prosecutors, judges, and jurors lacked the DNA evidence that ultimately led to the convicts' release; *they honestly believed the defendants to be guilty*. This possibility of being misled by appearances and incomplete evidence is why the symbol of justice—the lady with the scales—is always blindfolded.

The point of this discussion is not to criticize the justice system, but to emphasize the dangers inherent in presuming that a particular person does not deserve vigorous legal representation. Everyone is entitled to legal counsel and a *chance* at gaining justice—even one who might appear to be the "bad guy."

CONCERNS ABOUT THE CLIENT'S ETHICS

Dealings with the unethical client pose a difficult quandary. It is entirely possible for a paralegal to stumble across something that suggests that the client is not what the attorney believes her to be. The paralegal might even discover that the client has been lying to her own attorney or falsifying evidence. What can be done when an attorney suddenly finds himself representing an unethical client?

The action taken by the attorney will depend upon the nature of the client's unethical behavior and other circumstances. The attorney might ask the court to relieve him from the representation of that client—although the court is unlikely to consent unless the client is able to retain other legal counsel. He might inform the court that, unwittingly, he has misled the court with false evidence provided by the client. The exact remedy will depend upon the situation, the laws of that jurisdiction, and the professional code of ethics that governs the conduct of attorneys in that state. For the paralegal who comes across evidence of client misconduct, the duty is clear: Inform the attorney at once.

CONCERNS ABOUT AN ATTORNEY'S CONDUCT

A more difficult situation for a paralegal would be any concern about the ethical behavior of an attorney in his own office. If an attorney *were* to act unethically, there would be a number of serious considerations. Among those things at stake could be:

- the interests of justice,
- the client's interests,
- the attorney's reputation and career,
- the paralegal's sense of ethical responsibility, and
- the firm's reputation and the practices of other attorneys in the firm.

It would be a difficult situation in which to remain objective and to follow a course of action that is ethical, prudent, and fair to all concerned.

Part of the problem is that "unethical" is a *highly subjective* term, one which is far easier to use than to define. Discussed in the abstract, ethical rules often sound clear and unambiguous. But real-life situations often seem far less clear, and people find themselves pulled in opposite directions by conflicting values and/or loyalties.

Of course, it would be painfully difficult to question one's employer about ethical matters. Yet, for a variety of reasons many people feel that such a dialog is *absolutely essential*. A few such reasons are listed below:

- the very real possibility that the legal assistant's ethical doubts are unfounded
- the belief that ordinary decency requires one to permit the employing attorney to explain the situation
- the belief that the attorney should have an opportunity to correct the problem
- the importance of avoiding unwarranted damage to the attorney's reputation, which might result if others were told

The *unfounded accusation* made in good faith is a genuine and unnerving possibility, and is a persuasive reason for discussing the matter with the attorney. Although difficult, it might be possible to explore the issue with questions that do not appear accusatory and do not cause emotional defenses to be raised: "I think I must have misunderstood what you said to our client yesterday afternoon. Could you clarify that for me?" If the response demonstrates that the attorney has acted correctly, after all, the paralegal will be greatly relieved that she did not reach an unfounded conclusion.

Perhaps the most cautious approach would be to speak with an officer of the local bar association, without identifying the employing attorney. This type of consultation would offer the following benefits:

- an informed and objective evaluation of the situation
- information about the paralegal's rights and responsibilities under the law
- guidance in avoiding personal liability (e.g., for slander)
- information about laws that protect **whistle-blowers** who report employer misconduct to the authorities

Given the nature of the problem, many reputable attorneys would provide this type of consultation without charge to the paralegal, as a professional responsibility. Of course, client confidences must *never* be breached in such a discussion.

A **whistle-blower** is an employee who reports the misconduct of his employer.

WHEN NONLAWYERS PROVIDE LEGAL SERVICES TO THE PUBLIC

As mentioned in Chapters 1 and 2, the marketplace has created a haphazard "solution" of sorts to the high cost of legal services. Across the nation, thousands of non-attorney providers have set up shop to offer legal services directly to the public. They sometimes advertise themselves as "paralegals," or refer to their services as "self-help legal clinics" or "legal typing services." (See the "Case in Point" in Chapter 2.) These non-attorney providers are able to charge low fees because they are not supervised by attorneys and do not have the overhead or income expectations of attorneys.

These services are unlicensed, unregulated, and often operated in violation of state laws regulating the practice of law. Small landlords use their services for unlawful detainer (i.e., eviction) actions. Married couples call upon them to prepare simple wills or to obtain an uncomplicated divorce. Debtors use them to prepare bankruptcy petitions. The non-attorney legal providers might or might not have legal experience or paralegal education. Predictably, some have botched their work, doing great harm to clients.

Apparently, no one has completed a systematic study to evaluate the quality of the services offered by these unsupervised non-attorneys, nor of the frequency of consumer complaints about their services. A few non-attorney providers have been prosecuted in some states for practicing law without a license, and a small number have received jail terms.

The Practice of Law

Almost everyone recognizes that one must have a license to practice law. Although it can be a criminal offense to practice law without a license, it is not always easy to define the practice of law. Fundamentally, to practice law is to provide *to someone else* services that require special legal knowledge and skills—knowledge and skills that can be obtained only by completing a comprehensive curriculum in the law. The function of the state bar exams is to evaluate the legal knowledge and skills of each candidate for the bar. Because the practice of law involves providing services to another person, representing or "advising" oneself is not considered to be practicing law.

The courts in some states have held that one can be "practicing law" without appearing in court and without even claiming to be a lawyer. Filling out legal forms might require special legal knowledge, and, in many states, if it is done for another, that might be considered to be the practice of law. That seems most obviously true if the non-attorney says something like, "You don't need to go to a lawyer, I can help you with the necessary forms." The latter statement is a legal conclusion based (presumably) upon the non-attorney's assessment of the *legal implications* of the "client's" situation and is offered as legal guidance to that person. One danger is that through ignorance the non-attorney might fail to ask pertinent questions that would reveal important legal issues, thereby leaving the client vulnerable to serious legal harm. In many states, it makes no difference whether the services are provided for a fee or without charge, because the principle purpose of the prohibition is to protect the public from incompetence, not to prevent ill-gotten financial gain to non-attorneys.

The Unauthorized Practice of Law

The *unlawful* practice of law is often termed the unauthorized practice of law (UPL). In most jurisdictions it is illegal to practice law unless one *has a license* to practice law—that is, he has become an attorney by passing the state bar exam and taking the oath as an officer of the court.

Exceptions to the general rule against the practice of law by non-attorneys vary somewhat from state to state. Certain qualified professionals—real estate agents, tax accountants, insurance agents, and labor union officers, for example—may give *very limited* legal advice, draft legal documents, or provide some limited form of legal representation *within their narrowly defined fields of expertise:*

- Tax accountants often represent clients before the Internal Revenue Service.
- In employment grievances, labor union officers represent both the union and the employee in formal hearings before neutral arbitrators—who typically are attorneys—whereas the employers are usually represented by lawyers in those same hearings.
- Some government agencies (e.g., the Social Security Administration and some state worker compensation agencies) permit non-attorneys to represent clients in hearings before those agencies.
- Some states permit a non-attorney employee to represent her employer in small claims court (where attorneys are generally prohibited from practicing), provided that the non-attorney employee's appearance in court is incidental to her other employment duties.
- Real estate agents select and fill in the appropriate forms when preparing their clients' purchase offers and counteroffers. In that process they sometimes suggest the terms of those offers and also explain the legal meaning and tax effects of holding property as joint tenants, tenants in common, community property, and the like.

The foregoing exceptions to the UPL rule are considered to be lawful either because they are authorized by statute or government regulation or because they have been recognized by the courts to be *a lawful practice of long standing under the common law* of that state.

A most unusual example of unlicensed practice is the **jailhouse lawyer**. In *Johnson v. Avery*, 383 U.S. 483 (1969), the U.S. Supreme Court held that *an inmate's constitutional right* to legal counsel and effective access to the courts overrode a state law prohibiting the unlicensed practice of law. At issue was the jail inmate's access to the legal assistance offered by other, self-tutored inmates who served as "jailhouse lawyers."

A **jailhouse lawyer** is an inmate who assists other inmates with their legal defense.

Of course, that decision was based upon the actual unavailability of licensed attorneys for prison inmates. However, if adequate assistance by members of the bar had been readily available to prison inmates, those inmates would no longer have had a constitutional right to the assistance of the *unlicensed* jailhouse lawyers. It is important to recognize that the Supreme Court's decision in *Johnson v. Avery* was based upon the right of the "inmate-client" to *receive* legal counsel, *not* upon any constitutional "right" of the jailhouse lawyer to practice law without a license.

THE SEASONED PARALEGAL AS A PERCEIVED LEGAL "EXPERT"

Through constant exposure, it is not uncommon for a seasoned paralegal who performs sophisticated legal work to become something of an expert in a particular area of law. A paralegal specializing in bankruptcy, probate, or mechanic's lien law, for example, will within a few years know much more about both the substantive law and the procedures of routine bankruptcies, probate, or mechanic's liens (as the case might be) than will an attorney in general practice who rarely handles such matters. Although it would be illegal and unethical to do so, it is possible that an *expert* paralegal specialist could competently handle—unsupervised—a simple client matter within her specialty more efficiently and effectively than could the typical attorney in a general law practice. But therein lies a danger.

The danger for those who rely upon the "expert" paralegal lies in the narrow scope of the paralegal's knowledge and of her focus. Presumably, a generalist attorney will have a broader knowledge of the law and a broader focus when reviewing a client's situation. That can be important, because the facts in a particular client's situation might alert the generalist attorney to other significant legal issues (e.g., outside of the areas of bankruptcy or probate). If a paralegal who is expert in a particular field decides to leave the supervision of an attorney and set up shop to render advice and assistance directly to the public, she runs the risk of malpractice through her ignorance of other areas of the law—not to mention civil and/or criminal liability for the unauthorized practice of law.

THE DANGERS OF CASUAL ADVICE

It is entirely possible to practice law without being aware of that fact. Awareness depends, in large part, upon how the "practice of law" is defined in state law. If it is defined as *compensated* legal advice and/or representation, then very few people inadvertently practice law. But in most states, compensation is *not* required—free representation or legal advice given to others is sufficient. In those states, it is the rare adult (or teenager) who does not occasionally "practice law." Consider these examples:

- One neighbor advises another—whose landlord is unresponsive—to just have his water heater repaired and then enclose the bill and deduct the cost when he mails his next rent check.
- An employee tells a colleague to "get the boss' promise in writing," so that the boss cannot later claim that no salary increase was promised.
- A high school student tells a classmate that the teacher cannot suspend her from class without giving a reason and allowing her a chance to appeal that decision.
- An acquaintance tells a landlord that he doesn't need an attorney to evict nonpaying tenants—"Just take them to small claims court."
- A parent tells her grown son that he doesn't need to report tips from his restaurant job when he fills out his tax return.

The advice given in those situations falls within the practice of law because *it requires a legal conclusion* that:

- Tenants can make repairs on their own initiative and legally deduct the cost from their rent.
- Written promises are more easily enforced than oral promises.
- A high school student is entitled to an explanation and a hearing prior to being suspended.
- The landlord's situation is simple enough for a non-attorney to handle, and it can be effectively dealt with in small claims court.
- Tips are not considered to be earned income for tax purposes.

Common sense might tell us that the first and second conclusions are reasonable—although the first might not be supported by the law of that state. The third and fourth conclusions require a sophisticated understanding of the factual circumstances and of the law. The fifth conclusion, of course, is false. These examples illustrate why most laypersons are not knowledgeable enough to evaluate the free legal advice given by their neighbors, relatives, colleagues, classmates, and friends. Nor are they prepared to evaluate any advice that might be given by a paralegal.

As a practical matter, of course, nobody really cares about this sort of amateur "lunchroom" or "over-the-back-fence" legal advice—certainly not the local bar association or the county prosecutor. Unless those neighbors, classmates, and colleagues start charging legal fees, they are not likely ever to be prosecuted. And one might believe that anyone with any sense at all takes such free "legal advice" with a generous grain of salt. After all, how much can it be worth if it is given for free in the lunchroom at work or over a barbecue grill in someone's backyard?

But suppose the neighbor, colleague, or acquaintance giving advice is a paralegal? What if the advice is taken seriously? *Very* seriously. After all, paralegals are "trained in the law," aren't they? They work on legal matters every day. They are surrounded by attorneys and must surely absorb legal wisdom by osmosis. *They must know what they are talking about.*

Does this mean that qualified paralegals carry more responsibility than the neighborhood amateurs for any advice they might casually give? The answer is "yes." There are two reasons for that greater responsibility:

1. the *greater reliance* others place upon their comments or opinions, knowing they are paralegals
2. the *greater confidence* with which paralegals appear to speak, even casually, because of their knowledge and experience.

Imagine a circumstance in which someone has been told by a casual acquaintance, "You should sue your boss for firing you without any reason." Then that same person hears from an experienced paralegal that, as an "at-will employee"—one who can quit or be fired at any time, without any reason—he does not appear to have valid grounds for a lawsuit. Which statement will be given greater credence? The lesson here is that casual comments might be perceived as competent legal guidance when offered by a paralegal. That danger is not eliminated even if the paralegal informs everyone that she is not an attorney. Saying, "*I'm not an attorney, but . . .* " is about as effective a disclaimer as, "*I'm not prejudiced, but . . .* "

Even when an acquaintance does not take any *action* based upon a paralegal's comment, the acquaintance still can be harmed by having been given the advice. For example, satisfied that he now understands his legal situation, the acquaintance might fail to seek the advice of an attorney. Although he really needs competent legal advice, he relies instead upon the trusted paralegal's impression about his legal situation.

> **Ethics Watch**
>
> The safe response to casual legal inquiries is: "I can't offer legal advice, but if you are concerned, you should talk to an attorney." Then that individual can make his own decision about spending money for a legal consultation. Some attorneys will provide that initial consultation free of charge, as a method of attracting new clients. It often costs someone nothing to learn from a qualified legal expert that he really does not need an attorney, after all.

TALKING AND TEACHING *ABOUT* THE LAW

Giving legal advice and talking *about* the law are two very different things. When a layperson talks or writes about the law, he is not practicing law. If a high school civics teacher does his job properly, he talks about the law a great deal. In fact, at times he is *teaching law*. Listed below are examples of substantive and procedural law topics which are commonly taught in high school:

- constitutional law: freedom of speech, the right to remain silent, unreasonable search and seizure, trial by jury, and due process
- civic responsibilities: obeying the laws, voting, serving on juries, and paying taxes
- criminal procedures: arrest, indictment, trial, and appeal
- electoral law: qualifications to vote and hold public office, electoral fraud, and recall of public officials
- lawmaking procedures: legislation, veto, override of a veto, and the initiative process

But the civics teacher does not practice law unless he discusses the law *as it applies to the factual situation of a particular student to whom the point is addressed*. And, of course, well-meaning civics instructors sometimes do exactly that. This is simply one more example of the inadvertent, but pervasive, practice of law by unqualified laypersons.

> **Ethics Watch**
>
> For the paralegal who is not involved in teaching or writing about the law, the issue is where to draw the line in casual conversations. There is nothing wrong with talking or writing about legal principles or procedures *in the abstract*. But the paralegal must be alert to situations where the listener might rely upon the paralegal's comments or apply them to her own legal situation. Making that distinction is not always easy. The prudent paralegal will speak with great caution.

The **National Federation of Paralegal Associations (NFPA)**, a nonprofit organization founded in 1974, comprises some 55 state and regional paralegal associations (representing some 17,000 paralegals), as well as many individual sustaining members. In governance and policy decisions, each member association has one vote, regardless of size. The NFPA promotes ethical standards and professional development for the profession.

The **National Association of Legal Assistants (NALA),** a nonprofit organization founded in 1975, comprises some 18,000 legal assistant members and approximately 90 state and regional affiliates. In governance and policy decisions, each member has one vote. The NALA promotes ethical standards, certification, and professional development for the profession.

SECTION 3. VERIFYING PARALEGAL COMPETENCE

Across the nation, paralegals face an important crossroads. Within the next decade, it is likely to be determined whether some form of state regulation or national certification will emerge as the dominant influence for the profession. Important issues are at stake here—for paralegals, attorneys, and the public. The **National Federation of Paralegal Associations (NFPA)** and the **National Association of Legal Assistants (NALA)** have developed differing philosophies and policies related to these issues. Later in this chapter, the reasons underlying their differences will be discussed.

Before discussing the controversy regarding state regulation or certification of paralegals, it might be helpful to clarify some terminology. In this chapter, "paralegal" and "legal assistant" will continue to refer to non-attorney legal paraprofessionals who work under the supervision of attorneys—even if the latter are independent paralegals working for a number of different law firms. "Non-attorney provider" will refer to someone offering legal services directly to the public—probably illegally—without attorney supervision. "Legal technician" will refer to a non-attorney provider that, in the future, might be authorized by law to provide legal services directly to the public. As of this writing, legal technicians have yet to be authorized in any jurisdiction of the United States. Although the preceding terminology is somewhat arbitrary, it should minimize confusion for the reader.

"Regulation" implies government restrictions that would determine the qualifications for persons who could practice as paralegals (or, perhaps, legal technicians) and what services those paralegals (or legal technicians) could lawfully provide under attorney supervision (for paralegals) and without attorney supervision (for legal technicians). Regulation could involve state licenses and an examination process. For various practical and legal reasons, formal licensure is the more likely form for any state regulation that might come to pass.

Professional "certification" usually means accreditation of individual paralegals under the auspices of prestigious national, regional, or state associations. Because it lacks the force of law, nongovernmental certification depends upon public and professional recognition in order to be an effective influence. The NALA and the NFPA each have established a certification process. Their certificate programs are discussed later in this chapter.

It is entirely possible for state regulation and professional certification to exist simultaneously. Medical doctors, for example, must possess state licenses to practice medicine. However, they often become "board certified" in their specialty, as well. Real estate agents must be licensed, but many of them also seek professional certification as a Realtor®.

PROTECTING THE TITLES "PARALEGAL" AND "LEGAL ASSISTANT"

Many of the unsupervised non-attorneys who offer legal services to the public style themselves as a "paralegal." In fact, in many parts of the nation, their services are advertised in telephone company yellow pages under the heading "Paralegals." This use of the title has caused concern and distress to thousands of attorney-supervised paralegals and to their national organizations, but in most states nothing has been done to prohibit that misleading practice. Under the law, anyone may hang out his shingle as a self-styled "paralegal" or "legal assistant," even though he might lack any professional legal qualifications.

Although a number of states have adopted statutory definitions for "paralegal" and "legal assistant," in 1999, Maine became the first state to enact legislation *regulating* the use of the titles "paralegal" and "legal assistant":

Maine Revised Statutes

Title 4. Judiciary

Chapter 18. Paralegals and Legal Assistants

Section 921. Definitions
As used in this chapter, unless the context otherwise indicates, the following terms have the following meanings.
1. Paralegal and legal assistant. "Paralegal" and "legal assistant" mean a person, qualified by education, training or work experience, who is employed or

retained by an attorney, law office, corporation, governmental agency or other entity and who performs specifically delegated substantive legal work for which an attorney is responsible.

Section 922. Restriction on use of titles
1. Prohibition. A person may not use the title "paralegal" or "legal assistant" unless the person meets the definition in section 921, subsection 1.
2. Penalty. A person who violates subsection 1 commits a civil violation for which the forfeiture of not more than $1000 may be adjudged.

The Maine statute is too new to enable one to evaluate its impact upon the legal community and those unsupervised non-attorneys in Maine who have styled themselves as "paralegals." The statute might be challenged on constitutional grounds as an unreasonable restriction on First Amendment free speech rights. It might be challenged also on the grounds that the statutory definition for the titles is unconstitutionally vague and ambiguous. It will be interesting to see how many other states follow Maine's lead and in what ways their statutes might differ. California adopted a similar statute in 2000, with strictly defined qualifications for paralegals and legal assistants (*California Business and Professions Code* § 6450, et seq.).

STATE LICENSURE FOR "LEGAL TECHNICIANS"

To many lawmakers and consumer groups, a partial answer to the present high cost of legal services would be the *licensed and regulated* legal technician. The legal technician would not be required to complete three years of law school or take the bar exam—she would not be an attorney. Instead, the technician would have less extensive (and much less expensive) legal education and training, and would provide strictly limited legal services. The idea is to have the legal technician handle relatively *simple* matters that do not require a comprehensive legal education, such as completing court forms for personal bankruptcies, divorces, or adoptions; representing clients before government hearing officers and appeals boards; handling real estate closings; preparing and filing incorporation papers; and preparing wills. Note that all of the preceding matters would have to be simple and uncomplicated. It is unlikely that legal technicians would be authorized to handle *complex* bankruptcies, business transactions, wills, and so forth.

If legal technicians were licensed, it is probable that they would have to qualify for a specific area of law (e.g., bankruptcy) and would be limited to practicing within that area. Part of their training would enable them to recognize situations beyond their competence, so that clients would be referred to an attorney when appropriate.

Advocates and Opponents of Licensure for Legal Technicians

The drive for licensure of legal technicians comes largely from groups wanting to make basic legal services more affordable to people of limited means and, to a lesser degree, from groups seeking to protect the public from the mischief caused by unqualified (and, of course, unlicensed) non-attorneys. One very active group is HALT—An Organization of Americans for Legal Reform, which was discussed in Chapter 1. The NALA and the NFPA differ over the concept of legal technicians, just as they do over licensure for paralegals. Those differences will be discussed later in this chapter.

The strongest opposition to licensure of legal technicians has come from attorneys. Their prime argument is that such technicians would exceed their competence or, through ignorance, fail to recognize a problem requiring an attorney's expertise. It is as though medical ophthalmologists were to say—and perhaps some do—that optometrists should not be permitted to evaluate visual acuity and prescribe lenses because they might fail to recognize symptoms of an underlying disease that is causing the vision problem of the patient. HALT and other consumer groups supporting the legal technician option do not deny that many legal problems require the services of an attorney, but they suspect that the organized bars' opposition is motivated more by self-interest than by concern for consumer protection.

LICENSURE FOR ATTORNEY-SUPERVISED LEGAL ASSISTANTS

Licensure is one of the most controversial issues within the paralegal profession. Some of the arguments made by those who favor licensure are listed below:

- Licensure would establish clear qualifications for attorney-supervised paralegal practitioners.
- Licensure would reinforce the consumer protection currently provided by licensure of attorneys.
- Licensure would provide a mechanism for disciplining legal assistants who violate the law or professional ethics.
- Licensure would protect the "paralegal" and "legal assistant" titles from being used by unlicensed persons, particularly by unsupervised non-attorneys providing legal services to the public.
- Licensure would increase the public recognition and elevate the prestige of the profession.

Opponents offer the following arguments against licensure:

- There is no need for licensure, because attorney supervision ensures ethical conduct and competent legal work by legal assistants.
- Ethical standards have been clearly established by both major national paralegal organizations.
- Any ethical lapses are adequately disciplined by the employing attorney.
- Licensure would necessarily establish only minimum qualifications and would not elevate the profession above the level currently maintained by paralegals and their employers.
- Licensure might have the effect of discouraging or preventing the expansion of the paralegal role within the practice of law.
- The "paralegal" and "legal assistant" titles can be protected by statute from misuse by those who are unsupervised by attorneys.

PROFESSIONAL CERTIFICATION: NOT A SIMPLE ISSUE

If paralegals are to be certified, these questions must be answered:

- Why certify?
- Who certifies?
- What criteria will be used?

Certification has been discussed briefly in earlier chapters. Essentially, it means awarding a certificate of completion to someone who has performed either of the following:

- successfully completed a prescribed course of paralegal studies
- passed a qualifying examination administered by a recognized paralegal organization

Certification offers a number of benefits to the profession and the individual. Most obviously, it can contribute to the professional status of paralegals in those job markets where it is recognized. Potentially, it might offer paralegal organizations more influence over paralegal education—similar to that which the ABA now exerts. Individual certification offers one recognized standard for evaluating the individual paralegal.

To the extent that certification represents a high level of professional competence, it can contribute to more challenging assignments and higher salaries. Certification could be one criterion for promotion along the paralegal career track, in those law offices that have one. Because law firms could justify higher billing rates for certified paralegals, certification might have appeal for the employer, as well. Although some law firms currently prefer certificates from ABA-approved programs when hiring new paralegals, they realize that ABA approval tells them little about individual graduates of those programs. A recognized individual certificate would be helpful to law firms that wish to establish some reasonably objective criteria for employment.

There seems to be general agreement that the ABA and state bar associations should not certify paralegals, a position with which the ABA itself agrees. The common view is that there is too much potential conflict of interest for the bar associations to control certification of paralegals. Of course, although the ABA does not certify *individual* legal assistants, it does grant "approval" to those paralegal programs that apply for approval and meet its standards for quality. This has led to the misleading phrase "ABA-approved certificate," which often appears in advertisements for paralegal positions. The ABA's approval process validates educational programs and institutions—*not* the competence of individual graduates. The ABA also maintains that its approval process is not equivalent to academic accreditation of a paralegal program.

The Certified Legal Assistant Examination

For most professions, certification is offered by an organization of one's peers. The NALA established the first nationally recognized paralegal certificate, designated as the **Certified Legal Assistant® (CLA)**, in 1976. At this writing, just over 10,000 legal assistants—more than 50% of the NALA's membership—have received the CLA designation.

Before taking the written CLA examination, a candidate must have sufficient education and/or legal experience. Graduates of a bona fide (although *not* necessarily ABA-approved) legal assistant program are not required to have working experience as a paralegal. Basically, the NALA requires that the candidate possess *one* of the following qualifications in order to sit for the examination:

- graduation from a legal assistant program meeting NALA's standards
- a bachelor's degree plus one year's experience as a legal assistant
- a high school diploma, seven years' experience as a legal assistant, and completion of twenty hours of continuing legal education.

The two-day examination is based upon federal law and procedure. It includes such topics as substantive law, ethics, legal research, and judgment and analytical ability.

A Certified Legal Assistant ® may later sit for an advanced specialty examination in any of the following fields:

- bankruptcy
- corporations/business law
- real estate
- civil litigation

A **Certified Legal Assistant® (CLA)** is a legal assistant, meeting minimum standards of education and experience, who has successfully completed a written examination administered by the National Association of Legal Assistants (NALA).

- criminal law and procedure
- intellectual property
- probate and estates

Those who pass the advanced examination receive the **Certified Legal Assistant Specialist®** designation. More than 800 legal assistants have earned that designation. The NALA has also established advanced specialty certificate programs for California, Florida, and Louisiana.

The Paralegal Advanced Competency Exam

The National Federation of Paralegal Associations had been reluctant to establish a certification process on the grounds that self-regulation can be contaminated by self-interest. The NFPA's position was that, for certification to be acceptable, it must be controlled by a body that reflects various constituencies: paralegals, attorneys, paralegal educators, and the public. The NFPA also criticized the eligibility criteria used by the NALA to determine who might take the CLA examination, contending that candidates for certification should be required to have some minimum period of full-time paralegal employment in addition to the educational requirements.

In 1994, the NFPA announced its plans to develop a proficiency exam for *experienced* paralegals, the **Paralegal Advanced Competency Exam (PACE)**. Under the supervision of a task force of paralegals, paralegal educators, attorneys, and others, the examination was developed by an independent test development firm. The exam is divided into two tiers: The first tier tests general legal knowledge and ethics, and the second tier tests selected legal specialties. As of this writing, the specialties for the Tier II examinations have not been announced. Candidates for Tier I must meet one of the following criteria:

- They must have a minimum of four years of work experience as a paralegal, if application was made prior to December 31, 2000, or
- They must have a bachelor's degree; they must have completed a paralegal program in an accredited institution; and they must have a minimum of two years of work experience as a paralegal.

As can be seen, the NFPA is "grandparenting" most paralegals who entered their paralegal career prior to 1996, regardless of the extent of their post-high school education or academic legal preparation. Beginning in 2001, however, the NFPA's emphasis upon a four-year degree as a minimal entry qualification for the paralegal career becomes a requirement to sit for the PACE exam. Paralegals who receive a satisfactory score on the exam may use the designations "PACE–Registered Paralegal" or "RP."

NALA AND NFPA: TWO VISIONS FOR THE FUTURE

Attorney-supervised legal assistants are in a profession still being defined, although the rate of progress in that defining process has slowed somewhat in the past decade. Although paralegals and attorneys are less frequently discovering new possibilities and roles for the paralegal within the traditional law office setting all agree that the discovery process is not complete by any means. There are those who fear that, as the paralegal role becomes more clearly established, new opportunities for that role might become more difficult to explore, and exploration might encounter resistance from attorneys and paralegals accustomed to a more traditional paralegal role. This very complex issue underlies differing visions held by the NFPA and the NALA for the future of their profession.

This question of the legal assistant's role must be viewed within the larger context of other circumstances and events. One such circumstance is the growing

---

A **Certified Legal Assistant Specialist® (CLAS)** is a CLA who has successfully completed an advanced specialty examination in a particular area of the law.

The **Paralegal Advanced Competency Exam (PACE)** is an examination, established by the National Federation of Paralegal Associations, to determine general legal knowledge, ethics, and selected legal specialties.

Practice Tip

There is a hidden advantage in obtaining CLA and PACE certification. Both the NFPA and the NALA offer study guides and seminars to prepare for their respective examinations. The preparation process provides an excellent review of topics studied in one's paralegal education, and it might introduce other topics that were not part of that education. Completing the examination successfully will be a source of pride and satisfaction to the paralegal and can be a confidence booster. Once a paralegal has received the certificate, she can educate her employer about these efforts to establish a standard measure of paralegal competency. The NALA and the NFPA require that paralegals participate in continuing legal education in order to maintain their CLA and RP designations.

cadre of unsupervised, self-styled "paralegals" who offer legal services to the public. Some legal assistants are deeply concerned that their collective professional reputation might be diminished in the public's eyes if unregulated non-attorney providers sell inadequate or incompetent legal services while calling themselves "paralegals." As those unlicensed providers become more numerous and advertise their "paralegal" services more widely, the public might have difficulty distinguishing between them and the professionally qualified paralegals who work under the supervision of attorneys.

Another relevant circumstance is the increasing number of professionally qualified paralegals who work in government, corporate, and other settings *without* the direct, immediate supervision of an attorney. Typically, they perform substantive legal work for their employers, who may or may not have that work reviewed by either in-house or outside legal counsel. A paralegal in this group might interact regularly with the employer's legal counsel, receiving guidance from that attorney, even though she is not directly supervised by that attorney. Some professionally qualified paralegals working in these environments avoid using the titles "paralegal" or "legal assistant" precisely because they are not attorney-supervised.

These professionally qualified paralegals working without attorney supervision present ethical questions that trouble some members of the profession. Others believe that adequate professional and ethical standards can be maintained in these circumstances if the paralegal has a firm understanding of ethical concerns and recognizes the limitations of his own legal skills and knowledge. Still others believe that these paralegals are developing new frontiers in discovering the profession's future role.

At some risk of oversimplification, it might be said that the NALA sees the future of the legal assistant career as remaining firmly within the traditional context of an attorney-supervised, employer-regulated profession, with the NALA providing guidance on ethical standards and professional competence through CLA certification and continuing legal education. With the same caveat regarding oversimplification, it might be said that the NFPA sees the paralegal career as including more possibilities than simply direct attorney supervision and regulation, with paralegals assuming less restricted roles under state licensure. In that context, the NFPA sees it's role as supporting ethical and professional standards through PACE certification and continuing legal education.

A Case in Point

New Jersey Supreme Court

In re Opinion No. 24 of the Committee on Paralegal Education and Regulation

128 NJ 114 (1992)
[Summarized and Paraphrased]

Differing visions were evident when the NALA and the NFPA responded to the prospect of state regulation of legal assistants in New Jersey. The New Jersey Supreme Court had established a Committee on Paralegal Education and Regulation, with the charge to report back to the Supreme Court its recommendations regarding possible regulation of New Jersey legal assistants. In 1998, the committee report recommended that the supreme court "should establish a regulatory scheme to govern the practice of paralegals."

The NALA submitted a statement to the New Jersey Supreme Court respectfully disagreeing with the committee's recommendation for licensure.[1] The reasons stated by the NALA included the following:

- There has been no demonstrated public need to regulate paralegals.
- Regulation would increase costs to employers and their clients.
- The proposed licensure scheme would not allow for the growth of the paralegal profession.

The text of the NALA's statement emphasized the effectiveness of the current practice of attorney supervision in maintaining ethical conduct of and the quality of legal services provided by paralegals. It also argued that professional paralegal associations "offer [standards for entry into the career, ethical codes, and self-regulation as] viable alternatives to governmental regulation."

In its response to the committee's report,[2] the NFPA *supported* licensure for paralegals, although it expressed some qualifications regarding the particular scheme outlined by the committee. The NFPA stated that a key condition of its support is that licensure "enhance" the paralegal role. The intent of this qualification is made clear in another NFPA document, the *Statement on Issues Affecting the Paralegal Profession:* "NFPA members adopted a position to endorse regulation of paralegals as long as paralegals would be able to do more under the regulatory plan than they were previously doing."[3] The latter document also states as a necessity the revision of ethical rules to allow for "ultimate responsibility and accountability of a lawyer for paralegal work, rather than *under direct supervision.* . . ." [Italics in the original.]

In May 1999, the New Jersey Supreme Court announced its Administrative Determinations regarding the Report of the Committee on Paralegal Education and Regulation. The supreme court " . . . concluded that direct oversight of paralegals is best accomplished through attorney supervision rather than through a Court-directed licensing system."

Supreme Court of New Jersey Administrative Determinations: Report of the Committee on Paralegal Education and Regulation (May 24, 1999).

The different visions of the NFPA and the NALA appear also in other documents, policies, and statements that the two organizations have adopted or published. The NALA has published a compilation of state statutory and regulatory law that seems to indicate that licensure is called for only when stringent criteria are met—conditions that the NALA does not believe to exist. These conditions follow:

- need, evidenced by harm to the public under existing circumstances
- ineffective protection under existing circumstances
- a requisite for special skills, knowledge, and abilities
- an absence of alternatives that would adequately protect the public

In contrast, the NFPA supports the development of a licensure plan that would permit an "expanded role" for paralegals. The NFPA's position on regulation advocates provisions for the following:

- a two-tiered licensure system, with a license for general practice and an advanced license for specialty practice
- ethical and disciplinary standards
- standards for paralegal education
- definitions for paralegal tasks in specialty areas of law

The NFPA also recognizes the right of each state to determine the regulatory system—which might, or might not, include licensure—most appropriate to the needs of that state. NFPA has developed a detailed, thirteen-page *Model Act for Paralegal Licensure* that state legislatures could either adopt outright or modify to meet the particular needs of a given state.

In addition to the *Model Act*, described above, the NFPA has proposed another model act to exempt paralegals "retained or employed by a lawyer, law office, governmental agency, *or other entity* . . . who may be performing substantive legal work with the supervision of *or accountability to* an attorney . . ." from state laws prohibiting the unauthorized practice of law. [Emphasis added.] The words italicized here have been a cause for controversy, because they appear to contemplate that paralegals would legally and ethically perform substantive legal work without being under the direct supervision of an attorney, although some form of accountability to an attorney would exist.

THE AMERICAN BAR ASSOCIATION AS *DE FACTO* ARBITER OF PARALEGAL EDUCATION

Until the 1980s, the American Bar Association was the only national organization that had a major impact upon paralegal education and the hiring standards for paralegals. Without either state licensure or a *universally recognized* certification program, attorneys had few independent measures upon which they could rely when evaluating paralegal job applicants. In 1973, the ABA established standards for paralegal education programs. By establishing criteria for paralegal education and then granting formal "approval" to those schools that met the criteria, the ABA came to exert a strong influence upon paralegal education in this nation.

The ABA was in a unique position, because its members were (and are) the employers of the vast majority of supervised paralegals. So it appeared to be in the best interests of the ABA membership for the organization to assert its influence. Ironically, although the ABA partially filled the original vacuum, it did so with significant reluctance. In fact, in 1981 the House of Delegates—the governing body of the ABA—decided to withdraw from participation in any approval process for paralegal programs. This decision caused great consternation for those schools that had gone to substantial effort and expense to qualify for approval. The ABA later reversed that decision.

In reality, ABA involvement in paralegal education has contributed enormously to the profession. It has ensured that the approved programs have relevance to the real world of assisting attorneys in the practice of law. And, for paralegals, it has established a certain degree of credibility with the legal profession that might have been far more difficult to otherwise attain. There is no way to estimate with any accuracy how many attorneys might never have hired their first legal assistant, if it were not for the "ABA-approved" certificate.

Controversy over ABA Influence

Although ABA involvement brought tangible benefits to the paralegal profession, it also engendered substantial controversy. Many paralegal educators and practicing paralegals were (and are) concerned that a conflict of interest was inevitable if attorneys wielded a dominant influence over paralegal education. Who was to protect the public interest? Or the interests of paralegals?

In recent decades, three national organizations have gradually increased their influence upon paralegal education. In 1976, the NALA established the Certified Legal Assistant (CLA) examination, which is discussed earlier in this chapter. By 1986, however, the number of CLAs still numbered less than 2,000, and the CLA designation had yet to establish itself as a standard recognized by attorneys nationwide. In 1994, the NFPA established the PACE exam, as noted earlier.

At the present time, national certification programs can affect paralegal curriculum only indirectly. The examination passing rates for graduates of each paralegal program are not published, so that there is no clear pressure upon the programs to prepare their students for the certificate examinations. The influence of certification may soon increase, however, because more than 10,000 legal assistants have now earned the CLA designation.

In 1986, the NFPA established an Education Task Force and, in 1992, adopted a Suggested Curriculum for Paralegal Studies. In 1981, the American Association for Paralegal Education (AAfPE) was organized with the goal of promoting high standards for paralegal education. In 1997, the AAfPE adopted a Statement of Academic Quality that identifies key components of a quality paralegal education program (e.g., curriculum development, facilities, faculty, and program director). The statement identified ten topics (e.g., ethics, law-related computer skills, and substantive and procedural law) that are essential to a quality paralegal program. The AAfPE also offers model syllabi for twenty-two distinct courses commonly taught in paralegal programs.

The AAfPE's potential influence upon paralegal education is substantial, because its membership comprises almost exclusively practicing paralegal educators. Individual voting members must be faculty or advisory board members of schools that hold an institutional membership in the AAfPE. To qualify for full voting membership, schools must either be approved by the ABA or be in substantial compliance with ABA standards. This link to ABA standards has provoked controversy, with some paralegal educators believing it might diminish the independence and diversity of viewpoints expressed in AAfPE deliberations.

The ABA itself has recognized the controversy that grows out of its extensive influence over paralegal curriculum and instruction. In 1981, the ABA changed the make-up of the Approval Commission, which recommends approval of paralegal programs for consideration by the ABA Committee on Legal Assistants and the House of Delegates. The commission now includes representatives from the AAfPE, NALA, and NFPA. As a result, the commission now includes almost equal numbers of attorneys and of paralegals. Other commission members include a representative from the Association of Legal Administrators (ALA), a nonlegal educator, and a member of the general public.

A QUESTION OF ETHICS

Susan Payne is a former legal assistant who now is the assistant manager of the human resources department of a mid-sized manufacturing company. Her legal training and experience is highly valued by the firm, and she generally acts as the company's liaison with outside legal counsel.

The employees of the company are represented by the Teamsters' Union, and Susan is sometimes involved in labor-management disputes in the company. A recent grievance over the dismissal of an employee for alleged intoxication worked its way up the grievance-resolution hierarchy until Susan's boss ruled against the employee. The union has submitted the case to binding arbitration, as provided for in the collective bargaining contract.

Susan has been designated by the company to be its advocate before the arbitrator, an attorney with substantial experience in arbitration. She will have the responsibility of preparing the case, interviewing potential witnesses, questioning and cross-examining witnesses at the hearing, and making oral arguments on the facts and the application of the collective bargaining contract to the case. Susan will be opposed in the hearing by a regional labor relations representative of the Teamsters' Union.

Will Susan be violating her ethical duties as a legal assistant if she carries out all of the responsibilities described above? Will she be engaged in the unauthorized practice of law?

Chapter Summary

- Because attorneys have a special duty of loyalty to their clients and of responsibility to society, legal ethics have a special importance in the practice of law.
- The ABA promotes legal ethics through its model rules and its standards for accrediting law schools and approving paralegal programs.
- The mandatory rules of ethical conduct are state rules, and they are enforced primarily by state courts and state bar associations.
- Attorneys can be disciplined by a variety of methods, ranging from reprimands to disbarment.
- As can attorneys, legal assistants can be sued personally for many ethical violations, and they can be prosecuted for those that violate criminal laws.
- The attorney-client privilege protects all private communications between the client and the attorney or members of his staff.
- The attorney work product rule protects all notes, memoranda, theories, strategy, and other material prepared by the attorney or her staff in contemplation of litigation.
- Paralegals must avoid giving legal advice, even in casual conversation with friends and relatives, because their opinions might be given special weight when those persons make decisions about their own legal interests.
- The unauthorized practice of law is generally understood to be the unlicensed person's provision to others of services that require the knowledge and skills of an attorney.
- Unlicensed "paralegals" and "self-help legal clinics" provide legal services directly to the public without attorney supervision, but they usually operate in violation of the law against unauthorized practice.
- The National Association of Legal Assistants (NALA) and the National Federation of Paralegal Associations (NFPA) have established programs to certify paralegal competence.
- The NALA and the NFPA have differing visions for the future of the profession, particularly regarding licensure and the role of paralegals in providing legal services.

KEY TERMS

affirmative duty
attorney-client privilege
attorney-work product
Bates stamp
candor rule
censure
Certified Legal Assistant® (CLA)
Certified Legal Assistant Specialist® (CLAS)
commingling
conflict check
conflict of interest
contempt of court
crime-fraud exception
de novo
diligence
disbarment
discovery
exculpatory evidence
frivolous claim
imputed conflict of interest
jailhouse lawyer
jury tampering
legal technician
licensure
master
National Association of Legal Assistants (NALA)
National Federation of Paralegal Associations (NFPA)

obstruction of justice
officer of the court
Paralegal Advanced Competency
    Exam (PACE)
perjury
practice of law

pretrial discovery
quid pro quo
retainer
sanction
scope of employment
sexually hostile environment

suborning of perjury
subpoena
trust account
unauthorized practice of law
whistle-blower
work product rule

ACTIVITIES AND ASSIGNMENTS

1. Write an essay on the issue of billable quotas for paralegals. Determine whether it is possible to have a quota without jeopardizing either of the following:
   - the paralegal's income or job security
   - the integrity of the time billed to clients

   In your essay, propose an ethical system that includes a billable quota, but also safeguards the paralegal and the client. If you determine that such a system is an impossibility, explain why.

2. Survey newspaper and yellow pages advertisements for non-attorneys who offer legal services directly to the public. Prepare a chart showing the services advertised. Telephone or visit the office of several non-attorney providers to obtain and compare information about fees and services. Prepare a report on the information that you have gathered.

3. Interview a licensed real estate agent or broker (or a licensed insurance agent or broker) about the limits imposed by law on his rights to advise clients and prepare real estate, and insurance documents, respectively. Prepare a report on the "practice of law" by those non-attorney professionals. Where do they draw the line between appropriate professional services and the "unauthorized practice of law?" Do they advise clients about the tax consequences of various investment and insurance decisions?

4. In the opening scenario, Patricia gave Louise an update on the dental malpractice case while the checker was able to listen in. Did Patricia violate any ethical standards by doing so? If so, what standards did she violate? How should Patricia have responded to Louise's questions? Would it make any difference if they were in a part of the store where they could not be overheard? Would it make any difference if Patricia and Louise were both paralegals working in different departments of the same large law firm?

5. At the backyard barbecue, Patricia tried to avoid giving Alex any legal advice about his problem with his landlord. Did she violate any ethical rules in her response to Alex's questions? If so, which rules? Was there anything wrong with suggesting that Alex discuss the matter with Margaret, one of the new associates in Patricia's firm?

6. Eric and Hanh are legal assistants in the same firm. The firm has been putting a lot of pressure on the attorneys and legal assistants to exceed their annual quota of 1,700 hours. At lunch one day, Hanh complains about this pressure and the difficulty of meeting the quota, given all the interruptions and the nonbillable assignments he has been receiving. Eric responds by saying that the quota is "no problem." He explains that when he fills in his time sheets, he just adds 10% to the actual time he spends on each billable task, and that difference makes it easy to exceed his quota. If you were Hanh, what would you do?

7. You are a paralegal assigned to a major litigation case. One day, you are standing by the facsimile machine waiting for an urgent memorandum from an expert witness retained by your firm. But instead, the machine prints out a memorandum from the opposing attorney. The memorandum is addressed to *his* client—the cover sheet makes that clear—but has been transmitted in error to your law firm. Glancing at the memorandum, you realize immediately that it is the opposing counsel's analysis of an important legal issue in the case. The cover sheet contains a printed paragraph stating that the message is confidential and intended for the person to whom it is addressed and that anyone else receiving it is to notify the sender without reading the message. What should you do? What should your firm do? Would it make any difference if the cover letter did not contain that warning paragraph?

8. Carlos Carrillo has been working as a legal assistant for seven years, specializing in complex litigation cases involving defective motor vehicles. He has gradually learned a great deal about products liability law and trial procedures, in part because he has assisted in court during

five major trials. Recently, however, there has been a lot of turnover among the attorneys in the firm, and the partner he usually assists has just announced his retirement. Carlos realizes that the remaining products liability attorneys are difficult to work with, and he has begun to check the paralegal grapevine for job opportunities in other law firms. The timing is right, because the big case that Carlos has worked on for eighteen months is just about to go to the jury.

In the restroom during a trial recess, Carlos encounters one of the opposing attorneys. "I've been quite impressed by your work on this case, Carlos. We have an opening in our office right now for a senior litigation paralegal with your abilities. As soon as this case goes to the jury, why don't we have lunch and talk it over?"

Does this encounter raise any ethical questions? If Carlos is interested in the job, what should he do?

9. In this chapter, there is a "Case in Point" entitled "The Tobacco Papers." Review that section and then answer the following:

Was Merrell Williams a conscientious citizen and paralegal, simply blowing the whistle on possibly unethical or illegal conduct by a client of his law firm employer? Or, did he violate his fiduciary duty to his employer and the client, without just cause, revealing confidential client information for his own purposes?

ENDNOTES

[1] _____, *Response to the Report of the New Jersey Supreme Court Committee on Paralegal Education and Regulation* (National Association of Legal Assistants, 1999).

[2] _____, *Comments of the National Federation of Paralegal Associations, Inc. Regarding the Report of the Supreme Court of New Jersey Standing Committee on Paralegal Education and Regulation* (National Federation of Paralegal Associations, 1999).

[3] _____, *Statement on Issues Affecting the Paralegal Profession* (National Federation of Paralegal Associations [undated]).

[4] Supreme Court of New Jersey Administrative Determinations: Report of the Committee on Paralegal Education and Regulation (May 24, 1999).

PART II

Introduction to the Legal System

CHAPTER 4

The Law and The Courts

We are under a Constitution, but the Constitution is what judges say it is.

Charles Evans Hughes, Chief Justice of the U.S. Supreme Court, 1930–1941.

What, exactly, *is the law* in the American system of justice? Where is the law to be found? How is that law to be applied to the facts of any particular case?

Chapter 4 identifies the sources of law in the American legal system. It also describes the court systems—state and federal—and explains how it is determined which court should hear a particular case. This chapter also explains how trial court decisions are appealed to a higher court and describes the role of the U.S. Supreme Court. After careful study and review, the student should be able to answer these questions:

- What constitutes "the law"?
- Why is the law so uncertain?
- What is the difference between civil law and criminal law?
- What are the differences between constitutional, statutory, administrative, and common law?
- What is the source of the "common law," and how is it applied?
- Where do the state legislatures and Congress find their authority to enact laws?
- What is the highest law of the land?
- What happens when a law conflicts with the U.S. Constitution?
- Must states recognize and enforce the laws of other states?
- What determines which court should hear a case?
- How do state and federal courts exercise their jurisdiction?
- Can a state exercise jurisdiction over a person in another state?
- How does the appellate process work?
- Which cases can federal courts hear?
- Can nonjudicial government agencies also exercise judicial powers?

SCENARIO

A State Governor Defies the Constitution

A person charged in any State with treason, felony, or other crime, who shall flee from justice, and be found in another State, shall on demand of the executive authority of the State from which he fled, be delivered up, to be removed to the State having jurisdiction of the crime.

(*U.S. Constitution,* Article IV, Section 2)

The famous case of the "Scottsboro Boys" (as it was called by news media of that day) serves as an example of one state's refusal to surrender a fugitive sought by another state, in apparent defiance of the U.S. Constitution. In 1931, Haywood Patterson and seven other African American youths were convicted by juries in a state court in Scottsboro, Alabama, of raping two white women in a freight car as the train passed through that state. Although medical evidence contradicted the claims of the white women, Patterson and the seven other defendants were sentenced to the death penalty. However, the U.S. Supreme Court overturned those first convictions on **due process** grounds: the systematic exclusion of African Americans from Alabama juries.

At a second trial, in 1936, one of the two women recanted her prior testimony. Even so, Patterson was again convicted and sentenced to seventy-five years in prison. In 1948, Patterson escaped from an Alabama prison work gang and fled to Michigan. In 1950, Michigan Governor G. Mennen Williams refused to **extradite** Patterson to Alabama.

The last surviving "Scottsboro Boy" was pardoned by Alabama's governor in 1976.

The Scottsboro case raises several interesting questions: Why did Alabama not obtain a federal court order, compelling Michigan's governor to extradite Patterson? Does the mandate of Article IV, Section 2, apply even when the governor of the **asylum** state believes the fugitive has been unlawfully charged or convicted? Is each state in the federal union *sovereign,* so that it may ignore the mandates of the U.S. Constitution? This chapter will not provide explicit answers to all of these questions, but after reading the chapter, students might wish to propose their own answers. ■

Due process is the constitutional principle that government actions must be fair and reasonable when a person's substantial interests (e.g., life, liberty, or property) are at stake. Due process is required by the Fifth and Fourteenth Amendments to the U.S. Constitution.

Extradition is the involuntary removal of a criminal defendant from one jurisdiction to another state or nation that claims jurisdiction over the defendant based upon the crime allegedly committed.

An **asylum** is a place of refuge where fugitives from persecution seek safety.

SECTION 1. THE NATURE OF LAW

When used in the early chapters of this book, "the law" was used in a broad sense, meant to include the practice of law by attorneys, the operation of the court system, and legal procedures and principles. For the purposes of this chapter, however, the **law** will mean *the body of legal principles and standards applied by the courts in deciding the cases brought before them.*

What are these "legal principles" that the courts apply? Schoolchildren often receive the impression that every bit of the law has been written down, primarily by Congress and by the state legislatures. The news media might have reinforced this impression, perhaps adding some awareness of the fact that courts also determine part of the law. Many people have heard of something called the "common law," but some are under the impression that the **common law** is some kind of "unwritten law." Clearly, few people have an accurate understanding of what constitutes the law.

The **law** is the body of legal principles and standards that courts must apply in deciding the controversies brought before them.

Common law is the accumulation of legal principles found in court opinions. Common law is the law that courts apply when no constitutional, statutory, or administrative law governs under the facts in question.

THE IMPOSSIBLE TASK: KNOWING THE LAW

Do *lawyers* know what the law is? In general, yes, they do. In every detail, they never can. In law school, students learn the major principles of law and how to apply them to the facts of different situations. They learn to reason logically. They learn how to *find* the law: in the Constitution, in legislation and administrative regulations, and in court opinions. But they do not learn the law in its entirety. They *cannot* do so, for several reasons:

- The law is overwhelming in its scope and detail—no one individual can ever know all of it, as it exists at any given moment.
- Different legal theories can be applied to the same factual situation, so that competent and reasonable attorneys have honest disagreements about which legal principles should apply.
- The law is never complete—it is forever changing as court interpretations evolve and new laws are enacted and as the common experience of society changes.

The law is not static, something easily known—it is dynamic. That is one reason that legal analysis can be so intriguing and intellectually challenging.

The truth is that lawyers often do not know with certainty how the law will be applied in a particular case, and that is why there must be courts. Lawyers try to understand how the law will be applied, but they always know that *judges have the last word.* This chapter explores the sources of law upon which attorneys and judges rely, and the process used by the courts to determine the facts and to apply the appropriate law to those facts.

The Difficulty in Knowing Which Law to Apply

With the great multitude of laws already on the books, one might think that there must be an existing law to resolve every situation. Unfortunately, that is not true, because it is not even possible. The problem is that no one can foresee every situation, and even if legislators had such foresight, no one could write a law in specific language that would clearly apply to every situation. Human behavior is just too complex. Consequently, courts must derive legal principles from the entire body of law, including the legislative acts of Congress and the states, and prior decisions by the courts.

Oftentimes, the law is unclear because of a lack of precision, in the decisions written by courts and in the laws enacted by legislatures. Ambiguity, poor organization, and inconsistency—at times, even outright contradictions—sometimes bedevil those who try to discover what is intended in the law.

People often know that a particular law is on the books. Perhaps they can paraphrase it quite well. But locating that specific provision in the lawbooks can, at times, be quite daunting—like hunting for the proverbial needle in a haystack. And interested parties must locate that law if they are going to cite it to the court. It is not acceptable to state: "As your honor knows, the law requires a license." They must give the court an exact citation to that law.

When legal sources are inconsistent, several basic rules apply. For example, laws enacted by the legislature (known as **statutes**) take precedence over decisions by courts. (That will be discussed in more depth later in this chapter.) A difficulty arises, however, when it is unclear whether the court and the legislature were addressing the same legal issue. Simply reading the court opinion and the statute does not always resolve that uncertainty.

When several state statutes are inconsistent with one another, the most recently enacted governs. Also, a statute with specific language overrides one with general language on the same topic. The same rules apply to conflicts between

Laws enacted by Congress, a state legislature, or voters are known as **statutes**.

Legislative intent is the purpose that the legislature had in mind when it enacted the statute in question. When the purpose is not apparent from the plain language of the statute, the court determines the legislative intent by reviewing the statute's legislative history, including official reports by the legislature's committees when the proposed statute was voted upon.

federal statutes. But apparent inconsistencies between statutes often raise the question of **legislative intent:** It is possible that the legislature did not intend for the two statutes to govern the same exact issue. In such situations, the courts will attempt to discover the intent of the legislature when those apparently inconsistent laws were enacted. Suggestions for discovering legislative intent are discussed in Chapter 8.

The Difficulty in Understanding the Law

It would be helpful, of course, if all laws were clear and simple so that everyone could understand their meaning and application. But unfortunately, laws that *appear* to be stated in "clear and simple language" can be the most difficult of all to understand and apply. This difficulty can be illustrated by an issue familiar to most.

The First Amendment to the U.S. Constitution states, in part, that *"Congress shall make no law respecting an establishment of religion, or prohibiting the free exercise thereof. . . ."* This legal principle of religious freedom is a familiar one, yet its specific application can be puzzling in the extreme. Before someone can even understand the First Amendment's purpose, she must know the meaning of "religion"—or at least what the Founding Fathers thought it to be. Does "religion" mean a "recognized system" of religious belief? If so, recognized by whom? Does it mean "organized" religion, as in congregations that meet in synagogues, mosques, temples, or churches—or even witches in covens? Does the First Amendment protect a solitary individual's practice of a faith or belief that might be shared by no other person on Earth? Each of these questions returns the inquiry to the very intent of the First Amendment's religion clause. The court system *exists* to deal with exactly this type of uncertainty about the law and to resolve the competing interests that always arise between opposing parties.

To have a free society, there must be a *rule by law*—not by the prejudices or whims of public officials. That means courts should base their decisions upon established legal principles and sound logic. But, as already seen, that is not always easily done. If a legal assistant is to work effectively in the law, he must appreciate the importance of logical analysis and recognize how difficult it can be to know which legal principles should apply in a particular situation. Consequently, the paralegal should avoid any tendency to adopt the "simple" and "obvious" legal conclusion that first comes to mind.

DISTINGUISHING CIVIL AND CRIMINAL LAW

Criminal law defines crimes and establishes their punishment. Violations of criminal law can be punished by fine, imprisonment, or death.

The **plaintiff** is the person who initiates a lawsuit or criminal prosecution against another person. Private persons or the government may be the plaintiff in a lawsuit, but only the government may be the plaintiff in a criminal prosecution.

Civil law establishes the rights and obligations of each person in relation to other persons and the government. Civil law also establishes the powers and limitations of government authority.

There is a clear distinction between criminal and civil law, whether federal or state. In simple terms, **criminal law** is pretty much what everyone believes it to be: Criminal law prohibits and punishes conduct that is so serious that it offends society at large. Criminal offenses can be punished by imprisonment or death—violations of civil law cannot. A criminal act might have an easily identifiable victim (as in a theft), or it might simply injure the public at large (e.g., a legislator accepting bribes). But even when there is a single individual victim, the theory behind criminal law is that all of society is harmed by that act. Consequently, in every criminal case, the **plaintiff** is the government acting in the name of "the people."

Civil law governs "private" relationships between persons, such as contracts, property rights, marriage, parenthood, and a person's duty not to harm others. Civil law also regulates "public" relationships, including public education, the election of public officials, the licensing of medical doctors, and the operation of the court system. Civil law is often reinforced by criminal statutes—for example, the statutes providing criminal penalties for bigamy, fraud in private contracts, fraud in the election of government officials, or the practice of medicine without a license.

THE HIERARCHY OF LEGAL AUTHORITY

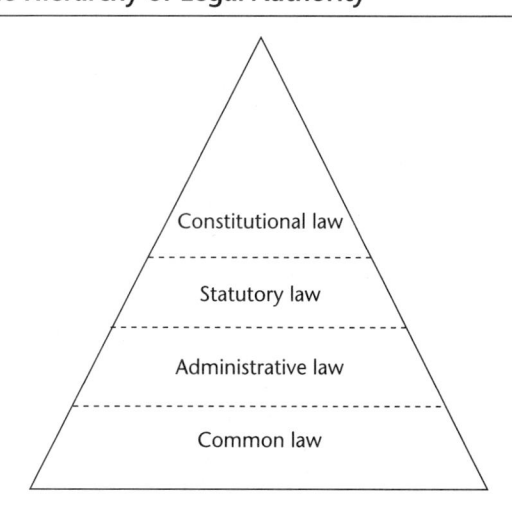

There is a general hierarchy of legal authorities, and there are four levels in that hierarchy. (See *Figure 4.1*.) Starting from the top, "constitutional law," each level of legal authority is superior to every authority below it. Therefore, the highest legal authority is **constitutional law**. A constitution is the most fundamental of human laws—it establishes a system of government and determines the powers and limitations of that government. All other laws and all governmental powers must be interpreted and applied in harmony with that constitution. The U.S. Constitution has established a federal republic with a *division of powers* between the central government authority (the "federal government") and the states. This division of powers has important implications for understanding the hierarchy of legal authorities, and it is discussed in a later section of this chapter. State constitutions, as well, provide part of this highest level of the hierarchy, constitutional law.

> **Constitutional law** is the law embodied in a constitution.

The next level of legal authority includes the statutes enacted by the state legislatures and by the Congress, and also treaties made between the United States and other nations. Federal and state statutes implement the powers granted by the U.S. Constitution and by the state constitutions, respectively. The federal and state constitutions establish basic principles, and the statutes spell out the details of the law. Court decisions interpret and apply both the constitutions and the statutes enacted under their authority.

Under the U.S. Constitution, federal treaties with other nations have the same legal authority as federal statutes—and when a statute and a treaty conflict, the *more recent* of the two governs. Consequently, within the United States the effect of any treaty provision can be overridden by enactment of a subsequent federal statute. Just like statutes, all treaties are subordinate to the U.S. Constitution.

The third level in the hierarchy is **administrative law**, composed of the regulations published by state and federal government agencies, and the court decisions that interpret them. Just as a statute must find authority in the constitution, administrative law must be based upon either constitutional or statutory authority. Most federal administrative law is established under authority delegated by Congress to the executive branch agencies. Every state government also issues regulations under the authority of its state constitution and state statutes. Finally, exercising their authority under the state and federal constitu-

> **Administrative law** comprises executive orders and the policies, regulations, decisions, and orders of government agencies. Administrative law is created and enforced at each level of government: local, state, and federal.

FIGURE 4.1 The Hierarchy of Legal Authority

- Constitutional law
- Statutory law
- Administrative law
- Common law

An **executive order** is a directive or statement of executive policy issued by the chief executive officer (e.g., President, governor, mayor) implementing her authority under constitutional or statutory law.

tions, respectively, state governors and the President issue **executive orders** that carry the force of law and therefore comprise part of the administrative law. This constitutional authority is often augmented by statutory authority to issue executive orders for particular purposes. Administrative law is discussed further in Chapter 5.

The lowest level of legal authority is *common law:* the accumulation of legal principles found in prior court decisions. Common law is often termed "judge-made" law, simply because it is found in the decisions written by judges. Although common law is at the bottom of the hierarchy of legal authority, it continues to have enormous importance in our legal system. That is because so many legal questions lie beyond the scope of existing statutes and administrative law. When that happens, the courts usually rely upon earlier court decisions to find a rule of law for modern situations. When a court follows the ruling in an earlier case, that earlier case is then known as a **precedent**. Of course, the rulings of the U.S. Supreme Court and the various state courts of last resort provide the most important precedents. A **court of last resort** is the highest appellate court in a given jurisdiction.

A **precedent** is an earlier court decision that states a legal principle that is used to resolve similar cases that follow.

The highest appellate court of any jurisdiction (e.g., a state) is known as the **court of last resort**. For the nation, the court of last resort is the U.S. Supreme Court.

Courts Apply the Hierarchy of Law

The courts always follow the highest legal authority that applies to the facts of any given case. Thus, a court will always apply constitutional law if it provides a clear resolution of the case at hand and will use common law only when no higher legal authority can be found. Regardless of the legal authority being applied, the court must always apply its own analysis to determine how that legal authority applies to the facts of the specific case before it. Because the court's own analysis is so important, even very specific and detailed statutory law eventually becomes stamped with the views of the judges who apply it to particular cases. The higher the court, the greater is its authority to interpret and state the law. It is not unusual for Congress or a state legislature to revisit a statute, and amend it, because it is displeased with the interpretation that the courts have applied to the original words of that statute.

The Supreme Law of the Land

> *This Constitution, and the Laws of the United States which shall be made in Pursuance thereof; and all Treaties made, or which shall be made, under the Authority of the United States, shall be the supreme Law of the Land; and the Judges in every State shall be bound thereby, any Thing in the Constitution or Laws of any State to the Contrary notwithstanding.*

(*United States Constitution,* Article VI, Section 2.)

The **Supremacy Clause** is Article VI, Section 2 of the U.S. Constitution, which states that federal law is supreme over all other laws in the United States.

This statement, known as the **Supremacy Clause** of the Constitution, might be one of the most powerful and important passages in the Constitution. It establishes *absolutely* that *valid* federal law is supreme over state law, and that the states do not have full sovereignty, but are subordinate components of the federal union. State constitutions and state laws must not conflict with the Supreme Law of the Land—which is federal law. Therefore, the meaning of "federal law" assumes great importance in the American legal system.

The U.S. Constitution, federal statutes and treaties, and federal regulations are the **Supreme Law of the Land**.

The **Supreme Law of the Land** comprises all *federal* constitutional, statutory, treaty, and administrative law. But look again at that opening phrase in Article VI, Section 2: *"This Constitution, and the Laws of the United States which shall be made in Pursuance thereof...."* That phrase means that, in order for federal laws to be supreme, they must be made "in pursuance of" the Constitution: that is, they must be in harmony with the Constitution. Thus, federal statutes, regulations, and policies that conflict with the U.S. Constitution are void. To be valid, an **act of Congress** (i.e., a statute enacted by the Congress) must conform to the Constitution. Any act of Congress that violates the Constitution is *not* part of the Supreme Law of the Land and is powerless to override state law. The same is true of federal treaties: They must be "*made . . . under the Authority of the United States,*" which authority obviously flows from the Constitution. Any treaty, also, that conflicts with the Constitution will be held by the courts to be invalid and therefore *not* part of the Supreme Law of the Land.

In the following "Case in Point," the U.S. Supreme Court considers whether Congress can authorize citizens to sue their own state government for violation of the federal *Fair Labor Standards Act.* In this case, the State of Maine claimed sovereign immunity from suit by its own citizens. The history of *Alden v. Maine* is summarized here.

A statute enacted by Congress is known as an **act of Congress**.

A Case in Point

Alden v. Maine

527 U.S. 706 (1999)

State probation officers filed suit in federal court against their employer, the State of Maine, seeking monetary damages for alleged violations of the overtime pay requirements of the federal *Fair Labor Standards Act of 1938.* The case was dismissed from federal court, based upon a prior ruling by the U.S. Supreme Court in *Seminole Tribe of Florida v. Florida,* 517 U.S. 44 (1996) that Congress does not have the power under the Constitution's commerce clause to subject state governments to lawsuits in federal courts. Although the Eleventh Amendment shields states against federal lawsuits only by citizens of another state or a foreign nation, the Court held that sovereign state immunity against its own citizens in federal court is inherent in our federal system of coexisting state and national governments.

The employees then filed suit in state court, but that suit was dismissed when the State of Maine claimed sovereign immunity. Because that action would have left the employees with no forum in which to press their claims under the federal statute, they appealed the dismissal to the Supreme Court.

The Supreme Court held that the State of Maine is immune also from any suit brought by its own citizens in state court, unless it consents to such lawsuits. It found that Congress' authority to regulate interstate commerce—the constitutional basis for enacting the *Fair Labor Standards Act*—does not empower it to abrogate state sovereign immunity. The Court stated that the Constitution's Supremacy Clause limits the power of congressional lawmaking by requiring that federal statutes be "made in pursuance [of]" the Constitution, and the Constitution embodies an arrangement of dual sovereignty. Any federal statute that exceeds the constitutional powers of Congress is void.

The analysis and argumentation of constitutional law in *Alden* is lengthy and complex, and received the support of only five justices among the nine who sit on the Supreme Court. But it is one of three Supreme Court decisions in the 1998–99 term that altered the balance of constitutional authority and sovereignty between the states and the national government. The other two cases were decided by the identical 5–4 split. In *Florida Prepaid Postsecondary Education Expense Board v. College Savings Bank,* 527 U.S. 627 (1999), and another closely related case decided at the same time, the Supreme Court held that the states may not be sued in federal court for state infringement of the *bona fide* patent or trademark rights held by others. Questions remain about the *extent* of state immunity and about whether citizens can sue their state governments for a pervasive "pattern" of discrimination that would violate federal law.

When a federal statute or treaty *is* constitutional, however, it is absolutely supreme over any contrary provisions of state law or acts of state governments. Thus, the constitutions and statutes of the fifty states must not violate the U.S. Constitution, nor conflict with federal statutes, nor with treaties between the United States and other nations. Not only are state constitutions and statutes subordinate to federal law, but so also are state administrative law and the actions of state courts, officers, and employees.

Actions of Federal Officials and Contrary State Law

What about the actions of federal officials and employees? Is an executive order by the President superior to a contradictory provision of state law? If the President is acting within his or her authority under the Constitution or a federal statute, the answer to the latter question is "yes." And because federal administrative law is an extension of federal constitutional and statutory law—that is, it is made under authority granted by the Constitution or by Congress—it also carries the force of federal law and is supreme over state law and the acts of state governments.

That principle applies to every federal officer and employee. To illustrate, not only are federal military convoys exempt from state traffic laws *when necessary for the efficient conduct of their duties,* but so too are Postal Service letter carriers. The rationale is that the military or Postal Service personnel are implementing federal law when they perform their duties. If state governments could frustrate the efficient implementation of federal law, the Supremacy Clause would be greatly weakened.

Cities, counties, and other local agencies are creatures of state government. That means that they must comply with the U.S. Constitution, of course. But it also means that they are subject to their state constitution and state laws. Consequently, city and county **ordinances** can be challenged under state statutes, the state constitution, the U.S. Constitution, and valid federal statutes.

Courts Exercise the Power of Judicial Review

One of the most important functions of the courts—particularly of the U.S. Supreme Court and the state courts of last resort—is their role in reviewing and resolving conflicts among laws. And, in resolving those conflicts, the courts apply the hierarchy of law. In this way, the courts have become the guardians of the Constitution and the rule of law.

It was in *Marbury v. Madison,* 5 U.S. 137 (1803), that the U.S. Supreme Court first asserted the authority of the courts to say "which law shall govern" when there is a conflict between the different levels of legal authority. In *Marbury,* the conflict was between the Constitution and an act of Congress. Ironically, in *Marbury,* the Supreme Court held that a congressional statute was unconstitutional because it would have given to the courts more power than the Constitution permitted. In rejecting an illegitimate gift of power from the Congress, the Supreme Court simultaneously claimed for itself the power to hold congressional acts to be unconstitutional.

The significance of that decision in *Marbury* was that the Supreme Court would no longer accept without question the legislative authority claimed by Congress under the Constitution. Instead, the Court would hold invalid any congressional acts that conflict with the Constitution. This role of the courts is called **judicial review**. Judicial review is not mentioned in the Constitution itself. It is the result of the Supreme Court's own interpretation of the judiciary's role under the Constitution.

The essence of judicial review is that a court often encounters two or more statements of the law on any given issue. One legal authority says "the law is

---

An **ordinance** is a local statute enacted by city or county government.

Practice Tip

Once the full case citation [Marbury v. Madison, 5 U.S. 137 (1803)] has been given, it is unnecessary—and also annoying to the reader—to repeat that full citation every time the case is mentioned, particularly when the case is mentioned repeatedly in a continuing discussion. In the latter situation, it is customary to refer to the case by naming a single party, as in "Marbury" or "Madison." Usually, the first party named in the citation is used to identify that case, so that Marbury v. Madison *would typically be referred to as "Marbury." Some exceptions to that practice will be introduced later.*

Judicial review is the power of the courts to void government actions that violate higher legal authority, such as constitutional law.

ABC," and the other legal authority says "the law is BCD." Although both authorities include "B" and "C" as part of the law, they differ over "A" and "D." Sometimes, two statements of the law are directly contradictory to each other. In either event, a court must decide which statement of the law should be applied to the case before it. In *Marbury,* the Supreme Court had to decide which of *two conflicting laws* it should apply and enforce: the Constitution or a contrary act of Congress. The Supreme Court concluded that it cannot apply a statute that conflicts with the Constitution.

Judicial Review Rests upon the Hierarchy of Law

The Supreme Court implicitly recognized the hierarchy of legal authority in which the Constitution is supreme over any contradictory statute. To have held otherwise would have permitted the Congress and the President to enact whatever laws they wished without regard for the Constitution. Without judicial review, the constitutional system of limited government might have disappeared as Congress and the President claimed ever greater powers. The *Marbury* court's holding in favor of judicial review, then, was a crucial decision for a "rule by law," rather than a "rule by men."

But this power of judicial review was itself claimed by imperfect men then sitting on the Supreme Court (no women being on the federal bench in the early nineteenth century). In theory, of course, those justices were independent, unswayed by the passions of public opinion, and had been selected from among the best legal minds in the nation. But, if one were to view the Supreme Court as an undisciplined and unaccountable group of self-anointed arbiters of constitutional law—and that point of view has been sincerely held by some critics—one could reach the opposite conclusion about the value of judicial review. Although human frailties and political bias might be as common to Supreme Court justices as to the rest of us, in the generations since the *Marbury* decision, the Supreme Court has developed a tradition of relative political independence, strong legal scholarship, and dedication to continuity in constitutional principles.

Reluctance to Overturn Established Precedent

The importance of continuity in constitutional principles is difficult to overemphasize. Without that continuity, no one could know from one day to the next what any part of the Constitution meant. One result of continuity has been that the Supreme Court has been extremely reluctant to overrule its own decision on abortion in *Roe v. Wade,* 410 U.S. 113 (1973), even though some subsequently appointed Supreme Court justices publicly criticized the constitutional theory for *Roe.* There are two reasons for this judicial self-restraint:

1. a belief that the Supreme Court's own authority and influence would be seriously diluted if its decisions fluctuated back and forth whenever a new "liberal" or "conservative" majority became dominant on the Court
2. a recognition that crucial constitutional principles should be articulated as a result of methodical legal analysis over a period of years and in light of the differing facts of many cases, rather than as a "snapshot" of the Court's legal philosophy at the moment when any single case is before it

As a result of this concept of continuity, once the Supreme Court has reached a fundamental interpretation of some part of the Constitution, it can be extremely difficult to persuade the Court to change that interpretation. This difficulty is illustrated by the Supreme Court's near-unanimous (7–1) holding in *Plessy v. Ferguson,* 163 U.S. 537 (1896). In *Plessy,* the Supreme Court ruled that racial segregation did not violate the Fourteenth Amendment's "equal

> **Practice Tip**
>
> The case citation to Brown v. Board of Education at the end of the paragraph informs the reader that it was in that case that the Supreme Court overturned its prior holding in Plessy v. Ferguson. End-of-paragraph citations are very common, and typically they provide the source of the legal principles contained in the paragraph(s) that they conclude. In court opinions, the student will even find citations following individual sentences, whenever more than one legal authority must be cited for several legal principles contained within a single paragraph.

protection" clause, so long as the segregated facilities were "equal." This ruling was followed fifty-eight years later by the Supreme Court's unanimous (9–0) holding that in public education, at least, racially segregated facilities are "inherently unequal" and therefore *do* violate the equal protection clause. *Brown v. Board of Education of Topeka, Kansas,* 347 U.S. 483 (1954).

If nothing else, the Supreme Court's reluctance to change course in its constitutional interpretations gives some measure of predictability to constitutional law. Without that predictability, the lower courts would always hesitate to take a stand on constitutional issues. That is an important concern, because all federal and state courts exercise judicial review and must apply the law of the U.S. Constitution.

Decisions on federal constitutional law by a state court or a lower federal court do not usually forge new territory, but simply apply prior Supreme Court decisions to the questions before them. Occasionally, however, these courts will go beyond the principles already stated by the Supreme Court and reach their own innovative holdings on a constitutional question. Understandably, that is done with some trepidation, because the possibility exists that a higher appellate court—or, perhaps the Supreme Court itself—will strike down their holdings as being *too* innovative and lacking sufficient foundation in the accumulated case law that has interpreted the Constitution.

THE AUTHORITY FOR STATE AND FEDERAL LEGISLATION

Not only must a statute not conflict with constitutional law, there also must be actual constitutional authority for government to legislate on the subject of that statute. That authority to legislate might be:

- explicitly *expressed* in the words of the constitution;
- *implied* by the provisions of the constitution; or,
- *inherent* in the nature of government.

For example, the U.S. Constitution gives express authority to Congress to define and punish crimes. The authority to regulate immigration is *not* expressed in the Constitution; however, it is implied by the express authority to grant citizenship and regulate foreign commerce. Although the Constitution *does* authorize Congress to raise an army and navy, if military forces had *not* been mentioned, it is likely that the Supreme Court would have upheld their establishment as an exercise of the inherent self-defense power of a sovereign nation.

Congress derives most of its legislative authority as expressed in Article I, Section 8, of the U.S. Constitution. Express authority to legislate is found also in some of the amendments to the Constitution. And legislative authority is implied in other articles of the original Constitution.

The legislative authority of the states is found primarily in the Tenth Amendment to the U.S. Constitution (the "reserved powers" clause, discussed below) and in the various state constitutions. A few specific state powers (e.g., to conduct elections for Congress and the presidency, and to approve constitutional amendments proposed by Congress) are set forth in other articles of the U.S. Constitution. Cities, counties, and other local governments enact ordinances under state authority. Although municipal ordinances are subordinate to state statutes, they are nonetheless part of statutory law.

State government must meet a constitutional authority test for all state statutes and policies. But that test is not too stringent, because the Tenth Amendment reserves to the states all powers "*not delegated to the United States by the Constitution, nor prohibited by it to the States....*" What powers remain for the states to exercise? All powers of government that the Constitution has not mentioned are reserved for the states. That fact gives enormous significance to the general police powers of the states.

The General Police Powers of State Government

The **general police powers** of the state governments encompass the protection of public health, safety, welfare, and morals. That broad scope has caused the courts to uphold a multitude of state laws that find no specific authority in either the U.S. Constitution or state constitutions. At issue here is a principle of **inherent powers** of government: the idea that any government of human society must possess certain powers or it fails to be capable of governing. Without the power to define and punish crimes, or to defend against invasion, for example, a government would be unable to continue in existence. Inherent powers also derive from the *fundamental purpose of government:* to preserve the peace and provide for the general welfare. (See, for example, the Preamble to the U.S. Constitution, in Appendix H.)

Because state police powers are so broad—even though vaguely defined—the courts tend to support any "reasonable" state policy that protects public health, safety, welfare, or morals, unless it clearly conflicts with a *guaranteed* individual freedom under the state or federal constitutions. State governments routinely do such things as regulating by statute the freedom of parents to educate their children at home rather than in a public school, dictating the retail price of a quart of milk, and requiring owners of oceanfront property to provide free public access—across their private property—to the beach. Each such statute is based upon the state government's exercise of its general police powers.

> The state governments possess broad **general police powers** that allow them to regulate public and private conduct in order to promote the public health, safety, welfare, and morals.
>
> **Inherent powers** are those powers of government that are essential to the fundamental functions of any government (e.g., to maintain public order, to defend against armed invasion) and thus derive from the nature of government rather than depending upon a grant of authority from any other source.

The Concurrent Powers of State and Federal Governments

Although federal law is supreme, that becomes important only when there is a conflict between state and federal law. In situations of **concurrent powers**—where both federal and state governments may legislate on the same subject matter—both state and federal laws are equally valid. The most obvious concurrent powers are to collect taxes, to define and punish crimes, to defend against armed invasion, and to expend public monies for the general welfare. But the states and Congress each, independently of one another, also regulate banks and the sale of securities (e.g., stocks and bonds), prohibit various forms of discrimination in employment, and establish pollution standards for motor vehicles. In the latter example, motor vehicle manufacturers must meet the stricter of the two standards in each state where they sell automobiles.

But there are some areas in which federal law **preempts** all state power to legislate. To "preempt" state power means to preclude any state regulation of some matter by claiming sole legislative authority for the federal government. For example, only Congress may establish a post office, or establish bankruptcy courts, because the Constitution reserves those functions to Congress and the federal government, exclusively. The Constitution preempts these powers for the federal government, and the states may not intrude.

> **Concurrent powers** are those that the federal and state governments both have (e.g., to tax, and to define and punish crimes).
>
> A higher legal authority (e.g., the federal government or the state government) might **preempt**—that is, claim for itself—all powers to regulate a particular issue, thereby barring any regulation of that issue by lower legal authorities (e.g., the state government or the local government). Thus, a state might preempt the regulation of alcohol, barring any regulation of alcohol by the cities or counties in that state.

SECTION 2. LAWS OF THE STATE GOVERNMENTS

The bulk of American law is found in state law. True, the U.S. Constitution establishes some parameters and limitations, but within that framework, the states have created the greater part of the law of this nation. Although, the Supremacy Clause makes federal law paramount—whenever state and federal law are in conflict—most state law never comes even close to conflicting with federal law. And, as recent decisions of the U.S. Supreme Court have made clear, Congress must watch its step when it attempts to regulate the behavior of state governments; without constitutional authority, Congress may not impinge upon the limited sovereignty that the fifty states possess.

In keeping with the hierarchy of legal authority discussed earlier in this chapter, the law of a given state is found in its constitution, its statutes, regulations, and common law. State courts have the final say on the *meaning* of state law. That doesn't mean that state law is immune to review by the federal courts—it simply means that state law *is* what the state courts say it is. If it turns out that the state law is unconstitutional, then that law will no longer govern.

THE UNIFORM ACTS

> The **Uniform Acts** are model statutes drafted by the National Conference of Commissioners on Uniform State Laws and subsequently enacted, essentially unchanged, by the various states.

The **Uniform Acts** are state laws based upon model statutes proposed jointly by legal scholars of the American Law Institute and the National Conference of Commissioners on Uniform State Laws. Examples include the Uniform Commercial Code, the Uniform Partnership Act, the Uniform Child Custody Jurisdiction Act, and the Uniform Anatomical Gifts Act. The purpose of the Uniform Acts is to establish common legal standards, rules, and procedures for matters that often cross state boundaries. This uniformity is accomplished when all (or nearly all) states enact the same uniform statute on any given issue, such as human organ donation. The Uniform Child Custody Jurisdiction Act reduces the likelihood of several states' claiming jurisdiction over the custody of a particular child, for example. A uniform act does not become the law of any state until it has been enacted by the legislature of that state.

These model statutes are drafted with the intention of making them acceptable to as many states as possible. This requires that the drafters consider the interaction of the model statutes with other existing state laws, as well as the business practices and social values found in the various states. Each state legislature is free to accept or reject each model statute, and often the model statutes are adopted in a somewhat modified form more acceptable to a particular state legislature. Even so, to the extent that the state laws are "uniform," the model statutes achieve their purpose.

> **Case law** is the accumulation of published court decisions that serve as a body of law upon which courts can rely in deciding later cases before them.

One benefit of the Uniform Acts is the body of **case law** that develops based upon them. Because the Uniform Commercial Code has been adopted, at least in part, by every state in the nation, there is case law from fifty states interpreting its provisions. Although case law from one state is only *persuasive* authority in the courts of another state, when the statutes are identical, the case law of the various states tends to develop a similar uniformity. It would defeat the purpose of the Uniform Acts if the courts of each state imposed their unique interpretation upon identical statutory language. For that reason, when considering the language of a uniform act, state courts give exceptional weight to the interpretations already made by the courts of other states.

THE COMMON LAW AND ITS APPLICATION

Except for Louisiana, which follows French legal tradition, the American system of law is based upon the English system that developed in medieval times. Before the English Parliament evolved, royal edicts and orders of the Crown's Privy Council (i.e., the king's or queen's council of ministers) were the precursors of modern statutes. Most ordinary civil disputes arose out of private relationships and were not covered by any form of written law. Local hereditary manor lords (e.g., a duke or an earl) often served as judges of such disputes, applying whatever sense of justice—or prejudice or whim—struck their fancy.

As the English political system evolved, Parliament gradually displaced the monarch and the Privy Council as the primary legislators, and a formal court system also developed. Still lacking statutory guidance for the settlement of most private disputes, the courts came to rely upon the decisions made in earlier cases. Those prior court decisions became precedents, establishing the rules of law to be followed when similar cases came before the courts in later years. Over time, the accumulation of precedents became known as the "common law," which was so called because it was intended to be "common" to the entire English nation. The common law determined rights and obligations in various situations: for example, under commercial contracts, between tenants and landlords, and among landowners who shared the water from streams flowing through their adjoining lands.

Courts of Equity and Courts of Law

These early English courts became known as **courts of law**. Although these courts served as a great improvement over the unpredictable decisions of hereditary lords, their decisions eventually became *too* predictable because of the inflexibility of the accumulated common law. The English common law courts continued to apply old legal principles even after they had little relevance to the realities of changing times, and the law became so rigid that it often bore little resemblance to justice, in any human sense. A landlord, for example, could be guilty of the most despicable conduct, yet win a case against his tenant so long as the landlord had not breached the "letter" of the old common law. As a result, a second, parallel court system was established to provide a remedy where the common law turned a blind eye to justice. These were known as the **courts of equity**. Their standard was fairness, rather than rigid adherence to precedent. In most of the United States, the functions of common law and equity have been combined within a single court system. The law of equity will be discussed in Chapter 6.

A **court of law** is a tribunal with authority to exercise judicial functions under the laws of its jurisdiction. In modern usage, "court of law" is commonly used to refer to a court holding both powers in law and powers in equity.

A **court of equity** is a tribunal with authority to administer justice according to the principles of equity (i.e., fundamental fairness), as opposed to traditional rules of early common law. In most of the United States, the courts of equity and courts of law have been merged.

Modern Day Common Law

The common law continues to be an essential part of the American system, and courts attempt to follow precedents closely, although not blindly. The obvious advantage of this is that people can know the general rules of law, as established in earlier court decisions, and thereby know in advance what their rights and obligations are likely to be in most situations. However, American courts will depart from precedent in particular situations where not doing so would cause a serious injustice, and they will move beyond existing precedent when changing circumstances require new legal principles—in effect, the creation of "new precedents." As a result, and in contrast to the old English system, American common law evolves continuously to accommodate the changing realities of modern times and to incorporate new concepts of justice.

In practice, this evolution is a very gradual process, so that the common law continues to be fairly predictable and people are not being constantly blindsided by dramatic changes in the law. In addition, departure from established precedent is rare in trial courts and unusual in the lower appellate courts. The most dramatic changes in common law usually occur in the decisions of the state courts of last resort. Because those are courts of the highest state jurisdiction, new precedents made there tend to stand undisturbed for many years.

Some commentators have stated that there is no such thing as a *federal* common law, distinct from state common law. In fact, the U.S. Supreme Court once stated, "there is no federal general common law." *Erie Railroad Co. v. Tompkins*, 304 U.S. 64, 78 (1938). This view assumes that federal courts will apply the common law of the various states, and that *is* the general practice to this day. However, the federal courts also operate as common law courts when they interpret statutory and constitutional law, relying upon earlier cases as precedents.

Practice Tip

Every beginning paralegal must be able to understand a **case citation**, which tells one exactly where to find the court's written decision in a particular case.

Figure 4.2 identifies the elements of the case citation for Erie Railroad Co. v. Tompkins.

The name of the case is *Erie Railroad Co. v. Tompkins*. The abbreviation "v." is read as "versus." (The "vs." form, so popular in sports, is not used in legal citations.) "U.S." identifies the case reporter as *United States Reports,* the official reporter for decisions of the U.S. Supreme Court. "304" identifies volume 304 of that reporter. The *Erie Railroad Co.* case begins on page 64 of that volume, and the words quoted here will be found on page 78. The court's decision was delivered in 1938.

A **case citation** is the information needed to identify a case (normally given in a standardized format) and to locate its published decision in a case reporter.

The **Full Faith and Credit Clause** is Article IV, Section 1 of the U.S. Constitution, which requires each state to recognize and accept the validity of statutes, public records, and judicial proceedings of the other states.

Jurisdiction is the authority of a court to determine the legal issues and the rights and obligations of the parties that are before it.

Public policy is the body of general principles of conduct, equity, and societal relationships that are so firmly established in law that no court will enforce contracts or administrative acts that violate those principles.

FIGURE 4.2 Description of a Case Citation.

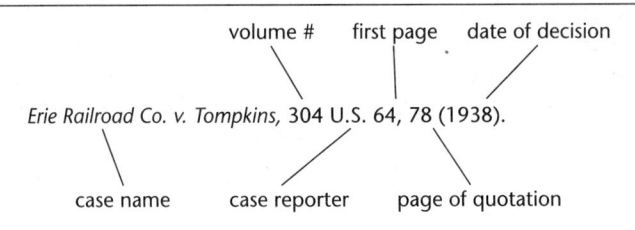

```
                      volume #    first page   date of decision
                           \          |           /
      Erie Railroad Co. v. Tompkins, 304 U.S. 64, 78 (1938).
                /                    |            \
          case name             case reporter    page of quotation
```

ENFORCING THE LAWS AND OFFICIAL ACTS OF OTHER STATES

When the U.S. Constitution was being drafted, a key concern was the sanctity of state laws and official state acts. Would the courts of one state try to overturn the marriages, wills, and contracts that another state had officially recognized? Would state court judgments in lawsuits be voided by the courts of another state? If that were to occur, chaos would reign. For that reason, the Full Faith and Credit Clause was included in the Constitution:

> *Full Faith and Credit shall be given in each State to the public Acts, Records, and judicial Proceedings of every other State. And the Congress may by general Laws prescribe the Manner in which such Acts, Records and Proceedings shall be proved, and the Effect thereof.*
>
> (U.S. Constitution, Article IV, Section 1.)

The **Full Faith and Credit Clause** means that, with very few exceptions, the courts of each state *must* recognize and uphold the statutes, administrative law, and court judgments of every other state of the Union. In 1790, the Congress exercised its authority under that clause, enacting statutory procedures for authenticating official state records. That statute provided that those records shall be recognized by every court in the nation, just as they are by the courts of the state where those records are kept. This statute applies to both federal and state courts. The federal statute is found in Title 28 of the *United States Code.*

Exceptions to Full Faith and Credit

A fundamental exception to the Full Faith and Credit Clause occurs when some state has acted without **jurisdiction**—that is, without legal authority—over the person or matter involved. A second exception occurs when to uphold a particular action would violate **public policy**—that is, the well-settled conscience of society regarding human relationships. For example, public policy concerns might cause a Utah court to refuse enforcement of a New Jersey judgment on a gambling debt incurred in a New Jersey casino, because gambling is illegal in Utah.

The U.S. Supreme Court has held that *state jurisdiction* may be examined by the courts of another state before giving full faith and credit to court judgments of other states. However, if a judgment appears to be the official record of a court of general jurisdiction—that is, a court of unlimited trial jurisdiction—there is a *presumption* that the court had proper jurisdiction. *Milliken v. Meyer,* 311 U.S. 457 (1940). But, of course, that presumption can be challenged by evidence that proper jurisdiction was actually lacking. If the presumption of jurisdiction cannot be overcome, the Full Faith and Credit Clause "precludes any inquiry into the merits of the cause of action, the logic or consistency of the decision, or the validity of the legal principles on which the judgment is based." *Id.,* at p. 462. In other words, the courts of one state may not exercise *judicial review* of the decisions made in the courts of another state.

Full faith and credit is routinely accorded to most administrative state actions: affidavits, notarizations, incorporation of businesses, certified copies of public records, and so forth. However, states are not required to accept professional licenses granted by other states; each state is free to establish its own licensing standards and procedures for attorneys, doctors, school teachers, and certified public accountants.

In *St. John v. Wisconsin Employment Relations Board,* 340 U.S. 411 (1951), the U.S. Supreme Court held that both state and federal courts must give full faith and credit to the judgments of the other jurisdiction. In other words, valid state judgments must receive full recognition in federal courts, and vice versa.

State Residency and Full Faith and Credit

A classic controversy over jurisdiction—and a controversy that is instructive about full faith and credit—involved so-called "quickie" or "easy" divorces granted by the courts of one state to residents of another state. To grant a divorce, the state must have personal jurisdiction over the spouse seeking the divorce. Because New York has sole jurisdiction to govern the marriage relationships of its own residents, it need not recognize a divorce granted to New York residents by the courts of a "foreign" state. Without exception, however, every other state must recognize a divorce that a state court grants to its own *bona fide* residents. This is a matter in which residency determines the jurisdiction of the court and, therefore, the validity of its judgment.

The picture becomes more complicated, however, if Nevada (for example) prescribes by statute a very brief period to establish legal residence in Nevada, following which it claims jurisdiction over the marriage relationship of its newly qualified resident and grants the divorce. If the person divorced in Nevada were to remain indefinitely in that state, the validity of the new Nevada residency would be clear, and Nevada's jurisdiction in the divorce proceedings would be unquestioned by the courts of other states.

What commonly occurred, however, was that people chose a state with a relatively short residency period and/or easy standards for granting a divorce. This standard by which to be granted a divorce was particularly important in earlier times when many states required proof of adultery as the only valid ground for divorce. The **petitioners** remained in the "foreign" state only long enough to establish "residency" and obtain the divorce, and then promptly returned to their true home states. In such a situation, the courts of some states treated the foreign state residency as a sham and refused to recognize the divorce on the grounds that a temporary absence from one's home state does not confer jurisdiction on the state where one actually is no more than a visitor. Because they based their objections upon a lack of jurisdiction, these states were conforming to their full faith and credit obligation, as stated by the Supreme Court in *Milliken v. Meyer,* 311 U.S. 457 (1940), which was discussed above.

Some states also objected to out-of-state divorces on grounds that public policy does not permit a resident to temporarily leave his home state for the purpose of evading the laws of that state and seeking another jurisdiction with laws more favorable to his circumstance. This practice is known as "jurisdiction shopping." The same legal theory is used by some states to collect "use taxes" (in lieu of sales taxes) on automobiles and other "big ticket" items purchased by its residents in nearby states that have lower sales tax rates—again, so that the state residents cannot escape the laws of their own states by temporarily traveling to a state with more favorable laws.

Practice Tip

The quotation at the end of the preceding paragraph is taken from Milliken v. Meyer, *for which a full citation already appears in the same paragraph. Rather than repeat the same citation or even refer to the case as "Milliken," the Latin word* idem *("the same") is used in its abbreviated form, "id."*

Id. *is used only when there are no intervening citations (e.g., for other cases). It is always accompanied by designation of the page, as in "at p. 462" here. It would be equally acceptable to use "Milliken" as the reference here, rather than "id."*

A **petitioner** is a person who seeks some action or remedy from a court.

STATE REGULATION OF INTERSTATE COMMERCE

Although only the federal government is permitted by the U.S. Constitution to regulate interstate or foreign commerce, the meaning of that restriction is not always clear. The *Uniform Commercial Code* (the **UCC**)—a standardized set of rules for conducting commercial transactions that has been enacted into law by every state of the Union—is a prime example of state governments' regulating interstate commerce. Most of the states enacting the UCC have modified it slightly—or, in some cases, significantly. Even so, the UCC provides remarkably uniform standards for commercial contracts for the sale of goods and merchandise. The UCC does not apply to other commercial transactions such as real estate or employment contracts.

But, without violating the U.S. Constitution, how can the state governments regulate contracts for the sale of goods and merchandise between and among the different states—which clearly involves **interstate commerce?** The answer has two parts:

1. Congress has not enacted a uniform law for commercial contracts in interstate commerce—which it clearly *could* do, if Congress thought it to be beneficial.
2. State laws affecting interstate commerce are usually valid if they do not impose excessive burdens on, or discriminate against, interstate commerce.

In the absence of federal legislation, the UCC actually fosters interstate commerce by making the terms and effects of commercial contracts more uniform and predictable nationwide. This is a situation in which coordinated state regulation—through a uniform code—contributes to the federal constitutional goal of a national economy.

Basically, it is the *interstate* or *foreign aspects* of commerce that states may not regulate. For example, the states may not restrict the interstate or foreign destinations of the airline or trucking industries. However, the states may impose highway speed limits on interstate truckers and specify the landing fees at public airports serving interstate flights, so long as those state actions do not impose an unreasonable burden on, or discriminate against, interstate commerce.

> The *Uniform Commercial Code* **(UCC)** is one of the Uniform Acts; it establishes the law of commercial contracts for the sale of goods and merchandise.

> **Interstate commerce** comprises all business transactions, communication, and transportation that cross state lines or that have a substantial impact on commercial activity among the states.

SECTION 3. THE STATE AND FEDERAL COURTS

There are two parallel court systems in the United States. The state courts—including county, parish, and local courts—apply state and local law, primarily, although they are bound to recognize and enforce the Supreme Law of the Land, as well. The federal courts apply state and/or federal law—whichever is appropriate to the case before them—but always give primacy to the Supreme Law of the Land. Both the state and federal courts hear civil cases—lawsuits, for example—and both hear criminal cases. Some types of cases arising under state law—probate and family law, for examples—rarely find their way into federal courts. A fundamental question before the court *in every case* is its authority to hear and decide that case.

JURISDICTION: THE AUTHORITY OF A COURT TO HEAR AND DECIDE A CASE

The authority of a court to hear and determine a case is called its "jurisdiction." There are three basic types of jurisdiction:

1. subject matter jurisdiction
2. *in rem* jurisdiction
3. personal jurisdiction

Under the Fifth and Fourteenth Amendments' due process clauses, a court must have subject matter jurisdiction and also personal jurisdiction over the defendant in order to hear and decide the case. Federal courts receive their jurisdiction from the U.S. Constitution and the federal statutes implementing its provisions. State courts receive their jurisdiction by implication of the Tenth Amendment, and from state constitutions and state statutes.

Subject matter jurisdiction generally refers to the court's authority to determine the type of case before it. Several federal courts have very narrow subject matter jurisdiction: the Bankruptcy Court, Tax Court, Court of International Trade, and so forth. A U.S. Court Martial has subject matter jurisdiction limited to crimes committed by military personnel subject to the *Uniform Code of Military Justice*. As mentioned earlier, courts with unrestricted subject matter jurisdiction are known as courts of general jurisdiction.

***In rem* jurisdiction** refers to the court's authority to determine the status of real or personal property located within its geographical territory. A common example is a suit to **quiet title** (i.e., a suit to resolve uncertainty about legal title to property). Obviously, such a lawsuit could determine the rights of a variety of persons who might have some claim to the property. For that reason, attorneys attempt to establish personal jurisdiction, as well, over likely claimants so as to preclude a later due process challenge to the court's order.

Personal jurisdiction (also known as *in personam* **jurisdiction**) is the authority of the court over the particular defendant being sued and its power to determine that defendant's legal rights, duties, and liabilities *in that case*. Plaintiffs automatically accept a court's jurisdiction when they file a lawsuit in that court, so that personal jurisdiction over the plaintiff is never an issue.

Personal jurisdiction over a civil defendant depends upon both geography and proper **service of process**. Service of process is the delivery of court documents (e.g., a summons or subpoena) to the person named therein, so that she might appear in court or respond by filing appropriate documents with the court. The usual method is **personal service**, done by hand delivering the documents to the defendant or (in some states) leaving them with a responsible person at her residence or office. Service of process is discussed further in Chapter 6.

Under the rules of personal jurisdiction, a resident of Ohio (for example) can be sued in that state's courts simply by being served with the complaint and summons. But a nonresident can also come under the jurisdiction of Ohio courts if he is served while physically present—even briefly—in that state. *Burnham v. Superior Court,* 495 U.S. 604 (1990). Service upon a temporary visitor is known as "tag service."

The Effect of Appearance on Personal Jurisdiction

An **appearance** occurs whenever a party or his attorney files written documents with the court or is physically present in court, for the purpose of affecting the outcome of the proceedings. A defendant who makes any **general appearance**

Subject matter jurisdiction is the authority of a court to hear and determine cases of a particular type (e.g., bankruptcy or family law).

***In rem* jurisdiction** is the authority of a court over particular property under its control.

An action to **quiet title** is brought before the court to resolve any uncertainty about who holds legal title to the real property in question.

Personal jurisdiction (also known as *in personam* **jurisdiction**) is the authority of the court over a particular defendant or responding party, and its power to determine that person's rights, duties, and liabilities in the case before the court.

Service of process is the delivery of legal papers to the person named in them, or to some other person authorized to receive them on her behalf.

Personal service is the physical delivery of legal papers, usually by handing them to the person named in them.

An **appearance** is coming before the court as an intended party to a legal controversy.

In a **general appearance**, a party or its attorney accepts the personal jurisdiction of the court by filing documents or being physically present to address the merits of the case.

has accepted the court's personal jurisdiction and cannot later challenge it. A "general appearance" before a court would include any appearance—whether made personally or through an attorney—to address the merits of the case. For that reason, defendants who intend to challenge the court's personal jurisdiction make **special appearances** for the limited purpose of that challenge. A special appearance for the sole purpose of challenging the court's jurisdiction does not constitute an acceptance of jurisdiction, as a general appearance would.

> A **special appearance** is made for the sole purpose of challenging that court's personal jurisdiction over the party appearing.

"Long Arm" Jurisdiction

Long arm statutes permit a state's courts to exercise jurisdiction over persons (both individuals and companies) that are located far beyond their geographical territory. Because the defendants are not physically present in the state, they must be served by **substituted service** of process. Substituted service is service by any method authorized by law, other than by personal service within that state: for example, by serving the defendant's agent within the state, by personal service outside of the state, or by mailing the documents to the person being served. Most states require out-of-state corporations that do business in their state to designate a local agent within that state for receipt of service of process.

> A **long arm statute** is a state law that establishes personal jurisdiction over persons outside of that state.
>
> **Substituted service** is any method of service authorized by law, other than by personal service within that state.

Long arm statutes assert a state's jurisdiction over an out-of-state defendant whose activities extend into that state. The U.S. Supreme Court has sanctioned "long arm" jurisdiction, provided that the defendants have "minimum contacts" in that state "such that the maintenance of the suit does not offend 'traditional notions of fair play and substantial justice.'" *International Shoe Company v. State of Washington,* 326 U.S. 310, 316 (1945), quoting *Milliken v. Meyer,* 311 U.S. 457, 463 (1940). The **minimum contacts** exist if the wrongful act (e.g., fraud, negligence, or breach of contract) occurs in the state claiming jurisdiction or if a company maintains offices or conducts business in that state. Advertising and selling products within the state is sufficient to meet the "minimum contacts" test. Because federal courts apply the civil law of the state where they sit, a state's long arm statute can also establish personal jurisdiction when suits are filed in a federal court within that state.

> **Minimum contacts** are the activities within a state that permit the courts to establish personal jurisdiction over a defendant.

Long Arm Jurisdiction over Criminal Defendants

A criminal defendant comes under the court's jurisdiction simply by being charged with a crime committed within that court's jurisdiction. So that criminals may not evade punishment by committing their crimes in international waters or international airspace, criminal jurisdiction is conferred by federal and international law on the state or nation where the vessel or aircraft next lands, as well as on the nation where the vessel or aircraft is registered. In addition, some federal statutes extend United States criminal jurisdiction to persons who participate in criminal activity outside of the United States that extends to American territory or otherwise substantially affects American national interests. Thus, former Panamanian dictator General Manuel Noriega was arrested by American troops in Panama (following the 1989 U.S. invasion of that nation) and was brought to the United States, where he was convicted in 1992 for his activities—*committed in Panama*—that aided the transportation of illegal drugs into the United States.

> ### Practice Tip
> In *International Shoe Company v. State of Washington, the Supreme Court quoted the words "traditional notions of fair play and substantial justice" from its earlier decision in* Milliken v. Meyer. *When a quotation from one case itself includes a quotation from an earlier case, that earlier case should be identified for the benefit of the reader, as has been done in the paragraph above:* "quoting Milliken v. Meyer, *311 U.S. 457 (1940)."*

Extradition of Fugitives

This chapter began with a scenario about the "Scottsboro Boys" case, in which Michigan's governor refused to return—that is, to extradite—an Alabama fugitive, in spite of the mandate in the Constitution to do so (Article IV, Section 2).

Extradition between the states is usually a routine judicial process. But the Scottsboro case is not unique. On a number of occasions state governors have refused to surrender to another state the person or persons charged with a crime. Such refusals were sometimes based upon the fact that subsequent to his crime and **unlawful flight** to evade justice, the fugitive had lived many years as a hard-working and law-abiding citizen in the state of his secret asylum. In other cases, the refusal has been the product of current public opinion about the nature of the crimes charged, or the perception that the fugitive would not receive a fair trial in the state seeking extradition. The latter perception was the motivating factor in the Scottsboro case. And at that time, when rebuffed by Michigan's governor and the courts of that "asylum state," the state seeking extradition (that is, Alabama) had no effective remedy.

Unlawful flight is leaving a jurisdiction for the purpose of avoiding arrest or prosecution.

Federal Powers to Compel Extradition

In *Kentucky v. Dennison,* 65 U.S. (24 How.) 66 (1861), the Supreme Court had held that the Extradition Clause of the Constitution is mandatory and that states may not refuse to surrender a fugitive simply on the basis that he was charged with acts that would not have been crimes in the asylum state. But the *Dennison* Court also held that *federal courts have no power* to order the governor of a state to surrender a fugitive under the Extradition Clause.

More than 100 years later, the Supreme Court finally changed its interpretation of the authority of federal courts to enforce the Extradition Clause. In *Puerto Rico v. Branstad,* 483 U.S. 219 (1987), the Supreme Court overruled part of its earlier decision in *Kentucky v. Dennison.* The *Branstad* court explained the 1861 decision in *Dennison* as a product of judicial thought in a period when the power of the federal government was at its weakest and civil war threatened the nation. Since the time of *Dennison,* the *Branstad* court stated, judicial interpretation of constitutional law had clearly swung in the opposite direction, and the authority of the federal courts to compel state officials to obey the Constitution was no longer questioned. The *Branstad* court also stated, "We reaffirm the conclusion [in *Dennison*] that the commands of the Extradition Clause are mandatory, and afford no discretion to the executive officers or courts of the asylum state." *Branstad,* 483 U.S. at 227. It would appear that *Branstad* has eliminated any question about an asylum state's absolute duty to surrender a fugitive under the Extradition Clause.

The decision in *Branstad* provides a glimpse of the Supreme Court's efforts to rationalize an earlier Supreme Court holding that can no longer withstand careful legal analysis. With the accumulation of case law between 1861 and 1987, the Supreme Court had no difficulty in concluding that—contrary to its holding in *Dennison*—the federal courts *can* compel a state official to comply with the Constitution. The *Branstad* court stated: "The fundamental premise of the holding in *Dennison*—'that the States and the Federal Government in all circumstances must be viewed as coequal sovereigns—is not representative of the law today.'" *Branstad,* 483 U.S. at 228, quoting *FERC v. Mississippi,* 456 U.S. 742, 761 (1982). The awkward part for the Supreme Court was to explain how it had earlier reached the opposite, erroneous conclusion—erroneous in hindsight, of course. The *Branstad* court "met" that challenge by evasion:

> If it seemed clear to the Court in 1861, facing the looming shadow of a Civil War, that the Federal Government, under the Constitution, has no power to impose on a State Officer, as such any duty whatever, and compel him to perform it, 24 How., at 107, basic constitutional principles now point as clearly the other way.

Branstad, at 227.

Practice Tip

Note the parenthetical "(24 How.)" in the citation for Dennison. *Until 1875, the official reporters for Supreme Court decisions were named after their editors. In* Kentucky v. Dennison, 65 U.S. (24 How.) 66 (1861), *Howard was the editor, and the case appeared in volume 24 of his series. Eventually, the editor-named series were republished in the official* United States Reports, *and the* Dennison *case now can be found in volume 65 of that reporter, beginning at page 66 (i.e., at 65 U.S. 66).*

> **Practice Tip**
>
> *As explained in an earlier Practice Tip, once a case has been fully cited, continuing references to that case are identified by the party first named in the citation:* "Marbury" *for* Marbury v. Madison, *for example. But here, both citations begin with the name of a government entity. Because Kentucky and Puerto Rico are parties to many thousands of cases, the name of the other party is used instead:* Branstad *and* Dennison, *respectively. The same practice applies if the first party named is an individual or a company with an unusually common name. Thus,* Brown v. Kopecky *would be referred to as* "Kopecky" *rather than as* "Brown," *and* ABC Co. v. Gilbert *would be referred to as* "Gilbert."

A modern scholar saw the earlier decision in *Dennison* less sympathetically:

> The [*Dennison*] case presented Chief Justice Roger B. Taney with a major dilemma. Taney was profoundly proslavery, deeply antagonistic toward the North, and desirous of settling all constitutional issues surrounding slavery in favor of the South. But with secession [by Southern states] already in progress, Taney was loathe to rule that the Supreme Court or the federal government might have the power to force state governors to act.[1]

The *Branstad* decision ignores entirely Chief Justice Taney's pro-slavery bias and his antagonism toward the concept of the supremacy of federal sovereignty. Of course, the *Branstad* Supreme Court can be excused for ignoring Taney's individual and philosophical dilemma: Although Taney had written the opinion in *Dennison,* he was supported by the vote of a unanimous court.

Most states have adopted the Uniform Criminal Extradition Act, which establishes uniform procedures for extradition of fugitives. Extradition between the United States and other nations is governed by the extradition treaties with those nations.

QUESTIONS OF VENUE AND FORUM

If it is clear that California courts have jurisdiction over a given lawsuit, in which county should it be filed? That is a question of **venue**, which is quite different from the question of jurisdiction. Suppose drivers from two California counties were involved in an automobile accident that occurred in a third county of that state. The California superior courts in all three counties could hear the case, because their jurisdiction extends statewide. Generally, the courts favor a venue that is not unduly harsh for defendants and is convenient for the greatest number of parties and witnesses. In this example, the plaintiff could file suit in any one of the three counties, but the defendant could petition the court for a **change of venue** based upon inconvenience for the defendant and/or witnesses. In emotionally charged criminal cases, defendants sometimes move the court for a change of venue in hopes of obtaining a jury that would be less biased than any that could be empaneled in the community where the crime occurred.

> **Venue** is the locality of a court in which a case is heard.
>
> **Change of venue** occurs when a case is transferred from one locality to another for the convenience of witnesses or the defendant, or to avoid the effect of pretrial publicity.
>
> When jurisdiction is available in both state and federal courts, the **forum** is the court in which the case is actually heard.

There also might be a question of **forum**: Should the suit be tried in state court or in federal court? If state and federal courts both have jurisdiction, the plaintiff may file suit in either one. For example, many states have nondiscrimination laws similar to the federal civil rights statutes. In that circumstance, the plaintiff may file under either the state or federal statute in state court—state courts having the authority *and constitutional duty* to enforce both state and federal law—or under the federal statute in federal court.

STATE COURT SYSTEMS

The courts of some states are organized on a three- or four-tier system, with the top tier being occupied by a single court of last resort. (See *Figure 4.3*.) In most states, the court of last resort is called the "supreme court," but in New York State the "supreme court" is a trial court of general jurisdiction.

This text will use "state court of last resort" or "state supreme court" to mean the highest court of that state. When "Supreme Court" is capitalized, it will refer to the U.S. Supreme Court. This chapter will not describe in detail the court system of each state, because doing so could fill nearly an entire book. The following discussion describes the features common to the majority of state court systems.

> A **trial court** hears and determines all questions of fact and applies the law to those facts.

Most states have one or two tiers of **trial courts**, which hear evidence and reach decisions about the *facts*—who did what to whom, for example—and

FIGURE 4.3 Typical State Court System

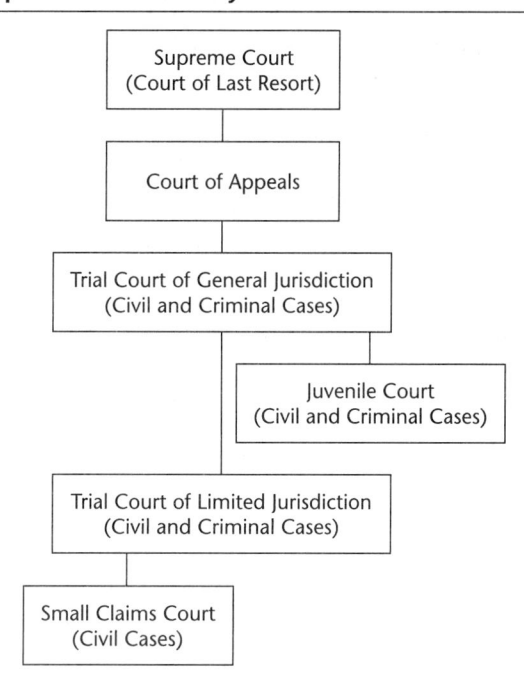

```
Supreme Court
(Court of Last Resort)
        │
Court of Appeals
        │
Trial Court of General Jurisdiction
(Civil and Criminal Cases)
        │
        ├── Juvenile Court
        │   (Civil and Criminal Cases)
        │
Trial Court of Limited Jurisdiction
(Civil and Criminal Cases)
        │
Small Claims Court
(Civil Cases)
```

about the *law* that applies to the case. Where two levels of trial courts exist, the lowest tier generally has limited jurisdiction. For example, **misdemeanor** trials might be heard in the inferior trial courts, whereas **felony** trials would be held in the superior trial courts. The civil jurisdiction for lawsuits in the inferior trial court might be limited to a maximum dollar amount (e.g., $25,000) that could be awarded to a successful plaintiff. The superior trial court would be competent to try civil lawsuits for any larger amount, without limitation.

Most states also have a small claims court that hears lawsuits for small sums. Because small claim procedures are so simple, there is no need for a long period of pretrial preparation, and cases can go to trial more quickly. Excepting a few states, plaintiffs and defendants in small claims courts may not be represented by attorneys, and they must argue the case for themselves. The purpose of that rule is to make the courts accessible even when the amount at stake would not justify the expense of legal fees. In most states, an attorney may represent *herself* as a defendant in a small claims action, but she may not represent clients. And no state permits an attorney to be the plaintiff in a small claims court where the defendant cannot be represented by counsel, because a lay defendant would be at a great disadvantage when facing an attorney-plaintiff.

Small claims courts are much less formal than ordinary trial courts, and the judge might conduct the proceedings somewhat as an exceptionally sophisticated English manor lord might have done in medieval times. The opposing parties typically have a poor understanding of the law and of court procedures, and the judge often rules on the basis of simple fairness rather than fine points of law. The defendant—that is, the one who did not make the decision to bring the suit in small claims court—usually has the right of appeal to the next level of trial courts. In many states, however, the plaintiff waives his right to appeal when he chooses to bring the lawsuit into the small claims court.

Some states still have **justice courts** for minor criminal offenses and lawsuits. Justice courts are usually found in very small communities. Their distinguishing feature is that some states permit non-attorneys to serve as the presiding justice, who often holds the title "justice of the peace" or "magistrate."

A **misdemeanor** is a less serious criminal offense, punishable by fine and/or imprisonment for a year or less.

A **felony** is a serious crime, punishable by fine and/or imprisonment for a year or more, or by death.

A **justice court** is an inferior trial court with very limited criminal and civil jurisdiction, presided over by a justice of the peace.

WHEN A COURT DECISION IS APPEALED

The losing party in a court case may usually request that the decision be reviewed by a higher court. In some court cases, neither party is fully satisfied with the decision, and both might appeal those parts of the decision that are unfavorable to them. The right to request a review, however, is no guarantee that a higher court will grant the review. If a higher court does review a lower court decision, its review is usually limited to legal and procedural issues.

Generally speaking, **questions of fact** are determined finally and forever in the trial court. A trial court's rulings on **questions of law**, however, are subject to appeal. In addition, a higher court might review the procedures followed in the lower court, in order to determine whether they comply with law. The party appealing the decision is called the **appellant** or **petitioner**. The opposing party is the **appellee** or **respondent**. Note that a party's status as petitioner or respondent has no relationship to being either the plaintiff or defendant at the trial stage of the case. The petitioner or appellant will be whichever party lost the case in trial court—either as defendant or plaintiff.

Before a party can obtain appellate review of the trial court's decision, usually that party must have raised in the trial court the same objection or legal argument that is to be the basis for appeal. This rule gives the trial court an opportunity to correct its own errors and contributes to the efficiency of the judicial system by limiting the number of unnecessary appeals. An unfortunate result of the rule is that attorneys are obligated (by their duty to clients) to raise numerous objections at trial, in order to preserve their right of appeal should they lose the case. The following are some of the common grounds for appeal of a trial court decision:

- lack of proper jurisdiction in the trial court
- incorrect application of the law to the facts of the case
- unreasonable or arbitrary action taken by the trial court without due consideration of the facts and the law (termed an "**abuse of discretion**")
- incorrect instructions to the jury about the law to be applied
- incorrect decisions on the admissibility of evidence
- premature dismissal of a lawsuit without permitting the plaintiff to revise his allegations and present evidence to support them

Vigorous Representation and the Risk of Frivolous Appeals

At times, attorneys must walk a fine line between their duty of vigorous representation and the risk of presenting a **frivolous appeal**. An appeal is considered to be frivolous when it fails to raise any relevant legal question that the court could resolve, or when an objective attorney would recognize that it is completely without merit and has no prospect of success. As discussed in Chapter 3, it can be difficult to distinguish between a frivolous claim, brought in bad faith, and a good faith appeal that is unorthodox, but also innovative—on the "cutting edge" of legal reasoning. The attorney's ethical duty to vigorously represent her client might cause her to suggest novel legal theories that most other lawyers would reject out of hand. If she succeeds in persuading the appellate court, she will win the case and participate in the making of new law. But if she fails to convince the appellate court, she and/or her client might be required to pay the opposing party's legal fees as the penalty for bringing a frivolous appeal. For fear of discouraging such vigorous representation, appellate courts are usually reluctant to impose severe penalties unless it appears obvious that the attorney acted in bad faith when she presented the appeal.

Sidebar definitions:

A **question of fact** is one of truth or falsity concerning past events.

A **question of law** is one regarding the meaning and application of the law.

An **appellant** or **petitioner** is the party asking a higher court to intervene in the case.

An **appellee** or **respondent** is the party against whom an appeal is taken.

A court decision that lacks any reasonable foundation, either in the evidence or in the law, or that exceeds the authority of the court, is termed an **abuse of discretion**.

A **frivolous appeal** is one completely without merit, lacking any reasonable basis under the facts and the law.

The appellate court hearing is very different from a trial. The facts of the case have already been established by the **trier of fact**—whether jury or judge. On appeal, the issues are legal, not factual. Harmless errors will not cause a reversal of the trial court's decision—the appealing party must have been denied justice by the trial court's error.

The **trier of fact** is the jury or judge, as the case might be; it is the person(s) who must determine all questions of fact in the case.

Discretionary Appellate Jurisdiction

Most states have two levels of appellate courts. Some intermediate state appellate courts have **discretionary jurisdiction**—meaning they can accept or reject any petition for appeal—but in most states there is an automatic right to be heard on appeal in the intermediate courts. The state courts of last resort generally possess discretionary appellate jurisdiction, although some states require automatic review by the state's highest court of all death penalty judgments.

If the state's highest court rejects a petition for review, the lower court decision will stand undisturbed. After the highest state court has ruled, therefore, the case normally is at an end, with no further appeal possible. The sole exception is a substantial **federal question** of law or due process, which makes an appeal to the U.S. Supreme Court theoretically possible, although unlikely. Unfortunately, the U.S. Supreme Court is inundated each year with some 5,000 petitions for review, and the Court and Congress have progressively narrowed the circumstances under which the Supreme Court will hear an appeal from state courts. In fact, only a very minuscule percentage of state cases ever reach the U.S. Supreme Court.

Discretionary jurisdiction is the authority of a court to accept or decline jurisdiction over a matter; in appellate procedure, it is the authority of an appellate court to accept or reject a petition for review.

A **federal question** is a question of federal law (constitutional, statutory, or administrative).

SCENARIO

Susan Mitchell works in the litigation section of a large law firm. She has twelve years of experience in civil litigation, the last four of those with her present firm. She is unusual for a legal assistant in a large firm, because she often does substantial legal research.

"This really happened by chance. When I joined this firm, I was assigned to one partner who supervised twelve associates. One of those associates was working alone on a small case that was taking forever to get to trial. Because I had so much litigation experience, Marta gave me almost the entire responsibility for managing the case. She made whatever appearances were necessary, and she was doing most of the research. But other than that, I did almost everything. She had plenty of other work to keep her busy. Anyway, after about six months, I knew that case about as well as she did.

"Then, Marta got in an auto accident and was out for about a month. The partner took over supervision of the case, with me continuing as before. Before the accident, Marta had started to research a major issue for a pretrial motion. The partner asked me to review her notes and cases, and to brief him on the status of the project. When I finished the briefing, he said that he and the associates were swamped with work, and he asked me whether I could continue the research on my own while Marta was out. I said, 'sure.' Secretly, I was delighted, because in my prior, smaller law firm, I had done lots of legal research and really enjoyed it.

"Cutting to the chase, when Marta returned to work I had a complete draft for the motion and photocopies of every case I had relied upon. She read my draft, made a few modifications, and asked me to do a bit more research on one issue. We won the motion and some of the attorneys started kidding me about being the 'new associate' in the firm. Ever since then, I've been doing research and drafting motions and oppositions and everything else. I love the intellectual challenge and I enjoy writing. So, it's great!"

THE FEDERAL COURT SYSTEM

The U.S. Constitution establishes a Supreme Court and authorizes Congress to establish trial courts and additional appellate courts. Acting on that authority, Congress has established the U.S. District Courts as the federal trial courts of general jurisdiction, and the Courts of Appeals as the intermediate appellate courts. In addition, Congress has established some special federal courts of limited trial jurisdiction (e.g., Bankruptcy Court, Tax Court, Claims Court), and also a completely separate military court system (the Courts Martial)—including its own appellate system—for the criminal prosecution of men and women in the military services. A simplified diagram of the federal court system appears in *Figure 4.4*. The following discussion is limited to the U.S. District Courts, the U.S. Courts of Appeals, and the U.S. Supreme Court.

Most civil and virtually all criminal federal trials are conducted in the U.S. District Courts, although particular types of civil cases (e.g., tax cases, bankruptcy cases) and military crimes are tried in one of the federal courts of limited jurisdiction. On appeal, a decision by the district court is reviewed by one of the U.S. Courts of Appeals. The next step up is the federal court of last resort—the U.S. Supreme Court, the only court with the power to reverse decisions made in the U.S. Courts of Appeals.

The Jurisdiction of Federal Courts

Under Article III, Section 2, of the Constitution, federal courts have trial jurisdiction over all actions, civil and criminal, brought under federal law. This is known as **federal question jurisdiction**. The statutes and actions of state and local government may be challenged in federal court if they conflict with the U.S. Constitution or other federal law. In those cases, the "federal question" is the conflict between state and federal law. A state law requiring public school pupils to recite an official prayer, for example, would conflict with the Fourteenth Amendment. In that example, conflict with the Fourteenth Amendment would be the federal question that establishes jurisdiction for the federal courts.

Federal question jurisdiction is based upon a question of federal law.

FIGURE 4.4 Basic Structure of the Federal Court System

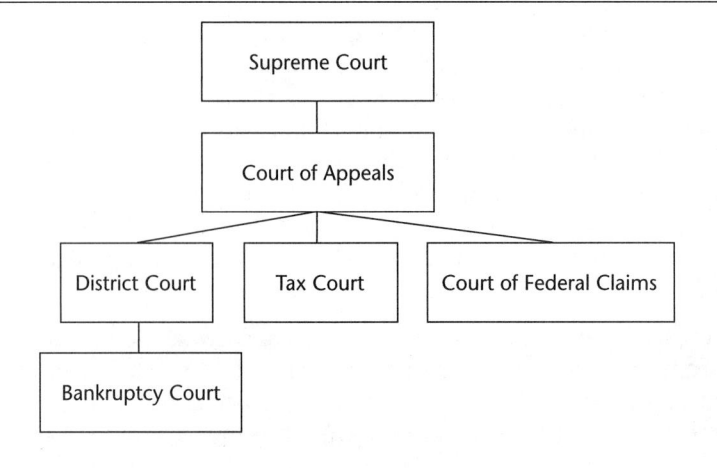

In addition to federal question jurisdiction, Article III of the Constitution provides for federal trial jurisdiction under the following circumstances:

- whenever the United States is a party to a lawsuit
- whenever a state is a party to a suit, and the opposing party is another state or the citizen of another state
- in lawsuits between a state or U.S. citizen and a foreign nation or a citizen of a foreign nation
- in all cases of maritime law (i.e., the law of shipping and navigation)
- when foreign diplomats are parties to the action
- in lawsuits under state law between citizens of different states

The latter jurisdiction, known as "diversity jurisdiction," is discussed below.

Federal Courts and Cases Arising Under State Law

Federal trial courts have **concurrent jurisdiction** (together with state courts) over lawsuits arising under state law in which **diversity of citizenship** exists and the amount in controversy exceeds a minimum amount set by Congress (currently $75,000). The original reason for providing federal jurisdiction in cases of diversity was the fear that the courts of one state might favor parties who were citizens of that same state. Federal jurisdiction was established to provide a neutral court for lawsuits between citizens of different states. Federal jurisdiction over cases arising under state law based upon diversity of citizenship is known as **diversity jurisdiction**. In diversity questions, it is not necessary to distinguish between individuals, corporations, partnerships, or unincorporated associations (e.g., churches, homeowner associations or labor unions), because personal jurisdiction may be asserted over each of them.

When there are multiple plaintiffs or defendants, *diversity will not exist if any one plaintiff and any one defendant are citizens of the same state.* If an individual defendant and a corporate plaintiff both reside in Wisconsin, for example, diversity jurisdiction will be defeated, even though all other plaintiff and defendant parties have unique states of residency (i.e., no other two parties are citizens of one state). Of course, diversity of citizenship is required only if the basis for the lawsuit arises under state law—it is *never* required for cases arising under federal law.

In diversity actions, the U.S. District Court must apply the law of whatever state would have concurrent jurisdiction. One exception involves an action in contract law when the contract itself specifies that it shall be interpreted under, and governed by, the laws of a particular state. On appeal, the circuit courts of appeals and the U.S. Supreme Court will apply the law of the same state, unless the district court erred in its choice of jurisdictional law. Federal court decisions (both trial and appellate) can be cited as precedents for the interpretation of state law, even in the courts of that state. However, a differing opinion by an appellate court of that state carries greater authority than would a federal court opinion for interpretation of the law of that state.

Concurrent jurisdiction exists when both state and federal courts have proper jurisdiction over a legal controversy.

Diversity of citizenship is the circumstance of all opposing parties in a case being citizens of different states.

Diversity jurisdiction is federal court jurisdiction based upon diversity of citizenship—the fact that no plaintiff and defendant in the case are citizens of the same state.

Pendent Jurisdiction over State Law Issues

When a case with a federal question is properly before the federal courts, they might also exercise **pendent jurisdiction** over a related claim under state law, even though no diversity of citizenship exists. Pendent jurisdiction, therefore, is an additional basis for federal court adjudication of state claims. Before pendent jurisdiction may be asserted, however, the federal and state claims must both arise from the same set of facts. Such a situation could arise, for example, if an

Pendent jurisdiction is federal court jurisdiction over a matter arising under state law, based upon the circumstance that the federal law matter and the state law matter both arise from the same set of facts.

airline refused to board a ticketed passenger based upon her race—a violation of federal statute—and if, in barring her entry onto the plane, the gate agent for the airline assaulted the passenger—a civil wrong under state law. The exercise of pendent civil jurisdiction over the assault would be at the discretion of the federal court.

Personal Jurisdiction in Federal Trial Courts

The personal jurisdiction of a U.S. District Court is limited to the geographical territory of the state in which it sits. This might be termed the court's "geographic" jurisdiction. Therefore, Michigan residents cannot, in most cases, be required to defend themselves against a lawsuit brought in federal courts sitting in Iowa. Under the state long arm statutes discussed above, however, there are important exceptions to that general rule.

It is not unknown for a U.S. District Court to apply the law of several states (and, perhaps, even the law of foreign nations) to a single case involving a number of activities, contracts, and parties, each of which presents issues under the laws of one or more of those jurisdictions. For example, imagine a single case in which each of the following had occurred:

- A contract entered into in Brazil specified that the laws of New York would govern.
- The contract provided that fraudulent conduct by any party to the contract would constitute a breach of the contract.
- An allegation has been made that the contract was itself induced by fraud committed in Brazil.
- The financing for the transaction was arranged in London, and the loan documents specified that British law would govern them.
- The contract was to be performed in Florida, and the defendant is a Florida corporation.
- The two plaintiffs are a New York corporation and a Brazilian company.
- The plaintiffs allege that the conduct of the defendant corporation constituted fraud under Florida law.

The Geographic Jurisdiction of Federal Appellate Courts

The United States and its overseas Commonwealth of Puerto Rico, as well as its territories and possessions (e.g., Guam, the U.S. Virgin Islands, and American Samoa), have been divided into eleven regions, each with a U.S. Court of Appeals. There also is a Court of Appeals for the District of Columbia. In addition to these twelve courts that hear appeals from the U.S. District Courts and from decisions by certain federal agencies (e.g., the National Labor Relations Board), there is a Court of Appeals for the Federal Circuit, which hears appeals from customs, patent, and trademark cases, and from cases involving claims against the federal government.

Of the thirteen courts of appeal, eleven are numbered (and are cited by number). These eleven courts serving distinct geographic regions are referred to as **circuits**, because in earlier centuries federal judges (including Supreme Court justices) once traveled by horse or wagon along a route known as a "circuit," holding court in various towns and cities as they went. The growth in population and litigation eventually led to permanently located district courts and courts of appeals, so that trial judges and appellate court justices no longer had to "ride" a circuit.

Even though the appellate justices no longer ride circuits, those courts are still referred to by circuit number, as in "the Seventh Circuit" (the U.S. Court of

> A **circuit** is the geographic area served by a federal court of appeals.

Appeals for Wisconsin, Illinois, and Indiana) or "the Eleventh Circuit" (for Alabama, Georgia, and Florida). Some of the more populous circuits are further divided into north, east, south, west, and central "districts," and their U.S. District Courts are then identified by the district in which they sit. For example, the most heavily populated area of Southern California (Los Angeles and Orange Counties) is served by the U.S. District Court for the Central District of California, which also includes five less populous counties; San Diego and Imperial Counties constitute the Southern District of California. A single district court might have several branch courts in major cities within the same judicial district. There is a minimum of one district court for each state, although a few larger states have as many as four. In addition, a single U.S. District Court might have many judges hearing cases in multiple courtrooms. Each judicial district has a **presiding judge** to assign cases and coordinate court activities.

The district courts within a given circuit are bound by the decisions of the court of appeals in that circuit. If neither the Supreme Court nor the court of appeals for that circuit has yet ruled on a particular legal issue, the district courts of that circuit are free to fashion their own interpretations of the law. In doing so, they often rely upon decisions on that issue that have been made in the courts of appeals of other circuits, but they are not required to do so. When the various circuits reach contradictory conclusions—that is, when they are in conflict on a legal issue—the law to be applied to a particular case depends upon the circuit in which the case is being tried. Only the Supreme Court can impose a single interpretation of the law to be applied nationwide.

> The **presiding judge** of a court assigns cases to particular judges, coordinates court activities, and supervises the court clerks and other employees.

Jurisdiction of the U.S. Supreme Court

The Supreme Court has **original jurisdiction** (i.e., trial jurisdiction) over cases involving foreign diplomats, as well as over lawsuits in which one of the states is a party. But it is very unusual for the Supreme Court to hear a case under its original jurisdiction. When that rare event occurs, the Court usually appoints a distinguished jurist to serve as a special master, hearing both evidence and legal argument and then rendering a report to the Supreme Court. The full Court then reviews the master's report in much the same manner as it reviews the record of a lower court case, and then issues its rulings.

> **Original jurisdiction** is trial jurisdiction, as opposed to appellate jurisdiction.

There are five ways for a case to come before the U.S. Supreme Court. Two of those are quite rare and will not be discussed here. The vast majority of cases come before the Court by writ of certiorari, mandatory appeal, and original jurisdiction—in that order of frequency.

Congress has, by statute, established categories of cases that will be heard on **mandatory appeal**. The Supreme Court has no discretion regarding those cases and must hear them. In the *Judicial Improvements and Access to Justice Act of 1988*, Congress greatly reduced the types of cases entitled to mandatory appeal, so that they are no longer a major factor in the Court's workload. The remaining mandatory appeal cases are primarily those arising under the *Voting Rights Act* and the various Civil Rights Acts.[2]

> A **mandatory appeal** is one that an appellate court (e.g., the Supreme Court) must hear, as a matter of law.

Petitions and Writs

Nearly all cases coming before the Supreme Court today are discretionary—the Court may accept or reject them at will. Would-be appellants file a **petition for review**, but the sheer number of petitions forces the Supreme Court to deny hearings to almost all of them. When the Supreme Court refuses to hear the case, the decision of the lower appellate court then stands undisturbed. The Court is more likely to grant review if a case raises a substantial new legal issue or offers the opportunity to resolve conflicts between the holdings of the various circuit

> A **petition for review** is a request that an appellate court hear an appeal from a lower court decision, or that it review and reverse some unlawful government action.

courts of appeals. Once the Supreme Court has issued its opinion resolving those conflicts, the trial and appellate courts of all circuits must then follow that holding. One study in the 1980s found that fewer than 2% of the decisions by the U.S. Courts of Appeals were ultimately reversed.[3]

If a petition for review is granted, the court issues a **writ of certiorari** to the court below, requiring it to certify the record and forward the case to the Supreme Court. The parties then submit written legal arguments (known as "appellate briefs") to the Court. The briefs are reviewed by the justices and their law clerks, who assist the justices with legal research and analysis of the case. When the case comes before the Court for oral argument, each side is usually permitted thirty minutes. During argument, it is common for the justices to question the attorneys and engage in brief discussion with them. Following oral argument, the justices meet in closed session to discuss the case. When they have reached a decision, the Chief Justice assigns one of the justices among the majority to write the opinion of the Court. Other justices often write separate **concurring opinions** or **dissenting opinions**.

> A **writ of certiorari** is an appellate court order to a lower court, directing it to "certify" the record of the case (i.e., verify the accuracy and completeness of the case record) and deliver it to the appellate court for review.

> In a **concurring opinion**, a justice states his or her own reasoning for agreeing with the majority decision of the court. A concurring opinion is counted as a vote for the majority decision.

> In a **dissenting opinion**, a justice states his or her own reasoning for disagreeing with the majority opinion. A dissenting opinion is a vote against the majority decision.

JUDICIAL IMMUNITY FROM LAWSUITS

Judges enjoy an extraordinary degree of independence: They are absolutely immune from *civil* liability for their official acts, no matter how injurious and reprehensible. The Supreme Court has ruled that such immunity applies even to judicial acts that are "in excess of their jurisdiction, and are alleged to have been done maliciously or corruptly." *Bradley v. Fisher,* 80 U.S. (13 Wall.) 335, 351 (1872). The reason for such blanket immunity is the chilling effect that civil liability would have on the judicial system. Without immunity, judges would be the constant targets of lawsuits brought by unsuccessful litigants, convicted criminals, and victims of crimes whose perpetrators were not adequately punished. Judges might be inclined to practice "defensive adjudication," with constant concern for those litigants most likely—and financially able—to "sue the judge." Of course, this judicial immunity has an unintended effect: It removes one possible deterrent to judicial misconduct.

Civil immunity for judges is "purchased" at the price of the occasional gross injustice, with no civil remedy available to those who are harmed. Unfortunately, a small number of individuals ultimately pay that enormous price so that society at large might have the benefit of judges who will decide the cases before them without fear of future retribution through harassment by litigation. The dilemma of judicial immunity is well illustrated by the U.S. Supreme Court decision in *Stump v. Sparkman,* 435 U.S. 349 (1977). Although the very lengthy opinion has been summarized here, a few key portions of the majority and dissenting opinions are quoted *verbatim*.

A Case in Point

Stump v. Sparkman

435 U.S. 349 (1977)

In 1971, Ora Spitler McFarlin petitioned the Circuit Court of DeKalb County, Indiana, to authorize a tubal ligation to be performed on her fifteen-year-old daughter, Linda Kay Spitler. In her petition, the mother stated under oath that her daughter was "somewhat retarded," and on several occasions had stayed out overnight with "older youth and young men." The petition further stated that the sterilization of her daughter was intended "to prevent unfortunate circumstances..." and would be in the best interests of the daughter.

[The foregoing quotations are from the mother's petition, that is reprinted in full as a footnote to the opinion of the U.S. Supreme Court (at page 351). Unless otherwise indicated, all following quotations will be the words of the Supreme Court in *Stump v. Sparkman*.]

The mother's petition was approved by Judge Harold Stump on the same day it was presented to the court. This occurred even though:

- no docket number was assigned to the petition,
- the petition was not placed in the files of the court clerk,
- the daughter was not informed of the petition,
- the daughter was not represented by any disinterested third party (i.e., a **guardian *ad litem***) acting to protect her interests as a minor, and
- no hearing was held prior to Judge Stump's approval.

Six days later, Linda Spitler was admitted to a hospital under the illusion that her appendix was to be removed. The tubal ligation was performed the following day, and Linda was released from the hospital without realizing the true nature of the surgery.

Two years later, Linda Spitler married Leo Sparkman. Their inability to conceive a child resulted in the discovery of her sterilization. The Sparkmans then filed suit in U.S. District Court against Linda's mother, the mother's attorney, the doctors who had performed the operation, the hospital, and Judge Harold Stump. The couple sought **damages** against Judge Stump for violation of Linda's constitutional rights. They alleged that the court's action had been arbitrary, in violation of the Fourteenth Amendment, and otherwise violated Linda's procedural due process rights. They further alleged that the sterilization violated Linda's privacy rights (presumably under the Bill of Rights and the Fourteenth Amendment) and the Eighth Amendment ban on cruel and unusual punishment.

The U.S. District Court held that Judge Stump was absolutely immune against civil liability, based upon the doctrine of **judicial immunity**. The U.S. Court of Appeals then **reversed** the district court, holding that Judge Stump had not acted within his jurisdiction and therefore lacked immunity.

The Supreme Court reversed the judgment of the U.S. Court of Appeals. Citing its earlier decision in *Bradley v. Fisher*, 80 U.S. (13 Wall.) 335 (1872), the Supreme Court again affirmed its holding in that case that judicial immunity applies "even when such acts are in excess of their jurisdiction, and are alleged to have been done maliciously or corruptly." *Bradley v. Fisher*, 80 U.S. at 351. However, the *Bradley* court had distinguished between "excess of jurisdiction and the clear absence of all jurisdiction over the subject-matter. Where there is clearly no jurisdiction over the subject-matter any authority exercised is a usurped authority, and . . . no excuse is permissible." *Bradley*, at 351. (Quoted in *Stump*, at pages 355–356.)

The Supreme Court in *Stump* continued: "A judge will not be deprived of immunity because the action he took was in error, was done maliciously, or was in excess of this authority; rather, he will be subject to liability only when he has acted in the 'clear absence of all jurisdiction.' 13 Wall., at 351." (At pages 356–357.) Under the principles established in *Bradley*, then, the complete absence of jurisdiction would deprive a judge of any civil immunity for his misdeeds. However, the Supreme Court found that the DeKalb County Circuit Court was a court of general jurisdiction, giving Judge Stump jurisdiction over the subject matter of the petition before him.

The Supreme Court stated:

We conclude that the Court of Appeals. . .erred in holding that he was not entitled to judicial immunity. Because the court over which Judge Stump presides is one of general jurisdiction, neither the procedural errors he might

---

In legal proceedings affecting the interests of a minor child, the child is represented by an adult **guardian *ad litem***—usually the parent, but sometimes another disinterested person appointed by the court.

Damages are financial compensation awarded by a court to the prevailing party in a lawsuit.

Judicial immunity is the doctrine that judges are absolutely immune from any civil liability for their official acts.

A lower court decision is **reversed** when a higher court voids that decision because it misstates the law or because improper procedures prevented the losing party from having a fair hearing.

have committed nor the lack of a specific statute authorizing his approval of the petition in question rendered him liable in damages for the consequences of his actions.

(At pages 359–360.)

The Supreme Court then considered whether Judge Stump's approval of the petition was a judicial act, because judges possess absolute immunity only for acts performed in their judicial capacity. The Court stated that an act by a judge is "judicial" if it is "a function normally performed by a judge . . . [and the parties] dealt with the judge in his judicial capacity. Here, both factors indicate that Judge Stump's approval of the sterilization petition was a judicial act. [Footnote omitted.]" (At page 362.)

The Supreme Court concluded:

> The Indiana law vested in Judge Stump the power to entertain and act upon the petition for sterilization. He is, therefore, under the controlling cases, immune from damages liability even if his approval of the petition was in error. Accordingly, the judgment of the Court of Appeals is reversed, and the case is remanded for further proceedings consistent with this opinion. (At page 364.)

In his dissenting opinion, Justice Potter Stewart criticized the majority opinion in sometimes scathing words:

> It is true that Judge Stump affixed his signature to the approval of the petition as "Judge, DeKalb Circuit Court." But the conduct of a judge surely does not become a judicial act merely on his own say-so. A judge is not free, like a loose cannon, to inflict indiscriminate damage whenever he announces that he is acting in his judicial capacity. [Footnote omitted.] (At page 367.)

Later in his dissent, Justice Stewart stated:

> There was no "case," controversial or otherwise. There were no litigants. There was and could be no appeal. And there was not even the pretext of principled decision-making. The total absence of *any* of these normal attributes of a judicial proceeding convinces me that the conduct complained of in this case was not a judicial act. [Emphasis in the original.] (At pages 368–369.)

Judges are *not* immune from criminal liability, however, and a small number have been removed or imprisoned for bribery, perjury, or other crimes. Of course, a criminal conviction by a court of law does not automatically remove any federal judge from the bench. Until the House of Representatives impeaches and the Senate also convicts and removes him, a federal judge may draw his salary even as he serves time in a federal or state penitentiary for a criminal abuse of his powers. Although criminal penalties might be powerful deterrents, the standard of proof for conviction—"beyond a reasonable doubt"—and the requirement for a unanimous verdict by the jury makes it a deterrent far less often applied than would be a civil suit for damages, where a less rigorous "preponderance of the evidence" is the standard of proof and a unanimous jury verdict is not required.

In addition to impeachment, some states empower the court of last resort to remove a lower court state judge for gross incompetence or egregious misconduct. The Supreme Court of the State of Washington used such a procedure in 1999. In a highly publicized and controversial case, the state Commission on Judicial Conduct found that a superior court judge had committed three serious disciplinary violations and recommended a four-month suspension without pay, completion of a course in judicial ethics, and revision of previously filed (but incomplete) judicial financial disclosure forms. The unanimous state supreme court found that suspension without pay was too lenient and ordered the judge's removal from the bench.[4] Some observers have suggested that the U.S. Supreme Court have similar removal power over lower federal court judges. Such a change, however, would require an amendment to the U.S. Constitution—seldom an easy accomplishment.

PUBLIC OPINION, PARTISAN POLITICS, AND THE COURTS

Presumably, most people would agree that politics and public opinion should not govern court decisions. The reality is that both politics and public opinion exercise significant influence—although indirectly—over the courts. In part, that is because the courts might lose credibility—and endanger their own independence—if the public were to see them as too isolated from the realities of modern times. And the public perception of "the realities of modern times" includes what people see on the evening news—even if in brief, misleading "sound bites." The other influential factor is the political process by which judges are nominated and confirmed.

The essence of judicial independence is freedom from partisan pressure once a judge is on the bench, but not necessarily freedom from all political bias that the judge might bring with her to the bench. Politics is a major consideration when the President or a governor appoints judges—most notably in appointments to the Supreme Court. Although the U.S. Senate usually confirms the overwhelming majority of judicial appointments—including those to the Supreme Court—it can reject an appointment for any reason whatsoever. Politics and differences over legal philosophy have been the primary considerations on those unusual occasions when the Senate has rejected the President's nominees to the Supreme Court.

It is safe to say, however, that once most federal judges have taken their oath of office, they have little concern for partisan reaction to their decisions. Because federal judges "*shall hold their Offices during good Behaviour...*" (*U.S. Constitution,* Article III, Section 1), none of them can be "fired" simply for making an unpopular decision. That postconfirmation immunity from easy removal is one reason that nominations to the Supreme Court have become so very controversial in recent decades. Practically speaking, the presidential appointment and Senate confirmation process are the only opportunities to influence, in a significant way, the legal philosophy and political bias of the federal courts. The great majority of federal judges remain on the bench until their retirement or death.

This discussion has focused upon the federal court system, but the basic themes apply to the state courts, as well. The states have generally followed the federal model, insulating their judges from political pressures after appointment to the bench. But, in those states where judges must periodically stand for reelection, their independence is potentially vulnerable.

A QUESTION OF ETHICS

Merle Redmont is a sole practitioner specializing in employment law and litigation. Her client wants to sue his employer and his immediate supervisor for age discrimination. The state's supreme court recently ruled that, under the *state's* antidiscrimination statute, employers are liable for illegal gender discrimination, but individual supervisors are not. The court's reasoning is that the employer can spread the costs of liability among all consumers in the marketplace, yet still have a motivation to avoid liability so that it can remain competitive and profitable. Individual supervisors, on the other hand, cannot spread the costs and could be financially devastated. Additionally, supervisors are acting in the interests of the employer, not their own interests. Finally, the court concluded that the supervisors should be able to exercise their discretion without constant fear of lawsuits, because employers can use their company policies and authority over managers to protect employees from arbitrary actions.

Merle is contemplating a lawsuit under the federal *Age Discrimination in Employment Act (ADEA)*. However, she believes the state court's reasoning is correct and should apply also under the *ADEA*—even though no federal court has reached that holding. The client is particularly angry at the supervisor and wants him named individually as a co-defendant with the employer. Merle believes the client has a strong case against the employer, but doesn't believe the supervisor should be sued. This dilemma has been troubling her for several days.

Merle approaches you, as her paralegal, to use you as a "sounding board" for her concerns—sort of "talking the issue through" with you. She is considering filing a suit as the client wishes, naming the supervisor as a co-defendant. But she expects that the court will then dismiss the case against the supervisor. She inquires about your opinion on the ethical question of pursuing a claim that she, as an attorney, doubts should be allowable under the law. How would you respond?

Chapter Summary

- Lawyers know most general legal principles and the specific law of some topics, but they can never know the entire body of the law.
- Criminal law defines and prohibits acts that are considered to be offenses against society, and it provides for punishments including fines, imprisonment, and death.
- Civil law establishes the legal rights and obligations of all persons, and also sets forth the powers and limitations of government.
- All law is organized in a hierarchy of legal authority, which determines which authority is superior when laws conflict.
- All authority to make law originates in the constitutions of the states and that of the United States.
- State law is subordinate to federal law, whenever the two conflict.
- The common law is based upon the early English system of law and incorporates the legal principles found in the accumulation of court decisions over the years.
- The Supreme Law of the Land is the U.S. Constitution and all federal law made under its authority.
- State courts are bound by the Supreme Law of the Land.
- A law that conflicts with the U.S. Constitution is void and will not be enforced by the courts.
- Each state must give full faith and credit to the official records and acts of every other state.
- The courts exercise judicial review over the actions of the legislative and executive branches of government.
- Judges are absolutely immune from civil liability for their official acts, provided that they have acted within their jurisdiction.

- A court must have both personal and subject matter jurisdiction in order to hear and determine a case.
- Long arm statutes provide jurisdiction over persons outside the geographic area of a court's jurisdiction.
- A court of original jurisdiction conducts the trial and determines all questions of fact and of law.
- On appeal, an appellate court determines questions of law and procedure, but not questions of fact.
- Appellate courts reach their decisions by majority vote of the justices hearing the appeal.
- Federal courts have jurisdiction over all actions brought under federal law.
- Federal courts may hear cases arising under state law if diversity of citizenship exists and the amount in controversy exceeds $75,000.
- The United States is divided into eleven regional circuits, each with a U.S. Court of Appeals.
- U.S. District Courts are bound by the decisions of the U.S. Supreme Court and of the U.S. Court of Appeals for their own circuit.
- When a petition for review is denied, the lower court judgment stands undisturbed.

KEY TERMS

(See the Glossary for definitions)

abuse of discretion	diversity jurisdiction	minimum contacts
act of Congress	diversity of citizenship	misdemeanor
administrative law	due process	ordinance
appearance	executive order	original jurisdiction
appellant	extradition	overrule
appellee	federal question	pendent jurisdiction
asylum	federal question jurisdiction	personal jurisdiction
case citation	felony	personal service
case law	forum	petition for review
change of venue	frivolous appeal	petitioner
circuit	Full Faith and Credit Clause	plaintiff
circuit court of appeals	general appearance	precedent
civil law	general police powers	preempt
common law	guardian *ad litem*	presiding judge
concurrent jurisdiction	*in rem* jurisdiction	public policy
concurrent powers	inherent powers	question of fact
concurring opinion	interstate commerce	question of law
constitutional law	judicial immunity	quiet title
court of equity	judicial review	respondent
court of last resort	jurisdiction	reversed
court of law	justice court	service of process
criminal law	law	special appearance
damages	legislative intent	statute
discretionary jurisdiction	long arm statute	subject matter jurisdiction
dissenting opinion	mandatory appeal	substituted service

Supremacy Clause	**trier of fact**	**unlawful flight**
Supreme Law of the Land	**Uniform Acts**	**venue**
trial court	**Uniform Commercial Code (UCC)**	**writ of certiorari**

ACTIVITIES AND ASSIGNMENTS

1. Study the first eight amendments to the U.S. Constitution. Prepare a chart with two columns. In the left column, list the civil liberties established by each amendment (e.g., "freedom of speech" under the First Amendment). In the right column, state a question about the interpretation or application of that civil liberty (e.g., "Does freedom of speech protect people who make bomb threats at an airport?"). Be prepared to give your opinion on each question during a class discussion. You do not need to do formal legal research unless your instructor directs you to do so.

2. The state governments possess "general police powers" to protect public health, safety, morals, and welfare. For each of the four police powers, identify five (5) actual state or local laws that are an exercise of that power. Try to rely upon your own general knowledge, doing research only if you must.

3. Working in groups of five students, prepare a joint list of *political rights* (often called "civil rights") that Congress has established by statute. Make your list from your own general knowledge, without further research.

4. Prepare three arguments for, and three arguments against, this proposition:

    "Federal judges should be limited to terms of twelve years."

5. Do some library research on the 1987 nomination of the Honorable Robert Bork, justice of the U.S. Court of Appeals, District of Columbia Circuit, to serve on the U.S. Supreme Court. Prepare a short essay describing the critical issues that caused his nomination to be so controversial. In your conclusion, summarize the reasons that his nomination was rejected by the U.S. Senate. If you wish, you might comment on the role of partisan politics in that nomination controversy.

6. Find out how appellate court justices are placed on the courts of your state. Prepare a short report on that procedure, including your evaluation of the procedure's possible effect upon the independence of the judiciary in your state.

7. If your state has something comparable to a small claims court, find out how individuals can file a claim or lawsuit. Prepare a report describing any limitations on the cases that can be heard, the procedures, any filing fees, and any right of appeal from the decision by that court. Include the right of clients to be represented by attorneys (if permitted), as well as the rights of an attorney to be either plaintiff or defendant in a small claims action.

8. The chapter opened with the story about the Scottsboro Boys. If you had been Michigan's governor at that time, would you have granted or withheld extradition of Haywood Patterson? Would you act differently today, if you were a governor and similar circumstances arose? Should a public official follow the law, even though she believes it will result in a grave miscarriage of justice?

ENDNOTES

[1] Paul Finkelman, "*Kentucky v. Dennison*" (Kermit L. Hall, ed.) *The Oxford Companion to the Supreme Court of the United States* (New York, N.Y.: Oxford University Press, 1992) p. 483.

[2] Congress has entitled a number of statutes as "Civil Rights Act of [year]," the best known being the Civil Rights Acts of 1875, 1964 and 1991.

[3] Rayman L. Solomon, "Courts of Appeals" (Kermit L. Hall, ed.) *The Oxford Companion to the Supreme Court of the United States* (New York, N.Y.: Oxford University Press, 1992) p. 205.

[4] Bob Van Voris, "The high cost of disclosure," *The National Law Journal* (January 20, 2000) pp. A1, A8–9.

CHAPTER 5

Administrative Law

> It would be a narrow conception of jurisprudence to confine the notion of "laws" to what is found written on the statute books.
>
> *Felix Frankfurter, Associate Justice of the Supreme Court (1939–1962)*

When most people think about the law, they probably envision the body of laws passed by Congress and the state legislatures—and some people might include local ordinances within their concept of law. Chapter 4 identified three other types of law: constitutional law, common law, and administrative law. Chapter 5 discusses administrative law. Administrative law plays an enormous role in the lives of ordinary people. It also serves to regulate the activities of businesses and professions.

This chapter will prepare the student to answer the following questions:

- What is administrative law?
- What are the functions of administrative law agencies?
- What is a regulation?
- How are rules and regulations made by administrative agencies?
- Where is the legal authority found to make administrative law?
- What is an administrative order?
- Are administrative agency records available to the public?
- What happens in the adjudication hearings by administrative agencies?
- What is the role of legal assistants in administrative law?
- Do the courts exercise judicial review over administrative law?

SCENARIO

In re: Maxwell Woodridge

Federal Aviation Administration

[March 14, 2000; Ronald Reagan Federal Building, Room 1327]

Excerpt from court reporter's transcript

Q. Captain Woodridge, what was the aircraft's altitude when the aviation safety inspector returned to the cockpit?

A. I believe we leveled off at flight level three-three-zero a few minutes before she returned.

Q. About thirty-three thousand feet, then. Where was the First Officer at that time—approximately zero-seven-fifteen Greenwich, wasn't it?

A. I'm not sure. Maybe he was in the other john.

Q. Could the First Officer have been sitting in the jump seat at that time?

A. No. Because as soon as the inspector returned to the cockpit, she took the jump seat.

Q. So, you were the only pilot at the controls . . . I mean, the only one in the cockpit at that time?

A. Not really. The inspector was rated and current for heavy jets.

Q. Well, I won't argue that point. But did you have personal knowledge that she was qualified and current in the seven forty-seven?

A. I didn't have personal knowledge of that, no.

Q. Anyway, this case isn't about the Boeing seven forty-seven—it's about a reg that applies to pilots operating all types of commercial jet aircraft.

A. So, what's your point, sir?

Q. When the inspector entered the cockpit, were you wearing your oxygen mask?

A. I don't recall.

Q. The inspector's report states that you were not wearing the mask, Mr. Woodridge.

A. Then I suppose I wasn't.

Q. You must be aware of the FAA regulation that requires you to wear an oxygen mask at that altitude whenever the other pilot is out of his seat.

A. Well, yeah. I know that. I guess I just forgot.

Q. You realize this is required in case a sudden depressurization or other emergency were to occur, don't you?

A. Yeah, I know that. But this was just a cargo flight, right? It's not as though passengers could be at risk.

Q. What about the potential risk to your first and second officers, Captain? What about you?

A. I suppose you're right. I should've had the mask on.

[The witness paused]

Can we resolve this without a suspension? Believe me, from now on I'll wear that mask whenever the regs require it.

[Maxwell Woodridge paid a civil fine of $1,000 for violating a regulation of the Federal Aviation Administration.]

SECTION 1. THE NATURE OF ADMINISTRATIVE LAW

On any given day, many thousands of people encounter administrative law in action. In the testimony above, the Federal Aviation Administration (FAA) is establishing the fact of a serious violation of FAA regulations by the captain of a large commercial cargo jet. As noted above, the pilot paid a civil fine—he also could have had his license suspended for a period of time.

The following examples illustrate the broad scope of administrative law, and the involvement of agencies at each level of government:

- The county assessor notifies a landowner that her property taxes will increase because of a rise in values; the owner submits a formal request for review by the assessment appeals board.
- The *Federal Register* publishes a "proposed rule and request for comments" issued by the Federal Communications Commission (FCC).
- A paralegal appears before an administrative law judge in the state department of motor vehicles, seeking restoration of the client's license, which was suspended for medical reasons.
- A fraternity at a state university is suspended, and its officers are put on probation, for violating rules regarding underage drinking at fraternity parties.
- The Federal Trade Commission (FTC) issues a *cease and desist order* against a national retailer, which is accused of false and misleading advertising.
- A public school teacher appears before a state administrative law judge to challenge a dismissal notice charging him with incompetency and unprofessional conduct.
- The state worker compensation appeals board hears a case in which a paramedic is seeking compensation for emotional and physical injuries caused by on-the-job stress, whereas her municipal employer alleges that her nightmares and heart attack actually were induced by severe marital problems.

Not one of the preceding situations occurs in court. In fact, at the present stage of administrative law, none of them involves a judicial court of law, in any way. Yet each situation invokes the legal authority of a government body. In most, questions of both fact and law will be determined; in most, the legal rights and responsibilities of business entities or individuals will be decided. And, in every instance, the formal decision of the government agency will carry the weight of law—provided, that it was properly reached and based on sound law, without an abuse of discretion—and it will be enforceable in a court of law. But, these seven situations provide no more than a glimpse into the enormous reach of *administrative law*.

Individuals and businesses typically encounter administrative law in the following ways:

- providing information and/or suggestions to agencies that are considering policy changes
- complying with administrative regulations that affect their activities
- seeking review of adverse decisions made by administrative agencies
- responding to charges that they have violated administrative regulations
- lodging complaints with an administrative agency against other individuals or organizations, alleging violation of statutory or administrative law

AGENCIES THAT CREATE ADMINISTRATIVE LAW

Generally speaking, administrative law is made by the executive branch of government, both state and federal. So, the president and the state governors, together with the many agencies they supervise, create administrative law. Under state authority, counties, parishes, cities, and other entities of local government also create administrative law in a similar fashion.

Administrative law comprises executive orders, agency-created regulations, and the body of executive agency decisions and orders that interpret and apply those regulations. But, note that policy making normally precedes the decisions and orders that follow. Most administrative agency orders and decisions are based upon specific administrative policies that implement statutory law. In some situations, a statute has already established the specific "rule"—which requires no augmentation by administrative rule making—and has placed the enforcement of that rule in the hands of an administrative agency, rather than a court of law.

The barebones function of an administrative agency—for example, the state department of motor vehicles, the U.S. Department of Agriculture, the county health department, the city library, or the FAA—is to carry out the existing policy of statutory law. Performing that basic function might appear to be a **ministerial act**—theoretically requiring minimal exercise of judgment or discretion. In reality, of course, only the most routine of official acts is purely ministerial, because government agencies must apply the statutory rules to real-life situations, and that often requires the exercise of substantial judgment and discretion.

A **ministerial act** is a clerical action implementing policy and procedures established by a higher government authority and does not require the exercise of judgment or discretion.

Independent Regulatory Agencies—A Special Class

An **independent regulatory agency** is one created by statute and is not subject to the control of the president or state governor.

In addition to the executive branch agencies under the president's direct control, Congress and some states have created a number of **independent regulatory agencies**—called "independent" because they are not directly answerable to the president or state governor. For example, many states have independent boards or commissions that regulate public utilities. As part of their regulatory function, such agencies publish regulations and adjudicate disputes over the utility rates that are charged to consumers and businesses. Typically, the state governor cannot overrule the actions of the independent agencies and may not dismiss the regulatory board members. Congress and some state legislatures have created these independent agencies to shield such regulatory activities from the interference of commercial and political influence.

Several of the situations described at the beginning of this chapter involve independent federal agencies: for example the FTC and the FCC. Other federal independent regulatory agencies that are heavily involved in administrative rule making and enforcement include the Interstate Commerce Commission (ICC), the National Labor Relations Board (NLRB), and the Securities and Exchange Commission (SEC). The president appoints the commissioners who control these agencies, but the president cannot fire them. In some independent agencies, the commissioners serve overlapping terms of twelve or fifteen years—far longer than the constitutional period any president is permitted to serve. The lengthy and overlapping terms normally would prevent any single president from being able to name all of the commissioners for any given agency. In the federal government, commissioners of independent agencies can be removed only by Congress through the impeachment process.

Independent agencies are in a "special class" not only because their commissioners and board members are not easily removed, but also because they exercise—although in a limited and proscribed fashion—all three forms of governmental authority: legislative, executive, and judicial. Some political scientists would argue that the independent agencies are true executive agencies, but exercise only "quasi-legislative" and "quasi-judicial" powers. That is because their rule-making authority is always subordinate to prior and subsequent Acts of Congress, and their judicial powers are far less broad than those of a court of law.

CREATING ADMINISTRATIVE LAW

One purpose of federal agency rule making is to relieve Congress and the president of the enormous burden of writing detailed legislation for complex and technical activities, such as aviation, prescription medications, nuclear power generation, genetically altered crops, and electronic communications. Presumably, the agencies that administer a statute or an executive function will have greater expertise in that area, resulting in more effective rules. Also, the agencies are believed to be relatively free of partisan politics when making rules and fine-tuning government policy—although they often are influenced by top-level agency officials who are political appointees rather than civil servants.

In administrative law, the administrative interpretations and application of a statute or an executive order are given official status as legal authority. In effect, *agency regulations, decisions, and orders become legal extensions of the statute or executive order upon which they are based.* Because the policies and detailed regulations are published, they diminish the opportunity for bureaucrats to inject their individual views into administration of the law. Rule making, enforcement, and the adjudication of disputes or violations are the principal administrative law activities of government agencies. Because administrative law varies from state to state, this text will focus on federal administrative law and procedure.

Executive Orders as Part of Administrative Law

Some legal commentators might not consider executive orders, first introduced in Chapter 4, to be part of administrative law. Yet, such orders have legal authority that often takes precedence over the administrative rules and orders issued by most executive agencies. It might be helpful to think of the Office of the President and a state governor's office as administrative agencies—which, in fact, they are. Other than their possible greater authority, executive orders are not qualitatively different from the rest of administrative law.

POLICIES, RULES, AND REGULATIONS

Administrative agencies establish policies to further the objectives stated in the statutes that they are implementing. In some instances, an agency establishes policies to further the purpose of an executive order. Formally, these policies are

> **Practice Tip**
>
> In the first citation to the Administrative Procedures Act, the symbol "§§" is used to indicate "Sections" (plural). If the citation were to a single section of the Act (e.g., Section 551(4)), the symbol "§" would be used.

The *Federal Register* is a daily publication of official announcements, proposed and adopted federal regulations, and other government documents.

The *Code of Federal Regulations (CFR)* contains all of the federal regulations that have been formally adopted (and not yet repealed). The code comprises some 50 "titles," each of which is devoted to a particular subject area (e.g., income tax or railroads). Each title is published in one or more volumes, depending upon its length, and is revised at least once each year.

A **regulation** is an agency-created rule that implements policies and procedures established by a higher government authority.

made through the rule-making process. Rule making by federal administrative agencies is governed by the *Administrative Procedures Act,* 5 U.S.C. §§ 551–559, 701–706. That act does not use the term "regulation." Instead, it speaks of "rules." However, "regulation" is a term often used conversationally by practitioners of administrative law, with the same *general* meaning ascribed to the word "rule" in the *Administrative Procedures Act*. Section 551(4) of that act provides, in pertinent part:

> "(4) 'Rule' means the whole or a part of an agency statement of general or particular applicability and future effect designed to implement, interpret, or prescribe law or policy. . . ."

Some rules, especially those of "particular applicability" to a specific case before the agency, will be published in the ***Federal Register*** (a compilation of official announcements and documents, published daily by the federal government), but are never codified by publication in the ***Code of Federal Regulations (CFR)***. When an attorney speaks of an "administrative regulation," she typically refers to one that appears in the *CFR*. Those are the **regulations** intended to have general application to the public. This text uses "regulation" in this same sense. Most states compile their own administrative regulations in a similar publication (e.g., the *Georgia Administrative Code*). A typical page from the *Federal Register* appears in *Figure 5.1*.

LEGAL AUTHORITY FOR ADMINISTRATIVE RULE MAKING

Every administrative rule, decision, and order must be based upon a higher legal authority. The *Administrative Procedures Act* governs the rule-making process—it does not grant rule-making authority. For example, the president issues executive orders based upon powers granted by the Constitution or delegated by an act of Congress. Similarly, state governors must find authority for their executive orders in their state constitutions and state statutes.

In 1948, when President Harry S. Truman ordered the armed forces to eliminate racial segregation of military units and personnel, he acted under his constitutional authority as commander in chief. When President Richard Nixon declared an economic emergency and froze all wages and prices in 1971, he was exercising powers granted by federal statutes.

A Case in Point

Youngstown Sheet & Tube Co. v. Sawyer

343 U.S. 579 (1952).

Because the president's constitutional authority is stated in such broad, general terms—as compared to the very specific authority granted by federal statutes—there often is some dispute over the extent of the president's constitutional authority in a given situation. For example, during the Korean War, President Truman ordered the secretary of commerce to seize and operate steel mills threatened by possible strikes. He cited his authority as commander in chief of the armed forces during a national emergency. However, the Supreme Court found no constitutional or statutory basis for extending the president's military authority to permit the seizure of private businesses, and it ordered that the mills be returned to their owners.

FIGURE 5.1   Sample Page from the *Federal Register*

Department of Transportation
Federal Aviation Administration
14 CFR Part 34
[Docket No. FAA–1999–5018; Amendment No. 34–3]
RIN 2120–AG68
Emission Standards for Turbine Engine Powered Airplanes
AGENCY: Federal Aviation Administration (FAA), DOT.
ACTION: Final rule.
SUMMARY: This document revises the emission standards for turbine engine powered airplanes to incorporate the current standards of the International Civil Aviation Organization (ICAO) for gaseous emissions of oxides of nitrogen (NO$_x$) and carbon monoxide (CO), and to adopt revised test procedures for gaseous emissions. This rule will bring the United States emissions standards into alignment with the standards of ICAO. Because, this rule is consistent with international standards, an emission certification test that meets U.S. requirements will meet ICAO requirements.
EFFECTIVE DATE: February 3, 1999.
The incorporation by reference of the publication listed in the rule is approved by the director of the Federal Register February 3, 1999.
FOR FURTHER INFORMATION CONTACT: Mr. Edward McQueen, Research and Engineering Branch (AEE-110), Office of Environment and Energy, Federal Aviation Administration, 800 Independence Avenue, SW., Washington, DC 20591, telephone (202) 267-3560.

SUPPLEMENTARY INFORMATION:
Availability of Final Rules
An electronic copy of this document may be downloaded, using a modem and suitable communications software, from the FAA regulations section of the Fedworld electronic bulletin board service (telephone: 703-321-3339), the Government Printing Office's electronic bulletin board service (telephone: 202-512-1661), or the FAA's Aviation Rulemaking Advisory Committee Bulletin Board service (telephone 800-322-2722 or 202-267-5948).
Internet users may reach the FAA's web page at **http://www.faa.gov/avr/arm/nprm/nprm.htm** or the Government Printing Office's webpage at **http://www.access.gpo.gov/nara/aces/aces140.html** for access to recently published rulemaking documents.

Any person may obtain a copy of this final rule by submitting a request to the Federal Aviation Administration Office of Rulemaking, ARM-1, 800 Independence Avenue, SW., Washington, DC 20591, or by calling (202) 267-9680. Communications must identify the amendment number or docket number of this final rule.
Persons interested in being placed on the mailing list for future Notices of Proposed Rulemaking and Final Rules should request from the above office a copy of Advisory Circular No. 11-2A, Notice of Proposed Rulemaking Distribution System, that describes the application procedure.

Small Entity Inquiries
The Small Business Regulatory Enforcement Fairness Act of 1996 (SBREFA) requires the FAA to report inquiries from small entities concerning information on, and advice about, compliance with statutes and regulations within the FAA's jurisdiction, including interpretation and application of the law to specific sets of facts supplied by a small entity.
If you are a small entity and have a question concerning this rule, contact your local FAA official. If you do not know how to contact your local FAA official, you may contact Charlene Brown, Program Analyst Staff, Office of Rulemaking, ARM-27, Federal Aviation Administration, 800 Independence Avenue, SW, Washington, DC 20591, 1-888-551-1594. Internet users can find additional information on SBREFA in the "Quick Jump" section of the FAA's web page at **http://www.faa.gov** and may send electronic inquiries to the following Internet address: 9-AWA-SBREF@faa.gov

Background
Section 232 of the Clean Air Act Amendments of 1970 (the Act), 42 U.S.C. 7401 *et. seq.*, requires the Federal Aviation Administrations (FAA) to issue regulations that ensure compliance with all aircraft emission standards promulgated by the Environmental Protection Agency (EPA) under Section 231 of the Act. The EPA has promulgated standards for engine fuel venting emissions, engine smoke emissions, and exhaust gaseous emissions of unburned hydrocarbons (HC), oxides of nitrogen NO$_x$, and carbon monoxide (CO). These emission standards are prescribed in 40 CFR part 87.
Since the promulgation of the initial U.S. standards in 1973 by the EPA, the FAA has worked with the International Civil Aviation Organization (ICAO) on the development of international aircraft engine exhaust emissions standards for NO$_x$, CO, HC, and smoke (SN).

Currently, the FAA regulations governing aircraft engine exhaust emissions do not include NO$_x$ and CO. This rule amends 14 CFR Part 34 to add the standards for NO$_x$ and CO that were adopted by the EPA in July 1997.

Analysis of the Rule as Adopted
Section 34.1

Section 34.1 is amended by expanding the definition of Class TF so that it would apply to new engine development programs such as propfan, unducted fan, and advanced ducted propfan (ADP) engines.

Section 34.2

Section 34.2 is amended by adding the abbreviations for Carbon Monoxide (CO) and Oxides of Nitrogen (NO$_x$), the two emissions standards being added to the regulations.

Section 34.21(d), (d)(1), and (e)(3)

In section 34.21, paragraphs (d), (d)(1) and (e)(3) are being amended to add CO and NO$_x$ standards for exhaust emissions as requirements for newly manufactured aircraft gas turbine engines of rated thrust greater than 26.7 Kilonewtons (kN). This change will make U.S. and international emissions standards and test procedures compatible.

Section 34.60(c)

Section 34.60(c) is amended to require a NO$_x$ measurement as part of the test procedures for engine exhaust gaseous emissions. This change is necessary to provide the data from which compliance with the new NO$_x$ standard may be demonstrated.

Section 34.61

Section 34.61 is amended by adjusting the allowable ranges of values in the properties of the fuel specifications to be used in aircraft turbine engine emission testing. This change will allow a wider band of test fuel acceptability without degradation in emission data quality and make U.S. and international emissions standards and test procedures compatible.

Section 34.62(a)(2)

Section 34.62(a)(2) is amended by adding CO emissions to the taxi/idle operating modes of the test procedure. This change is necessitated by the addition of the CO standard, and will make U.S. international emissions test procedures for engine exhaust gaseous emissions compatible.

Federal administrative agencies must have a valid grant of authority from either the president or the Congress, if they are to create administrative law. In either case, that authority is effectively a *delegation* of presidential or legislative authority. Without such a delegation of executive or legislative authority, an administrative agency has no legal basis upon which to make and enforce substantive rules (as opposed to procedural rules) affecting the material rights of businesses or individuals. The same principle applies at the state level: Governors and state legislatures delegate authority under their respective state constitutions.

Typically, Congress or a state legislature enacts an **enabling statute** that sets forth fundamental policy, establishes parameters for administrative rules and regulations, and authorizes an administrative agency to establish specific rules

> Congress or a state legislature enacts an **enabling statute** to authorize a government agency to create specific policies and issue regulations implementing that statute.

> **Practice Tip**
>
> Many paralegals employed in corporations review each day's issue of the *Federal Register* to identify anything that might affect the activities of that company. Of course, paralegals working in law firms that practice administrative law often have that same responsibility.
>
> Because the *Register* is written in such formal language—in "bureaucratese" some might say—and includes a substantial amount of legal and technical language, a paralegal needs to have a strong legal and technical vocabulary, as well as excellent reading speed and comprehension. If the paralegal is expected to prepare a summary of pertinent items and/or an evaluation of their potential effect upon the company, she will be performing a very sophisticated legal and technical analysis.

Separation of powers is the constitutional principle that prohibits one branch of government (either executive, legislative, or judicial) from assuming the powers of the other branches.

and regulations consistent with the policy and parameters set forth in the statute. The same statute often authorizes the agency to issue decisions and/or orders, and provides penalties for violation of the authorized administrative regulations and orders. The penalties might be civil, criminal, or both. The agency itself is often authorized to impose the civil penalties, but never criminal penalties—only a court can impose criminal penalties.

Limitations on Rule-Making Authority

This is a topic of unending legal controversy. Administrative regulations, decisions, and orders are constantly challenged on three general grounds:

1. that the administrative agency has exceeded the authority granted it
2. that even the grantor (e.g., the president or the Congress) lacked the authority ostensibly granted to the agency and, therefore, could not delegate it
3. that the very act of *delegating* the authority was unconstitutional

The latter objection usually argues that the Congress has attempted to delegate an authority that it possesses under the Constitution, but cannot properly delegate. In these cases, the argument is that the delegation erodes the independence and authority of the legislative branch of government, in violation of the **Separation of Powers** doctrine. But the U.S. Supreme Court has only twice—in 1935—invalidated a delegation of rule-making authority by Congress on that basis.

In basic terms, anything that would be unconstitutional if done by the president or Congress cannot be legitimized by authorizing an administrative agency to do the same thing. Thus, administrative law is subject to the U.S. Constitution, just like all other law. An administrative agency cannot receive a "blank check" for rule-making authority; there must be some recognizable boundary between the authority that is granted and that which is withheld. Otherwise, there might be judicial uncertainty about whether the agency is intended to have *any* authority in a particular instance.

The most common challenge to administrative law is that the agency has exceeded the authority granted to it. The resolution of that issue is a straightforward analysis of the enabling statute—usually a routine task for the courts.

PUBLIC PARTICIPATION IN AGENCY RULE MAKING

Generally, administrative agencies must provide ample opportunity for public participation in rule making. Occasionally, the first opportunity occurs when an agency invites public comment on a perceived problem, before any regulatory solution has been drafted. Individuals, companies, and other interest groups may submit written commentary on the problem, and in some cases public hearings are held. Following such public commentary, the agency staff usually drafts a proposed rule.

More commonly, public commentary is first invited after the agency has already drafted a proposed rule. Again, written commentary is always accepted, and for the more important or controversial issues public hearings are often held. Some corporate paralegals and those working in firms that practice administrative law often participate in preparing the written materials to be submitted to the government agency. A paralegal might attend a hearing and later prepare a summary of the information and views presented to the agency, as well as the reactions of agency staff.

ADMINISTRATIVE ORDERS

Section 551(6) of the *Administrative Procedures Act* defines an "order" as a final disposition of a matter, other than a rule. In other words, the adjudication of a particular case might result in either a "rule" or an "order." As explained above, a rule that is published in the *Code of Federal Regulations* generally becomes a regulation applicable to the public at large. An "order" does not become a regulation. However, like any decision in the common law, it might serve as precedent and impact the activities of many members of the public. The *Administrative Procedures Act* defines "adjudication" as the process for arriving at an order, whereas "rule making" is the process resulting in agency rules.

MANDATORY RECORD KEEPING AND THE SUBPOENA OF RECORDS

Because information is so crucial to regulation, businesses can be required to keep and submit records to the agencies that regulate them. An agency often prescribes forms that a business must fill out, so that all businesses will organize and present the same information in a similar manner. So long as the information is reasonably related to the agency's function, an agency may require a company to keep records that it would not otherwise keep in the ordinary course of business.

An agency must have statutory authority to issue a subpoena. Subpoenas are not authorized by the *Administrative Procedures Act*, but often they are authorized by the agency's enabling act. The use of subpoenas is not limited to formal hearings. They are generally permitted during prehearing investigations to determine whether the agency should invoke its rule-making or adjudication powers. For example, when Orange County, California, filed for bankruptcy protection in 1994, its financial losses of $1.6 billion—the largest municipal bankruptcy ever—involved both the purchase and the sale of various types of securities. The Securities and Exchange Commission (SEC) served subpoenas on the county government and various brokerage houses to discover whether federal securities laws had been violated.

The Supreme Court has repeatedly upheld very broad subpoena powers for administrative agencies. The Court has even rejected the argument that the entity served must be within the regulatory jurisdiction of the agency issuing the subpoena. Efforts to oppose subpoenas are so rarely successful that an attorney doing so risks the imposition of sanctions for bringing a frivolous action. A good rule of thumb is to regard an agency subpoena with the same respect one would accord to a subpoena issued by a court.

SECTION 2. ACCESS TO PUBLIC RECORDS

For many generations, public agencies routinely claimed that large portions of their records were confidential and refused to release them except upon court order. But, in recent decades, the Congress and most state legislatures have enacted public records statutes to ensure that the public's business is truly public. Each of these statutes provides exceptions, of course, so that the Central Intelligence Agency, local police departments, public hospitals, and other selected agencies do not have to open every archive and file to public inspection.

> **Practice Tip**
>
> *Obtaining public records is a very common assignment for legal assistants. For example, a law firm involved in litigation over an aircraft accident will need to obtain all of the relevant FAA airworthiness directives and safety bulletins for the type of aircraft involved in the accident. Accident reports for aircraft of the same type can be obtained from the National Transportation Safety Board (NTSB). (In some cases, a subpoena may be required for the latter.) The* Freedom of Information Act (FOIA) *provides the primary means for obtaining documents from all federal agencies. General information about the* FIOA *can be obtained from the Department of Justice Web site, and specific procedures can be obtained from the Web sites of other agencies.*

The federal *Freedom of Information Act (FOIA)* requires most federal records to be available to the public, subject to specified exceptions for national security, privacy, and so forth.

The federal *Freedom of Information Act (FOIA)* exemplifies these "public records" statutes and was enacted by Congress as an amendment to the *Administrative Procedures Act*.

Internet Access

U.S. Department of Justice — http://www.usdoj.gov

Enacted in 1966, the *FOIA* requires each federal agency to disclose, upon request, any information that is not specifically exempted by that statute. If the agency claims such an exemption, it carries the burden of proof in any court review of that claim. The result is a *statutory presumption* that agency records are public records and not confidential. The *FOIA* and similar state laws have brought about a profound change, making it far more difficult for agencies to conceal abuses of power, corruption, waste, and mismanagement. Although it can still be expensive and time-consuming for individuals to pry information from the hands of reluctant bureaucrats, the news media and special interest groups have had the resources to force many involuntary disclosures.

Most of the exemptions provided in the *FOIA* are common sense ones, such as the following:

- classified military and foreign intelligence information
- commercial trade secrets obtained by government agencies
- personnel and medical files of individuals
- records of on-going (i.e., not yet completed) law enforcement investigations

For obvious reasons, the Defense Department, federal intelligence agencies (e.g., the CIA and the National Security Agency), State Department, and federal law enforcement agencies have the broadest range of exemptions under the *FOIA*. However, even exempted documents may still be obtained by subpoena.

USING THE *FREEDOM OF INFORMATION ACT*

Each agency is required to publish in the *Federal Register* its guidelines for obtaining information under the *FOIA*. One simply addresses a letter to the official identified as that agency's *FOIA* officer (or fills out a form provided by the agency), describing with reasonable precision the information being requested. No justification needs to be given, because the records are now presumed to be public in nature. The requesting person might be required to pay search and copy fees, so it is wise to be as specific as possible in identifying the information needed.

Within ten days, the agency must respond with an acceptance or rejection of the request. A rejection can be based upon an *FOIA* exemption, the vagueness of the request, or a statement that the agency has no such records. In the event the request is rejected, the requesting party may appeal that denial, and the agency has twenty days to process the appeal. Unfortunately, there are no similar timelines for actual production of the information. The statute states only that it will be provided "promptly."

If an agency denies the *FOIA* request, the requesting party may file an action in the U.S. District Court to compel disclosure. In that event, the court will hear the full matter *de novo,* as though the prior agency hearing had not occurred. Although the judge might examine the documents in his chambers to determine their eligibility for exemption, that issue is usually decided based upon testi-

---

Practice Tip

Most federal agencies—and many state offices, as well—now maintain Web sites on the Internet. The Web sites of federal agencies often provide guidance and forms for making an FOIA request. Some agencies even permit the requests to be submitted electronically, by simply filling in a blank form online.

mony by agency personnel regarding the nature of the documents. Interestingly, in litigation between former intelligence officers and the CIA, some officers have used their right of access to secret documents—as litigants, not under the *FOIA*—to pressure the CIA into making financial settlements to end the litigation. Similarly, former CIA officers have used their access to secret documents—again, as litigants—to fend off government lawsuits aimed at preventing the publication of memoirs about their intelligence careers.

PRIVACY RESTRICTIONS UNDER THE *FREEDOM OF INFORMATION ACT*

Privacy concerns became a major issue in the decade following enactment of the *FOIA*. In particular, individuals and businesses became apprehensive that properly confidential information—once obtained by a federal agency—would be subject to disclosure because of inadequate exemptions under the *FOIA*. An unintended consequence of the *FOIA* was a greater reluctance to provide information to government agencies.

A Case in Point

Department of Air Force v. Rose

425 U.S. 352 (1976).

A law school student planned to write a law review article on disciplinary proceedings at the U.S. Air Force Academy. He requested copies of summaries of "honor board" decisions, which were routinely posted at the academy. The air force rejected the request, claiming that the *FOIA* exempted those records as personnel files whose release would constitute an invasion of privacy for the individuals who had been charged with infractions of academy regulations.

The U.S. Supreme Court determined that the requested records concerned matters of public interest. The Court then considered whether release of the records would constitute a "clearly unwarranted invasion of personal privacy," which is grounds under the *FOIA* for rejecting a request for information. The Court concluded that the public interest must be balanced against the potential invasion of privacy. Under the facts in this case, the Supreme Court held that deletion of identifying data about individual cadets would provide sufficient protection against an "unwarranted invasion," even though their contemporary classmates and instructors might recognize their identity from the facts of each case—as they would have when the summaries were earlier posted at the academy. The deletions of identifying data protected the former cadets from general public knowledge of their involvement in the disciplinary proceedings, so that there was no basis in law to withhold the summaries requested by the law student.

Concerns about the *FOIA* eventually led to passage of the *Federal Privacy Act* in 1974. The effect of the *Privacy Act* was to place a check against the operation of the *FOIA* as it applies to information about individuals. The general presumption for public disclosure under the *FOIA* was now limited by a specific presumption for *non*disclosure of information about private citizens. In addition, the *Privacy Act* regulates the collection of personal information and provides criminal and civil penalties for unlawful use or disclosure of that information. It also requires government files to be accurate and provides a procedure for a citizen to correct or supplement personal information in federal files that is inaccurate or incomplete.

Adjudication is the resolution of disputes through a hearing process before an impartial hearing officer.

SECTION 3. ADJUDICATING ADMINISTRATIVE LAW DISPUTES

Adjudication takes many forms, and it includes the judgments and decrees of state and federal courts. In administrative law, an adjudication is the determination of some particular matter pending before the agency. Administrative adjudication usually occurs in a hearing before an agency hearing officer. Although similar in many respects to a court proceeding, administrative hearings are less formal.

The *Administrative Procedures Act* has carefully separated the functions of investigation and prosecution by an agency from those of hearing and adjudicating the matter in dispute. Agency employees involved in investigation or prosecution of a case may not participate or advise during the adjudication of that matter. State laws do not always make this separation; therefore, state agency decisions might offer more occasion for challenge on grounds of bias.

DUE PROCESS IN ADMINISTRATIVE LAW

Whether in court or in an administrative law hearing, each person is entitled to receive reasonable due process of law. The Fifth Amendment to the Constitution requires the federal government to honor due process, and the Fourteenth Amendment imposes the same obligation upon the states. In addition, some state constitutions include their own due process clauses. The question of what constitutes constitutionally required "reasonable" due process is a complex one that the courts continue to refine. Due process requirements are more extensive when someone's substantial property interest—for example, his livelihood—is affected than when only minor or peripheral interests are involved.

The fundamental concept of due process is that no one should lose personal freedom or suffer criminal penalties unless fair procedures have been followed. Even property rights are protected by due process, so that agencies must use due process before they suspend or revoke anyone's driver's license or deny that person benefits provided by law (e.g., public schooling for children).

A CASE IN POINT

Goldberg v. Kelly

397 U.S. 254 (1970).

A watershed case in administrative due process involved the termination of welfare benefits. The State of New York had terminated benefits to a number of families for various reasons, such as the parent's refusal to enter a drug rehabilitation program. The practice in New York was to issue a seven-day termination notice and give the recipient an opportunity to submit a written protest. There was no provision for a pretermination hearing. The U.S. Supreme Court found that New York's administrative procedure violated the due process requirements of the Fourteenth Amendment.

The Supreme Court held that welfare benefits are a statutory entitlement and that their termination jeopardizes the health and safety of the recipients. Therefore, the Court set forth specific due process rights that must be observed:

- reasonable notice
- right to legal counsel

- right to examine and cross-examine witnesses
- an impartial decision maker
- a finding based upon law and the evidence

The *Goldberg* court's holding, although not **overruled**, appears to have been qualified by the Supreme Court's subsequent decision in *Mathews v. Eldridge,* 424 U.S. 319 (1976). In *Mathews,* the Social Security Administration terminated disability benefits after giving notice and an opportunity to protest in writing. No pretermination hearing was offered, although a later *post*termination hearing was available. The Supreme Court found those procedures to be constitutionally sufficient, **distinguishing** the welfare recipient's life on the edge of survival from a situation presumably less precarious for the disabled. However, *Mathews* established three factors that courts must consider when reviewing administrative actions for reasonable due process:

1. the importance of the property interest affected
2. the risk of mistake in the agency's procedures
3. the burden on the agency of implementing more protective procedures

The decision in *Mathews* makes clear that the more extensive due process required by *Goldberg* is not an automatic right in all administrative actions. Instead, the amount of process due the complainant must be determined by balancing the potential harm of denying greater due process against the burden of providing greater due process.

Informal administrative hearings often do not produce any written record, other than the result. In more formal hearings, there will be a record of documents submitted for consideration and, possibly, of oral testimony (if any is allowed). In the most formal hearings, there might be verbatim transcripts of all testimony and proceedings, and the parties and witnesses might be cross-examined under oath. The latter form of hearing is very similar to a civil court proceeding, except that strict rules of evidence are not generally followed.

Formal hearings in an administrative agency are usually heard by an **administrative law judge** who is an employee of that agency. That employment status might appear to foster a bias on the part of the administrative judges, but it is minimized by the fact that all personnel matters affecting an administrative judge are handled by the Federal Office of Personnel Management—*not* by the agency that employs the judge. Such judges are protected from arbitrary discipline or dismissal by rules of the Merit System Protection Board.

The administrative law judge has the power of subpoena, as well as the powers needed to control the administrative hearing—much as a judge controls proceedings before a court. The administrative judge determines the admissibility of evidence, but she does so under rules far less stringent than those found in the *Federal Rules of Civil Procedure* that govern federal court proceedings. After all written and oral evidence and argument have been received, the administrative law judge writes the preliminary findings in adjudication of that matter. Those findings can be overruled within the agency, but they will become final if not appealed. In almost every instance, the final adjudication is subject to court review. (Judicial review of administrative agency actions is discussed later in this chapter.)

The *Administrative Procedures Act* imposes strict limitations on *ex parte* **contacts** with administrative law judges, and even with other agency employees involved in the decision-making process. If an *ex parte* contact occurs, the agency must conduct a "show cause" hearing to determine if sanctions should be imposed or a claim dismissed.

A case is **overruled** when the same court renounces its own earlier statement of the law, made in that earlier case, and adopts a different rule of law to apply in the case now before the court.

A court **distinguishes** one case from another by finding that the differing facts require the application of a different legal principle.

An **administrative law judge** is the hearing officer of an administrative agency, with power to issue subpoenas, require testimony, rule on the admission of evidence, reach findings of fact and law, and impose authorized civil (i.e., noncriminal) penalties for violations of administrative law.

An *ex parte* **contact** occurs when only one party communicates with a court or administrative law judge, without participation by other interested parties.

Practice Tip

Most legislative acts of Congress are identified as "public laws"—that is, an act intended to have general application to the public, as opposed to a "private law" intended to apply to a specific person or entity. The public laws are numbered first by congressional term, then in numerical sequence. Public Law 94-409, the Government in Sunshine Act, was the 409th **public law** *enacted by the 94th Congress. The first public law enacted by the 94th Congress was Public Law 94-1. The Government in Sunshine Act, like many public laws, amended various portions of the United States Code, so that it is not found in a single, discreet portion of that Code. If a legal assistant wanted to read Public Law 94-409 in its entirety, he would best find it published in its original form, as passed by Congress.*

The 94th Congress met in the 1975–77 term, and the 95th Congress met in 1977–79. Each two-year term of Congress is numbered in that manner, beginning with the First Congress in 1789–91. Citation by term and number (e.g., Public Law 99-103) to a public law enacted by Congress is an acceptable alternative, when citation to the United States Code is impossible or awkward.

A **public law** is a statute intended to have general application to the public at large, as opposed to a private law intended to apply to a particular person or entity.

A CASE IN POINT

Gibson et al. v. Berryhill et al.

411 U.S. 564 (1973)

The Alabama state licensing board for optometrists was composed entirely of optometrists in individual, private practice. The Alabama Optometric Association had filed charges with the licensing board against a number of optometrists, charging them with unprofessional conduct (a ground for the suspension or revocation of optometric licenses). The basis for that charge was their employment by a corporation, Lee Optical Company.

All members of the licensing board were also members of the complaining Optometric Association, which excluded from its membership those optometrists who were employed by corporations. Two days after the Alabama Optometric Association filed its charges, the licensing board brought suit in state court against Lee Optical Company and thirteen of its employee-optometrists, charging the latter with aiding and abetting the company in its unlawful practice of optometry. Gibson and the other twelve defendants in the state court action then filed their own suit in the U.S. District Court, alleging violation of their due process rights under the Fourteenth Amendment to the U.S. Constitution.

The plaintiffs in *Gibson* alleged a bias on the part of the licensing board. Nearly half of all practicing optometrists in Alabama were employed by other persons or entities. Yet, only *self*-employed optometrists in private practice—including *all* members of the state licensing board—would fall heir to the business of the plaintiffs in *Gibson* whose licenses were to be suspended or revoked.

The U.S. District Court agreed that the board's immediate lawsuit against the employed optometrists evidenced its prejudgment of the Alabama Optometric Association's charges against them. That prejudgment, and the board members' apparent financial interest in the outcome of those charges, deprived the employed optometrists of their property right (i.e., to practice their profession) without due process of law. A unanimous Supreme Court upheld the district court decision.

ADMINISTRATIVE AGENCY HEARINGS AND PUBLIC ACCESS

In 1976, Congress enacted the *Government in Sunshine Act*, Public Law 94–409, which amended the *Administrative Procedures Act* to require most deliberative federal bodies to open their meetings to the public. 5 U.S.C. § 552(b). There are, however, exemptions from that requirement; essentially, they are similar to those for the *Freedom of Information Act*. Furthermore, some critics charge that bodies that do not welcome public scrutiny often turn the public rule-making meetings into pro forma "rubber stamp" sessions, having already arrived at their decisions through informal prior consultations. Adjudication hearings are less susceptible to "rubber stamp" sessions, because the prohibition against *ex parte* contacts with the hearing officer makes it difficult to arrive at a decision prior to the hearing itself.

Most states have similar sunshine statutes, many with similar exceptions. Probably the greatest benefit of sunshine laws are prior notice to the public, so that persons opposed to an official action can put their objections on the record before the vote is taken. Alabama's sunshine act appears in the following sidebar.

ADMINISTRATIVE LAW PENALTIES

As already mentioned, no administrative agency can impose a criminal penalty; thus, an administrative law judge cannot convict someone of a crime. But she can find someone guilty of a civil offense and impose a civil fine. Any penalty imposed by an administrative agency must be authorized by statute if it would affect a substantial interest or right of the person being penalized.

Many agencies are authorized to impose monetary penalties for violations of specified statutes or for violation of agency regulations. In most cases, the statute authorizes a penalty "not to exceed" a specified maximum for each offense. For certain types of violations—the continuous dumping of toxic wastes into streams, for example—a daily maximum penalty is established by statute and continues to accumulate each day the violation continues.

Some agencies are authorized to issue injunction-like orders, usually called **cease and desist orders**. Agencies that grant licenses or permits might deny, suspend, or revoke such licenses or permits. If Congress or the state legislature has made it a crime to violate agency regulations, the agency might refer the violator to the Justice Department or state prosecutors for criminal prosecution.

JUDICIAL REVIEW OF ADMINISTRATIVE ACTIONS

Most enabling acts that authorize administrative rule making and adjudication also provide for judicial review. The general rule is that administrative law is subject to judicial review under the same circumstances as any other governmental action, whether executive, legislative, or judicial. Furthermore, Section 702 of the *Administrative Procedures Act* establishes a statutory right to judicial review for any "person suffering legal wrong because of agency action, or adversely affected or aggrieved by agency action within the meaning of a relevant statute...." The federal courts generally presume that all administrative actions are subject to judicial review unless "clear and convincing evidence" of a contrary legislative intent is shown. *Abbott Laboratories v. Gardner*, 387 U.S. 136 (1967).

Just as appellate courts try to find a basis for **affirming** the actions of lower courts, there is a similar presumption that administrative law actions are valid. This presumption is based in part upon the underlying reason for authorizing administrative rule making and adjudication in the first place: An agency is presumed to be better qualified to regulate the activities placed within its purview. Also, policy making is not supposed to be a judicial function. So, in order to successfully challenge most administrative law actions, one must challenge its procedures, the scope of its authority, or its exercise of discretion.

Obstacles to Judicial Review

One obstacle to judicial review can be an explicit statutory preclusion (relatively rare) or a preclusion by the fact that Congress has "committed" an issue to the sound discretion of a particular agency. Both preclusions are based on the Constitution, which grants appellate jurisdiction to the Supreme Court "with such Exceptions, and under such Regulations as the Congress shall make" (Article III, Section 2). The committed-to-agency-discretion preclusion often is the more problematical, because it sometimes requires the courts to read between the lines of enabling statutes, thereby finding a preclusion to be *intended,* even where not explicitly stated by Congress. The courts sometimes find the latter preclusion where Congress has entrusted an exceedingly complex decision to a qualified agency—the courts lack any comparable expertise enabling them to review the soundness of the agency's decision, even under criteria set forth in the statute.

Alabama Criminal Code

§ 13A-14-2. Executive or secret sessions of certain boards.

(a) No executive or secret session shall be held by any of the following named boards, commissions or courts of Alabama, namely: Alabama Public Service Commission; school commissions of Alabama; board of adjustment; state or county tax commissions; any county commission, any city commission or municipal council; or any other body, board or commission in the state charged with the duty of disbursing any funds belonging to the state, county or municipality, or board, body or commission to which is delegated any legislative or judicial function; except, that executive or secret sessions might be held by any of the above named boards or commissions when the character or good name of a woman or man is involved.

(b) Any person or persons violating any of the provisions of this section shall be guilty of a misdemeanor, and, upon conviction, shall be fined not less than $10.00 nor more than $500.00. Any person who remains in attendance upon any meeting of any of the above named boards or bodies which is being held in secret or executive session shall be deemed guilty of violating the provisions of this section.

A **cease and desist order** is issued by an agency directing some person or entity to halt the specified illegal conduct and to refrain from such conduct in the future.

When a higher court **affirms** the decision of an administrative agency or of a lower court, it is validating that decision as being a proper conclusion under the law.

The same principle causes the courts to refuse intervention where an agency has, in its discretion, decided *not* to issue a regulation. Unless Congress has mandated the regulation in question, the courts generally leave that decision to the discretion of the agency. The same applies to discretionary enforcement activities. Unless a statute authorizes *ordinary citizens* to bring an enforcement action before the agency, the courts will not compel the agency to prosecute one.

Other obstacles to judicial review include standing, ripeness, and exhaustion of remedies. **Standing** is a party's genuine legal interest that is at stake in a case and that is sufficiently substantial as to require a court to hear the case. **Ripeness** refers to the legal maturity of a case, so that an actual controversy that a court may resolve can come before it. **Exhaustion of remedies** means that all administrative (i.e., nonjudicial) remedies have been exploited to their full potential without a satisfactory result. Standing will be discussed in Chapter 6; this discussion will consider only ripeness and exhaustion of remedies.

A case is not "ripe" for court action if the factual and/or legal issues are unclear or uncertain, and therefore do not establish a genuine "present controversy" for judicial determination. It may fail the ripeness standard also if it is based upon a hypothetical or speculative assumption that administrative proceedings will end unsatisfactorily. This standard is based upon two concerns: avoidance of unnecessary interference in agency proceedings, and conservation of the time and resources of the courts. In a case before the Supreme Court, Justice John Harlan wrote:

> Without undertaking to survey the intricacies of the ripeness doctrine it is fair to say that its basic rationale is to prevent the courts, through avoidance of premature adjudication, from entangling themselves in abstract disagreements over administrative policies, and also to protect the agencies from judicial interference until an administrative decision has been formalized and its effects felt in a concrete way by the challenging parties. [Footnote omitted.]
>
> *Abbott Laboratories v. Gardner,* 387 U.S. 136, 148–149 (1967)

Courts generally reject petitions for review if the petitioner has not yet "exhausted" all nonjudicial remedies. In this sense, administrative remedies are considered exhausted when all available agency proceedings have been concluded without a determination in the petitioner's favor. Thus, if the administrative agency has any internal level of appeal not yet used, the court might refuse to exercise judicial review. The rationale of judicial efficiency and unnecessary interference, which require "ripeness" prior to judicial review, also underpin the requirement that administrative remedies be exhausted prior to court review.

An exception to the latter requirement is a challenge to the adequacy of the administrative remedies that are available. A petitioner who can show that those remedies cannot reasonably protect his rights and interests might be able to obtain earlier judicial review on that basis. The latter argument is known as the **futility doctrine**. For example, if the record demonstrates that the agency has effectively made a decision that precludes a fair hearing for the petitioner, it clearly is futile to further pursue administrative remedies.

Judicial Review on the Merits

The first basis for a review on the merits of an agency action is that agency's enabling statute, which might establish specific criteria or parameters for judicial review. The second basis is found in Section 706 of the *Administrative Procedures Act.* That section states:

> To the extent necessary to decision and when presented, the reviewing court shall decide all relevant questions of law, interpret constitutional and statutory

---

Standing is a party's legal interest (in the outcome of a case) sufficient to require the court to hear and resolve the controversy.

Ripeness is the existence of an actual (as opposed to a prospective or hypothetical) legal controversy ready for determination.

The **exhaustion of remedies** rule requires one to go through all of the administrative procedures that are available, without success, before bringing a matter to the courts.

The **futility doctrine** is the principle that one should not be required to pursue administrative procedures when there is no reasonable expectation that a remedy could be available through such procedures.

provisions, and determine the meaning or applicability of the terms of an agency action. The reviewing court shall—

1. compel agency action unlawfully withheld or unreasonably delayed; and
2. hold unlawful and set aside agency action, findings, and conclusions found to be—
   a. arbitrary, capricious, an abuse of discretion, or otherwise not in accordance with law;
   b. contrary to constitutional right, power, privilege, or immunity;
   c. in excess of statutory jurisdiction, authority, or limitations, or short of statutory right;
   d. without observance of procedure required by law;
   e. unsupported by substantial evidence in a case subject to sections 556 and 557 of this title or otherwise reviewed on the record of an agency hearing provided by statute; or
   f. unwarranted by the facts to the extent that the facts are subject to trial *de novo* by the reviewing court.

In making the foregoing determinations, the court shall review the whole record or those parts of it cited by a party, and due account shall be taken of the rule of prejudicial error.

Section 706, quoted above, does not provide for a *de novo* review by the court—that is, a full hearing conducted as though the case had never been heard in the administrative agency. Instead, it calls for a "review [of] the whole record or those parts of it cited. . . ." But the Supreme Court has said, in **dictum**, that the *de novo* hearing is permitted only if some statute other than the *Administrative Procedures Act*—most likely the enabling statute—authorizes it. *Citizens to Preserve Overton Park, Inc. v. Volpe,* 401 U.S. 402 (1971). Although the *Overton* case was decided on other grounds, the Supreme Court's *dictum* is a helpful instruction on its understanding of law. Very few statutes explicitly authorize hearings *de novo,* so that, in most cases, a court review *de novo* is out of the question. As already mentioned, the *Freedom of Information Act* authorizes *de novo* review by the courts, making it an exception to that general rule.

In considering the bases for reversal in Section 706, the Supreme Court has generally trod a rather narrow path, clearly favoring deference to the administrative agencies. This was illustrated by the Court's opinion in *Chevron USA v. Natural Resources Defense Council, Inc.,* 467 U.S. 837 (1984). In that case, the Court held that any *unambiguous* statutory provision on the policy issue at hand must govern both the agency and the courts. But, if the statute is ambiguous, the courts are to defer to an agency interpretation as long as it is a reasonable one. The Supreme Court recognized that Congress might properly avoid deciding a difficult issue and place its resolution before an agency with expertise in that field of policy.

As a practical matter, few agency actions are struck down by the courts. The power of judicial review does not often overcome the presumption that agencies have acted within their proper discretion. The reality of judicial review of agency decisions is well summarized by Professor William F. Fox, Jr.:

> If an agency record is appallingly incomplete, or if some bad evidence or impermissible ex parte contract [sic] has totally poisoned a case, or if there are points of view not fully considered or drastic changes in agency policy not fully explained, a court might possibly reverse and remand; but as we shall see, the grounds on which agency action might be reversed are so narrow that the party who loses before the agency has precious little hope of prevailing in court. More importantly, . . . the normal disposition of a case in which the courts find a reversible defect is simply to remand to the agency for corrective proceedings.

William F. Fox, Jr., *Understanding Administrative Law (2d ed. 1992),* Matthew Bender, p. 287.

Practice Tip

In the preceding paragraph, a brief quotation from Section 706 includes a word in brackets ("[of]"). The brackets indicate to the reader that the word "of" has been inserted and is not present in the original text being quoted. This was done here because this textbook has quoted the word "review" as though it were a noun. (It is a verb in the statute quoted.) This type of editorial change is made for clarity—in this instance because the textbook did not quote the entire sentence from Section 706 and the brief quotation better fits within the sentence in which it is included if "review" is used as a noun, rather than a verb.

Another situation where brackets might be used is when the writer substitutes a proper name ("[Justice Harlan]") where the original text used "He":

"[Justice Harlan] stated that the case was not ripe for judicial determination."

Without the insertion of Justice Harlan's name in that brief quotation, the reader might wonder who "He" was.

Dictum is a statement about the law which the court did not need to make in order to reach the decision that the court has made. Dictum has no legal authority, because a court is permitted to decide only those legal controversies before it and might not determine the law on other issues.

Practice Tip

In the quotation from Professor Fox (bottom of page 165), "[sic]" has been inserted following the term "ex parte contract." This notation alerts the reader to the fact that the word "contact" was misspelled in the original text being quoted, as "contract." In other words, "sic" means that the error is in the original, not in the quotation. The notation of "sic" is always set within brackets, never within parentheses. An additional use of this notation is explained in a later Practice Tip.

THE ROLE OF LEGAL ASSISTANTS IN ADMINISTRATIVE LAW

As already noted, legal assistants can participate in the practice of administrative law in a variety of ways:

- representing clients before government agencies that permit non-attorneys to assume that role
- reviewing each day's issue of the *Federal Register* and preparing memoranda of items that affect the employer or the law firm's practice
- preparing written materials about a proposed agency rule, or for a hearing on an issue of importance to the law firm or corporate employer
- obtaining public records under the *Freedom of Information Act* and similar state laws.

In addition, administrative adjudication hearings provide an opportunity for legal assistants to support their supervising attorneys' practice in the field of administrative law. This latter role is quite similar to a legal assistant's civil litigation practice, which is described in Chapter 6.

The Paralegal as Advocate in an Executive Agency Proceeding

> Section 555(b) of the *Administrative Procedure Act* states, in part:
>
> A person compelled to appear in person before an agency or representative thereof is entitled to be accompanied, represented, and advised by counsel, or, if permitted by the agency, *by other qualified representative*. A party is entitled to appear in person or by or with counsel or other qualified representative in an agency proceeding . . . This subsection *does not grant or deny a person who is not a lawyer* the right to appear for or represent others before an agency or in an agency proceeding. [Emphasis added.]

The question of qualification is determined by the agency itself. The Internal Revenue Service (IRS), for example, has established qualification standards and procedures for non-attorneys to become "enrolled agents" for the purpose of representing clients on tax matters before the IRS. Approximately half of all representation before the IRS is by enrolled agents or certified public accountants.

Some law firms that specialize in administrative law assign legal assistants to appear on behalf of clients in hearings before agencies that permit non-attorney advocates. Naturally, this is done most often for procedural matters and with less complex cases that require minimal expertise in substantive law. Some experienced paralegals later transition to an independent, unsupervised practice of administrative law before those agencies that permit non-attorneys to do so. In that event, this text would no longer describe them as "paralegals," because they are not working under attorney supervision.

However, the typical paralegal in an administrative law practice will have attorney supervision, and responsibilities and assignments that are similar to those of a litigation paralegal. Many administrative law matters involve more paperwork and routine procedures than substantive issues. In that respect, an administrative law paralegal will assume a more prominent role and perform tasks similar to those practicing in fields such as bankruptcy and probate.

Administrative Adjudication Procedures

Although administrative agency adjudication is somewhat similar to a court proceeding, it also is markedly different. Witnesses will be under oath, but the rules of evidence (which apply in court proceedings) will not be strictly followed. The parties will be allowed to learn something of each other's case prior to the hearing, but not nearly as much as they would in pretrial discovery before a court trial. The hearing officer will be independent of the agency involved, but she is likely to participate much more actively in questioning witnesses and discussing with the parties the contested issues than would a judge in formal court proceedings. This discussion of adjudication procedures is based upon federal administrative law practice.

Initiating an Adjudicatory Hearing

Most adjudicatory hearings are initiated by the agency itself. In any event, the most important first step is to serve (i.e., deliver) a notice of the hearing to all parties involved. Typically, this is a form that the legal assistant will prepare. The party who causes the proceeding to occur has this responsibility. The notice must identify the date, time, and location of the hearing. It must also identify the parties involved, the statute or regulation under which the hearing is being held, and the issues to be determined. The notice may be delivered by messenger to the other parties, or mailed to them by certified mail.

Learning About the Opponent's Case

In civil trials, there is a process known as "pretrial discovery" that allows each party to conduct an exhaustive inquiry into their opponent's case. In administrative hearings, discovery is less free-wheeling and invasive. Parties may obtain a list of the witnesses and exhibits that the opposing party proposes to present. In some situations, a party may have a witness give prehearing testimony under oath (known as a "deposition"). Legal assistants usually prepare the documents that are exchanged prior to a hearing. If a deposition is taken, the legal assistant will probably prepare a summary of that testimony for the attorney's use.

The Administrative Hearing

At the hearing, the hearing officer—usually an administrative law judge (ALJ)—will review any documents that the parties want to introduce and will rule on their admissibility. In this process, the ALJ typically is much more flexible than a judge in a court of law, and questionable documents are often "allowed into evidence" although later "disallowed" (i.e., given little credence) when the judge makes his decision.

In a court of law, the judge often takes a very active role in questioning potential jurors. But, during the presentation of testimony, the same judge often appears to play a more passive role, simply ruling on objections and enforcing courtroom decorum. In an administrative hearing, by contrast, the ALJ tends to take a more active role throughout the proceedings. The ALJ might actively question the witnesses—perhaps even before the attorneys are permitted to do so—and engage in a dialogue with both counsel about the factual and legal issues of the case.

The Administrative Law Judge's Decision

The opposing parties might file posthearing briefs—written summaries of the evidence and arguments about the applicable law. Oral closing arguments are unusual. When the hearing is concluded, the ALJ will "take the matter under consideration"—just as most judges do in a court of law. After reviewing the testimony and other evidence, the ALJ will issue her "initial order," which will become binding if neither party files an objection. If an objection is filed, the ALJ will consider that objection and then issue her final order.

SCENARIO

Margaret Kreider is a paralegal and labor relations representative in the legal department of a large national labor union. When she first started working in labor relations, she was employed by a local union representing supermarket employees. In that job, she gained experience as a lay advocate for the union in grievance arbitration hearings. "It was a real thrill the first time an arbitrator found in favor of our union, even though I was up against an experienced attorney who put on the employer's case," Margaret recalls. "I had to question our own witnesses and also cross-examine [the witnesses called by the employer], too, and I would argue [to the arbitrator] that the facts demonstrated that the employer had violated the collective bargaining contract. It was really challenging! I wasn't working with direct attorney supervision then, but we relied heavily on our outside legal counsel for help in preparing our cases."

Margaret eventually went to work for a union representing state employees. In addition to grievance arbitrations, she eventually began representing the union in hearings before the state's government employee relations board. Under state law, union officials were permitted to appear before the board without legal counsel being present, and Margaret's previous litigation experience as a paralegal made her a natural for the role. "The board would hear the charges of unfair labor practices [i.e., illegal actions under state collective bargaining law] that we brought against the state [as the employer]. But we didn't win many of those, because the governor's appointees on the board were pretty conservative and sympathetic to management."

After ten years in that public employees' union, Margaret was hired to work in the legal department of a national labor union in the private sector. "Now, I really am working as a paralegal under the supervision of our in-house counsel. I still serve as an advocate in arbitration hearings and sometimes go up against attorneys. But in the private sector, the counterpart of the state government employee relations board is the National Labor Relations Board [NLRB], and our union has never used a lay advocate to argue a case before the NLRB—although that agency does permit non-attorneys to do so. Most of the NLRB cases are pretty complex, so I might never have that opportunity. But assisting the attorney in these cases is very much like being a litigation paralegal in a law firm. And I enjoy the feeling that I am on the side of working people—I guess I always empathize with the underdog." ■

A QUESTION OF ETHICS

Martina Monrovia is a former legal assistant who now represents Social Security applicants in hearings before that agency. Prior to going into her own private practice, Martina worked six years for a sole practitioner who specialized in administrative agency law, including appeals from Social Security rulings. After about three years in that firm, Martina began to appear on the less complicated cases that went before an administrative law judge.

Martina has been successful in her private practice and prides herself upon her professionalism. But recently she has been deeply troubled about the practices of a non-attorney colleague who also serves as an advocate in Social Security administrative hearings. Actually, the colleague is a friend and former paralegal whom Martina has known for ten years. The troubling issue is that the friend recently confided to Martina that he confines his role to actual appearances before administrative law judges. He relies upon another former paralegal to interview his clients, research the regulations, and prepare a case summary. Although he always reviews the client's case summary, often he doesn't meet his client until just a few minutes before the hearing.

Martina wonders if her friend is being ethical in his representation of clients. Also, she suspects that her friend's ex-paralegal assistant might be practicing law without a license (i.e., UPL), because she consults, evaluates, and advises clients without actually appearing before the Social Security Administration. Are Martina's concerns well-founded? If so, what should she do about them?

Chapter Summary

- Administrative law comprises executive orders, agency-created regulations, and the body of decisions that interpret and apply that body of law.
- Rule making, enforcement, and adjudication of disputes or violations are the principle functions of administrative law agencies.
- Congress and the state legislatures enact enabling statutes that authorize administrative agencies to make rules and adjudicate disputes.
- Agency-created rules with general application are codified in the *Code of Federal Regulations* and similar state regulatory codes.
- The Administrative Procedures Act establishes the federal procedures for creating administrative regulations and for adjudicating disputes and violations under administrative law.
- Administrative law is made by the president and state governors, by executive branch agencies that they supervise, and by independent regulatory agencies created by statute.
- Independent agencies are not subject to the direct authority of the president or state governor.
- The president and state governors create administrative law by promulgating executive orders that implement their authority under constitutional and statutory law.
- All federal administrative law must be based upon authority delegated by the president or by Congress.
- If an administrative agency has statutory power to issue subpoenas, that power will be construed broadly by the courts.
- The Freedom of Information Act (*FOIA*) makes all federal records, with certain specified exceptions, available to the public.
- The Federal Privacy Act limits the collection of personal information by government agencies and creates a presumption that personal information is not to be disclosed.
- Adjudication hearings are similar to civil court proceedings, except that they are less formal and do not follow strict rules of evidence.
- Persons are entitled to due process when administrative agency actions might deprive them of their property rights.
- With certain exceptions, all deliberative federal bodies must open their meetings to the public.
- Unless exempted by statute, administrative law actions are generally subject to judicial review under the same circumstances as any other governmental action.
- The courts seldom reverse administrative agency actions.

KEY TERMS

adjudication
administrative law judge (ALJ)
affirm
cease and desist order
Code of Federal Regulations (CFR)
de novo
dictum
distinguish
enabling statute
ex parte contact
exhaustion of remedies
Federal Register
Freedom of Information Act (FOIA)
futility doctrine
independent regulatory agency
ministerial act
overrule
public law
regulation
ripeness
separation of powers
standing
subpoena

ACTIVITIES AND ASSIGNMENTS

1. Go to a law library and locate the *Code of Federal Regulations*. Find the title for regulations published by the Social Security Administration. Within that title, locate the provision that allows non-attorneys to represent applicants for benefits. (Note: The provision may not use words such as "lawyer" or "non-attorney.") Photocopy that provision.

2. In a law library, find the regulatory code for the agencies of your state. Find the title that establishes the hearing procedures for state agencies. If there is no such title, look for the hearing procedures in the title for one of these agencies:
   - department of motor vehicles
   - worker compensation agency
   - unemployment insurance/compensation agency

   Find out whether the procedures identify the license or other qualifications required for someone who represents persons appearing in those hearings.

3. In a law library, locate the *Federal Register*. Find a notice of a forthcoming public hearing to be held by a federal agency. Write a brief report on the nature of the hearing, the issue(s) to be considered, and the opportunity for public participation.

4. Go to one of the following agencies, and request a copy of written procedures for appealing a decision by that agency:
   - state department of motor vehicles
   - state unemployment insurance/compensation agency
   - state workers' compensation agency
   - Social Security Administration
   - Internal Revenue Service

5. Attend a meeting of the city council or the governing body of the local school system. Obtain a copy of the agenda, and prepare a report on the actions taken at the meeting. Identify those actions that established policy, those that established rules or regulations, and those that did not have any general effect upon the entire school system.

6. Attend an adjudication hearing in one of the agencies listed in number 4, above. Prepare a written report on the procedures followed, the opportunity for submitting written or oral testimony, and the degree of objectivity demonstrated by the administrative law judge(s).

7. On the Internet, the Web sites for many federal agencies are identified by the acronym for the agency. For example, the Social Security Administration's Web site is found at http://www.ssa.gov. Locate the Web sites for the following federal agencies:
   - Internal Revenue Service
   - Department of Transportation
   - Interstate Commerce Commission

   Find instructions (on the Web site of one of the above agencies) for submitting a request under the Freedom of Information Act.

CHAPTER 6

Civil Litigation and Alternative Dispute Resolution

> We have created here in America the most litigious society in the history of mankind.
>
> *Lewis F. Powell, Jr., Associate Justice, U.S. Supreme Court, 1972–1987*

Civil litigation is the specialty of more than 70% of all paralegals employed in law firms. Others practice in specialties where litigation commonly occurs, even if it is not the primary focus—intellectual property, bankruptcy, and probate quickly come to mind. Many corporate paralegals support litigation activities as a substantial part of their work.

Because the great majority of practicing legal assistants work in civil litigation, all legal assistants should have a general understanding of this practice. The more a legal assistant knows about what goes on during trial—jury selection, admission of evidence, direct examination, cross-examination of witnesses, and instructions given by the judge to jurors—the better prepared that legal assistant will be to support the attorney who will present the client's case in court. For that reason, chapter 6 will present trial procedures as a conceptual framework for the work that litigation paralegals do.

One issue that sometimes troubles new paralegals is the court's exclusion of certain potential evidence that common sense might suggest that a jury should receive. This can be particularly troubling to someone who has actually served on a jury that did *not* hear evidence that it assumed to exist. Working in a real-life litigation case, that paralegal might be instructed to find legal authority for excluding evidence in the client's case. This chapter provides an introduction to some of the reasons that courts do *not* permit jurors to hear all of the potential evidence, all of the time.

Finally, the chapter introduces alternative dispute resolution (ADR) as a quicker, more economical way to settle disputes that otherwise might end up in court.

After reading this chapter, the student should be able to answer the following:

- Is litigation all that the civil courts do?
- Who can bring a lawsuit?

- What remedies can a court provide to a damaged party?
- How do the rules of evidence determine what is heard during trial?
- How does a plaintiff start a lawsuit?
- How does a defendant respond to a lawsuit?
- How do the parties prepare for trial?
- What happens during the trial?
- What is the burden of proof in civil trials?
- How are judgments enforced?
- How do mediation and arbitration resolve disputes more quickly, and at substantially less expense?

SCENARIO

"Say... You're a lawyer...."

Casual acquaintances are enjoying a friendly conversation when one of them suddenly changes the subject: *"Say.... You're a lawyer.... My neighbor's trees are blocking our view, and the jerk refuses to trim 'em. Can I sue him?"*

If there is an attorney anywhere who has never encountered this kind of fishing for free advice, it must be a lawyer who keeps his occupation a deep, dark secret—perhaps one who works for the CIA.

But some attorneys have a ready response for this type of question: *"Sure, you can.... As long as you pay a hundred and eighty bucks and file a complaint."*

SECTION 1. THE NATURE OF CIVIL LITIGATION

The fact is, *anyone* can "sue" any other person *about anything*; they need only to file the complaint and pay the filing fee. The real questions should be: "Will the judge throw the case out of court? And if she doesn't, what are my chances of winning?"

Filing a lawsuit is not difficult, but it is only the first step in litigation. Winning a lawsuit requires many more procedural steps, and it requires that the facts and the law be in the plaintiff's favor. An extraordinary number of the lawsuits filed in this nation are completely useless because they lack any viable basis under the facts or the law, or both. Of course, most of these groundless lawsuits are quickly dismissed by the courts. The courts sometimes term them "frivolous," especially when plaintiffs with a personal grudge against the defendant try to use the court system as a tool of harassment.

Litigation is the process of using the courts to resolve controversies about someone's rights and responsibilities. Litigation is termed "civil" when it is prosecuted under civil law, rather than criminal law. Any person (i.e., individual, corporation, partnership, etc.) may submit to the appropriate court any genuine controversy over that person's legal rights or responsibilities under the law. The government prosecutes civil cases on its own behalf—to enforce its rights or to recover damages when it is harmed—or on behalf of the people when the public is being harmed by someone's wrongful conduct.

WHY PEOPLE SUE

Although there are various types of lawsuits, most of them are brought to court for the following reasons:

- to assert a legal right
- to obtain a remedy for breach of contract
- to obtain a remedy for the harm caused by another person's wrongful act or omission
- to terminate a legal relationship

The first category often involves title to property. In some rural areas, property boundaries are still defined by natural features, such as hilltops, large boulders, or streambeds. If an unusually wet winter causes a stream to change its course, neighboring landowners might get into a dispute over the ownership of the land lying between the original streambed and the new one. Typically, the landowner who appears to have "lost" some land to the stream's shifting course might ask the court to determine new boundaries and thus preserve his ownership of land that now lies on the other side of the streambed. That would be a suit to assert an existing right—his ownership of the land. Except for parental rights regarding children, lawsuits to assert rights are relatively unusual.

Breach of contract is a very common cause of lawsuits, particularly among business enterprises. Economic hard times can cause a business to be overwhelmed with debts and other obligations it had assumed when business was brisk. For example, a company's move to larger quarters might become unexpectedly impractical and financially impossible—in spite of having already broken ground for construction of the new building. Often, there is a dispute over the meaning of contract language—especially when changing circumstances cause a "minor" contract provision to take on unexpected importance. Of course, breach of contract sometimes results from bad faith.

The third cause for lawsuits is someone's "wrongful act" or "wrongful omission." In other words, the plaintiff claims that the defendant either did something wrong—that harmed the plaintiff—or *failed* to do something he *should* have done to prevent harm to the plaintiff. Wrongful acts or omissions that harm others are known as "torts." Torts are the stuff of lawsuits over such things as automobile accidents, injuries on theme park rides, sexual harassment, medical malpractice, assault and battery, and supermarket tabloids that make up lurid stories about movie stars. Chapter 12 (on the Web site for this textbook) is devoted to the law of torts and the issues that arise in their litigation.

Some legal relationships cannot easily be terminated without court approval. The most obvious of these is the marriage relationship. Although most states now permit court-approved marital dissolutions without assigning fault to either marriage partner, a few states still require allegations of misconduct by one spouse against the other—and permit the accused spouse to contest those allegations in court. When business partners cannot agree upon a dissolution of their partnership, it may be necessary to have a court dissolve that partnership and determine each partner's residual rights after the partnership ceases to exist. Occasionally, a juvenile seeks emancipation from his legal status as a minor, and that motion is often opposed by his parent or guardian. The courts, then, must resolve these contested issues. Each of these situations involves litigation of the parties' respective rights and obligations.

COURT PROCEEDINGS OTHER THAN LITIGATION

Litigation occurs when there is a controversy over legal rights or obligations. But people sometimes use the courts when there is no controversy, but the court's approval is required for some action—uncontested adoptions and divorces, for example. People sometimes go to court to change their legal names. (However, some states permit a person to use any name he prefers for any purpose that is neither fraudulent nor criminal.) Some states require court approval for contracts to employ a minor child in specified capacities (e.g., a contract to appear in a commercial film), in order to ensure that the parent or guardian does not neglect the child's best interests. But, unless contested, none of these matters is litigation.

Court approval is needed also to obtain a discharge from one's debts in bankruptcy or to settle an estate in probate. Probate matters involve litigation when someone challenges the validity of a will or the proposed action of an administrator of the estate. Larger bankruptcy cases quite often involve litigation, usually when creditors oppose some action proposed by the bankrupt debtor (including, of course, his discharge from debts), or when other parties must be forced to pay debts owed to the bankruptcy estate.

THE ADVERSARY SYSTEM OF JUSTICE

The opponents in a contested court proceeding are known as the **parties** to the case; in litigation, the usual parties are the plaintiff(s) and the defendant(s)

The **adversary system** of justice relies upon the opposing parties to present all relevant evidence and legal argument so that the court can arrive at a just resolution of their controversy.

The American judicial system is based upon the idea that the opposing **parties** will present all relevant evidence and legal arguments, and the court will then reach a decision based upon that evidence and the law. This method for resolving legal conflicts is called the **adversary system**. The theory is that if opposing advocates present their best evidence and legal arguments, the court will surely hear everything it needs to reach a just decision. This premise is reinforced by the ethical obligation of attorneys, under the candor rule, to inform the court of any law that is unfavorable to their own clients.

Fundamentally, the adversarial process assumes that each opposing party and its attorney will learn of the facts and the law favorable to his or her side, and will present it effectively in court. In practice, relevant evidence and favorable legal authorities sometimes go unheard in court because they are difficult to find, or because the party that would benefit from them is totally unaware that they even exist (e.g., a subsequent will that has been stored in a shoebox). The adversary system does not guarantee perfect justice—only a reasonably fair and effective process to *seek* justice.

STANDING TO SUE

Both the facts and the law must be on the side of a plaintiff if he is to win a lawsuit. The most fundamental question in a lawsuit is the *standing* of the plaintiff. If the plaintiff lacks standing, the suit will be dismissed—that is, thrown out of court. Standing requires a factual and legal basis for the plaintiff to bring a claim against the defendant. The victim of a physical assault has standing, because she is the one who suffered the assault. The victim's spouse, also, might have standing to sue for his damages—loss of companionship, for example—but not for the physical injuries his wife sustained.

If a corporation cheats the federal government by falsifying test results for military pilot-ejection seats, does every taxpayer in the nation have standing to sue? Does the pilot injured by the defective ejection seat have standing? Or, is the federal government itself the only "person" with standing to sue? Clearly, the taxpayers, the pilot, and the government were all damaged by the falsified tests, but "standing" to sue will be determined as a question of law. In this example, the government would have standing, but taxpayers would not—unless they were the individuals who first discovered the fraud and had brought a whistleblower's suit under the federal *False Claims Reform Act*, which authorizes such lawsuits. If the ejection seat met the Defense Department design requirements for that particular product, the injured pilot's suit might be barred by the government contractor defense—a common law immunity for companies that manufacture products to the specifications of the federal government.

THE STATUTE OF LIMITATIONS FOR ASSERTING A CLAIM

Every jurisdiction has a **statute of limitations** that requires a plaintiff to file her lawsuit within a prescribed period of time. A plaintiff who allows that statutory period to expire is generally barred from filing a lawsuit. For example, Ohio requires a lawsuit for fraud to be commenced within four years (*Ohio Revised Code*, Section 2305.09). If a limitation period is not specifically provided for a particular **cause of action**, there usually is a "catchall" statute prescribing a limitation period for miscellaneous causes of action.

There are different limitation periods for various causes of action. Some actions must be filed within one year from the date the potential plaintiff was harmed by another person's negligence or misconduct. Other types of actions must be filed within two, three, or four years, respectively. The statutory limitation periods differ from one state jurisdiction to the next. The limitation period has several purposes. Potential witnesses move, or even die. Memories fade and become less reliable. Various kinds of evidence might be lost, or business records eventually destroyed. Potential defendants—including those who are actually innocent of any misconduct—must live with the anxiety of potential litigation hanging over their heads. The idea is that justice is not well served by indefinite delay.

When does the "clock begin to run" on the statutory limitation period for a particular cause of action? That point in time is set by the statute of limitations. Generally speaking, a cause of action **accrues** at the time a person or his property is harmed, and the statutory limitation period begins to run on that date. Some injuries, however, are not apparent to the victim at the time of the wrongdoer's misconduct. Some states specify that certain causes of action (e.g., fraud, structural defects, or medical malpractice) accrue at the time that the victim actually learned—or *should* have learned—of his injury.

Where the statute of limitations does not "stop the clock" for such hidden injuries, some state courts have held that a strict enforcement of the statutory limitation period would be contrary to public policy, because the purpose of a limitation period is not to conceal injury from the victim. Those courts have adopted the "discovery doctrine" of limitations, under which accrual occurs—and the limitation period begins to run—upon the victim's *discovery* of his injury. However, if his failure to discover the injury results from his own negligent inattention, courts are less likely to apply the discovery doctrine of limitations.

> The **statute of limitations** establishes a maximum time period within which a plaintiff must initiate a lawsuit or lose all rights to sue the defendant under that cause of action.

> The set of facts that create the basis for a viable lawsuit against another person is known as a **cause of action.**

> A cause of action **accrues** when the facts would permit the filing of a viable lawsuit, or other court action, under the laws of that jurisdiction. Accrual establishes the beginning of the statutory limitation period for that cause of action.

Ethics Watch

If the statutory deadline to file a complaint is missed, the client's case is probably lost. If the law firm is at fault, it might be liable for legal malpractice. Depending upon state law, the client might be able to collect from the law firm monetary damages equal to those she would have been entitled to had she won the lawsuit that was not filed within the limitation period.

THE DOCTRINE OF LACHES

In some circumstances, it is not sufficient to initiate a lawsuit within the statutory limitation period. The limitation period is not intended to give license to all sorts of unnecessary delay. Once the injury and most relevant facts are known to the plaintiff, justice is best served by initiating the lawsuit promptly. Procrastination invites the very problems a limitation period is intended to prevent in the first place: missing witnesses or evidence, failing memories, and so forth. Consequently, courts have adopted the doctrine of **laches**.

Under the doctrine of laches, a plaintiff may not initiate litigation if her own unreasonable and unnecessary delay has left the defendant less able to defend himself against the lawsuit. This is most clearly the case when vital witnesses or evidence—which would have been available had litigation been started promptly—are no longer available. The doctrine of laches applies most often when the statutory limitation period is quite long—say, four or six years. It is rarely applied when a plaintiff files on the 364th day under a one-year statute of limitation.

> The doctrine of **laches** bars a plaintiff from unreasonably delaying the filing of a lawsuit if her delay leaves the defendant less able to defend himself.

MONETARY AND EQUITABLE REMEDIES

The person harmed by someone's misconduct or negligence usually seeks **civil damages** (a court judgment for payment of money). There are several types of civil damages. **General damages** are those that are the direct and necessary result of the defendant's unlawful conduct. They include such things as the cost of repairs to damaged property and compensation for disfigurement or loss of a body function (e.g., walking). General damages also include compensation for past and future pain and suffering resulting from the injury.

Special damages are those that actually result from the defendant's conduct, but are not direct or necessary consequences of that conduct: medical expenses, cost of hiring household help, and loss of wages or business profits, for examples.

An unsettled question of damages is the loss of the quality of life that was enjoyed by the plaintiff prior to injury. Although **loss of consortium** (the companionship, affection, sexual relations, loyalty, and care given by a marriage partner) has long been recognized as a ground for damages when the plaintiff's spouse has been killed or seriously injured, most courts have not extended this concept of damages beyond the marital relationship to the loss of a general "quality of life." The frequency of severely disabling injuries (e.g., resulting in quadriplegia) and the success of modern medicine in preserving life, however diminished by disabilities, might lead to a future change in the law of damages.

> **Civil damages** are monetary damages awarded by the court to the injured party.
>
> **General damages** are monetary damages to compensate the victim for the natural and necessary consequences of someone's wrongful act or omission.
>
> **Special damages** are monetary damages that arise from the plaintiff's particular circumstance; they are not the inevitable result of the wrongful act, but result from the circumstance in which the wrongful act occurred.
>
> **Loss of consortium** is the impairment of the benefits of the marital relationship, including affection, companionship, care, and sexual relations.

Equitable Remedies

In addition to monetary damages, trial courts can also provide **equitable remedies**. An equitable remedy is some type of relief other than money damages: for example, injunctions, writs of mandate, orders for specific performance, and declaratory judgments. As explained in Chapter 4, specific performance is a common equitable remedy in contract disputes.

An **injunction** is a court order that prohibits some anticipated or continuing action, or that requires someone to reverse a wrongful action. For example, a city might seek an injunction to prohibit a strike by police officers. A homeowners' association might ask for an injunction against the development of a new airport (or the expansion of an existing one). A **temporary restraining order** (often referred to as a "TRO") is an "emergency injunction" *used to maintain the status quo* until the court can properly review the facts and hear legal arguments

> An **equitable remedy** is any judicial remedy other than monetary damages.
>
> An **injunction** is a court order to stop doing, or refrain from doing, some action that harms another.
>
> A **temporary restraining order** (or **TRO**) is a temporary form of the injunction, intended to maintain the status quo until the court can rule on the merits of the situation.

by the concerned parties. Temporary restraining orders are used to prevent irreparable harm that might result if an injunction were delayed. A homeowner can seek a temporary restraining order to prevent a neighbor from cutting off a tree limb that might crush the petitioner's garage. TROs are commonly used in family law proceedings to prevent the improper disposition of community property or the removal of a child from that state's jurisdiction. After issuing a TRO, the court will soon conduct a full hearing to determine whether the temporary order should become a permanent injunction.

A **writ of *mandamus*** (also known as "writ of mandate") is an order compelling a public official to do her duty under the law. For example, the governor of one state might seek a federal writ of mandate to compel the governor of an asylum state to surrender a fugitive. A citizen might seek such a writ if election officials refused to register him to vote simply because he is blind.

A **declaratory judgment** is a court determination of the legal rights and obligations of the parties to a dispute that the court could properly decide. A unique feature of this remedy is that the court does not award money damages or any other equitable remedy, such as an injunction. Usually, a person seeks a declaratory judgment when he is uncertain of his rights and obligations. The judgment has the advantage of providing guidance so that he does not try to assert presumed rights that he does not actually have under the law, and also does not—through ignorance—invade the lawful rights of others. A declaratory judgment binds the parties involved, and the same issues cannot be litigated again. Most states have adopted the Uniform Declaratory Judgments Act, and Congress has enacted a federal Declaratory Judgment Act for actions brought in federal court.

A **writ of *mandamus*** (or writ of mandate) is a court order commanding a public official to do her duty.

A **declaratory judgment** establishes the legal rights and obligations of the parties to a controversy, without awarding damages or issuing any order.

SECTION 2. THE RULES OF EVIDENCE AND THE SEARCH FOR JUSTICE

Everyone agrees that judges and juries should consider only that evidence that helps them to reach a just conclusion about the facts, under the law that applies to that case—but which evidence *is* that? Some critics argue that the **rules of evidence** cripple the adversary system by excluding information that a jury should consider in the interests of justice. Of course, the very purpose of those rules is to provide the jury with sufficient evidence while excluding evidence that would *prevent* either party from receiving a fair trial. Those twin objectives of the rules of evidence can be very difficult for the court to balance.

The admission of evidence is determined primarily by the test of **relevance**. Relevant evidence tends to prove or disprove a material fact. And a **material fact** is one that can influence the outcome of a case.

Whether a fact is material, or not, depends upon the law. To illustrate: Under the law, in order to convict someone of premeditated murder, a motive must be established. Thus, romantic jealousy—if proved—is a material fact, because it is a plausible motive for murder. An angry letter from the defendant accusing the deceased lover of carrying on another relationship would be relevant evidence to establish that material fact of jealousy. The linchpin of this entire rationale is the law: motive as a required element of murder.

Under the relevancy test, a judge will exclude evidence when the fact it tends to prove or disprove is *not* material—that is, under the law that fact will make no difference in the case. For example, in criminal trials, evidence of prior convictions

The **rules of evidence** are established by statute or the courts to govern the admissibility of evidence, so that all parties will receive a fair hearing.

Evidence is **relevant** when it tends to prove or disprove a material fact.

A **material fact** is one that can influence the outcome of a legal proceeding.

is excluded because it can neither prove nor disprove who committed the most recent crime in question. Of course, if the defendant is finally convicted, many states have a postverdict penalty phase in criminal trials, during which the jury may be told of prior convictions before recommending an appropriate sentence.

In jury trials, the court must balance the relevance of proffered evidence against its possible **prejudicial effect**. Evidence is prejudicial if it is likely to cause the jury to decide an issue—for example, the credibility of a witness, or the guilt or liability of a defendant—on an improper basis. Because jurors are more susceptible to passion, sympathy, and prejudice than are the case-hardened and learned judges—or so the theory goes—some evidence that would be admissible in a **trial by court** (i.e., a trial without a jury) is excluded from a jury trial. Consider the following example.

In a trial for rape, should the jury hear evidence that the defendant possesses a collection of pornography, some of which depicts violence against women? A judge might consider the violent pornography to be relevant to the question of motive (e.g., a possible hostility toward women), yet exclude that evidence for fear that the jury would focus on that inflammatory issue alone and simply conclude that if such a "depraved person" has been charged with rape, "he must be guilty." When the sensibilities and moral values of jurors are greatly offended by one piece of evidence, the court will be concerned that they might lose their ability to evaluate *all* of the evidence in an objective manner.

BALANCING PROBATIVE VALUE AGAINST PREJUDICIAL EFFECT

But relevant evidence is not automatically excluded just because it might be prejudicial. Instead, the court also weighs that prejudicial effect against the **probative value** of the evidence. Evidence has probative value if it establishes a material fact that tends to prove or disprove an issue that is properly before the court. One must remember that the court is in search of the truth, and evidence with probative value contributes to that search. Evidence that is potentially prejudicial might still be so highly probative—that is, so important to the issues of the case—that the jury should consider it. The court must ask itself: Which party is exposed to the greater risk of injustice by the court's ruling—the one party if the evidence is excluded or the other party if the evidence is admitted?

The result of that balancing test, of course, is that juries sometimes see a somewhat "sanitized" body of evidence so that their passions and prejudices will not interfere with their obligation to fairly evaluate all evidence presented, whereas judges will hear all relevant evidence in a trial by court. Defense attorneys sometimes request a trial by jury for the very reason that it offers an opportunity to have excluded some prejudicial, although relevant, evidence. Once again, the conflicting interests of justice must be balanced, one against the other: the constitutional or statutory right to a trial by jury—a jury untainted by prejudice or bias—and the right of the other party to prove its case.

OTHER REASONS FOR EXCLUDING EVIDENCE

Lack of relevancy and potential prejudice are not the only reasons for excluding evidence. Certain types of evidence are excluded from *both* jury trials and trials by court. These exclusions are based upon a variety of grounds, such as privileged communications, hearsay, public policy, or due process rights.

It is commonly known that information given to one's attorney is privileged; usually, neither the client nor his attorney can be compelled to reveal that information. But other communications also are protected by a **privilege of confidentiality**:

Evidence has a **prejudicial effect** when it tends to cloud the jurors' minds with bias or prejudice, so that they cannot dispassionately weigh all of the evidence before them.

In a **trial by court,** there is no jury, and the judge acts as the trier of both fact and law.

Evidence has **probative value** when it establishes a material fact that tends to prove or disprove an issue affecting the outcome of the case.

A **privilege of confidentiality** exists for communications within legally protected relationships, in which society's interest in protecting that relationship outweighs society's interest in obtaining evidence that might be relevant to a particular legal proceeding.

- clergy-penitent communications
- doctor-patient communications
- spousal communications

Generally speaking, the court cannot require these communications to be revealed, or introduced as evidence, unless the client, penitent, patient, or spouse waives that privilege. Of course, these privileges are not absolute. For example, a plaintiff suing for whiplash injuries may not claim a privilege for communications with his doctor about those particular injuries, or prior similar injuries, because he has placed the very nature and cause of his injuries in legal controversy. In some jurisdictions, a psychiatrist or treating psychologist must reveal threats against others made by her patient. And, in some circumstances, a court might order the revelation of an otherwise privileged communication.

Public policy requires the exclusion of certain pretrial discussions between the plaintiff and the defendant. For example, it is common for the parties to attempt to negotiate pretrial settlements so that they can avoid the uncertainty, risk, and expense of going to trial. Defendants—even those innocent of any wrongdoing—often find it in their best interest to substitute a moderate financial settlement for the ordeal and expense of a trial.

But settlement negotiations sometimes break down. In that event, **offers of compromise** made during the unsuccessful settlement negotiations may not be introduced at trial as evidence of an admission of liability. The primary reason is that, otherwise, defendants would be reluctant to negotiate out-of-court settlements. The public policy objective of early compensation for victims, with minimum legal expense, would be frustrated. In addition, settlement negotiations should be encouraged so that the court system is not bogged down in unnecessary litigation. If every dispute went to trial, many persons would be denied justice because of the overtaxed courts and the resultant delays in getting one's "day in court." For these and other reasons, offers of compromise are not admissible.

Evidence of postaccident remedial measures generally is not admissible. For example, if someone falls on a poorly lit staircase, the fact that the landlord later improved the lighting cannot be introduced to show that he could have prevented the accident by making that improvement a month earlier. If evidence of remedial measures were admitted in lawsuits against them, many landlords would be inclined to risk additional accidents rather than improve the lighting. That same rule of evidence applies also to the postaccident measures taken by manufacturers to improve the safety of consumer products. Public policy clearly favors the encouragement of postaccident remedial measures so that other innocent persons can be protected from similar injuries.

An **offer of compromise** is made to settle a dispute, but without admission of fault or liability by the party making the offer.

THE "BEST EVIDENCE" RULE

The **best evidence rule** carries a misleading name. The rule does not apply to all evidence, only to **writings**. A "writing" is data or communication recorded in a paper document, photograph, sound recording, computer disk, or other medium. The best evidence rule requires that the original of some writing—rather than a copy—be presented as evidence of the communication it contains. The rule is intended to prevent fraud and any unintended distortion of the communication.

If the original writing is not available, then a copy might be admitted into evidence. However, it might be necessary to present testimony establishing the reliability of the copy. Modern technology has led to a modification of the rule. The *Federal Rules of Evidence* permit introduction of duplicates produced by a process "which accurately reproduces the original," without establishing that the original is not available (FRE 1001(4)).

The **best evidence rule** requires that a party offer the original writing (rather than some photographic or xerographic copy of the original, for example).

A **writing** is a tangible recording of something, in the form of a document, photograph, tape recording, computer disk, or other medium; a writing might be a latent or digital image if it is retrievable in a form that the physical senses can observe and comprehend.

WHY HEARSAY EVIDENCE IS EXCLUDED

Hearsay evidence is *secondhand knowledge* offered in the form of testimony or a written document *about* an out-of-court statement made by someone else. Although there are a number of exceptions, the general rule is that hearsay evidence may not be admitted (the **hearsay rule**). The essence of hearsay is that the original speaker is not present in court, and yet his out-of-court statement is offered as proof of some fact. Because the original speaker is not present in court, he cannot be cross-examined. Because hearsay evidence is always secondhand knowledge, it might be inaccurately reported in the document or the testimony being offered. Consequently, hearsay evidence is suspect on two grounds: the truth and accuracy of the original out-of-court statement, and the truth and accuracy of the document or testimony presented in court to establish that out-of-court statement. In addition, the opposing party is denied due process, because the original speaker is not subject to **cross-examination** under oath.

In spite of these deficiencies, hearsay evidence is admissible under a number of specific exceptions to the hearsay rule. It is beyond the scope of this textbook to consider all of the exceptions. However, among the more common exceptions are the following:

- admissions by a party to a lawsuit that are inconsistent with her position in litigation
- spontaneous declarations in a moment of excitement
- routine business records

> **Hearsay evidence** is secondhand information offered to establish some oral or written statement that previously was made out of court.
>
> The **hearsay rule** excludes hearsay evidence from admission in legal proceedings.
>
> In a **cross-examination**, a witness called by the other party is questioned to test the accuracy, thoroughness, and credibility of his testimony.

> *Practice Tip*
>
> *A paralegal who enjoys both research and litigation should learn as much as possible about the rules of evidence, because a significant portion of litigation research concerns those rules and their application to particular cases.*

SECTION 3. PRETRIAL PROCEDURES

The preceding two sections have established the legal principles and framework within which civil litigation occurs. Sections 3 through 6 will describe the civil litigation process and the legal assistant's role in civil litigation. The litigation procedures described here will differ somewhat from those followed in some jurisdictions. As mentioned at the beginning of this chapter, civil litigation is a significant part of their practice for the great majority of legal assistants. Especially for new legal assistants, the pretrial phase of litigation provides an opportunity for making a major contribution to the work of the litigation team.

THE PLAINTIFF INITIATES THE LAWSUIT

A lawsuit begins when the **complaint** is filed with a court of proper jurisdiction. The complaint sets forth the factual basis and legal theories for the lawsuit. The facts are presented as **allegations** (i.e., as statements of fact that are yet to be proved true). In a breach of contract action, for example, the complaint would allege the following:

- A contract was entered into.
- The plaintiff and defendant are parties to the contract.
- The defendant has a duty under the terms of the contract.
- The plaintiff has fulfilled all of her duties under the contract.

> A **complaint** is the legal document that begins a lawsuit, stating the allegations (to be proved at trial) that establish a cause of action and the court's jurisdiction and asking the court to grant an equitable or monetary remedy.
>
> An **allegation** is a statement claiming that something is true. However, the allegation must be proved in court to establish personal jurisdiction, a valid cause of action, or an affirmative defense.

- The defendant has breached a material (i.e., substantial) duty under the contract.
- The plaintiff has been damaged by the defendant's breach of the contract.

Those are the allegations necessary to establish a cause of action for breach of contract. The complaint alleges all of the known relevant claims so that the court will have a "picture" of the case and can recognize the legal issues involved. The complaint must also state (as allegations) the facts that would establish the court's personal jurisdiction over the defendant. But the complaint proves nothing. It is not evidence—only allegations that set the stage for the lawsuit. In *Figure 6.1*, jurisdiction is supported by the allegations in paragraphs 1 through 4.

Service of Process

There is an additional step that must be completed before the case can go forward. The defendant has a right to know that he is being sued and on what grounds, because no one can defend themselves against a secret lawsuit. Giving formal **notice** to the defendant that he is being sued is absolutely essential.

Notice to the defendant is accomplished by delivering a **summons** and a copy of the complaint to each defendant named in the complaint. The court clerk will "issue" a summons after the complaint has been filed. The summons sets forth the names of the plaintiff(s) and the defendant(s), identifies the court where the complaint has been filed, and sets a deadline for the defendant to respond to the suit. In some states, a paralegal in the office of the plaintiff's attorney usually prepares the summons form, and the court clerk validates it by signature or rubber stamp. Delivery of the summons or other court documents (such as a writ or a notice of hearing) to a party in the lawsuit is known as "service of process." The rules regarding service of process are quite strict—especially regarding service of the summons and complaint, because that is the first official notice to the defendant that she is being sued. Once the defendant has responded to the lawsuit, the rules of service are generally less restrictive—for example, allowing either party to serve the other (or her attorney) by mail.

It is the responsibility of the plaintiff's attorney to ensure that the summons and complaint are served on each defendant, although the sheriff or marshal might perform the actual service in some jurisdictions. Many jurisdictions permit any adult who is not a party to the lawsuit to perform service of process. In those jurisdictions, an **attorney service** is often used to serve legal papers and file documents with the court.

In some states, the summons must be delivered by personal service to the defendant. The statutes and court rules of each jurisdiction determine what method constitutes "personal service." The most strict standard is hand delivery to the defendant in person. In some states, however, hand delivery to the defendant's apparent agent—for example, the defendant's spouse or personal secretary—is adequate. In other jurisdictions, the summons may be served by registered mail addressed to the defendant's last known address.

THE DEFENDANT RESPONDS

After being served with a lawsuit, the defendant has three choices:

1. to ignore the lawsuit
2. to file an answer with the court
3. to file a demurrer or a motion to dismiss the lawsuit

Practice Tip

New paralegals usually do not have the immediate opportunity to draft complaints and other court pleadings; their writing skills are usually first tested with correspondence or discovery requests and responses. Because pleadings involve legal issues, a paralegal might have to demonstrate strong research skills before he will be given the chance to draft a complaint. Once the paralegal has demonstrated those skills, an attorney will be more confident in asking the paralegal to draft pleadings.

Notice is information or knowledge that would cause a prudent person to make inquiry or take further action to protect his interests; in litigation, "giving notice" is performed by serving legal papers to the person receiving notice.

A **summons** is an order commanding a defendant to appear and answer the complaint in a lawsuit.

An **attorney service** is a company that specializes in delivery and messenger services for law firms. Law firms retain the attorney service to deliver and file documents with courts and county recorder offices, and as a messenger service. Where the law permits, the company serves legal notices on defendants and other persons, and certifies that the service of process has been properly completed.

Practice Tip

When a complaint or other document is filed with the court clerk, it is customary to send along an extra copy. The clerk will date-stamp the extra copy to indicate when the original was filed with the court. This "conformed" copy is then returned to the law firm, where it becomes part of the case file and also serves as a type of "receipt" for the filing.

Practice Tip

A common task for legal assistants is to create a "service list" for everyone who must be served with legal documents in a pending case. The service list provides the name and address at which service will be made, either in person or by mail. For all parties represented by legal counsel, it is the attorney who will be served. In addition to this list for "official" service, the law firm might maintain a second list for informal service by facsimile or e-mail. It is likely that many jurisdictions will soon permit formal service by the latter methods, as well.

FIGURE 6.1   Sample Complaint

Sure, Swift & Profit
Attorneys at Law
701 Nutmeg Street
San Diego, California 92104
(619) 221-3400

IN THE UNITED STATES DISTRICT COURT
FOR THE SOUTHERN DISTRICT OF CALIFORNIA

GEORGE ABLE, an individual,)) Plaintiff,)) v.)) CYBERMAXIM COMPANY, a Delaware) corporation,)) Defendant.) _____)	Civil Action No. 99-76542

COMPLAINT FOR BREACH OF CONTRACT

1. Plaintiff George Able ("Plaintiff") is a citizen of the State of California.
2. Defendant Cybermaxim Company ("Defendant") is a corporation organized under the laws of the State of Delaware.
3. Defendant maintains its corporate headquarters in Wilmington, Delaware. Plaintiff is informed and believes, and based upon such information and belief alleges that at all times mentioned herein Defendant was authorized to conduct business in the State of California, and maintained its principal business office in California at 12014 Trade Center Drive, Suite 1244, San Diego, California.
4. The matter in controversy herein exceeds the sum of Seventy-Five Thousand Dollars ($75,000.00).
5. On or about January 4, 1997, Plaintiff and Defendant entered into a written contract, whereby Defendant designated Plaintiff to be its sole and exclusive agent for the marketing and sale of Cybermaxim computer software within the State of California (the "Contract"). A true and correct copy of the Contract appears as Exhibit "A" to this Complaint and is incorporated herein by reference.
6. Paragraph 2 of the Contract provides that the agency created by the Contract shall continue until January 4, 2002.
7. The Contract was made, entered into and to be performed within the State of California. Paragraph 17 of the Contract provides that it shall be interpreted under and governed by the laws of the State of California.
8. Plaintiff is informed and believes, and based upon such information and belief alleges that on or about September 1, 1998, Defendant entered into a contract with WebNet Marketing Corporation, a California corporation ("WebNet"), to market and sell Cybermaxim computer software in WebNet Computer Marts located in various cities of California ("WebNet Mart"). Plaintiff is informed and believes, and based upon such information and belief alleges that, in or about October 1, 1998, and continuing through December 31, 1998, WebNet sold Cybermaxim computer software at various WebNet Mart locations in California.
9. Under the terms of the Contract, Defendant had a duty to honor, preserve and protect Plaintiff's exclusive agency to market and sell Cybermaxim computer software in California, and to refrain from authorizing any other person to market or sell Cybermaxim computer software in California.
10. By entering into an agreement with WebNet for the marketing and sale by WebNet of Cybermaxim computer software at WebNet Mart locations in California, Defendant has breached Defendant's obligations under the Contract.
11. Plaintiff has duly performed all terms and conditions of the Contract to be performed on his part, excepting only those terms and conditions which have been excused by reason of Defendant's breach as herein alleged.
12. As a direct and proximate result of Defendant's breach of the Contract, Plaintiff has been damaged in an amount to be proved at trial, said amount exceeding Fifty Thousand Dollars ($50,000.00), exclusive of interest and costs.
13. By reason of Defendant's breach, Plaintiff has been required to retain the law firm of Swift, Sure & Profit to commence and prosecute this action, and Plaintiff is entitled to recover from Defendant his attorneys' fees and costs of suit incurred herein.

WHEREFORE, Plaintiff prays for judgment against Defendant as follows:
1. Compensatory damages in an amount to be proved at trial;
2. For cost of suit incurred herein;
3. For attorneys' fees; and,
4. For such other and further relief as the Court may deem just and proper.

Dated: January 2, 1999   SWIFT, SURE & PROFIT

                                          _____
                                          Susan Sure, Attorneys for Plaintiff
                                          George Able

The first choice can be disastrous, no matter what the merits of the case might be. If the defendant does not file a response to the lawsuit—or fails to respond within the period allowed by statute—the plaintiff can obtain a **default judgment**, which means that the plaintiff has won the case because of the defendant's failure to respond. Defendants should ignore a lawsuit *only* if an attorney advises that they have no chance of defeating the complaint and should not waste money trying to raise a defense. (A second legal opinion might well be advised.) Even in those circumstances, a negotiated settlement is often preferable to accepting a default judgment. Because the plaintiff cannot be certain that the defendant will not go to trial, the defendant can file an answer and then try to negotiate a compromise that is far preferable to accepting a default.

A default judgment may be set aside for **good cause**, but it might be exceedingly difficult to convince a court to do so. The strongest ground for setting aside a default is evidence showing that the plaintiff did not properly serve the summons and complaint—in other words, the defendant was not legally informed of the lawsuit and was, therefore, denied the opportunity to respond.

In response to a complaint, most defendants file an **answer**. The answer usually denies all allegations in the complaint. A **general denial** of "each and every allegation" in the complaint is a legally sufficient answer, and forces the plaintiff to prove at trial each and every allegation necessary to sustain his cause(s) of action. Often, the answer also raises one or more affirmative defenses. An **affirmative defense** is an allegation by the defendant of some fact or legal principle that insulates the defendant against allegations in the complaint. In a breach of contract action, for example, a common affirmative defense is that the *plaintiff* was the first to breach the contract, thereby relieving the defendant of any further duties under the contract. Affirmative defenses are not required in every answer, but the failure to raise an affirmative defense might constitute a permanent waiver of that defense.

Failure to Allege a Valid Cause of Action

The third alternative for the defendant is to file a **demurrer**, or a **motion to dismiss**. The demurrer (or motion to dismiss) states, in effect: *"Even if every single allegation in the complaint is true, the complaint still fails to state any valid cause of action."* For example, suppose a complaint was filed in which the only misconduct alleged was, "You don't love me anymore." The demurrer would say, in effect: "Even if that's true, so what? I have no legal duty to love you." Although absurd, this example illustrates our point. In addition, it is no more outlandish than some complaints that are occasionally filed in the courts! The demurrer is not an admission that the allegations are true—it is simply saying, *"So what?"* If the court **sustains** the demurrer **with prejudice**, the case is dead, because the plaintiff is not allowed to rework his complaint.

But when the courts do sustain a demurrer, they usually do so **without prejudice**, which permits the plaintiff to revise the complaint so that it does state a valid cause of action. In the example above, the plaintiff might add these allegations:

- You promised to marry me if I would support you while you were in medical school.
- I did support you all through medical school.
- You have successfully completed medical school.
- You have refused to marry me, despite your promise.

Depending upon the law of that jurisdiction, the amended complaint might now state a valid cause of action, because promises to marry might be enforceable

---

A **default judgment** is one entered in favor of the plaintiff, because of the defendant's failure to respond to the lawsuit.

A legally sufficient reason for excusing a failure to comply with a procedure or timeline established by statute or court rule is known as **good cause.**

The **answer** is the defendant's pleading that responds to the plaintiff's complaint.

A **general denial** is the defendant's denial of "each and every" allegation in the complaint.

An **affirmative defense** is a legal defense that would overcome allegations by the plaintiff, even if those allegations were true.

A **demurrer** is a pleading in which the defendant claims that the plaintiff has failed to state a valid cause of action, even if all allegations in the complaint were true.

A **motion to dismiss** is a request (usually by the defendant) that the court finally dispose of a controversy without a trial on the merits, or entry of any judgment.

To **sustain** is to approve and uphold.

To dismiss a matter **with prejudice** is to deny any right or opportunity to amend or revive the matter dismissed; to sustain a demurrer with prejudice is to deny the plaintiff any further opportunity to amend or revive the complaint.

To dismiss **without prejudice** is to allow the matter dismissed to be amended and/or revived; to sustain a demurrer without prejudice is to allow the plaintiff to amend and refile the complaint.

FIGURE 6.2 Sample Answer

Adamson, Teshima, Álvarez & Gaum
Attorneys at Law
1723 Embarcadero Boulevard, Suite 1200
San Diego, California 92104

IN THE UNITED STATES DISTRICT COURT
FOR THE SOUTHERN DISTRICT OF CALIFORNIA

GEORGE ABLE, an individual,
 	
                               Plaintiff,
 	
                      v.
 	
CYBERMAXIM COMPANY, a Delaware
    Corporation,
 	
                               Defendant.
	Civil Action No. 99-76542

**ANSWER OF CYBERMAXIM COMPANY TO COMPLAINT FOR
BREACH OF CONTRACT**

    Defendant, Cybermaxim Company, by its attorney, answers the Complaint filed by Plaintiff, George Able, as follows:

1. Defendant admits the allegations in Paragraphs 1, 2 and 3 of the Complaint.
2. Defendant has no information or belief as to Plaintiff's alleged damages. Based on said lack of information or belief, Defendant denies the allegations in Paragraph 4 of the Complaint.
3. Defendant admits that Plaintiff and Defendant entered into the written contract appearing as Exhibit "A" to the Complaint in this action (the "Contract"). Defendant denies that Plaintiff was granted, by the Contract or otherwise, a sole and exclusive agency for marketing and selling Cybermaxim software in California.
4. Defendant admits the allegation(s) in Paragraph 6.
5. Defendant admits the allegation(s) in Paragraph 7.
6. Defendant denies that it has, by entering into a contract with WebNet Marketing Corporation, breached the Contract. Defendant further denies that it has breached the Contract by any other act or omission of Defendant.
7. Defendant denies that Plaintiff has performed all terms and obligations of the Contract.
8. Defendant denies that Plaintiff has been damaged by any act or omission of Defendant.
9. Defendant denies that any act or omission of Defendant has required Plaintiff to retain legal counsel or prosecute the within lawsuit. Defendant further denies that Plaintiff is entitled to recover from Defendant any attorneys' fees or costs of suit.

FIRST AFFIRMATIVE DEFENSE

Plaintiff has failed to use his best efforts to market and sell Cybermaxim computer software, as required by Paragraph 4 of the Contract. By Plaintiff's acts and omissions, Plaintiff has breached the Contract.

SECOND AFFIRMATIVE DEFENSE

Although Defendant denies that it agreed to designate Plaintiff its sole and exclusive agent for marketing and selling Cybermaxim computer software in California, if there is a contestable issue, Defendant alleges that Plaintiff's agency was lawfully and justifiably terminated due to his inability and failure to perform his obligations under the alleged agency.

THIRD AFFIRMATIVE DEFENSE

Plaintiff has failed to mitigate his damages, if any.

WHEREFORE, Defendant prays for judgment against Plaintiff as follows:
1. That Plaintiff receive and take nothing by way of his complaint;
2. For attorneys' fees; and
3. For such other and further relief as the Court may deem just and proper.

Dated: January 15, 1999   ADAMS, TESHIMA, ÁLVAREZ & GAUM

                                                              Anthony Westrom, Attorneys for
                                                               Cybermaxim Company

FIGURE 6.3 Sample Motion to Dismiss

Adamson, Teshima, Álvarez & Gaum
Attorneys at Law
1723 Embarcadero Boulevard, Suite 1200
San Diego, California 92401

IN THE UNITED STATES DISTRICT COURT
FOR THE SOUTHERN DISTRICT OF CALIFORNIA

GEORGE ABLE, an individual,	)	
Plaintiff,	)	Civil Action No. 99-76542
v.	)	
CYBERMAXIM COMPANY, a Delaware Corporation,	)	
Defendant.	)	

DEFENDANT CYBERMAXIM COMPANY'S MOTION TO DISMISS THE COMPLAINT

Defendant Cybermaxim Company ("Defendant") hereby moves the Court to dismiss Plaintiff George Able's Complaint herein, and states:
1. That the Complaint fails to state a cause of action against Defendant.
2. That the amount in controversy is less than Seventy-Five Thousand Dollars ($75,000.00).
3. That there are no facts to show that Defendant granted a sole and exclusive agency to Plaintiff to market and sell Cybermaxim computer software in California.

WHEREFORE, for lack of a sufficient Complaint, Defendant prays judgment that the Complaint of the plaintiff be dismissed.

Date: January 24, 1999   ADAMS, TESHIMA, ÁLVAREZ & GAUM

Anthony Westrom, Attorneys for Defendant
Cybermaxim Company

---

under some circumstances. Because courts usually allow plaintiffs to revise their defective complaints, many attorneys do not bother with the time and expense of filing a demurrer. Occasionally, however, demurrers are used because they put the case on a temporary "hold" while the plaintiff revises the complaint; meanwhile, the defense has some additional time to prepare the answer.

In some jurisdictions, including all federal trial courts, a motion to dismiss is used in lieu of the demurrer. The motion to dismiss might be based on a number of grounds: failure to state a valid cause of action, improper service of the complaint and summons, expiration of the statute of limitations, lack of jurisdiction, and so forth. In the example above, it would be a "motion to dismiss for failure to state a cause of action" (or, "failure to state a claim"). *Figure 6.3* provides an example of a motion to dismiss for failure to state a cause of action.

MOTIONS FOR JUDGMENT ON THE PLEADINGS

After the complaint and answer are on file, either party might file a motion for **judgment on the pleadings**. When granted by the court, this judgment is based upon the documents filed with the court: the complaint, the answer, the motion for judgment on the pleadings, and the written opposition to that motion. However, two types of evidence might be found in the written documents. Exhibits (e.g., copies of contracts) might be attached to any of the documents already mentioned, as can be **declarations** or sworn **affidavits** by anyone having personal knowledge of relevant facts. A declaration—unsworn, but signed under penalty of perjury—typically is a factual narrative. An affidavit is similar, but the

---

A **judgment on the pleadings** is a finding by the court that no controversy of material fact exists and that one party is entitled to prevail as a matter of law.

A **declaration** is a written statement that includes an affirmation that it is made under penalty of perjury.

A sworn **affidavit** is a written statement made under oath before a person authorized to administer such an oath.

author takes an oral oath that it is a true statement. Although no oral testimony is heard, the court usually permits oral arguments on the law.

Motions for judgment on the pleadings are granted only when there are no questions of fact to be decided—that is, when the plaintiff and the defendant do not dispute the material facts of the case. The only issues before the court must be questions of law. When one party files a motion for judgment on the pleadings, the other party usually argues that some questions of material fact do remain to be determined at trial and that the motion should not be granted. Courts do not often grant contested motions for judgment. Sometimes, however, the plaintiff and defendant agree to **stipulate** to all relevant facts and then jointly submit the case to the court for judgment on the legal issues.

> To **stipulate** is to mutually agree upon some factual or legal issue; stipulations may be in writing or orally acknowledged before the court.

The steps in the early stages of litigation appear in *Figure 6.4*. As already explained, everything starts with the filing of a complaint. The defendant then determines the next step: He can file an answer (the most common decision), or he can file a demurrer or motion to dismiss which attacks the very basis of the lawsuit. For that reason, the diagram provides alternative paths. For example, if the court denies a demurrer, the defendant will file an answer—which he could have done at the beginning. A similar choice awaits both parties after the answer has been filed. Usually, the case continues without either party filing a motion for judgment on the pleadings.

DISCOVERY AND PREPARATION FOR TRIAL

Once an answer has been filed and no judgment on the pleadings has been requested, the case now enters the stage where both parties prepare for trial. A vitally important phase of trial preparation is called **discovery**. Under the right of discovery, each party has a legal right to obtain information from the other side about his case, including evidence in his possession, factual and legal contentions he intends to put forward at trial, the identity of persons possessing certain information or evidence, and so forth. This right of discovery is given by statute or court rules in the interests of both justice and the efficiency of the courts.

> **Discovery** is the pretrial process during which litigating parties obtain information and documents from each other.

The theory behind discovery is that justice is seldom best served by courtroom surprises. Discovery also allows the parties to prepare their cases more

FIGURE 6.4 Litigation—from Complaint to Judgment on the Pleadings

```
                        Plaintiff files Complaint
                           /            \
                  Defendant files Demurrer
                    (motion to dismiss)
                    /            \
        Demurrer sustained    Demurrer denied
            by court             by court
                |                   \
          Case closed                \
                                      Defendant files Answer
                                      /
                        Defendant or Plaintiff files
                        Motion for Judgment on the Pleadings
                           /                \
            Judgment on the Pleadings    Judgment on the Pleadings
              granted by court              denied by court
                    |                             \
               Case Closed                         \
                                                Case Continues
```

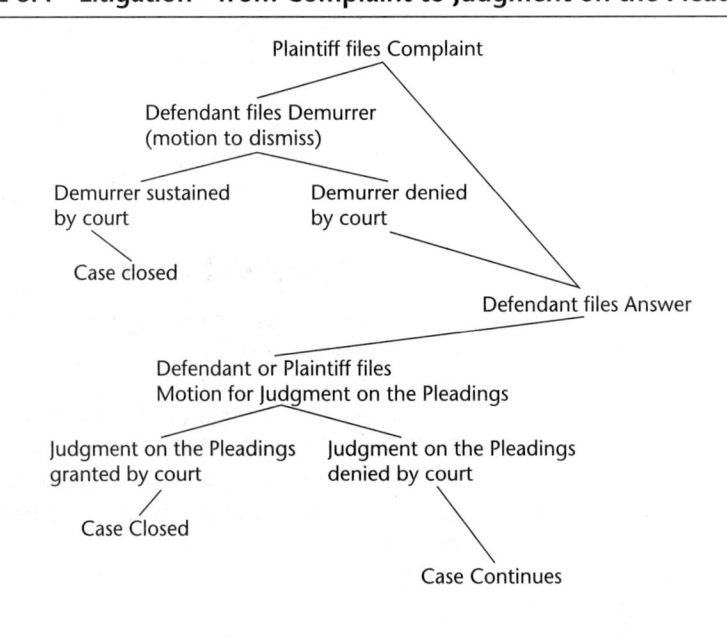

thoroughly, which means that they can present them more efficiently in court. Discovery not only shortens the length of trials, it often leads to out-of-court settlements when both parties have learned the true strengths and weaknesses of their respective cases. Discovery is intended also to prevent a guilty party from concealing "smoking gun" evidence.

In the following "Case in Point," an internal Ford Motor Company memorandum—obtained by the plaintiffs during pretrial discovery—became a proverbial "smoking gun" piece of evidence. The memorandum, which became Exhibit No. 125 at trial, provided vital corroboration for the testimony of a former Ford executive. That former executive testified about Ford's decision to forgo relatively inexpensive "fixes" for an automobile design that it already knew to be vulnerable to gas tank failure in a rear-end collision. Excerpts from the court's lengthy 41-page decision are quoted here *verbatim*. Information enclosed in brackets is taken from other portions of the court's own opinion—portions that have not been reprinted here—and have been inserted to clarify the court's discussion of the evidence.

> **Practice Tip**
>
> *More than any other single task, litigation paralegals prepare discovery requests and responses. They draft the interrogatories, requests for admission, and requests for production—which are explained below—and they respond to those discovery requests by the opposing party. At times, the discovery process appears to be almost clerical, but it often requires the use of sound judgment. This is particularly true in responding to discovery, because one often must analyze the client's file to determine what is truly responsive, what is protected by attorney-client privilege, and what is really irrelevant.*

A CASE IN POINT

Grimshaw v. Ford Motor Company

California Court of Appeal

119 Cal.App.3d 757, 174 Cal.Rptr. 348 (1981)

* * * *

A 1972 Ford Pinto hatchback automobile unexpectedly stalled on a freeway, erupting into flames when it was rear ended by a [Ford Galaxie] proceeding [28 to 37 MPH] in the same direction. Mrs. Lilly Gray, the driver of the Pinto, suffered fatal burns and 13-year old Richard Grimshaw, a passenger in the Pinto, suffered severe and permanently disfiguring burns on his face and entire body.

* * * *

It was later established that [a carburetor malfunction caused] the engine to flood and stall.

* * * *

Ordinarily marketing surveys and preliminary engineering studies precede the styling of a new automobile line. Pinto, however, was a rush project, so that styling preceded engineering and dictated engineering design to a greater degree than usual. Among the engineering decisions dictated by styling was the placement of the fuel tank. . . . The Pinto's styling . . . required the tank to be placed behind the rear axle leaving only 9 or 10 inches of "crush space"—far less than in any other American automobile or Ford overseas subcompact . . . [T]he Pinto was designed so that its bumper was little more than a chrome strip, less substantial than the bumper of any other American car produced then or later. The Pinto's rear structure also lacked reinforcing members . . . [which] rendered the Pinto less crush resistant than other vehicles. Finally, the differential housing . . . had an exposed flange and a line of exposed bolt heads . . . sufficient to puncture a gas tank driven forward against the differential upon rear impact.

* * * *

During the development of the Pinto, prototypes were built and tested. . . . These prototypes as well as two production Pintos were crash tested by Ford to determine, among other things, the integrity of the fuel system in rear-end accidents.

* * * *

The crash tests revealed that the Pinto's fuel system as designed could not meet the 20-mile-per-hour . . . standard [proposed by the federal government].

* * * *

Tests conducted by Ford on other vehicles, including modified or reinforced mechanical Pinto prototypes, proved safe at speeds at which the Pinto failed.

* * * *

When a prototype failed the fuel system integrity test, the standard of care for engineers in the industry was to redesign and retest it. The vulnerability of the production Pinto's fuel tank at speeds of 20 and 30-miles-per-hour [in] fixed barrier tests could have been remedied by inexpensive "fixes," but Ford produced and sold the Pinto to the public without doing anything to remedy the defects.

* * * *

Equipping the car with a reinforced rear structure, smooth axle, improved bumper and additional crush space at a total cost of $15.30 [per vehicle] would have made the fuel tank safe in a 34 to 38-mile-per-hour rear-end collision by a vehicle the size of the Ford Galaxie. If, in addition to the foregoing, a bladder or tank within a tank [at an additional cost of $8.00] were used or if the tank were protected with a shield [at a cost of $4.00], it would have been safe in a 40 to 45-mile-per-hour rear impact. If the tank had been located over the rear axle [at a cost of $9.95], it would have been safe in a rear impact at 50 miles per hour or more.

* * * *

Harley Copp, a former Ford engineer and executive in charge of the crash testing program, testified that the highest level of Ford's management made the decision to go forward with the production of the Pinto, knowing that the gas tank was vulnerable to puncture and rupture at low rear impact speeds creating a significant risk of death or injury from fire and knowing that "fixes" were feasible at nominal cost. He testified that management's decision was based on the cost savings which would inure from omitting or delaying the "fixes."

* * * *

Mr. Copp's testimony concerning management's awareness of the crash tests results and the vulnerability of the Pinto fuel system was corroborated by . . . a report (Exhibit 125) prepared by Ford engineers pertaining to the financial impact of a proposed federal standard on fuel system integrity and the cost savings which would accrue from deferring even minimal "fixes." [Footnote omitted.]

* * * *

Exhibit No. 125 was a report presented at a Ford production review meeting in April 1971. . . . The report recommended, *inter alia,* deferral from 1974 to 1976 of the adoption of "flak suits" or "bladders" in all Ford cars, including the Pinto, in order to realize a savings of $20.9 million. The report stated that the cost of the flak suit or bladder would be $4 to $8 per car. The meeting at which the report was presented was chaired by Vice President Harold MacDonald and attended by Vice President Robert Alexander and occurred sometime before the 1972 Pinto was placed on the market.

* * * *

Punitive damages (also known as "exemplary damages") are awarded to punish the defendant for outrageous conduct and to deter others from similar conduct.

The jury awarded plaintiff Grimshaw $2.5 million in compensatory damages, and $125 million in **punitive damages** against Ford Motor Company. The trial court reduced the punitive damage award to $3.5 million. The heirs of Mrs. Gray were awarded $559,680 in compensatory damages against Ford. The court of appeal affirmed the trial court's judgment.

Why Litigants Do Not Destroy Damaging Evidence

One might wonder why Ford Motor Company did not simply shred all copies of the "smoking gun" report (Exhibit No. 125) that played such a significant role in the *Grimshaw* case. First of all, it would have been unethical and illegal for Ford Motor Company to do so. In fact, under some circumstances, it is a criminal offense to destroy potential evidence in civil litigation. In addition, there are *practical* reasons that make it extremely risky to attempt a surreptitious destruction of evidence:

- In most companies, there are multiple copies of any given document.
- Most companies do not have accurate records of all authorized copies.
- There is no way to be sure that unauthorized copies do not exist.
- There is no way to be sure that copies (authorized or not) have not found their way into the hands of the company's business partners, consultants, or attorneys.
- An ethical (or simply disgruntled) employee might decide to "blow the whistle" if she knows that evidence is being destroyed.
- Courtroom revelations that evidence has been destroyed can compound many times over the legal and financial damage that the destroyed evidence itself would have caused.

Therefore, for ethical, legal, and practical reasons, attorneys tell their clients *never* to destroy any potential evidence. And major corporations have recognized the wisdom of that advice. In the late 1990s, thousands of damaging documents were surrendered by tobacco companies in litigation brought against them by various state governments. Those surrendered documents were instrumental in the companies' decisions to settle—for the first time ever—lawsuits charging that cigarettes are a serious health hazard.

Tools of the Discovery Process

Most discovery between the parties is accomplished using interrogatories, requests for admissions, requests for production of documents, and the taking of depositions—each of which is explained below. Less frequently, parties request scientific analysis of some piece of evidence, physical inspection of some location (e.g., a factory), or medical examination of the plaintiff. But the four methods first mentioned are the most common, by far.

Any information or document clearly identified and requested in discovery that is not provided by the responding party may not later be used by that nonresponsive party during trial. For example, if copies of specified contracts are requested by the plaintiff, but are not produced by the defendant, the court can prohibit that defendant from later introducing as evidence any contract "inadvertently omitted" in his response to discovery. Exclusion of evidence is a common sanction for failure to respond fully to the discovery request, but the court may impose more severe sanctions if warranted. If the *requesting party* somehow obtains a copy of that same contract by other lawful means, however, he would *not* be barred from introducing it at trial, because he did not violate any duty under the rules of discovery. Of course, the rules of discovery apply equally to plaintiff and defendant, regardless of which is the requesting or responding party in discovery.

Interrogatories

Interrogatories are written questions that the other party must answer in writing and under oath. Of course, the questions must be sufficiently specific and

Interrogatories are written questions delivered to another party in a lawsuit, and to which that party must respond in writing and under oath.

FIGURE 6.5 Sample Interrogatories

Adamson, Teshima, Álvarez & Gaum
Attorneys at Law
1723 Embarcadero Boulevard, Suite 1200
San Diego, California 92401

IN THE UNITED STATES DISTRICT COURT
FOR THE SOUTHERN DISTRICT OF CALIFORNIA

GEORGE ABLE, an individual,	)	
	)	
Plaintiff,	)	Civil Action No. 99-76542
	)	
v.	)	
	)	
CYBERMAXIM COMPANY, a Delaware Corporation,	)	
	)	
Defendant.	)	

**DEFENDANT CYBERMAXIM COMPANY'S INTERROGATORIES
TO PLAINTIFF GEORGE ABLE**

The plaintiff, GEORGE ABLE ("Plaintiff"), and his attorney of record are requested to answer the following interrogatories separately and fully, in writing and under oath, pursuant to *Federal Rules of Civil Procedure* 33(a). It is requested that the answers be signed under oath by the party making such answers and that they be served upon the defendant, Cybermaxim Company ("Defendant"), within thirty (30) days of the service of these interrogatories.

In answering these interrogatories, please furnish all information which is available to you, including information in the possession of Plaintiff's attorneys, investigators, employees, representatives and designated expert witnesses.

1. State the basis of Plaintiff's contention that Cybermaxim Company granted to Plaintiff a sole and exclusive agency to market and sell Cybermaxim computer software in California.
2. State the basis of Plaintiff's contention that Plaintiff has fully performed all terms and conditions of the contract identified as Exhibit "A" to the Complaint in this action.
3. State the full name and last known address of every person known to Plaintiff to have seen or heard the Plaintiff make any statement or statements regarding any of the events or facts alleged in the Complaint in this action.
4. State the basis of Plaintiff's contention that Plaintiff has suffered damages in excess of Seventy-Five Thousand Dollars ($75,000.00).
5. State the name, last known address and job title of any person who has personal knowledge in support of the damage claims of the Plaintiff.

Date: March 27, 1999   ADAMSON, TESHIMA, ÁLVAREZ & GAUM

George Teshima, Attorneys for Defendant
Cybermaxim Company

---

clear so that they can be answered without having to speculate about their meaning. Generally speaking, interrogatories should be the first discovery tool used, because the responses often identify witnesses to be deposed later and documents to be included in a request for production of documents. Interrogatories are also inexpensive, compared to document production and depositions. An example of interrogatories appears in *Figure 6.5* and a sample response in *Figure 6.6*.

In many states the total number of interrogatory questions is limited by statute or court rules. The *Federal Rules of Civil Procedure* permit twenty-five interrogatories by each party to each other party in a lawsuit. However, under *FRCP* 26(b)(2), the local rules of a federal district court might permit more than twenty-five interrogatories. The purpose of limiting the number of interrogatories is to prevent any one party from overwhelming another party—especially one with fewer financial resources—with unnecessary and burdensome in-

FIGURE 6.6 Sample Response to Interrogatories

Sure, Swift & Profit
Attorneys at Law
701 Nutmeg Street
San Diego, California 92104
(619) 221-3400

IN THE UNITED STATES DISTRICT COURT
FOR THE SOUTHERN DISTRICT OF CALIFORNIA

GEORGE ABLE, an individual,)) Plaintiff,)) v.)) CYBERMAXIM COMPANY, a Delaware) Corporation,)) Defendant.))		Civil Action No. 99-76542

**PLAINTIFF GEORGE ABLE'S RESPONSE TO
DEFENDANT CYBERMAXIM'S INTERROGATORIES**

Plaintiff George Able responds to Defendant Cybermaxim's first set of Interrogatories as follows:

Answer to Interrogatory No. 1:
The plain language of the contract between Plaintiff and Defendant, which appears as Exhibit "A" to the Complaint herein (the "Contract"), states that the Plaintiff shall be the "sole and exclusive agent for the marketing and sale of Cybermaxim computer software" within the State of California.

Answer to Interrogatory No. 2:
Plaintiff was obligated by the Contract to perform the following:
a. Market Cybermaxim software to small businesses in California;
b. Call in person on at least sixty (60) small businesses each month; and;
c. Fill all orders received from small businesses in California.

Plaintiff has, in fact, performed each and all of these obligations. Plaintiff's performance is demonstrated by such actions as the following:
a. Plaintiff has placed advertisements in the "business" yellow pages of every metropolitan area in California.
b. Since January 1997, and continuing until the month preceding the filing of the Complaint herein, Plaintiff called in person in excess of eighty (80) small businesses each month.
c. Plaintiff has filled all orders received from small businesses in California until Cybermaxim ceased delivery of Cybermaxim software to Plaintiff's place of business, in or about the first week of August 1998.

Answer to Interrogatory No. 3:

Melissa Able	Mark Ericson	Susan Sure, Esq.
2034 Redwood Street	554 Thyme Avenue	Swift, Sure & Profit
San Diego, CA 92105	San Diego, CA 92104	701 Nutmeg Street
		San Diego, CA 92104

Answer to Interrogatory No. 4:
Under the terms of the Contract, Plaintiff was to continue until January 4, 2002 as the sole and exclusive agent for the marketing and sale of Cybermaxim software within the State of California. In the period from January 1997 until August 1998, Plaintiff was clearing in excess of eight thousand dollars ($8,000.00) per month in commissions on the sale of Cybermaxim software. At that rate, Plaintiff's total commissions under the Contract for the period September 1998 until January 2002 would be approximately two hundred thirty-two thousand dollars ($232,000.00). As the result of Defendant Cybermaxim's breach of the Contract, Plaintiff will not receive those commissions.

Answer to Interrogatory No. 5:
Marianne Mollard, Certified Public Accountant
4523 Embarcadero Blvd.
San Diego, CA 92104

Dated: April 16, 1999   SWIFT, SURE & PROFIT

                                      Susan Sure, Attorneys for Plaintiff
                                      George Able

VERIFICATION

**STATE OF CALIFORNIA
COUNTY OF SAN DIEGO**

    I, George Able, declare and state:
    I am the plaintiff in the within action;
    I have read the foregoing RESPONSE TO INTERROGATORIES and know the contents thereof; and I certify that the same is true of my own knowledge, except as to those matters which are herein stated upon my information and belief, and as to those matters I believe them to be true.
    I declare, under penalty of perjury under the laws of the United States, that the foregoing is true and correct.

    Executed on April _____, 1999, at _____, California.

George Able

quiries. When the number of interrogatories is limited, the attorney must craft her discovery plan with care so that the maximum amount of useful information can be obtained. Interrogatories cannot be served on nonparty witnesses, who must be **deposed**, instead.

> To **depose** a person is to take his testimony under oath and out of court.

Requests for Admissions

Requests for admissions are a list of statements, each of which the responding party must admit or deny, in writing and under oath. They often are used to narrow the issues before the court by getting the uncontroverted facts into evidence. If a party fails to respond to a request for admissions, the facts stated therein are treated as though the nonresponding party had actually admitted their truth; consequently, such admissions implied by silence cannot later be disputed at trial. Upon a showing of "good cause," a court might permit a nonresponding party to respond at a later time, but it can be exceedingly difficult to show good cause. The most common ground for permitting a late response is evidence that the requests were not properly served.

> **Requests for admissions** is a discovery device in which one party asks the other party to admit or deny, in writing and under oath, certain facts.

As with interrogatories, requests for admissions are addressed only to parties to the litigation, not to other witnesses. The *Federal Rules of Civil Procedure* do not limit the number of admissions requested, although local court rules and some state jurisdictions might impose limits. A sample request for admissions appears in *Figure 6.7*.

Production of Documents

Requests for production of documents ask for specified documents or categories of documents (e.g., "any and all correspondence between A and B in the year 1992 that refer or relate to ZZZ") that must be made available for inspection and copying. The request for production of documents can be entitled a "demand for production" or a request or demand for "inspection of documents." In most cases, the responding party simply provides photocopies of all documents that match the request, although the requesting party has the legal right to inspect the originals. All documents must be produced that are in the custody, possession, or control of the responding party. That includes documents in the possession, custody or control of that party's attorneys, employees, agents, and so forth.

> A **request for production of documents** is a demand that one party permit the examination and copying of relevant documents.

Requests to inspect evidence or materials are essentially the same as requests for production of documents, except that they do not necessarily require the responding party to turn over the documents or materials (or copies of them) to the requesting party. For example, an automobile rim and tire that failed in an accident might be inspected by the defendant's expert witness at a properly equipped laboratory; the plaintiff's expert witness, also, can be present during the inspection and retain custody of those articles. Requests to inspect, rather than to produce, are generally used when it is impossible or inconvenient to produce an accurate copy of the original document or article. This type of request is used also to enter into a building (e.g., hospital operating room, factory, or repair shop) for the purpose of making visual observations, measurements, photographs, and so forth. The request to inspect is also used to obtain nondestructive metallurgical or chemical testing of objects that might be used as evidence during trial.

Requests to produce or inspect are served on parties only, never on nonparties. If relevant documents or objects are in the possession of nonparties, a **subpoena *duces tecum*** is used to gain access to them. There is no limit on the number of documents or objects to be produced or inspected, and that sometimes leads to abuse of discovery by a party that tries to bury an opponent under reams of paper while the legal fees mount exponentially. The remedy against that abuse is to file an objection to the request, and let the court determine

> A **subpoena *duces tecum*** requires the person served to appear and bring specified documents or other evidentiary items.

FIGURE 6.7 Sample Request for Admissions

Adamson, Teshima, Álvarez & Gaum
Attorneys at Law
1723 Embarcadero Boulevard, Suite 1200
San Diego, California 92401

IN THE UNITED STATES DISTRICT COURT
FOR THE SOUTHERN DISTRICT OF CALIFORNIA

GEORGE ABLE, an individual,	)	
	)	
Plaintiff,	)	Civil Action No. 99-76542
	)	
v.	)	
	)	
CYBERMAXIM COMPANY, a Delaware Corporation,	)	
	)	
Defendant.	)	

REQUEST FOR ADMISSIONS

The plaintiff, GEORGE ABLE ("Plaintiff") and his attorneys are requested to answer the following requests for admissions separately, in writing and under oath, pursuant to Federal Rules of Civil Procedure § 33(a). It is requested that the answers be signed under oath by the person making such answers and that they be served upon the defendant, Cybermaxim Company ("Defendant") within thirty (30) days of the service of this Request for Admissions.

 1. Admit that at the time you entered into the contract identified as Exhibit "A" to the Complaint, you knew that Defendant intended to enter marketing and sales agreements with other businesses in California.
 2. Admit that you have never sold Cybermaxim computer software to customers located outside of the fifteen southernmost counties of California.
 3. Admit that you have made no substantial effort to market Cybermaxim computer software in California.
 4. Admit that your total cumulative sales of Cybermaxim computer software have not exceeded $10,000.00 gross revenue during the period from the date the parties entered into the contract identified as Exhibit "A" to the Complaint, and up to the time said Complaint was filed in this action.

Dated: March 10, 1999   ADAMSON, TESHIMA, ÁLVAREZ & GAUM

                                 _____
                                 George Teshima, Attorneys for Defendant
                                 Cybermaxim Company

---

whether the requests are excessive. Unfortunately, objections result in legal fees, as well. A sample request for production appears in *Figure 6.8*.

Depositions

As already mentioned, a deposition is oral testimony by a witness (known as the **deponent**); this testimony is taken out of court (usually in an attorney's office) but under oath. A court reporter swears the witness and then records the testimony stenographically just as would be done in court. After the transcript has been prepared, the deponent makes corrections to the transcript and then signs it to verify its accuracy. Just as the deposition testimony itself was made under penalty of perjury, so are any corrections to the transcript. Corrections by the deponent are usually few in number, and they seldom amount to an outright contradiction of the testimony as recorded by the court reporter. Typical corrections are of the following nature:

- changing "would" to "could," or "hassled" to "harassed"
- correcting misspellings of proper names
- correcting simple misstatements of fact ("The computers had Intel Pentium III II processors")
- inserting a word that was missed by the court reporter ("Mr. Backus and I met in West Covina, in 1978")

Practice Tip

In most states, the highest appellate court—or a judicial council of appellate court justices—establishes procedural rules that apply to all courts in that state. The federal courts are governed by the Federal Rules of Civil Procedure, adopted by the U.S. Supreme Court. Compliance with court rules is very important, and serious consequences can sometimes follow if they are ignored or inadvertently violated. Ignorance of the rule is never an acceptable excuse.

In both federal and state courts, local rules are adopted by the courts in a particular jurisdiction. These, too, must be carefully followed. A copy of the local rules can be obtained from the office of the court clerk. State and federal rules—usually including local court rules—are available on Westlaw and LEXIS-NEXIS, as well.

Finally, individual judges often establish their own standards and procedures that apply only to those matters heard in that judge's courtroom. When a case is assigned to a particular judge, it is a good idea to call the clerk in that courtroom to inquire about any requirements of the judge that would apply to that type of case.

The **deponent** is the person whose testimony is taken in a deposition.

FIGURE 6.8 Sample Request for Production

Adamson, Teshima, Álvarez & Gaum
Attorneys at Law
1723 Embarcadero Boulevard, Suite 1200
San Diego, California 92401

IN THE UNITED STATES DISTRICT COURT
FOR THE SOUTHERN DISTRICT OF CALIFORNIA

GEORGE ABLE, an individual,　　　　　　)
　　　　　　　　　　　　　　　　　　　　)
　　　　　　　　　　　　Plaintiff,　　　)　　　　Civil Action No. 99-76542
　　　　　　　　　　　　　　　　　　　　)
　　　　　　v.　　　　　　　　　　　　　)
　　　　　　　　　　　　　　　　　　　　)
CYBERMAXIM COMPANY, a Delaware　　　　)
　Corporation,　　　　　　　　　　　　　)
　　　　　　　　　　　　　　　　　　　　)
　　　　　　　　　　　　Defendant.　　　)
　　　　　　　　　　　　　　　　　　　　)

REQUEST FOR PRODUCTION OF DOCUMENTS

The plaintiff, GEORGE ABLE ("Plaintiff") and his attorneys are requested to identify and produce for inspection each and every document described below, pursuant to Federal Rules of Civil Procedure § 33(a). It is requested that Plaintiff respond to this request in writing, and that said response be served upon the defendant, Cybermaxim Company ("Defendant") within thirty (30) days of the service of this Request for Production of Documents.

In responding to this request, please identify and produce all described documents which are in the possession or control of Plaintiff, Plaintiff's attorneys, employees, representatives and/or agents.

1. All documents, including but not limited to, invoices and receipts, which refer or relate to the sale of Cybermaxim computer software by the Plaintiff.
2. All documents which refer or relate to efforts by the Plaintiff to market Cybermaxim computer software in California.
3. All correspondence between the Plaintiff and any other person regarding Plaintiff's alleged sole and exclusive agency for the marketing and sale of Cybermaxim computer software in California.

Dated: March 10, 1999　　　　　　　　　　ADAMSON, TESHIMA, ÁLVAREZ & GAUM

　　　　　　　　　　　　　　　　　　　　George Teshima, Attorneys for Defendant
　　　　　　　　　　　　　　　　　　　　Cybermaxim Company

To **lodge** a document is to formally place it in the court records for reference at a later time.

To **impeach** a witness is to use probing questions or other evidence to raise doubts about the credibility of that witness' testimony.

If a deponent makes corrections that change the substance of her testimony, during the trial she might be questioned at length about those changes.

The deposition transcript becomes part of the case record and might be **lodged** with the court or read aloud in the trial. Depositions are extremely useful, because an attorney can learn in advance how a witness will respond to questions during trial. Equally important, depositions can be a cornucopia of unexpected new information about the case. Occasionally, the testimony of a witness in court ("I don't remember the time") is contrary to, or inconsistent with, her testimony in deposition ("I'm sure it was just before the Miami-Denver game came on TV"). In that event, an attorney might use the deposition testimony to **impeach** the credibility of an opposing witness. Attorneys also use depositions to discover the theories of opposing expert witnesses. Excerpts from two deposition transcripts appear in Appendix A.

VIDEOTAPING DEPOSITIONS

Depositions might be recorded by either audio- or videotape. There is a Uniform Audio-Visual Deposition Act that has been adopted in some jurisdictions. Under that act, there is no requirement to have a stenographer simultaneously record the testimony, although that can be an advantage if equipment problems occur. The witness must be sworn, however, and that oath must be recorded or officially noted on the videotape. Under the uniform act, the videotape is an official record, along with any stenographic record made concurrently (or made subsequently from the tape).

Because all parties normally want a stenographic transcript of deposition testimony, it is an additional expense to create a videotape as well. This expense might be justified, however, when the videotape permits a jury to see the demeanor of the witness. Certainly, videotaped testimony is more effective with a jury than is a stenographic transcript that is read aloud in court. Videotape gives the jury a far greater opportunity to judge the reliability of a witness based upon facial expression, body language, tone of voice, and so forth. The audio recording of a deposition allows one to listen to a word or sentence multiple times, should there be a dispute over the accuracy of the stenographic record.

Another advantage of videotape is the opportunity to include visual demonstrations as an additional component of the testimony—just as is done in live courtroom testimony. Similarly, drawings, photographs, physical objects, and other exhibits can be displayed on the screen as they are being discussed by the deponent. Depositions can be taken at a remote location where the physical environment adds meaning and clarity to the testimony: a factory floor or a highway intersection, for example.

Expense and equipment problems are the greatest disadvantages of videotaped depositions. However, some critics also believe that witnesses, and especially attorneys, tend to play to the camera in a way that alters their demeanor and words. Those critics also contend that a camera is more intrusive upon one's thoughts and emotions than is the presence of a court reporter.

Obtaining Evidence from Third Parties

Parties to a lawsuit can obtain testimony from *nonparty witnesses* through the use of a subpoena. In most jurisdictions, an attorney representing a party to the suit may sign the subpoena; in other states, the court clerk must issue the subpoena. The subpoena might be for a witness to appear at trial or for a pretrial deposition. If a witness is asked to bring documents, those must be clearly described in the subpoena *duces tecum*. Technically, none of this is considered to be "discovery," because that term defines the right of opposing litigants to obtain pretrial information from each other, but nonparty witnesses should be considered when the attorney develops her strategy and schedule for discovery.

Objections to Discovery

Regardless of the method of discovery being used, the responding party has the right to object to certain types of requests or questions. In general, discovery must be calculated to discover relevant evidence or to lead to the discovery of relevant evidence. But, in some jurisdictions, the scope of discovery is limited to information "necessary" to prepare for trial. The latter limitation is not much different from the apparently more liberal rule, because it is reasonably "necessary" to uncover all possible leads to relevant evidence.

Requests or questions that do not meet those tests are improper, and a response can be refused. It is common practice, however, for counsel to state the objection and then have the deponent respond "without waiving the objection" made. In that way, the objection is preserved and might be raised again in court to exclude the testimony being sought. A great deal of time and money is conserved by not dueling in court over every objection at the time it is first raised in pretrial discovery. In addition to questions of relevance, objections are often made on the grounds that the request would violate the attorney-client privilege or the attorney work product rule.

> **Practice Tip**
>
> Paralegals are not permitted to examine or cross-examine a deponent. Although a paralegal might attend a deposition to handle exhibits, usually that is not the case. Paralegals play an important role, however, in preparing questions and assembling relevant documents prior to the deposition, and in preparing summaries of the deposition transcripts. These summaries are used by attorneys for a quick review of the deponent's testimony and as a type of "index" to locate the deponent's testimony on a particular topic. Appendix A provides sample deposition testimony and a sample of a legal assistant's summary of testimony.

FIGURE 6.9 Typical Objections to Discovery Requests

Question Request	Objection
"What did you tell your attorney about that?"	Attorney-client privilege
State the name and address of each person who has knowledge or information relevant to this lawsuit.	Vague and ambiguous
Identify the person whose negligence caused the accident.	Requires a legal conclusion
Produce all correspondence between yourself and your ex-wife referring or relating to the application for the loan.	Privileged marital communication
Produce all loan applications received by Plaintiff since its incorporation.	Burdensome and oppressive
State the destination of your trip during which the traffic accident occurred.	Not relevant
Produce all notes and memoranda prepared by the investigator retained by the Plaintiff's attorneys.	Attorney's work product rule
"How fast was the other vehicle traveling when it collided with your truck?"	Calls for a conclusion
Admit that Defendant offered to settle this lawsuit by paying $5,000 to Plaintiff.	Offer of compromise inadmissible
Admit that since Plaintiff was injured, Defendant installed new lighting fixtures in the stairwell where Plaintiff was injured.	Post-accident remedial measures inadmissible
State the date, name of the physician, and name of the hospital, if any, for each occasion in which you have sought treatment for or been diagnosed as having any mental illness.	Physician-patient privilege (provided that responding party has not placed his mental health in legal controversy)

There are some limitations upon a party's right to object during discovery. For example, one must respond to all parts of a question or request that are *not* objectionable. Objections must be raised in a timely manner—which is the reason why counsel routinely "preserve" their objections even when permitting the deponent to respond, as discussed above. Finally, the grounds for objections must be stated in specific terms so that their basis is clear. Typical objections to discovery requests appear in *Figure 6.9*.

In some cases involving business activities or defective consumer products, parties might seek **proprietary trade secret** information (e.g., manufacturing blueprints or confidential customer lists). In those cases, it is common for the responding party to ask the court for **protective orders** that bar the use of the information for any purpose other than the lawsuit and that also prohibit disclosure of the information outside of the lawsuit.

A **proprietary trade secret** is information developed and owned by a business enterprise, which it uses to gain competitive advantage.

A **protective order** is a court order limiting an opposing party's access to, and use of, proprietary trade secrets.

SCENARIO

Four months ago, Elena D'Angela completed her paralegal studies with a certificate in civil litigation. During her final semester, she participated in an internship program at a medium-sized law firm that handles bankruptcy and civil litigation matters. At the conclusion of the internship, she received a letter of recommendation to the law firm where she now works. "That internship really made a difference. If I hadn't done that, I doubt I would have this job now. It wasn't just the letter of recommendation from one of the partners in that firm, it also was the hands-on experience that it gave me."

Since joining her current firm, Elena has been involved in a variety of tasks for a case that will go to trial within a few months. "I've been working on this lawsuit about the crash of a small aircraft. The passenger suffered burns, but she's going to be O.K. The pilot died on impact. The pilot's husband and the passenger are suing our client, which manufactured the plane. They claim that a fuel system failure caused the accident."

Elena has been working on the discovery phase of the lawsuit. "At first, all I did was sort through the client's documents and prepare copies of everything that had been requested in the plaintiffs' demand for production. Then, one of the senior paralegals showed me how to draft our response to that demand. I was surprised at how many documents we objected to providing, but then provided anyway without waiving our objections. Right now, though, the attorneys are in a big dispute over some blueprints for the plane's fuel system. We are insisting that they are proprietary trade secrets, but the attorney says we'll probably turn them over if we get a protective order from the court."

"Now that most of the 'paper' discovery process is completed, we are starting to take depositions. I've been given the job of preparing summaries of the deposition testimony. Although I did that once during my internship, I'm still pretty nervous about the chance that I might leave out something really important when I do the summary. Fortunately, Jack—he's the senior paralegal on the case—has agreed to read the transcript and then check my first 'depo' summary. And he suggests, 'if in doubt, include it.' That sounds like a good idea."

"Last week, I summarized the passenger's deposition. It was really interesting, and I was impressed with the way my attorney questioned her in such a gentle, understanding way. It wasn't at all like the sort of grilling you see in movie trial scenes. Of course, he was trying to get as much information from her as he could, and there wasn't any jury to influence. I'm looking forward to some of the expert witness depos. Both sides have retained a pilot and an engineer as 'testifying' experts, so that's four depos right there. It's going to be interesting to see how much my engineering degree helps when I do the summaries. Of course, I don't know anything about flying, so those two depos might be more challenging." ■

Discovery Cutoff and Pretrial Conferences

At some point before trial, the court might order a **discovery cutoff date**, by which time all discovery must be completed. Opposing counsel sometimes stipulate to continued discovery beyond the cutoff date, although court approval would be required if the stipulated extension would delay the trial or any scheduled hearing in the case. Upon a showing of good cause by either party, the court might authorize continued discovery. In some jurisdictions, these issues are resolved by the attorneys and the judge in a **status conference** while discovery is still in progress.

After the conclusion of discovery, a final **pretrial conference** is generally held to determine scheduling for the trial and deal with other procedural issues. Each party estimates the length of the trial. If a party desires a trial by jury, it will request one at or before the pretrial conference. The attorneys will discuss with the judge any concerns they have about the management of the trial (e.g., juror challenges or the sequence in which multiple plaintiffs and defendants will present their cases). The judge might require the attorneys to lay out their cases in brief oral summaries, including their evidence and legal arguments. At the pretrial conference, attorneys usually submit written **trial briefs** that analyze and argue all key legal issues likely to arise during trial.

The final pretrial conference can turn into a **settlement conference**, in which the judge attempts to mediate a resolution agreeable to all sides. If the judge

The **discovery cutoff date** is the deadline, set by statute or the court, by which all pretrial discovery must be completed.

The **status conference** is a meeting between the court and counsel to evaluate the progress of the case toward trial and to resolve discovery disputes.

The **pretrial conference** is a meeting between the court and counsel to schedule the trial and related pretrial hearings, to determine if a jury is to be empaneled, and to resolve other procedural matters.

A **trial brief** is a memorandum of points (i.e., statements of the law) and authorities (i.e., statutes, court cases, etc.) that argues all of the legal issues expected to be decided by the court during trial.

A **settlement conference** is a postdiscovery meeting between the court and all parties and their counsel to attempt an out-of-court settlement and avoid trial.

> A **settlement agreement** is a contract, often requiring court approval, that permanently disposes of the controversy between the parties.

succeeds, the case will not go to trial and the opposing parties will later sign a formal **settlement agreement** that will be approved by—and usually made an order of—the court. Of course, negotiation of the settlement agreement language can break down, requiring another settlement conference with the judge, or perhaps even a trial.

Some jurisdictions require a mandatory settlement conference with the court prior to any case going to trial. The judge wields such great discretion over the conduct of a trial and can influence the outcome substantially by exercising her power to admit or exclude evidence—as well as by her rulings on legal and procedural issues. As a result, she holds great leverage at the settlement conference. Judges frequently apply not-so-gentle persuasion to reach a settlement of the case without going to trial. The attorneys must be accompanied at the mandatory settlement conference by the litigating parties. Parties other than individuals must be represented at the mandatory settlement conference by a partner, corporate officer, or other person (*not* just their legal counsel) with full authority to reach a binding settlement. *Figure 6.10* continues the sequence of pretrial litigation.

PRETRIAL MOTIONS

Before a trial begins, either party may present motions requesting the court's order or ruling regarding the conduct of the trial and certain legal issues expected to arise during the trial. Examples of pretrial motions include:

- motions *in limine* to exclude particular issues or evidence;
- motions to request judicial notice of facts; and,
- motions to strike undisclosed evidence.

Motions *in Limine*

> A **motion *in limine*** proposes to limit or exclude from trial certain evidence or legal issues.

Before the trial—and sometimes during trial—plaintiffs and defendants introduce motions to exclude certain issues or evidence that they anticipate the opposing party will try to introduce. These are known as **motions *in limine*.** Motions *in lim-*

FIGURE 6.10 Litigation—Complaint through Discovery

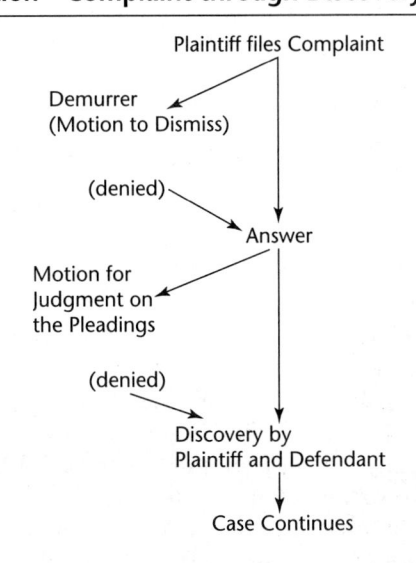

Plaintiff files Complaint → Demurrer (Motion to Dismiss) → (denied) → Answer → Motion for Judgment on the Pleadings → (denied) → Discovery by Plaintiff and Defendant → Case Continues

ine usually are made on the basis of relevance, hearsay, privilege, or prejudicial effect on the jury. Motions are also made to exclude trade secrets, prior criminal convictions, subsequent remedial measures, and offers of compromise. In very unusual circumstances, the motion to exclude might be based upon an allegation that the party introducing the evidence obtained it improperly—for example, by illegal eavesdropping, bribery, or burglary.

Requests for Judicial Notice of Facts

Courts are permitted to take judicial notice of certain types of factual information without the necessity that evidence be introduced to establish those facts. Judicial notice is based upon the idea that such facts are universally recognized and are incontrovertible by any plausible evidence. The purpose of judicial notice is judicial efficiency. Examples of such facts include the following:

- the geographic boundaries of the State of Michigan
- the relationship between Greenwich Mean Time (GMT) and the local time at Boise, Idaho
- the date of John F. Kennedy's assassination
- the name of the current governor of New York
- the provisions of the United Nations Charter

> **Practice Tip**
>
> Motions in limine are supported by legal memoranda justifying the exclusion of the evidence in question. Opposing parties then file memoranda in opposition to the motions. These memoranda are based upon a substantial amount of legal research, which can be conducted by experienced paralegals with strong analytical and research skills. An experienced paralegal might also draft the motion in limine.

Motions to Strike Undisclosed Evidence

A motion to strike undisclosed evidence is intended to exclude evidence that was requested (but not provided) during discovery or that was not disclosed as otherwise required by law or court rules. Often, this motion prompts a heated dispute between opposing parties about the adequacy of the discovery request (in identifying what was requested) and/or the characteristics of the proffered evidence that might distinguish it from the evidence requested. As a practical matter, the courts tend to admit evidence that has been tardily disclosed unless the objecting attorney can demonstrate substantial prejudice to his client's case.

PRETRIAL BRIEFS AND STIPULATIONS

Each party usually submits to the court its analysis and arguments about the legal issues that the court will have to decide. This is done in the pretrial brief, which carries the title of "memorandum of points and authorities." The brief is based upon thorough legal research and is written as a persuasive document. Its purpose is to convince the court that each significant legal issue should be decided in favor of the party presenting the memorandum. Naturally, the opposing party will present a brief arguing for different legal conclusions by the court.

The pretrial stipulation is a joint submission by all parties to the case. In the stipulation, the parties inform the court about the following:

- facts agreed upon, and facts contested
- matters of law agreed upon and matters contested
- witnesses to be called and exhibits to be introduced

The purpose of the stipulation is to provide the court with a clear statement of the case and an outline of how each party will present its case. All attorneys in the case sign the stipulation before it is submitted to the court.

SECTION 4. TRIAL PROCEDURES

With discovery completed, trial briefs and stipulations filed, and pretrial motions disposed of, the case is now ready for trial. If either party desires a trial by jury, that request will have been filed with the court well before the date set for trial. In some jurisdictions, a party requesting a jury must post a bond for payment of the daily juror fees before a pool of prospective jurors will be called for that case.

JURY SELECTION

Juries continue to be popular with civil litigants, and jury selection can be a critical phase of the trial. The size of civil juries varies between six and twelve jurors, depending upon the jurisdiction. It is common for several alternate jurors to be chosen, especially for lengthy trials. The alternate juror hears all evidence, but does not participate in deliberations or voting unless she must replace one of the original jurors.

Members of juries must be intellectually competent to serve in that capacity, but competence does not depend upon education. Ordinary intelligence is sufficient. Even the ability to speak and understand English must be considered with care, because no objective standard exists for the degree of English fluency required for jury service. The exclusion of non-native speakers could be challenged as ethnic discrimination. Sign language interpreters will be provided by the court for jurors who are hearing impaired or deaf. Fortunately, all parties usually agree in their desire to exclude anyone who appears to suffer from a serious intellectual or emotional disability, and the court can excuse such a person **on its own motion**.

> When a court acts **on its own motion,** it acts on its own initiative rather than in response to the petition or motion of a litigating party.

Assuming minimal competency, the most important standard for jury selection *should* be objectivity toward the parties and the issues. In reality, both plaintiffs and defendants try to exclude jurors who might favor their opponent and, at the same time, try to include those who would favor their own side. In theory, at least, their opposing efforts will cancel out, leaving a jury of reasonable balance, if not complete objectivity.

The process of probing for possible bias or incompetency in prospective jurors is called *voir dire*. Usually the judge begins by asking general questions of the jurors en masse. Then attorneys for each party ask more specific questions, directing some questions to the jurors en masse, but most to individual jurors. In major cases, attorneys employ psychologists or other consultants to advise them in jury selection.

> *Voir dire* is the process of examining prospective jurors in order to determine their qualification to serve.

In complex cases, it is common to have prospective jurors respond to a written questionnaire. The attorneys and the court then review those written responses to prepare questions for individual members of the jury pool. Questionnaires offer several advantages:

- They save time in court.
- They permit more thorough questioning of each prospective juror.
- They permit the prospective juror to respond in relative privacy to questions that might carry strong emotional significance.

Each party is allowed to challenge prospective jurors. A **challenge for cause** must be based upon the juror's prior experience (e.g., personal involvement in a similar situation or case), or some behavior or statement by the juror that indicates a likely bias or other disqualification. There is no limit on the number of challenges for cause, although the court will overrule those challenges that lack

> A **challenge for cause** is based upon good reason, stated to the court, to doubt a prospective juror's qualification to serve impartially; it asks the court to excuse that juror from service.

merit. Each party also has a limited number of **peremptory challenges**, which may be made without any explanation or justification: *"The plaintiff asks the court to thank and excuse juror number 17."* It is not unusual for attorneys, paralegals, and police officers to be excused in this manner, perhaps because the attorneys do not want a juror with legal background to substitute his own understanding of the law for the instructions of the court nor to exercise a dominant influence during jury deliberations. Because they are limited in number, attorneys avoid using peremptory challenges until the last stage of jury selection. It is a rare attorney who is completely satisfied with the jury finally seated, but he usually understands that it could have been much worse.

> A **peremptory challenge** is a request that the court excuse a prospective juror from service, without stating any reason for that request.

OPENING STATEMENTS

After the jury is sworn by the judge or court clerk, the judge usually explains to the jury something of the nature of the case, trial procedures, and their responsibilities as jurors. The judge normally instructs the jury that the **opening statements** by the attorneys are not to be considered as evidence, but rather they are two divergent "road maps" indicating what each attorney believes the evidence in the case will show. Because opening statements are not evidence, the attorneys are permitted substantial latitude in their remarks.

The plaintiff presents her opening statement first, and the defendant follows. Each attorney summarizes the evidence he intends to present and the ultimate facts he believes that evidence will prove. The attorneys also discuss the law that the jury will apply to the facts of the case. Of course, the judge's instructions on the law—given at the end of the trial—must govern the jury's deliberations.

Attorneys also use the opening statement to introduce themselves to the jury. They want to be seen as honest, intelligent, and sincere—interested only in justice for their client. They also want the jury to lose its initial curiosity about them so that the jurors will concentrate on the witnesses once testimony begins. The attorneys also use the opening statements to continue their assessment of the jury, noting any reactions the jurors might have.

> The **opening statement** is an attorney's explanation to the jury of the nature of the case, the evidence to be presented, and the issues to be proved by that evidence.

THE PLAINTIFF'S CASE IN CHIEF

Following both opening statements, the plaintiff's attorney presents her **case in chief**. During this stage of the trial, the plaintiff will present all testimony and other evidence necessary to establish the ***prima facie* case** and, hopefully, convince the jury that the plaintiff should prevail. The primary feature of the plaintiff's case in chief is the **direct examination** of witnesses called by the plaintiff. Because the plaintiff's case is presented first, it can have the enormous advantage of shaping the jury's early impressions of the case.

The purpose of the testimony—particularly if it is a trial by jury—is to tell a clearly understandable and credible story. There always is a danger that the jury will be overwhelmed and confused by an onslaught of facts that do not appear to fit into any understandable pattern. To prevent that, the attorney should have given the jury a preview of the case as part of her opening statement. During the case in chief, she must be careful to present the witnesses and evidence in a sequence and manner that clarifies the case.

> The **case in chief** is the plaintiff's initial presentation of evidence.
>
> The plaintiff's evidence before the court—which is sufficient to prevail, unless later contradicted by more persuasive evidence offered by the defendant—establishes a ***prima facie* case** in favor of the plaintiff.
>
> **Direct examination** is the first questioning of a witness by the party who called her.

Preparing Witnesses to Testify

Each witness will have been carefully rehearsed for direct examination so that both the witness and attorney know the questions and answers well. It is common, also, to take important witnesses through a mock cross-examination so

> **Practice Tip**
>
> When the testimony of a witness is not expected to cover complex matters, an experienced trial paralegal might be assigned to provide the preliminary preparation for that witness. The paralegal will focus on the same potential problems that an attorney would emphasize. Once the paralegal has completed that task, the attorney can take the witness through a final rehearsal, with the paralegal taking notes on any remaining problems.
>
> Some trial attorneys use office staff, including paralegals, as a mock jury for their own rehearsal of opening and closing statements. They can also use this mock jury to evaluate their examination of witnesses on critically important testimony.

that they will be prepared for questions likely to be asked by opposing counsel. An ethical attorney will never encourage the witness to be dishonest, but she will suggest alternative, *equally honest* ways to respond, if the witness is inclined to respond poorly. This preparation is intended to eliminate a variety of problems that commonly occur with inexperienced witnesses:

- unresponsive answers
- answers that tell more than the question requires
- rambling, incoherent answers
- answers that assume knowledge of information that the jury does not have
- unfamiliar jargon or unnecessarily technical language
- nonverbal answers that the court reporter cannot hear and transcribe
- excessively rapid or slow speech

Another vitally important reason for rehearsing the testimony is to ensure that the witness does not provide unexpected answers during trial. Attorneys attempt to adhere to this cardinal rule: *Never ask a question unless you know the answer that will follow.*

Conducting the Direct Examination

During direct examination, the attorney should lay a foundation for the testimony of each witness: What circumstances made it possible for the witness to have first-hand knowledge of the facts in this case? What special or unique knowledge does the witness have about the facts of the case?

The attorney will pose questions that permit the witness to feel comfortable and demonstrate self-confidence. Usually, this begins with questions about the background of the witness and how he came to be involved in the case. Although some of these introductory questions might be irrelevant, the court usually permits them, especially if they put the witness at ease and allow the jury to gain some sense of the witness' personality.

As each witness is questioned, she will be asked to identify any exhibits of which she has direct personal knowledge: checks she has written or cashed; photographs she has taken; physical evidence that she found at the scene of an event; a calendar that she has kept of her daily appointments and activities; and so forth. Once it is shown that she has personal knowledge of the exhibit and that the exhibit has some relevancy to the case (a process known as **laying foundation**), the exhibit can be admitted into evidence and the witness can testify further about its significance.

To **lay foundation** is to present testimony that establishes the admissibility of other evidence to follow.

The sincerity and credibility of the witness can be reinforced by asking on direct examination the very questions that the defense might later use to undermine the witness' credibility or knowledge. Potentially "damaging" statements can be defused when they are brought out under a less hostile direct examination.

Cross-Examination of the Plaintiff's Witnesses

As each witness completes his testimony, the plaintiff's attorney will say something like, "Your witness," to inform the court, jury, and defense attorney that the direct examination of that witness has been concluded. At that point, the defense attorney will begin his cross-examination of that witness.

Perhaps the single most important rule about cross-examination is that, in most jurisdictions, *it is restricted to the scope of direct examination.* If the witness has testified only about what he saw on July 4, 1995, he cannot be asked in cross-examination about an unrelated topic or event. If the defense wishes to question him on other topics, it will have to call him as a defense witness when it puts its own case before the court. This restriction applies to cross-examination of witnesses by both parties; it does not matter which side conducted the direct examination—generally, the cross-examination cannot go beyond the scope of the direct examination. One exception to the "scope of direct" limitation is the examination of the witness' credibility. Thus, a witness might be asked on cross-examination about prior instances in which he has lied under oath.

Cross-examination has a purpose exactly opposite that of direct examination. Whereas the direct examination attempted to show the witness as honest, sincere, and knowledgeable, the cross-examination attempts to show that same witness as being unsure of his facts and generally unreliable. This purpose of cross-examination is called impeachment. It is intended to cause the jury and/or judge to doubt and disallow the testimony of the witness.

Impeachment is accomplished by a variety of methods, including the following:

- causing the witness to retract testimony given under direct examination or to admit that it was inaccurate or incomplete
- causing the witness to appear confused and uncertain of the facts
- showing that the witness has some bias in favor of the opposing party
- showing that the witness has some prejudice against the client
- showing that, in deposition, the witness testified differently about the same facts

When the plaintiff has presented all witnesses and evidence for its side, it will **rest its case**, which means that the defense now has its turn to present the defendant's case.

THE MOTION FOR NONSUIT OR DIRECTED VERDICT

Although unusual, it sometimes happens that a plaintiff rests her case without establishing a *prima facie* case. As previously explained, a *prima facie* case is established by presenting evidence that—if believed by the trier of fact—establishes each required element of the case. In an action for breach of contract, for example, the plaintiff must present evidence showing that she was damaged by the breach—damage being an essential element of a cause of action for breach of contract. If she rests her case without doing so, there is no *prima facie* case and the defendant is entitled to win the lawsuit without presenting any evidence.

For this reason, at the conclusion of the plaintiff's case in chief, the defense usually asks the court to dismiss the case by declaring that the plaintiff did not establish the required *prima facie* case; the defense makes this request in the form of a motion for **directed verdict** or a motion for **nonsuit**. A directed verdict orders the jury to find in favor of the moving party (in this example the defendant). A nonsuit is a court judgment for the defendant. Courts are reluctant, however, to grant these motions unless the plaintiff's case is unmistakably deficient. The trial court's ruling on these motions is subject to reversal on appeal.

PRESENTING THE DEFENDANT'S CASE

The plaintiff typically puts on *two* cases: his case in chief and his case in rebuttal (described below); but the defendant presents only one case. Because the defendant does not have the burden of proof, her presentation of evidence is not referred to as her "case in chief." In this regard, it is helpful to remember that the

A party **rests its case** when it has presented all evidence it intends to offer (excepting any rebuttal evidence to be offered later).

A **directed verdict** is an instruction by the court that the jury is to return a verdict against the party having the burden of proof, without considering the evidence; a directed verdict is required, as a matter of law, when the plaintiff fails to present a *prima facie* case.

Nonsuit is a court judgment for the defendant, based upon the plaintiff's failure to present a *prima facie* case.

civil defendant need not "prove" her innocence of any wrongdoing unless the plaintiff first establishes a *prima facie* case.

The goals of the defendant are as follows:

- to cast doubt upon key elements of the plaintiff's case (or better yet, to demolish the plaintiff's entire case)
- to make the defendant appear to be the innocent victim of the plaintiff's unjustified prosecution

It might be possible for the defense to tell a different story that will lead the judge or jury to reject the plaintiff's version of events. This strategy presents a *Rashomon* defense—named after the famous Japanese tale in which each witness to a single event recounts a different version of that event. The trier of fact must then decide which version is more believable.

A different strategy is to continue undermining the credibility of key plaintiff witnesses—a process that began with cross-examination during the plaintiff's case in chief—without offering any particular alternative scenario for what actually occurred. For example, the defense might call credible witnesses who offer information that puts the testimony by plaintiff witnesses in a different light, with different implications. Defense witnesses might be able to portray plaintiff witnesses as being biased or less than honest. A defense witness might, for example, testify that the plaintiff witness is his former employee, and that he had caught the ex-employee in numerous lies about events in the workplace.

Of course, every defense witness is subject to cross-examination by the plaintiff, and to redirect examination by the defendant's attorney. The process is essentially identical to the examination of plaintiff witnesses during the plaintiff's case in chief. When the defendant's attorney has completed presentation of his evidence, he will rest the case for the defense.

THE PLAINTIFF'S REBUTTAL EVIDENCE

Evidence in rebuttal is offered by the plaintiff to contradict or impeach the evidence already offered by the defense.

Evidence in rebuttal is presented by the plaintiff, after the defense has rested its case, to defeat the defendant's case. Because the plaintiff's case in chief goes first, the defense is able to present its own "rebuttal" evidence when the defense first calls witnesses and presents its evidence so that the defense has no need to later present a separate case in rebuttal.

However, when the plaintiff presented its case in chief, it did not yet know exactly what testimony the defense would present, or in what manner. Therefore, despite the pretrial discovery that had been done, it is entirely possible that the defense would present evidence in its case that the plaintiff had not anticipated or that would require some type of response beyond a cross-examination of the defense witnesses. In that event, the plaintiff will present its case in rebuttal.

In its rebuttal, the plaintiff might recall witnesses who testified during its case in chief, and/or it might call entirely new witnesses. Each of those witnesses is subject to cross-examination and to redirect examination. Once the plaintiff has completed presentation of rebuttal evidence and the defense has completed cross-examination, the case is almost ready to go to the jury. First, however, come the closing statements.

CLOSING STATEMENTS

As with opening statements, closing statements are not evidence, and the jury will be so instructed by the court. Just as the opening statements presented two different "road maps" to show where the evidence would lead, closing statements present two different summaries to explain what the evidence has shown.

In effect, closing statements are summations of testimony, and they are arguments about how the law should be applied to the evidence. Although counsel are permitted wide latitude in their closing statements, they are forbidden to misstate the evidence that has been presented to the jury.

The plaintiff is usually permitted to reserve a portion of her closing statement for rebuttal of the defense closing statement. But the defense does not have a similar privilege, for essentially the same reason that the defense has no need to put on rebuttal evidence—he has heard the plaintiff's closing statement before he makes his own. Consequently, the plaintiff has the opportunity to be heard first (in opening statement, case in chief, and closing statement) and also last (in rebuttal evidence and rebuttal closing statement). The same advantage is held by prosecuting attorneys in criminal cases.

SECTION 5. VERDICTS AND JUDGMENTS

At the beginning of a simple trial (i.e., one plaintiff, one defendant), the plaintiff is seeking enforcement of some right or remedy for some wrong. The plaintiff needs a decision by the court. The defendant, in contrast, needs nothing from the court. If the plaintiff fails to show up or asks the court to dismiss the entire action, the defendant has "won" the case. To obtain a favorable verdict, the plaintiff must present evidence that meets the standard of proof.

THE STANDARD OF PROOF FOR CIVIL LAWSUITS

The **standard of proof** in criminal trials is well known: "beyond a reasonable doubt." Depending upon jurisdiction and the legal issue at stake, the standard in civil cases is either by a **preponderance of evidence** or by **clear and convincing evidence**.

Basically, "preponderance" means that the weight of the evidence causes the trier of fact to lean one way more than the other—what might be called a "50%-plus" standard. Preponderance means that a fact that must be proved has been shown more likely to be true than not. But it does *not* mean that there is any certainty that the alleged fact is true. Preponderance results from consideration of all of the evidence, the believability of that evidence, and its persuasive nature. However, some studies have shown that many jurors subjectively believe that legal "preponderance" should be significantly more convincing than just a 50%-plus preponderance; those jurors might believe that it should be convincing.

Clear and convincing proof, on the other hand, requires a reasonable *certainty* that the fact to be proved is true. This standard falls somewhere between "preponderance of the evidence" and "beyond a reasonable doubt." Clear and convincing proof permits some reasonable doubt about the certainty of the alleged fact, but it requires evidence that is reasonably convincing, not just persuasive. *Figure 6.11* summarizes the various standards of proof.

The **standard of proof** is the degree of persuasion that evidence must achieve in order to sustain a verdict.

Preponderance of evidence requires that evidence presented by the prevailing party must outweigh, in credibility and/or materiality, the evidence presented by the other party; the slightest margin of difference is sufficient.

Clear and convincing evidence requires that persuasive evidence show the facts necessary in order to reach the ultimate verdict as being highly probable.

THE DIFFERENCE BETWEEN A VERDICT AND A JUDGMENT

A useful thing to remember is that *the jury returns a verdict* and *the court enters a judgment*—and the judgment is what really counts. In civil cases, the verdict need not be unanimous. Most states permit a civil jury to reach a verdict by

FIGURE 6.11 Standards of Proof

Standard Proof	Jury's State of Mind
Proof beyond a reasonable doubt	Convinced to a moral certainty
Clear and convincing proof	Convinced to a *reasonable* certainty; reasonable doubt permissible
Preponderance of the evidence	Verdict supported by the greater weight of evidence; result more likely than not

FIGURE 6.12 Sample Jury Instructions

Extreme and outrageous conduct is conduct which goes beyond all possible bounds of decency so as to be regarded as atrocious and utterly intolerable in a civilized community.

Extreme and outrageous conduct is not mere insults, indignities, threats, annoyances, petty oppressions or other trivialities. All persons must necessarily be expected and required to be hardened to a certain amount of rough language and to occasional acts that are definitely inconsiderate and unkind.

Extreme and outrageous conduct, however, is conduct which would cause an average member of the community to immediately react in outrage.

Superior Court of Los Angeles County, California, *California Jury Instructions--Civil, Book of Approved Jury Instructions [BAJI]* (Paul G. Breckenridge, Jr., ed., 8th ed., 1994) BAJI 12.74.

> **Practice Tip**
>
> *Experienced paralegals sometimes do much of the research for jury instructions. It is customary for the parties to present proposed jury instructions to the court well before the end of the trial. These are supported by legal memoranda based upon research by the attorney and/or paralegal.*

---

three-fourths vote; thus with the typical jury of twelve persons, nine votes would be sufficient to return a verdict. Together with the less stringent standard of proof in civil cases, that makes it relatively easy for civil juries to reach a verdict. Jury deadlocks (e.g., a 6–6 or 8–4 split vote) seldom cause mistrials in civil cases. The exact vote required for a civil verdict varies with jurisdiction and with the total number of jurors for that case.

Before retiring for deliberations, the jurors receive instructions from the court regarding their duties and the law to be applied to the case. Those **jury instructions** are of great importance, and many judgments have been overturned on appeal because the appellate court held that the trial judge gave incorrect instructions on the law—that is, the trial court incorrectly stated the legal standards that the jury must apply to the facts before it. During deliberations, the jury might request clarification or additional instructions from the court. Such requests are transmitted through the court bailiff. An example of jury instructions appears in *Figure 6.12*.

Jury instructions are the court's explanation of the legal principles that the jury must apply to the facts before it.

FIGURE 6.13   Sample Special Verdict Form

SPECIAL VERDICT

We, the jury in the above entitled action, find the following special verdict on the questions submitted to us:

Question No. 1:   Were the defendants negligent? Answer "yes" or "no" after the name of each defendant.

		Yes	No
Answer:	Defendant XYZ, Inc.	___	___
	Defendant Whistles, Ltd.	___	___

If you answer Question No. 1 "no" as to each defendant, sign and return this verdict.

If you answer Question No. 1 "yes" as to any defendant, then answer Question No. 2 as to such defendant.

Question No. 2:   As to each defendant that you answered "yes" to in response to Question No. 1, was such negligence a cause of injury to the plaintiff?

Answer "yes" or "no" after the name of [each] such defendant.

		Yes	No
Answer:	Defendant XYZ, Inc.	___	___
	Defendant Whistles, Ltd.	___	___

Superior Court of Los Angeles County, California, *California Jury Instructions--Civil, Book of Approved Jury Instructions [BAJI]* (Paul G. Breckenridge, Jr., ed., 8th ed., 1994) Adapted from BAJI 16.00.

General and Special Verdicts

In cases involving complex facts and legal issues, the court might require the jury to return a **special verdict**. A special verdict requires the jury to reach findings of fact only, without applying the law to those facts. (The latter task is left to the court.) In such a case, the jury receives a list of written questions, each of which must be answered. (See *Figure 6.13*). In effect, the jury is returning its verdict on the facts in piecemeal fashion. That simplifies the task for the jury and allows the parties and the court to better understand the jury's deliberations and ultimate verdict. A special verdict permits the court to discover inconsistencies in the

A **special verdict** is one in which the jury answers a number of questions about its factual conclusions based upon the evidence.

conclusions of the jury. Inconsistent findings of fact can be grounds for the court to set aside the verdict of the jury.

In some jurisdictions, the jury returns a single **general verdict**, together with responses to a series of "interrogatories" about its conclusions of fact. Because the responses to interrogatories must be consistent with the general verdict, they have much the same effect as a special verdict. However, the jury returning a general verdict will also apply the law—as instructed by the court—to its findings of fact when it reaches its general verdict.

A **general verdict** is one in which the jury decides the entire case in a single finding, after applying the law as instructed by the court.

THE MOTION FOR JUDGMENT NOV

When the jury returns its verdict, the court might poll the jurors to confirm the accuracy of the reported verdict. The court will enter judgment in accordance with the verdict if the court is satisfied that:

- the jury has deliberated in good faith;
- the verdict is supported by substantial evidence; and,
- there is no appearance of serious juror misconduct.

A losing party might present a motion for **judgment NOV**, also known as **judgment notwithstanding verdict**. This might occur, for example, when a jury has returned incompatible special verdicts. In that case, the court might enter a judgment that removes such incompatibility. *When a court reverses a general verdict by the jury, the circumstances must be such that the court could properly have ordered the jury to return a directed verdict—that is, the only verdict possible under the law*. A court may not reverse a general verdict simply because the judge considers that the jury believed the wrong evidence.

A **judgment notwithstanding verdict** (a **judgment NOV**) is a judgment entered by the court, contrary to the jury verdict.

Before the court enters its judgment, the losing party might also move for a new trial, arguing that some fatal defect invalidated the trial just then concluding. A court might set aside a civil verdict and declare a mistrial for the following reasons:

- because of the court's own judicial errors
- when a jury verdict is clearly contrary to the evidence
- if the court learns that serious juror misconduct has occurred

Motions for a new trial are not often granted, however.

THE CASE BEFORE THE APPELLATE COURT

The losing party—either defendant or plaintiff—might decide to appeal the judgment to a higher court, in which case that party is known as the appellant and the opposing party as the appellee. Because civil trials often involve numerous plaintiffs and defendants, and a mix of related facts and issues, it may be that neither side wins completely. Consequently, several parties might be dissatisfied with the result of the trial and decide to appeal, in which case each is an appellant on different issues. When monetary damages have been awarded, the losing party who appeals usually has to post a financial bond to guarantee payment in case the appeal fails.

The appellate court receives a complete transcript of the trial and copies of all exhibits. Although the record on appeal reveals the evidence heard by the trial court and the court's findings of fact, *questions of fact do not go on appeal*. Unless there was a serious violation of procedure or abuse of discretion by the trial court, the factual questions have been decided once and for all. If a serious violation did occur (e.g., the improper admission or exclusion of evidence), the case will be **remanded** by the appellate court for new proceedings in the trial court, perhaps even a new trial. If the appellate court affirms the trial court's

When an appellate court **remands** a case, it returns it to the lower court for appropriate further action in keeping with the appellate court's decision.

FIGURE 6.14 Litigation—Complaint through Judgment

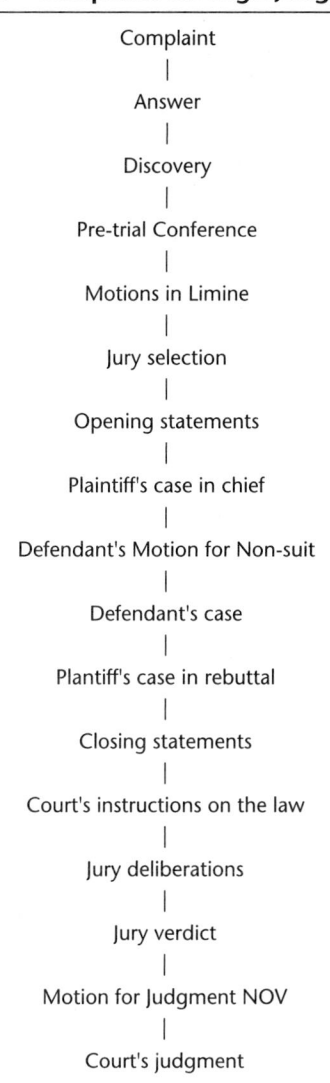

```
                Complaint
                   |
                 Answer
                   |
                Discovery
                   |
            Pre-trial Conference
                   |
             Motions in Limine
                   |
              Jury selection
                   |
            Opening statements
                   |
          Plaintiff's case in chief
                   |
        Defendant's Motion for Non-suit
                   |
             Defendant's case
                   |
          Plantiff's case in rebuttal
                   |
             Closing statements
                   |
        Court's instructions on the law
                   |
             Jury deliberations
                   |
               Jury verdict
                   |
          Motion for Judgment NOV
                   |
              Court's judgment
```

judgment, the case is usually remanded to the trial court for final disposition (e.g., the entry of a final judgment). If the appellate court *reverses* the trial court on errors of law, the trial court's findings of fact still stand, and the case will be remanded to the trial court for a new judgment conforming to the holding of the appellate court on issues of law.

The questions of law that go before the appellate court will be viewed in a light most favorable to the trial court's judgment. In other words, the appellate court must try to sustain the decision of the trial court. In effect, the appellant is entitled to a fair trial, but not necessarily a perfect trial. To obtain reversal, the appellant will have to convince the appellate court that a serious error of law or procedure clearly occurred *and* that the error was not harmless but actually damaged the legal interests of the appellant. A trial court judgment will not be reversed because of a **harmless error**, as the interests of justice do not require it. The admission of improper evidence is a common example of harmless error, where the result at trial would have been the same even without the improper introduction of evidence.

Also, an appellate court will let a lower court judgment stand—so long as the result is legally correct—even though the lower court reached that judgment based upon an incorrect understanding of the law. To illustrate: A manufacturer

Harmless error by the trial court does not jeopardize any substantial right or interest of the appealing party and therefore does not require reversal.

incorrectly held liable by the trial court under the doctrine of strict products liability could have been correctly held liable—based upon the evidence presented at trial—under a different legal theory, for example a breach of implied warranty. If the evidence clearly supports the latter liability, the appellate court will not disturb the judgment, even though the trial court reached its holding under the wrong legal theory. It may, however, remand the case for further consideration of the damages that might be properly awarded for breach of implied warranty.

When a case is heard on appeal, there are no witnesses, no testimony, no evidence. If any litigating party attends the hearing, she does so as an interested observer—not as an active participant in the hearing. The entire appellate proceeding is in the hands of the parties' attorneys and the court. Most appellate court hearings are held before a quorum of three appellate justices, sitting together. If the hearing is of extraordinary importance or if it is a rehearing by that same court to reconsider a particularly difficult legal issue, all justices of that appellate court might sit *en banc* (as a "full bench") to hear the appeal. Because appellate court decisions are made by majority vote, it is customary to have an odd number of justices to hear the case.

> An appellate court sits *en banc* when all justices of that court hear an appeal.

Prior to the hearing, each party submits an appellate brief that summarizes the facts and history of the case and also argues the law to be applied. Those appellate briefs will have been studied and the law researched by the appellate justices with the assistance of the court's research attorneys or law clerks (the latter usually being recent law school graduates awaiting admission to the bar). The purpose of the appellate hearing is to allow the attorneys for both sides to make oral arguments and for the court to question them on points of law.

After hearing oral arguments, the appellate justices will take the case under submission, perhaps doing additional research on issues raised at that hearing. Eventually, the justices will discuss the case among themselves and vote on the outcome. One of the justices will be designated to write the opinion of the court.

As discussed in Chapter 4, an appellate court has three basic choices: (1) It may affirm (i.e., sustain) the trial court's decision; (2) it may reverse (i.e., declare void) the trial court's decision; or, (3) it may affirm in part and reverse in part. If a new trial is not ordered, a reversal of the trial court decision means that the party that "won" the case at trial has actually *lost* the case—and the original "loser" has won, after all.

ENFORCING COURT JUDGMENTS

Obtaining a judgment is not the end of the client's case. The judgment establishes the respective legal rights and responsibilities of the parties, but it does not automatically change things. The most common problem with enforcing judgments involves the payment of damages or the surrender of property. There are various ways to enforce judgments. Only the most common are summarized below.

> A **writ of execution** is an order implementing an earlier judgment of the court; it is a writ ordering that particular property of the defendant be sold to satisfy a money judgment.

The winning party can apply to the court for a **writ of execution** against property owned by the losing party. This writ is a court order authorizing the sheriff or marshal to take possession of the property and sell it at auction. The proceeds of the auction are then used to satisfy the money judgment. If the auction brings more than necessary to pay the judgment, the excess is returned to the **judgment debtor**.

> A **judgment debtor** is a defendant against whom a money judgment has been entered.
>
> A debtor is **insolvent** if she lacks sufficient assets or income to satisfy a judgment.
>
> A debtor is **judgment proof** if she is insolvent, or if her assets are protected by statute or are beyond the jurisdiction of the court.

Occasionally, a judgment debtor will be **insolvent**—that is, lacking any substantial assets or source of income with which to pay the judgment. Such a debtor is said to be **judgment proof**. If that truly is the case, it usually is not worthwhile to pursue collection, and the judgment debt can be written off as a bad debt.

> An **automatic stay** is the immediate suspension of all legal proceedings affecting the assets of the debtor in bankruptcy.

If the judgment debtor files a bankruptcy petition, that invokes an **automatic stay** by the bankruptcy court, which bars any legal action to enforce

CHAPTER 6   Civil Litigation and Alternative Dispute Resolution   **211**

a debt or collect on a court judgment. If it can be shown that the bankruptcy filing is unwarranted, however, the bankruptcy court will dismiss the petition, thereby stripping the debtor of any protection under bankruptcy laws. If the bankruptcy filing is valid, it is possible that the judgment debtor will be discharged by the bankruptcy court, permanently relieving him of any obligation to pay the judgment.

The law governing enforcement procedures is the law of the jurisdiction where the judgment debtor's assets (real property, bank accounts, etc.) are located, not the jurisdiction where the judgment was won. The first step in enforcement is to identify and locate the assets of the judgment debtor. If the judgment debtor is unscrupulous, this can be a challenging task: Personal property can be moved or hidden and legal title to both personal and real property can be transferred to friends or relatives, either to conceal the property or at least complicate the collection efforts. Title might be transferred to a trust or corporation controlled by the judgment debtor or his relative or accomplice. Those transfers of title might be **fraudulent transfers** under the law, but they can be difficult and expensive to set aside.

Real property records and motor vehicle records can be searched, often by using computer databases. If the judgment debtor can be located, he can be served with a summons for a **judgment debtor examination**, during which he must answer questions under oath and must reveal the identity and location of his assets. When the judgment debtor cannot be located—or if he lies about his assets—private investigators can be used to track down his assets.

A **judgment lien** can be filed against property owned by the judgment debtor. Although judgment creditors usually prefer to force a sale by writ of execution, there are situations in which the judgment debtor's property interest is uncertain or only prospective. A beneficiary or heir, for example, has only a prospective or unperfected interest in the real property still in probate. Recording a judgment lien against that property would put potential future purchasers on notice of the judgment creditor's claim against that property interest and would establish priority over other claims or mortgages recorded at a later date. Another prospective property interest would be money owed by a third party *to the judgment debtor*. In some jurisdictions, the judgment creditor can serve that third party with notice of a judgment lien against those monies due, so that the judgment creditor's claim will be paid before any money passes into the hands of the judgment debtor.

If the judgment is for possession of specific property (e.g., a house), rather than for general damages, a judgment debtor might be served with a court order to turn over that property, and that order can be enforced through the court's **contempt powers**. A judgment creditor can also **garnish** the wages of the judgment debtor, in which case the employer must pay a portion of those wages (subject to a statutory limit) directly to the judgment creditor. Obviously, garnishment is a slow way to collect any sizeable sum. Garnishment procedures can be legally exacting, much as unlawful detainer procedures are, and a procedural misstep can prevent success.

SECTION 6. PARALEGAL RESPONSIBILITIES IN LITIGATION

Paralegals have become an essential part of the litigation team in law firms today. Their litigation assignments have become more diverse, and their responsibilities greater, as attorneys have learned to provide high-quality, cost-

---

Practice Tip

Paralegals play a key role in the enforcement of money judgments. Often it is necessary to track down assets of the judgment debtor, and sometimes the judgment debtor herself must be located so that she can be served with a summons for a judgment debtor examination.

Paralegals typically prepare the following enforcement documents for the attorney's review and signature, and then arrange to have them served, filed, and/or recorded:

- writ of attachment (before judgment)
- writ of execution (after judgment)
- summons for judgment debtor exam
- judgment lien
- order for garnishment of wages

A **fraudulent transfer** is a debtor's unlawful disposal of his assets to defraud creditors.

A **judgment debtor examination** is a proceeding in which the judgment debtor appears before the court to be questioned under oath concerning his assets.

A **judgment lien** is an encumbrance upon real or personal property of a judgment debtor, recorded in the jurisdiction where the property is located.

The court has **contempt powers** to punish persons who disobey the orders of the court or hinder its proceedings.

To **garnish** is to attach a portion of a debtor's wages or bank accounts, so that funds are paid directly to the creditor.

effective service to their clients. In many law offices, the most experienced paralegals perform assignments that, a decade or so ago, were thought to require the expertise of associate attorneys: sophisticated legal research; drafting legal memoranda for submission to the court, and preparing witnesses for their appearance in court. Of course, new paralegals will spend several years working on less complex assignments before they are ready for these advanced responsibilities.

INFORMATION: THE INDISPENSABLE FOUNDATION OF LITIGATION

Before a complaint is ever filed, potential plaintiffs and defendants often anticipate the *possibility* of a lawsuit. Several questions logically arise:

- What are the client's provable damages—or affirmative defenses?
- How strong is the opposing party's case?
- Should a settlement offer be made before a lawsuit is filed?
- What are the chances of losing if no settlement is possible and the case goes to trial?
- Would going to trial harden the litigants' positions and preclude a last-minute settlement?

The answers to these questions are dependent upon each party who is collecting, analyzing, and understanding critical information.

TYPICAL ASSIGNMENTS FOR NEW LEGAL ASSISTANTS

As already mentioned, new legal assistants will not be expected to take on the very challenging and sophisticated assignments that some senior legal assistants receive. If it were otherwise, it would be unfair to the legal assistants and to the clients. New legal assistants need time to absorb an enormous range of information about law and legal procedures, and to develop the necessary advanced skills before they attempt the more challenging assignments. This section discusses typical litigation assignments for new legal assistants.

Preparing, Filing, and Serving Court Documents

Most new litigation paralegals are introduced immediately to the preparation, filing, and serving of court documents. These are tasks that legal secretaries have long assumed, and some firms continue to rely upon secretaries to handle pleadings, summonses, and discovery documents. However, many firms prefer that paralegals assume those responsibilities, in part because paralegals should require less attorney supervision and in part because their time can be billed to the client. Statutes or court rules generally establish strict guidelines for the format and content of pleadings and discovery documents, so that a new legal assistant needs to become very familiar with those requirements.

Coordinating with the Court and Other Counsel

When court proceedings are imminent, coordination with the court clerk becomes extremely important. Legal secretaries and paralegals typically handle a large portion of this coordination. Because it requires an understanding of civil procedure and court rules, coordinating the litigation process is not a routine matter for the new paralegal.

Practice Tip

Information is the common thread of the paralegal's role in litigation. This role is exemplified by the following tasks, among others:

- *interviewing clients and witnesses*
- *screening public records*
- *coordinating with outside investigators and expert consultants*
- *managing and reviewing discovery*
- *organizing and maintaining files of all kinds*
- *reviewing numerous cartons of documents in search of the missing "needle in the haystack"*
- *preparing and managing exhibits for trial (and sometimes in court)*

Practice Tip

The rules identifying which documents must be served on which party can be quite complicated. Occasionally, even experienced legal assistants will be uncertain. Although cases have been lost for failure to serve a particular document on the opposing party, no one ever lost a case by serving a document unnecessarily. Therefore, the best rule is: If in doubt, serve.

In coordinating with the court, the paralegal will:

- schedule hearing dates;
- determine the court's requirements for *ex parte* notice to the opposing party; and,
- inquire about any other special conditions or procedures required by the judge of that court.

This process is most efficient in the federal court system and in those states that have one judge handle all court proceedings for a given case. In states that do not assign a case to a single judge "for all purposes," even more coordination will be required. Of course, the paralegal will rarely, if ever, be speaking to the judge—he will be speaking with the court clerk.

COOPERATION BETWEEN OPPOSING COUNSEL

Most litigating attorneys understand that opposing parties are better off if they cooperate in moving the litigation process forward. They also recognize that some clients pay a lot of money for—but receive little benefit from—frequent courtroom battles over the *process* of bringing a case to trial. It might seem unnatural for attorneys who are adversaries to cooperate with one another, but in fact it can be to the mutual benefit of their opposing clients. One purpose of a cooperative relationship is to increase the chances of a pretrial settlement. Trials and preparation for trials can be exorbitantly expensive. Often it is in the best financial interests of all parties to reach a settlement at the earliest possible date. But because settlement decisions can be difficult to make before each side has enough information to evaluate the strength of its case and that of its opponent, the early stages of trial preparation (e.g, discovery) might be unavoidable. Even while both sides are conducting discovery, the opposing attorneys can establish a cooperative and intelligent approach to the dispute without violating their clients' respective interests in the case. This cooperation between opposing counsel often takes a form known as "professional courtesy."

A common gesture of professional courtesy is permitting an opposing party to serve a pleading by mail or facsimile when personal service is normally required under the rules. Another example is extending a deadline that the opposing party is required to meet. In many jurisdictions, a defendant has only thirty days within which to file its answer or demurrer to the complaint. Yet plaintiff counsel commonly grant extensions to defendants. It might appear that granting the extension would violate the plaintiff attorney's obligation to vigorously prosecute her client's

> **Practice Tip**
>
> If given this authority by their supervising attorneys *(and when permitted by court rules)*, paralegals and legal secretaries often arrange timeline extensions and coordinate other procedural matters between the offices of opposing counsel without the two attorneys' ever communicating directly with each other. This coordination is often done through informal telephone conversations. Quite literally, one legal assistant calls the other attorney's secretary or paralegal to ask, "Can we have a ten-day extension on our opposition to your motion for summary judgment?"

Ethics Watch

The crucial point is that ethical attorneys generally consider themselves bound by the timeline extensions granted on their behalf by paralegals or legal secretaries, and judges will look very critically upon any attorney's effort to disavow such a commitment. However, it is customary and extremely important for the paralegal requesting the extension to write a confirming letter to the opposing attorney:

> "This letter will confirm the telephone conversation I had today with your legal assistant, Daryl Koenig, during which your office granted a ten-day extension for our opposition to your . . . ."

The confirming letter is an important protection of the client's interests. It has become customary to transmit that letter of confirmation by facsimile in order to allow the opposing attorney an immediate opportunity to raise any objections to the informal understanding already reached.

case, but that is not necessarily so. If the extension is refused, the defendant can almost always come up with a legally adequate answer to file before the deadline and later file a carefully amended answer. Therefore, the opportunity to get that "easy default" is often an illusion. In addition, by granting the extension, the plaintiff counsel has taken the first step toward establishing a positive working relationship with the opposing counsel. And, who knows—next time it might be the plaintiff counsel who needs an extension for an important deadline.

COMPLYING WITH DEADLINES

In lawsuits, there are numerous deadlines established by statute, by court rules, and by stipulation between the litigating attorneys. Failure to comply with some deadlines can compromise the client's case and also result in malpractice claims. Paralegals are often responsible for the firm's timeline management system (known as a **tickler system**), which ensures that attorneys are reminded *in advance* as each deadline approaches and that each document is received on time, or timely served on other parties and filed with the court.

*Law firms use a **tickler system** to alert attorneys and paralegals to imminent deadlines.*

Although computer programs are the predominant tickler system for law firms today, some small firms might still use what is essentially a paper calendar system. When the attorney or paralegal identifies the date when a document must be filed with the court or served on another party, he fills out a small form in at least two copies: one copy for the due date itself and another copy for a date typically three to ten days in advance of the due date. The tickler form identifies the case, the document, the final due date, and the "early warning" tickle date. The appropriate copy of the form will be placed on the attorney's desk the evening before each designated date.

The early warning tickle is both a reminder and an opportunity to confirm that the document is being prepared and will be ready to file or serve on time. Many attorneys prefer to schedule their work so that they file or serve a document at least two days before its actual deadline—that leaves time for corrective measures in case some last-minute problem arises.

DRAFTING DISCOVERY REQUESTS AND RESPONSES

Neophyte legal assistants working in litigation will soon be involved in drafting discovery documents. The attorney should brief the paralegal, providing a summary of the facts and legal issues involved in the case. The paralegal will then be asked to prepare a discovery request—interrogatories, for example—or a response to discovery.

Referring to the complaint and other pleadings, and to her notes from the attorney's briefing, the legal assistant can draft a list of questions. A new paralegal will want to accumulate sample interrogatories from other cases of a similar type for her form book. Those examples will suggest questions to be included and will provide examples of the careful, thorough language that must be used in order to avoid leaving loopholes for the party who must answer the interrogatories. Equally important, referring to the sample interrogatories will bolster the new paralegal's confidence as she drafts her own document. If these are the paralegal's first set of interrogatories, she might want to ask another paralegal or legal secretary in the office to review them and offer suggestions. Finally, the attorney will review and revise the discovery document.

Responses to discovery are drafted in a similar fashion. For a response to a request for inspection and production of documents, for example, responses from similar cases will be an invaluable guide. Grounds for objecting to the request are of special importance in drafting responses. The paralegal should have a list of common objections at hand. (A listing of typical discovery objections appears earlier in this chapter.) If an objection seems well-based, the paralegal should include it. The attorney can always delete the objection.

A common practice is to state the objection, followed by this statement: "Without waiving said objection, the following documents will be produced." Then one lists those documents. This technique "preserves" the objection that later can be asserted in court, if necessary, and it also avoids an expensive and time-consuming fight over the discovery process. This method of handling objections is a common practice also when the parties are hoping to work out a settlement as soon as all sides have the information needed to evaluate the case.

Paralegals are often responsible for drafting interrogatories, requests for production, and the responses to them. It is less common for paralegals to draft requests for admissions, demands for medical or psychiatric examination, and the like. The request for admissions requires a sophisticated understanding of the legal issues—more than most paralegals would have, unless they are working in a field in which they have special expertise. Demands for medical and psychiatric examinations are rather uncommon, except in particular types of practice (e.g., personal injury, worker's compensation, and medical malpractice).

NOTICES TO APPEAR FOR DEPOSITION

The paralegal often coordinates deposition schedules with the client's witnesses and with opposing counsel for deposition of its witnesses. In most cases, there is no problem in arranging depositions, because a court order can be obtained to compel a witness to appear. For all depositions, a notice to appear for deposition (or a subpoena) is sent to the deponent, with copies served on all other parties. If the deponent is a party to the lawsuit or is another witness represented by counsel, the notice must be sent to that attorney. The paralegal normally prepares the deposition notice or subpoena and serves it by mail or arranges for personal service, if that is required. In some jurisdictions, the paralegal will also prepare an **affidavit of service** (or **proof of service**), verifying that the notice or subpoena has been properly served. Depending upon court rules, the affidavit of service might be filed with the court.

SUMMARIZING DEPOSITIONS AND OTHER DISCOVERY INFORMATION

Another typical task for a new paralegal is summarizing depositions. It usually is not a difficult task, unless the deponent is an expert witness. Depositions of expert witnesses sometimes involve highly technical concepts and vocabulary, and for that reason litigation paralegals with specialized training and experience in technical fields (e.g., medicine, construction, accounting, or engineering) are often in high demand.

The attorney will use the deposition summary to review the highlights of a witness' testimony. Because the summary is easy to scan, the attorney can quickly find a topic of importance. The summary is also an index that identifies the pages where that testimony appears in the transcript. When the trial testimony of a witness differs from his testimony in deposition, the attorney will challenge the witness to explain the discrepancy. Impeachment is used to shake a witness' confidence and to cause the jury or court to doubt his credibility.

In complex cases, the paralegal might prepare a table summarizing the information obtained through all forms of discovery. It would be organized by key facts and legal issues. Using the table, the paralegal or attorney can quickly identify discovery documents that provide that information. Discovery information might also be summarized in memorandum form.

> **Practice Tip**
>
> *The court clerk has a very important position, coordinating all of the paperwork that passes through the judicial system, managing the court's calendar, and coordinating with the lawyers who have cases pending. In most jurisdictions, the court clerk is able to issue important legal documents (e.g., abstract of judgment, summons, and default judgment) based upon court records and without seeking specific approval from the judge.*
>
> *Any paralegal who is so ill-advised as to treat the court clerk as a "clerical" employee will come to regret it and hope that the case is reassigned to a different courtroom. A court clerk is in a position to smooth the way for an inexperienced paralegal or attorney—or to chastise even the most experienced litigator for every minor misstep in preparing and filing paperwork with the court.*

An **affidavit of service** is a declaration made under penalty of perjury affirming that documents have been properly served on another person.

A **proof of service** is equivalent to an affidavit of service.

> **Practice Tip**
>
> When the attorney needs documents copied or served in a distant city, how will the legal assistant manage to have that done? The answer, of course, is to contact an attorney service in that city. Usually, such services can be located using "yellow page" sites on the Internet. The legal assistant can also identify law firms in that city, using a print directory such as Martindale-Hubble or a Web site such as http://www.westlaw.com. A phone call to the receptionist at several law firms should easily obtain the telephone number for the attorney service that those firms use. Arrangements with that attorney service can then be made over the phone.

An **exemplar** is a single sample that serves as a model or example of a larger number of essentially identical things.

The **custodian of records** in a business or government agency is the person responsible for maintaining the records of that business or agency.

To **certify** a public record is to authoritatively verify a copy of that record to be true and correct.

To **cite check** is to verify the accuracy of all citations to legal authority found in a memorandum and the accuracy of all quotations from legal authority.

The computer age is revolutionizing the management of discovery information. New software allows the computer to create a database containing summaries of all discovery information, pleadings, and legal memoranda. The database can even contain the full text of every single document (letters, invoices, pleadings, deposition transcripts, etc.) in the case, and the computer can search that database in seconds to locate key facts or testimony. In complex cases, paralegals are increasingly brought to the counsel's table in court so that they can use notebook computers that contain that entire database of information, providing the attorney in trial with instant access to any information needed. (See Chapter 9 for a discussion of the use of computers in litigation.)

PREPARING TRIAL EXHIBITS

An exhibit at trial can be any physical object: a spark plug, letter, receipt, photograph, chart, audio tape, and so on. But most exhibits are paper documents. Even in fairly simple lawsuits, an attorney might use a substantial number of exhibits—perhaps as many as 100. In large, complex cases, the exhibit list might extend into the thousands. Whether 100 or 3,000, those exhibits need to be prepared for use and indexed so that they can be quickly located.

Paralegals often work with expert witnesses and consultants in preparing specific exhibits, such as photographic blow-ups, charts, videotapes, and computer simulations. The paralegal will coordinate with the court clerk to ensure that sufficient copies of paper exhibits are available for use by the court, witnesses, and counsel for all parties.

In some cases, the object that caused an injury or death was destroyed in that event or was so severely damaged that the jury would be unable to understand its original design, shape or structure. In that circumstance, a duplicate article might be used as an **exemplar**—that is, an article that is identical in all material features to the original article that was damaged or destroyed. In a trial resulting from an auto accident, for example, an identical tire (same brand and model) might be presented as an exemplar for the tire that disintegrated in the accident. The exemplar allows the jury to better understand expert testimony about the tire's design and structure.

OBTAINING GOVERNMENT AND BUSINESS RECORDS

Records maintained by business and government agencies are often pivotal to the outcome of a lawsuit. As explained in Chapter 5, most government records in the United States are public documents available to anyone. Business records of any litigating party can be obtained through discovery; records of other businesses are not generally available to the public. However, those nonparty business records can be obtained by serving a subpoena *duces tecum* on the **custodian of records**—the employee responsible for maintaining those records. If the custodian of records cannot appear to testify in court, she can be deposed so that the authenticity of the records can be established by sworn testimony. Copies of government records can be **certified** by the agency's custodian of records to be true and correct copies of the original.

CITE CHECKING

A very important research task for paralegals is **cite checking**. Before an attorney submits his memorandum of points and authorities to the court, he wants to be absolutely certain that every citation and every quotation is accurate. The paralegal will verify the accuracy of each citation: case name, date, volume and page numbers, and citation format. Every quotation will be checked *verbatim*, and comma for comma, and *italics* for *italics,* to ensure absolute literal accuracy. Although computer software is available that automatically cite checks for much of the foregoing, some attorneys are reluctant to trust a computer to do this very important task.

Up to this point, the cite check assignment has not required the paralegal to actually understand a court decision that the attorney has cited. But when the legal assistant is asked to confirm that each court opinion actually stands for the exact proposition for which it is being cited, a clear understanding of that opinion is indispensable. Someone must verify that the attorney's paraphrasing or summarization accurately reflects the court's holding on the legal issues in each case being cited. This phase of cite checking becomes much more challenging and interesting.

> **Ethics Watch**
> It is impossible to stress too strongly the importance of attending to detail when cite checking. An incomplete or inaccurate cite check leaves the attorney exposed to great professional embarrassment before the court. Worse yet, it could result in losing a motion and conceivably, the case. Liability for legal malpractice is a very genuine danger if cite checking is carelessly done.

LOCATING CASE LAW ON A PARTICULAR ISSUE

Similar to the second phase of cite checking described above, locating case law on a particular issue—the next level of legal research—requires some legal analysis. The attorney will usually offer one case on that issue, as a starting point, or will direct the paralegal to a discussion of the issue in a law review article, legal treatise, or legal encyclopedia. Using the methods described later (in Chapter 8), the paralegal will then "follow the paper chase" in pursuit of additional cases that will assist the attorney in her analysis of the issue.

PREPARING THE TRIAL NOTEBOOK

An important litigation tool is the **trial notebook**, which serves the attorney as a reference and resource manual during trial preparation and during the trial itself. Although some attorneys organize the "notebook" in a series of manila folders, others prefer to use one or more three-ring binders. The purpose of the trial notebook is to have essential information easily at hand while preparing the case and also in court. Although some attorneys prefer to set up and maintain the trial notebook themselves, others rely heavily upon paralegals and legal secretaries to share this task. As attorneys and paralegals become more comfortable with computer support for litigation, laptop or notebook computers have been replacing the bulky notebooks and cardboard boxes that countless legal assistants have had to load into automobile trunks and haul up courthouse stairs.

A **trial notebook** is a collection of essential information about a case going to trial, used both for pretrial preparation and as a reference during trial.

The following are typical components of a trial notebook:

- case outline—a summary of the key facts and issues that must be addressed during trial, and a chronological plan for presentation of the client's case
- pleadings—the complaint, answer, and all other pleadings in the case
- trial brief—the memorandum of points and authorities that identifies the legal issues that the trial court is expected to decide, provides a summary of the evidence to be presented, and argues those issues of law

FIGURE 6.15 Preparing the Trial Notebook

Task	Typical Responsibility
CASE OUTLINE	Attorney
PLEADINGS	Attorney, assisted by paralegal
TRIAL BRIEF	Attorney, possibly assisted by paralegal's research
STATEMENT OF DAMAGES	Paralegal, assisted by client (attorney will review with client)
MOTIONS IN LIMINE	Attorney, possibly assisted by paralegal's research
EXHIBITS	Paralegal, assisted by client and/or expert witness
JURY SELECTION PLANS	Attorney, possibly assisted by paralegal
WITNESS LIST	Attorney
DEPOSITION SUMMARIES	Paralegal
PROPOSED JURY INSTRUCTIONS	Attorney, possibly assisted by paralegal's research
DIRECTORIES FOR COUNSEL AND WITNESSES	Paralegal

- statement of damages—an itemized list of all financial damages and costs incurred by the plaintiff as a result of the defendant's misconduct
- motions *in limine*
- pretrial motions to exclude or limit certain evidence and issues that opposing parties might present to the court
- oppositions to the motions *in limine* that opposing counsel is expected to present
- exhibit list
- jury selection—criteria for selection of jurors and questions to be asked during the *voir dire* examination
- witness list
- deposition summaries—summaries tabbed for key issues and possible impeachment testimony
- proposed jury instructions—instructions on the law to be given by the court for the jury's guidance during deliberations
- directories for counsel and witnesses—addresses and phone numbers for all counsel representing each party to the litigation and a directory of witnesses (including expert witnesses) for the client

WORKING WITH WITNESSES

Paralegals coordinate with the client's witnesses so that each will know when and where to appear. It is advisable to serve each witness who is not a party with a subpoena, so that last-minute jitters do not result in the witness not appearing. The paralegal will be responsible for keeping witnesses informed of scheduling changes, as the unpredictable pace of the trial can require witnesses to appear earlier or later than first anticipated.

Legal assistants might be responsible for preparing witnesses by going over their deposition testimony with them, including any exhibits about which they will testify. An experienced legal assistant might review with the witness the questions likely to be asked and the witness' answers to those questions. In exceptional circumstances, it might be necessary for the legal assistant to remain outside the courtroom with a witness, soothing his anxieties while he waits to be called to the stand.

LEGAL ASSISTANTS IN THE COURTROOM

Although not an assignment for a new legal assistant, assisting at trial can be one of the more interesting and rewarding experiences that a litigation paralegal will have. It is briefly discussed here to give the paralegal student a sense of the possibilities ahead.

As attorneys become more accustomed to relying upon paralegals for trial preparation, paralegals are assisting in court with increasing frequency. Paralegal assistance at trial makes good sense, financially and professionally. The cost to clients is substantially less than having an associate attorney present at the trial, and the associate—who otherwise would be sitting **second chair** to the lead attorney at trial—is free to assist the lead counsel in other ways (e.g., by doing legal research) or can be working in the office on other client matters. With an experienced legal assistant present in court, an attorney sitting second chair might be unnecessary.

Paralegal assistance at trial offers practical benefits as well. The paralegal often has personal knowledge of the "trivia" of the case that surpasses that of any attorney who has not been intimately involved with the case—and what appears to be trivia can take on unexpected importance during trial. Some attorneys find that a paralegal's view of the trial is different from an attorney's perspective, and they rely upon the paralegal to offer a perspective that is closer to a juror's reaction as the trial progresses. A legal assistant who maintains an objective view of the trial can be extremely valuable to the attorney trying the case. For that reason, paralegals and other firm personnel are sometimes asked to sit in the spectator seating of the courtroom, so that they can report their observations during breaks in the trial.

Depending upon the court rules and the law firm's policy, a paralegal might be permitted to sit with the attorney at the counsel table. This is the most efficient arrangement, because it makes it easier for the paralegal to hand off exhibits and pass or receive notes as the trial progresses. If a paralegal does sit at the counsel table, it is helpful if the attorney introduces her to the jury as a paralegal—not an attorney—and explains that she will not address the court or question witnesses. One benefit of that approach is to avoid the perception among jurors that the client is bringing several high-priced attorneys to trial. In the eyes of the jury, a lone attorney assisted by one or two paralegals might present a favorable contrast to an opposing party that is represented by two or more attorneys.

Jury Selection

During jury selection, the paralegal will take notes about the prospective jurors, particularly about their responses to the questions posed by the judge and the attorneys during *voir dire*. Jury selection is based upon carefully planned criteria; but it is also based on the intuitive perceptions of the attorney. The paralegal can contribute an additional perspective to this process. For example, the paralegal should observe body language and facial expressions, because a juror's tendency to be receptive or aloof can influence his role as a trier of fact. In addition, the legal assistant should note how prospective jurors respond to the personalities of the attorneys who are trying the case, because a juror's reaction to an attorney can color his attitude toward the client. In similar fashion, the paralegal

---

> **Practice Tip**
>
> The subpoenas for witnesses typically require each of them to appear on the very day and hour at which the case is scheduled to begin. Obviously, they cannot all testify at that time—or perhaps even on that day. Nor are the witnesses generally allowed to sit in the courtroom to hear the testimony of others. To avoid keeping a witness waiting for hours or days in the courthouse hallway, the attorney can send an **on-call letter** for each witness to sign. The on-call letter states that the witness has been served with a subpoena to appear at a given place and time, but that for the convenience of the witness he agrees to remain "on-call"—constantly available by phone—and will appear in court within a defined period of time (e.g., within two hours of being notified). The legal assistant usually explains the arrangement to each witness and prepares the on-call letters. Copies of all subpoenas and on-call letters should be included in the trial notebook.

An **on-call letter** is signed by a witness under subpoena, who thereby agrees to remain available by phone and to appear in court within a defined period after being notified.

An attorney who sits **second chair** at the counsel's table in court assists the lead attorney who has primary responsibility for trying the case.

should observe the jury's reactions to the opening statement of each attorney, because those reactions might reveal issues that are confusing or offensive to the jury. The observation process should continue throughout the trial.

In effect, the paralegal becomes the attorney's surrogate observer: another set of eyes and ears. During testimony, the paralegal should take careful notes—particularly during the attorney's direct and cross-examination, because it is difficult for the attorney to question witnesses and simultaneously take notes. If the court permits, it can be helpful for the paralegal to attend discussions with counsel in the judge's chambers, as issues requiring further legal research are often raised in such discussions.

Managing Exhibits during Trial

The case outline in the trial notebook will contain a chronology of the testimony and exhibits to be presented on behalf of the client. If the court clerk has informed the legal assistant that it is permissible to prenumber all exhibits, that will have been done. Otherwise, the legal assistant should have prepared a temporary system using numbered folders, envelopes, or removable tabs. That numbering system should be reflected in the case outline, so that the legal assistant can follow the progress of the case and have the exhibits readily at hand as they are needed.

If the exhibits have not been prenumbered, the court clerk will assign an identifying letter or number (e.g., "Exhibit 17") as each exhibit is admitted into evidence. From then on, the exhibit is the "property" of the court and must be handled in accordance with court rules and the policy of that particular judge. Plaintiff's and defendant's exhibits might have separate numbering sequences (e.g., "Plaintiff's Exhibit 17"), or all exhibits might be numbered consecutively, regardless of which party has offered them. Computer software is available to track the status of all anticipated and admitted exhibits.

As the attorney presents her case, the paralegal locates the exhibits and keeps them ready for introduction into evidence. It is equally important to keep track of all exhibits presented into evidence by the opposition, because any exhibit admitted in evidence can be used by any party for direct and cross-examination of witnesses. The court might require all parties to exchange exhibit lists prior to trial (the most efficient practice); otherwise, the legal assistant will be responsible for creating a list of opposition exhibits, numbered to match the exhibit numbers assigned by the court clerk. This list will make it far easier for the attorney to locate an opposition exhibit when she needs it.

SECTION 7. ALTERNATIVE DISPUTE RESOLUTION

Because litigation is so expensive and time-consuming, an increasing number of litigants are choosing to resolve their disputes through **alternative dispute resolution (ADR)**. ADR includes a variety of nonjudicial processes (e.g., conciliation, neutral evaluation, and fact finding), but the more common are negotiation, mediation, and arbitration. In some jurisdictions, ADR is mandatory for specified classes of disputes. Although statutes or court rules might require the parties to attempt ADR, their ultimate right to a trial by court cannot be denied. This section will emphasize mediation and arbitration, although negotiations might also occur before, during, and/or after either mediation or arbitration.

Practice Tip

Many judges have specific preferences regarding the handling of exhibits once they have been introduced and marked by the court clerk. In some courtrooms, the attorneys or legal assistants are permitted to handle exhibits during breaks, or even to keep them on or near the counsel table for use during examination of witnesses. In other courtrooms, the clerk retains strict possession and control of all exhibits admitted into evidence, and they must be retrieved from him and returned to him each time they are used. It is important to discuss this policy with the court clerk prior to the start of the trial, so that neither the legal assistant nor the attorney incurs the displeasure of the judge or the court clerk.

Alternative dispute resolution (ADR) is the disposition of legal controversies through nonjudicial proceedings, such as negotiation, arbitration, or mediation.

ADVANTAGES OF ALTERNATIVE DISPUTE RESOLUTION

Time and expense have already been mentioned as factors that motivate litigants to use ADR. Because there is no formal discovery process and there are no crowded court dockets to wait behind, timelines are greatly shortened in mediation and arbitration. It is not unusual for a dispute to reach final resolution through ADR within three or four months. The resulting reduction in legal fees can be a substantial savings. Other advantages of ADR over litigation include the following:

- The parties have much greater control over the process.
- The parties can select a neutral with expertise in the subject matter of their dispute.
- The proceedings are confidential, rather than a public record.
- There is a greater likelihood of preserving a positive on-going relationship after the dispute has been resolved.

MEDIATION

Mediation is the process in which a neutral third party acts as a facilitator, consulting with each party to find out what its needs and demands are, and trying to find a possible compromise between the parties. Because the **mediator** keeps all information confidential—revealing to the opposing party only what the confiding party has authorized—the litigating parties are able to immediately place all of their cards on the table. The mediator's only interest is to find a solution that the parties can live with—he is not particularly concerned with who is the victim and who is the villain of the case.

Mediation is the resolution of disputes with the assistance of a neutral who helps the disputing parties to find a mutual resolution of their differences.

A **mediator** is the neutral third party who facilitates mediation.

In addition to the general advantages of ADR, listed above, mediation offers some advantages unique to this process:

- Either party can pull out of mediation at any time, so that there is less opportunity for tactics of intimidation or manipulation.
- The parties are more likely to honor the spirit, as well as the letter, of an agreement they have mutually crafted.
- The parties can create solutions that a court might lack the power to impose upon either of them.
- Mediation tends to reduce barriers to communication and mutual understanding, and can provide a first step toward establishing better communication between parties who want (or need) to remain in an on-going relationship.
- Even where mediation fails to resolve *all* differences, often it can narrow the issues that then must be resolved by the court.

Two Stages of Mediation

In some disputes, the parties have developed so much hostility and distrust that it is impractical to immediately bring them together in a single room for a discussion of their differences. The more intimate the relationship—marriage or a close business partnership, for example—the more likely this is to be true. When spouses or business partners are ready to take each other to court, the relationship is inevitably volatile and the hard feelings are deeply personal. One attorney has written:

> "It is often harder to get disputing parties to agree to talk than it is to reach agreement once the talks have started. Getting to 'Maybe' can be harder than Getting to 'Yes.' "[1]

This is one reason that mediators usually start by making *ex parte* contact with each party to explore the situation. In these preliminary contacts, the mediator will do the following:

- explain the process, if the parties are not already familiar with mediation
- assure the parties of her neutrality
- assure the parties of the confidentiality of the process
- inquire about the issues and needs important to each party
- determine whether the dispute is one appropriate to the mediation process
- determine how much "separate room" (i.e., remote mediation) is necessary before face-to-face mediation can begin

The initial form of mediation often is "shuttle diplomacy" (via telephone, e-mail, or *ex parte* meetings) to be followed later by same-room mediation with all parties present. In this shuttle diplomacy stage, the mediator is an attentive listener and occasional questioner, until she has a clear understanding of the dispute and the perceived needs of each party. After she has gained their trust, she might begin to explain to each party the perspective of their opponent, without endorsing or validating either perspective. Her objective is to bring the parties to the point where they can sit with her and each other in the same room and engage in constructive discussion of their problems.

In the second, face-to-face stage, the mediator will facilitate an exchange between the parties about their respective viewpoints and grievances. When both parties fully understand the other's complaints, concerns, and needs, the mediator will begin to explore options for resolution. Because both parties now trust her, they will be far more receptive to compromises that she suggests than they would be to any proposals from their opponent.

If agreement is reached, the mediator will help the parties to craft a written settlement agreement. Once signed by both parties, the agreement becomes a binding, enforceable contract. A good settlement agreement will include a process for resolving future disagreements over the same or related issues, or over implementation of the settlement itself. If the parties were referred to mediation by a court and the court still retains jurisdiction over that matter, it might be necessary to obtain formal court approval of the settlement. Court approval would *always* be necessary for certain types of settlements, for example:

- settlements determining child custody and parental rights
- settlements between heirs determining the distribution of the decedent's estate

ARBITRATION

In contrast to a mediator, an **arbitrator** acts as a judge might and bases her decision upon the law as it applies to the facts at hand. Consequently, an **arbitration** hearing is similar to a trial, although much less formal. The rules of evidence are less rigidly applied in arbitration, and the arbitrator often takes a more active part in questioning witnesses than a judge typically would. If the parties have not agreed to final and binding arbitration (discussed below), the arbitrator's decision is merely advisory, and either party may reject it and pursue litigation.

Many contracts include clauses that call for arbitration of any disputes that arise under those contracts. These clauses are intended to protect the parties from the cost and delay of litigation, and also to make a continuing, positive relationship between the parties more likely. In most contracts, these clauses provide for binding arbitration of the dispute. Arbitration clauses are especially common in the following contracts:

Practice Tip

Mediation is a an alternative career that an experienced paralegal might wish to consider. Training in mediation is offered by some colleges, as well as by regional associations of mediators. Some Legal Aid Societies and other nonprofit agencies offer mediation services to low-income clients as a solution to disputes with landlords and merchants, and for marital problems. Newly trained mediators often can gain practical experience by doing pro bono mediation for such organizations.

An **arbitrator** is the neutral third party who conducts an informal hearing on the merits of a dispute and renders a decision (the "award").

Arbitration is the resolution of disputes with the assistance of a neutral party who receives evidence, hears argument, and renders a decision.

- construction industry contracts
- collective bargaining contracts
- insurance policies
- securities dealer/client contracts
- physician/patient contracts
- international trade contracts

Advisory and Binding Arbitration

As mentioned earlier, a person's right to trial by court cannot be summarily taken from him. But when parties submit a dispute to **binding arbitration**, they are voluntarily surrendering their right to a court trial. The arbitrator's decision will be final, and it will be enforced by the courts, if necessary. Courts are reluctant to overturn an award even if the arbitrator reached conclusions of fact that are not supported by any substantial evidence, or reached conclusions of law that were incorrect. Only in rare cases do courts overturn an arbitrator's award, and then only if:

- the objecting party was induced by fraud to agree to the arbitration clause;
- the arbitrator's award was obtained by fraud or corruption;
- the arbitrator exceeded his authority; or
- the award violates public policy.

Binding arbitration imposes a final and enforceable decision on the parties who submit a dispute to the arbitrator.

To illustrate the latter point (by extreme example), if an arbitrator resolved an employment dispute by requiring the employee to become an indentured servant of the employer, no court would permit that award to stand in violation of public policy.

In **advisory arbitration**, the arbitrator effectively *recommends* to the disputing parties a resolution that his understanding of the evidence and the law would dictate. It is the same decision that he would impose if he heard the matter under binding arbitration. Because this arbitration is only advisory, either party may reject it and pursue litigation. But the advisory award might be indicative of how a court of law would rule, based upon the same evidence. So, a dissatisfied party might decide that it is not worth risking the expense of contesting the same issue in a court of law and therefore accept the arbitrator's nonbinding decision.

Advisory arbitration results in a nonbinding decision based upon the evidence and applicable law.

Hawaii has one of the more progressive policies calling for advisory arbitration. Rule 2.1 of the *Rules of Professional Conduct* requires an attorney to inform the client that ADR is an alternative to litigation. In addition, court rules provide that a case will not be set for trial until the parties (or their attorneys) have met face-to-face for consideration of alternative dispute resolution. The parties must then inform the court of the ADR methods that they selected—and if nonbinding ADR is not agreed to, they must inform the court of which party has objected, and why. In spite of such objection(s), the court may order the parties to participate in ADR prior to the case coming to trial. As is the case with all nonbinding processes, participation does not guarantee successful resolution.

Binding Arbitration Clauses in Contracts

If there is a binding arbitration clause in a contract, it might be impossible to bring a contractual dispute before the courts. Both federal and state arbitration statutes (discussed below) reflect a public policy interest in the encouragement of arbitration in lieu of litigation. This public policy interest is based upon the following:

- supporting and enforcing the contractual agreements—including arbitration clauses—that the interested parties have made

- requiring the parties to exhaust other available remedies for a final resolution before bringing the dispute before the courts
- shielding the courts from the burden of unnecessary litigation
- avoiding the expense that additional litigation would impose upon the taxpayers

If a contract provides only advisory arbitration, however, the courts are far more receptive to hearing the case. Although some courts have required even the advisory process to first be completed before hearing the case, other courts have accepted disputes without requiring advisory arbitration. The latter practice is based upon the apparent futility of pursuing a nonbinding process that might offer no real prospect for final resolution of the dispute.

Federal and State Arbitration Acts

The *Federal Arbitration Act of 1925* (9 U.S.C. §§ 1, *et seq.*) applies to arbitration of contractual disputes in interstate commerce. The act states that arbitration agreements are enforceable and that federal courts must compel parties to arbitrate disputes covered by those agreements. Ruling in a multitude of cases regarding various interstate commerce issues, the U.S. Supreme Court has recognized a broad authority for Congress to regulate even those activities that are tenuously related to business activities among the states. So, it appears that the federal act applies to the overwhelming majority of commercial arbitrations in the United States, even between individual and corporate citizens of a single state.

Thirty-five states have adopted the *Uniform Arbitration Act.* Similar to the federal act, the *Uniform Arbitration Act* requires state courts to compel arbitration if a contract includes an arbitration clause. Both federal and state courts share the reluctance to overturn an arbitrator's award, as described above. Because so many arbitrations are subject to the concurrent jurisdiction of the state and federal acts, they would be enforceable in either state or federal court on the basis of either state law or federal law. Of course, if there is a conflict between the state and federal acts, the federal act will govern.

Arbitration Procedures

Generally, the parties to an arbitration will select the arbitrator. If they cannot agree upon the person to serve as arbitrator, typically that person is then selected in one of the following ways:

- The parties request a list of available arbitrators from some organization of neutrals and then alternately strike names from that list until only one name remains.
- Each party names one arbitrator, and the two named arbitrators then select a third.

In the latter instance, the third arbitrator selected either serves alone or the three compose a tripartite panel that decides all issues by majority vote.

As explained earlier, the arbitration hearing is similar to a trial, but less formal. Witnesses are customarily placed under oath, but the rules of evidence are not strictly followed. Each party presents its own evidence and argues any legal issues that must be decided. If the arbitration arises under an arbitration clause in a contract, most arbitrators limit themselves to applying the terms of that contract and will not take it upon themselves to enforce statutory law that has not been explicitly incorporated into that contract. If there is no contractual arbitration clause and the parties have chosen arbitration to resolve all differ-

---

Practice Tip

Names of arbitrators or mediators may be obtained from the Federal Mediation and Conciliation Service (FMCS). Some state governments have their own counterpart to the FMCS. Names may also be obtained from some local or state bar associations.

The American Arbitration Association (AAA) is the nation's largest private organization of neutrals, and it will provide lists of available arbitrators or mediators. The association has adopted detailed arbitration procedures that the parties may agree to use. The advantage of adopting the AAA rules is that they are totally neutral and anticipate most problems likely to arise in arbitration.

ences between them, the arbitrator usually applies whatever statutory and common law is applicable to the dispute.

The Role of the Legal Assistant in Arbitration

To some degree, the role of legal assistants in arbitration is similar to that in litigation. A key difference is the absence of discovery, if ADR has been chosen before discovery would normally begin. Of course, in some cases it is the information gained during discovery that leads the parties to consider ADR. Other than discovery, however, the need for investigation, interviewing witnesses, legal research, and other information-gathering processes exists in arbitration just as it does in litigation. So, there's plenty of work for the legal assistant in the early development of an arbitration case. There are no formal pleadings in arbitration, and memoranda of points and authorities are less often submitted to an arbitrator.

> **Practice Tip**
>
> Arbitration is another career option for legal assistants; however, it is a more difficult field for the non-attorney to enter. Most arbitrators are attorneys—many of them, former judges. Arbitration training is provided by some of the colleges that offer mediation training. For the non-attorney, an established reputation as an effective mediator is probably the most promising entrée to arbitration, although training in arbitration law and procedure would be essential.

A QUESTION OF ETHICS

Elsa Banks is a litigation paralegal in a Chicago law firm. She currently is working on a lawsuit in which the firm's client is a small manufacturer of gasoline-powered lawnmowers. The plaintiff alleges that a defect in a mower gasoline tank resulted in an explosion, severely burning the plaintiff. Elsa has spent several days in the client's offices reviewing documents for a response to the plaintiff's request for production. The client company's owner (and CEO) has been working with Elsa to locate the documents needed for the response.

Late one afternoon, just after the owner had left for the day, Elsa came across an internal memorandum written by the company's engineer. She had difficulty understanding the memorandum because of the technical terms and engineering issues. But it appeared to Elsa that it might indicate a possible problem with the gas tank design. Elsa placed the memorandum with a small stack of documents on the owner's desk, with a note indicating that they should review and discuss the documents in the morning.

When Elsa arrived at the company at nine the next morning, the owner was already at his desk. The two began reviewing the documents Elsa had left the evening before. It took about forty-five minutes to go through the stack. When they finished, Elsa asked, "Where's the memorandum from your engineer?" The owner replied, "What memorandum?" A slight chill went down Elsa's back.

Although the owner's desk was always meticulously neat, they searched the desk and office for the missing memorandum, with no luck. "Perhaps it fell on the floor, and the cleaning lady threw it out," the owner suggested. Elsa could not escape the suspicion that the owner had found the memorandum before she arrived and removed it from the stack on his desk.

What should Elsa do about her suspicions?

CHAPTER SUMMARY

- Anyone can file a complaint, but a court might dismiss the case for lack of standing or for failure to state a valid cause of action.
- Standing to sue requires that the plaintiff have a valid factual and legal basis for bringing that controversy before the court.

- People sue to assert a legal right, obtain a remedy for breach of contract, or obtain a remedy for harm caused by another.
- The courts rely upon the adversary system to bring all relevant evidence and law before the court.
- Relevance and materiality generally govern the admissibility of evidence.
- Because of the danger of prejudicial effect, juries sometimes do not hear all relevant evidence.
- Courts award either monetary damages or equitable remedies.
- Lawsuits are initiated by filing a complaint and serving the complaint and a summons upon the defendant.
- Defendants respond to complaints by filing an answer, a demurrer, or a motion to dismiss.
- Litigating parties prepare for trial by using pretrial discovery.
- Depositions, interrogatories, requests for production, and requests for admissions are the most commonly used methods of discovery.
- The standard of proof in civil cases is generally a preponderance of the evidence or clear and convincing proof.
- After closing statements, the court instructs the jury on the law to be applied in that case.
- The court might direct the jury to return a verdict required by law and might set aside a verdict that is contrary to law.
- In civil litigation, legal assistants typically:
  - prepare and file court documents,
  - coordinate with the court and counsel for other parties,
  - monitor deadlines to ensure they are met,
  - draft discovery requests and responses,
  - coordinate depositions,
  - summarize depositions and discovery information, and
  - prepare trial exhibits.
- Litigating parties often submit their dispute to alternative dispute resolution (ADR).
- Mediation and arbitration are the most common forms of ADR.

KEY TERMS

(See Glossary for definitions.)

accrues	**answer**	**certify**
adversary system	**arbitration**	**challenge for cause**
advisory arbitration	**arbitrator**	**cite check**
affidavit	**attorney service**	**civil damages**
affidavit of service	**automatic stay**	**clear and convincing evidence**
affirmative defense	**best evidence rule**	**complaint**
allegation	**binding arbitration**	**contempt powers**
alternative dispute resolution (ADR)	**case in chief**	**cross-examination**
	cause of action	**custodian of records**

CHAPTER 6   Civil Litigation and Alternative Dispute Resolution   **227**

declaration	judgment NOV	remands
declaration judgment	judgment on the pleadings	request for admissions
default judgment	judgment proof	requests for production of documents
demurrer	jury instructions	rests its case
depondent	laches	rules of evidence
depose	lay foundation	second chair
deposition	litigation	settlement agreement
direct examination	lodge	settlement conference
directed verdict	loss of consortium	special damages
discovery	material fact	special verdict
discovery cutoff date	mediation	standard of proof
en banc	mediator	status conference
equitable remedy	motion *in limine*	statute of limitations
evidence in rebuttal	motion to dismiss	stipulate
ex parte hearing	nonsuit	subpoena
exemplar	notice	subpoena *duces tecum*
fraudulent transfer	offer of compromise	summons
garnish	on-call letter	sustain
general damages	on its own motion	temporary restraining order (TRO)
general denial	opening statement	tickler system
general verdict	parties	trial brief
good cause	peremptory challenge	trial by court
harmless error	prejudicial effect	trial notebook
hearsay evidence	preponderance of evidence	verdict
hearsay rule	pretrial conference	*voir dire*
impeach	*prima facie* case	with prejudice
injunction	privilege of confidentiality	without prejudice
insolvent	probative value	writ of execution
interrogatories	proof of service	writ of *mandamus*
irreparable harm	proprietary trade secret	writing
judgment debtor	protective order	
judgment debtor examination	punitive damages	
judgment lien	relevance	

ACTIVITIES AND ASSIGNMENTS

1. The United States is widely regarded as a "litigious society." What does that mean? What are some causes for pervasive litigation in the United States? Do attorneys instigate or provoke unnecessary litigation? If so, how? What are the costs (economic and social) of pervasive litigation? Can or should anything be done to reduce the tendency to litigate? If so, what? Does the legal profession have any responsibility to reduce the level of litigation? Prepare yourself to discuss these questions, based upon your general knowledge of the problem.

2. Appendix A includes:
   - an excerpt from the deposition of Elizah Walsh, in *ABX Memory Corp. v. InsureAll & Co.;*
   - a sample summary for the deposition excerpt of Elizah Walsh; and
   - an excerpt from the deposition of Matilda Bollen in *Price v. Ephrin, et al.*

   Prepare a summary of the deposition excerpt for Bollen, using the sample summary for Walsh as an example. In doing so, consider the type of important issues of fact and law that have been revealed in the deposition of Walsh. Of course, the issues in *Price v. Ephrin, et al.* will be different, but you should try to identify several. Your instructor might provide guidelines for treating various aspects of the deposition (e.g., deponent's education and objections by counsel).

3. Research your state's statute of limitations to determine the limitation periods for the following torts:
    - fraud
    - assault
    - legal malpractice
    - medical malpractice

    For each tort listed, cite the statute number (or state code section) that establishes the limitation period.

4. Research the procedures in your state for obtaining a temporary restraining order (TRO) against someone who is stalking the client. Prepare a short report on those procedures, and include any standard court forms that are used in your jurisdiction.

5. Collect news clippings about a major controversy that is likely to result in litigation. Assume that you are a legal assistant in the law firm representing potential plaintiffs in that litigation. Identify a likely defendant in such litigation. Draft a simple set of *interrogatories* to the defendant, based upon the information you find in the news clippings.

6. Go to a local court and observe an actual trial in progress (a civil case, preferably). If possible, select a case that can be completed in a day or two, so that you can observe as many portions of the trial as possible. (Court bailiffs can often predict the approximate duration of a trial.) Prepare a report on your observations, emphasizing the following:
    - the conduct of jury selection (if any)
    - the degree to which the judge interacted with prospective jurors and/or testifying witnesses
    - the use of leading questions during direct and cross-examination of the same witness
    - the conduct of attorneys toward adverse witnesses

    In your observations, comment on what made an impression upon you and on things you learned about the trial process.

7. Prepare a report on how prospective jurors are selected for the courts in your community. What exemptions from jury service are permitted by state law or local court rules? How long must prospective jurors remain available if not immediately selected to serve?

8. Observe an actual jury selection in progress, and include your observations in your report. Did it appear that any prospective jurors were excused for arbitrary reasons? If you were the attorney trying the case, would you have used a peremptory challenge to excuse any of the jurors who ultimately were retained? Be specific, and give reasons.

9. If you could change the jury selection system, what changes would you make? Explain why you would make those changes.

ENDNOTES

[1] James K. Hoenig, J.D., Ph.D, *Getting to "Maybe."* Hawaii State Bar Association, October 6, 1997 (at http://library.findlaw.com).

CHAPTER 7

Criminal Law and Procedure

> We have to choose, and for my part I think it a less evil that some criminals should escape than that the Government should play an ignoble part.
>
> *Oliver Wendell Holmes, Associate Justice of the U.S. Supreme Court, 1902–1932*

Crime is a major concern of the American people. Compared to the other industrialized nations of the world, the United States has a remarkably high proportion of its population in prisons. Although crime rates for most serious offenses were falling significantly in the 1990s, especially among juveniles, the prison populations continued growing.

There is a perception among some Americans that the criminal justice system has failed to control crime and that criminals are treated too leniently. Many believe that court decisions have given criminals more rights than their victims have. Under this pressure, the state and federal governments continue to enact tougher anticrime legislation.

The criminal courts and the criminal defense bar find themselves inundated with cases and defendants. Prosecutors and defense attorneys alike are turning to legal assistants to help shoulder the enormous workload of criminal prosecution and defense. Criminal law offers many career options for legal assistants, including the opportunity to advance into positions of substantial responsibility in public agencies. Whether working for the prosecution or the defense, legal assistants make a vital contribution to the criminal justice system.

Chapter 7 will provide a conceptual framework for the work of legal assistants in criminal law practice, as was done for civil litigation in Chapter 6. Trial procedures will be given less emphasis, however, because in many ways they are substantially similar to civil trial procedures. Those areas where criminal procedures differ from civil litigation will be emphasized. After studying this chapter, the student should be able to answer the following questions:

- What is a crime?
- How are crimes classified?
- What are the due process rights of accused persons?

- Do crime victims have rights?
- What are the roles of grand juries and trial juries in criminal law?
- What are the typical steps in a criminal prosecution?
- What is the role of the legal assistant in criminal law?

SCENARIO

The Case of the Winter Solstice

As the hushed courtroom audience strained to hear, the witness spoke in a barely audible voice: "Inside the garage, Reginald was standing over Fiona's body with a bloody knife in his hand. He had a weird look in his eyes, and . . . and . . . he was sobbing quietly." In spite of her soft voice, the expression in the witness' eyes suggested firm determination.

The famous defense attorney pondered these words for only a moment, but it seemed an eternity before he spoke. "Miss Brannard, what time was it when you returned to the garage?"

"It was a little after six-thirty. The evening news had just started. I always watch Walter Cronkite."

"Didn't you already testify that you couldn't do the laundry that afternoon because the electricity in the garage wasn't working?"

"Well . . . yes."

"Miss Brannard, the murder occurred in the early evening on December 22nd, the shortest day of the year. Without electricity, that garage was in total darkness at six-thirty. How could you see the blood on the knife or the strange expression in Reginald's eyes?"

Suddenly numbed, the witness stared at the brilliant attorney. "What I meant to say. . . . What I meant was. . . ." Her unfinished sentence lingered in the deafening silence.

But her stumbling words were answered by the attorney's resonant, demanding voice: "You were *jealous* of Fiona, weren't you, Miss Brannard? And you were angry at Reginald—*bitterly* angry. He had jilted you for that younger woman—isn't that true?"

The prosecution's star witness stared at the attorney, her previously confident mouth now only a thin, crimson slash across her pale face. She did not answer.

"Just before you left the kitchen, Miss Brannard, what were you doing?"

The witness visibly struggled to regain her composure. "I . . . why . . . I was carving the turkey for dinner! The three of us were going to have a nice dinner and talk things over."

"Miss Brannard, isn't it true that Reginald and Fiona had left the living room while you were preparing dinner? You saw their silhouettes through the kitchen window as they embraced on the back porch. You then left the kitchen—*still holding the carving knife*—and went outside intending to confront them. But when you reached the porch they were nowhere in sight, isn't that true? Did you hear their voices coming from the garage, Miss Brannard, or did you surprise them in more intimate circumstances?"

Her face suddenly florid, Eloise Brannard began to weep convulsively. The courtroom murmur raced to a roar as the judge's gavel pounded for order. But, above the din, her scream was clearly audible: "*I hated them both when I saw them together, and I hate him still!*"

The shock of her words did what the judge's gavel could not, and the courtroom suddenly fell into silence. Her next words were spoken in a quiet, but bitter tone: "The electric chair's *too good* for Reginald, after what he's done to me."

The attorney looked first into the jurors' eyes and then turned to the witness with a mixture of scorn and pity. "No further questions, Your Honor." ■

SECTION 1. THE NATURE OF CRIMINAL LAW

Most people realize that courtroom scenes like "*The Case of the Winter Solstice*" do not really happen. Spontaneous confessions and similar courtroom histrionics are the creations of Hollywood and pulp fiction, of course. And, as much as they might have enjoyed Angela Lansbury in her television series, *Murder, She Wrote*, most viewers realized that authors of mystery novels do not actually solve **capital crimes** in real life—at least, not each week.

For the courts, prosecutors, and criminal defense attorneys, perhaps the most significant difference in the real world is that very few formally charged criminal defendants ever go to trial. The primary reason is that about 90% of all defendants formally charged actually plead guilty instead of going to trial. Some other defendants are initially charged, but never brought to trial because the prosecuting attorney has later determined that the evidence against them is insufficient. Sometimes charges against lesser offenders are dropped simply because there are too many defendants and too few prosecutors (and courtrooms) to handle all of the cases.

A **capital crime** is one punishable by death.

AT LEAST TWO VICTIMS FOR MOST CRIMES

For most crimes, there is only one plaintiff, but two victims. Always, the plaintiff is the people. The first victim, of course, is the individual directly harmed by the crime. The second victim is society at large. Acting on behalf of the people—and the individual victim—the government prosecutes the crime. The individual victim cannot bring a criminal action, but he can file a parallel civil lawsuit against the criminal.

Criminal law is clearly distinguished from civil law by four features:

1. Society is always the plaintiff in criminal actions, whether one individual has been murdered or tens of thousands have been cheated.
2. The penalties for criminal offenses can include imprisonment or death.
3. The standard of proof for criminal offenses is much higher than in civil litigation.
4. The standard for due process is higher in criminal cases than in civil cases.

Crimes are defined and criminal penalties prescribed by law when the prohibited actions are considered to be threats to the safety, good order, or well-being of the community at large—not just to those individuals immediately harmed. Society declares the offending act to be a crime when any of the following are true:

- ■ Civil liability is an inadequate deterrent to the offending conduct that harms others.

- Private conduct (e.g., bigamy) shocks the moral sensibilities of society.
- Private conduct (e.g., injecting heroin) is believed to lead to offenses against others.
- Society wants retribution for an offense against another.

State governments define a multitude of crimes under the broad police powers, which are discussed briefly in Chapter 4. Of course, many harmful actions (e.g., slander or breach of contract) are not defined as crimes, and the victims must sue in civil court to recover damages. Despite these differences between criminal and civil law, the identical act (e.g., drunk driving) can result in both a criminal prosecution and a civil lawsuit for any injury to others.

THE CRIMINAL ACT AND CRIMINAL INTENT

All crimes involve a forbidden act or a forbidden *refusal* to act. Drunk driving is an example of the former; failure to file an income tax return is an example of the latter. The law requires most crimes to have an additional element, **mens rea** (criminal intent). But some crimes do *not* require criminal intent—it is enough that the prohibited act occurred. An example of the latter is "negligent homicide." A driver who maintains a speed of 37 miles per hour on a rain-slicked highway might be well under the posted speed limit and yet be driving negligently fast for the road conditions. There is no criminal intent in the driver's mind, because she fails to recognize the risk inherent in her speed under those conditions. In some jurisdictions, however, she would be criminally culpable for any death that her misjudgment causes.

For an act to be criminal, it must be voluntary. An otherwise criminal act might be excused if committed under substantial duress or threat of harm. A voluntary act under threat of harm does not have genuine criminal intent, *mens rea,* because the motivation is self-protection, not harm to others. Thus, the ill-prepared hiker who breaks into a mountain cabin to avoid freezing to death in a subzero blizzard would not have the requisite *mens rea* for the crime of breaking and entering.

True criminal intent requires the criminal to voluntarily *and willfully* commit the forbidden act, either for unjustified self-benefit or out of malice toward another. When someone fires a gun into the air on New Year's Eve, he intends no specific harm to anyone else. But he has committed the forbidden act for his own entertainment and with a reckless disregard for the possible consequences to others. This illustrates a **general intent** to violate the law.

When the criminal's action demonstrates an intent to cause the specific, actual harm that results, that is known as **specific intent**. Specific intent is always present in crimes such as premeditated murder, bank robbery, and arson. Many other crimes also require specific intent, including:

- burglary;
- attempted murder;
- assault with intent to rape; and
- possession of marijuana with intent to sell.

Some jurisdictions now legally impute (i.e., attribute) specific intent to people who willfully violate the criminal laws with reckless disregard or indifference to the harm likely to result. Drunk drivers, for example, are being charged with second degree (i.e., unpremeditated) murder when their intoxication results in fatal accidents. Without the imputation of specific intent, these crimes probably would be prosecuted as manslaughter actions. The imputation of specific intent reflects a society's determination to hold drunk drivers strictly liable for the foreseeable consequences of their decisions.

Mens rea is the intention to commit a prohibited act for an unlawful purpose.

The voluntary and willful decision to commit a prohibited act constitutes **general intent**, even though no harmful result is intended.

When a willful, prohibited act is intended to cause harm, **specific intent** exists.

Practice Tip

Of course, most members of a typical jury are not likely to care that much about the complexities of the law of criminal intent. They might not even understand the court's instructions on that issue. But, they will apply their own life experience, common sense, and bias to the evidence that they hear. Ultimately, the jury will determine its own intuitive standard for criminal intent. In a trial by jury, the attorney must never forget the perspective of a jury of ordinary people.

What is the criminal liability of the person who attempts one crime with specific intent, but inadvertently causes an injury to an unintended victim? This situation arises with distressing frequency in drive-by shootings, when an innocent victim is killed by bullets aimed at a rival gang member. Under a principle known as **transferred intent**, the law treats this crime as one with specific intent, just as though the shooter had intended to kill, say, the three-year old child rather than the actual twenty-two-year old target. The criminal's inaccurate aim does not relieve him of the full consequences of his intended crime and actual murder. In the example given, the shooter could be convicted of *premeditated* murder of the three-year old victim.

Many crimes fall within the category of *strict liability*. These crimes do not require that actual harm result from the illegal act—it is enough that the forbidden act occurs. Running a red light is one example of a crime of strict liability. Another is the failure to get a building permit for a room addition that would have been legal if the permit had been obtained. The purpose of strict liability is to deter the forbidden conduct.

> Under the principle of **transferred intent,** a perpetrator's intent to harm is legally "transferred" from the intended victim of his willful, prohibited act to the actual (although unintended) victim of that act.

Criminal Liability for Attempted Criminal Acts

For most crimes, the prosecutor must demonstrate by evidence that a forbidden act was committed and that harm resulted. One cannot be convicted of perjury if one attempts to lie under oath, but by inadvertent omission of a single word actually tells the truth. Nor is someone a criminal if she secretly takes her recently deceased mother's jewelry, not realizing that her mother had bequeathed the jewelry to her.

Society has a powerful interest in deterring conduct undertaken with criminal intent before it succeeds in its purpose. For that reason, state laws make it a criminal offense to possess the particular array of tools commonly used by burglars. Cultivating marijuana plants is forbidden even if they are intended solely for the manufacture of clothing or rope. Attempted assault, rape, and murder are criminal acts even if there is no physical contact or injury to the intended victim. For these offenses, also, strict criminal liability is imposed.

Some crimes of this nature are known as **inchoate crimes**. They include:

- failed attempts to commit a crime;
- solicitation of a crime by another; and,
- conspiracies to commit a crime.

> An **inchoate crime** is a prohibited act, which if continued to its intended end, would result in another crime.

One occasionally reads of an arrest for solicitation of murder, in which one spouse unwittingly tries to hire an undercover police officer to kill the other spouse. This example would appear to be both a failed attempt at murder-for-hire *and* a solicitation of murder.

If *attempted* crimes were not themselves a crime, police would be powerless to intervene before the criminal has accomplished his purpose. For example, an armed criminal could lie in wait, intending to shoot when his victim appears, but then abandon the effort with impunity if he were prematurely detected. By making the attempt—in this case, lying in wait with intent to kill—also a crime, society achieves an added deterrent to the intended crime itself.

Solicitation is an attempt to induce another person to commit a crime. Most jurisdictions make it a crime to solicit the commission of a criminal act. Solicitation of murder and solicitation of prostitution are the most familiar examples. The solicitation is a crime separate from the intended crime (e.g., murder or prostitution) to be committed by another person or in collaboration with the person soliciting the crime.

When two or more persons agree to a joint effort to commit a crime, they commit the crime of **conspiracy**. A telephone conversation in which two per-

> **Solicitation** is the crime of inducing another person to commit a crime; the solicitation is itself criminal even if the other person does not commit the intended crime.

> Two or more persons commit the crime of **conspiracy** when they agree to a joint effort to commit some other crime.

sons agree to meet at a specified place and time so that one can buy illegal drugs from the other constitutes a conspiracy. The conspiracy is a crime separate and distinct from the ultimate crime—the drug deal—that the conspiracy is intended to further. So, if a police officer interrupts their meeting before the illegal transaction is begun, the telephone conversation still stands as a criminal conspiracy. The conspiracy need not be successful to be a crime.

Each coconspirator is equally guilty of the conspiracy, regardless of which of them would be the principal actor(s) in the ultimate crime. However, each must have specific intent to enter into the conspiracy *and* to cause the commission of the ultimate crime being planned. In some jurisdictions, a voluntary and unequivocal withdrawal from the plan before the ultimate crime is committed can be offered as a defense to the crime of conspiracy. But such withdrawal must be sufficiently early so that the remaining coconspirator(s) can also decide to abandon the plan. Public policy favors allowing a legal defense of "voluntary withdrawal," because one conspirator's withdrawal might precipitate the collapse of the entire conspiracy.

Vicarious Liability for the Criminal Acts of Others

The general rule is that one is criminally responsible only for one's own actions. But, like so many other rules of law, there are important exceptions. Most of these exceptions are based upon either of the following:

- a person's contribution to a criminal act by another person
- a person's failure to prevent a crime that he could have prevented

Vicarious criminal liability is responsibility for the crimes actually committed by another person.

An **accessory before the fact** is one who encourages or assists another person to commit a felony but is not present during that felony.

An **accessory after the fact** is one who has knowledge that a felony has been committed and assists the felon in avoiding punishment.

Responsibility for the crimes of others is known as **vicarious criminal liability**. The most familiar example is acting as an accessory to someone else's criminal act. One can be an **accessory before the fact**—for example, furnishing the gun that a friend needs to rob a gas station. Or, one can be an **accessory after the fact**—for example, lying to investigators about where the friend is hiding after the holdup. The vicarious criminal liability of accessories to a crime arises from the crime the other person actually commits. In our example, without the occurrence of a crime (the holdup, or an attempted holdup) there generally would be no crime in giving a friend a gun, nor in lying about where the friend is staying. Although one cannot be an accessory to a crime never committed, one still might be criminally culpable as a coconspirator.

Another common form of vicarious criminal liability is the culpability of criminals for the acts of their cofelons. For example, if one criminal murders a guard during a "takeover robbery" of a bank, the other persons participating in the robbery can be charged with murder, as well. It doesn't matter that they did not fire a single shot. In some jurisdictions, the same principle would apply if someone—perhaps even one of the robbers—were killed in a traffic accident during a postrobbery pursuit. This vicarious criminal liability is known as "felony murder," which is based upon an old common law rule. Today, of course, this rule is found in the statutes of many states.

Less common, perhaps, is the vicarious liability of a corporation for the crimes committed by its employees to further that company's business enterprise. In recent years, some corporations have been found criminally culpable for actions such as dumping pollutants, price fixing, and bribery. At first thought, it might seem pointless to convict a corporation of a crime. Obviously, the corporation cannot be imprisoned or executed—it can only be fined. But establishing criminal liability gives the government additional leverage for reforming the corporation's conduct and preventing future crimes on its behalf. By establishing criminal liability, the government is able to more easily obtain civil penalties, injunctions, and other court orders.

Also, a criminal conviction can create extremely bad press, and possibly shareholder problems, for the corporation. Criminal liability can be a powerful deterrent to careless supervision of corporate employees, as well as a deterrent to management's actual direction or encouragement of criminal activities for the corporation's benefit.

Vicarious criminal liability never shields the original actor from the legal consequences of his crime—it simply creates a separate criminal liability for those vicariously responsible—the accessories, cofelons, employers, and so forth.

Habitual Offender Laws

Some jurisdictions invoke a **three-strikes rule** when the defendant is convicted of her third serious felony. Typically, the third felony conviction carries a mandatory prison term of exceptional length—perhaps life. In one highly publicized case, the three-strikes rule was invoked in California when a criminal with a long record (including two felony convictions) was charged with felonious robbery for stealing a slice of pizza from a teenager. Typically, three-strikes statutes prohibit plea bargaining the most recent felony charge—which would become the third strike, if the defendant is convicted—down to a misdemeanor.

The **three-strikes rule** is a statute requiring a lengthy prison sentence (in some states, as much as life in prison) for a person convicted of a third serious or violent felony.

In three-strikes jurisdictions, defendants facing their second or third felony prosecution are more likely to insist on a jury trial. Because criminal defendants are entitled to a speedy trial, civil cases must be delayed to make courtrooms available for criminal trials. Consequently, the backlog of civil cases is growing in some three-strikes jurisdictions. These states also face a substantial increase in prison costs as the three-strikes rule adds thousands of long-term inmates to an already growing prison population.

COMMON LAW CRIMES AND STATUTORY CRIMES

In medieval England, criminal law developed in much the same way as civil law—from the decisions of noble lords sitting in judgment of lesser nobles, peasants, and serfs. Instead of simply imposing civil liability for the victim's damages, the defendant was sometimes adjudged to have offended the lord's authority or the "Crown's peace." With the development of a court system and appointed judges, those decisions on criminal law became part of the common law of the land—that is, the law that was "shared in common" by all regions of England. Punishments (which included fines, imprisonment, banishment, torture, dismemberment, and execution) were imposed for crimes under the common law, as well as for those prohibited by royal decree. Today, *statutory* criminal law has almost completely replaced common law crimes, but in some jurisdictions **criminal contempt** of court survives as a common law offense.

Criminal contempt is conduct that obstructs the essential functions of a court or legislative body and is sufficiently serious to be punished as a criminal offense.

Common law crimes placed great latitude in the hands of judges, because there was no single, clearly stated definition of the crime, nor any uniform standards for punishment. In the extreme, judges could simply say that a crime of old was no longer a crime of that day—or vice versa. People were put to death for such minor crimes as picking pockets. The advantage of a crime defined by statute is that there is a fixed definition, which courts can overrule only if it is found to be unconstitutional. Of course, the courts can *interpret* that statute, but they are always forced to deal with the words of the statute. Only the legislature can change the statute.

But the statutory definition of crimes also places more responsibility upon the individual. There is less excuse—*legally, no excuse*—for ignorance of the law. But, of course, the complexity of statutory law still makes understanding the law difficult for many. Even learned attorneys disagree about the meaning and effect of various statutes. But, everyone shares a common starting point in the criminal statute.

Laws Unconstitutional for Vagueness

Sometimes criminal statutes are intended to prohibit a broad range of activities that are difficult to describe with precision. Many communities still have on their books ordinances that prohibit "vagrancy," sometimes defined as lacking a "fixed place of residence" or "visible means of support." Most of these statutes are probably unconstitutional for vagueness. A statute is **unconstitutionally vague** when the acts prohibited by it are not clearly defined and a person cannot know with reasonable certainty what is prohibited. Punishing a person for acts that she cannot know are prohibited is a denial of due process of law under the Fifth and Fourteenth Amendments. Vague statutes also tend to encourage arbitrary and discriminatory enforcement by police officers, and weigh most heavily against those who are poor or unpopular. [See, for example, *Papachristou v. City of Jacksonville,* 405 U.S. 156 (1972).]

In the following "Case in Point," the U.S. Supreme Court found unconstitutional a California statute requiring people who "loiter" or "wander" on the streets to provide "credible and reliable" identification to any peace officer who requested such identification. Failure to provide satisfactory identification constituted "disorderly conduct, a misdemeanor" under the statute. A key issue in searching or arresting a person is the existence of **probable cause** to believe a crime has been committed. In *Kolender v. Lawson,* the court mentions "probable cause" a number of times. Probable cause will be discussed further later in this chapter.

> A statute is **unconstitutionally vague** when the acts it prohibits are not clearly defined and a person cannot know with reasonable certainty what acts are prohibited.

> **Probable cause** is established by facts that suggest to a reasonable mind that a person has more likely than not committed a crime, and it is the legal basis for conducting a search or an arrest.

A CASE IN POINT

Kolender v. Lawson

461 U.S. 352 (1983)

Justice O'CONNOR delivered the opinion of the Court.

This appeal presents a facial challenge to a criminal statute that requires persons who loiter or wander on the streets to provide a "credible and reliable" identification and to account for their presence when requested by a peace officer under circumstances that would justify a stop under the standards of *Terry v. Ohio,* 392 U.S. 1, 88 S.Ct. 1868, 20 L.Ed.2d 889 (1968). [Footnote omitted.] We conclude that the statute as it has been construed is unconstitutionally vague within the meaning of the Due Process clause of the Fourteenth Amendment by failing to clarify what is contemplated by the requirement that a suspect provide a "credible and reliable" identification. Accordingly, we affirm the judgment of the court below.

Appellee Edward Lawson was detained or arrested on approximately 15 occasions between March 1975 and January 1977 pursuant to Cal. Penal Code § 647(e). [Footnote omitted.] Lawson was prosecuted only twice, and was convicted once. The second charge was dismissed.

Lawson then brought a civil action in the District Court for the Southern District of California seeking a declaratory judgment that § 647(e) is unconstitutional, a mandatory injunction seeking to restrain enforcement of the statute, and compensatory and punitive damages against the various officers who detained him. The District Court found that § 647(e) was overbroad because "a person who is stopped on less than probable cause cannot be punished for failing to identify himself." Juris. Statement, at A-78. The District Court enjoined enforcement of the statute, but held that Lawson could not recover damages because the officers involved acted in the good faith belief that each detention or arrest was lawful.

* * * *

As generally stated, the void-for-vagueness doctrine requires that a penal statute define the criminal offense with sufficient definiteness that ordinary people can understand what conduct is prohibited and in a manner that does not encourage arbitrary and discriminatory enforcement. [Multiple citations omitted.] Although the doctrine focuses both on actual notice to citizens and arbitrary enforcement, we have recognized recently that the more important aspect of vagueness doctrine "is not actual notice, but the other principal element of the doctrine—the requirement that a legislature establish minimal guidance to govern law enforcement." [Citation omitted.] Where the legislature fails to provide such minimal guidelines, a criminal statute may permit "a standardless sweep [that] allows policemen, prosecutors, and juries to pursue their personal predilections." [Bracketed pronoun (within the quotation) in the original.] [Citation omitted.]

Section 647(e), as presently drafted and construed by the state courts, contains no standards for determining what a suspect has to do in order to satisfy the requirement to provide a "credible and reliable" identification. As such, the statute vests virtually complete discretion in the hands of the police to determine whether the suspect has satisfied the statute and must be permitted to go on his way in the absence of probable cause to arrest. An individual, who police may think is suspicious but do not have probable cause to believe has committed a crime, is entitled to continue to walk the public streets "only at the whim of any police officer" who happens to stop that individual under § 647(e). Shuttlesworth v. City of Birmingham, 382 U.S. 87, 90, 86 S.Ct. 211, 213, 15 L.Ed.2d 175 (1965). Our concern here is based upon the "potential for arbitrarily suppressing First Amendment liberties...." Id., at 91, 86 S.Ct., at 213. In addition, § 647(e) implicates consideration of the constitutional right to freedom of movement. See Kent v. Dulles, 357 U.S. 116, 126, 78 S.Ct. 1113, 1118, 2 L.Ed.2d 1204 (1958); [following citation omitted]. [Footnote omitted.]

* * * *

At oral argument, the appellants confirmed that a suspect violates § 647(e) unless "the officer [is] satisfied that the identification is reliable." [Bracketed verb (within quotation) in original.] Tr. of Oral Arg. 6. In giving examples of how suspects would satisfy the requirement, appellants explained that a jogger, who was not carrying identification, could depending upon the particular officer, be required to answer a series of questions concerning the route that he followed to arrive at the place where the officers detained him [Footnote omitted.] or could satisfy the identification requirement simply by reciting his name and address. See id., at 6-10.

It is clear that the full discretion accorded to the police to determine whether the suspect has provided "credible and reliable" identification necessarily "entrust[s] lawmaking 'to the moment-to-moment judgment of the policeman on his beat.'" [Citations omitted.] Section 647(e) "furnishes a convenient tool for 'harsh and discriminatory enforcement by local prosecuting officials, against particular groups deemed to merit their displeasure,'" [citations omitted] and "confers on police a virtually unrestrained power to arrest and charge persons with a violation." [Citation omitted.] . . . .

We conclude that § 647(e) is unconstitutionally vague on its face because it encourages arbitrary enforcement by failing to describe with sufficient particularity what a suspect must do in order to satisfy the statute. Accordingly, the judgment of the Court of Appeals is affirmed, and the case is remanded for further proceedings consistent with this opinion.

DEFENSES TO CRIMINAL CHARGES

The most fundamental defense to any criminal charge is the defendant's plea of "not guilty." That imposes upon the prosecution the entire burden of proof for each element of the crime charged. Just as each element of a cause of action must be proved in civil litigation, each element of a crime must be proved to establish guilt in a criminal prosecution.

As in civil litigation, there are affirmative defenses that the defendant can raise against a criminal charge. An affirmative defense *admits the acts* alleged, but attacks the legal basis for holding the defendant criminally liable. An affirmative defense says, in effect, "I shot the sheriff—but it was no crime under the circumstances." Common affirmative defenses include:

- self-defense;
- incompetency;
- entrapment; and
- coercion or necessity.

Although self-defense is a concept familiar to all, as a legal defense it is widely misunderstood. The law sets strict limits upon the circumstances that permit the use of deadly force in self-defense. The fundamental principle is that only *reasonable* force may be used in defending oneself or others, or in protecting one's property. Far too many people have mistakenly thought that they could use deadly force against someone who was burglarizing their home—only to find themselves charged with murder.

Incompetency as an affirmative defense is the claim that the defendant was mentally incapable of forming the necessary *mens rea,* or criminal intent. Incompetency may be based upon age (e.g., under seven years), intellectual deficiency (i.e., developmentally disabled), legal insanity, or diminished capacity. "Syndrome" defenses (e.g., battered spouse syndrome and traumatic stress syndrome) generally fall into this category.

Legal Insanity and Diminished Capacity

Legal insanity is an affirmative defense that claims that the defendant was suffering from a mental defect of reason that prevented him from forming criminal intent.

It is important to distinguish **legal insanity** from a psychiatric diagnosis of mental illness—although the latter might aid in establishing the legal basis for an insanity plea. Insanity is a legal term, not a medical term. Particular psychiatric illnesses that cause the patient and relatives great suffering do not necessarily create the legal basis for insanity. The underlying concepts for the affirmative defense of legal insanity are as follows:

- Criminal penalties are incapable of deterring the insane from committing criminal acts.
- Insane persons cannot understand the reasons for the criminal penalties they would receive.
- Society receives no benefit from applying criminal law to insane behavior.

Insanity might be temporary, existing during a relatively brief period when the crime occurs, or it can be on-going and apparently permanent. In addition, a person who was sane at the time of the crime may be found incapable, by reason of insanity, to stand trial afterward. The reason for this finding is that the defendant is mentally incapable of assisting in her own defense. Legal insanity is a changing, very controversial legal issue, and it is beyond the scope of this textbook to discuss insanity in any great depth.

In some jurisdictions, insanity means that the defendant did not understand the nature of his act, or the difference between right and wrong. The law of these jurisdictions is based upon some variation of the M'Naghten Rule. This rule derives from a nineteenth-century case in which M'Naghten killed the British prime minister's secretary, believing that the victim was actually the prime minister himself. His acquittal by jury was based upon his evident mental illness, not on the mistake in identity.

Some jurisdictions have modified the M'Naghten Rule to include an "irresistible impulse" resulting from mental illness, even if the defendant understood his action and/or understood the difference between right and wrong. The very controversial "syndrome" defenses are variations on the irresistible impulse concept and diminished capacity.

Diminished capacity is the inability to form specific criminal intent, because of mental illness, intoxication, or emotional trauma. Although not relieving the defendant from *all* criminal liability—as legal insanity would—diminished capacity reduces that liability in proportion to the diminishment. Typically, a finding of diminished capacity results in a conviction for a lesser offense (e.g., manslaughter rather than murder).

Diminished capacity is the inability to form specific criminal intent, because of mental illness, intoxication, or emotional trauma.

Entrapment

The basic concept of **entrapment** is very easy to illustrate. If an undercover officer tells a sales clerk that he will pay her "under the table" half of the retail price for a digital camera that he intends to steal from the store—and the clerk agrees to take the money and not report the theft—that is entrapment. Entrapment is an effective defense in this case because it claims the following:

- The intention to commit a crime never entered the sales clerk's head until the police officer suggested it.
- The crime would not have occurred *but for* the police officer's suggestion.

Entrapment is any action by a government agent intended to induce the commission of a crime for which the perpetrator will then be prosecuted.

Entrapment prosecutions are improper because it is against public policy for law enforcement officers to:

- encourage the commission of crimes that otherwise might never occur or
- convert otherwise law-abiding citizens into criminals.

If a defendant can establish that entrapment occurred, the court will dismiss the charges against her. Judges and jurors must accept any reasonable interpretation of the evidence that suggests innocence—and thus raises a reasonable doubt about guilt. So, it can be easier for the defendant to establish possible entrapment than for the prosecution to establish the defendant's *independent* criminal intent. As with any *defense*, entrapment does not require proof beyond a reasonable doubt.

Coercion or Necessity

Just as the ill-prepared hiker seeking refuge from a subzero blizzard does not have the criminal intent normally present when breaking and entering a mountain cabin, a hostage with a gun at his own head does not have criminal intent when his captor says, "Shoot the sheriff or I'll blow *your* brains out!" The law does not require that one sacrifice one's own life to preserve that of another. If the law were to impose such a duty, it would be futile in almost every case, because our survival instinct is so very powerful. There is no benefit to society in imposing such an unspeakably onerous duty. Those who refuse to shoot the sheriff would most likely act out of moral revulsion, not out of a legal duty.

THE THREE CATEGORIES OF CRIMINAL OFFENSES

Although the legal standards are not precisely uniform among the fifty states, criminal offenses are generally categorized into felonies, misdemeanors, and infractions. All three categories may be punished by fines, but they differ markedly in the degree of personal confinement that may be imposed. Most criminal statutes explicitly categorize an offense as a felony, a misdemeanor, or an infraction. If not, the general rule is that the maximum punishment authorized by law determines the category in which an offense falls (see *Figure 7.1*). In some jurisdictions, the statute might authorize the prosecutor to file a case as either a felony or a misdemeanor, although the court can reduce a felony charge to a misdemeanor at its discretion. In some jurisdictions, a statute might authorize a range of penalties, and *the penalty actually imposed* by the court on a particular defendant then determines whether that offense was a misdemeanor or a felony.

In addition to fine or imprisonment, conviction for felonies and misdemeanors might deprive the criminal of certain rights and privileges under the law. In most states, a felony conviction disqualifies an individual from holding public office, and might deprive her of the right to vote. A felony conviction might preclude a person from obtaining government employment or from obtaining a professional license as a teacher or an attorney.

In most jurisdictions, a felony is punishable by a term of one year or more in prison, or by death. Fines may be imposed for felony convictions in addition to or in place of a prison term. Many **crimes against persons** (murder, rape, robbery, and kidnaping) and some **crimes against property** (e.g., burglary, arson, and grand theft) are felonies. Nonviolent crimes might be classified as felonies because they deprive the victim of some fundamental right (e.g., the security of one's home or the protection of a constitutional right). Other nonviolent felonies pose serious dangers to society even though an individual victim cannot be identified in each instance (e.g., income tax evasion, fraud in government contracts, bribery of public officials, and false statements under oath).

Misdemeanors are less serious offenses that do not merit the death penalty or long prison sentences. The penalty for a misdemeanor is typically confinement for one year or less. Fines also may be imposed for misdemeanors, either in addition to or in place of the jail term. Actually, fines are imposed far more often than jail terms for misdemeanors.

Infractions are minor crimes (or civil offenses) for which the *only* authorized penalty is a fine. Familiar examples are minor traffic offenses and parking violations, but some jurisdictions have a broad range of other minor offenses classified as infractions. These might include possession of small quantities of marijuana for personal use, minor building code violations, or playing the radio too loudly after 10:00 P.M. Most infractions are violations of city or county ordinances.

> A **crime against persons** is a criminal offense that injures a person or deprives him of his right to be left in peace.

> A **crime against property** is a criminal offense that takes or damages property belonging to another.

> An **infraction** is a minor criminal offense punishable only by fine.

FIGURE 7.1 Crimes and Punishments

	Fine	Jail—1 Year or Less	Prison— 1 Year or More	Death
Felony	Yes		Yes	Yes
Misdemeanor	Yes	Yes		
Infraction	Yes			

Because both criminal infractions and civil offenses are punishable by fines only, they are distinguished from each other primarily by the procedures used for their enforcement. A **citation** (commonly called a "ticket") is customarily issued for all infractions. The individual cited must sign a statement promising to later appear in court to answer the charge. If the individual refuses to sign the citation, the officer might choose to make a formal arrest. If the person cited fails to appear in court as promised, she will be subject to additional penalties.

For civil offenses, a citation or "notice to appear" might be handed—or simply mailed—to the offender. Generally, the civil offender is not required to sign the citation under penalty of arrest for refusal to sign. Failure to appear as directed, however, can subject the civil offender to penalties. Criminal infractions are administered by the courts; civil infractions are often administered by nonjudicial administrative agencies.

A **citation** (known as a "ticket") is a written notice of violation of the law and a notice to appear in court.

CIVIL AND CRIMINAL OFFENSES

In addition to minor infractions, there are numerous noncriminal **civil offenses** that can be punished by fines or by the revocation of some privilege granted by government (such as a license). The opening scenario for Chapter 5, "Administrative Law," illustrated such an offense—a commercial pilot's failure to don an oxygen mask. The disbarment of an attorney or the temporary suspension of her license to practice normally occurs in civil proceedings, rather than criminal. An extraordinary exception to the "no confinement" rule for civil offenses can occur in cases of civil contempt of court. A court can compel a reluctant witness to sit in a jail cell until the witness "purges" himself of the contempt charge by answering the questions posed to him by the court or a grand jury.

A **civil offense** is a noncriminal offense against society that is punishable only by fine or the suspension or revocation of a license or other privilege.

Civil offenses generally require no more than proof by a "preponderance of the evidence." Some jurisdictions require "clear and convincing proof" for certain civil offenses—a stricter standard than preponderance of the evidence. These standards of proof under civil law are discussed in Chapter 6.

But in criminal cases, the standard is **proof beyond a reasonable doubt**. Criminal proceedings also require a higher degree of legal due process, giving the criminal defendant greater protection than a civil defendant would receive. Because both the standard of proof and the due process requirements are less stringent under civil law, government agencies often prefer to bring civil rather than criminal charges.

In criminal cases, the standard is **proof beyond a reasonable doubt,** requiring evidence that convinces a reasonable and prudent person to believe, to a moral certainty, that an accused person did commit the crime charged.

GRAND JURIES AND TRIAL JURIES

One of the most cherished institutions inherited from the English system of law is trial by a jury of one's peers. Today, a jury is meant to be a reasonable cross-section of the community. In practice, juries seldom match that ideal—especially in lengthy trials—and tend to be composed of retired persons, government employees, students, and employees of large companies that will continue their salary during jury service. Attorneys, law enforcement officers, and paralegals are not often seated as jurors, especially in criminal cases.

A trial jury is also known as a **petit jury** (i.e., a "small" jury). Usually it comprises twelve persons, but might have fewer than twelve. Trial juries were originally intended to prevent judicial tyranny. Even now, juries remain an important part of the legal system. They bring common sense, pragmatism, and personal values to a judicial process that is often absorbed by legal technicalities. In that regard, juries are both valuable and dangerous: They can (and often do) give weight to relevant but improper testimony that they have heard, even though the judge has instructed the jury to disregard it; they can be (and often are) swayed by passion and prejudice; they can (and often do) substitute their own

A **petit jury** is a trial jury (usually of twelve persons).

collective sense of justice in place of the instructions the judge has given on the law. In a positive sense, however, juries sometimes do for the criminal justice system what the courts of equity did for the inflexible common law system of England: They can inject a human sense of justice where the law is too rigid, unable to accommodate unique circumstances.

Grand juries were originally established to restrain unwarranted prosecutions. Their function is to hear evidence and determine whether a criminal prosecution is justified. If prosecution is justified, the grand jury returns an indictment (sometimes called a **true bill**) that is presented to the court. An **indictment** is a formal written accusation that there is probable cause to believe someone has committed a crime. A grand jury is usually composed of between twelve and twenty-three citizens. The Fifth Amendment requires a grand jury indictment for serious federal offenses. However, states may use grand juries or any other accusatory process that meets the constitutional requirements of due process.

In modern practice, most grand juries tend to be under the substantial influence of the prosecuting attorney, and they can be powerful tools in his hands. Prosecutors have this kind of influence because grand jurors hear only what the prosecutor chooses to present to them. The prosecutor alone decides upon the witnesses and evidence to be presented. There is no cross-examination. If the potential defendant is subpoenaed to appear, her attorney is excluded from that grand jury hearing. Although she may be permitted to leave the room to ask him for counsel, she is left to her own resources to determine when that is appropriate.

It is possible for the entire grand jury proceedings to occur without the potential defendant even being aware of them—or of the fact that he is the target of any investigation or contemplated prosecution. Grand juries sometimes meet in total secrecy and return indictments that are sealed by the court until the defendant has been taken into custody. This is extremely useful, of course, when suspected criminals are likely to flee and evade arrest. Even when they know of the proceedings, neither the potential defendant nor his attorney is permitted to be present while others testify.

The importance of the grand jury's role varies from state to state. In some states, the prosecutor's **information** and a subsequent **preliminary hearing** in court are used as an alternative to a grand jury indictment. The prosecutor's "information" is a sworn affidavit prepared by the prosecutor. In a preliminary hearing, the court reviews the evidence and determines whether there is probable cause to hold the defendant for trial. Some states use grand jury indictments, but do not require preliminary hearings by the court after the indictment. Grand jury indictments, prosecutors' informations, and preliminary hearings are discussed further later in this chapter.

THE PRESUMPTION OF INNOCENCE

A basic principle of criminal justice is the presumption that an accused person is innocent of the crime. That **presumption of innocence** means that the burden of proof lies with the prosecution. The accused is not required to prove his innocence, because his innocence is already *presumed* as a matter of law. Although rare, a defense attorney might "rest her case" without calling a single witness or presenting any evidence to establish her client's innocence. If the prosecution has failed to establish a *prima facie* case for guilt beyond a reasonable doubt, the judge or jury is compelled under the law to find the defendant "not guilty," even though no defense case whatsoever has been offered.

The accused person receives a second advantage from the presumption of his innocence: the benefit of any doubt. The judge or jury must view the evidence in the light most favorable to the accused. If the evidence allows *any* rea-

---

A **grand jury** (a "large" jury, usually twenty-three jurors) inquires into criminal accusations to determine whether there is probable cause to bring an accused person to trial, in which case it returns a criminal indictment.

An **indictment** (or **true bill**) is a formal, written criminal accusation presented to the court by a grand jury.

An **information** is a written, sworn accusation by a prosecutor, which serves as the basis for bringing the accused person to trial without involving a grand jury.

A **preliminary hearing** is held before a court to determine if probable cause exists to bring a defendant to trial.

The **presumption of innocence** is a legal presumption that the defendant is innocent until proven guilty, placing the entire burden of proof in criminal trials on the prosecution.

sonable interpretation inconsistent with guilt, the legal presumption of innocence requires a verdict of "not guilty." This is because any reasonable interpretation that would suggest innocence *must inevitably* create a "reasonable doubt" about the accused person's guilt—but a guilty verdict must be based upon proof beyond a reasonable doubt.

In criminal cases, most states require the trial jury to reach a unanimous verdict. Because guilt must be proved beyond a reasonable doubt, any juror not so convinced must vote "not guilty." (It is important to remember that innocence need not be proved, at all.) If all jurors are convinced of guilt beyond a reasonable doubt and to a moral certainty, the jury will return a verdict of guilty. If all are *un*convinced of guilt beyond a reasonable doubt, the jury will return a verdict of not guilty. If some are convinced of guilt, but other jurors are not, the trial jury will be a hung jury, unable to return a verdict. A hung jury results in a mistrial, which means that no valid trial has occurred at all.

RIGHTS OF THE VICTIMS AND RIGHTS OF THE ACCUSED

Section 2 of this chapter discusses the due process of law that every criminal defendant must receive. Due process in criminal law troubles some people, who feel that our criminal justice system has been compromised. Three common perceptions contribute to this concern:

1. that the justice system is "tilted" in favor of acquittal for the criminal
2. that criminals (and the attorneys who defend them) "work" the justice system to the criminal's own advantage
3. that the justice system cares more about criminals than it does about the victims of crime

Public support for the criminal justice system has been eroded by such perceptions. Attorneys who represent criminal defendants are sometimes the targets of public and political criticism, and this issue can present a morale problem for paralegals working for criminal defense attorneys. Any paralegal contemplating criminal defense work should consider the stress this public controversy might induce. The following discussion is intended to stimulate thoughtful reflection on these issues.

First, it must be noted that the three perceptions listed above refer to "criminals," not "defendants." Stated in that manner, there appears to be an implication that the criminal defendant is assumed to be guilty. It might be useful to consider whether substituting the word "defendant" would change the way these issues are perceived.

With that caveat, there clearly is a factual basis underlying the first two perceptions. The justice system does operate under *constitutional imperatives* to protect the rights of an accused person—but there are no corresponding constitutional imperatives to protect the rights of victims. And criminal defendants and their attorneys *do* "work" the justice system, in the sense that they exploit every due process right (which some critics term "technicalities") to avoid conviction and punishment. In fact, criminal defense attorneys believe it is *their ethical duty* to do so.

The Constitution emphasizes safeguards (i.e., due process) for criminal defendants because in earlier centuries—even in earlier generations of the twentieth century—defendants were sometimes condemned to prison, or even to death, with little regard for objective proof of their guilt. Faked evidence and perjured testimony were not unusual. In unspoken reality, defendants often were *presumed guilty*—the legal presumption of innocence being regarded as an annoying technicality. It wasn't that difficult for many police officers, prosecutors, and judges to believe that most defendants were undeserving of any effective legal defense.

Due process was not the invention of the Supreme Court—it was a firmly held conviction of our nation's Founding Fathers, who were neither career criminals nor criminal defense attorneys. The Founding Fathers expanded upon the very limited due process rights already established under English law. But they also recognized that even those "established" rights were routinely violated in the English legal system. Due process rights were included in the Bill of Rights *precisely because* the Founding Fathers had observed pervasive abuses by British police, prosecutors, and courts.

Why does the Constitution not also require due process for the *victims* of crime? Once again, the answer lies in history and also hinges upon this premise: Crime victims are best protected by strict enforcement of the laws against criminal behavior. And, in the days of the Founding Fathers, criminals were *very* vigorously prosecuted, indeed. In fact, eighteenth-century America was so "prosecution-oriented" that a constitutional mandate for the protection of victims would have seemed superfluous.

For more than a century, due process rights for defendants did not create serious obstacles to prosecution and punishment, because the constitutional protections in the Bill of Rights restrained the federal government only and did not apply to the states. The fact is that state governments had much less concern for due process, and the U.S. Supreme Court rarely interfered with state court decisions on due process. Some state constitutions had their own due process guarantees, but in practice those protections generally were not strictly enforced by most state courts. Not until 1868, when the Fourteenth Amendment was added, did the U.S. Constitution require the states to provide due process. But several generations were to pass before even that requirement was clearly defined and enforced by the court system.

Society faces a dilemma: how to offer greater protection for victims without returning our legal system to the "presumed guilty" mind-set of the eighteenth-century, or to the nineteenth-century practices under which no one "policed" the police? Few of us would favor a return to such an unjust system. But a genuine solution to the problem of protecting the rights of victims will take many years and a great deal of trial and error. Certainly, legislative efforts to establish an appropriate balance will be struck down by the Supreme Court if they run afoul of the Constitution, and those rulings might further inflame public discontent over the issue.

Ethics Watch

Criminal defendants do not need to prove their innocence, although an airtight alibi is always helpful—instead, the prosecution must prove their guilt. Because circumstances can so easily make an innocent person *appear* to be guilty, the justice system relies upon a vigorous defense to test the sufficiency and accuracy of the prosecutor's case. Consequently, defense attorneys and their legal assistants have an *ethical obligation* to zealously defend their clients, no matter how unpopular that cause might be with the news media, politicians, or the public.

SECTION 2. DUE PROCESS IN CRIMINAL PROCEDURE

In the context of criminal law, "due process" means procedures that are required by fundamental standards of fairness and justice that have developed under the Anglo-American legal tradition. Although some features of criminal due process have been created by state constitutions and by state and federal statutes, most have developed as court interpretations of the U.S. Constitution. As was explained in Chapter 4, the state governments are prohibited by the Fourteenth Amendment from depriving any person of due process of law:

> "... [N]or shall any State deprive any person of life, liberty or property, without due process of law...."

The federal government must satisfy the same due process requirements under the Fifth Amendment to the Constitution. So, regardless of the court, every criminal defendant is entitled to due process of law.

In 1833, the U.S. Supreme Court held that the Bill of Rights (Amendments 1–10) restrict only the federal government, not the states. *Barron v. Baltimore,* 32 U.S. 243 (1833). That remained the law of the land even after the Fourteenth Amendment was added to the Constitution in 1868. Finally, in a series of decisions beginning in the late nineteenth century, the U.S. Supreme Court began to *incorporate* procedural rights under the Bill of Rights within the meaning of "due process of law" required of the states by the Fourteenth Amendment. In a sense, the Supreme Court has "nationalized" most of the protections under the Bill of Rights, through its interpretation of the Fourteenth Amendment's Due Process Clause. Technically, it is still that Due Process Clause—not the Eighth Amendment—that forbids the states to impose "cruel and unusual punishment." But it is common practice to reference one of the first ten amendments when speaking or writing of their specific prohibitions that have been incorporated into the Fourteenth Amendment.

In defining "due process of law," the Supreme Court has not followed a clear path, nor has it even adopted a consistent philosophical basis. Its decisions have wavered between differing concepts of liberty and limited government. But the overall trend has been a broadening of due process rights, and the Supreme Court has never overruled an earlier decision and removed any protection it had once held to be part of due process under the Fourteenth Amendment. In its more recent decisions, the Court has held that the Due Process Clause incorporates any right that is both fundamental and essential to the concept of "ordered liberty." Those protections that are found in the Bill of Rights are given special weight by the Court when it determines which rights are both "fundamental" and "essential."

As of this writing, the Supreme Court has held that each of the following procedural protections under the Bill of Rights is also valid against the states under the Fourteenth Amendment's Due Process Clause:

- freedom from unreasonable search and seizure
- freedom from double jeopardy
- freedom from compulsory self-incrimination
- right to a speedy and public trial
- right to trial by an impartial jury
- right to notice of all accusations
- right to confront witnesses
- right to subpoena witnesses
- right to assistance of legal counsel
- freedom from excessive bail or fines
- freedom from cruel and unusual punishment

The only procedural protections under the Bill of Rights that have *not* been incorporated within the Fourteenth Amendment's Due Process Clause are:

- jury trials in civil cases and
- indictment by grand jury for all serious crimes.

> **Practice Tip**
>
> Many criminal defense attorneys are sole practitioners or members of small law partnerships. Lacking the assistance of associate attorneys, they must either bear the entire burden of all legal research for their cases or rely upon legal assistants to share that load. Criminal cases often involve disputes over detention, search and seizure, arrests, incriminating statements, and so forth. Applying the constitutional principles to the facts of each situation can require extensive legal research. Small criminal defense firms, then, offer good research opportunities for legal assistants who enjoy that type of work.

The **Miranda warning** informs a criminal suspect that he has the right to remain silent and the right to the counsel of an attorney.

Self-incrimination includes actions or words that cause the actor or speaker to appear to be guilty of some crime.

In addition, the right to a twelve-person jury in federal trials (under the Sixth Amendment) has not been extended to the states under the Fourteenth Amendment, and some states continue to use smaller juries for misdemeanor trials. Of course, state constitutions can establish additional due process protections that apply in the courts of that state. But state constitutions may not limit or reduce the protections under the U.S. Constitution.

THE MIRANDA WARNING

The best-known statement of criminal due process is found in the **Miranda warning** that arresting officers routinely recite to persons taken into custody. However, the Miranda warning is not a comprehensive summary of all due process rights. It focuses upon the Fifth Amendment right against **self-incrimination** (i.e., making oneself appear to be guilty) and, to a lesser extent, the Sixth Amendment right to assistance of counsel.

There is a common misconception that an *arrest* is not valid if the Miranda warning is not given to the arrestee, but that is incorrect. The warning is not needed to validate the arrest, but rather to make any statements or confessions made while in custody admissible as evidence against the accused. If an arrestee makes a voluntary statement in spite of being told that she has the right to remain silent and to obtain legal counsel, then her statement is generally admissible as evidence against her. If she was not informed of her Miranda rights, the arrest would be valid but her statement might be inadmissible.

The Miranda warning is based upon *Miranda v. Arizona,* 384 U.S. 436 (1966), in which the U.S. Supreme Court linked the Sixth Amendment right to legal counsel to the Fifth Amendment right against self-incrimination. Although the court was primarily concerned with self-incrimination, it recognized that the right to counsel was an essential protection against an uninformed waiver of the Fifth Amendment right. The Supreme Court recognized that a person in custody might not only be ignorant of her right to remain silent—that is, to not incriminate herself—but also might fail to understand the gravity of statements made without the advice of an attorney. The Court also recognized the right of the arrestee to waive (i.e., to surrender) her rights both to remain silent and to obtain advice of counsel. But the Supreme Court held that such a waiver must be voluntarily and intelligently made by the arrestee, after she has been informed of her Miranda rights.

The development of the Miranda warning provides an excellent illustration of the evolution of procedural due process. The post–Civil War Fourteenth Amendment laid the foundation with its Due Process Clause, restricting the actions of state governments. Because a person in custody is, by definition, a person deprived of "liberty," he must be accorded due process. The question then became, what procedures must be followed to meet the due process requirement? In a long series of decisions, the Supreme Court has answered (and continues to answer) that question.

In *Miranda,* the Supreme Court faced two important questions:

1. Is a statement made by an arrestee who is ignorant of his right to remain silent and his right to have legal counsel a "voluntary" statement under constitutional standards?
2. If such a statement fails the constitutional test, should it be excluded as evidence at trial?

The Supreme Court held that such statements do *not* meet constitutional standards for voluntary statements, and that they must be excluded as evidence. In an unusual further step for Supreme Court decisions, the Court then spelled out the actual content of a "Miranda warning" that would meet constitutional standards:

- The suspect has the right to remain silent.
- Any statements made by the suspect will be used against her.

- The suspect has the right to have an attorney present.
- If the suspect cannot afford an attorney, one will be appointed for her.

The Miranda warning accomplishes two purposes, then: (1) It informs the person in custody of his constitutional rights, and (2) it preserves the admissibility of any incriminating statements made subsequent to the warning.

The Supreme Court Revisits *Miranda*

Within two years after the Supreme Court's *Miranda* decision, Congress enacted a statute intended to override that decision in federal prosecutions. The statute states, in part: "In any criminal prosecution brought by the United States or by the District of Columbia, a confession . . . shall be admissible in evidence if it is voluntarily given." 18 U.S.C. 3501. The essence of Section 3501 was to make the test for admissibility the "voluntary" nature of the statement—not compliance with the Miranda warning. Believing that statute to be unconstitutional, however, a succession of U.S. Attorneys General—under four Republican and two Democratic administrations—had refused to use it in their prosecution of criminal defendants. The congressional "override" of *Miranda* appeared to be a dead issue.

But, in 1999, the Fourth Circuit Court of Appeals placed the conflict between *Miranda* and Section 3501 squarely before the nation's judicial system. When the Supreme Court then agreed to reconsider *Miranda v. Arizona, supra,* many observers wondered if the Court's conservative majority saw this as an opportunity to overrule *Miranda.* The case presenting this opportunity involved an accused bank robber, Charles Dickerson, who had confessed his crimes to a Federal Bureau of Investigation (FBI) Special Agent. Prior to trial, Dickerson asked the U.S. District Court to suppress (i.e., rule inadmissible) the confession. At the hearing on the motion to suppress, the FBI agent testified that Dickerson had made the confession voluntarily, and *after* being read (and having waived) his Miranda rights. Dickerson testified that he confessed *prior to* being read his Miranda rights.

Documentary evidence (a search warrant and an "advice-of-rights" form) were consistent with Dickerson's testimony, but not with that of the FBI agent. The district court found the defendant's testimony more credible than that of the FBI agent and suppressed the confession. Later, the government asked the district court to reconsider its decision, offering additional evidence to support the FBI agent's testimony. The district court refused that request for reconsideration, and the government then appealed that decision to the U.S. Court of Appeals.

On appeal, the government did not argue that the enactment of 18 U.S.C. 3501 had superseded the *Miranda* decision in federal prosecutions, thereby making a tardy Miranda warning irrelevant. In *United States v. Dickerson,* 166 F.3d 667 (1999) the Fourth Circuit repeatedly refers to the government's "refusal" to make that argument. An obviously frustrated Fourth Circuit insisted upon considering Section 3501 on the appellate court's own initiative. The court of appeals held that the Supreme Court's holding in *Miranda* was *not* a conclusion of constitutional law, and that Congress had the authority to enact Section 3501 as a statutory rule of evidence. In effect, the appellate court held that Section 3501 superseded *Miranda.* On that basis, it reversed the district court's suppression of Dickerson's confession. Dickerson then filed a petition for *certiorari* with the U.S. Supreme Court.

The Supreme Court granted *certiorari* in a procedural order at *Dickerson v. United States,* 528 U.S. 1045 (1999). That brief order reads as follows:

Case below, 166 F.3d 667.

Motion of petitioner to proceed in forma pauperis granted. Petition for a writ of certiorari to the United States Court of Appeals for the Fourth Circuit granted limited to Question 1 presented by the petition. Paul G. Cassell, Esquire, of Salt

---

Practice Tip

The Supreme Court's brief order in 528 U.S. 1045 contains several interesting features. The essence of the order ("writ") is to direct the Fourth Circuit Court of Appeals to certify (i.e., authenticate) and forward to the Supreme Court the record of the "case below" (here, United States v. Dickerson, *166 F.3d 667) for review by the Supreme Court. (The writ of* certiorari *is an order used by the Court to select those cases it wishes to review.)*

Note that in the court of appeals, the case name begins with the appealing party, United States, *and in the Supreme Court with the petitioning party,* Dickerson. *The name of the party bringing a matter before the court— whether as plaintiff, petitioner, or appellant—customarily appears first.*

The Supreme Court granted Mr. Dickerson, the petitioner, permission to proceed in forma pauperis, which means that he will not have to pay any court costs for the Supreme Court review. Although not shown in this order, the Supreme Court subsequently appointed a distinguished Virginia attorney to represent Dickerson and argue his case before the Court. Because prison inmates rarely have the financial resources to employ expert appellate counsel—and because the Supreme Court wants the benefit of argumentation by the best available legal minds—it is not unusual for the Court to appoint counsel for those few inmates whose cases it agrees to hear.

Finally, the Supreme Court's order invites a Utah professor of law, Paul G. Cassell, not only to submit a brief, but to actually participate in oral argument

> **Practice Tip (continued)**
>
> before the Court. (Note that the professor is invited to argue in support of the Fourth Circuit's decision that Dickerson asks the Court to overturn.) Although it is not unusual for the Supreme Court to entertain written amicus curiae ("friend of the court") briefs, it is exceptional for the court to invite both written brief and oral argument by a named individual who is not a party to the case. (Professor Cassell, as amicus curiae, had argued the Dickerson case before the Fourth Circuit, as well—arguing, in fact, that *Miranda* was *not a constitutional imperative*.)

Lake City, Utah, is invited to brief and argue this case, as amicus curiae, in support of the judgment below.

U.S., 1999
Dickerson v. U.S.

The issue before the Supreme Court in *Dickerson* was whether the Miranda warning is a constitutional requirement or just a court-crafted remedy. The Supreme Court's 7–2 opinion in *Dickerson v. United States*, ____ U.S. ____, 120 S.Ct. 2326, 147 L.Ed.2d 405 (2000) was written by the conservative Chief Justice William Rehnquist. The Supreme Court's key holding states:

> We hold that Miranda, being a constitutional decision of this Court, may not be in effect overruled by an Act of Congress, and we decline to overrule Miranda ourselves. We therefore hold that Miranda and its progeny in this Court govern the admissibility of statements made during custodial interrogation in both state and federal courts.

Later in his opinion, the Chief Justice writes:

> The Miranda opinion itself begins by stating that the Court granted certiorari "to explore some facets of the problems ... of applying the privilege against self-incrimination to in-custody interrogation, and to give concrete constitutional guidelines for law enforcement agencies to follow." [Citation omitted.] In fact, the majority opinion is replete with statements indicating that the majority thought it was announcing a constitutional rule. [Footnote omitted.] Indeed, the Court's ultimate conclusion was that the unwarned confessions obtained in the four cases before the Court in Miranda "were obtained from the defendant under circumstances that did not meet constitutional standards for protection of the privilege." [Footnote omitted.] [Citation omitted.]
>
> * * * *
>
> Congress retains the ultimate authority to modify or set aside any judicially created rules of evidence and procedure that are not required by the Constitution. [Citations omitted.]
> But Congress may not legislatively supersede our decisions interpreting and applying the Constitution. [Citation omitted.]
>
> * * * *
>
> In sum, we conclude that Miranda announced a constitutional rule that Congress may not supersede legislatively. Following the rule of stare decisis, we decline to overrule Miranda ourselves. The judgment of the Court of Appeals is therefore Reversed.

> **Practice Tip**
>
> In the citation to the Supreme Court's opinion in *Dickerson*, the official citation is incomplete (i.e., volume and page numbers missing). This situation occurs when citing a recent action by the Supreme Court, because the official reporter is published much later than the unofficial reporters. Once the Dickerson case appears in *United States Reports*, the official citation will be available.

In the following "Case in Point," the Supreme Court had carved out an interesting exception to the usual requirement for a Miranda warning. *Illinois v. Perkins*, 496 U.S. 292 (1990), presents this question to the Court: Does the Constitution require a Miranda warning when an undercover officer becomes an apparent fellow convict and the cellmate of a murder suspect—and then induces the suspect to implicate himself in the murder?

A CASE IN POINT

Illinois v. Perkins

496 U.S. 292 (1990)

Justice KENNEDY delivered the opinion of the Court.

An undercover government agent was placed in the cell of respondent Perkins, who was incarcerated on charges unrelated to the subject of the agent's investigation. Respondent made statements that implicated him in the crime that the agent sought to solve. Respondent claims that the statements should be inadmissable because he had not been given Miranda Warnings by the agent. We hold that the statements are admissible. Miranda Warnings are not required when the suspect is unaware that he is speaking to a law enforcement officer and gives a voluntary statement.

I

In November 1984, Richard Stephenson was murdered in a suburb of East St. Louis, Illinois. The murder remained unsolved until March 1996, when one Donald Charlton told police that he had learned about a homicide from a fellow inmate at the Graham Correctional Facility, where Charlton had been serving a sentence for burglary. The fellow inmate was Lloyd Perkins, who is the respondent here. Charlton told police that, while at Graham, he had befriended respondent, who told him in detail about a murder that respondent had committed in East St. Louis. On hearing Charlton's account, the police recognized details of the Stephenson murder that were not well known, and so they treated Charlton's story as a credible one.

. . . The police wanted to investigate further respondent's connection to the Stephenson murder, but feared that the use of an eavesdropping device would prove impracticable and unsafe. They decided instead to place an undercover agent in the cellblock with respondent and Charlton. The plan was for Charlton and undercover agent Parisi to pose as escapees from a work release program who had been arrested in the course of a burglary. Parisi and Charlton were instructed to engage respondent in casual conversation and report anything he said about the Stephenson murder.

Parisi, using the alias "Vito Bianco," were placed in the cellblock with respondent at the Montgomery County Jail. The cellblock consisted of 12 separate cells that opened onto a common room. Respondent greeted Charlton who, after a brief conversation with respondent, introduced Parisi by his alias. Parisi told respondent that he "wasn't going to do any more time" and suggested that the three of them escape. Respondent replied that the Montgomery County Jail was a "rinky-dink" and that they could "break out." The trio met in respondent's cell later that evening, after the other inmates were asleep. Respondent said that his girlfriend could smuggle in a pistol. Charlton said: "Hey, I'm not a murderer. I'm a burglar. That's your guys' profession." After telling Charlton that he would be responsible for any murder that occurred, Parisi asked respondent if he had ever "done" anybody. Respondent said that he had and proceeded to describe at length the events of the Stephenson murder. Parisi and respondent then engaged in some casual conversation before respondent went to sleep. Parisi did not give respondent Miranda Warnings before the conversations.

Respondent was charged with the Stephenson murder. Before trial, he moved to suppress the statements made to Parisi in the jail. The trial court granted the motion to suppress, and the State appealed. The Appellate Court of Illinois affirmed. 176 Ill.App.3d 443, 126 Ill.Dec. 8, 531 N.E.2d 141 (1988), holding that Miranda v. Arizona, 384 U.S. 436, 86 S.Ct. 1602, 16 L.Ed.2d 694 (1966), prohibits all undercover contacts with incarcerated suspects that are reasonably likely to elicit an incriminating response.

II

In Miranda v. Arizona, supra, the Court held that the Fifth Amendment privilege against self-incrimination prohibits admitting statements given by a suspect during "custodial interrogation" without a prior warning. Custodial interrogation means "questioning initiated by law enforcement officers after a person has been taken into custody. . . ." The warning mandated by Miranda was meant to preserve the privilege during "incommunicado interrogation of individuals in a police-dominated atmosphere." Id., at 445, 86 S.Ct., at 1612. That atmosphere is said to generate "inherently compelling pressures which work to undermine the individual's will to resist and to compel him to speak where he would not otherwise do so freely." Id., at 467, 86 S.Ct., at 1624. "Fidelity to the doctrine announced in Miranda requires that it be enforced strictly, but only in those types of situations in which the concerns that empowered the decision are implicated." Berkemer v. McCarty, 468 U.S. 420, 437, 104 S.Ct. 3138, 3148, 82 L.Ed.2d 317 (1984).

Conversations between suspects and undercover agents do not implicate the concerns underlying Miranda. The essential ingredients of a "police-dominated atmosphere" and compulsion are not present when an incarcerated person speaks freely to someone whom he believes to be a fellow inmate. . . .

* * * *

Miranda was not meant to protect suspects from boasting about their criminal activities in front of persons whom they believe to be their cellmates. This case is illustrative. Respondent had no reason to feel that undercover agent Parisi had any legal authority to force him to answer questions or that Parisi could affect respondents's future treatment. Respondent viewed the cellmate-agent as an equal and showed no hint of being intimidated by the atmosphere of the jail. In recounting the details of the Stephenson murder, respondent was motivated solely by the desire to impress his fellow inmates. He spoke at his own peril.

* * * *

We hold that an undercover law enforcement officer posing as a fellow inmate need not give Miranda Warnings to an incarcerated suspect before asking questions that may elicit an incriminating response. The statements at issue in this case were voluntary, and there is no federal obstacle to their admissibility at trial. We now reverse and remand for proceedings not inconsistent with our opinion.

It is so ordered.

DOUBLE JEOPARDY

The Double Jeopardy Clause of the Fifth Amendment states:

> ". . . [N]or shall any person be subject for the same offence to be twice put in jeopardy of life or limb. . . ."

Although this principle derives from ancient Greek and Roman law, it is not well understood even today. The courts have interpreted the clause to prohibit two prosecutorial abuses:

1. a second prosecution following an acquittal for the identical offense
2. a second prosecution following conviction for the identical offense

The meanings of "same offence" and "twice put in jeopardy" have been controversial, and the Supreme Court has found it difficult to resolve these issues with any unanimity. Interestingly, the courts have not been equally troubled by the meaning of "life or limb," and have invoked the double jeopardy protection when no more than a fine or imprisonment could be imposed—as opposed to the death penalty or dismemberment.

Once a valid trial has been completed—or when the improper conduct of the prosecution or the court has invalidated a trial in progress—the protection against **double jeopardy** becomes *absolutely effective*. That makes possible the situation where one can confess one's guilt after an acquittal and even sell a book entitled "*How I Got Away With Murder,*" yet still be immune from a second

---

Double jeopardy is being tried again for the same criminal offense following an earlier trial on that charge.

prosecution for that murder. A subsequent prosecution is *not* barred by an appellate court's reversal of a completed trial in which a defendant was convicted. Reversal means that a valid trial was never completed.

Mistrials and Double Jeopardy

But, in many circumstances, because no valid trial has occurred, the defendant may be tried again. For example, a mistrial can be declared because of juror misconduct (e.g., a juror conducting his own investigation to determine the facts of the case or a juror who has placed a bet on the outcome of the case). A **mistrial** is a determination by the trial judge that the proceedings have been irretrievably compromised so that either the defendant or the plaintiff cannot receive a fair, impartial hearing. A mistrial bars a second prosecution when either of the following is true:

- The mistrial results from prosecutorial misconduct.
- The mistrial results from serious error by the court.

A mistrial does *not* bar a subsequent prosecution if either of the following is true:

- The mistrial occurs with the consent of the accused (e.g., on his own motion).
- The mistrial results from some "manifest necessity" that is beyond the court's control (e.g., juror misconduct).

On the other hand, if an appellate court determines that the trial court has declared a mistrial without sufficient grounds to do so, the defendant may not be tried again.

The most common form of mistrial occurs when the jury is unable to reach a unanimous verdict. A criminal jury that is hopelessly deadlocked is called a **hung jury**. This is an example of a circumstance beyond the court's control. Because a hung jury cannot reach a unanimous verdict on the criminal charges, the court must declare a mistrial and no valid trial is completed. Consequently, a hung jury does not preclude the prosecutor from trying the same criminal case again.

In rare instances, criminal defendants must go through three or four trials because two or three juries have been unable to reach a unanimous verdict in the earlier trials—and, thus, no valid trial has been concluded. One obvious danger is the ability of the government to use its inexhaustible resources to wear down a particular criminal defendant until he submits (i.e., bargains to plead guilty for a reduced sentence) by forcing him to go through a series of mistrials. If abused, the government's financial and legal resources could overwhelm the defendant.

> A **mistrial** is an invalid trial, declared by the court when some misconduct or procedural problem prevents the completion of a valid trial.

> A **hung jury** is a deadlocked jury, one that is unable to deliver the required number of votes for a verdict.

Multiple Crimes and Double Jeopardy

Another exception to the double jeopardy rule is when multiple crimes occur. More than one offense can result from the same action, and a defendant can be tried for each of those offenses. For example, a bank robbery might result in state charges for armed robbery; but if that bank belongs to the Federal Reserve System, a robbery would also violate federal criminal statutes protecting the integrity of the national banking system. As a result of separate convictions in state and federal courts, the convict could be sentenced to separate prison sentences in both state and federal penitentiaries.

A member of the U.S. armed forces accused of murder can be convicted of violating the *Uniform Code of Military Justice* and can also be convicted of state laws against murder. Separate prosecutions in a state court and a court martial would not violate the double jeopardy rule. The violation of federal law and the violation of state laws—even though resulting from a single act—are legally separate offenses.

A nationally televised video of an arrest led to two criminal trials arising from one event in 1993. Four Los Angeles police officers were prosecuted in state court on the charge of using excessive force against Rodney King during his arrest—an offense under state law. Following their acquittal on the state charges, the officers were then prosecuted in federal court for violating the civil rights of Mr. King—an offense under federal law. Although all four officers had been acquitted in state court, two of them were subsequently convicted in federal court on the civil rights charges and served time in federal prison.

In all three of the preceding examples, the state and federal criminal statutes were serving specific purposes—protecting different state and national interests. In the state court actions, the purposes were to protect the public and bank employees, and to prevent unnecessary police violence. In the federal prosecutions, the purposes were, respectively, to protect the national banking system, to maintain good order and discipline in the armed forces, and to protect the constitutional rights of the public. Because there were different public interests at stake, there were multiple harms resulting from a single act.

A SPEEDY TRIAL

The Sixth Amendment requires a "speedy" trial. Of course, it is not easy to say how fast "speedy" actually must be. In fact, a common defense objection is to trials that proceed too rapidly, depriving the defendant's attorney of the time needed to prepare an effective defense. The constitutional restriction exists for the protection of the defendant, not for the convenience of the prosecution or even the safety of the community. So courts often delay trials at the request of the defense, but seldom accelerate them at the request of the prosecution. In reviewing objections to delays, the courts evaluate both the reason for delay and any harm actually caused to the defendant. But a defendant who fails to object to delays when they occur would have a difficult time convincing an appellate court that she was denied a sufficiently speedy trial.

A PUBLIC TRIAL

The actual words of the Sixth Amendment are "a speedy *and public* trial" [emphasis added]. That right has been incorporated by the Supreme Court within the meaning of the Due Process Clause of the Fourteenth Amendment. "History has proven that secret tribunals were effective instruments of oppression." *Estes v. Texas,* 381 U.S. 532 (1965). A public trial protects not only the particular defendant charged, but also the community. The public at large has an interest in justice that is administered fairly and openly. Open courtrooms help to engender public confidence in the justice system.

That said, there is no absolute right to a public trial any more than there is an absolute right to unrestricted free speech. For extraordinary good cause, a court may close its proceedings to the public and to the press. A common cause for this is the protection of a witness: young victims of sexual crimes or persons testifying in the face of death threats, for example. Fortunately, the constitutional principle of public hearings is so firmly established in American jurisprudence that a trial court would be held strictly accountable by the appellate courts for any improper exclusion of the public.

In a related matter, courts have the authority to seal their records from public scrutiny. This is done for a variety of reasons: criminal indictments prior to an arrest of the person indicted; testimony or affidavits that might expose the witness to danger; testimony that would reveal national security matters or compromise on-going criminal investigations; affidavits offered to obtain search or arrest warrants; and so forth. The court's decision to seal a record may be appealed to a higher court.

IMPARTIAL JURY

Trial by jury was first instituted to prevent a biased and sometimes corrupt English judiciary from depriving criminal defendants of a fair trial. Of course, an English jury of one's "peers" originally was a jury comprising noblemen—not a particularly sympathetic audience for the trial of a commoner accused of poaching deer in the Crown's forests. But it might have offered some protection to a nobleman accused of treason against the king. At any rate, the right to be a juror is no longer limited to citizens of wealth or title.

A defendant has a right to trial by an impartial jury. Impartiality is the major reason for the *voir dire* process described in Chapter 6. Because the consequences of a conviction are so severe, impartiality takes on even greater importance in criminal trials. The Supreme Court has struck down convictions in which particular groups have been systematically excluded from the jury. In *Batson v. Kentucky,* 476 U.S. 79 (1986), the U.S. Supreme Court held that a prosecutor's peremptory challenge to prospective jurors—a prerogative that is held also by the defendant—must be "color-blind," not arbitrarily based upon the race of the prospective juror. In *Batson,* all African American prospective jurors were removed from the jury pool by the prosecution's peremptory challenges. The defendant, Batson, was African American.

Of course, that decision in *Batson* appears to suggest that peremptory challenges might not be fully "peremptory"—that is, subject to no question—after all. If peremptory challenges fall disproportionately upon jurors who are members of minority groups, they can be suspect and might be the basis for reversal on appeal.

SELF-INCRIMINATION

The Fifth Amendment states, in part, that no person "... *shall be compelled, in any criminal case, to be a witness against himself.*" As discussed earlier, the Miranda warning is based primarily on this guarantee against self-incrimination. The courts have held that this protection applies to any governmental proceeding in which a person is compelled to testify, not just to testimony given as a defendant in a criminal trial. Thus, in a civil lawsuit, or in a state legislature committee hearing, or in testimony given under subpoena before any administrative agency, an individual has the same constitutional right to refuse to make any statement, or answer any question, if the statement or answer would be self-incriminating. This is often referred to as "taking the Fifth."

Self-incrimination does not require an actual confession or any overt claim to involvement in a crime. Self-incrimination means *self-implication* in criminal conduct—anything one does or says from which a natural inference could be drawn that one was criminally involved. Consequently, the protection is rather broad. In practice, a court must determine when the Fifth Amendment privilege is justified and when a witness should be compelled to answer. It is not unusual for a judge to hear the requested testimony *in camera* (i.e., privately and in chambers) before ruling on the right to a Fifth Amendment privilege. If the judge rules against the witness, refusal to testify can result in a finding of contempt of court.

Fingerprints, body tissue, and body fluids (hair, blood, saliva, skin cells, etc.) are not considered to be testimony and cannot be withheld under the Fifth Amendment. Similarly, the Fifth Amendment does not protect a suspect from

A proceeding *in camera* is conducted in the judge's chambers, beyond public view.

being photographed or placed in a line-up. Even involuntary voice samples and handwriting samples can be required.

A novel application of the Fifth Amendment occurred when Congress once enacted a statute requiring all persons possessing a machine gun to purchase a tax stamp from the Treasury Department. Failure to purchase the tax stamp was a crime. But it was already a crime to possess the type of gun to which the statute applied. Consequently, when the federal government attempted to prosecute for failure to purchase the tax stamp, a federal court held that purchasing the stamp would constitute a self-incriminating statement by the purchaser. On that basis, the statute requiring purchase of the stamp was held to be unconstitutional.

In some situations, witnesses are given **immunity** so that they can testify without fear of any prosecution. It is even possible for a competent body (e.g., a court or a committee of Congress) to compel testimony by granting immunity from prosecution, because the immunity eliminates the Fifth Amendment basis for remaining silent.

> **Immunity** is a special exemption from prosecution, granted by a court or legislative body.

There are two types of immunity: use immunity and transactional immunity. If a person is granted **transactional immunity**, he cannot be prosecuted for the crime in question, no matter how or where evidence is obtained about that crime. Not only may the government not use *his testimony* to prosecute him for the crime, it may not prosecute him for that crime, period. In legal effect, transactional immunity is tantamount to a judicial "pardon."

> When **transactional immunity** (or blanket immunity) is granted, the immunized person may not be prosecuted for the underlying crime (the "transaction"), regardless of the source of any evidence that might be used against him.

In contrast, **use immunity** only prevents the government from using a person's testimony—and any other evidence which that testimony might lead them to discover—in any prosecution for the crime in question. Evidence obtained from other sources may be used without limitation. One problem for prosecutors is that at times it can be difficult to demonstrate that they would have learned of the other evidence even if the immunized testimony had not first been given. In other words, the defendant might claim that the other evidence was somehow "forbidden fruit" of the immunized testimony.

> A grant of **use immunity** means that the witness' own testimony may not be used against her, nor any evidence identified or discovered as a result of her immunized testimony.

As one might imagine, transactional immunity is rarely given. Some argue that it is contrary to public policy to "purchase" testimony at such a high price—absolute criminal immunity. In addition, if use immunity is granted, it is possible to compel the testimony or to hold the person in contempt of court if he refuses to testify. Consequently, some say, transactional immunity is unnecessary.

CONFRONTING AND CROSS-EXAMINING ADVERSE WITNESSES

The Sixth Amendment speaks of the defendant's right to be "*confronted with the witnesses against him.*" Those words might appear to mean that a defendant has the right to *hear* their accusations in court, but no more. However, the courts have recognized that the entire Sixth Amendment was intended to be a protection for criminal defendants. Consequently, that phrase has been understood to mean that a defendant has a constitutional right to challenge the witnesses against him.

The defendant challenges prosecution witnesses in two ways:

1. by cross-examining those prosecution witnesses
2. by presenting rebuttal evidence to impeach the witnesses' credibility and reliability

The first of these is the more important by far, because the Sixth Amendment specifically guarantees the defendant's right to call witnesses in his defense. On the other hand, if it were not for this right of confrontation, it is conceivable that a court might rule a defense witness' testimony inadmissable for lack of relevance if it did no more than impeach the testimony of a prosecution witness, without addressing the criminal allegations of the prosecution.

There are limited exceptions to the defendant's right to confront witnesses, usually to protect particularly vulnerable witnesses. Children, for example, are accorded special protection by the court against excessively aggressive or intimidating cross-examination. Victims of sexual offenses generally may not be questioned about their prior sexual activities—although this limitation is grounded also in the same rule of relevance that precludes allusion to a criminal defendant's prior convictions. Finally, the right to confront witnesses does not prevent the admission of evidence under various exceptions to the hearsay rule: deathbed statements, business records, and so forth.

THE RIGHT TO LEGAL COUNSEL

The right to legal counsel is one of the most fundamental of all rights in criminal procedure. In federal court, this right is guaranteed by the Sixth Amendment:

"In all criminal prosecutions, the accused shall . . . have the Assistance of Counsel for his defence."

In state court, the right to counsel is required under the Due Process Clause of the Fourteenth Amendment. But does this right to counsel mean that:

- the government must pay an attorney to represent the indigent defendant; and
- the defendant is entitled to counsel at all stages of criminal procedure?

As with all procedural rights, these questions are answered gradually, case by case, over a period of many years.

Overall, the U.S. Supreme Court has approached these issues with great concern for the criminal defendant, and it has adopted a broad interpretation of this right to legal counsel. In the first Scottsboro Boys case decided by the Supreme Court (see the opening scenario to Chapter 4), *Powell v. Alabama,* 287 U.S. 45 (1932), the Court held that the state must appoint legal counsel for indigent defendants in all capital cases. Only ten years later, however, the Supreme Court rejected a petitioner's claim that a state must appoint counsel for indigent defendants in *non*capital felony trials. *Betts v. Brady,* 316 U.S. 455 (1942). This remained the law of the land for the succeeding twenty-one years until, in 1963, the Supreme Court overruled *Betts* in *Gideon v. Wainwright,* 372 U.S. 335 (1963). Excerpts from the Court's opinion in *Gideon* appear in the "Case in Point," below.

A CASE IN POINT

Gideon v. Wainwright

372 U.S. 335 (1963)

Mr. Justice BLACK delivered the opinion of the Court.

Petitioner is charged in a Florida state court with having broken and entered a poolroom with intent to commit a misdemeanor. This offense is a felony under Florida law. Appearing in court without funds and without a lawyer, petitioner asked the court to appoint counsel for him, whereupon the following colloquy took place:

'The COURT: Mr. Gideon, I am sorry, but I cannot appoint Counsel to represent you in this case. Under the laws of the State of Florida, the only time the Court can appoint Counsel to represent a Defendant is when that person is charged with a capital offense. I am sorry, but I will have to deny your request to appoint Counsel to defend you in this case.

'The DEFENDANT: The United States Supreme Court says I am entitled to be represented by Counsel.'

Put to trial before a jury, Gideon conducted his defense about as well as could be expected from a layman. He made an opening statement to the jury, cross-examined the State's witnesses, presented witnesses in his own defense, declined to testify himself, and made a short argument 'emphasizing his innocence to the charge contained in the Information filed in this case.' The jury returned a verdict of guilty, and petitioner was sentenced to serve five years in the state prison. Later, petitioner filed in the Florida Supreme Court this habeas corpus petitioner [sic] attacking his conviction and sentence on the ground that the trial court's refusal to appoint counsel for him denied him rights 'guaranteed by the Constitution and the Bill of Rights by the United States Government.' [Footnote omitted.] Treating the petition for habeas corpus as properly before it, the State Supreme Court, 'upon consideration thereof' but without an opinion, denied all relief. Since 1942, when Betts v. Brady, 316 U.S. 455, 62 S.Ct. 1252, 86 L.Ed.1595, was decided by a divided Court, the problem of a defendant's federal constitutional right to counsel in a state court has been a continuing source of controversy and litigation in both state and federal courts. [Footnote omitted.] To give this problem another review here, we granted certiorari. 370 U.S. 908, 82 S.Ct. 1259, 8 L.Ed.2d 403. Since Gideon was proceeding in forma pauperis, we appointed counsel to represent him and requested both sides to discuss in their briefs and oral arguments the following: 'Should this Court's holding in Betts v. Brady, 316 U.S. 455, 62 S.Ct. 1252, 86 L.Ed.1595, be reconsidered?'

The facts upon which Betts claimed that he had been unconstitutionally denied the right to have counsel appointed to assist him are strikingly like the facts upon which Gideon here bases his federal constitutional claim. Betts was indicted for robbery in a Maryland state court. On arraignment, he told the trial judge of his lack of funds to hire a lawyer and asked the court to appoint one for him. Betts was advised that it was not the practice in that county to appoint counsel for indigent defendants except in murder and rape cases. He then pleaded not guilty, had witnesses summoned, cross-examined the State's witnesses, examined his own, and chose not to testify himself. He was found guilty by the judge, sitting without a jury, and sentenced to eight years in prison....

* * * *

... Since the facts and circumstances of the two cases are so nearly indistinguishable, we think the Betts v. Brady holding if left standing would require us to reject Gideon's claim that the Constitution guarantees him the assistance of counsel. Upon full reconsideration we conclude that Betts v. Brady should be overruled.

* * * *

... The fact is that in deciding as it did—that 'appointment of counsel is not a fundamental right, essential to a fair trial'—the Court in Betts v. Brady made an abrupt break with its own well-considered precedents. In returning to these old precedents, sounder we believe than the new, we but restore constitutional principles established to achieve a fair system of justice. Not only these precedents but also reason and reflection require us to recognize that in our adversary system of criminal justice, any person haled into court, who is too poor to hire a lawyer, cannot be assured a fair trial unless counsel is provided for him. This seems to us to be an obvious truth. Governments, both state and federal, quite properly spend vast sums of money to establish machinery to try defendants accused of crime. Lawyers are everywhere deemed essential to protect the public's interest in an orderly society. Similarly, there are few defendants charged with crime, few indeed, who fail to hire the best lawyers they can get to prepare and present their defenses. That government hires lawyers to prosecute and defendants who have the money hire lawyers to defend are the strongest indications of the wide-spread belief that lawyers in criminal courts are necessities, not luxuries. The right of one charged with crime to counsel may not be deemed fundamental and essential to fair trials in some countries, but it is in ours. From the very beginning, our state and national constitutions and laws have laid great emphasis on procedural and substantive safeguards designed to assure fair trials before impartial tribunals in which every defendant stands equal before the law. This noble ideal cannot be realized if the poor man charged with crime has to face his accusers without a lawyer to assist him. . . .

* * * *

The judgment is reversed and the cause is remanded to the Supreme Court of Florida for further action not inconsistent with this opinion.

Reversed.

It is interesting to note that the *Gideon* court found representation by counsel to be a right both "fundamental" and "essential" to a fair trial. In subsequent cases, the Supreme Court held that the right to counsel applies during the following:

- custodial interrogations (the Miranda right)
- lineups for identification by witnesses
- arraignments
- preliminary hearings
- sentencing

Since the *Gideon* decision, virtually all levels of government have established public defender offices for the specific purpose of representing those who cannot afford an attorney. In addition, some private foundations and other nonprofit organizations provide free representation for those appealing their death sentences.

This is a continuing issue in constitutional law, particularly regarding attorneys appointed by the trial court who lack adequate time and resources to prepare a defense. It is no exaggeration to state that some public defenders have such overwhelming caseloads that they meet with some clients for less than fifteen minutes—in total—before representing them at felony arraignments. At the time of this writing, there are jurisdictions that pay court-appointed counsel in capital cases as little as $75.00 per hour and provide no additional funds to pay for private investigators, expert witnesses, and other services that privately retained defense lawyers consider essential.

The Supreme Court has not established any criteria for determining indigence, so that matter has been left in the hands of Congress, the state legislatures, and the courts. Obviously, a defendant who easily could pay an attorney for a trial lasting two days might be hopelessly "indigent" if the trial were to extend into several months—as often happens with high-profile capital cases.

The *Gideon* decision did not address another important aspect of that representation—the competency of the defendant's representation by counsel. That issue has been before the courts in other cases, however.

This right to legal counsel is more than a perfunctory right—the representation must be at least minimally adequate. Convictions can be overturned because of the incompetent defense mounted by the defendant's attorney, although the defendant must show that an acquittal would have been probable with competent representation. State appellate courts have overturned convictions where the defendant's attorney was impaired by alcoholism. Convictions have also been overturned for failure to raise obvious and critically important defenses.

> **Ethics Watch**
>
> Because a criminal defendant has a constitutional right to effective representation, legal assistants practicing in the field of criminal law bear a very heavy responsibility. It is entirely possible for the acts or omissions of a legal assistant to diminish the effectiveness of a defense at trial. Because the client faces such extreme consequences if the case is lost, the defense attorney and her paralegals bear a proportionate responsibility to the client.

THE RIGHT TO SELF-REPRESENTATION

In *Faretta v. California,* 422 U.S. 806 (1975), the Supreme Court held that a defendant's right to choose his counsel overrides any constitutional imperative for competent representation. The Court upheld the right of a criminal defendant to represent himself, even though he could not do so as effectively as a trained attorney.

The defendant, Anthony Faretta, was accused of grand theft, a felony. He informed the court well before trial that he wished to conduct his own defense. The trial judge advised the defendant that if he represented himself he would, nonetheless, have to conform to all of the "ground rules" of trial procedure. In effect, the court advised Faretta that no special exception would be made for him. The court initially granted Faretta's request, but then required that a court-appointed attorney present the defendant's case during trial. A jury convicted the defendant. On review, the U.S. Supreme Court held that the defendant has a constitutional right to self-representation, and that the state may not force him to be represented by a lawyer.

SCENARIO

Finding Challenge and Satisfaction in the Public Defender's Office

For the past three years, Mary Nguyen has been a paralegal in a public defender's office in California. Prior to her present position, she was a litigation paralegal in a large San Diego law firm. Mary made the job change for two reasons: job satisfaction and challenge. "The litigation firm I worked for represented clients who were wealthy and powerful. They could afford whatever it took to get the very best legal representation. I come from an immigrant family that had to struggle just to put my two brothers and me through college. I guess I just naturally feel for the underdog. So, I was looking for a way to help the less fortunate."

Eventually, Mary came down to a choice of working for a Legal Aid Society or going into a public defender's office. "I had done some *pro bono* work for Legal Aid and several other outreach organizations, but their funding was always uncertain. I'm a single parent, so when I decided to leave the litigation firm, job security and benefits were major issues for me. The public defender's job offered that security together with the chance to make a difference in the lives of those less fortunate than I."

Mary's second motivation was to find more challenge in her work. "In the particular law firm where I worked, there was a very strong sense of hierarchy that affected the type of assignments paralegals could get. In addition to new associates, they always had law clerks and 'summer associates' [law students who are hired each summer to do legal research]. So, the paralegals were pretty much confined to traditional paralegal assignments. I could have moved to another law firm with broader opportunities, but that wouldn't satisfy my other objective.

"In the public defender's office, a paralegal can take on almost anything that doesn't breach the boundary of practicing law. The attorneys in the office have such incredible caseloads, they can't possibly do all of the things a criminal defense attorney in private practice normally does: thorough witness interviews, field investigations, extensive legal research, and so on. They have very limited funds for hiring private investigators or expert witnesses. The two staff investigators they have concentrate on the capital cases, although occasionally they can spare some time for other really 'dicey' cases. Our office has no choice other than to use its paralegals to the *n*th degree. And I love it."

Mary acknowledges that there are some negative aspects of her job. "It's really tough to see the look in a victim's eyes when he knows you are helping to defend the person accused of assaulting him. Sometimes I feel quite sure that a particular client *should* be found guilty—but I deal with that. And then there are those clients who seem like the scum of the earth, and you feel like they deserve to rot on 'Devil's Island.' Just as troubling though, is when I become really convinced that our client is innocent, and then see him convicted anyway. You can't imagine what it's like to see someone like that go to prison."

Mary seems to have come to terms with these issues—at least, most of the time. "If I start to waiver, I remind myself that I have no right to appoint myself judge and jury and deprive these people of a vigorous defense. And then there's the prosecutor's office, with staff and resources *our* office will never have, to "pin the tail" on the one who did the crime. I also remind myself of the really deserving clients we have proved to be innocent—not many, but just one's enough to make it all worthwhile. I keep a cork bulletin board on the wall by my desk, and it is covered with news clippings about death row inmates who have been released after umpteen years because new DNA technology has finally proved they were not the killers. I wonder how many of their own defense attorneys believed them to be guilty when they were on trial."

And what about the scumbags? "Even a scumbag could be innocent of *this* particular crime. But even if he's the one, we have a system of justice that presumes his innocence, but still goes after him with a vengeance! It would be a terrible thing to surrender that system to our personal passions of bias and disgust. I'm part of that system of justice, and I'm proud to be. I know, I must come across as a 'bleeding heart' liberal. But, what can I say?" ■

THE EXCLUSIONARY RULE

As discussed earlier, the purpose of the Miranda Warning is twofold:

1. to protect the suspect from making careless, prejudicial statements
2. to make admissible the postarrest statements made *after* the person in custody has been informed of his rights

But the true authority of the *Miranda* ruling is found in its enforcement tool: the exclusion of statements improperly obtained without giving the warning.

The **exclusionary rule** is a lawyer's term for the legal tool that puts real teeth into both the *Miranda* ruling and the constitutional prohibition against unreasonable search and seizure. The theory behind the exclusionary rule is that police officers are not often prosecuted or disciplined for violating the privacy and due process rights of suspects. If the police are not subject to effective discipline, will their personal integrity be enough to restrain them from violating

The **exclusionary rule** prohibits the introduction of evidence that was obtained in violation of constitutional protections.

> **Practice Tip**
>
> In criminal cases, admissibility of evidence is one of the most frequent, and contentious, controversies. Whether working for the prosecutor or the defending attorney, a paralegal will encounter these disputes in case after case. An understanding of the law of criminal evidence makes any paralegal in criminal law practice far more useful to the supervising attorney.

the due process rights of suspects? In *Mapp v. Ohio,* 367 U.S. 643 (1961), the Supreme Court concluded that, too often, it was not. In his opinion for the court, Justice Clark observed that, although the courts of some states had adopted their own exclusionary rule, those states that had not done so had been unable to establish any effective way to limit unreasonable police searches.

Before *Mapp,* confessions by beating and illegally seized evidence were routinely admitted at trial on the theory that the criminal should not be protected by "technicalities" and because the Constitution did not speak explicitly of excluding such ill-gotten evidence. A common premise was that the criminal should not go free just because the police also broke the law. As a result, the constitutional "protections" were largely meaningless. Because criminal prosecution of police abuses was virtually nonexistent, the Supreme Court imposed the exclusionary rule as the only practical means for enforcing constitutional protections. This does not mean that the issue is settled, for each term of the Supreme Court brings new cases attempting to expand or limit the exclusionary rule. The usual testing ground for the exclusionary rule is the Fourth Amendment:

> *The right of the people to be secure in their persons, houses, papers, and effects, against unreasonable searches and seizures, shall not be violated; and no Warrants shall issue, but upon probable cause, supported by Oath or affirmation, and particularly describing the place to be searched, and the persons or things to be seized.*

Compared to the other amendments in the Bill of Rights, the Fourth Amendment is unusual in its detail. It speaks not only of "persons" and "houses," but also "papers, and effects." It states that warrants must be based upon "probable cause, supported by oath or affirmation." It requires search warrants to be specific in describing what is to be searched and what is to be seized. This is in great contrast to the lack of detail in the First Amendment, or the Eighth. Of course, if probable cause is shown, a warrant may be issued and the search will not violate the Fourth Amendment. The facts supporting this belief in probable cause must be stated in an affidavit by the officer requesting the search warrant.

The Fourth Amendment forbids only *unreasonable* searches and seizures, and a great many Supreme Court cases have dealt with the meaning of "unreasonable" in a variety of circumstances. Also troublesome has been the application of eighteenth century concepts of privacy to modern day reality. Who could have dreamed, in the eighteenth century, of telephone wiretaps, or of "bugs" planted in a suspect's mattress, or of optical antennae that can enable an eavesdropper to monitor conversations inside a building through the vibrations they induce in the exterior window panes? What, indeed, is an "unreasonable" search? There is no easy answer, and the parameters of permissible searches without warrants will continue to be defined by the courts as new technology provides ever more ways to invade one's privacy.

In the following "Case in Point," the Supreme Court considers whether the Fourth Amendment requires a search warrant prior to aerial surveillance of a person's backyard to see if marijuana plants are being cultivated. In its opinion, the Court speaks of the "curtilage" of a home. Curtilage is a legal concept, and describes land and buildings immediately adjacent to one's home. In an earlier case, the Supreme Court defined curtilage as "the area to which extends the intimate activity associated with the 'sanctity of a man's home and the privacies of life.' " *Oliver v. United States,* 466 U.S. 170, 180, 104 S.Ct.1735, 1742, 80 L.Ed.2d 214 (1984), quoting *Boyd v. United States,* 116 U.S. 616, 630 (1886). Curtilage is significant in the following case because it indicates a possible expectation of privacy.

A Case in Point

California v. Ciraolo

476 U.S. 207 (1986)

[All footnotes omitted.]

Chief Justice BURGER delivered the opinion of the Court.

We granted certiorari to determine whether the Fourth Amendment is violated by aerial observation without a warrant from an altitude of 1,000 feet of a fenced-in backyard within the curtilage of a home.

On September 2, 1982, Santa Clara police received an anonymous telephone tip that marijuana was growing in respondent's backyard. Police were unable to observe the contents of respondent's yard from a ground level because of a 6-foot outer fence and a 10-foot inner fence completely enclosing the yard. Later that day, Officer Shutz, who was assigned to investigate, secured a private plane and flew over respondent's house at an altitude of 1,000 feet, within navigable airspace; he was accompanied by Officer Rodriguez. Both officers were trained in marijuana identification. From the overflight, the officers readily identified marijuana plants 8 feet to 10 feet in height growing in a 15- by 25-foot plot in respondent's yard; they photographed the area with a standard 35mm camera.

On September 8, 1982, Officer Shutz obtained a search warrant on the basis of an affidavit describing the anonymous tip and their observations; a photograph depicting respondent's house, the backyard, and neighboring homes was attached to the affidavit as an exhibit. The warrant was executed the next day and 73 plants were seized; it is not disputed that these were marijuana.

After the trial court denied respondent's motion to suppress the evidence of the search, respondent pleaded guilty to a charge of cultivation of marijuana. The California Court of Appeal reversed, however, on the ground that the warrantless aerial observation of respondent's yard which led to the issuance of the warrant violated the Fourth Amendment. 161 Cal.App.3d 1081, 208 Cal.Rptr. 93 (1984). That court first held that respondent's backyard marijuana garden was within the "curtilage" of his home, under Oliver v. United States, 466 U.S. 170, 104 S.Ct. 1735, 80 L.Ed.2d 214 (1984). The court emphasized that the height and existence of the two fences constituted "objective criteria from which we may conclude he manifested a reasonable expectation of privacy by any standard." 161 Cal.App. 3d, at 1089, 208 Cal.Rptr., at 97.

Examining the particular method of surveillance undertaken, the court then found it "significant" that the flyover "was not the result of a routine patrol conducted for any other legitimate law enforcement or public safety objective, but was undertaken for the specific purpose of observing this particular enclosure within [respondent's] curtilage." Ibid. It held this focused observation was "a direct and unauthorized intrusion into the sanctity of the home" that violated respondent's reasonable expectation of privacy. Id., at 1089–1090, 208 Cal.Rptr., at 98 (footnote omitted). The California Supreme Court denied the States' petition for review.

We granted the State's petition for certiorari. [Citation omitted.]

We reverse.

The State argues that respondent has "knowingly exposed" his backyard to aerial observation, because all that was seen was visible to the naked eye from any aircraft flying overhead. The State analogizes its mode of observation to a knothole or opening in a fence: if there is an opening, the police may look.

. . . Respondent contends that he has done all that can reasonably be expected to tell the world he wishes to maintain the privacy of his garden within the curtilage without covering his yard. Such covering, he argues, would defeat its purpose as an outside living area; he asserts he has not "knowingly" exposed himself to aerial views.

The touchstone of Fourth Amendment analysis is whether a person has a "constitutionally protected reasonable expectation of privacy." Katz v. United States, 389 U.S. 347, 360, 88 S.Ct. 507, 516, 19 L.Ed.2d 576 (1967).... Katz posits a two-part inquiry: first, has the individual manifested a subjective expectation of privacy in the object of the challenged search? Second, is society willing to recognize that expectation as reasonable? See Smith v. Maryland, 442 U.S. 735, 740, 99 S.Ct. 2577, 2580, 61 L.Ed.2d 220 (1979).

Clearly—and understandably—respondent has met the test of manifesting his own subjective intent and desire to maintain privacy as to his unlawful agricultural pursuits. However, we need not address that issue, for the State has not challenged the finding of the California Court of Appeal that respondent had such an expectation....

* * * *

We turn, therefore, to the second inquiry under Katz, i.e., whether that expectation is reasonable. In pursuing this inquiry, we must keep in mind that "[t]he test of legitimacy is not whether the individual chooses to conceal assertedly 'private' activity," but instead "whether the government's intrusion infringes upon the personal and societal values protected by the Fourth Amendment." Oliver, supra, 466 U.S., at 181–183, 104 S.Ct., at 1742–1744.

* * * *

That the area is within the curtilage does not itself bar all police observation. The Fourth Amendment protection of the home has never been extended to require law enforcement officers to shield their eyes when passing by a home on public thoroughfares. Nor does the mere fact that an individual has taken measures to restrict some views of his activities preclude an officer's observations from a public vantage point where he has a right to be and which renders the activities clearly visible. E.g., United States v. Knotts, 460 U.S. 276, 282, 103 S.Ct. 1081, 1085–1086, 75 L.Ed.2d 55 (1983). "What a person knowingly exposes to the public, even in his own home or office, is not a subject of Fourth Amendment protection." Katz, supra, 389 U.S., at 351, 88 S.Ct., at 511.

The observation by Officers Shutz and Rodriguez in this case took place within public navigable airspace, see 49 U.S.C.App. § 1304, in a physically nonintrusive manner; from this point they were able to observe plants readily discernable to the naked eye as marijuana. That the observation from aircraft was directed at identifying the plants and the officers were trained to recognize marijuana is irrelevant....

* * * *

... The Fourth Amendment simply does not require the police traveling in the public airways at this altitude to obtain a warrant in order to observe what is visible to the naked eye.

Reversed.

In spite of its explicit proscription, the Fourth Amendment protection has been qualified to a remarkable degree by Supreme Court decisions. Moveable "scenes of crime" (e.g., an automobile, a boat, or an airplane) have been held to have less protection than fixed premises. Searches without warrant may be made of a suspect's person, office, or house if they are made at the conclusion of a **hot pursuit** of the suspect.

Searches may be made of a room within a house if the officers observe through a window what appears to be criminal conduct. In that latter circumstance, a critical issue can be whether the observing officers were in an "area open

Hot pursuit is the physical act of closely, vigorously, and continuously pursuing a person suspected of committing a crime.

to the public"—for example, the sidewalk or front walkway—or were going across lawns and through shrubbery where the public is not usually "invited." As the Court's opinion in *Ciraolo* indicates, aerial surveillance may be undertaken without a warrant, and evidence observed from the air may be used in a prosecution.

It is unlikely that the definitions for "reasonable" and "unreasonable" will become clear and definite standards within the foreseeable future. And that makes it difficult for the courts and the police—and for innocent citizens who happen briefly to be under suspicion.

Internet Access

National District Attorneys Association	http://www.ndaa.org
National Association of Criminal Defense Lawyers	http://www.criminaljustice.org
National Criminal Justice Reference Service	http://www.ncjrs.org

---

SECTION 3. CRIMINAL LAW PROCEDURES

The states are not uniform in their sequence for criminal court procedures. The sequence of criminal procedures can vary also, within a single jurisdiction, depending upon circumstances in any given case. For example, it makes a major difference if:

- the arrest occurs spontaneously, at or shortly after the time a crime is committed; or
- the arrest occurs after an extensive investigation of suspected criminal activity.

In the latter case, police and prosecutors would be ready to present formal charges to the court shortly after arrest. The following discussion offers only one sequence as a possible exemplar, and the paralegal needs to familiarize himself with the procedures of his own state and locale.

INQUIRY, DETENTION, AND ARREST

The *circumstances* under which police obtain an accused person's statements and other types of evidence can determine whether those statements and evidence will be admissible in a prosecution of the alleged crime. For this reason, the law of inquiry, detention, and **arrest** is of great importance for both prosecutors and defense attorneys. In addition, an officer making an arrest can incur civil liability for **false arrest** if she exceeds her legal authority in a given situation. False arrest is actually a form of false imprisonment, and it occurs when an arrest is made without proper legal authority—for example, without probable cause to believe the arrested person has committed a particular crime. Indeed, under unusual circumstances, an officer can even be *criminally* liable for a false arrest made under "**color of law**" for an ulterior motive. For example, an arrest made to afford the officer an opportunity to initiate a sexual advance toward the person in custody would be "false arrest under color of law."

An arrest occurs when a law enforcement officer indicates his intention to subject the suspect to the control and custody of the arresting officer based upon a probable cause to believe that the suspect has committed a specific crime. In some jurisdictions, a person may not be arrested for a misdemeanor

An **arrest** occurs when an officer, believing that a crime has been committed, uses her legal authority to deprive a person of his liberty to go on about his way.

False arrest (or *false imprisonment*) is an unlawful detention of a person, depriving her of liberty without legal grounds.

Color of law is the appearance of some legal authority or right that does not, in fact, exist; an abuse of authority made possible by the offender's status as a public officer.

unless the crime was committed in the presence of the person making the arrest. The dividing line between a brief detention and an arrest is not always clear.

Ordinary citizens have the power to make an arrest—a **citizen's arrest**—for offenses committed in their presence. The usual practice following a citizen's arrest is to call a police officer, who then takes custody of the suspect based upon that citizen's arrest. Of course, citizens and police officers alike are subject to lawsuit for false arrest; therefore, a citizen's arrest is a power that should be used with great caution.

> A **citizen's arrest** is made by one who is not a sworn peace officer, usually for a crime committed in their presence.

Short of making an arrest, a police officer might briefly **detain** a person. A detention is the accosting of a person, limiting that individual's freedom to go on about his business, while the police officer asks questions of the detained person, checks for outstanding warrants, or observes the immediate vicinity for evidence of a crime. Although there are no clearly defined parameters, extending a detention beyond a reasonably brief period might transform it into an arrest. By the same token, a person is not necessarily detained just because an officer asks her to identify herself and explain her presence. The encounter rises to a detention when the person believes that she is not free to leave or when the questions asked suggest a specific suspicion of criminal conduct. The authority of the officer increases as the situation rises first to a detention, and then to an arrest. At the same time, the due process rights of the individual increase. At some point, the officer must provide the Miranda warning if she wants the suspect's subsequent answers to be useable as evidence. The determination of this threshold point has been the crux of many Supreme Court cases in recent decades.

> A person is **detained** when he is stopped for a brief inquiry, based upon a reasonable suspicion that a crime has been committed or is imminent.

Before a police officer detains a person, he must have a **reasonable suspicion** that the detained person has engaged in, or is about to engage in, a criminal act. That suspicion may not rest on intuition—the officer must be able to state facts that would lead a reasonable officer of his experience to suspect criminal activity. This degree of suspicion is not enough to justify an actual arrest or a full search, but it can justify an exterior pat-down of the clothing to ensure that the person has no concealed weapons. This is known as the "stop and frisk" rule.

> A **reasonable suspicion** is based upon facts that can be stated and that would cause a reasonable officer of equivalent experience to suspect criminal activity.

If the officer's inquiry develops facts sufficient to support a finding of probable cause to believe the person has committed a crime, the officer may then arrest that person. Probable cause is significantly more than the reasonable suspicion that justifies a brief detention. **Probable cause** requires facts and circumstances that would lead a reasonable person to believe that an actual crime has been—or is being—committed by the suspect. Although an officer might briefly detain a person on reasonable suspicion that he is *contemplating* an imminent criminal act, no such prospective authority exists for an arrest. An arrest is permitted only for *actual criminal conduct,* not for a presumed future intention.

> **Probable cause** is established by facts that suggest that a crime has been committed.

The U.S. Supreme Court's decision in *Florida v. Royer,* 460 U.S. 491 (1983) concerned the authority of police to detain a suspect and search his luggage. The exclusionary rule was applied in that case, because police lacked probable cause to search the luggage, in which they found marijuana. (In the Court's opinion, the alternative spelling "marihuana" is used.) Excerpts from the *Royer* decision appear below as "A Case in Point."

A Case in Point

Florida v. Royer

460 U.S. 491 (1983)

[All footnotes omitted.]

JUSTICE WHITE announced the judgment of the Court and delivered an opinion, in which JUSTICE MARSHALL, JUSTICE POWELL, and JUSTICE STEVENS joined.

We are required in this case to determine whether the Court of Appeal of Florida, Third District, properly applied the precepts of the Fourth Amendment in holding that respondent Royer was being illegally detained at the time of his purported consent to a search of his baggage.

I

On January 3, 1978, Royer was observed at Miami International Airport by two plainclothes detectives.... Detectives Johnson and Magdalena believed that Royer's appearance, mannerisms, luggage, and actions fit the so-called "drug courier profile." Royer, apparently unaware of the attention he had attracted, purchased a one-way ticket to New York City and checked his two suitcases, placing on each suitcase an identification tag bearing the name "Holt" and the destination "La Guardia." As Royer made his way to the concourse which led to the airline boarding area, the two detectives approached him, identified themselves as policemen working out of the sheriff's office, and asked if Royer had a "moment" to speak with them; Royer said "Yes."

Upon request, but without oral consent, Royer produced for the detectives his airline ticket and his driver's license. The airline ticket, like the baggage identification tags, bore the name "Holt," while the driver's license carried respondent's correct name, "Royer." When the detectives asked about the discrepancy, Royer explained that a friend had made the reservation in the name of "Holt." Royer became noticeably more nervous during this conversation, whereupon the detectives informed Royer that they were in fact narcotics investigators and that they had reason to suspect him of transporting narcotics.

The detectives did not return his airline ticket and identification but asked Royer to accompany them to a room, approximately 40 feet away, adjacent to the concourse. Royer said nothing in response but went with the officers as he had been asked to do. The room was later described by Detective Johnson as a "large storage closet," located in the stewardesses' lounge and containing a small desk and two chairs. Without Royer's consent or agreement, Detective Johnson, using Royer's baggage check stubs, retrieved the "Holt" luggage from the airline and brought it to the room where respondent and Detective Magdalena were waiting. Royer was asked if he would consent to a search of the suitcases. Without orally responding to this request, Royer produced a key and unlocked one of the suitcases, which one detective then opened without seeking further assent from Royer. Marihuana was found in that suitcase. According to Detective Johnson, Royer stated that he did not know the combination to the lock on the second suitcase. When asked if he objected to the detective opening the second suitcase, Royer said "[n]o, go ahead," and did not object when the detective explained that the suitcase might have to be broken open. The suitcase was pried open by the officers and more marihuana was found. Royer was then told that he was under arrest. Approximately 15 minutes had elapsed from the time the detectives initially approached respondent until his arrest upon the discovery of the contraband.

Prior to his trial for felony possession of marihuana, Royer made a motion to suppress the evidence obtained in the search of the suitcases. The trial court found that Royer's consent to the search was "freely and voluntarily given," and that, regardless of the consent, the warrantless search was reasonable because "the officer doesn't have the time to run out and get a search warrant because the plane is going to take off." Following the denial of the motion to suppress, Royer changed his plea from "not guilty" to "*nolo contendere,*" specifically reserving the right to appeal the denial of the motion to suppress. Royer was convicted.

The District Court of Appeal, sitting en banc, reversed Royer's conviction. The court held that Royer had been involuntarily confined within the small room without probable cause; that the involuntary detention had exceeded the limited restraint permitted by *Terry v. Ohio,* 392 U.S. 1 (1968), at the time his consent to the search was obtained; and that the consent to search was therefore invalid because tainted by the unlawful confinement.

* * * *

. . . We granted the State's petition for certiorari, 454 U.S. 1079 (1981), and now affirm.

II

Some preliminary observations are in order. First, it is unquestioned that without a warrant to search Royer's luggage and in the absence of probable cause and exigent circumstances, the validity of the search depended upon Royer's purported consent. Neither is it disputed that where the validity of a search rests on consent, the State has the burden of proving that the necessary consent was obtained and that it was freely and voluntarily given, a burden that is not satisfied by showing a mere submission to a claim of lawful authority. [Citations omitted.]

Second, law enforcement officers do not violate the Fourth Amendment by merely approaching an individual on the street or in another public place, by asking him if he is willing to answer some questions, by putting questions to him if the person is willing to listen, or by offering in evidence in a criminal prosecution his voluntary answers to such questions. [Citations omitted.] . . . The person approached, however, need not answer any question put to him; indeed, he may decline to listen to the questions at all and may go on his way. *Terry v. Ohio,* 392 U.S., at 32-33 (Harlan, J., concurring); *id.,* at 34 (WHITE, J., concurring). He may not be detained even momentarily without reasonable, objective grounds for doing so; and his refusal to listen or answer does not, without more, furnish those grounds. *United States v. Mendenhall, supra,* [446 U.S. 544 (1980)] at 556 (opinion of Stewart, J.). If there is no detention—no seizure within the meaning of the Fourth Amendment—then no constitutional rights have been infringed.

Third, it is also clear that *not all seizures of the person must be justified by probable cause to arrest for a crime.* [Emphasis added.] Prior to *Terry v. Ohio, supra,* any restraint on the person amounting to a seizure for the purposes of the Fourth Amendment was invalid unless justified by probable cause. *Dunaway v. New York, supra,* [442 U.S. 200 (1979)] at 207-209. *Terry* created a limited exception to this general rule: certain seizures are justifiable under the Fourth Amendment if there is articulable suspicion that a person has committed or is about to commit a crime. In that case, a stop and frisk for weapons were found unexceptionable . . . . Although not expressly authorized in *Terry, United States v. Brignoni-Ponce,* 422 U.S. 873, 881-882 (1975), was unequivocal in saying that reasonable suspicion of criminal activity warrants a temporary seizure for the purpose of questioning limited to the purpose of the stop. In *Brignoni-Ponce,* that purpose was to verify or dispel the suspicion that the immigration laws were being violated, a governmental interest that was sufficient to warrant temporary detention for limited questioning. Royer does not suggest, nor do we, that a similar rationale would not warrant temporary detention for questioning on less than probable cause where the public interest involved is the suppression of illegal transactions in drugs or other serious crime.

* * * *

Fourth, *Terry* and its progeny nevertheless created *only limited exceptions* to the general rule that seizures of the person require probable cause to arrest. [Emphasis added.] Detentions may be "investigative" yet violative of the Fourth Amendment absent probable cause. In the name of investigating a person who is no more than suspected of criminal activity, the police may not carry out a full search of the person or of his automobile or other effects. Nor might the police seek to verify their suspicions by means that approach the conditions of arrest....

* * * *

III

The State ... [has] submitted that the entire encounter was consensual and hence Royer was not being held against his will at all. We find this submission untenable. Asking for and examining Royer's ticket and his driver's license were no doubt permissible in themselves, but when the officers identified themselves as narcotics agents, told Royer that he was suspected of transporting narcotics, and asked him to accompany them to the police room, while retaining his ticket and driver's license and without indicating in any way that he was free to depart, Royer was effectively seized for the purposes of the Fourth Amendment....

... We agree with the State that when the officers discovered that Royer was traveling under an assumed name, this fact, and the facts already known to the officers—paying cash for a one-way ticket, the mode of checking the two bags, and Royer's appearance and conduct in general—were adequate grounds for suspecting Royer of carrying drugs and for temporarily detaining him and his luggage while they attempted to verify or dispel their suspicions in a manner that did not exceed the limits of an investigative detention.... We have concluded, however, that at the time Royer produced the key to his suitcase, the detention to which he was then subjected was a more serious intrusion on his personal liberty than is allowable on mere suspicion of criminal activity.

... What had begun as a consensual inquiry in a public place had escalated into an investigatory procedure in a police interrogation room, where the police, unsatisfied with previous explanations, sought to confirm their suspicions. The officers had Royer's ticket, they had his identification, and they had seized his luggage. Royer was never informed that he was free to board his plane if he so chose, and he reasonably believed that he was being detained. At least as of that moment, any consensual aspects of the encounter had evaporated.... As a practical matter, Royer was under arrest.... [T]he State's brief in this Court interprets the testimony of the officers at the suppression hearing as indicating that had Royer refused to consent to a search of his luggage, the officers would have held the luggage and sought a warrant to authorize the search. Brief for Petitioner 6.

* * * *

The State's ... final argument is that Royer was not being illegally held when he gave his consent because there was probable cause to arrest him at that time.... The facts are that a nervous young man with two American Tourister bags paid cash for an airline ticket to a "target city." These facts led to inquiry, which in turn revealed that the ticket had been bought under an assumed name. The proffered explanation did not satisfy the officers. We cannot agree with the State, if this is its position, that every nervous young man paying cash for a ticket to New York City under an assumed name and carrying two heavy American Tourister bags may be arrested and held to answer for a serious felony charge.

V

Because we affirm the Florida District Court of Appeal's conclusion that Royer was being illegally detained when he consented to the search of his luggage, we agree that the consent was tainted by the illegality and was ineffective to justify the search. The judgment of the Florida District Court of Appeal is accordingly

Affirmed.

Notice of Arrest

It is not necessary for the arresting officer to verbally state that an arrest is being made, although such a statement *is* legally effective as an arrest. An arrest might be accomplished by directing a suspect to accompany the officer to another location under circumstances that indicate he is not free to leave (as in the *Royer* case, above), by tackling a fleeing person, by placing the suspect in a police car or other confining space, or by handcuffing the suspect—and these are just a few examples of what can constitute an arrest. When an officer pulls a driver over in a routine traffic stop, it is considered a detention rather than an arrest, unless the officer takes further action to escalate the encounter into an arrest. However, a driver who ignores a patrol car's red lights and siren and attempts to elude pursuing officers can be presumed to be under arrest when he is finally stopped for the crime of **evasion of arrest**.

Evasion of arrest is attempting to elude a pursuing police officer who has signaled one to halt.

Booking a suspect creates a formal record of the arrest.

Bookings

For felonies and serious misdemeanors, an arrested person is usually **booked** at a police station, jail, or courthouse. The booking creates a formal, written record of the arrest. In addition to the arrestee's name, address, description, and the offense charged, the booking record usually includes the arrestee's fingerprints and photograph. It is customary to book all arrested persons placed in jail custody, but many arrestees are released immediately after being booked, without being jailed. They might be released on **bail**, or on their **own recognizance**.

For very serious felonies, the accused will be held until he can appear in court. At that time, the court will establish the required bail amount based upon the particular circumstances of the alleged crime, and upon the accused's history and connection with the community. The bail hearing is discussed later in this chapter.

Bail is a pledge of personal or real property to the court, made to guarantee a person's appearance in court at a later date.

Release on one's **own recognizance** means a release on the arrestee's personal promise to appear in court, without any pledge of money or property as guarantee.

An **arrest warrant** is a court order authorizing the arrest of a person.

A **bench warrant** is a court order authorizing the arrest of a person for failure to appear in court, or for some other contempt of court.

Warrants

In some situations, the court will issue an **arrest warrant**. This sometimes happens when a grand jury returns an indictment, but it also occurs when law enforcement officers or prosecutors present sworn affidavits showing probable cause to believe that a suspect has committed a crime. A court may also issue a **bench warrant** for arrest on its own initiative when an accused person fails to appear in court when ordered to do so, or for some other contempt of court. *Figure 7.2* illustrates an arrest warrant for issue by a federal court.

BAIL HEARING

Any person arrested and not released within twenty-four to seventy-two hours (depending upon jurisdiction) must be brought before a court for a bail hearing. This hearing is sometimes referred to as a "first appearance," and in some jurisdictions it is similar to an arraignment in which the defendant is asked to enter a plea. At this time the charges are stated, the defendant is informed of his due process rights, and bail is set. If the defendant cannot afford to hire an attorney, the court can appoint a **public defender** or other private counsel to represent him.

A **public defender** is an attorney employed by the government to represent criminal defendants who cannot afford to retain an attorney.

A **bail bond** is a written guarantee by a bonding company to pay the court a defined amount of money if the accused fails to appear as ordered.

In nearly all jurisdictions, the courts have established a "bail schedule" that lists the required bail for all offenses, except for the most serious felonies. If the arrested person can post the required amount, she can be released immediately, without waiting for a court appearance. Although it is difficult for most people to quickly raise several thousand dollars, they often can raise enough cash to purchase a **bail bond**. Bail bonds are sold by private businesses that locate

FIGURE 7.2 Warrant for Arrest

United States District Court
Central District of California

United States of America
             Plaintiff   **WARRANT FOR ARREST**
v.
                                   Case Number:

            Defendant

TO: The United States Marshal and
     Any Authorized United States Officer

     YOU ARE HEREBY COMMANDED to arrest _____
                                                         (Name)
and bring him or her forthwith to the nearest magistrate judge to answer a(n):
☐ Indictment   ☐ Information   ☐ Complaint   ☐ Order of Court   ☐ Violation Notice   ☐ Probation Violation Petition
charging him or her with (brief description of offense):

in violation of Title _____ United States Code, Section(s) _____

_____SHERRI R. CARTER_____   _____CLERK OF COURT_____
Name of Issuing-Office   Title of issuing Officer

/s/ Sherri R. Carter   _____, CA
Signature of Issuing Officer   Date and Location
Bail Fixed at $ _____   By _____
                                                                             Name of Judicial Officer

RETURN	
This warrant was received and executed with the arrest of the above-named defendant at _____	
DATE RECEIVED	NAME AND TITLE OF ARRESTING OFFICER	SIGNATURE OF ARRESTING OFFICER
DATE OF ARREST		

themselves conveniently near the jail or courthouse. Depending upon a person's criminal record (or lack thereof), a bond can be purchased for about 10% to 20% of the full amount. The bonding company then guarantees the accused's appearance in court. If the accused fails to show up, the bond is forfeited to the court.

Individuals with no family or employment ties to the community, and those with significant criminal records, must post a substantially higher bail to obtain release from jail. If the defendant has a passport, the court might require him to surrender it to the court clerk until all proceedings in the case are completed.

The Eighth Amendment prohibits "excessive bail," but courts actually have a very wide latitude within which they may set bail without fear of reversal on appeal. Bail amounts in excess of one million dollars are not unknown in extraordinary circumstances. Normally, bail is denied entirely for persons accused of murder. For other very serious crimes, bail might be set very high or even denied because the defendant is considered to be a "flight risk"—one who is unlikely to appear when ordered.

INDICTMENT OR PROSECUTOR'S INFORMATION

If the prosecutor believes that probable cause exists, he may seek a grand jury indictment. Alternatively, in most states, the prosecutor can present a sworn **information** to the court with trial jurisdiction for the offense charged. Where permitted, prosecutors more often present the information rather than seeking a grand jury indictment. Some states require a preliminary hearing (discussed below) to follow either an indictment or an information; other jurisdictions require the preliminary hearing only for cases charged in a prosecutor's information.

> A prosecutor's **information** is a sworn criminal complaint against the accused.

An indictment is returned by the grand jury if a majority (but no less than twelve) vote to indict the accused. Indictment requires that *probable cause* be established to believe that the accused committed the crime with which she is charged. Although jurors are permitted to ask questions of any witness, they seldom do so. As explained earlier, the grand jury will hear only one version of the case—the prosecutor's. For this reason, it is unusual for indictments to be denied. When they are, it usually indicates a very weak case that the prosecutor felt compelled to pursue—often for political reasons. If the grand jury refuses to indict, the prosecutor can publicly place the responsibility for that decision on the jury. A subpoena to testify appears in *Figure 7.3*.

It is a criminal offense to disclose grand jury proceedings and testimony, although the result of the jury's deliberations may be announced. This became an issue during the Clinton administration when federal grand juries were investigating the so-called Whitewater scandal and subsequently the alleged perjury by the president during an unrelated deposition. The court supervising the latter grand jury ordered an investigation into alleged leaks to the news media by the office of the independent counsel, Kenneth Starr. The alleged leaks from the independent counsel's office came in the midst of President Clinton's impeachment trial in the U.S. Senate.

Anyone subpoenaed to appear before the grand jury can invoke the Fifth Amendment privilege against self-incrimination. As already explained, however, that privilege can be overcome by granting use immunity to the witness. The supervising judge can hold recalcitrant witnesses in contempt for refusal to answer questions or for refusal to appear before the grand jury.

SCENARIO

From Bankruptcy Fraud to the District Attorney's Office

Marvin Mullard is a senior legal assistant in the office of the district attorney (D.A.) in a large Midwestern city. He coordinates assignments for six other legal assistants in the office and works on some of the major cases that are being prepared for prosecution. Prior to joining the district attorney's office, Marvin spent five years as a bankruptcy paralegal in a medium-sized law firm.

"I actually became interested in criminal work as the result of working in bankruptcy. Our firm usually represented the court-appointed trustee in Chapter 11 reorganizations. A good deal of our work was in recovering assets that the debtor had fraudulently transferred or tried to conceal from creditors and the bankruptcy court. We even had some cases that were so outrageous that the trustee or the court referred the debtors to the U.S. Attorney's office for prosecution. When

FIGURE 7.3 Subpoena to Testify Before Grand Jury

United States District Court
Central District of California

United States of America
        Plaintiff
v.
        Defendant

SUBPOENA IN A CRIMINAL CASE

Case Number:

TO:

☐ YOU ARE HEREBY COMMANDED to appear in the United States District Court at the place, date and time specified below to testify in the above case.

PLACE	COURTROOM
	DATE AND TIME

☐ YOU ARE ALSO COMMANDED to bring with you the following document(s) or objects(s):

U.S. MAGISTRATE JUDGE OR CLERK OF COURT	SHERRI R. CARTER	DATE
(BY) DEPUTY CLERK	CLERK OF COURT	

ATTORNEY'S NAME, ADDRESS AND PHONE NUMBER:

SUBPOENA IN A CRIMINAL CASE

that happened, part of my job was to work with that office to bring them up to speed on the case. If I had been involved in developing evidence of fraud, I would prepare an affidavit recounting how all of the information had been obtained, what people had stated to me in interviews, and so forth. It was really quite intriguing. Anyway, I always felt a little disappointed that I wasn't in on preparing the criminal case for prosecution."

Marvin thought initially about trying to get a job with the U.S. Attorney's office, perhaps specializing in fraud cases. But, before he had really explored that possibility, he learned of an opening in the district attorney's office and applied for that position. "It occurred to me that if I was getting a little tired of bankruptcy work, eventually I might feel that way about criminal fraud. Also, the idea of getting away from the sea of paper that bankruptcy and fraud involve was really appealing. So, when the D.A.'s office offered me the job, I took it."

Marvin has been in the district attorney's office now for four years, and he really enjoys his work. "There are three things that I especially like about my job. Number one, is the variety. I work on different kinds of felony cases, and the circumstances of each are really unique. I'm constantly learning new things about criminal law. Number two, there is a tremendous amount of satisfaction in bringing the bad guys to justice. That's particularly true when the crime has left a lot of innocent victims. Number three, our supervising prosecutor really lets us take on new challenges. One of my favorites is doing the research and then drafting our opposition to motions to suppress evidence. You can't imagine the outrageous arguments some defendants try to use to keep evidence out. One guy claimed that it was unconstitutional for the cops to go through the stuff he put out for pickup on trash day. He said he had a right to the privacy of his discards! Can you *believe* it?"

Does Marvin ever worry that his office might succeed in convicting an innocent person? "Not really. You know all this publicity about a few guys getting out 'cause DNA tests have proved they didn't do it, those are just the tiniest fraction of people who have been convicted. Of course, human error is going to happen. There's no way we will ever have a perfect justice system. Know what that means? Some of the real crooks we prosecute end up walking. And then they commit more crimes against more innocent victims. So, that's why we use the adversary system of justice. And when we know who the crook is, it's my job to help the prosecutor prove it. It's up to the defense counsel and the court to prevent us from convicting the wrong person." ■

ARRAIGNMENT

At the arraignment, the defendant is informed of the exact charges on which she is to be tried. If new evidence has been developed, the charges might have changed since the bail hearing, if one was held. The defendant enters her **plea** to the charges, as modified. If the defendant refuses to enter a plea, the court will enter a plea of "not guilty" on the defendant's behalf. With the approval of the court, the defendant can change a "not guilty" plea to "guilty" at any point in the case.

A **plea** is the defendant's answer to a criminal charge: guilty, not guilty, or no contest.

If the defendant pleads guilty, the court will question her to ensure that she understands the consequences and that her plea is being entered voluntarily. If the court accepts the guilty plea, it might impose sentence immediately, although that is unusual for serious offenses. If for any reason the court rejects the guilty plea, the court will enter a plea of not guilty.

A plea of *nolo contendere* (or **no contest**) accepts all of the consequences of a guilty plea (including imprisonment) without actually admitting guilt.

As an alternative to guilty or not guilty, the defendant might plead ***nolo contendere*** (often referred to as a **no contest** plea). The court must consent to the entry of a no contest plea. A no contest plea means that the defendant accepts full punishment without admitting criminal culpability. If accepted by the court, that plea is treated as a conviction in every way except one: It may not be used later in a civil lawsuit as proof that the defendant committed that act. By contrast, if a defendant pleads guilty or is convicted after pleading not guilty, the plaintiff in a civil lawsuit can simply cite that plea or conviction as conclusive proof that the defendant was guilty of that act (e.g., drunk driving), and there can be no effective defense on that point. But a *nolo contendere* plea does not give the civil plaintiff that advantage—he will have to prove "from scratch" that the defendant was driving under the influence, even though the defendant pleaded

FIGURE 7.4 Criminal Procedure: Arrest through Sentencing

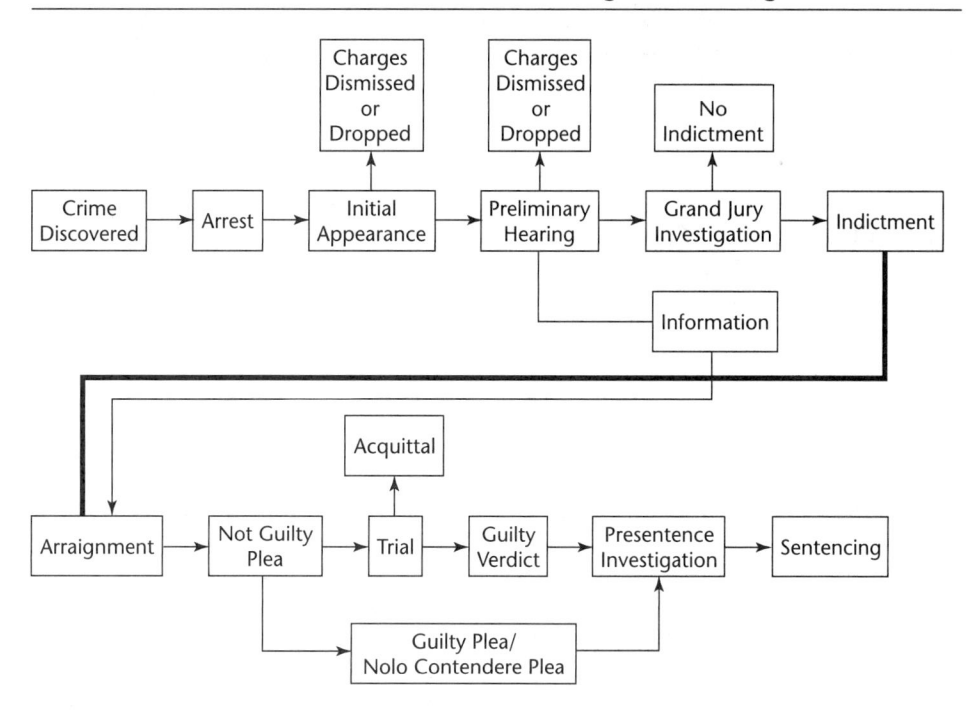

```
Crime Discovered → Arrest → Initial Appearance → Preliminary Hearing → Grand Jury Investigation → Indictment
                              ↓ Charges           ↓ Charges              ↓ No Indictment
                              Dismissed           Dismissed
                              or Dropped          or Dropped
                                                  → Information →

Arraignment → Not Guilty Plea → Trial → Guilty Verdict → Presentence Investigation → Sentencing
                                 ↑ Acquittal
              → Guilty Plea/Nolo Contendere Plea →
```

no contest and served jail time for drunk driving. *Figure 7.4* charts the stages in a criminal case from discovery through sentencing.

PLEA BARGAINING

At this time, or during any other stage of the prosecution, the defendant and prosecutor might engage in **plea bargaining**. Plea bargaining occasionally occurs even in the final stage of a trial, while the jury is deliberating its verdict. This is a controversial process in which the two sides attempt to agree on a guilty plea, usually to a lesser offense (e.g., to trespassing in lieu of burglary, or to misdemeanor reckless driving in lieu of felony drunk driving). Plea bargaining can also address the prosecution's recommendation for sentencing, the place of detention, restitution to victims, procedural issues related to sentencing, and other matters. Of course, the court must approve any plea bargain arrangement. If the court rejects the bargain, it is either renegotiated to the satisfaction of the court or the case goes to trial.

The defendant agrees to such a plea in order to avoid the risk of heavier punishment if convicted on the original, more serious charge. The prosecutor agrees to a lesser offense in order to avoid the possibility of an acquittal at trial, which would allow the defendant to "walk." Prosecutors also plea bargain when caseloads would overwhelm the justice system's capacity to conduct trials. A plea bargain might be struck after a hung jury has caused the first trial to end in mistrial, because that result brings into question the strength of the prosecution's case.

Critics of plea bargaining object to defendants' escaping the full penalty for their actual crimes. But plea bargaining appears unavoidable, because prosecutors and public defenders are understaffed and court calendars are overloaded. Prosecutors point out that the entire criminal justice system could collapse under the sheer number of cases if every defendant went to trial.

Perhaps the most famous plea bargain in American history occurred in 1973 (coincidentally, in the midst of the unrelated Watergate scandal), when Vice

A **plea bargain** results in a guilty plea, usually to a lesser offense, in exchange for a reduced sentence, thus avoiding the expense and uncertain result of a trial.

President Spiro Agnew agreed to enter a plea of *nolo contendere,* resign from the office of vice president, and pay a fine of $10,000. He was also sentenced to three years' probation. The charge was evasion of federal income taxes on illicit payments that Agnew had accepted while holding state office in Maryland. In 1981, a Maryland court ordered Agnew to pay Maryland more than $248,000 for the bribes he had accepted.

PRELIMINARY HEARINGS FOR FELONY COMPLAINTS

Preliminary hearings are used primarily for felony cases. Misdemeanor cases do not require preliminary hearings in most jurisdictions. The hearings are heard by the court, without a jury. The purpose of a preliminary hearing is to determine whether sufficient cause exists to have the defendant **bound over** for trial. It is not necessary to prove guilt in a preliminary hearing—only that there is *probable cause* to believe that the defendant committed the charged crime. In other words, the preliminary hearing either confirms or rejects the indictment by the grand jury or the charges in the prosecutor's information.

In a preliminary hearing, prosecution witnesses can be cross-examined by the defense, and in some jurisdictions the defendant is permitted to present his own witnesses and **exculpatory evidence** (i.e., evidence that tends to establish the defendant's innocence, or nonculpability). Most jurisdictions permit hearsay evidence and illegally obtained evidence to be heard in the preliminary hearing—as they also do in grand jury proceedings—although such evidence probably would be excluded during trial.

A prosecution stops dead in its tracks if the judge finds there is no probable cause. The court then dismisses the charges, and the defendant is released. That is one reason prosecutors often prefer the grand jury process in those jurisdictions that do not require a preliminary hearing in addition to a grand jury indictment. Because grand jury witnesses are never cross-examined by the defense and an indictment usually may issue upon a simple majority vote, it is far easier to establish probable cause with a grand jury than in a preliminary hearing before a judge.

> A criminal defendant is **bound over** for trial when a court orders him to appear for trial at a later date.

> **Exculpatory evidence** tends to establish the defendant's innocence.

PRETRIAL DISCOVERY

Similar to civil litigation, the government and the defendant have a mutual right of discovery. However, this right is far more limited in criminal law, and it varies widely among the states. In most jurisdictions, the defense must inform the court and the prosecution if it intends to use affirmative defenses, such as insanity or self-defense. The government must reveal to the defense certain evidence *that the defense requests*—such as prior statements by the defendant when interviewed by the police or prosecutor. The defense is entitled to receive copies of laboratory reports that the prosecution intends to use.

Pretrial discovery has been highly controversial, with civil libertarians demanding almost unlimited discovery by the defense, and get-tough-on-crime advocates arguing that criminals will find a way to escape justice if they know the government's case before trial. However, discovery also raises constitutional issues, and the U.S. Supreme Court has held that exculpatory evidence must be provided by the prosecution *at the request of the defense.* That rule was stated in the "Case in Point" that appears below. The Supreme Court here affirms the holding of the Maryland Court of Appeals, the case having come before the Supreme Court on appeal.

A Case in Point

Brady v. State of Maryland
373 U.S. 83 (1962)

Opinion of the Court by Mr. Justice DOUGLAS, announced by Mr. Justice BRENNAN.

Petitioner and a companion, Boblit, were found guilty of murder in the first degree and were sentenced to death, their convictions being affirmed by the Court of Appeals of Maryland. 220 Md. 454, 154 A.2d 434. Their trials were separate, petitioner being tried first. At his trial Brady took the stand and admitted his participation in the crime, but he claimed that Boblit did the actual killing. And, in his summation to the jury, Brady's counsel conceded that Brady was guilty of murder in the first degree, asking only that the jury return that verdict 'without capital punishment.' Prior to the trial petitioner's counsel requested the prosecution to allow him to examine Boblit's extrajudicial statements. Several of these statements were shown to him; but one dated July 9, 1958, in which Boblit admitted the actual homicide, was withheld by the prosecution and did not come to petitioner's notice until after he had been tried, convicted, and sentenced, and after his conviction had been affirmed.

Petitioner moved the trial court for a new trial based on the newly discovered evidence that had been suppressed by the prosecution. Petitioner's appeal from a denial of that motion was dismissed by the Court of Appeals without prejudice to relief under the Maryland Post Conviction Procedure Act. 222 Md. 442, 160 A.2d 912. The petition for post-conviction relief was dismissed by the trial court; and on appeal the Court of Appeals held that suppression of the evidence by the prosecution denied petitioner due process of law and remanded the case for a retrial on the question of punishment, not the question of guilt. 226 Md. 422, 174 A.2d 167. The case is here on certiorari, 371 U.S. 812, 83 S.Ct. 56, 9 L.Ed.2d 54. [Footnote omitted.]

* * * *

We agree with the Court of Appeals that suppression of this confession was a violation of the Due Process Clause of the Fourteenth Amendment. The Court of Appeals relied in the main on two decisions from the Third Circuit Court of Appeals—United States ex rel. Almeida v. Baldi, 195 F.2d 815, 22 A.L.R.2d 1407, and United States ex rel. Thompson v. Dye, 221 F.2d 763—which, we agree, state the correct constitutional rule.

* * * *

In Pyle v. Kansas, 317 U.S. 213, 215-216, 63 S.Ct. 177, 178, 87 L.Ed.214, we phrased the rule in broader terms:

'Petitioner's papers are inexpertly drawn, but they do set forth allegations that his imprisonment resulted from perjured testimony, knowingly used by the State authorities to obtain his conviction, and from the deliberate suppression of evidence favorable to him. These allegations sufficiently charge a deprivation of rights guaranteed by the Federal Constitution, and, if proven, would entitle petitioner to release from his present custody. Mooney v. Holohan, 294 U.S. 103, 55 S.Ct. 340, 79 L.Ed.791.'

* * * *

We now hold that the suppression by the prosecution of evidence favorable to an accused upon request violates due process where the evidence is material either to guilt or to punishment, irrespective of the good faith or bad faith of the prosecution.

The principle of Mooney v. Holohan is not punishment of society for misdeeds of a prosecutor but avoidance of an unfair trial to the accused. Society wins not only when the guilty are convicted but when criminal trials are fair; our system of the administration of justice suffers when any accused is treated unfairly. An inscription on the walls of the Department of Justice states the proposition candidly for the federal domain: 'The United States wins its point whenever justice is done its citizens in the courts.' [Footnote omitted.] A prosecution that withholds evidence on demand of an accused which, if made available, would tend to exculpate him or reduce the penalty helps shape a trial that bears heavily on the defendant. That casts the prosecutor in the role of an architect of a proceeding that does not comport with standards of justice, even though, as in the present case, his action is not 'the result of guile,' to use the words of the Court of Appeals. 226 Md., at 427, 174 A.2d, at 169.

PRETRIAL MOTIONS

When a criminal case has been set for trial, the defense and prosecution may present motions to the court regarding the conduct of the trial, evidence to be admitted or excluded, and so forth. These are very similar to pretrial motions in civil litigation. The more common pretrial motions in criminal cases include the following:

- motion to suppress unlawfully obtained evidence
- motion for severance of the trials of codefendants
- motion for change of venue

Special hearings are normally held to dispose of the pretrial motions. However, the court might deny a motion to suppress evidence and tell counsel to raise that objection again when the evidence is proffered at trial. For obvious reasons, the last two motions listed above must be disposed of before trial.

A motion for severance will be granted if a joint trial would deprive any codefendant of a fair trial. This might occur if one codefendant intends to present a defense shifting blame to the other codefendant. Permitting that to happen in a joint trial would have one codefendant collaborating in the people's prosecution of the other. Of course, either defendant might agree to testify against the other in separate trials, in exchange for a plea bargain. Severance might be granted if only one of the codefendants committed particularly horrendous acts during the crime. Unless the other codefendant is charged with vicarious responsibility for those acts, the court might anticipate that the jury could be prejudiced against the one defendant by the evidence about those acts committed by the other.

If pretrial publicity makes it unlikely that a defendant can receive a fair trial in the county where the crime occurred, that defendant would move for a change of venue to the court of another county. Venue can be changed, also, for the convenience of witnesses.

TRIAL

Only a small fraction of criminal cases ever go to trial—although that trend is changing somewhat for felony cases in three-strikes jurisdictions. The weaker cases are dismissed on the prosecutor's motion, and most other cases are plea bargained. The few cases that go to trial follow a court process that is similar to that of civil lawsuits:

- jury selection
- opening statements
- prosecutor's case in chief
- defendant's case

- prosecutor's case in rebuttal
- closing statements
- court's instructions on the law
- jury deliberations and verdict
- judgment entered

The equivalent steps in civil litigation are discussed in Chapter 6.

The major difference in a criminal trial is the prosecutor's greater burden of proof: beyond a reasonable doubt, as compared to preponderance of the evidence or clear and convincing proof. Another difference: The court may set aside a guilty verdict in a criminal trial—and either dismiss all charges against the defendant or order a new trial—but the court may not disturb a jury's verdict of *not* guilty. In civil cases, the court may set aside any verdict, whether the jury found in favor of the plaintiff or the defendant, and enter the court's judgment "notwithstanding the verdict" of the jury.

Sentencing

If a defendant pleads guilty or no contest, or is convicted, the court usually sets a later date for sentencing. For serious felonies, there might be a presentencing hearing at which evidence is presented to guide the court in imposing a sentence. In the presentencing hearing, some evidence inadmissible at trial (e.g., prior convictions) may be heard. In many jurisdictions, the crime's victims are permitted to address the court on the question of an appropriate sentence.

The prosecutor will make a recommendation for sentence, and the court usually receives a sentencing recommendation from probation authorities. The recommendation by probation authorities is usually based upon a review of the case and an evaluation of the defendant's amenability to rehabilitation. Evidence of the defendant's remorse or lack thereof is considered relevant to the prospect for rehabilitation. Whatever sentence is imposed, it must be one authorized by statute. In recent years, there has been a trend toward limiting the discretion of judges, both to gain greater consistency and to preclude discriminatory sentencing practices.

The court may impose a **suspended sentence**, which usually means that the convicted person may remain free on **probation** for a set term of good behavior. Any subsequent probation violation could then result in actual imprisonment. With prisons overcrowded and expensive to maintain, many courts now sentence nonviolent criminals to extended periods of unpaid community service. Some courts sentence defendants to home detention (a form of "house arrest") that is monitored by means of tamperproof electronic devices worn around the clock by the convict. Prisoners who appear to be good candidates for rehabilitation might be housed in jail, but released each day to report to their regular jobs.

A **suspended sentence** is imposed by the court, but held in abeyance for a period of time (probation) while the convict demonstrates good behavior.

Probation is the release of a convicted person, without prior confinement, on condition of good behavior for a specified period of time.

APPEALS

The general appellate process is similar for criminal and civil cases, and it is discussed briefly in Chapters 4 and 6. However, a criminal *verdict* may be appealed only by the defendant, never by the prosecutor. That is because an appeal by the prosecutor of a not guilty verdict would result in double jeopardy to the defendant. The double jeopardy rule does not, however, prevent the prosecution from appealing the following:

- a pre-verdict dismissal of the case
- a post-verdict reversal of a conviction
- the sentence imposed by the court

Any appeal from the judgment of the court must be filed promptly, or the right to appeal might be lost altogether. As in civil cases, the appellate court reviews questions of law and procedure, but not the merits of the evidence. As a matter of law, however, the judgment must be supported by some evidence, however questionable. The appellate court will not set a judgment aside because it believes the jury or judge believed the wrong evidence.

WRIT OF *HABEAS CORPUS*

A **writ of *habeas corpus*** is a court order commanding the person having custody of someone in confinement to bring that prisoner to court and show cause why the prisoner should not be released from all custody.

A petition for a **writ of *habeas corpus*** attacks the legal basis for a person's detention. It is available in both state and federal courts, under the Fourteenth Amendment and Article I, Section 9 of the Constitution, respectively. The writ, if granted by the court, commands the authority having custody to bring the detainee to court and show cause why she should not be released. In practice, the parties usually appear through counsel, although a detainee might attend if her testimony is needed.

There is a constitutional presumption that all persons are entitled to their liberty, unless there is good and necessary cause for their confinement. Because that presumption endures for their entire lives, a petition for *habeas corpus* may be filed at any time during their confinement. Thus, when the time for appeals has passed, a prisoner may still seek release by filing such a petition. For example, when DNA evidence has belatedly demonstrated the innocence of some prison inmates, *habeas corpus* has been the vehicle for obtaining their release. A petition for the writ may be based upon any substantial defect in the legal basis for continued confinement. The court must determine whether the defect—if one is established—requires the prisoner's release.

Outside of criminal law, the writ can be used to obtain release from civil confinement to a mental institution. It also has been used to release minor children from unlawful confinement by their parents and to obtain release from the military services.

A QUESTION OF ETHICS

Myrick Dennison is a legal assistant in the office of the independent counsel (sometimes called the "special prosecutor") appointed to investigate possible crimes by a member of the president's cabinet. Myrick previously worked for seven years in the office of the U.S. Attorney for the District of Columbia.

Attorneys in the office of the independent counsel have been interviewing a number of potential witnesses who might have knowledge of the activities of the cabinet member under investigation. Myrick is responsible for coordinating background investigations by the FBI on potential witnesses, and he is often present when the attorneys interview those witnesses. His duties also include setting up and maintaining files on witnesses, which contain the FBI reports, transcripts of their interviews, news clippings, and sundry other information.

By sheer chance, Myrick is an acquaintance of one of the potential witnesses, Jack Heller. Myrick and Jack were in graduate school at the same time, at the University of Michigan, Myrick studying political science and Jack, chemistry. They encountered each other occasionally at various campus events and seemed to share many interests. After graduate school, they went their separate ways, with no thought of ever meeting again.

In the current investigation, Jack's name has come up, and Myrick has set up a file on his former acquaintance. As time passes, the attorneys seem to focus more attention on Jack's relationship with the cabinet member's daughter. It turns out that the cabinet member brought Jack into her staff as a consultant on environmental issues, and over a period of six months he spent a substantial amount of time in her Washington, D.C., office.

Finally, Jack is interviewed by an attorney in the independent counsel's office. Several days later, the transcript arrives for Myrick to place in Jack's file. Naturally, Myrick is curious and reads the transcript. The interview doesn't turn up anything major about the cabinet officer, but Myrick is stunned by one statement Jack makes: "I've never been charged with any crime." Myrick remembers distinctly that in one somewhat inebriated statement, years before, Jack told him that he had been charged with shoplifting, but an influential political friend had managed to have the records expunged. Then Jack said, "I shouldn't have told you about this, because I might want to run for political office some day. You'll keep this between us, won't you?" Myrick had assured Jack that he would.

Should Myrick tell the attorneys about this apparent deception, even though it appears to be irrelevant to the subject of the ongoing investigation?

Chapter Summary

- Society is a victim and the sole plaintiff in all criminal actions.
- Criminal acts are categorized as felonies, misdemeanors, and infractions.
- Civil offenses are noncriminal offenses punishable by fines or denial of professional privileges.
- Criminal defendants are entitled to due process of law.
- Failure to give the Miranda warning might bar introduction of statements by the accused, but it does not invalidate the arrest.
- There are various exceptions to the double jeopardy rule.
- The exclusionary rule prohibits admission of evidence obtained in violation of the Fourth Amendment.
- An arraignment is a court proceeding in which the defendant is charged and offered an opportunity to enter a plea.
- A preliminary hearing determines whether there is sufficient cause to hold the defendant for trial on a felony charge.
- Defendants are neither represented nor present during grand jury deliberations, which can be conducted without the accused's knowledge.
- The grand jury indictment is a formal accusation of criminal conduct.
- Criminal proceedings may be initiated by either an indictment or a prosecutor's criminal complaint.
- A criminal jury verdict must be unanimous.
- A hung jury results in a mistrial.

KEY TERMS

accessory after the fact	bound over	criminal contempt
accessory before the fact	capital crime	detain
arraignment	citation	diminished capacity
arrest	citizen's arrest	double jeopardy
arrest warrant	civil offense	entrapment
bail	color of law	evasion of arrest
bail bond	conspiracy	exclusionary rule
bench warrant	crime against persons	exculpatory evidence
booking	crime against property	false arrest

felony	Miranda warning	public defender
general intent	misdemeanor	reasonable suspicion
grand jury	mistrial	self-incrimination
hot pursuit	*nolo contendere*	solicitation
hung jury	own recognizance	specific intent
immunity	petit jury	suspended sentence
in camera	plea	three-strikes rule
inchoate crime	plea bargain	transactional immunity
indictment	preliminary hearing	transferred intent
information	presumption of innocence	unconstitutionally vague
infraction	probable cause	use immunity
legal insanity	probation	vicarious criminal liability
mens rea	proof beyond a reasonable doubt	writ of *habeas corpus*

ACTIVITIES AND ASSIGNMENTS

1. Working with several of your fellow students, prepare a list of specific offenses (*excluding* offenses under the state motor vehicle code) that you believe would be *infractions* under the laws of your state and local governments. Prepare a second list of specific offenses that you believe are "moving violations" subject to *misdemeanor* penalties under the state motor vehicle code.

2. Draft a specific proposal for improving "victims' rights" without violating the due process rights of defendants in criminal prosecutions. Be prepared to justify and defend your proposal.

3. Review again *Florida v. Royer*, 460 U.S. 491 (1963), which is excerpted in this chapter. Do *you* think that the police officers had "probable cause" to arrest Royer, *before* he unlocked his suitcase? If so, why? If not, why not?

4. Discuss the following issues:
   - Does it make good sense for a person to simply walk away and not even listen to any questions police might ask—as the Supreme Court suggests in *Florida v. Royer* they may do?
   - Why did the Supreme Court conclude that Royer was as a "practical matter . . . under arrest" at the time he unlocked one of his suitcases?
   - Would it have made any difference—under the Fourth Amendment's bar against unreasonable searches and seizures—if Royer had thought he was free to leave at any time, but unlocked his suitcase anyway?

5. Review the discussion about plea bargaining. Then prepare to discuss the following issues:
   - Should plea bargaining be prohibited? If so, why? If not, why not?
   - What would be the practical consequences of eliminating plea bargaining?
   - How could those consequences that are harmful be minimized?
   - Should public officials (e.g., Vice President Spiro Agnew) be prohibited from plea bargaining charges of official misconduct? What would be the rationale—for and against—treating public officials differently from those who steal hub caps, burglarize apartments, or commit murder?

6. If you were to enter a criminal law practice as a paralegal, would you prefer to work in prosecution or in criminal defense? Prepare a short statement explaining your preference. Identify the values important to you that would influence your preference.

7. Discuss the grand jury's role and procedures as they relate to the following:
   - the presumption of innocence
   - the right to confront witnesses
   - the pursuit of justice for society and the accused

8. Review the discussion of the exclusionary rule. Develop a proposal for protecting individuals from compulsory self-incrimination and unreasonable search and seizure that would make the exclusionary rule unnecessary. In effect, your proposal must allow the admission of evidence without regard for the Fourth and Fifth Amendments, but it must also provide effective protection against abuse of those constitutional rights.

PART III

PARALEGAL SKILLS AND PROCEDURES

CHAPTER 8

Legal Analysis, Research, and Writing

You, however, can easily correct this bill to the taste of my brother lawyers, by making every other word a "said" or "aforesaid," and saying everything over two or three times, so that nobody but we of the craft can untwist the diction, and find out what it means. . . .

Thomas Jefferson, 3rd President of the United States, 1801–1809

Chapter 1 emphasized the importance of communication skills in a paralegal's practice—in particular, writing skills. Legal research and writing are closely related, both requiring strong verbal and analytical abilities. A fact well known to educators is that the best writers are usually avid readers, and weak writing skills can be improved by reading, and modeling after, the work of good writers. In addition, people who read and write a great deal tend to develop a richer vocabulary, which improves their ability to speak articulately and persuasively.

In a similar way, analytical skills can be improved by reading well-written, well-reasoned analytical essays. Before the age of law schools, people became lawyers by "reading the law" as an apprentice to a practicing lawyer, which is how Abraham Lincoln studied the law. In the modern-day law school, students hone their analytical skills by reading the work of legal scholars (much of that in court opinions) and by subjecting their own efforts to the scrutiny of their professors and fellow students. Of course, outside of mathematics, all reasoning is done in words, and the effective use of language is crucial to success.

The significance of the preceding two paragraphs is that verbal and analytical skills can be improved, even at the age of 34 or 64. Unfortunately, those skills can also atrophy from nonuse, like muscles held motionless in a plaster cast. The paralegal student who has been continually exercising those skills will probably find legal research and writing much easier than the student who has permitted those skills to lie unchallenged for a period of years.

After reading this chapter, the student should be able to answer the following questions:

- How does a paralegal analyze a legal question?
- What are the three major purposes of legal research?

- When is a court opinion "on point"?
- How does the researcher avoid irrelevant tangents?
- How are court opinions briefed?
- What is the difference between *primary* and *secondary* legal sources?
- What is the difference between *mandatory* and *persuasive* authority?
- How can the paralegal locate the court opinion for a specific case?
- Which components of a published opinion must never be quoted?
- How can one court opinion be used to locate other cases on the same legal issue?
- How is *Shepard's Citations* used?
- How can the legal assistant avoid the common mistakes of poor legal writing?
- How does a memorandum of points and authorities differ from a memorandum of law?

SCENARIO

Clear Legal Writing—an Oxymoron?

"I read briefs prepared by very prominent law firms. I bang my head against the wall, I dash my face with cold water, I parse, I excerpt, I diagram, and still the message does not come through. In addition, the structural content is most often mystifying."

From a letter by Los Angeles Superior Court Judge Ronald E. Swearinger to Professor Robert W. Benson, quoted in Robert W. Benson, "The End of Legalese: The Game Is Over," 13 *New York University Review of Law and Social Change* 519, 529 (1985)

"Things are changing. It has become apparent to growing numbers of people that criticizing legal language is not just a game. . . . To dismiss criticism of legalese as a mere game is to pretend that there are no real stakes. But just as it is obvious to every school child who has scrawled a dirty word on the chalkboard that language is power, so it ought to be obvious to all of us that lawyers' language is power exercised by a power elite and that the stakes in it are very real and very high. . . ."

Robert W. Benson, "The End of Legalese: The Game Is Over," 13 *New York University Review of Law and Social Change* 519, 520 (1985). Reprinted by permission of the author. ■

SECTION 1. LEGAL ANALYSIS

Legal analysis is the skill and process that links legal research with legal writing. Of course, attorneys and paralegals write ordinary correspondence and memoranda that do not involve legal analysis—and that writing, too, is important in the practice of law. Portions of this chapter address skills and techniques that contribute to effective business correspondence. But the more challenging task for new paralegals and attorneys is to write memoranda and court documents that present a clear and effective analysis of the legal issues related to a given situation.

Research provides the legal principles that will shape that analysis. Good legal writing makes the analysis understandable and persuasive. Thorough research, sound analysis, and effective writing—each is essential to the final result. To explain each of these components, this chapter will use hypothetical situations that present legal issues that might arise in a typical law practice.

THE PURPOSES OF LEGAL RESEARCH

Research is the foundation for sound legal analysis. The fundamental purposes of legal research are to accomplish the following:

- to answer specific legal questions
- to find legal principles and authorities that can affect the client's interests
- to provide guidance for the client to deal with some situation in a lawful and beneficial manner

Perhaps a simple example of each purpose would be helpful.

- In a civil litigation case, the attorney wants to know whether postmortem evidence that the pilot used cocaine within the twenty-four hours preceding the aircraft accident is admissible in trial.
- The attorney wants legal arguments to support the client's right to recover compensation from the county after a rainstorm overwhelmed the storm drains and the resulting flood seriously damaged his home.
- The client owns a shopping mall and wants guidance on the right of the public to solicit signatures for political petitions on private mall property, and guidance on the mall management's right to prohibit or regulate such activities.

The first example involves an interpretation of the rules of evidence. The second example might be more challenging, because it probably requires greater use of analogy (discussed later in this chapter) to compare the application of law to situations that have factual differences. The third example requires the development of written guidelines based upon constitutional law, any applicable statutes, and court decisions.

UNDERSTANDING THE ASSIGNMENT

No one can do competent research if she does not understand her objective. Before sending a paralegal off on a research assignment, the attorney should provide a thorough briefing on the relevant facts and the legal issues to be studied. Most attorneys recognize the importance of this briefing. At times, however, the attorney might be so intimately familiar with the case that she forgets that the paralegal needs to be brought up to speed.

It might be helpful to explain why paralegals are occasionally "in the dark" about legal issues in a major case. In a large firm, it is not unusual for several attorneys to meet with the client when a major case is first accepted. As the case proceeds, several attorneys might sit in on various conferences with the client, some of them lengthy and detailed. Similar conferences might occur with witnesses and consultants, and occasionally with opposing counsel. When important legal questions arise, attorneys in the office might confer for extended periods. Although many law firms use attorney-paralegal teams and often include the paralegal in substantive discussions, in other firms the paralegal would be working on other assignments during many of these dialogues. In some cases, the paralegal might be familiar with little more than the **pleadings**, correspondence, and other

In litigation, **pleadings** are the documents (e.g., the complaint and the answer) filed with the court in which the parties state their respective allegations, claims, and defenses.

> **Practice Tip**
>
> It is a good practice to verify one's understanding by repeating the research assignment to the attorney before beginning to work on it. That can be done orally for a simple assignment or in writing for a complex one. Another good technique is to restate the attorney's assignment at the beginning of the legal assistant's memorandum about the research results.

A **nuisance** is any unreasonable or unlawful activity (or thing) that deprives another person of the reasonable use and enjoyment of his land (a private nuisance) or that interferes with the rights of the general public (a public nuisance).

A **primary source** is a statement of the law found in a constitution, an act of the legislature, a court decision, or a government regulation.

Mandatory authority is legal authority (from a primary source) that is binding upon the court.

documents in the case file, and some incidental phone conversations with the client, consultants, and possibly some witnesses. In this circumstance, the attorney might not recognize the effect of not participating in many of the substantive discussions. It might be necessary for the attorney to spend twenty or thirty minutes briefing the paralegal for a single research assignment.

In litigation, *pleadings* are the documents (e.g., the complaint and the answer) filed with the court in which the parties state their respective allegations, claims, and defenses.

DEFINING THE ISSUES

When the legal assistant understands the context for the research assignment, the next step is to define the legal issues that are to be researched. This discussion will use a hypothetical situation to demonstrate this process of defining legal issues.

Assume for a moment that an attorney wants to know whether damages can be recovered against a county government on the legal theory of "nuisance." A **nuisance** is any use of one's property that unlawfully interferes with the right of a neighbor to enjoy the use of his own property. By looking up "nuisance" in a legal dictionary, the paralegal will learn that there are both *private* and *public* nuisances, and that a nuisance might be either *permanent* or *continuing* in nature. The legal assistant should realize at this point that a good deal of time could be wasted if she plunges right into the research without knowing the character of the nuisance in the client's case. If she does not have the facts, she must get them.

In response to a request for clarification, the attorney explains that the client lives near a county storm drain inlet that must accept the runoff from a large area of watershed. Until recently, most of the watershed was undeveloped land that absorbed much of the rainfall. However, new residential development on higher terrain has created rooftops, streets, and sidewalks that do *not* absorb water, and the amount of downhill runoff has increased dramatically. The storm drain inlet near the client's home is no longer adequate, and the homes of the client and several neighbors have been flooded twice in a period of eighteen months. A consulting hydrologist (an expert on soil absorption of water) has estimated that the client's home is now likely to be flooded an average of once every two years. A real estate broker has informed the client that his home is virtually unmarketable, because state law requires him to disclose the flooding problem to any prospective buyer. The attorney believes the county might be liable for permitting new upslope development without improving the storm drain system.

The immediate question is whether the inadequate storm drain can be characterized as a nuisance. The attorney did not ask whether the client's fear of future flooding and his anxiety over the property's decline in value constitute "emotional distress" for which damages might be recovered, so that, at this point, that is not an issue. However, as the legal assistant studies the law, she should be alert for any cases that might suggest whether the client can recover emotional distress damages for fear and anxiety under those circumstances, an issue that might arise later. She should also be alert for any statutory or case law that states that a government facility cannot be considered a nuisance.

UNDERSTANDING LEGAL SOURCES AND LEGAL AUTHORITY

One finds the law by going to various sources of legal authority. A **primary source** is any statement *of* the law: a constitution, statute, court opinion, regulation, and so forth. Primary sources are **mandatory authority**—that is, they are binding upon the courts—*when they state the law of that jurisdiction.* A New Jersey statute or appellate court ruling is therefore mandatory authority for the public officials and the courts of that state. But primary sources for Texas law would *not* be binding upon the courts of New Jersey.

Although not mandatory authority in New Jersey, Texas law might be persuasive authority in the courts of that state, just as New Jersey law might be persuasive in Texas courts. **Persuasive authority** is legal authority that may be considered or ignored, in the court's own discretion.

There are special circumstances, however, that can make the law of another jurisdiction mandatory. When a court in one jurisdiction is applying the law of another jurisdiction, the case law of that other jurisdiction is mandatory authority. For example, if a North Dakota court is interpreting a contract that states that it shall be governed by the laws of Florida, the North Dakota court must follow the decisions of Florida courts on the interpretation and implementation of contracts. In other words, a North Dakota court may *not* conclude that the Florida courts have misstated the law of Florida on contracts.

The courts of each state are the final authority on the law of that state. This principle is recognized by both state and federal courts. In federal courts, most lawsuits require the application of state law. Where state court precedents from that jurisdiction are available, the federal courts treat them as mandatory authority. If state court precedents in that jurisdiction cannot be found, the federal courts apply persuasive authority (which often is primary authority from other state jurisdictions). Even the U.S. Supreme Court considers itself bound by the decisions of state courts on the law of their respective jurisdictions. The judges on the federal bench are so highly respected that the opinions of federal courts—both trial and appellate—on the interpretation of state law are regarded as excellent persuasive authority.

A **secondary source** is any statement *about* the law. Legal encyclopedias and scholarly articles in legal periodicals are examples of commonly cited secondary sources. Because it is a statement *about* the law—not a statement *of* the law—a secondary source is never binding on the courts. It is only persuasive, just like the primary sources from other jurisdictions (e.g., other states). Nonetheless, a court often cites a secondary source in its decision, and at times it is the only authority cited. This might occur because the court could not find primary sources to resolve the issue before it, or because it has been persuaded by secondary sources that prior common law decisions were incorrect. *Figure 8.1* illustrates the relationship of legal sources to mandatory and persuasive authority.

> **Persuasive authority** is legal authority that is not binding upon the court.

> A **secondary source** is a statement *about* the law (e.g., a scholarly article written by a recognized legal authority).

FIGURE 8.1 Mandatory and persuasive legal authority

Primary Sources	Secondary Sources
Constitution Statutes Regulations Case Law	Treatises Encyclopedias Law Reviews etc.

Primary Sources For Same Jurisdiction ← Mandatory Authority

Primary Sources For Other Jurisdictions / Secondary Sources ← Persuasive Authority

Citing Appropriate Legal Authority

In legal research, a paralegal should always cite *mandatory* authority whenever it can be found. Persuasive authority should be cited *only* when one of the following occurs:

- Mandatory authority cannot be found.
- Mandatory authority is unfavorable to the client's position.
- Persuasive authority clarifies the application of mandatory authority.

But, in a memorandum to the attorney, the paralegal should cite mandatory authority, even when it is unfavorable to the client's position; that is, the attorney *must* be informed of the bad news along with the good. In a memorandum submitted to the court, unfavorable mandatory authority is often acknowledged to demonstrate intellectual honesty, although the attorney often tries to minimize its impact by arguing that it is not applicable to the case at hand. In some situations, the ethical rule of candor requires disclosure of unfavorable authorities. (The rule of candor is discussed in Chapter 3.)

Sometimes the attorney cannot find a case in his own jurisdiction that has addressed the legal issue he is researching. It is possible that the client's case is a **case of first impression**, which means that the issue has never been decided by the appellate courts. In other words, there is no precedent. It is also possible that he has been unable to locate those appellate decisions that have addressed that issue. Without an appellate decision in that jurisdiction, what authority should be cited?

In a case of first impression, attorneys can cite the type of authority that the courts often cite to resolve such cases: persuasive authority. As already mentioned, case law from other jurisdictions is persuasive, not mandatory; however, at times, it can be highly persuasive and therefore well worth citing. Decisions by the courts of several states, in particular, have exerted a strong influence on the nation's common law. For example, the Delaware courts are generally followed by other state courts on issues of corporate law (e.g., the fiduciary duties of a board of directors to the corporate shareholders when a buyout offer is received). Texas and California courts have been unusually influential on issues of **tort law**, which governs the duty to avoid injury to other persons.

ANALYZING A LEGAL QUESTION

One approach to legal analysis is called the IRAC method, which most attorneys learn in law school. "IRAC" stands for:

- issue
- rule
- application
- conclusion

The IRAC approach simply assures that the paralegal approaches the problem in a systematic and productive manner. It breaks down the process of legal analysis into four basic steps. Although this method can be applied mentally in simple matters, this explanation assumes that it will be used to prepare a written report to the attorney.

The first step is to clearly define the issue: "Does a public school teacher have the authority to require a fourth grade student to stand in the corner for minor misbehavior?"

The second step is to locate the rule—that is, a statement of the law governing that issue. It is possible that the answer to the question posed above will be

---

Practice Tip

If the legal assistant cannot find primary sources on point, she should continue her research in secondary sources. If she cannot find the answer in secondary sources, it is time to present a status report to the attorney. The attorney might have suggestions for more effective research, or he might decide that continuing the chase is not worth the effort.

A **case of first impression** presents a novel legal question that cannot be answered based upon precedent.

Tort law is the law governing civil wrongs that injure another person (e.g., fraud, slander, negligence, and assault).

found in the statutes governing public schools. If not, it will be necessary to find an applicable common law rule in a court case.

The third step is to apply that rule to the facts of the case at hand. The paralegal must be prepared to explain why the rule has application under those facts. When the rule has been derived from case law, this might require substantial analysis.

The final step is to state the conclusion of the paralegal's analysis: "The state Education Code authorizes a teacher to use reasonable, appropriate and necessary punishment to correct a student's misbehavior. Courts have held that a temporary exclusion from class activities is reasonable when the student's conduct has been disruptive."

In the hypothetical example above, the researcher first found a statute that addressed the issue and then found court decisions that applied that statutory rule. Sometimes, however, one cannot find a statute or court opinion that clearly applies to the issue at hand. In that circumstance, she might need to fashion a "new" rule based upon the legal principles that apply to similar (though not identical) circumstances. Those related legal principles are usually found in statutes or case law.

APPLYING A STATUTE TO SPECIFIC FACTS

Assume that the client is a small corporation that has filed a petition for reorganization under Chapter 11 of the *Bankruptcy Code*—which means that it is not going out of business, but plans to continue operation during and after the bankruptcy proceedings. The client has filed with its bankruptcy petition several lists of customers who owe money to the corporation, but wants the court to **seal** the court record of those lists, because competitors might approach those customers to take away their business.

Section 107 of the *Bankruptcy Code* states:

> **§ 107. Public access to papers**
> (a) Except as provided in subsection (b) of this section, a paper filed in a case under this title and the dockets of a bankruptcy court are public records and open to examination by an entity at reasonable times without charge.
> (b) On request of a party in interest, the bankruptcy court shall, and on the bankruptcy court's own motion, the bankruptcy court may—
> (1) protect an entity with respect to a trade secret or confidential research, development, or commercial information; or
> (2) protect a person with respect to scandalous or defamatory matter contained in a paper filed in a case under this title.

A court may **seal** some portion of its records to prevent any person from examining them without obtaining prior permission of the court.

Clearly, subsection (a) creates a presumption that the customer lists are open to inspection by the public, including competitors of the debtor. The issue, then, is whether the client can qualify for the exception provided in §107(b)(1).

To apply subsection (b) to the facts of the client's situation, the paralegal must identify each element of that subsection. Those elements are as follows:

- a party in interest
- requests that the bankruptcy court
- protect an entity with respect to
- a trade secret, or
- confidential research, or
- confidential development, or
- confidential commercial information

It is not absolutely clear that the word "confidential" in § 107(b)(1) modifies each of the nouns that follows in that phrase—perhaps "confidential research" is a

> **Practice Tip**
>
> When doing legal research, the legal assistant should not make assumptions about the meaning of ambiguous syntax in a statute—unless the ambiguity does not affect the client's interests. In the example given here, it is commercial information that the client wants protected. Therefore, the legal assistant should try to find case law that clarifies which terms are modified by the word "confidential" in § 107(b)(1).

category distinct from "development" and "commercial information." But, in outlining the elements of that subsection, this textbook assumes the syntax to mean that "development" and "commercial information" must also be "confidential" in nature to qualify for protection. This appears reasonable, because there is no obvious reason that Congress would require research to be confidential, yet permit *non*-confidential development and commercial information to qualify for the statutory protection. It would be necessary to review case law to see how the courts have interpreted that same syntax.

Now, the paralegal must go down the list of statutory elements to determine whether the customer list is entitled to protection. Certainly, the client is a party in interest, because it is the debtor in the bankruptcy case. The law firm will immediately file the request, if it appears that the customer list qualifies. The client corporation is an entity (as would be an individual, partnership, city, church, etc.). So, the critical question becomes: Does the customer list qualify as "a trade secret" or "confidential commercial information?"

Because those two terms are not defined in the *Bankruptcy Code*, the paralegal will have to research case law interpreting Section 107. If that research does not reveal an interpretation of those terms, the paralegal will probably research their definitions under state law (either statutory or case law). Without actually conducting the research, it is reasonable to expect that the customer lists would qualify as confidential commercial information. They probably qualify as trade secrets as well, because there is substantial case law holding that customer lists can be "trade secrets."

WHEN A COURT OPINION IS "ON POINT"

A case is **on point** when it presents the same legal issue that is being researched or argued.

A case is **on all fours** when it presents the identical legal issue and substantially similar material facts.

For a case to be **on point**, it *must* confront the same legal issue—and each case the attorney cites to the court as precedent should be on point, or the court might reject it out of hand. The ideal precedent is one that is "on all fours." To be **on all fours**, the case must confront the identical legal issue *and* must be substantially similar in all material facts. As explained in Chapter 6, a material fact is one that could determine the outcome of the case. Differences in *non*material facts are not relevant, because they cannot affect the outcome of the case. It is not unusual to find cases that raise the identical legal issue, but it can be extremely difficult to find a case that is on all fours, with substantially similar material facts. But then, a case on all fours—although ideal—is seldom necessary to win the client's case.

If there are a number of cases on point, it is a good idea to determine which is the "leading" case on the issue. Usually, it will be the case most often cited in other court opinions or the one decided by the higher appellate court. All other factors being equal, the more recent case is likely to be more influential than earlier cases. In addition, any case with facts similar to the client's situation will be a key case—even if it isn't quite on all fours.

USING ANALOGY IN LEGAL ANALYSIS

Analogy is a process of reasoning by which legal principles that apply to one set of facts are then applied to differing, but similar, facts.

Because cases on all fours are so rare, usually one must rely upon analogy. **Analogy** is a method for applying legal principles to different *but similar* factual situations. Analogy works well when the similarities between two cases are more relevant to the legal issue than are the factual differences between the two cases. Consider the following example. Assume that a bus has been involved in an accident that resulted in injuries to some passengers, and there is some question about the bus driver's failure to avoid the accident. Perhaps there is a court opinion that addresses the level of driving skill that a bus driver is reasonably expected to exercise.

Now, there are likely to be cases that state that a taxi driver is held to a higher standard of skill than is the nonprofessional driver because paying passengers rely upon her to have superior skills. Can one analogize that principle to a bus driver with paying passengers? Clearly, one can. Bus passengers also pay fares and reasonably rely upon the driver to have superior driving skills. The similarity of the paying passengers' reliance upon a professional driver is more significant than the difference between a taxi cab and a bus. If the bus had been a church bus driven by a parent volunteer, however, the analogy would not work. The parent volunteer illustrates a frequent problem with analogy: the "distance" between factual "similarities."

Here is another example: If employers are held liable for the negligence of their employees, can parents be held equally liable for the negligence of their teenage children? Is that a convincing analogy? Probably not. Clearly, the bus driver analogy is closer and easier to argue than is this second analogy. That is because there are more similarities between taxi drivers and bus drivers than there are between employers and the parents of teenagers.

The attorney can try to make a good argument for the validity of the second analogy, but the court might find that the analogy does not apply. It is true that neither employers nor parents can directly supervise and control their employees or teenagers 100% of the time; in that respect, they are similar. But an employer is operating in the marketplace and can spread the financial risk for his liability among all of his customers, through higher prices, whereas the parent has no comparable mechanism for passing on the financial risk resulting from his child's negligence. Also, an employer can selectively hire and discharge employees to achieve a less accident-prone workforce, whereas parents have no such opportunity. These differences might argue for imposing greater liability upon employers for the negligence of their employees than upon parents for the negligence of their teenagers.

The paralegal must keep analogy in mind even when he reads cases with differing fact patterns. He cannot reject every case with differing facts, because that would reject the very use of analogy itself and would require him to either produce a precedent on all fours or have no precedent at all.

CONCURRING AND DISSENTING OPINIONS

As mentioned in prior chapters, only the majority opinion of a court can be cited as precedent, but that does not require the researcher to completely ignore dissenting and concurring opinions. Although concurring and dissenting opinions are not the official opinion of the court and cannot be cited as precedent, they sometimes include citations that lead the researcher to other cases that are useful in his research. Finally, a dissenting opinion in a case decided many decades ago might now be adopted, in a new case, as the correct statement of the law, if legal thinking has been changing in the intervening years.

The conclusion of the majority opinion might be determined largely by the *facts* of the particular case at hand. The appellate justices might be in general agreement about the principles of law, but they might differ on how those principles (or *which* of those principles) should be applied under the facts of the case. Such disagreements often become the substance of dissenting opinions. Or, the justices might be in agreement on the holding of a case, but might reach that same result by applying different legal principles and reasoning. That difference in legal analysis results in concurring opinions.

In the following "Case in Point," Justice Louis Brandeis wrote a stinging dissent to the decision of the Supreme Court in *Olmstead v. United States*, 277 U.S. 438 (1928). The case involved bootleggers who were apprehended and convicted during prohibition days on the basis of government wiretaps. No search warrant had been obtained, so that the question before the Court was whether a wiretap implemented without physical entry into one's home or office constituted a "search" under the Fourth Amendment. The Court held, five to four, that it did not.

In addition to the constitutional issue, Justice Brandeis argued that the government should not be permitted to commit crimes in order to catch a criminal, and that the wiretap evidence obtained in violation of Washington state law should be excluded on that ground as well. In 1967, the Supreme Court effectively adopted Brandeis's views when it established the "reasonable expectation of privacy" standard for unreasonable warrantless searches. *Katz v. United States*, 389 U.S. 347 (1967).

A Case in Point

Olmstead v. United States

277 U.S. 438 (1928)

Mr. Chief Justice TAFT delivered the opinion of the Court.

These cases are here by certiorari from the Circuit Court of Appeals for the Ninth Circuit. [Citations omitted.] . . . They were granted with the distinct limitation that the hearing should be confined to the single question whether the use of evidence of private telephone conversations between the defendants and others, intercepted by means of wire tapping, amounted to a violation of the Fourth and Fifth Amendments. [Citations omitted.]

The petitioners were convicted in the District Court for the Western District of Washington of a conspiracy to violate the National Prohibition Act (27 USCA) by unlawfully possessing, transporting and importing intoxicating liquors and maintaining nuisances, and by selling intoxicating liquors. Seventy-two others, in addition to the petitioners, were indicted. Some were not apprehended, some were acquitted, and others plead guilty.

* * * *

The information which led to the discovery of the conspiracy and its nature and extent was largely obtained by intercepting messages on the telephones of the conspirators by four federal prohibition officers. Small wires were inserted along the ordinary telephone wires from the residences of four of the petitioners and those leading from the chief office. The insertions were made without trespass upon any property of the defendants. They were made in the basement of the large office building. The taps from house lines were made in the streets near the houses.

The gathering of evidence continued for many months. Conversations of the conspirators, of which refreshing stenographic notes were currently made, were testified to by the government witnesses. . . .

* * * *

. . . The Fourth Amendment may have proper application to a sealed letter in the mail, because of the constitutional provision for the Postoffice [sic] Department and the relations between the government and those who pay to secure protection of their sealed letters. . . .

The United States takes no such care of telegraph or telephone messages as of mailed sealed letters. The amendment does not forbid what was done here. There was no searching. There was no seizure. The evidence was secured by the use of the sense of hearing and that only. There was no entry of the houses or offices of the defendants.

* * * *

The judgments of the Court of Appeals are affirmed. The mandates will go down forthwith under rule 31.

Affirmed.

Mr. Justice BRANDEIS (dissenting).

The defendants were convicted of conspiring to violate the National Prohibition Act (27 USCA). Before any of the persons now charged had been arrested or indicted, the telephones by means of which they habitually communicated with one another and with others had been tapped by federal officers....

The government makes no attempt to defend the methods employed by its officers. Indeed, it concedes that, if wire tapping can be deemed a search and seizure within the Fourth Amendment, such wire tapping as was practiced in the case at bar was an unreasonable search and seizure, and that the evidence thus obtained was inadmissible. But it relies upon the language of the amendment, and it claims that the protection given thereby cannot properly be held to include a telephone conversation.

When the Fourth and Fifth Amendments were adopted, 'the form that evil had theretofore taken' had been necessarily simple. Force and violence were then the only means known to man by which a government could directly effect self-incrimination. It could compel the individual to testify—a compulsion effected, if need be, by torture. It could secure possession of his papers and other articles incident to his private life—a seizure effected, if need be, by breaking and entry. Protection against such invasion of 'the sanctities of a man's home and the privacies of life' was provided in the Fourth and Fifth Amendments by specific language. [Citation omitted.] But 'time works changes, brings into existence new conditions and purposes.' Subtler and more far-reaching means of invading privacy have become available to the government. Discovery and invention have made it possible for the government, by means far more effective than stretching upon the rack, to obtain disclosure in court of what is whispered in the closet.

Moreover, 'in the application of a Constitution, our contemplation cannot be only of what has been, but of what may be.' The progress of science in furnishing the government with means of espionage is not likely to stop with wire tapping. Ways may some day be developed by which the government, without removing papers from secret drawers, can reproduce them in court, and by which it will be enabled to expose to a jury the most intimate occurrences of the home. Advances in the psychic and related sciences may bring means of exploring unexpressed beliefs, thoughts and emotions. 'That places the liberty of every man in the hands of every petty officer' was said by James Otis of much lesser intrusions than these. [Footnote omitted.] ...

* * * *

The evil incident to invasion of the privacy of the telephone is far greater than that involved in tampering with the mails. When a telephone line is tapped, the privacy of persons at both ends of the line is invaded, and all conversations between them upon any subject, and although proper, confidential and privileged, may be overheard. Moreover, the tapping of one man's telephone involves the tapping of every other person whom he may call, or who may call him. As a means of espionage, writs of assistance and general warrants are but puny instruments of tyranny and oppression when compared with wire tapping.

* * * *

... It is, of course, immaterial where the physical connection with the telephone wires leading into the defendants' premises was made. And it is also immaterial that the intrusion was in aid of law enforcement. Experience should teach us to be most on our guard to protect liberty when the government's purposes are beneficent. Men born to freedom are naturally alert to repel invasion of their liberty by evil-minded rulers. The greatest dangers to liberty lurk in the insidious encroachment by men of zeal, well-meaning but without understanding. [Footnote omitted.]

Independently of the constitutional question, I am of the opinion that the judgment should be reversed. By the laws of Washington, wire tapping is a crime. [Footnote and citation omitted.] To prove its case, the government was obliged to lay bare the crimes committed by its officers on its behalf. A federal court should not permit such a prosecution to continue. [Citation omitted.]

* * * *

Decency, security, and liberty alike demand that government officials shall be subjected to the same rules of conduct that are commands to the citizen. In a government of laws, existence of the government will be imperiled if it fails to observe the law scrupulously. Our government is the potent, the omnipresent teacher. For good or for ill, it teaches the whole people by its example. Crime is contagious. If the government becomes a lawbreaker, it breeds contempt for law; it invites every man to become a law unto himself; it invites anarchy. To declare that in the administration of the criminal law the end justifies the means—to declare that the government may commit crimes in order to secure the conviction of a private criminal—would bring terrible retribution. Against that pernicious doctrine this court should resolutely set its face.

When the majority opinion is unfavorable to the position of the client, it is especially important to read carefully any dissenting or concurring opinions. The factual differences between the appellate case and the client's situation could possibly lead to a different legal conclusion. When the majority opinion of an appellate court recognizes the effect of such factual differences, it *distinguishes* the case at hand from prior appellate decisions that reached a different conclusion. The court is saying, in effect, "That earlier decision was correct under the facts of that case, but this case is different and requires a different legal conclusion." Perhaps the attorney can successfully argue that the facts of the client's case are substantially different from those cases that reached legal conclusions that would be unfavorable to the client.

AVOIDING IRRELEVANT TANGENTS

In legal research, it is important to remain focused on the issue being researched. The first step in avoiding tangents is to establish a clear focus from the beginning. That is why a thorough briefing is so essential before the paralegal begins her research. If she is hazy about the facts or the legal question presented, she cannot establish and maintain a clear focus. As the research progresses, the paralegal might encounter unexpected complexities in the legal issue under study. There might be subissues of the issue, or even subissues of subissues. Before launching off in a new direction, it might be wise to go back to the attorney and obtain additional guidance.

KNOWING WHEN TO STOP

One of the more difficult decisions for a neophyte researcher can be the decision to stop the "paper chase." The following paragraphs offer a few guidelines for that decision.

At some point, the legal assistant might realize that each newly found case seems to provide the same answer to the issue she is researching. In other words, it becomes apparent that the law is "well settled" on that issue. This is likely to occur when she is able to find a good number of cases on point.

In other situations, she might not find any cases clearly on point, but she might succeed in finding cases with holdings that can be applied to the client's situation through the process of analogy. If she has done rather exhaustive research and is fairly well convinced that no case on all fours is likely to be found, it might be time to stop.

If she has found the answer she has been searching for, it is time to verify the authorities she has found. This is done primarily through a process known as "Shepardizing" (explained in Section 2 of this chapter). That process will alert her to any cases that are no longer considered "good law"—that is, to no longer be a correct statement of the law.

SCENARIO

A Legal Assistant "Works Her Way" into Research and Legal Writing

Delaine Kohlbeck has worked five years as a legal assistant in a small partnership. The firm's eight lawyers do a variety of legal work. The firm's practice includes litigation, real estate, bankruptcy, business transactions, and estate planning. Delaine's assignments have become progressively more challenging, and now she spends about one-fourth of her time in legal research, preparing memoranda on the results of that research, and drafting motions for submission to the court. Her research assignments are mostly in litigation and bankruptcy.

Delaine started with the firm shortly after completing her paralegal certificate. During the first two years, her assignments were primarily in litigation. "I spent untold hours in the client's office going through the files to identify documents that were relevant to the lawsuit. The client's staff would make photocopies of those I selected, and I would take the copies back to the firm for the attorney to review. In the firm office, I spent much of my time organizing and cataloging documents for delivery to the opposing counsel who had requested them."

As a trial date approached, Delaine would assist the attorneys with research on the admissibility of various kinds of evidence, jury instructions, and other issues related to the trial. "Finally, when this really important case was coming to trial, the attorney realized that I was just as familiar as he was with most of the factual issues and the documents. So, he asked me to be in court during the trial. It was a complicated wrongful death case, and arguments about the admission of evidence kept coming up as the trial progressed. The judge would even entertain new arguments on evidentiary issues that he had ruled on before trial as motions *in limine*. So, the attorney began sending me across the street—literally, across the street—to the county law library to research these issues while court was in session. I think that's when the firm really began to have confidence in my research abilities."

When that trial was over, several attorneys in the office began giving more research assignments to Delaine. "I really liked that, because it demonstrated that I had earned their respect and confidence. It also helped that I discovered a love for legal research—the more challenging, the better. It's amazing, when I think now of how intimidating legal research seemed when I was getting my certificate."

Delaine describes how she proceeds with a major research assignment: "Usually, the attorney will spend about ten or fifteen minutes briefing me—more, if the assignment is somewhat complicated. Then I am off to the law library. I find that it is more efficient to hit the books [rather than use a computer] when I am familiarizing myself with a general topic. Then, later, when I have my 'sea legs,' so to speak, I might develop a plan for using Westlaw to continue my research on well-defined issues. I always have to make an assessment of the efficiency and cost of online research balanced against what I can accomplish in the law library."

Practice Tip

If the legal assistant is uncertain about the "answers" his research has produced, he can prepare an outline for a memorandum on the legal issue he has researched. As he constructs his logical analysis in outline form, any gaps in the reasoning should reveal themselves. The outline will prepare him to discuss his progress with the attorney and will make it easier for her to provide guidance if additional research is needed.

A former English teacher, Delaine's writing and analytical skills are highly valued by the firm. "I have prepared a lot of memoranda summarizing my research results, but the real challenge came when one of the attorneys proposed that I draft the appellate brief for a fairly uncomplicated case going up to the court of appeals. I had already done a lot of the research on that case before it went to trial, and I had assisted the attorney in court during the entire trial. So, I was very familiar with the facts and the legal issues. It was enormously gratifying when the attorney filed the appellate brief with very little modification of my draft—and doubly so when we won that case on appeal!" ■

SECTION 2. LEGAL RESEARCH

Let the reader be clear about the meaning of "essential skills" for legal research. This section will introduce the skills needed to "test the waters" of legal research, but doing so is more like dipping a toe than taking the plunge. The skills presented here are used at all levels of legal research. But, in order to become competent even in *basic* legal research, a paralegal student will need to complete a separate course in legal research.

There is no doubt that computers are rapidly increasing in their importance for legal research; in fact, the future of legal research belongs to the computer, on-line databases, CD-ROMs and the Internet. The contents of law libraries are increasingly available on CD-ROM, and almost every print source for legal research—including all of those discussed in this chapter—can be accessed in computer databases, such as Westlaw and LEXIS-NEXIS. (The role and uses of computers for research are discussed in Chapter 9.) However, this chapter focuses upon the traditional methods using materials in print form.

FINDING A STARTING POINT

It can be most intimidating to receive a research assignment and have no clue about where to begin. If a paralegal finds herself in that situation, the solution is: Ask for guidance. The attorney or a senior paralegal should be able to provide suggestions for starting points.

The attorney might suggest a case that discusses the legal issue in question. A relevant court opinion is a useful starting point, because it can lead to other cases discussing the same or related legal issues. But, suppose the attorney does not know of a relevant case. In that event, the paralegal will have to find a starting point in other sources. The most common "other sources" are listed below:

- annotated statutes
- case annotations
- digests
- treatises
- legal encyclopedias

Each of these sources for research clues will be discussed in this chapter.

IDENTIFYING KEY TERMS

Before going to these sources, however, it is a good idea for the paralegal to identify several key terms related to the client's case. These key terms will become valuable research tools. In the residential flooding case mentioned earlier in this chapter, the attorney has decided to allege **negligence**, as an alternative cause of action to his nuisance theory. He has asked his legal assistant to find out whether the county government can be held negligent for approving the uphill development without increasing the capacity of the storm drain. By looking up the legal definition of "negligence," the legal assistant learns that it is an act or omission that violates a duty of care to avoid unreasonable risk of harm to others. This duty requires the degree of care that a reasonable and prudent person would use under the circumstances. From this one source, he can identify several key terms: negligence, duty of care, reasonable, and prudent person. As he defines the issues for his research, he will relate these key terms to the facts of the case at hand. For example, what is the "duty of care" owed by a government agency to existing homeowners at lower elevations, when approving additional up-slope development? Is a government planning agency required to exercise a *higher* degree of care than is the ordinary reasonable and prudent neighbor?

Legal dictionaries are not the only place to find key terms. As the paralegal studies treatises on tort law or negligence, he will discover other key terms for his research. Court opinions are a particularly valuable source of key terms, because the courts in a given jurisdiction tend to use a common vocabulary as a form of shorthand. The courts of some jurisdictions, for example, use "emotional distress" as a catchall for inconvenience, annoyance, fear, anguish, anxiety, and discomfort.

Once the paralegal has found a key term, it will be useful in locating sources and in understanding the relevance of the cases he finds. Treatises and legal encyclopedias have extensive indexes. By looking under "negligence," for example, he probably will find a subheading for "duty of care."

Negligence is the failure to use the care a reasonable person would use under the same circumstances, so that others will not be harmed.

Practice Tip

Some terms of art (e.g., "negligence") can be too broad in scope to prove useful in locating cases. This quickly becomes apparent—especially when it is used for an on-line search in Westlaw or LEXIS, and many hundreds of cases are instantly identified. The legal assistant needs to find subheadings (e.g., "duty of care") or other related terms that will yield a more manageable number of cases.

USING STATUTORY CODES

A **code** is a collection of statutes organized by topic, and a single code might comprise one or more volumes. The statutes of the United States have been compiled into a statutory code, and most state statutes are similarly organized. For example, most states have both a **penal code** (sometimes called a "criminal code") and a **code of civil procedure**. The statutes defining and prohibiting criminal acts (and establishing penalties for their violation) typically appear in the penal code. The laws governing general court procedures and the prosecution of civil lawsuits usually appear in the code of civil procedure.

Although their titles might vary, other typical state codes include the following sections:

- tax
- insurance
- education
- corporation
- commercial
- government
- labor

The *United States Code* includes "titles" for the following:

- transportation
- internal revenue
- foreign relations
- shipping
- Indians

A **code** is a compilation of statutes or administrative regulations organized by subject.

The **penal code** defines crimes and prescribes their punishment.

The **code of civil procedure** establishes the procedures that are used in civil litigation and other civil court proceedings.

FIGURE 8.2 Statutory Codes

- public contracts
- national defense
- education

The federal codes are identified by title numbers. For example, the *Internal Revenue Code* is identified as Title 26 of the *United States Code.*

A code typically contains numbered **sections** or paragraphs, which are the smallest subdivisions of that code. Numbered sections might be organized into larger "chapters" within the same code. Chapters might be organized into larger "titles" or "divisions," depending upon the practice of each state. Within each code, these subdivisions (i.e., divisions, titles, chapters, articles, etc.) bring together the statutory sections (or paragraphs) on particular legal topics. In *Figure 8.2*, the volumes for *West's Illinois Compiled Statutes, Annotated* appear on the shelf of a law library.

In a statute, a **section** is a discrete provision, of one or more paragraphs, that is to be read and interpreted as a whole.

Locating a Specific Code Section

The legal assistant might have the citation for a statute, either provided by the attorney or found in some source, such as a court opinion or a treatise. With that citation, it is not difficult to find the statute itself. If the citation is not known, published codes are usually accompanied by a topic index that allows the researcher to find the relevant code section.

It is not unusual, however, to find nothing in the index under what one believes is an "obvious" topic heading. The researcher must think of much more than just synonyms for the obvious headings—she must approach the index in both logical and innovative ways. For example, if the legal issue concerns the rights of public school students, the researcher might have to check the index for responsibilities and duties of public schools and public school teachers. Topic headings to be consulted would *begin* with "public school," "school," "school teachers," "teachers," and "students." If the right in question relates to discrimination, that would suggest additional headings.

One complication is the variety of citation formats required by the different jurisdictions. As mentioned above, the *United States Code* is organized into num-

FIGURE 8.3 Example of a Pocket Part

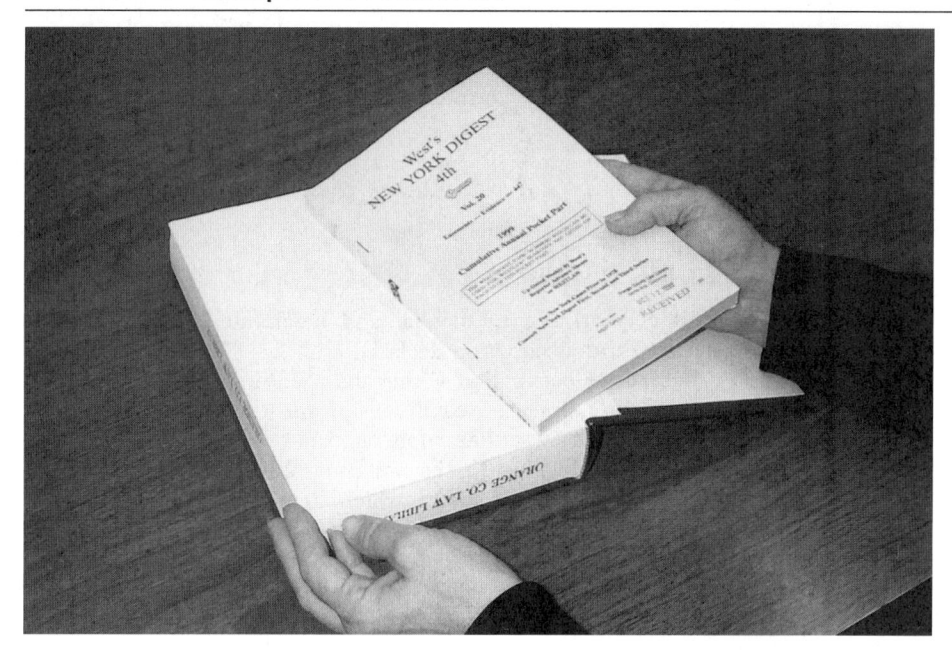

bered "titles." Each title will take up one or more volumes of the code. If the citation is 11 U.S.C. § 101, the paralegal must find the volume for Title 11 (clearly marked on the spine of each volume) that contains Section 101. The sections included in each volume are also marked on the spine. The rest is easy, because the sections appear in numerical sequence within each volume.

Suppose, however, that the citation is to *Hawaii Revised Statutes*, § 572-1. The paralegal will find that the statutory volumes for Hawaii are organized by chapter numbers. The correct volume is located by checking the volume spines to find the one that contains Chapter 572. State jurisdictions using this form of organization might also segregate the volumes by topic, so that all laws governing family law, for example, appear in a single volume.

In a jurisdiction that organizes its statutes into named codes, a citation might take the form of *Education Code* § 1205.3. The legal assistant must find the volumes devoted to the *Education Code*, and then locate Section 1205.3. That is quite simple, because the sections appear in numerical sequence, just as they do in the titles of the *United States Code*.

Using Annotated Codes to Find Case Law

When enacted, a statute might comprise one (or any number of) sections or paragraphs. If a state publishes an "official" set of statutes, it usually includes no more than the exact words of the statute itself, and the dates of enactment and amendment of that statute. Although useful for the actual statutory language (which is always mandatory authority within that jurisdiction), official statute books are not very helpful in legal research. To really understand the statutory language and to find cases that interpret and apply it in varying circumstances, the paralegal usually consults an **annotated code**.

Annotated codes are published by companies such as West Group, Bancroft-Whitney Company, and Lawyers Co-operative Publishing Company. (Bancroft-Whitney is part of the West Group.) The annotated codes include the complete statutes, word for word, that are found in the official codes. Because they are unofficial, the annotated codes may include whatever additional information and commentary the publisher believes to be useful. *Figure 8.4* shows a page found in *West's Arizona Revised Statutes Annotated*.

Practice Tip

Like many legal sources published in hardbound editions, statutory codes are kept current by inserts known as "pocket parts." A **pocket part** is a pamphlet that is physically inserted in a "pocket" inside the back cover of the volume (see Figure 8.3). Therefore, when the researcher has a code citation, it is wise to look first in the pocket part; if it is found there, she knows that she is reading the current version of that statute. If the section she is looking for is not in the pocket part, the version in the hardbound volume is still current. If the hardbound volume is so new that there is no pocket part, there should be an insert in the pocket that states that fact. If nothing at all is found in the pocket, the pocket part might have been lost or misplaced.

Overlooking the pocket parts can lead to major grief!

Pocket parts are paperbound inserts, placed in a cardboard pocket of the binding of individual volumes in statutory codes, treatises, legal encyclopedias, and so on; they contain revisions made since the bound volume was published.

An **annotated code** contains the codified statutes, with notes about court decisions applying or interpreting those statutes, references to related law review articles, and references to recognized legal treatises or encyclopedias; these annotations are prepared by the commercial publisher of the annotated code.

FIGURE 8.4 Arizona Revised Statutes Annotated, §23-802

ARIZONA REVISED STATUTES ANNOTATED

EMPLOYERS' LIABILITY LAW § 23–802
Ch. 5 Note 3

Liability Law, § 23–801 et seq. Nunez v. Arizona Mill. Co. (App. 1968) 7 Ariz.App. 387, 439 P.2d 834.

§ 23–802. Declaration of policy

Labor and services of workmen at manual and mechanical labor in the employment of a person in an occupation declared by § 23–803 to be hazardous is service in a hazardous occupation within the meaning of the terms of § 23–801. By reason of the nature and conditions of and the means used and provided for doing the work in a hazardous occupation, such service is especially dangerous and hazardous to the workmen because of risks and hazards inherent in such occupations and which are unavoidable by the workmen therein.

Historical and Statutory Notes

Source:
Laws 1912, Ch. 89, § 3.
Civ.Code 1913, § 3155.
Rev.Code 1928, § 1385.
Code 1939, § 56–802.

Notes of Decisions

Dangerous work 2
Mining operations 3
Negligence, generally 1

1. Negligence, generally

The Employers' Liability Law gave the injured servant a right of recovery regardless of negligence of the master, in view of Civ.Code 1913, § 3155 (now this section). Arizona Copper Co. v. Burciaga (1918) 20 Ariz. 85, 177 P. 29.

2. Dangerous work

Under Const. Art. 18, § 7, providing for the enactment of the Employers' Liability Law contained in Civ.Code 1913, §§ 3154 to 3158 (see, now, § 23–801 et seq.), and its provisions making the employer liable for the death or injury of employee caused by any accident due to conditions of a hazardous occupation, the employer was liable when the injury was caused by an accident due to conditions of the employment, which conditions need not have been inherent in the occupation, but could have arisen from the manner in which the business was carried on, the word "hazardous" having been defined as "exposed to; exposing to; or involving danger; risk of loss or calamity; perilous; risky;" and the word "condition" having been defined as "mode or state of being; state or situation with regard to external circumstances; essential quality; property; attribute." Consolidated Arizona Smelting Co. v. Egich (1920) 22 Ariz. 543, 199 P. 132.

The means employed to do the work can cause it to be dangerous. Arizona Eastern R. Co. v. Matthews (1919) 20 Ariz. 282, 180 P. 159.

3. Mining operations

In view of Civ.Code 1913, § 3147 (see, now, § 23–282), which provided that employment in all underground mines, underground workings, open workings, open pit workings, in or about, and in connection with, the operation of smelters, reduction works, stamp mills, concentrating mills, chlorination processes, cyanide processes, cement works, rolling mills, rod mills and at coke ovens and blast furnaces, was declared to be injurious to health and dangerous to life and limb, laws enacted which reasonably regulated the employments enumerated were within the police powers of the state. Inspiration Consol. Copper Co. v. Mendez (1917) 19 Ariz. 151, 166 P. 278, affirmed 39 S.Ct. 553, 250 U.S. 400, 63 L.Ed. 1058, motion denied 40 S.Ct. 12.

In view of Const. Art. 18, § 7, directing the legislature to enact laws "to protect the safety of employes in all hazardous occupations," a superintendent of a construction company injured by a delayed blast, while in such employment, was entitled to recover for such injuries under the Employers' Liability Law, Civ.Code 1913, § 3153 to 3162 (see, now, § 23–801 et seq.) as the words "workman" and "employe" were used therein interchangeably and with the same meaning, and a superintendent was included in the term "employe." Deyo v. Arizona Grading & Const. Co. (1916) 18 Ariz. 149, 157 P. 371.

395

Arizona Revised Statutes Annotated, Copyright by West Group. Reprinted by permission.

The commentary is often derived from authoritative sources, such as reports by the responsible committees in the state legislature that enacted the statute, or by official state law review commissions. For example, when a committee of the state legislature issues its report on a bill, it typically explains the purpose of that bill. That legislative purpose is referred to as the "legislative intent." Courts often give great weight to explanations by a legislative committee that has reviewed and shaped the language of the statute.

In some states, official law review commissions recommend legislation that is then enacted by the state legislature (often with few substantive changes). Again, the commission's comments upon the intent and meaning of the proposed legislation are very persuasive for the courts, especially when the legislature has adopted the commission's recommendations without substantial change.

Other important **annotations** to a particular code section are references to court opinions that have interpreted and/or applied that code section. In each annotation, the court's comment or ruling is summarized in a brief paragraph, followed by the case citation. Annotations related to a particularly significant code section can take up scores of pages (with ten or fifteen annotations per page), making them a rich source of clues for research. The case annotations for each code section are often grouped under topic headings that indicate the particular legal issue (e.g., the constitutionality of the statute) discussed in that group of cases. The paralegal can review the annotations to identify cases that appear to be relevant to the issue being researched and then use the citations to locate the full court opinions.

There are two publishers of annotated codes for federal statutes. West publishes the *United States Code Annotated*, and the Lawyers Co-operative Publishing Company and the Bancroft-Whitney Company jointly publish the *United States Code Service, Lawyers' Edition*. These companies publish annotated codes for many state jurisdictions, also.

> An **annotation** is a commentary or supplemental information about a case, statute, or regulation.

USING CASE REPORTERS

Court opinions are found in case **reporters**, which are bound volumes containing the published opinions of a court, or of a number of courts. The *United States Reports*, for example, is the **official reporter** for opinions of the U.S. Supreme Court. Those Supreme Court decisions also appear in unofficial reporters, the *Supreme Court Reporter* (published by West Publishing Company) and the *United States Supreme Court Reports, Lawyers' Edition* (published jointly by the Lawyers Co-operative Publishing Company and the Bancroft-Whitney Company). The **unofficial reporters** contain every word of the Supreme Court opinions published in the official reporter, *United States Reports*. However, the unofficial reporters include editorial commentary that is not found in the official reporter. Another difference is that the unofficial reporters do not publish all of the many procedural orders of the Supreme Court that appear without any written opinion in the *United States Reports*. *Figure 8.5* is an example of such procedural orders, found in *United States Reports*. *Figure 8.6* shows two opposing pages from *Dowling v. United States*, 493 U.S. 342 (1990) as they appear in *United States Reports*.

Regardless of which reporter one is using to research U.S. Supreme Court cases, only the official reporter should be cited to the courts. This practice is followed even though the Supreme Court, in its own published opinions, includes parallel citations along with the official citation to its prior court opinions. For that reason, the unofficial reporters contain pagination indicators that correspond to the official reporter. Thus, in *Figure 8-7*, the "inverted T" symbol in the *Supreme Court Reporter* identifies the "page break" found in the official *United States Reports*, so that the first word following that symbol is also the first word on that page in the official reporter. This system makes it possible to provide a

> A **reporter** is a series of volumes containing the complete decisions of the courts in a particular jurisdiction.
>
> An **official reporter** is the series published at the direction of the court or legislature; cases cited to a court must include the official citation if an official reporter exists.
>
> An **unofficial reporter** is a series published by a commercial publisher.

FIGURE 8.5 Procedural orders in *United States Reports*

ORDERS 1011

514 U. S. March 6, 9, 17, 20, 1995

No. 94–6992. Pizzo v. Whitley, Warden, et al., 513 U. S. 1116;

No. 94–6993. Mizkun v. Widnall, Secretary of the Air Force, et al., 513 U. S. 1099; and

No. 94–7043. Baez v. Douglas County Commission et al., 513 U. S. 1117. Petitions for rehearing denied.

No. 94–6177. Ridings v. United States, 513 U. S. 976. Motion for leave to file petition for rehearing denied.

March 9, 1995

Dismissal Under Rule 46

No. 94–1251. Farron v. Dun & Bradstreet, Inc. C. A. 11th Cir. Certiorari dismissed under this Court's Rule 46. Reported below: 36 F. 3d 95.

March 17, 1995

Certiorari Denied

No. 94–8465 (A–660). Williams v. Gramley, Warden, et al. C. A. 7th Cir. Application for stay of execution of sentence of death, presented to Justice Stevens, and by him referred to the Court, denied. Certiorari denied. Reported below: 50 F. 3d 1356 and 1358.

March 20, 1995

Certiorari Granted—Vacated and Remanded

No. 93–1907. Shalala, Secretary of Health and Human Services v. Mother Frances Hospital of Tyler, Texas. C. A. 5th Cir. Certiorari granted, judgment vacated, and case remanded for further consideration in light of *Shalala* v. *Guernsey Memorial Hospital, ante,* p. 87. Reported below: 15 F. 3d 423.

Certiorari Granted—Reversed. (See No. 94–898, *ante,* p. 115.)

Miscellaneous Orders

No. ———. Bilzerian v. Securities and Exchange Commission;

No. ———. Will v. Will;

---

precise official citation for a quotation, even when using the unofficial reporter. The use of the inverted "T" symbol is explained further under "Understanding the Parts of a Court Opinion," below. Many attorneys use unofficial reporters exclusively, never opening a single volume from an official reporter.

The decisions of the U.S. District Courts and the U.S. Courts of Appeals are published in the *Federal Supplement* and the *Federal Reporter*, respectively, both published by West Publishing Company. There are no official reporters for these courts. U.S. District Court decisions construing the *Federal Rules of Civil Procedure* and the *Federal Rules of Criminal Procedure* are published by West in the *Federal Rules Decisions*.

FIGURE 8.6 Sample pages from *U.S. Reports*

---

342 OCTOBER TERM, 1989

Syllabus 493 U. S.

DOWLING v. UNITED STATES

CERTIORARI TO THE UNITED STATES COURT OF APPEALS FOR THE THIRD CIRCUIT

No. 88-6025. Argued October 4, 1989—Decided January 10, 1990

Petitioner Dowling was convicted of robbing a Virgin Islands bank while wearing a ski mask and carrying a small pistol. Relying on Federal Rule of Evidence 404(b)—which provides that evidence of other crimes, wrongs, or acts may be admissible against a defendant for purposes other than character evidence—the Government introduced at trial the testimony of one Henry, who stated that a similarly masked and armed Dowling had been one of two intruders who had entered her home two weeks after the bank robbery. Although Dowling had been acquitted of charges in the Henry case, the Government believed that Henry's description of him strengthened its identification of him as the bank robber and that her testimony linked him to another individual thought to be implicated in the bank robbery. The District Court permitted the introduction of the testimony and twice instructed the jury about Dowling's acquittal and the limited purpose for which the testimony was being admitted. The Court of Appeals affirmed the conviction, ruling that, although the Government was collaterally estopped by the acquittal from offering Henry's testimony at trial and the testimony was inadmissible under the Federal Rules of Evidence, its admission was harmless because it was highly probable that the error did not prejudice Dowling. The court declined to apply the more stringent standard of *Chapman v. California*, 386 U. S. 18, 24, applicable to constitutional errors because the District Court's error was evidentiary and not of constitutional dimension.

Held:

1. The admission of the testimony did not violate the collateral-estoppel component of the Double Jeopardy Clause. The collateral-estoppel doctrine prohibits the Government from relitigating an issue of ultimate fact that has been determined by a valid and final judgment, *Ashe v. Swenson*, 397 U. S. 436, but does not bar in all circumstances the later use of evidence simply because it relates to alleged criminal conduct for which a defendant has been acquitted. Here, the prior acquittal did not determine the ultimate issue in the bank robbery case because in the second trial the Government was not required to show beyond a reasonable doubt that Dowling was the man who entered Henry's house. This decision is consistent with other cases where this Court has held that an

---

342 DOWLING v. UNITED STATES 343

Opinion of the Court

acquittal in a criminal case does not preclude the Government from relitigating an issue when it is presented in a subsequent action governed by a lower standard of proof, *United States v. One Assortment of 89 Firearms*, 465 U. S. 354, 361-362; *One Lot Emerald Cut Stones v. United States*, 409 U. S. 232, 235. Even if the lower burden of proof at the second trial did not serve to avoid the collateral-estoppel component of the Double Jeopardy Clause, Dowling failed to satisfy his burden of demonstrating that the first jury determined that he was not one of the men who entered Henry's home. Pp. 347-352.

2. The introduction of the evidence did not violate the due process test of "fundamental fairness." Especially in light of the trial judge's limiting instructions, the testimony was not fundamentally unfair, since the jury was free to assess the truthfulness and significance of the testimony, since the trial court's authority to exclude potentially prejudicial evidence adequately addresses the possibility that introduction of such evidence will create a risk that the jury will convict a defendant based on inferences drawn from the acquitted conduct, since inconsistent verdicts are constitutionally tolerable, and since the tradition that the Government may not force a person acquitted in one trial to defend against the same accusation in a subsequent proceeding is amply protected by the Double Jeopardy Clause. Pp. 352-354.

855 F. 2d 114, affirmed.

WHITE, J., delivered the opinion of the Court, in which REHNQUIST, C. J., and BLACKMUN, O'CONNOR, SCALIA, and KENNEDY, JJ., joined. BRENNAN, J., filed a dissenting opinion, in which MARSHALL and STEVENS, JJ., joined, *post*, p. 354.

Robert L. Tucker argued the cause and filed briefs for petitioner.

Stephen L. Nightingale argued the cause for the United States. With him on the brief were *Solicitor General Starr, Assistant Attorney General Dennis, Deputy Solicitor General Bryson,* and *Joseph C. Wyderko.**

JUSTICE WHITE delivered the opinion of the Court.

At petitioner's trial for various offenses arising out of a bank robbery, testimony was admitted under Rule 404(b) of the Federal Rules of Evidence, relating to an alleged crime

---

**Steven E. M. Hartz* filed a brief for the National Association of Criminal Lawyers as *amicus curiae* urging reversal.

Many states have official reporters designated by statute or by order of the supreme court of those states, and some form of unofficial reporter exists for all states. The unofficial reporters for the courts of most states are organized regionally or by jurisdiction. Thus, West's *Southern Reporter* includes decisions by the courts of Louisiana, Mississippi, Alabama, and Florida, and is part of the *National Reporter System* published by West Publishing Company. That system is composed of seven regional reporters, plus West's reporters for the federal courts, and it includes separate West reporters for the courts of California, Illinois, and New York. Those state reporters are published separately because of the quantity of court opinions from those populous states, as well as the extraordinarily large market offered by the many thousands of attorneys who practice in those states. Opinions from those three states also appear in their respective regional reporters, the *Pacific Reporter* and the *North Eastern Reporter*, both published by West.

FIGURE 8.7 Sample pages from *Supreme Court Reporter*

West's Supreme Court Reporter, Copyright by West Group. Reprinted by permission.

As with federal cases, West's *National Reporter System* prints every word of the state court opinions it publishes. However, a West regional reporter does not necessarily include every state appellate court case, unless it is the designated official reporter for that state.

Locating a Specific Court Case

Assume that the paralegal has found this case citation in an annotated state code: *Mobile v. Bolden*, 446 U.S. 55 (1980). She might recognize this to be a U.S. Supreme Court case, because of its official citation to the *United States Reports*. In the law library, the paralegal must find where that official reporter is shelved and then locate volume 446. The case entitled *Mobile v. Bolden* begins on page 55 of that volume.

The names of case reporters (e.g., *United States Reports*) are always abbreviated in case citations. It is simply a custom that might have begun as a method of conserving space on the printed page. In any event, it is the custom, and the paralegal must learn to recognize and use the accepted abbreviations. The names of most state reporters are easily recognized, because the standard citations suggest the state names: e.g., Ala. (Alabama), Del. (Delaware), and, R.I. (Rhode Island). The abbreviations for some of West's regional reporters are not always so transparent: e.g., P.2d (*Pacific Reporter, Second Series*) and A. (*Atlantic Reporter, First Series*). The abbreviation for the *Federal Reporter* is also obscure: F. or F.2d (for the first and second series, respectively). U.S. District Court decisions are found in F.Supp. (*Federal Supplement*). The publisher, West, is not to be faulted, however, because it was not West that adopted or prescribed these rather obscure abbreviations.

Most secondary sources (such as treatises and encyclopedias) print a list of reporter abbreviations in the front matter of each volume. By checking that list, the paralegal can make a note of the full name of the reporter—or a more recognizable abbreviation of her own invention—when she makes a note of the case citation. Lists of recognized abbreviations for case reporters appear also in most books on legal research. A paralegal new to legal research should arm herself with a copy for ready reference.

> **Practice Tip**
>
> *Occasionally, the publisher of a case reporter decides to publish that reporter in a new "series." That might occur, for example, when the publisher decides to change the page format or volume size. The volumes of each series are numbered consecutively, beginning with volume one. Thus, one will find volumes 1, 2, 3, and so forth, in the* Atlantic Reporter, Second Series *(abbreviated as A.2d), as well as in the first series of that reporter.*

USING DIGESTS TO LOCATE CASE LAW

One of the major challenges of legal research is locating case law that addresses the legal issue at hand; digests are designed to help the researcher do exactly that. A **digest** is a multi-volume publication that groups cases by topic (i.e., by the legal issues determined in those cases). If the legal assistant is researching an issue in bankruptcy law, for example, one volume of a digest would organize brief summaries of the many thousands of cases in bankruptcy law according to particular subtopics (e.g, "pre-petition fraudulent transfers"). The volumes of a digest are organized alphabetically, so that the first volume includes legal topics beginning with the letter "A" (e.g., agency, aliens, and attorney-at-law).

A **digest** contains brief summaries of court decisions, organized by topic.

A digest does not reprint the entire opinion in a case, but it provides a brief paragraph summarizing the court's holding on the legal issue before it. These case summaries are similar to the annotations found in annotated codes. When the legal assistant finds a case that appears useful, the citation leads him to the reporter in which the full opinion is printed. Annotations found in digests must *never* be cited or quoted as legal authority.

Federal court decisions are digested in *West's Federal Practice Digest*. In addition, there are two digests that contain only Supreme Court cases: the *U.S. Supreme Court Digest* (West Publishing) and the *U.S. Supreme Court Reports Digest* (Lawyers Co-operative Publishing).

West's Key Number System

When using a digest published by West, the researcher will notice that each discrete legal topic is identified by a **key number**. These key numbers relate to West's alphabetical outline of legal topics in all fields of the law. All West publications, including the *National Reporter System*, use the identical key number for that particular legal issue, so that it becomes a research tool to locate additional authorities on a discrete legal issue (e.g., Negligence 28, Care Required in General). That means that a legal assistant can identify the key number for any issue in a particular court opinion published by West—or in any other West publication—and then use it to locate case summaries on that same topic in other publications.

A **key number** is a discrete number associated with a particular legal topic, and it is used to identify material about that topic in case reporters, digests, and other publications of the West Group.

For example, if the paralegal has found a pertinent legal topic in *West's Missouri Digest*, she can use the corresponding key number to find summaries of cases treating that same legal issue in *West's New York Digest*. West publishes separate key number digests for most state jurisdictions, as well as regional digests corresponding to most of the regional reporters published by West. A few other publishers provide digests for some state jurisdictions, but those do not

FIGURE 8.8 Sample page from West's *Missouri Digest*

5 Mo D 2d—149 **ATTORNEY & CLIENT** ⚖︎11(1)

For references to other topics, see Descriptive-Word Index

Mo.App. 1940. A person must be of good moral character before he is eligible for admission to the bar.

In re Block, 136 S.W.2d 358.

Mo.App. 1937. Restrictions on practice of law are not primarily for benefit of attorneys, but for benefit of society.

Clark v. Reardon, 104 S.W.2d 407, 231 Mo.App. 666.

⚖︎5–6. *For other cases see earlier editions of this digest and the decennial digests.*

Library references

C.J.S. Attorney and Client.

⚖︎7. **Determination of right to admission.**

Library references

C.J.S. Attorney and Client §§ 19–22.

D.C.Mo. 1981. Petitioner, alleging that he had been denied his request to take Missouri bar examination by state board pursuant to Missouri Supreme Court rule on basis that he was not graduated from an American Bar Association approved law school, was required to exhaust his state administrative remedies completely before his access to federal court was created. V.A.M.R. Crim. Rules 8.03(a)(2), 8.12; U.S.Dist.Ct.Rules E.D.Mo., General Rule 2.

West v. Missouri Bd. of Law Examiners, 520 F.Supp. 159, affirmed 676 F.2d 702.

D.C.Mo. 1978. Federal district court is without jurisdiction to review denial of a license to practice law with respect to particular applicants absent showing that denial was predicated on a constitutionally impermissible reason. 28 U.S.C.A. § 1343.

Newsome v. Dominique, 455 F.Supp. 1373.

Allegations of arbitrary cutoff scores on state bar exam and retesting procedures were insufficient to justify federal judicial intervention into matters entrusted to the state judiciary; likewise, claim that requests for reconsideration were routinely denied was also not cognizable in federal court; applicants' only remedy lay with the state Supreme Court, as the body having power to grant a license, and the United States Supreme Court. 28 U.S.C.A. § 1343; V.A.M.R. Bar and Judiciary Rules 8.02, 8.08.

Newsome v. Dominique, 455 F.Supp. 1373.

⚖︎8–9. *For other cases see earlier editions of this digest and the decennial digests.*

Library references

C.J.S. Attorney and Client.

see Vernon's Annotated Missouri Statutes

⚖︎10. **Admission of practitioners in different jurisdiction.**

Library references

C.J.S. Attorney and Client §§ 26–28.

D.C.Mo. 1972. Motions of plaintiff and defendant to permit visiting lawyers who were members of foreign state bars in good standing to appear in suit for alleged violations of the Sherman Act, which motions had not been opposed in the pleadings, would be granted. Sherman Anti-Trust Act, § 1, 15 U.S.C.A. § 1; Clayton Act, § 4, 15 U.S.C.A. § 15.

Gerecht v. American Ins. Co., 344 F.Supp. 1056.

Mo. 1975. Fact that a person is admitted to or disbarred from bar of one state does not compel any other state to admit or disbar that person to or from its own bar. V.A.M.R. Bar and Judiciary Rule 5.19.

In re Weiner, 530 S.W.2d 222, 81 A.L.R.3d 1272, supplemented 547 S.W.2d 459.

⚖︎11. **Practitioners not admitted or not licensed.**

Corporation practicing law, see Corporations ⚖︎377½. Enjoining unauthorized practice of law, see INJUNCTION.

Library references

C.J.S. Attorney and Client § 30.

⚖︎11(1). **In general.**

Mo. 1961. The Supreme Court has inherent power to regulate and discipline the Bar, to define and declare what is the practice of law, and to prevent practice of law by laymen or other unauthorized persons.

Hoffmeister v. Tod, 349 S.W.2d 5.

The Legislature may, in exercise of its police power, aid a court by providing penalties for unauthorized practice of law, and for that purpose may define the practice of law, but the Legislature may in no way hinder, interfere with or frustrate the court's inherent power to prevent practice of law by laymen or other unauthorized persons.

Hoffmeister v. Tod, 349 S.W.2d 5.

Mo. 1940. Missouri has adopted a policy that practice of law and doing of law business, both in and out of its courts, shall be limited to persons with special qualifications and duly licensed as attorneys. R.S.1939, §§ 13313, 13314 (V.A.M.S. §§ 484.010, 484.020).

De Pass v. B. Harris Wool Co., 144 S.W.2d 146, 346 Mo. 1038.

Mo. 1939. While a layman may represent himself in court, he cannot, even on a single occasion, represent another, whether for a

West's Missouri Digest, 2d, Copyright by West Group. Reprinted by permission.

CHAPTER 8 ⚖ Legal Analysis, Research, and Writing 307

compare to the scope of the West system for state jurisdictions, and they do not use West's proprietary key number system. In *Figure 8.8*, a sample page from West's *Missouri Digest*, case annotations appear for "Attorney & Client."

If the legal assistant does not have a key number, it is still possible to effectively use a digest. In bankruptcy law, for example, the researcher can use the "descriptive word index" volumes of a digest to locate a topic heading for "fraudulent transfers." If the index search is not productive, the legal assistant can review the table of contents for the volume on bankruptcy until a relevant subtopic is located. In a West digest, the key numbers appear in both the index and the table of contents.

UNDERSTANDING THE PARTS OF A COURT OPINION

The appellate court's decision in *Roozen v. Ramstead*, 124 Cal. App.3d 332, 177 Cal. Rptr. 276 (1997), appears in *Figures 8.9* and *8.10*. It is reprinted here from West's *California Reporter*, an unofficial reporter for the California appellate courts. As the official citation indicates, the same opinion can be found in volume 124 of *California Appellate Reports, Third Series*, at page 332.

At the top of each right-hand page, the case citation for the *California Reporter* appears immediately below the case name. On the first page of the case, the citation to the official reporter ("124 Cal. App.3d 332") appears immediately above the case name. The numeral "124" identifies the volume, and "332" is the page on which that case is reported. The citation to the unofficial reporter, "177 Cal. Rptr. 276," follows the same sequence: volume number, reporter name, and first page. "Cal. Rptr." is the approved abbreviation for West's *California Reporter*.

The published case name gives more information than is needed to correctly cite this case. That portion of the full case name that appears in ALL CAPS identifies what is needed for a correct citation: *Roozen v. Ramstead*. The plaintiff's or appellant's name always appears first in the case name. In this particular instance, the plaintiff Roozen also happens to be the appellant—the one who has appealed the trial court decision. (See *Figure 8.11* on page 311.)

The "case number" appears immediately below the case name. One can tell that *Roozen* is a civil case because "The People" are not the plaintiff, and the case number is "Civ. No. 60930." ("Civ. No." means "civil case number.") In place of a case number, some courts list a "docket number," which also identifies the specific case.

Below the case number, the appellate court deciding this case is identified as the Court of Appeal for the Second District in California. "Division 5" identifies the particular three-justice appellate panel in the Second District that heard this case. Next, the date of the appellate decision is given: October 6, 1981. The date is important because it allows one to compare appellate decisions that reach different legal conclusions. Generally, a recent case is likely to be a more accurate statement of the law than is an earlier case that reached a different conclusion.

The Case Summary and Headnotes

Next comes the "case summary." The **summary** (sometimes called a **syllabus**) provides an opportunity to learn what the case is about without reading the entire opinion. The summary of the case is *not* part of the court's opinion. In the official reporter, the summary is written by the "reporter of decisions," an attorney authorized by the court of appeal to prepare the summary. Summaries in unofficial reporters are written by the editorial staff of their publishers. If the reader were to compare the summaries published in the official and unofficial reporters, he would find that they are different. Because it is not part of the court's opinion, the summary should *never* be quoted and should

The **summary** of a court decision comprises one or more paragraphs summarizing the key issues and holdings of the court in that case; the summary is unofficial, is provided for the convenience of the reader, and must *never* be quoted or cited as a statement of the law in that case.

A **syllabus** can be a summary of the case, although the term sometimes includes the headnotes, as well.

FIGURE 8.9 Roozen v. Ramstead, 177 Cal.Rptr. 276

ments can be added (e. g. 12022, 12022.5, 12022.7) decidedly leaves the impression that not all felonies in which a firearm is used are to be enhanced.

This vexing inconsistency with respect to enhancements simply does not exist with regard to the 5 year lid on nonviolent felonies, contained in the fourth sentence of Penal Code § 1170.1(a). That sentence reads: "In no case shall the subordinate terms for such consecutive offenses which are not 'violent felonies' as defined in subdivision (c) of Section 667.5 exceed five years." Looking at the express language of the 5 year lid, it is apparent that the legislative intent was to exclude all "violent felonies" specified in section 667.5(c) from the operation of the 5 year lid. Section 667.-5(c)(8) refers to any felony with an enhancement under section 12022.5. This is precisely the kind of crime defendant pled guilty to 32 counts of.[1]

In spite of this express language, *People v. Childs*, 112 Cal.App.3d 374, 169 Cal.Rptr. 183 applied *Harvey* to this situation. We do not find the analysis in *Childs* persuasive.[2] We find no ambiguity nor any "close and subtle" question presented. We decline to interfere with the clear cut decision of the Legislature that the 5 year lid simply does not apply to those having been convicted of using a firearm in the conviction of a felony. To us, the legislative intent is clear. There is no reason for judicial interpretation and no possible excuse for applying the rationale of *Harvey* to this situation. It is obvious that the Legislature takes a dim view of dangerous, assaultive, armed criminals and has afforded trial courts the opportunity to imprison these individuals for prolonged periods of time for the protection of society. On the other hand and with a recognition of human frailty involved in offenses which do not necessarily endanger the victim physically, the Legislature has put a lid on time to be served. Thus, a defendant who passes 100 bad checks can only receive 5 years in consecutive sentences. An armed robber who endangers the lives of his victims by the use of a deadly weapon may receive as many consecutive sentences as the court finds reasonably required for the protection of innocent members of society. As we indicated earlier, it was clearly not the legislative intent that as a matter of state policy all armed robberies after the first 6 are free and unpunishable.

Judgment affirmed.

TAMURA and MORRIS, JJ., concur.

---

124 Cal.App.3d 332

Marie ROOZEN, Plaintiff and Appellant,

v.

Christopher RAMSTEAD and Robert Ramstead, Defendants and Respondents.

Civ. 60930.

Court of Appeal, Second District, Division 5.

Oct. 6, 1981.

Appeal was taken from a judgment of the Superior Court, Los Angeles County, Richard F. C. Hayden, J., dismissing negligence action. The Court of Appeal, Stephens, Acting P. J., held that negligence

---

1. According to Winston Churchill, a preposition is something one should never end a sentence with.

2. Neither did Division One of this court in *People v. Hernandez*, 120 Cal.App.3d 500, 175 Cal.Rptr. 22. Unfortunately, *Hernandez* reached the same conclusion that *Childs* did but under an even more troublesome analysis. It concluded that since the Supreme Court had denied a hearing in *Childs* and ordered *In re Rodriguez*, 114 Cal.App.3d 287, 171 Cal.Rptr. 832 and *People v. Harvey*, 114 Cal.App.3d 252, 170 Cal.Rptr. 577 (cases which went the other way) decertified, that somehow this created an ambiguity which they resolved in favor of the defendant. Then the Supreme Court granted a hearing in *Hernandez*. The remaining contestants are *Childs* and this court.

We assume, as did the Court of Appeal in *Hernandez*, that Rule of Court 977, prohibiting the citation of an unpublished opinion, does not bar our mentioning these opinions in this context.

West's California Reporter, Copyright by West Group. Reprinted by permission.

FIGURE 8.10 *Roozen v. Ramstead, 177 Cal.Rptr. 276*

124 Cal.App.3d 305   HERITAGE PUB. CO. v. CUMMINS   277
Cite as, App., 177 Cal.Rptr. 277

action, which was not brought to trial within five years after it was filed, was properly dismissed, notwithstanding that before expiration of the five-year limitation the parties orally agreed to submit the case to arbitration, where the limitation expired prior to plaintiff's execution of a stipulation to that effect and submission of the stipulation to defendants.

Judgment affirmed.

Pretrial Procedure ⇐590

Negligence action, which was not brought to trial within five years after it was filed, was properly dismissed, notwithstanding that before expiration of the five-year limitation the parties agreed orally to submit the case to arbitration, where the limitation expired prior to plaintiff's execution of a stipulation to that effect and submission of the stipulation to defendants. West's Ann.Code Civ.Proc. § 583.

Robert S. Gibbs, Westake Village, for plaintiff and appellant.

John F. Cobb and James H. Baggaley, Los Angeles, for defendants and respondents.

STEPHENS, Acting Presiding Justice.

Plaintiff filed a negligence action on November 18, 1974. It was transferred from the municipal court to the superior court on March 23, 1976. In October, 1979 plaintiff and defendants discussed submission of the case to arbitration and orally agreed to do so. Plaintiff signed a stipulation to that effect on December 17, 1979, but defendants at no time signed. The five-year limitation under Code of Civil Procedure section 583 had run prior to the execution of the stipulation by plaintiff and its submission to defendants.

The court concluded there was no reason, estoppel or otherwise, not to grant the motion for dismissal in accordance with section 583. We concur, there being no authority to justify a different result.

Code of Civil Procedure, section 583, subdivision (b), provides: "Any action heretofore or hereafter commenced shall be dismissed by the court in which the same shall have been commenced or to which it may be transferred on motion of the defendant, after due notice to plaintiff or by the court upon its own motion, unless such action is brought to trial within five years after the plaintiff has filed his action, except where the parties have filed a stipulation in writing that the time may be extended."

Code of Civil Procedure section 1141.17 states:

"Submission of an action to arbitration pursuant to this chapter shall not toll the running of the time periods contained in Section 583 as to actions filed on or after the operative date of this chapter. Submission to arbitration pursuant to a court order within six months of the expiration of the statutory period shall toll the running of such period until the filing of an arbitration award."

The trial court was correct in holding that the delay herein involved was not occasioned by defendant.

Judgment affirmed.

ASHBY and HASTINGS, JJ., concur.

---

124 Cal.App.3d 305

HERITAGE PUBLISHING COMPANY, a California Corporation, Plaintiff and Respondent,

v.

Joseph J. CUMMINS, et al., Defendants and Appellants.

Civ. 60302.

Court of Appeal, Second District, Division 3.

Oct. 6, 1981.

As Modified on Denial of Rehearing Nov. 4, 1981.

Hearing Denied Dec. 30, 1981.

Libel action was brought by a Jewish weekly newspaper against another Jewish

West's California Reporter, Copyright by West Group. Reprinted by permission.

Published court opinions are often preceded by brief paragraphs called **headnotes**, each summarizing the holding of that court on a discrete legal issue before it.

The **holding** of a court is its statement of the law on an issue before it.

Practice Tip

As explained, the summary and headnotes are not *part of the court's official opinion, and they* must not *be quoted or cited as authority. Nonetheless, these unofficial statements can be very useful to the researcher who must review scores of cases. Often, there is not enough time to read each of those cases in its entirety, but the summaries and headnotes can help the paralegal to quickly screen the cases for relevancy.*

never be relied upon as a statement of the law in that case. (Read that statement *again*, because it highlights one of the most common and serious errors committed by paralegal students.) At the end of the summary in *Roozen*, it notes that the court of appeal affirmed the decision of the trial court.

Following the summary, there usually appears a series of paragraphs known as **headnotes**. As will be explained shortly, the headnote paragraphs are extremely useful for legal research. The headnotes briefly summarize the **holdings** (i.e., legal conclusions) of the appellate court on the legal issues before it and often the holdings from other cases that this court has relied upon to reach its conclusion in the case at hand. In *Figure 8.12* on page 313, we see a headnote preceding the court's opinion in *Roozen v. Ramstead*. Like the summary, headnotes are *not* part of the court's opinion and must never be cited or quoted.

Occasionally, headnotes summarize statements in the opinion that were not essential to reaching the court's holding in that case. Such statements are known as *dicta*, and they may not be cited as legal precedent. However, *dicta* in the opinions of the U.S. Supreme Court (and of the various state supreme courts) receive close attention as possible indications of how the court might rule if that issue *were* officially before the court.

Each headnote is about a separate legal issue. The *Roozen* case is quite unusual in that the appellate court had only one legal issue to decide—hence, there is a single headnote. In cases with more than one headnote, each is usually numbered (e.g., from "1" to "17", if there are seventeen headnotes). Because *Roozen* has only one headnote, the headnote is not numbered. Later in this chapter, a New York criminal case with several headnotes will be used to illustrate their value in locating other cases that address the same legal issues.

Following the headnotes, the appearances by counsel are listed. This information can be very helpful to someone researching the same legal issues that are discussed in the case being read. Occasionally, an attorney will contact the counsel who appeared for the appellant or respondent in a published case to discuss those legal issues. As a professional courtesy, attorneys often share their knowledge and analysis with other attorneys who are working on similar cases. They might even provide a copy of their appellate briefs. That courtesy sometimes results in referrals that bring them new clients.

The Court's Opinion

Make no mistake about where the court's opinion actually starts. *Only the opinion itself may be quoted or relied upon as a primary source or mandatory authority.* In *Roozen*, the acting presiding justice of the court of appeal wrote the court's opinion. The opinion begins with the words that follow "STEPHENS, Acting Presiding Justice":

"Plaintiff filed a negligence action on November 18, 1974. It was transferred from...."

Nothing prior to those words may be quoted or relied upon as precedent.

Within the body of the opinion, bold numerals within brackets are usually found, identifying the starting point for the discussion of each legal issue decided by the court. These bold numerals correspond directly to the headnote numbers. Because *Roozen* had only a single legal issue in question, there was no need to include a "[1]" at the beginning of that discussion. Although that case involved only one issue, it is not unusual for cases to have ten or twenty legal issues, and an equal number of corresponding headnotes. *Grimshaw v. Ford Motor Company*, 119 Cal.App.3d 757, 174 Cal.Rptr. 348 (1997), which is excerpted in Chapter 6, has eighty-five headnotes! The corresponding bold numbers within the body of the opinion make it easy to locate quickly the court's discussion on issues identified in the headnotes.

FIGURE 8.11   *Roozen v. Ramstead*, p. 276

---

ments can be added (e. g. 12022, 12022.5, 12022.7) decidedly leaves the impression that not all felonies in which a firearm is used are to be enhanced.

This vexing inconsistency with respect to enhancements simply does not exist with regard to the 5 year lid on nonviolent felonies, contained in the fourth sentence of Penal Code § 1170.1(a). That sentence reads: "In no case shall the subordinate terms for such consecutive offenses which are not 'violent felonies' as defined in subdivision (c) of Section 667.5 exceed five years." Looking at the express language of the 5 year lid, it is apparent that the legislative intent was to exclude all "violent felonies" specified in section 667.5(c) from the operation of the 5 year lid. Section 667.-5(c)(8) refers to any felony with an enhancement under section 12022.5. This is precisely the kind of crime defendant pled guilty to 32 counts of.[1]

In spite of this express language, *People v. Childs*, 112 Cal.App.3d 374, 169 Cal.Rptr. 183 applied *Harvey* to this situation. We do not find the analysis in *Childs* persuasive.[2] We find no ambiguity nor any "close and subtle" question presented. We decline to interfere with the clear cut decision of the Legislature that the 5 year lid simply does not apply to those having been convicted of using a firearm in the conviction of a felony. To us, the legislative intent is clear. There is no reason for judicial interpretation and no possible excuse for applying the rationale of *Harvey* to this situation. It is obvious that the Legislature takes a dim view of dangerous, assaultive, armed criminals and has afforded trial courts the opportunity to imprison these individuals for prolonged periods of time for the protection of society. On the other hand and with a recognition of human frailty involved in offenses which do not necessarily endanger the victim physically, the Legislature has put a lid on time to be served. Thus, a defendant who passes 100 bad checks can only receive 5 years in consecutive sentences. An armed robber who endangers the lives of his victims by the use of a deadly weapon may receive as many consecutive sentences as the court finds reasonably required for the protection of innocent members of society. As we indicated earlier, it was clearly not the legislative intent that as a matter of state policy all armed robberies after the first 6 are free and unpunishable.

Judgment affirmed.

TAMURA and MORRIS, JJ., concur.

---

124 Cal.App.3d 332

Marie ROOZEN, Plaintiff and Appellant,

v.

Christopher RAMSTEAD and Robert Ramstead, Defendants and Respondents.

Civ. 60930.

Court of Appeal, Second District, Division 5.

Oct. 6, 1981.

Appeal was taken from a judgment of the Superior Court, Los Angeles County, Richard F. C. Hayden, J., dismissing negligence action. The Court of Appeal, Stephens, Acting P. J., held that negligence

---

1. According to Winston Churchill, a preposition is something one should never end a sentence with.

2. Neither did Division One of this court in *People v. Hernandez*, 120 Cal.App.3d 500, 175 Cal. Rptr. 22. Unfortunately, *Hernandez* reached the same conclusion that *Childs* did but under an even more troublesome analysis. It concluded that since the Supreme Court had denied a hearing in *Childs* and ordered *In re Rodriguez*, 114 Cal.App.3d 287, 171 Cal.Rptr. 832 and *People v. Harvey*, 114 Cal.App.3d 252, 170 Cal.Rptr. 577 (cases which went the other way) decertified, that somehow this created an ambiguity which they resolved in favor of the defendant. Then the Supreme Court granted a hearing in *Hernandez*. The remaining contestants are *Childs* and this court.

We assume, as did the Court of Appeal in *Hernandez*, that Rule of Court 977, prohibiting the citation of an unpublished opinion, does not bar our mentioning these opinions in this context.

West's California Reporter, Copyright by West Group. Reprinted by permission.

In the *Roozen* decision reprinted above (see *Figure 8.11*), the reader will find the inverted "T" symbol appearing in the left margin. For each symbol in the margin, there is a corresponding symbol in the body of the text. The marks in the margin are accompanied by a number. For example, in *Figure 8.10* on page 309, just before the *Roozen* opinion begins with the identity of Justice Stephens as its author, the marginal inverted "T" is accompanied by the number "333." That means that the words following the inverted "T" in the text appeared on page 333 in the official reporter. Oftentimes, the inverted "T" is embedded in the middle of a line, as can be seen in the first column on page 276 from the *California Reporter* (*Figure 8.9* on page 308). That indicates exactly where the page break occurred in the official reporter. The page break notations in an unofficial reporter can be used by the researcher to provide a correct official citation for any quotation.

At the very end of its opinion, the court states its **disposition** of the case. As mentioned in Chapter 4, the decision of the lower court might be affirmed (i.e., held valid), reversed, or both affirmed in part and reversed in part. Alternatively, the decision of the lower court might be **modified** by the appellate decision. The appellate court often remands (i.e., sends back) a case to the lower court for further proceedings in conformity with the appellate court's decision. Following the court's disposition of the case, the names of justices concurring in and/or dissenting from the opinion of the court will be listed.

> The court's final resolution of a controversy before it is known as the **disposition** of that controversy.

> An appellate court might **modify** the disposition of a case decided by a lower court without reversing its holdings on the legal issues before it.

In the *Roozen* case, the court of appeal's three justices reached a unanimous decision. This is indicated by this statement at the end of the court's opinion:

"ASHBY and HASTINGS, J.J., concur."

The reader might wonder why Justice Ashby's first and middle initials are omitted, whereas those of Justice Hastings appear to be given. But actually, Justice Hastings' initials are not necessarily "J.J." The latter is, instead, a notation standing for "Justices [of the court]." If Hastings had been the only justice to concur in the opinion written by Justice Stephens, the statement would have been:

"HASTINGS, J., concurs."

It is not unusual for a justice to write a separate concurring opinion in which she agrees with the result of the court's opinion but gives different or additional reasoning for reaching that result. It is common also for a justice to write a dissenting opinion in which she disagrees with both the result and the reasoning of the court's opinion. Note an important reminder: Although concurring and dissenting opinions may be cited or quoted for *persuasive* argument, they are never a primary source or mandatory authority. Only the court's majority opinion can be mandatory authority. If concurring or dissenting opinions are ever referred to, they *always* must be identified as such to avoid misleading the reader.

FOLLOWING THE PAPER CHASE

Virtually all court opinions cite legal authority to support their own legal conclusions. Most often, those citations are to prior case law, although statutes and other legal authorities are commonly cited, as well. Citations to earlier cases as precedents illustrate the very important doctrine of **stare decisis** ("let the decision stand"), under which courts do not casually disturb well-settled law but apply it to later cases presenting similar facts and issues.

> **Stare decisis** is the doctrine of following established case law (i.e., precedent) in deciding other cases that later come before the courts.

Court opinions always cite clear precedents when they are available. If no precedent directly on point can be found, the opinion usually cites decisions on related issues and then draws analogies to reach a decision on the particular legal issue before it. At times, the courts must rely upon secondary sources for

FIGURE 8.12   Headnote in *Roozen v. Ramstead*

---

124 Cal.App.3d 305   HERITAGE PUB. CO. v. CUMMINS   277
Cite as, App., 177 Cal.Rptr. 277

action, which was not brought to trial within five years after it was filed, was properly dismissed, notwithstanding that before expiration of the five-year limitation the parties orally agreed to submit the case to arbitration, where the limitation expired prior to plaintiff's execution of a stipulation to that effect and submission of the stipulation to defendants.

Judgment affirmed.

Pretrial Procedure ⬅ 590

Negligence action, which was not brought to trial within five years after it was filed, was properly dismissed, notwithstanding that before expiration of the five-year limitation the parties agreed orally to submit the case to arbitration, where the limitation expired prior to plaintiff's execution of a stipulation to that effect and submission of the stipulation to defendants. West's Ann.Code Civ.Proc. § 583.

Robert S. Gibbs, Westake Village, for plaintiff and appellant.

John F. Cobb and James H. Baggaley, Los Angeles, for defendants and respondents.

⌐233 ⌐STEPHENS, Acting Presiding Justice.

Plaintiff filed a negligence action on November 18, 1974. It was transferred from the municipal court to the superior court on March 23, 1976. In October, 1979 plaintiff and defendants discussed submission of the case to arbitration and orally agreed to do so. Plaintiff signed a stipulation to that effect on December 17, 1979, but defendants at no time signed. The five-year limitation under Code of Civil Procedure section 583 had run prior to the execution of the stipulation by plaintiff and its submission to defendants.

The court concluded there was no reason, estoppel or otherwise, not to grant the motion for dismissal in accordance with section 583. We concur, there being no authority to justify a different result.

⌐234 ⌐Code of Civil Procedure, section 583, subdivision (b), provides: "Any action heretofore or hereafter commenced shall be dismissed by the court in which the same shall have been commenced or to which it may be transferred on motion of the defendant, after due notice to plaintiff or by the court upon its own motion, unless such action is brought to trial within five years after the plaintiff has filed his action, except where the parties have filed a stipulation in writing that the time may be extended."

Code of Civil Procedure section 1141.17 states:

"Submission of an action to arbitration pursuant to this chapter shall not toll the running of the time periods contained in Section 583 as to actions filed on or after the operative date of this chapter. Submission to arbitration pursuant to a court order within six months of the expiration of the statutory period shall toll the running of such period until the filing of an arbitration award."

The trial court was correct in holding that the delay herein involved was not occasioned by defendant.

Judgment affirmed.

ASHBY and HASTINGS, JJ., concur.

---

124 Cal.App.3d 305
⌐HERITAGE PUBLISHING COMPANY, a California Corporation, Plaintiff and Respondent,

v.

Joseph J. CUMMINS, et al., Defendants and Appellants.

Civ. 60302.

Court of Appeal, Second District, Division 3.

Oct. 6, 1981.

As Modified on Denial of Rehearing Nov. 4, 1981.

Hearing Denied Dec. 30, 1981.

Libel action was brought by a Jewish weekly newspaper against another Jewish

---

West's California Reporter, Copyright by West Group. Reprinted by permission.

guidance on a particular issue. When a court explicitly adopts a legal principle found in a secondary source, that has the effect of declaring that principle to be the common law of that jurisdiction. Thereafter, that case can be cited as primary authority for that principle.

The "paper chase" is the process of following clues found in annotated codes, digests, court opinions, and other sources until the researcher has either found authority that can be cited or determined that the chase is no longer worth the effort. Those "clues" are usually citations to case law on the same or related issues. If the researcher begins with a relevant case—say, *ABC v. XYZ,*—he should also look at all cases *cited* in *ABC v. XYZ* that appear relevant to the issue being researched.

USING TREATISES

Over time, a particular treatise might be cited by the courts with increasing frequency and thereby gain a certain status for its persuasive authority. Examples include *McCormick on Evidence* and *Prosser and Keeton on the Law of Torts.* Of particular value is a recognized treatise on the law of one's own jurisdiction (e.g., Witkin's *California Evidence*).

Courts often cite the *Restatements of the Law* published by the American Law Institute. The *Restatements* comprise dozens of volumes that have attempted to unofficially "codify" the common law of the United States in all major areas of the law. They have been written by distinguished judges, law professors, and attorneys, and therefore they have been given great weight by the courts. The *Restatements* are considered to be highly persuasive authority.

EVALUATING LARGE NUMBERS OF POTENTIALLY USEFUL CASES

When a large number of cases must be reviewed, the paralegal should start with those of her own jurisdiction. Those should then be divided into groups: opinions of the highest appellate court, followed by opinions of each appellate level below. Each group should then be listed chronologically, beginning with the most recent cases. The reason for organizing the citations in this manner is to look for the *most recent* court decisions at the *highest appellate level.* In other words, the highest appellate court cases, if any, will be reviewed in reverse chronological order, beginning with the most recent. Then, the opinions of the next lower appellate level are reviewed in the same way, and so on.

As this process continues, the researcher never knows when—or even if—significant cases will be found. When faced with far more cases than can be read, it is essential that one sort, or identify, those cases according to their apparent value. A case that appears to be a strong candidate can be read immediately. Of course, some "strong candidates" might turn out to be of little use when they have been read. Any case that clearly has no value can be crossed off the list. Cases that appear to be of uncertain value (based upon the summary and headnotes) can be marked with a question mark. If the strong candidates do not provide the answer, the paralegal can then read the cases that appeared somewhat less promising. In effect, this is a method for prioritizing the use of valuable research time.

USING CASE CITATORS

For obvious reasons, no attorney wants to rely upon a case that is no longer good law—or, worse yet, cite that case to a court. Therefore, the attorney's first concern is whether the case is still good law—or has been overruled or re-

> **Practice Tip**
>
> Although law review articles can be very persuasive secondary sources, that is true only if they are authored by a distinguished jurist (e.g., perhaps a law school professor or a judge). Because law reviews publish many articles written by law students, the legal assistant must use caution when citing an article from a law review as persuasive authority.

versed. A case is overruled when the *same* court adopts a contrary rule of law in a later case. A case is reversed when a *higher* court holds that a lower court's ruling in that case was in error. The U.S. Supreme Court only occasionally *overrules* its own prior decisions, but it frequently *reverses* the decisions of lower courts. Other state and federal appellate courts can overrule their own decisions and reverse those of lower courts, as well.

One can learn whether a case has been reversed or overruled by using a citator. A **citator** provides citations to subsequent cases or publications that have cited or ruled upon the case in question. If the case has been overruled or reversed, the citator will indicate that fact by a notation (together with the citation to the court opinion in which that overruling or reversal occurred).

The most commonly used print citator is a publication called *Shepard's Citations*. Shepard's/McGraw-Hill, Inc. publishes a set of these volumes for every official reporter and for all unofficial reporters of major importance. A variety of notations are used to provide information about a given case and about later cases that have cited it. In addition to the print volumes, *Shepard's Citations* are available on computer, using the LEXIS-NEXIS database. These and several other on-line citators are discussed in Chapter 9.

Attorneys and paralegals use *Shepard's Citations* to determine whether a given case is still good law, or not. This is such an integral part of legal research that the legal profession has transformed the publication's very name into a verb: "to Shepardize." When one **Shepardizes** a case, she is looking for other useful cases and also checking to make sure that the case being Shepardized has not been overturned by a higher court. One Shepardizes a case by checking its official or unofficial citation in *Shepard's Citations*.

A second reason for Shepardizing is to locate other cases that discuss the same legal issues. Shepardizing the headnote numbers of a case can lead to other useful cases, and it is an important part of following the paper trail of legal authority. The mechanics of using *Shepard's* for this purpose will be illustrated below.

In addition to subsequent court cases, *Shepard's* lists citations to legal periodicals that have mentioned the case in question. Because legal periodicals often publish long, detailed, and scholarly articles on important legal issues, *Shepard's* can lead the paralegal to a veritable goldmine of legal analysis and case citations on the question at hand.

Using *Shepard's Citations*

This chapter introduces the print version of *Shepard's Citations*, which is found in law libraries. A New York state criminal case, *People v. Rossey*, 89 N.Y.2d 970, 678 N.E.2d 473 (N.Y. Ct. App. 1997), will serve as an exemplar for this discussion.

The appellant, Rossey, was convicted of second-degree murder in a trial before the Supreme Court for Queens County, New York. On appeal to the appellate division of the supreme court, the conviction was reversed. The State of New York appealed that reversal to the New York Court of Appeals. The court of appeals then reversed the appellate division—in effect, "reversing the reversal" by the lower court—and remitted the case to the appellate division for further consideration. The opinion of the court of appeals appears in *Figure 8.13*.

For this discussion of Shepardizing, assume that the legal issue of interest is identified in headnote number 2 in *Rossey*: whether evidence of the kind heard in *Rossey* is sufficient to support a conviction for second-degree murder. The court of appeals held that it was sufficient.

The opinion of the court of appeals in the *Rossey* case appears in three reporters: the official reporter, *New York Reports, Second Series*; West's *New York Supplement, Second Series*; and West's *North Eastern Reporter, Second Series*. The

---

Practice Tip

*Although a case might not have been overruled or reversed, it still should not be cited as precedent if a rehearing or hearing on appeal has been granted and is still pending. A **rehearing** is a second chance before the same court that has already decided the case; a **hearing on appeal** is one held before a higher court. If either type of hearing has been granted, Shepard's will indicate that fact by notation.*

A **citator** provides citations to subsequent cases or publications that have cited the case in question.

To **Shepardize** a case, the legal researcher uses *Shepard's Citations* to determine whether the court's decision in that case is still valid or whether it has been reversed or overruled. *Shepard's Citations* also identify later cases that mention the case being Shepardized.

A **rehearing** occurs when a court permits new arguments and reconsiders its own decision in that case.

A **hearing on appeal** occurs when an appellate court agrees to review a lower court decision.

FIGURE 8.13 The Court's Opinion in *People v. Rossey*

PEOPLE v. ROSSEY
Cite as 678 N.E.2d 473 (N.Y. 1997)

89 N.Y.2d 970

₉₇₀The PEOPLE of the State of New York, Appellant,

v.

Jose ROSSEY, Respondent.

Court of Appeals of New York.

Feb. 13, 1997.

Defendant was convicted in the Supreme Court, Queens County, Demakos, J., of second-degree murder, and criminal possession of weapon in second and third degree, and he appealed. The Supreme Court, Appellate Division, 222 A.D.2d 710, 635 N.Y.S.2d 970, reversed. People appealed. The Court of Appeals held that sufficient evidence supported determination that defendant had intent to kill victim, who was shot by defendant's companion.

Reversed and remitted.

1. Criminal Law ⇐1144.13(3), 1159.2(7), 1159.6

Standard of appellate review in determining whether evidence before jury was legally sufficient to support finding of guilt is whether evidence, viewed in light most favorable to People, could lead rational trier of fact to conclude that elements of crime had been proven beyond reasonable doubt; test is same for both direct and circumstantial evidence.

2. Homicide ⇐234(5)

Determination that defendant had intent to kill victim, who was shot by defendant's companion, as required for conviction for second-degree murder, was supported by evidence that defendant drove companion and another person to area of crime, drove around apparently looking for victim, engaged victim in heated verbal conversation on street, turned and waved his arms as though giving signal, at which point companion got out of car and killed victim, and then drove companion away from crime scene. McKinney's Penal Law § 125.25, subd. 1.

₉₇₁Richard A. Brown, District Attorney of Queens County, Kew Gardens (Johnnette Traill and John M. Castellano, of counsel), for appellant.

Carlos G. Manalansan and Daniel L. Greenberg, New York City, for respondent.

OPINION OF THE COURT

MEMORANDUM.

The order of the Appellate Division should be reversed and the case remitted to that Court for consideration of the facts and other issues raised but not considered on the appeal to that Court.

Defendant was convicted of murder in the second degree (Penal Law § 125.25[1]) and criminal possession of a weapon in the second and third degrees (Penal Law § 265.02[4]; § 265.03). The Appellate Division reversed the conviction and dismissed the indictment, concluding that the evidence "when viewed in the light most favorable to the People, fails to establish beyond a reasonable doubt that the defendant acted in concert with Ocasio to intentionally cause Guerra's death" (222 A.D.2d 710, 712, 635 N.Y.S.2d 970). The Court further noted that the evidence did not prove beyond a reasonable doubt or to a moral certainty that the defendant shared the intent to kill Guerra and that the evidence does not exclude the " 'fair inference' " that the defendant did not share in Ocasio's intention to kill Guerra (*People v. Rossey, supra*, at 711, 635 N.Y.S.2d 970). This standard was erroneous.

[1] Generally, including a circumstantial evidence case, "the standard of [appellate] review in determining whether the evidence before the jury was legally sufficient to support a finding of guilt beyond a reasonable doubt is whether the evidence, viewed in the light most favorable to the People, could lead a rational trier of fact to conclude that the elements of the crime had been proven beyond a reasonable doubt" (*People v. Cabey*, 85 N.Y.2d 417, 420, 626 N.Y.S.2d 20, 649 N.E.2d 1164; see also, *People v. Norman*, 85 N.Y.2d 609, 620, 627 N.Y.S.2d 302, 650 N.E.2d 1303). Although the evidence that defendant shared Ocasio's intention to kill

FIGURE 8.13 (continued)

474 N.Y. 678 NORTH EASTERN REPORTER, 2d SERIES

was circumstantial, the test for appellate review on the issue of the legal sufficiency of the evidence is |₃₇₂the same for both direct and circumstantial evidence (*People v. Cabey, supra,* at 421, 626 N.Y.S.2d 20, 649 N.E.2d 1164).

[2] Viewed in a light most favorable to the People, the evidence indicated that the defendant drove the actual shooter and another person to the area of the crime, drove around apparently looking for the victim, engaged the victim in a heated verbal conversation on the street, and turned and waved his arms as though giving a signal. At that point the shooter got out of the car and killed the victim. The defendant then drove the shooter away from the crime scene. This evidence allows a rational trier of facts to conclude that the defendant was acting in concert with the shooter. Therefore, under the correct appellate standard of review, the evidence is legally sufficient to sustain the conviction beyond a reasonable doubt.

KAYE, C.J., and BELLACOSA, SMITH, LEVINE, CIPARICK and WESLEY, JJ., concur.

TITONE, J., taking no part.

Order reversed, etc.

---

89 N.Y.2d 506

|₅₀₆In the Matter of NEW YORK COUNTY DES LITIGATION.

Susan WETHERILL, Respondent,

v.

ELI LILLY & COMPANY et al., Defendants,

and

Emons Industries, Inc., Appellant.

Court of Appeals of New York.

Feb. 11, 1997.

Plaintiff brought action against manufacturers of drug diethylstilbestrol (DES) to recover damages for personal injuries suffered as result of in utero exposure to DES which her mother had ingested. The Supreme Court, New York County, Gammerman, J., granted defendants' motions for summary judgment, dismissing complaint as time barred. Plaintiff appealed, and the Supreme Court, Appellate Division, reversed, 225 A.D.2d 372, 639 N.Y.S.2d 40. After leave to appeal was granted, the Supreme Court, Titone, J., held that discovery of the injury occurs under toxic tort statute of limitations when injured party discovers primary physical condition on which claim is based.

Reversed.

Smith, J., dissented and filed opinion.

1. Limitation of Actions ⚖=95(5)

"Discovery of the injury" occurs for purposes of toxic tort statute of limitations, and time for bringing action begins to run, when injured party discovers primary physical condition on which claim is based, and not at time of more complex discovery of both condition and nonorganic etiology of that condition; abrogating *Cochrane v. Owens–Corning Fiberglas Corp.,* 219 A.D.2d 557, 631 N.Y.S.2d 358, and *Scherrer v. Time Equities,* 218 A.D.2d 116, 634 N.Y.S.2d 680. McKinney's CPLR 214–c.

See publication Words and Phrases for other judicial constructions and definitions.

2. Limitation of Actions ⚖=95(5)

For all intents and purposes, discovery that plaintiff's symptoms were attributable to injury inflicted by outside force is the same as "discovery of the cause of the injury" within meaning of toxic tort statute of limitations. McKinney's CPLR 214–c.

3. Limitation of Actions ⚖=95(5)

Toxic tort statute of limitations was enacted to overcome effect of line of decisions holding that toxic tort claims accrue upon "impact" or exposure even though resulting illness may not be manifested for a long time

---

West's North Eastern Reporter, Copyright by West Group. Reprinted by permission.

Practice Tip

Shepard's Citations uses the following symbols to indicate the history of the case being Shepardized:

a	affirmed
cc	connected case
D	appeal dismissed
m	modified
r	reversed
s	same case, different court or proceeding
S	substitution of new opinion
v	vacated
*	certiorari or appeal denied or dismissed
US cert den	certiorari denied by U.S. Supreme Court
US cert dis	certiorari dismissed by U.S. Supreme Court
US reh den	rehearing denied by U.S. Supreme Court
US reh dis	rehearing dismissed by U.S. Supreme Court

The symbols that indicate the treatment in a later court opinion of the case being Shepardized are listed below:

c	criticized
d	distinguished
e	explained
f	followed
h	harmonized
j	mentioned in dissenting opinion
L	limited holding to precise issues of that case
o	overruled
p	parallel in facts and issues to case at hand
q	questioned

These symbols are listed and explained in the frontmatter of each volume of *Shepard's Citations.*

FIGURE 8.14 Page 580 from *Shepard's Citations for West's Northeastern Reporter, 2d Series*

Shepard's Northeastern Citations, Vol. II, Supplement 1995–1999, Copyright 1999 by Shepard's Company. Reproduced by permission of Shepard's. Further reproduction of any kind is strictly prohibited

latter two reporters are unofficial reporters. One can Shepardize the court of appeals' decision using the citation for any one of these reporters. The following discussion will use the citation for West's *North Eastern Reporter* to illustrate the Shepardizing process.

In *Figure 8.14*, the reader will see page 580 reprinted from *Shepard's Citations for the Northeastern Reporter, 2d Series.* Before using any page in *Shepard's*, it is

FIGURE 8.15 Excerpt from *Shepard's Citations* for 678 N.E.2d 473

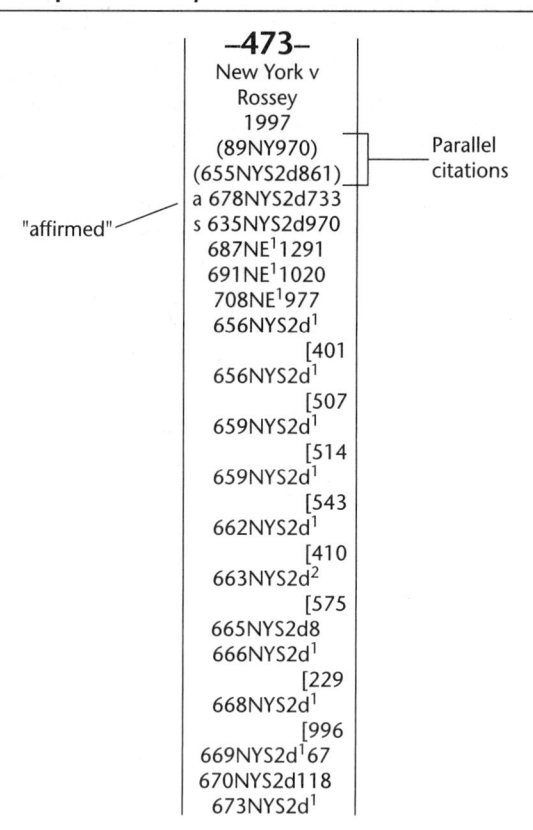

```
                    –473–
                  New York v
                    Rossey
                     1997
                  (89NY970)      ⎤ Parallel
                 (655NYS2d861)   ⎦ citations
  "affirmed"    a 678NYS2d733
                s 635NYS2d970
                  687NE¹1291
                  691NE¹1020
                  708NE¹977
                  656NYS2d¹
                    [401
                  656NYS2d¹
                    [507
                  659NYS2d¹
                    [514
                  659NYS2d¹
                    [543
                  662NYS2d¹
                    [410
                  663NYS2d²
                    [575
                  665NYS2d8
                  666NYS2d¹
                    [229
                  668NYS2d¹
                    [996
                  669NYS2d¹67
                  670NYS2d118
                  673NYS2d¹
```

Shepard's Northeastern Citations, Vol. II, Supplement 1995–1999, Copyright 1999 by Shepard's Company. Reproduced by permission of Shepard's. Further reproduction of any kind is strictly prohibited

vitally important to check the reporter name and the volume number at the top of that page. At the top of page 580 from *Shepard's*, one finds the full name of the reporter in which *People v. Rossey* appears in bold ("**Northeastern Reporter, 2d Series**"). Note that *Shepard's* uses "Northeastern" as one word, although the title of the West Group reporter is actually *North Eastern Reports, Second Series*.

Having confirmed that this volume of *Shepard's* is for the correct reporter, the next step is to check the volume number that appears at the top of the page. It is possible to make a grievous error, because another volume of the *North Eastern Reporter, 2d Series*, might also have a case beginning at page 473. This danger becomes more acute when checking the paperback supplements to *Shepard's*, as will be explained below.

Now that the legal assistant has confirmed that she is on the right page of *Shepard's* for the citation to *People v. Rossey*, she will find the pertinent citations listed by the beginning page numbers for each case. Because the *Rossey* case is published at 678 N.E.2d 473, the citations appear immediately below "**-473-**" printed in bold. (See *Figure 8.15*).

A **parallel citation** (i.e., a citation for the identical court opinion in *People v. Rossey*, but published in a different reporter) is always listed first, and in parentheses. Thus, the first citation listed is for 89 N.Y.2d 970, the citation for *People v. Rossey* in the official reporter, *New York Reports, 2d Series*. If a case is published in three reporters, there will be two parallel citations in parentheses, one below the other. Notice that, for space reasons, *Shepard's* does not use the approved abbreviations for reporter names, which must be used when filing papers with the court.

Following the two parallel citations in parentheses, the next entry—"a 678NYS2d733"—is a citation to 678 N.Y.S.2d 733. The lowercase "a" that precedes the volume number indicates that the Appellate Division of the Supreme

A **parallel citation** is a citation to the same court opinion in another case reporter.

Court for Queens County subsequently affirmed the trial court's judgment in *Rossey*, following the holding in the court of appeals opinion.

Headnote numbers can be very useful for finding other cases on the same or related issues, because headnote numbers often appear in *Shepard's Citations*. For example, if headnote number two in *Rossey* identifies the legal issue in question, the legal assistant can check *Shepard's* to see if other cases have cited the opinion in *Rossey* on that same issue.

Glancing down the list of citations under "-**473**-" in *Shepard's* (see *Figure 8.16*), the legal assistant will find this entry: 663NYS2d^{2}575. The superscript numeral "2" that precedes the page number identifies the headnote in *Rossey* for which another court has cited that case. Note that the superscript numeral identifies the headnote number for that legal issue in *Rossey*—not the headnote number in the citing court's opinion. If the issue of interest were found in headnote number one in *Rossey*, there would be many cases citing *Rossey* on that point. This example illustrates one of the most valuable features of *Shepard's Citations*: The researcher can quickly locate other cases that address the legal issue at hand.

FIGURE 8.16 *Shepard's Citations* **for 678 N.E.2d 473**

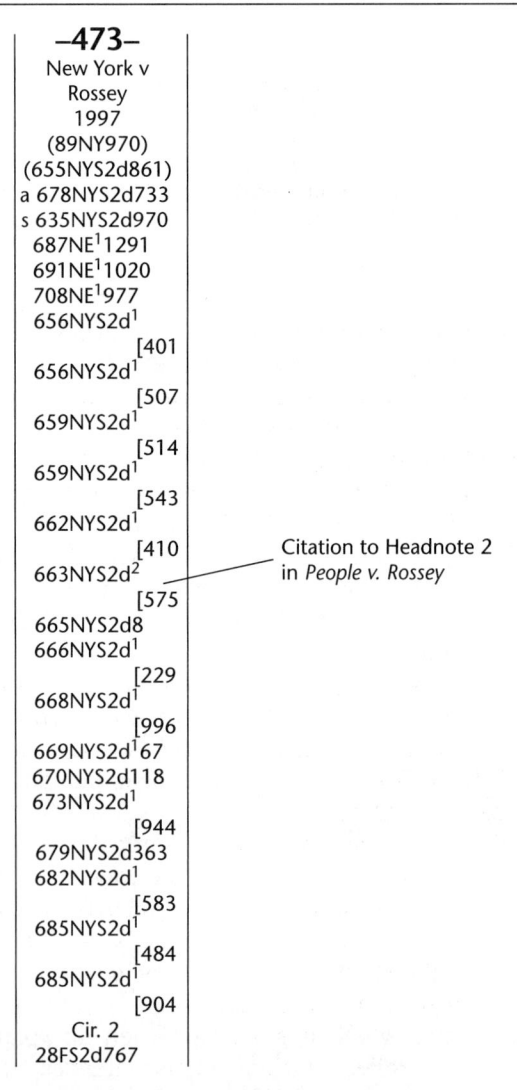

```
        -473-
      New York v
        Rossey
         1997
       (89NY970)
     (655NYS2d861)
    a 678NYS2d733
    s 635NYS2d970
      687NE¹1291
      691NE¹1020
      708NE¹977
      656NYS2d¹
              [401
      656NYS2d¹
              [507
      659NYS2d¹
              [514
      659NYS2d¹
              [543
      662NYS2d¹
              [410
      663NYS2d²         ——— Citation to Headnote 2
              [575         in People v. Rossey
      665NYS2d8
      666NYS2d¹
              [229
      668NYS2d¹
              [996
      669NYS2d¹67
      670NYS2d118
      673NYS2d¹
              [944
      679NYS2d363
      682NYS2d¹
              [583
      685NYS2d¹
              [484
      685NYS2d¹
              [904
        Cir. 2
      28FS2d767
```

Shepard's Northeastern Citations, Vol. II, Supplement 1995–1999, Copyright 1999 by Shepard's Company. Reproduced by permission of Shepard's. Further reproduction of any kind is strictly prohibited

CHAPTER 8 — Legal Analysis, Research, and Writing

If the United States Supreme Court had cited *People v. Rossey* in any opinion, a citation to that U.S. Supreme Court opinion would immediately follow the parallel citation, before any other citations to state court cases. As of the publication date for our sample page from *Shepard's Citations*, the researcher knows that the U.S. Supreme Court had not cited *Rossey*, because a citation to a New York court is the first entry following the parallel citations in parentheses.

But, on the same page from *Shepard's*, there is a case that *has* been acted upon by the U.S. Supreme Court. (See *Figure 8.17*.) The citations for 678 N.E.2d 482 appear under "**-482-**" in the far right column on page 580 of *Shepard's*. Following the parallel citations, there are three citations to the official and unofficial reporters for the U.S. Supreme Court. Each of these citations is preceded by the notation "US cert den"—indicating that the U.S. Supreme Court denied the petition for review in *New York v. Vasquez*, 678 N.E.2d 482 (N.Y. Ct. App. 1997). "522US846" refers to the official Supreme Court reporter, *United States Reports*. The next citation is to *United States Supreme Court Reports, Lawyers' Edition, Second Series*, an unofficial reporter. "118SC131" refers to West's *Supreme Court Reporter*, also an unofficial reporter.

FIGURE 8.17 Excerpt from *Shepard's Citations* for 678 N.E.2d 482

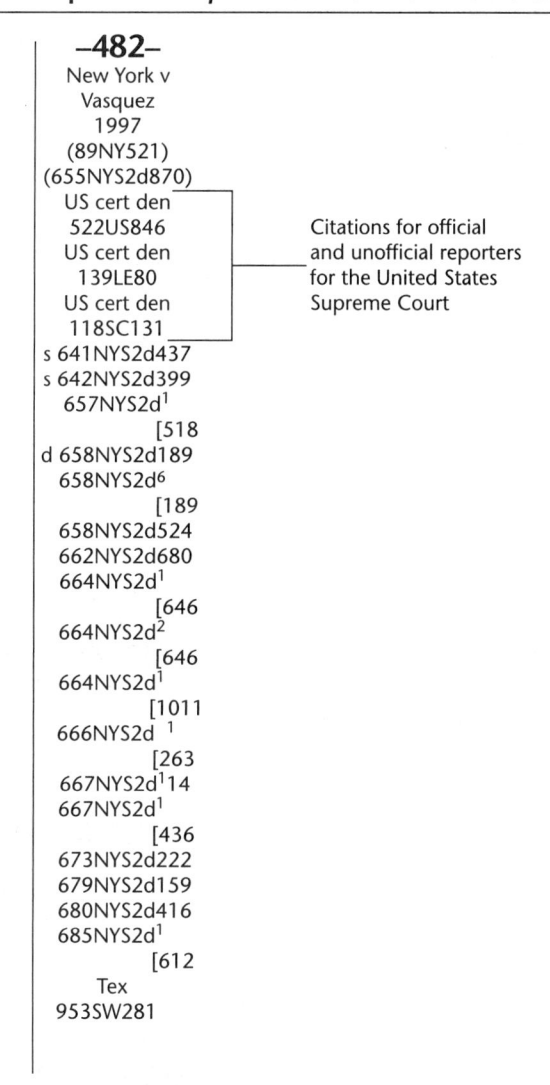

```
            -482-
         New York v
           Vasquez
             1997
          (89NY521)
        (655NYS2d870)
         US cert den   ┐
         522US846      │
         US cert den   │  Citations for official
         139LE80       ├─ and unofficial reporters
         US cert den   │  for the United States
         118SC131      ┘  Supreme Court
       s 641NYS2d437
       s 642NYS2d399
         657NYS2d¹
              [518
       d 658NYS2d189
         658NYS2d⁶
              [189
         658NYS2d524
         662NYS2d680
         664NYS2d¹
              [646
         664NYS2d²
              [646
         664NYS2d¹
              [1011
         666NYS2d ¹
              [263
         667NYS2d¹14
         667NYS2d¹
              [436
         673NYS2d222
         679NYS2d159
         680NYS2d416
         685NYS2d¹
              [612
            Tex
         953SW281
```

Shepard's Northeastern Citations, Vol. II, Supplement 1995–1999, Copyright 1999 by Shepard's Company. Reproduced by permission of Shepard's. Further reproduction of any kind is strictly prohibited

Supplements *to Shepard's Citations*

There is an additional step in Shepardizing *People v. Rossey*. The sample page in *Figure 8.14* was taken from the hardbound volume of *Shepard's Citations*, published in 1999. How can the researcher learn what has happened since 1999? Is it possible that *Rossey* has been reversed or overruled since the hardbound volume was published? Are there additional recent cases that have cited *Rossey*?

The answers to these questions lie in the paperback supplements to the bound volumes of *Shepard's* (and, occasionally, in hardbound supplements to the original bound volumes). These supplements are published as frequently as every month for some reporters, but less often for others. To clarify your understanding of this system of supplements, imagine a new hardbound volume of *Shepard's Citations for the Northeastern Reporter, 2d Series* that was typeset this morning. It would contain the entire accumulation of citations to all court opinions published in *West's North Eastern Reporter, 2d Series*. But, within a month, additional new court opinions would be released that cite some of the cases already included in the brand new volume of *Shepard's*. Because those most recent citations to the *North Eastern Reporter, 2d Series*, cannot be found in the hardbound volume, *Shepard's* will publish a thin white paper supplement.

Each month, that white supplement grows thicker. Whenever a new white supplement comes out, the prior white supplement is discarded. When the white supplement becomes about one-eighth-inch thick, *Shepard's* will change the supplement cover from white to red. That red supplement will not be republished every month, so that the law library must now keep it for some time. But the month after that red paperback supplement is published, a new white supplement will appear containing all citations *subsequent to* the recent red supplement.

This process continues. Eventually, the red supplement becomes thick (a half inch or more). At that point, it is republished in a yellow/ochre cover. At some point, the *Shepard's* series will include a yellow/ochre supplement containing older citations, plus a red supplement containing newer citations and a thin white supplement containing the most recent citations—all supplementing the original bound volume.

Shepardizing is not complete until all current supplements have been checked. The most recent supplement will list on its cover the bound volumes and paper supplements that constitute a complete set of *Shepard's* for that reporter. The possibility of the most recent supplement's being misplaced presents a small risk that the paralegal will be unable to do a complete Shepardization: The supplements found—usually those in yellow and red covers—appear to be up-to-date, so that the paralegal will not realize that a new white supplement has been published and should be checked. That is one of the attractions of using LEXIS-NEXIS for Shepardizing, because that computer database displays all *Shepard's* volumes and supplements in a contiguous format.

A CLOSER LOOK AT A CASE THAT HAS BEEN REVERSED OR OVERRULED

The usual significance of reversing or overruling a case is that it is no longer a valid statement of the law and may not be:

- relied upon as precedent, or
- cited as authority for the legal principle(s) stated in the opinion.

But, sometimes it is not that simple. Many court opinions decide more than a single legal issue. Each discrete legal issue will be identified in a separate headnote—which might number one, or in the dozens, in any single case. Where an opinion has stated

---

Practice Tip

Every paralegal must be able to competently Shepardize a case, and "competently" means zero errors. Carelessness in Shepardizing can be potentially devastating: It could lose a client's case, and it could cost a paralegal his job. Fortunately, Shepardizing is not difficult—in fact, it is quite easy once one has learned the ropes. The key is concentration and attention to detail: The legal assistant must be meticulous when Shepardizing case law.

FIGURE 8.18 Checklist for Shepardizing

- Identify the reporter (e.g., West's *California Reporter*) which included the opinion we are Shepardizing, *Roozen v. Ramstead*, 177 Cal.Rptr. 276 (1981).
- Select the earliest volume of *Shepard's Citations* for that reporter.
- In *Shepard's,* find the volume number (and series) of that reporter where the opinion appears (e.g., **177**).
- On the page in *Shepard's,* find the beginning page number for that opinion (e.g., -**276**-) in the reporter we have used.
- Verify again that the page in *Shepard's* displays the correct reporter, volume number and series for the case we are Shepardizing.
- Identify the parallel citation in parentheses; make a note of it for citation purposes.
- Carefully scan all citations listed in *Shepard's* for that case, noting especially any which are preceded by **r** (for reversed) or **o** (for overruled); *make a note of those citations.*
- Note any citations preceded by **d** (for distinguished), **e** (for explained) or **f** (for followed).
- If the case being Shepardized has not been overruled or reversed, make a photocopy of the page in *Shepard's* for further research.
- Highlight any citations to a headnote number (from the original case) which is of interest.
- Repeat the above steps in the white, red and ochre supplements to the hardbound volume.
- Check the cover of the most recent supplement to ensure that a complete set is available and has been reviewed.

the law on multiple issues, it might be reversed or overruled on one or more of those issues, but it might be affirmed on other issues. That is why one sometimes comes across the statement "reversed on other grounds" when a case has been cited as valid authority in a later court opinion. Consequently, one should never assume that a reversed or overruled decision has no value whatsoever. One must read the appellate opinion (which reversed or overruled) in order to determine whether the original decision might still be valid for the particular issue in question. If the case has been reversed (or overruled) on any issue, *Shepard's* will indicate that fact by showing an **r** or **o** in boldface preceding a citation to the case in which that occurred. *Figure 8.18* provides a checklist for Shepardizing the print editions of *Shepard's Citations*.

SECTION 3. LEGAL WRITING

If popular perceptions are to be believed, the writing of all doctors is unreadable and the writing of all lawyers is incomprehensible. Of course, these are unfair stereotypes, for there are many doctors with good penmanship and lawyers who write with clarity. That said, however, there has been a continuing problem with legal writing that sometimes is dense and difficult to understand. The brief commentaries by Judge Swearinger and Professor Benson quoted in the opening scenario for this chapter are not unusual observations.

Surprisingly, the most prevalent problem in legal writing is not the use of legal jargon—although that is problematic enough—but a disregard for the ordinary rules of good writing. Some judges, lawyers, and legal assistants tend to make the same mistakes as other inept writers, and then they compound that problem by using legalese. Most obscure and ineffective legal writing results from the following:

- poor organization
- excessive use of the passive voice
- unnecessary and ineffective compound sentences
- excess verbiage
- inadequate editing and revision

The result is writing that is difficult to follow and understand. Throw in an arcane legal term ("connubial state") where simple English ("marital relationship") would do, and one quickly reaches the level of incomprehensibility for which the legal profession is too often criticized:

> "There can be no great uncertainty that plaintiff's claim has validity, since his rights within the connubial state are indisputably established under the common law as being those which are customary and usual for such persons in such circumstances."

See how easy it is to be obscure? The same argument certainly could be made more clearly—perhaps like this:

> "There is no question that the plaintiff has a valid claim, because his marital rights are well established under common law."

CLEAR LEGAL WRITING: *NOT* AN OXYMORON

The beginning of clear writing is good organization, and the beginning of good organization is knowing what one is trying to accomplish. Is the purpose just to convey the facts, or is the writer trying to persuade? Is the intended audience a court, an attorney, the client, or some other party? Is the document one that might affect the legal rights of a client—a contract or pleading, for example—or is it routine correspondence? Once the objective is clear, the next step is the opening. In journalism, the opening is the headline or title of an article. In legal writing, the opening might be the heading for a section within a pleading, or it might be the opening paragraph of a memorandum. In either case, the opening should hook the reader's interest and communicate the purpose of the document. Countless pleadings and letters have been doomed to insignificance by a meandering, unfocused opening.

Assume for the moment that a paralegal is drafting a memorandum to the court, which means that she is trying to persuade the court. With her opening already decided upon, she should then outline the steps by which she will lead the reader (i.e., the judge) to the desired conclusion. Her outline is like a road map. If the opening has told the judge that evidence of cocaine use by the pilot should be excluded from the trial, how can she get the judge to agree? A simple outline of the relevant facts and the legal arguments should be constructed before another paragraph is written.

Each major heading in the outline should become either an entire section or a paragraph—the decision will depend upon the complexity and total length of the memorandum. If each heading requires an entire section, then subheadings can be prepared for the paragraph development. Paragraph by paragraph, the memorandum should lead the reader through the logical development of the

FIGURE 8.19 Sample Outline for Memorandum

OUTLINE FOR MEMORANDUM

GROWING CROPS AND HARVEST BY FORMER LESSEE

I. Facts
   A. 10-year lease of 240 acres to farmer
   B. Lessor can terminate lease on 90-day notice
   C. Lease gives right to harvest "growing crop" in event of early termination
   D. Client gave notice after 3 years 8 months
   E. At time of notice, 197 acres planted in alfalfa
   F. Lessor claims right to harvest annual crops for period of 4 years

II. Definition of "growing crop"
   A. Not defined in lease or by statute
   B. California Supreme Court held alfalfa not to be a "growing crop" in context of property taxation law (*Miller v. County of Kern*, 137 Cal. 516)
   C. Supreme Court distinguished between annual and perennial crops
   D. Court of Appeal held turf grass not to be a growing crop, relying upon *Miller* (*Nunes Turfgrass v. County of Kern*, 111 Cal. App.3d 855)

III. Right of former lessee to harvest
   A. Tenant has "right of emblements" to harvest crop when lease of uncertain duration is terminated
   B. The right to harvest fruit from trees has been limited to fruit that was mature at the termination of the tenancy, all work having been done upon the crop for that year (*Blaeholder v. Guthrie*, 17 Cal. App. 297)
   C. No California case has decided the comparative rights of landowners and former tenants to multiple annual harvests subsequent to termination of the lease

IV. Conclusion

writer's legal analysis. Excessively long paragraphs obscure that logic and deprive the reader of the visual signals (i.e., paragraph breaks) that alert her to the topic development and that help her to organize her own mental understanding of the memorandum. The writer should use headings and subheadings in the finished document—they aid the reader's comprehension by alerting her to the topic or purpose of the passage she is about to read. They also make it easier to locate a particular section for later review.

Remember: The court might not be familiar with the case, and certainly is not as familiar with the legal analysis that the writer will present in the memorandum. In addition, the judge probably is working under an overwhelming caseload. Poor paragraph organization can severely weaken the readability and persuasiveness of the memorandum. Why should a busy judge spend precious time deciphering an obscure memorandum of legal arguments? Good paragraph organization is indispensable to effective pleading!

Is the writer now satisfied with the paragraph organization? Then the writer should test it against her own objective: Does the memorandum inform and persuade the reader as intended? If the writer is confident that it does, she may have done a great job. Except for unfamiliar legal concepts (e.g., "strict products liability"), any educated layperson should be able to understand and follow the general concepts without any prior knowledge of the case or the law.

Using Active Language

Active language uses the active voice and action verbs. The active voice, remember, makes the subject of the sentence *do* something, whereas, in the passive voice, the subject has something *done to it*. Write, "the plaintiff learned that . . ." (active voice) instead of, "the plaintiff was informed that . . ." (passive voice). Most often, the subject of the sentence should be the actor, not the target of someone else's action. The active voice offers several advantages: It draws the reader's attention to the subject of the sentence, and it expresses more energy and seems livelier to the reader. As a general rule, stick to the active voice.

There are exceptions to this general rule, of course. If one wishes to portray the client as an innocent victim of someone else's misconduct, it might be effective to have the client be the subject of the sentence but to use the passive voice to emphasize the idea that *she* did not do anything wrong: "While the plaintiff was proceeding through the intersection with the green light, she was struck broadside by the defendant's vehicle." The passive voice can also soften the impact of any statement—and sometimes that is exactly what the writer wants. It can also focus the reader's attention on what was done. The point is to use the passive voice for a purpose—and not to fall into a habit of writing in that voice.

In addition to using the active voice, the effective writer uses active verbs rather than nouns or noun substitutes. In place of words ending in "-ion," "-ing," or "-ance" (e.g., protection, determining, and resistance), wherever possible use the verbs from which they were derived (i.e., protect, determine, and resist). The sentence, "This letter is written in protection of my client's interests," combines an inactive noun ("protection") with the passive voice ("is written"). A more effective sentence would be, "I am writing this letter to protect my client's interests." Active verbs give life and authority to their sentences.

Managing Sentence Length

Many short sentences will cause the writing to be choppy. Combining two short, closely related sentences into one can make one's writing read more smoothly. As a general rule, however, brief sentences are a virtue because they force the writer to be concise. Run-on sentences, which ramble without clear focus or even a conclusion, are the worst of all sentences. Consider the following example:

> "The question before the court is whether evidence that the pilot used cocaine shortly before the flight should be admitted into evidence, and if so, what restrictions should be placed upon that evidence, since it could be highly prejudicial to the defendant if no restrictions were imposed by the court and the plaintiff were allowed to introduce evidence of prior cocaine usage which had nothing whatsoever to do with the accident in this case."

Although the preceding example is extreme (and includes other offenses against good writing), it is no worse than the style of some documents actually submitted to courts. That run-on sentence of seventy-four words could be rewritten in three tight, readable sentences (fifty-five words, total) that would communicate far more effectively:

> "The question before the court is whether evidence that the pilot used cocaine shortly before the flight should be admitted into evidence. Such evidence should be excluded because it would be highly prejudicial to the defendant. Any evidence of prior cocaine usage that is unrelated to the accident must be excluded because it is irrelevant."

Using Concise Language

Among the worst characteristics of "lawyer-like" writing is verbiage—excess words. Some lawyers never write a letter "about" anything—it is always "in regard to" something. Although widely accepted and used, the latter phrase simply adds clutter where concise language would serve. Worse yet, such phrases are symptomatic of a tendency to clutter every page with excess verbiage. (See how easy it is? "Verbiage" means excess wordiness—so "*excess* verbiage" is a redundancy.)

There is no problem with excess words in a first draft; but there is no excuse for keeping most of them in the final version. An essential goal of the rewriting process is to express the same thing in fewer words without omitting any important content. But which words are "excess"? Even good writers add words when they clarify meaning or enrich the tone of their writing. There are two basic tests for recognizing verbiage: Which words and phrases can be eliminated entirely without sacrificing essential meaning or tone? Which phrases can be more concisely stated without sacrificing essential meaning or tone? Many times it is best to scrap the first effort completely and start again from scratch. There are a number of Web sites devoted to good legal writing. Most of them are maintained by law schools or bar associations.

Internet Access

University of Arkansas, Little Rock http://www.ualr.edu/~cmbarger
American Bar Association http://www.abanet.org/lpm/bp160_front.shtml

---

WRITING "LIKE A LAWYER"

If the writing of lawyers is sometimes incomprehensible, it is usually because they tend to forget *why* they write, and instead try to make their writing "sound" lawyer-like. New paralegals might think that their writing should conform to that stilted legal style affected by some. Imitating that style might lend a false sense of security for the uncertain neophyte, but it is a temptation that should be resisted.

"Legalese," as it is known—even among attorneys—usually obscures meaning and therefore is an obstacle to effective communication. This is not to suggest that legal **terms of art** should never be used—every profession has its own special vocabulary, and terms of art are sometimes the most efficient way to communicate a very specific concept. Among attorneys and judges, for example, the term "constructive fraud" conveys a concept that could easily require several paragraphs to explain in ordinary English. But ordinary English should be used whenever it can provide efficient communication. There is no need to say "the contract should be *avoided*," because "the contract should be *nullified*" means exactly the same thing and is more commonly understood. Attorneys will understand the jargon, but most clients will not. Another feature of legalese is a stiff style, often "achieved" by omitting articles, as in the example below:

"Plaintiff objects to . . ."

Standard English would do, with no threat to the client's legal interests, as shown below:

"The Plaintiff objects to . . ."

All legal writing has at least this purpose: to convey information. Often, there is a second major purpose: to persuade. The information one wants to convey

> A **term of art** is a word or phrase that carries a meaning peculiar to a particular profession (e.g., a "shave" in dermatology or "constructive fraud" in law).

might be "these are the facts" or "this is our view of the law"—but, either way, it is still information. Persuasive writing says, "follow me through this line of thought, and you will come to agree with me." Incomprehensible writing cannot accomplish either purpose. *The most important lesson of legal writing is to write clearly, succinctly, and correctly: Get to the point, make no mistakes, and avoid unnecessary "legalese."*

A professor of law at Howard University has established a Web site devoted to the recognition of clear, effective legal writing. The "Legal Writing Hall of Fame" provides outstanding examples of legal memoranda, briefs, and correspondence—most written by attorneys, but some written by law students.

Internet Access

Legal Writing Hall of Fame — http://www.law.howard.edu/faculty/pages/berry/goodwork/goodwork.htm

---

EDITING AND REVISION

Second only to organization, rewriting is the most important part of good writing. Paragraphs (and even sentences) need to be restructured and rephrased. A highly skilled writer might revise an important document three or four times. The average writer might need to make twice that many revisions.

LEGAL CORRESPONDENCE

Every legal assistant must be able to write letters that communicate effectively and correctly, and that reflect favorably on the employer and the client. That requires a good deal more than correct spelling, grammar, and punctuation. The effective letter should be clear and unambiguous. It should minimize the need for follow-up phone calls or correspondence. Most letters should have a professional but friendly tone. Writing letters that meet these criteria is a combination of both skill and art. A legal assistant who can consistently produce correspondence of high quality will be prized by the attorneys with whom he works. It is beyond the scope of this book to teach the art of correspondence, but the general comments already presented apply to letters just as they do to pleadings and other legal writing.

A new paralegal will generally begin with cover letters for the transmission of documents (e.g., responses to discovery), letters requesting information, and letters informing clients and others of calendar matters (e.g., hearing dates and meeting times). Eventually, the paralegal might be called upon to prepare more substantive correspondence, either for her own signature or for that of the supervising attorney. Letters for the signature of the attorney might include demand letters or opinion letters.

Demand Letters

A **demand letter** asks someone to do something that the client wants done: the debtor to pay overdue bills; the tenant to vacate the premises; the bill collector to "cease and desist" from harassing the client; the insurance company to pay a disputed insurance claim; and so forth. If the target of the demand letter is represented by counsel, the letter will be addressed to that person's attorney. An example of a demand letter appears in *Figure 8.20*.

Practice Tip

The final product can always benefit from another revision—it is never perfect. One obstacle to good editing is a deadline imposed by the court or the attorney. Whenever possible, the legal assistant should draft a document well in advance of any deadline, so that he has an opportunity to set it aside and return to it several times with a new perspective for each revision.

Another key to good editing is "peer review," otherwise known as relying upon a fresh pair of eyes. Someone who has never seen a document will quickly identify ambiguities, contradictions, and outright errors that the document's author often overlooks.

A **demand letter** is written by an attorney to obtain someone's compliance with a legal obligation to the client.

FIGURE 8.20 Sample Demand Letter

Adamson, Teshima, Álvarez & Gaum
Attorneys at Law
1723 Embarcadero Boulevard, Suite 1200
San Diego, California 92104
(619) 445-3000

June 23, 2000

Kate Truesdale
2654 Nutmeg Street   CERTIFIED MAIL
San Diego, California 92104

Re: Installment purchase Loan No. Z-4231
      South Bank of San Diego

Dear Ms. Truesdale:

This firm represents South Bank of San Diego (the "Bank"). The Bank holds your promissory note for $12,500.00 securing a loan to you for the installment purchase of a 1994 Plymouth Voyager.

The Bank has previously notified you by letter dated April 12, 2000, that you were, at that time, three months behind on your payments. An additional two months have passed and the Bank has received no response from you. Nor has it received any further payments since your last payment of $257.19, which was received on January 10, 2000. On May 15, 2000, the Bank sent you a letter by Certified Mail demanding immediate payment of your remaining debt of $7,092.17, and informing you of its intent to repossess the Plymouth Voyager should that sum not be paid by June 1, 2000. In the same letter, the Bank stated its intent to take any necessary further action to recover the money which you owe the Bank. The Bank subsequently retained Joe's Midnight Tow to recover the Plymouth Voyager, but that company has been unable to locate the vehicle.

The Bank has directed us to inform you that it has frozen your savings account, with a balance of $3,513.69, as permitted by your loan agreement with the Bank. In addition, if full repayment is not received by July 1, 2000, the Bank will file suit against you in Superior Court. As provided in your loan agreement, you will be liable for all attorneys' fees and court costs necessitated by your default on the loan.

If you have any questions, feel free to call me at (619) 445-3000.

Sincerely,

Joan Adamson, Esq.

> **Practice Tip**
>
> *Sometime back in the dark ages of legal writing, someone apparently thought legal pronouncements became more powerful when stated twice in the same sentence. Thus, contractual agreements under attack were said to be "null and void," even though either adjective alone would suffice without the other. "Cease and desist" is a similar redundancy, as are "free and clear" and "true and correct." Unfortunately, although "party of the first part" and many other anachronisms have gradually disappeared from most legal writing, redundant expressions persist even today. In the pursuit of clear writing, it is best to eliminate them.*

One might anticipate that all demand letters are threatening in tone, like the typical collection agency letter that states that the account will be turned over to an attorney if not paid within ten days. In most situations, however, the tone of the demand letter should be persuasive, rather than threatening. That is particularly true when it is addressed to legal counsel. Attorneys are generally aware of potential legal consequences; however, they might need to be persuaded that there are sound legal reasons that their client should comply with the demand. A threatening tone could be counterproductive.

Opinion Letters

An **opinion letter** is written by an attorney—either to the client or to a third party—to communicate the attorney's formal evaluation of a legal issue submitted by the client.

Due diligence is the degree of professional effort, attention, care, and good judgment that is expected of a reasonable and prudent person under the circumstances at hand. In business transactions, *due diligence* is the party's efforts to become adequately informed prior to making a final commitment.

The **in-house general counsel** is an attorney employed within a company to serve as its primary legal advisor.

The **opinion letter** is written to the client or to others whom the client wishes to inform regarding some legal matter. A confidential opinion letter to the client should be completely objective in addressing any legal issues, because its purpose is to inform the client of potential liabilities, claims, consequences, options, and the like. Opinion letters of this type concern such matters as the client's powers and duties as the executor of an estate or the likelihood of recovering damages for wrongful discharge from one's job. In business dealings, an opinion letter is often written on behalf of the client, but addressed to someone else. The letter might state, for example, that the client has exercised **due diligence** prior to reaching a decision to enter into the transaction in question. The latter type of opinion letter might be somewhat persuasive in tone.

A very brief example of an opinion letter appears in *Figure 8.21*. Although much less detailed than usual, it illustrates the content and style of such letters. In this example, outside legal counsel is writing to the **in-house general counsel** of the client corporation.

FIGURE 8.21   Sample opinion letter

Adamson, Teshima, Álvarez & Gaum
Attorneys at Law
1723 Embarcadero Boulevard, Suite 1200
San Diego, California 92104

July 1, 1999

Jeffrey S. Doenitz, Esq.
WorldWeb Pacific, Inc.
3 World Trade Center, Suite 1700
Montrose, California 92679

    Re: Employment of former employee of TransPac Services, Inc.

Dear Mr. Doenitz:

I understand that WorldWeb Pacific, Inc. ("WorldWeb"), wishes to employ Ms. Audrey Maltesian, the former Vice President for Business Development ("Maltesian") of TransPac Services, Inc. ("TransPac"), a competitor with WorldWeb in providing Internet consultation and support services for companies engaged in trade among the Pacific Rim nations.

You have asked for my opinion about the non-compete agreement which Maltesian signed when she accepted her position with TransPac in 1987 (the "Agreement"). Specifically, you have asked whether that Agreement would prohibit Maltesian from accepting the employment you wish to offer her, as Vice President for Far East Services, and whether WorldWeb could be liable for any damages to TransPac.

I have reviewed the Agreement, and I assume that Maltesian has no other agreement(s) with TransPac which would restrict her employment by TransPac. In the Agreement, I find the following provisions to be especially relevant to your inquiry:
    1) the Agreement shall be governed by California law;
    2) the Agreement has no expiration date, and purports to prohibit specified conduct by Maltesian--including her employment by a competitor--for an indefinite period; and,
    3) the Agreement specifically states that it shall apply to subsequent employment of Maltesian in the United States, or in any country in the Western Hemisphere.

FIGURE 8.21 (*continued*)

> California case law on this issue is clear: public policy favors the right of a person to pursue a career and to make a living, and a "non-compete" agreement which substantially interferes with this right is unlawful. In determining whether particular non-compete agreements violate that public policy, California courts have considered the duration of the non-compete agreement, its geographical limitations, and its effect upon the prospective livelihood of the employee. Of course, the cases have also considered the actual or potential damage to prior employers when a valued employee is hired by a competitor.
>
> In particular, California courts have voided non-compete agreements which are not reasonably limited in their effect by time and geography. In the situation submitted for my opinion, the Agreement appears to be clearly unreasonable in its limitations upon Maltesian's future employment, and I believe that WorldWeb would prevail on those counts if its employment of Maltesian were challenged by TransPac. In addition, computer database and on-line communication systems, such as the Internet, are changing so rapidly that TransPac would be hard pressed to show actual damages resulting from Maltesian's "defection" to WorldWide with any technical knowledge she acquired while an employee of TransPac, particularly since her duties with WorldWeb will be in the areas of customer development and service.
>
> I suggest that WorldWide require Maltesian to sign an agreement, concurrent with her employment by WorldWeb, providing that she will not bring with her from TransPac any document, file, or recording which contains trade secrets belonging to TransPac, and that she will not use or disclose in the course of her employment with WorldWeb any personal knowledge of any TransPac trade secrets.
>
> I further suggest that Maltesian provide written notice to TransPac of her intention to accept employment with WorldWide and that she ask TransPac to identify information which they believe to be proprietary trade secrets.
>
> Please feel free to contact me if you have any questions about this matter.
>
> Sincerely,
>
> Anthony Westrom
> Attorney at Law

PLEADINGS: "MAY IT PLEASE THE COURT..."

Pleadings are the fundamental documents filed with the court in a lawsuit. These documents contain the parties' allegations of facts, and any legal claims or defenses. However, in common usage, the term "pleading" is often applied to any document filed with the court for the purpose of influencing the court's management of the case or the ultimate outcome of the litigation. Thus, motions and oppositions to motions are sometimes referred to as "pleadings." This chapter uses the term in that broader sense.

Statutes and rules of court sometimes require pleadings to follow a particular formula and to conform to a particular format. For example, a complaint must always allege facts that give the court jurisdiction over the defendant and the subject matter of the lawsuit. This is done by alleging the nature of the parties (i.e., individual, corporation, partnership, etc.) and the facts that establish jurisdiction (e.g., residency or the state in which incorporated). A particular cause of action requires allegations to support that cause of action. A complaint for breach of contract, for example, fails to state a valid cause of action if there is no allegation that a contract existed between the plaintiff and defendant—the existence of the contract is one of the essential elements of a cause of action for breach. Each essential element must be pleaded (i.e., alleged). Consequently, well-drafted complaints often follow a legal "formula" to be certain of pleading valid jurisdiction and sound causes of action. These formulas for complaints usually cannot be avoided, and other pleadings might require similar formulas.

> **Practice Tip**
>
> *Before drafting a pleading, the paralegal should review the rules of court for that jurisdiction, including local rules for current format and procedural requirements. These rules typically govern the spacing, content, and arrangement of information: name of court; case name and number; attorney's name, address, and signature; line spacing; margins; and so forth. The court clerk might refuse to accept a pleading that does not conform to those rules.*

> **Practice Tip**
>
> When using sample pleadings from someone else's form file, the legal assistant should make two photocopies of each pleading: one to serve as a "working" copy and one to retain as an exemplar. The working copy can be marked up as the legal assistant adapts its language to the facts and issues of the case at hand. After the attorney has revised the draft, the legal assistant should make a photocopy of the final version for his own form files. Of course, today's exemplar is more likely to be kept on a computer, rather than in three-ring binders.
>
> During the first year or so, every paralegal must depend upon other paralegals and attorneys for examples of pleadings. It is perfectly routine and nothing to be hesitant about. A word of caution, however: Old pleading samples might no longer conform to current court rules.

A **form file** (or **form book**) is a collection of sample pleadings that serve as models for drafting similar pleadings in the future.

A **case brief** is a summary of a court opinion that is prepared by an attorney or legal assistant for use within the law firm.

The wording of the allegations can be important, because they will be evaluated under strict rules of law and procedure. The unfortunate result is that attorneys tend to rely upon tried and true wording that has withstood challenges in court, even though it is not a model of clarity: "The plaintiff is informed and believes, and on the basis of such knowledge and belief, alleges that the defendant is, and at all relevant times herein was, a resident of the County of Shasta."

The Paralegal's Form File

A new paralegal should always use pleadings from other cases as models when drafting a complaint, motion, and the like. Even experienced attorneys use examples from old cases. It is also wise to start one's own **form file**, (or **form book**), which can be carried along should one move to a different law firm.

> **Ethics Watch**
>
> If the legal assistant intends to take a form file along when leaving employment with the law firm, the file should contain copies only of those pleadings that are *part of the public record*—e.g., on file with a court. Otherwise, confidential client information could be compromised if seen by someone in the legal assistant's new law firm.

Because pleadings are of such great importance, this is not the appropriate occasion for a new paralegal to strike a critical blow in the battle against legalese—leave that decision to the attorney. Until the paralegal has gained substantial experience and legal sophistication, it is safer to stick to the traditional wording even though it might seem obscure. The danger of simplifying the obtuse language of earlier pleadings is that the neophyte might not recognize an essential term of art. "Simplifying" that expression might destroy the message that it communicates to the court. Of course, the reviewing attorney should catch such errors. However, attorneys are notoriously busy people, and horrendous mistakes have been known to appear in documents filed with the courts.

BRIEFING A COURT OPINION

When analyzing a single, discrete legal question, often it is necessary to evaluate five or ten different appellate decisions that might contribute to the determination of that legal issue. Reading and evaluating those cases can be a very time-consuming task. Associate attorneys and paralegals are sometimes asked to prepare a **case brief** of each opinion so that the responsible attorney can more efficiently analyze the legal question at hand. The case brief not only saves the supervising attorney's time, but it also provides an organized written summary for future reference.

In preparing the case brief, the paralegal should understand the legal issues and relevant facts in the client's case, so that he can recognize the significance of each part of the appellate court's opinion in the case to be briefed. Although it is entirely feasible to brief any court opinion without such an understanding, there is always the chance that the paralegal will overlook something of significance because he is not well-informed about the client's case.

A case brief usually contains the following sections:

- factual background
- procedural history (if provided in the opinion)
- legal issue

- holding of the lower court (if stated in the appellate opinion)
- holding of the appellate court
- reasoning of the appellate court

The *factual background* helps the attorney to compare that case to the facts of the client's case. Factual differences can determine which legal principles apply to a case, or they can change the way in which the same legal principles apply in two different cases. When the paralegal is familiar with the facts of the client's case, she can usually recognize significant facts in the court opinion. However, the paralegal must be cautious about substituting her own judgment for that of the attorney. Despite the implication of the term "brief," it is better to risk erring on the side of more detail than necessary.

A short *procedural history* provides an understanding of how the case came before the appellate court. This can be quite significant. For example, the attorney needs to know whether the trial court decided the case on its merits, or whether it dismissed the complaint for some procedural reason, preventing the case from going to trial. Some appellate court decisions, however, omit the procedural history of the case. In that situation, the paralegal can simply state that the procedural history does not appear in the opinion being briefed.

The *legal issue* in the appellate case might be the identical issue that is in question in the client's case; more often, however, it is a related issue that is relevant to the client's case. To evaluate the significance of the appellate decision, the attorney should know exactly which issue was before the appellate court. A single appellate case might have a dozen or more legal issues before it. The legal issues to be emphasized in the brief are those relevant to the client's case.

The *holding of the lower court* is simply a brief statement of its conclusion on the law that governs the issues before it. Many times, however, the appellate opinion says next to nothing about a trial court's holding. The legal assistant can include in his brief only the information that is available. If the lower court is also an appellate court, or a U.S. District Court, its opinion might have been published.

The *holding of an appellate court* is always found in its own opinion. The "holding," does not mean "affirmed," "reversed," or "remanded." Rather, the holding is the conclusions of law that led the court to affirm, reverse, or modify the lower court's ruling; "The passengers in an automobile do not assume a duty to pedestrians by virtue of their status as car-pool members."

The final section of a typical case brief is the *reasoning of the court*. This is the most important part of the brief. It will be a summary of the legal arguments and critical facts that led the court to its holding on the legal issue. The student should note that the legal issue and the court's holding have been summarized in earlier sections of the brief; this section on the reasoning of the court should answer the question, "*Why* did the court reach that holding on this issue?" Because of its great importance, this section of the brief is often the longest portion, followed in length by the section on the factual background.

Students often wonder about including the case citations they find in the opinion being briefed. As a general rule, citations should be included only if it is clear that they have great importance for the issue that is of concern to the attorney. If the attorney wants to know the authorities cited by the court on some point of law, she can always ask for those citations. A sample brief of an appellate court opinion appears in Appendix B.

THE MEMORANDUM OF LAW

An internal **memorandum of law** is a document prepared for use within the law firm, or within the corporate legal department. It is not filed with a court, nor given to opposing counsel. Although in some jurisdictions, a memorandum of

---

Practice Tip

When paralegal students brief a court opinion, their most common mistakes are the following:

- *making the factual summary more than half of the entire brief*
- *omitting the line of logical reasoning that led the court to reach its conclusions on questions of law*
- *including dozens of case citations found in the opinion being briefed*
- *injecting their personal opinions or interpretations into the body of the brief*

A **memorandum of law** is an objective written report of research and analysis on one or more legal issues, prepared by an attorney or paralegal for use within the law firm.

An **intraoffice memorandum** one is prepared for internal use within the law firm.

Practice Tip

When drafting an intra-office memorandum of law, the most common mistakes by paralegal students include the following:

- *omitting material facts*
- *failing to state clearly the question(s) presented*
- *making the "brief" answers almost as long as the conclusion of the memorandum*
- *failing to present a thorough legal analysis*
- *failing to develop the legal analysis in a logical progression*
- *quoting from the summary or headnotes of a case*
- *minimizing the importance of unfavorable legal authorities*
- *transforming the memorandum into a partisan document advocating the client's case*

points and authorities is sometimes termed a "memorandum of law," this text uses the latter term to mean an **intraoffice memorandum**—one not intended for submission to the court. (Memoranda to be submitted to the court are discussed below.) The memorandum of law analyzes a legal issue, relying on all relevant statutes and case law, both favorable and unfavorable to the client's case. Except for a conclusion that might propose a partisan analysis for use in court, the memorandum should be completely objective. The objectivity of the memorandum is *essential* to ensure that the attorney will anticipate the arguments of opposing counsel and to address potential weaknesses in the client's case.

Although memoranda of law are prepared in a variety of formats, the following one is common:

- summary of facts
- legal question(s) presented
- brief answer(s)
- legal analysis
- conclusion(s)

The summary of facts should be short, presenting only those facts relevant to the legal question at issue. The legal question presented is usually very succinct; subtleties can be addressed in the legal analysis section. The brief answer should be stated in a short paragraph, at most. The major portion of the memorandum is in the legal analysis section.

The *legal analysis* is often written in the style of an appellate court decision. Statutes, cases, and secondary sources are always cited so that the attorney can evaluate the weight of those authorities and can use them for further research. It is vitally important that the memorandum state both the arguments that support and those that undermine the client's legal position, and identify those that lead the legal assistant to the ultimate conclusion (favorable or unfavorable) on the legal question presented.

The *conclusion* will state in summary form the result of the legal analysis. It might also recommend related issues for further research. When an attorney writes a memorandum of law, he sometimes proposes in the conclusion a partisan line of argument that could be argued to the court, even if the attorney expects the court to reach a contrary conclusion. In that event, the conclusion should clearly state the ruling reasonably anticipated, based upon the law, in addition to proposing a partisan argument. A sample memorandum of law appears in Appendix C.

THE MEMORANDUM OF POINTS AND AUTHORITIES

An **appellate brief** is a memorandum that argues the law on the matters that have been submitted on appeal.

A **memorandum of points and authorities** is a persuasive memorandum on one or more legal issues, prepared by an attorney or paralegal for submission to the court.

Attorneys often prepare memoranda intended to persuade the court to adopt the client's position on some question of law or procedure. In advance of a trial, for example, the attorney will prepare a trial brief that addresses all of the major legal and procedural issues that the court will decide in the course of the trial. If a case is later appealed to a higher court, the attorneys for all parties will prepare **appellate briefs** that argue the law on the matters that have been submitted on appeal.

Trial briefs and appellate briefs are examples of **memoranda of points and authorities**. In a memorandum of points and authorities, the attorney argues the law as it applies to the facts of the case. In fact, *partisanship is the distinguishing* *characteristic of memoranda of points and authorities*, although they are otherwise similar to the intraoffice memoranda of law discussed in the preceding section. The "points" are legal propositions (i.e., arguments) favorable to the client's position, and the "authorities" are primary and secondary sources that support those propositions.

A memorandum of points and authorities begins with a summary of the relevant facts. Of course, those facts are stated in a manner designed to lead the court to apply the law that is favorable to the client. Next comes a legal proposition. The legal proposition appears as a paragraph or section heading, and it states a legal principle favorable to the client: "It is within the discretion of the court to permit the jury to view the scene of the accident." A legal analysis supporting that proposition follows. As in the memorandum of law, the legal sources relied upon are cited—but the writer emphasizes those *favorable* to the client's legal proposition.

The typical memorandum continues with a series of propositions, designed to lead the reader to a final conclusion favorable to the client. A challenging task in drafting the memorandum is to present the facts and the law in a persuasive fashion without being so partisan as to lose all credibility with the court. One helpful technique is to anticipate the arguments of opposing counsel (e.g., "The plaintiff might argue that . . .") and explain why those arguments should not apply to the case at hand. This contention can be supported by pointing out differences between the factual situation in the client's case and the factual situation in court opinions that appear to favor the anticipated arguments by the opposing counsel.

As discussed earlier, primary sources for the writer's jurisdiction (i.e., mandatory authority) should be cited for each argument supporting the proposition stated. If there is no mandatory authority that can be cited for a particular proposition, the opinions of other jurisdictions might be cited to the court for their very persuasive effect. As the paralegal gains experience with legal research, he will come to know the types of secondary sources most frequently cited by appellate courts in their own opinions.

Making the Memorandum Persuasive

A good portion of most legal writing aims to persuade (e.g., pleadings, trial briefs, and letters to opposing counsel). One cannot always succeed in that effort, because some things are beyond the writer's control. No one can change the facts of his client's case. The writer cannot erase the personal biases of the judge. He cannot change the body of legal precedent that governs the law of the case. He can only do his best under the circumstances. Fortunately, the presumably "best effort" often can be improved.

Here are a few guidelines for effective persuasion:

- Write clearly and concisely.
- Start with a statement or position agreeable to the reader.
- Soften any bold statements that are likely to arouse an unfriendly bias.
- Lead the reader gently and methodically toward the desired conclusion.
- Anticipate objections, and refute them without antagonizing the reader.
- Quote authority that the reader cannot ignore.
- Avoid any hint of arrogance, condescension, or antagonism.
- Remember that the reader should feel good about adopting the client's position.

Practice Tip

Persuasion is an exercise in human relationships, not simply cold logic. Forgetting the importance of human nature can defeat the best of logicians. For that reason, a writer must use care, even in choosing a title or caption. If she anticipates that the judge is a vehement opponent of illegal drug use, she should avoid a caption like: "Motion to Exclude Evidence of Cocaine Use." Instead, she can try something like, "Motion to Exclude Prejudicial Evidence." The more strongly she anticipates an unfriendly bias in the court, the more important it is to support her position with authority the court cannot easily dismiss.

Practice Tip

When the attorney has finalized the memorandum of points and authorities and the paralegal is preparing to file it with the court, she should consider how she can make things easier for the judge. Human nature being what it is, many judges prefer that counsel attach photocopies of all cases, statutes, and other authority they cite in a motion or brief. This saves the court's time and trouble in looking them up. It is an excellent idea to call the judge's clerk and inquire about his honor's preference in that regard.

Ethics Watch

Credibility is extremely important in litigation. An attorney needs credibility not only with the judge, but also with opposing counsel. It is very important to keep the attorney's credibility in mind when drafting persuasive documents. Credibility is best achieved by acting with ethical and intellectual integrity at all times. Credibility can be irretrievably destroyed by any one of the following:

- distorting the facts
- distorting or misquoting the law
- citing case authority that is no longer good law
- any appearance of intellectual dishonesty

This does not mean that one must trot out every single case unfavorable to his client—he might omit unfavorable law that is arguably inapplicable; but he must *never* misrepresent the law. Although it might be wise to write:

"The Court of Appeals for the Second District stated in *ABC v. XYZ* that trustees must not engage in self-dealing. That case can be distinguished because . . . ," one must *never* imply that the court of appeals stated anything other than what it actually did state.

CITING LEGAL AUTHORITIES

The court rules of most jurisdictions follow the citation format prescribed in *The Bluebook: A Uniform System of Citation,* published by the Harvard Law Review Association. *The Bluebook* has been compiled by the law review editors of four university law schools. As of this writing, it is in its sixteenth edition. Although the complexity of its rules can appear extraordinarily daunting to the neophyte researcher, most of those rules are never needed for the typical memorandum of law or points and authorities. Every legal assistant needs a copy of it on her desk, but most will refer to it only occasionally. In fact, the most common forms of citation have already appeared in this text.

The Association of Legal Writing Directors (ALWD) has published a new citation manual that has attracted a great deal of interest. *The ALWD Citation Manual* provides a single citation system for all legal writing, including court documents, law review articles, and so forth. Because the association members teach legal writing in law schools, this new manual could become an influential force in future legal writing. At this writing, the association claims that its manual has been adopted by professors at more than sixty law schools and "at least twenty paralegal education programs."

Internet Access

Association of Legal Writing Directors   http://www.alwd.org

A QUESTION OF ETHICS

Jon Greenbaum has been working many months on a major civil litigation case that is about to go to trial. Because of his extensive experience and advanced skills, he has the confidence of the three attorneys working the case, and he has done extensive legal research on the issues likely to arise during the trial. Jon will be sitting with the firm's attorneys at the counsel table during trial, managing the exhibits, taking notes, and observing jurors' reactions.

Today, attorneys for all parties are in court. The trial will begin in two days, so no jury has been seated. The attorneys are arguing motions by various parties to exclude or admit certain types of evidence. At one point, the court interrupts opposing counsel, who has been arguing for exclusion of some correspondence as being inadmissible hearsay evidence. The judge says, "But, counselor, didn't the court of appeals hold in *Cheever v. Thompson* that such correspondence is an exception to the hearsay rule?" The opposing counsel appears stunned and says, "I believe so, your honor." The judge states, "Your motion to exclude is denied. The correspondence will be admitted."

Jon glances at Jill Marchant, the attorney from his firm who is arguing the motions in today's hearings. Her face is calm, and she appears satisfied with the court's characterization of the *Cheever* case. But Jon remembers coming across *Cheever v. Thompson* in the course of his pretrial research. And his memory is that the *Cheever* court's holding was not really on point for the issue the parties have been arguing today. In fact, Jon believes that it wouldn't support the decision just made by the court. What should Jon do?

Chapter Summary

- The fundamental purposes of legal research are to achieve the following:
    - to answer specific legal questions
    - to provide legal arguments to support the client's position
    - to provide guidance to the client
- Primary sources are statements *of* the law; secondary sources are statements *about* the law.
- Mandatory authority is binding upon the court; persuasive authority might be considered or disregarded by the court, in its own discretion.
- Annotated codes often lead the researcher to relevant cases.
- Unofficial reporters print every word of the court's opinion; they also add editorial material written by the editorial staff of the publisher.
- The summary and headnotes that precede the court's opinion must never be quoted or cited.
- If a court explicitly adopts a statement about the law in a secondary source, that statement becomes part of the common law of that jurisdiction.
- Cases are Shepardized to ensure that they are still good law and to locate additional cases that treat the same legal issues.
- The IRAC method is a mode of legal analysis which calls upon the researcher to define the *issue*, identify the legal *rule*, *apply* that rule to the facts, and draw a *conclusion* based upon that application.
- A case is on point when it confronts the same legal issue.
- A case is on all fours when it confronts the identical legal issue and all material facts are substantially similar.
- Every legal assistant should accumulate a form file of sample pleadings, memoranda, and letters.
- A memorandum of law is an objective analysis of the question presented, generally prepared for internal office use, or for the client.
- A memorandum of points and authorities is a persuasive document that presents legal arguments and the authorities that support those arguments.

KEY TERMS

analogy	holding	persuasive authority
annotated code	in-house general counsel	pleading
annotation	intraoffice memorandum	pocket part
appellate brief	key number	primary source
case of first impression	mandatory authority	rehearing
case brief	memorandum of points and authorities	reporter
citator		seal
code	memorandum of law	secondary source
code of civil procedure	modify	section
demand letter	nuisance	Shepardize
dictum	official reporter	*stare decisis*
digest	on point	summary
disposition	on all fours	syllabus
due diligence	opinion letter	term of art
form file	overrule	tort law
headnote	parallel citation	unofficial reporter
hearing on appeal	penal code	

ACTIVITIES AND ASSIGNMENTS

1. Photocopy the complete opinion from a case in an official or unofficial reporter. It can be any state or federal case—even a case chosen at random—provided that it has at least three headnotes. On the photocopy, highlight the *first sentence* of the court's opinion (not the case summary or headnotes). Then, highlight the first sentence where the court begins its discussion of the legal issue found in headnote 2. Highlight also the court's *disposition* of the case.

2. Using the same case that you photocopied for the above assignment, provide the following information:

    - the number of legal issues decided by the court
    - the name of the justice who wrote the opinion of the court
    - the names of the justices, if any, who joined in the opinion of the court
    - the justices who wrote concurring opinions, if any
    - the justices who wrote dissenting opinions, if any

3. Find a statute—on any topic whatsoever—in either the annotated codes for your state, or in the *United States Code Annotated.* (A single section of a code qualifies as a "statute.") In selecting the statute, make sure that it is followed by five or more annotations (which usually appear as a series of numbered "notes"). Photocopy the pages that include the statute and a few annotations that follow that statute. Do not photocopy more than two pages of annotations.

    Select just one annotation for a case that you can easily locate in an unofficial or official reporter. Read the case that is cited in that annotation. Prepare a brief memorandum in which you verify or dispute the accuracy of the *annotation* in the annotated code. Does the case really say what the annotation suggests that it does?

4. From the case you read for the preceding activity, select one legal issue from among the headnotes. Then, using the topical index to the annotated code, try to locate a statute related in some way to that legal issue. (Use your imagination for alternative topic headings in the index.) You might have to try several legal issues from that case before you are able to find a related statute.

    Photocopy the page in the index that led you to that statute, and highlight the topic heading. Photocopy also the page with the statute you found. Attach those photocopies to a photocopy of the page with the headnote (highlighted) that identified the legal issue you selected.

5. Rewrite this sentence to improve its clarity without sacrificing its content or purpose:

    "This court cannot but reach the obvious conclusions necessarily required by the documents and testimony submitted to it: to wit, that the plaintiff has not proved his case."

6. Select a court opinion, between ten and twenty pages in length, from an official or unofficial reporter. (Select an opinion *without* concurring or dissenting opinions.) Following the guidelines in this chapter, prepare a brief of that court opinion. (See the example in Appendix B.) Attach a photocopy of that case.

7. Your instructor will give you a very simple legal issue to research, together with the facts from a hypothetical client's situation. You are to research the law on that issue and then *apply* the law to the facts in the client's situation. You will do this in a "memorandum of law." Remember, you are *not* an attorney, and this is *not* a course in legal research and writing—keep it simple! (See Appendix C for a sample memorandum of law.) Attach photocopies of all cases and statutes cited in the memorandum.

8. Assume that your firm has missed yesterday's deadline for responding to the request for production of documents propounded by the opposing party. Those requests were served on your firm by mail. However, they did not arrive until seventeen days after the date of their mailing (leaving only thirteen days to comply with the deadline). Also, the attorney was out of the office for three days, suffering from the flu. Unfortunately, the firm's computer system "crashed," taking with it the tickler system (which reminds attorneys and legal assistants of all deadlines); the deadline for responding "fell through the cracks," without your office's requesting an extension. Draft a letter to opposing counsel explaining the circumstances and requesting an additional ten days for the response to his request.

CHAPTER 9

Computers in the Law Office

> Computers have just one function in law firms, and that is keeping track of our billables and our firm accounts. All this nonsense about using computers in the courtroom is just that—nonsense. The day I use a computer to practice law will be the day I resign from the bar.
>
> *Written by an attorney who now wishes to remain anonymous.*
> *(It is untrue that his grandfather refused to use a telephone in his law practice—that was another lawyer with a similar name.)*
>
> Intelligence and hard work can substitute for a hard drive almost any time. But none of us has unlimited reservoirs of intelligence or hard work.
>
> *George P. Field, "Using a Computer at Counsel Table," 28* Trial *30 (September 1992).*

One of humankind's more difficult challenges is to accept and embrace new and profoundly different ways of working, communicating, and thinking. For many legal professionals, today's most disconcerting challenges are the changes being wrought by means of the microchip and the Internet. Although the transition has been difficult for some, others in the profession are beginning to wonder how they ever managed to practice law without word processors, e-mail, and on-line research.

Chapter 9 addresses the evolving role of computers and related technologies in the practice of law. It is organized into three sections. Section 1 discusses the increasing importance of computers in the practice of law and in the work of paralegals. Section 2 introduces computer-assisted legal research using CD-ROMs, Westlaw, and LEXIS-NEXIS. Section 3 considers the Internet as a rapidly developing medium for research, both legal and factual.

Upon completing this chapter, the student should be able to answer these questions:

- How are computers commonly used in the practice of law?
- How are computers used in the courtroom?

- What degree of computer literacy is expected of new paralegals?
- What are the features of word processing software that make it so valuable to law firms?
- What is a database manager, and how is it used by law firms?
- How does a spreadsheet differ from a database?
- How is legal information organized by the on-line services?
- How are Westlaw and LEXIS-NEXIS used for on-line research?
- What kinds of research can be accomplished on the Internet?
- How are on-line search engines and directories used?
- How does one locate reliable legal materials on the Internet?
- How can one find discussion groups for legal issues and research?

SCENARIO

Legal Assistant with Computer Saves the Day in Court

On the last day of trial in my client's bad-faith employment termination case, a defense witness testified, "Because of [the plaintiff's] poor sales efforts, the entire company dropped in market share throughout the region."

The answer produced immediate dyspepsia at our counsel table. The defense had never before contended that my client had been fired for his negative effect on sales results.

We had anticipated, and refuted, the defense position that complaints from customers and "failure to adapt" to new company policies justified the firing. But now, with trial almost over, we had a new defense to counter, and it was one so potentially damaging that in a different sort of case it could have been the basis for a damages counterclaim.

* * * *

Fortunately, as in every recent case, our computer was with us in the courtroom. My legal assistant searched the deposition transcripts in the case for the word "market" within five words of the word "share" . . .

Within seconds (while the unsuspecting defense witness had gone on to another subject), the laptop had retrieved and indexed every transcript reference to "market share" or any close variant . . .

After another 30 seconds of skimming results, my assistant had found just what we needed: the witness' own deposition testimony that in the year my client had been fired "the volume of business was deteriorating . . . all the regions were doing less business . . . the drop in market share was pretty much a condition of the market." The dread prospect of cross-examination had just become a delight.

George P. Field, "Using a Computer at Counsel Table," 28 *Trial* 30 (September 1992). ■

The preceding testimonial to the value of computers in the courtroom offers only a narrow glimpse of their potential role in the practice of law. It also demonstrates how valuable it can be to have a paralegal at the counsel table, able to pull up on-screen the full text of documents—even as the trial proceeds. This chapter will discuss some of the many ways in which computers can make the practice of law more effective and cost-efficient.

SECTION 1. THE IMPACT OF COMPUTERS ON THE PRACTICE OF LAW

The arrival of the computer and the Internet is not the first time that the legal profession has struggled with technological change. Around the turn of the century—that is, circa 1900, *not* 2000—lawyers struggled with the unwelcome intrusion of *two* mechanical devices: the telephone and the typewriter:

> Future Secretary of State John Foster Dulles recalled that when he joined the large New York law firm of Sullivan & Cromwell in 1911, neither telephones nor stenographers were widely accepted as part of the traditional law practice. He remembered that "[s]ome of the older partners felt that the only dignified way of communication between members of the legal profession was for them to write each other in Spencerian script, and to have the message thus expressed [*sic*] delivered by hand." In fact, Sullivan & Cromwell did not obtain a telephone until 1887, nearly a decade after the invention became available, and that telephone was a wall phone located in the outer office, which the clerks were forbidden to touch except when it rang.[1]

Of course, times soon changed, and all law firms found that the telephone and typewriter were wonderful devices to aid in the practice of law. And just as telephones and typewriters soon became indispensable tools, so have computers become indispensable in today's modern law office.

Beginning in 1985, the Chicago-Kent Center for Law and Computers conducted an annual survey of computer use in the nation's 500 largest law firms. In 1985, only 7% of the attorneys in the nation's largest firms had computers on or near their desks; by 1994—the last year for which the survey has been published—that figure had risen to 83%.[2] That represents an *average annual increase of more than 30%*. At that rate of growth, the figure for large-firm attorneys with a computer close at hand would have reached 100% before the end of the following year, 1995. Although common sense suggests that 100% is unlikely ever to be achieved among the generation of attorneys who entered their professional careers prior to the computer age, that pace of technological adaptation was remarkable, indeed.

It is possible that some smaller firms have been significantly slower in making the investment in computer technology. But, in 1998, the Wisconsin State Bar's Law Firm Technology Survey was distributed to firms of all sizes in that state. That survey found that 71% of the firms had Internet access—compared to only 50% in the preceding year.[3] If that astounding *rate* of change—a 42% increase in a single year—were to continue, the remaining 29% of Wisconsin law firms would have established Internet access within the following year. As for the future, by subsidizing law school access to their services, LEXIS-NEXIS and Westlaw have ensured that the current generation of law school graduates will enter practice with the full expectation of using this technology.

COMPUTER USE IN LAW FIRMS

In spite of the growth in on-line research and Internet access, the primary functions of computers in law firms continue to be word processing, billing and accounting, and e-mail. Correspondence is pervasive in all fields of law, and litigation and many other specialities generate an incredible quantity of documents. The importance of the computer for word processing will increase as paper documents gradually disappear from the practice of law, to be replaced by computer files. Eventually, almost all documents will be filed electronically with the courts, and law firms will replace a large portion of their file cabinets with electronic storage media that require only a tiny fraction of the former space.

Law firms depend upon computers to record billable hours and generate fee statements for clients. Specialized software programs tailored to the needs of law firms allow attorneys and paralegals to record their billable time on their desktop computers. Typically, the firm's computers are linked together in a local area network (LAN) so that the accounting department automatically receives each day's billable time. Monthly statements for each client (complete with detailed descriptions of the services being charged) can then be automatically generated. And virtually all firms—even sole practitioners—use computers to keep the firm's own financial records. The use of computers for billing and accounting is discussed in Chapter 11.

A rapidly growing use for computers is legal research. This includes the use of on-line legal information services (e.g., Westlaw and LEXIS-NEXIS—discussed later in this chapter) and legal materials on CD-ROM compact disks. Computer-assisted legal research offers many advantages, especially if the law firm does not have a large library of print materials. Research for factual information (e.g., real property records, plaintiff-defendant case indices, motor vehicle registrations, credit reports, and Security and Exchange Commission filings) is rapidly growing on-line. Increasingly, legal assistants are going to their computers to locate newspaper articles, medical research, government statistics, expert witnesses, and missing (or elusive) persons. (See Chapter 10.) Data that once were obtained by telephone, mail, or time-consuming travel to government offices, are now available on-line.

Computers are rapidly taking over the management of all documents in large-scale litigation, and eventually they will be used to manage all but the smallest of lawsuits. Correspondence, discovery documents, exhibits, and full deposition transcripts can all be stored, organized, tracked, and searched in a litigation database on a notebook computer.

Another common use for computers is the tickler system, sometimes known as "docket control." This is a variation on the calendar software used by many executives in the business world. In addition to appointments and meetings, the tickler system monitors such events as court dates and discovery deadlines. (Tickler systems are discussed in Chapter 11.)

When a law firm uses appropriate software for all of the preceding functions, it establishes a comprehensive information system that supports both its legal functions and its business functions. Of course, a highly desirable feature of an information system is the ability to transfer data easily from one part of the system to another. For example, the Westlaw software makes it easy to download documents from Westlaw directly into a WordPerfect or Word document. *Figure 9.1* summarizes the features of a comprehensive information system.

COMPUTERS IN THE COURTROOM

Computer technology is about to revolutionize the courtroom itself, as it is introduced into almost every aspect of court proceedings. Although true computer-integrated courtrooms are still few in number, they clearly are the wave of the future. The most familiar use of courtroom computers is for docket management by the court clerk. In most large court systems today, all courtroom computers are connected to a computer in the central clerk's office, and data are easily transferred between them. This makes it possible for the presiding judge or court administrator to track the caseload of each judge and simplifies the assignment of

FIGURE 9.1 The Main Components of a Law Firm Information System

```
COMPUTER
HARDWARE
- - - - - - - - - - - - - - - -
SOFTWARE
word processing
desktop publishing
database
spreadsheet
timekeeping and billing
calendar and docket control
Westlaw or LEXIS
browser
```

new cases as they are filed. Once a case has been assigned to a particular court, the computer can provide its status and the date of any scheduled proceeding in that case.

But the real revolution in trial procedures is driven by the use of computers to present demonstrative evidence, to immediately transcribe and display testimony, and to make available legal authorities for immediate consideration by the judge. In a computer-integrated courtroom, the court reporter's stenographic notes are almost instantly transcribed by computer software and displayed on computer screens available to counsel, the judge, and (sometimes) the jury. Prior testimony in the case can be searched and selected portions rapidly displayed on the screen, which makes it possible to quickly terminate disputes over what counsel or witnesses said earlier in that case.

In an article in *Trial* magazine, Judge Frank Andrews of the 116th Judicial District Court of Texas cited some of the advantages of real-time transcription:

- Everyone involved is much more conscious of what they say and how they say it.
- The judge can easily refer to the exact wording of a question before ruling on an objection.
- Attorneys can review testimony during trial, during breaks, and in the evening, using unedited transcripts stored on diskettes.
- Pretrial rulings can be easily reviewed, even if multiple judges and attorneys have been involved in the case.
- Hearing-impaired litigants, witnesses, attorneys, and jurors can participate in a way that was previously impossible.[4]

Illustrating the latter point, Judge Andrews describes the case in which a hearing-impaired defendant—previously convicted of a felony and sentenced to 25 years in prison—was able, using real-time transcripts, to assist in his own defense during a new trial of his case, and was acquitted. It is important to note that real-time transcription of the reporter's notes can occur with or without a video camera in the courtroom. Thus, the judge's first-mentioned advantage, above, does not result from "playing to the camera," but from the realization that the testimony is available in immediate transcription.

Of course, some court proceedings *are* being videotaped. The court reporter's real-time transcript can be marked with time signals that correspond to identical markings on the videotape of the testimony. This allows the transcript to be searched for particular testimony and then the corresponding portion of the videotape to be located and played on a courtroom monitor. The controversy over "playing to the camera" is likely to be a continuing issue.

During trial, computer-generated video simulations can reenact—either in slow motion or at normal speed—the events leading to, say, an automobile accident and can also illustrate the effects of trauma on a victim's body. Computer graphics can demonstrate the operation of hidden, internal components of machinery or illustrate the disintegration of an automobile tire that fails because of a manufacturing defect. This type of illustration falls within the same evidentiary category as diagrams on a courtroom easel, prepared by an expert witness for use during his testimony. But it has the capacity to be far more informative and, therefore, much more effective with a judge or jury.

A potential problem with computer-generated video is the opportunity to manipulate the images to produce a desired—although misleading—image. The same potential problem exists with once-ordinary still photography, which now can be altered by computers to produce virtually any image desired. The type of photographic evidence that once carried great credibility for the accuracy of the image is destined to be examined with great caution in future trials. The validation of photographic evidence will be a growing specialty among some expert witnesses.

PARALEGALS BEARING NOTEBOOKS

Even small laptop or notebook computers have the capacity to store the full text of many thousands of pages of documents. And, they are available with CD-ROM drives, which virtually removes *any* limits upon the quantity of documents that can be accessed on a computer right in the courtroom. In his standard-size briefcase, a legal assistant can easily carry CD-ROMs holding the equivalent of ten file cabinets.

Using special database software, such as Summation Blaze or Discovery/Magic, the legal assistant can do a full-text search during trial and retrieve deposition testimony or exhibits that relate to an issue that has just arisen during testimony. As in the scenario at the beginning of the chapter, this capability can allow the attorney to immediately compare pretrial discovery information with the evidence being offered by opposing counsel in trial. The legal assistant can also use the computer during trial to easily manage and locate all exhibits—an otherwise gargantuan task in large-scale, complex litigation.

A common responsibility for legal assistants during trial has been note taking. Although real-time transcription—if available—will reduce that need, there will continue to be a need to make note of comments, jury reactions, possible questions for cross-examination, and so on. And, in the vast majority of courtrooms today, real-time transcription is not yet a reality. The legal assistant can use a word processor to take notes, although some attorneys and legal assistants prefer to use outlining software, such as GrandView. The advantage of outlining software is that it automatically numbers each entry, and it makes later editing easier by automatically renumbering the entries, as any are deleted, added, or moved.

COMPUTER LITERACY FOR ENTRY-LEVEL PARALEGALS

As with many professions, computer literacy has become a necessity for paralegals. But which skills and knowledge are implied by "computer literacy"? For paralegals it usually means, *at the minimum*, an ability to use word processing software—usually Corel WordPerfect or Microsoft Word—and an operating system such as Microsoft's Windows or Apple's OS. Of course, the law firms using Apple's Macintosh computer are not nearly as numerous as the majority of firms using IBM-compatible personal computers (also known as "PCs").

Although it is currently known as "keyboarding," computers require the same typing skill as typewriters do. At the time of this writing, voice-recognition software (discussed below) has not yet achieved the accuracy necessary to completely replace keyboarding skills. And, although some people find that voice recognition is effective for creating first drafts, they prefer to make most of their revisions manually. Entry-level legal assistants should be prepared to create their documents without depending upon voice-recognition software. "Hunt and peck" keyboarding doesn't meet that standard—something in the range of 35 to 55 words per minute is likely to be expected.

Computer literacy implies the ability to accelerate one's own learning and efficiency curves with new software programs by applying the computer skills one already has. A computer-literate paralegal will not be intimidated by on-screen icons or menus or by the keyboard shorthand that is used for some computer-based legal research—nor by the manuals that explain how to use computer programs. Although particular software programs predominate in the practice of law, it is not essential that a new paralegal already know those specific programs.

For example, Corel's WordPerfect currently is the predominant word processing program in smaller law firms, whereas Microsoft's Word is more widely used in large firms and corporate legal departments. But a paralegal familiar with a different word processor, such as WordPro, is "computer literate" in the sense that he has already made the transition from a typewriter to the sophisticated, interactive word processing power of a computer. The level of computer literacy that most law firms are seeking is the ability to do basic word processing and to learn other computer applications. Computer "literacy" does not mean computer expertise. After all, new computer programs appear, and familiar programs change, with great frequency—it is the ability to learn and adapt that is important.

If a paralegal student can learn only one software program, however, either Corel WordPerfect or Microsoft Word is perhaps the better choice because they are used by paralegals more than any other **application programs**. It would be an advantage, also, to be proficient in a database manager such as Paradox, Approach, or Access, and possibly a spreadsheet such as Lotus 1-2-3 or Excel. Although spreadsheets are not so often used by most paralegals, database applications are—and they are becoming pervasive in litigation and some other specialties. There are other types of software applications created specifically for law firms, but they really need to be learned on the job. As with word processing, familiarity with one database or spreadsheet program makes it easier for a paralegal to learn a new, competing program.

An **application program** is a computer program for performing complex operations (e.g., a word processor, database manager, or spreadsheet).

THE E-MAIL CHALLENGE

As any experienced user knows, the first challenge of e-mail is how to keep up with it. It is distressingly easy to get behind, with 153 unread e-mails waiting to be reviewed, so that checking e-mail has to be a disciplined routine each day. Particularly for the e-mail neophyte, it is wise to be cautious about placing her name on any list (e.g., the local paralegal association's e-mail list) that daily broadcasts mail on subjects of common interest to everyone on that list. One can quickly find herself on ten or twelve lists, screening 153 e-mail messages *every day!*

> **Ethics Watch**
> An attorney has an ethical obligation to apply herself diligently to her clients' legal matters. Unread and unanswered e-mail can lead to ethical problems. If a client is harmed by this lack of diligence, the attorney might be subject to bar discipline and/or malpractice liability. Of course, all legal assistants share this ethical responsibility for diligence.

Practice Tip

Although e-mail generally is not a substitute for formal correspondence, and a more casual tone is common, that does not excuse the use of sloppy syntax or incorrect grammar and spelling. Because e-mail tends to be composed on the fly without careful editing, one must be careful not to write something that will be regretted later. Remember, also, that the recipient can forward the message to someone else by simply typing an address and hitting the "forward" button on her screen.

If it is necessary to send a lengthy document by e-mail, it is better to make it an attachment that the receiving party can open as a document and download or print out. The e-mail message itself should be short enough so that the recipient can read it easily on the monitor screen.

Even if a new legal assistant has never used e-mail, it is not difficult to learn the basics. So, there should be no apprehension on that point. E-mail with clients and other law firms is rapidly becoming an important mode of communication, and clients are coming to appreciate—and often demand—rapid turnaround on their queries and requests. In fact, responsiveness to e-mail has become a marketing tool for law firms. Thus, there is no way for the legal assistant to avoid jumping into the e-mail pool with everyone else.

A growing use of e-mail is the sharing of documents that can be revised and then retransmitted by the receiving party. It is not unusual for contract negotiations to proceed in this "ping-pong" manner of e-mail. So, legal assistants need to learn how to integrate word processing with e-mail and to use "attachments" with e-mail messages. One should be able to compose a message in a word processor and then dump that message into the e-mail software for transmission to the intended recipient. Recent versions of word processing software are making that transition easier, and sometimes virtually seamless. A potentially more complicated task is dumping *incoming* e-mail attachments into the computer's word processor. That is because the sender might be using different e-mail and word processing software, which can create some compatibility problems. As the software becomes more sophisticated, however, these processes will become seamless even when the sender and receiver are using different products.

E-Mail Privacy

As attorneys increase their use of the Internet, a number of ethical issues have arisen. How secure and private is e-mail? Is it any more—or less—secure than the telephone, facsimile transmissions, or the U.S. Postal Service? What are the implications of e-mail for client confidences and attorney malpractice?

The use of e-mail to discuss client matters has been widely debated. Some have argued that **encryption software** should be used to protect against electronic eavesdropping on e-mail. However, in 1999, the American Bar Association (ABA) issued Formal Opinion 99-413 on "Protecting the Confidentiality of Unencrypted E-Mail." The opinion concluded: "Lawyers have a reasonable expectation of privacy in communications made by all forms of e-mail, including unencrypted e-mail sent on the Internet." The opinion compared the risk of e-mail interception to the vulnerability of other forms of communication, including U.S. Mail and land-line telephone communications.[5]

The ABA opinion acknowledged that some state bar associations had earlier reached different conclusions, particularly regarding the need for client consent to the use of e-mail. But the opinion stated that ". . . more recent opinions reflecting lawyers' greater understanding of the technology involved approve the use of unencrypted Internet e-mail without express client consent." But the opinion then advised consultation with the client when ". . . the lawyer reasonably believes that confidential client information being transmitted is so highly sensitive that extraordinary measures to protect the transmission are warranted. . . ."[6]

Encryption software converts plain text into code, so that one must have a "key" to decode and read the encrypted text.

> **Practice Tip**
>
> *An electronic version of a document might contain more than meets the eye. Whether viewed on the monitor's screen or printed out, the document one sees is only the latest version—but in the computer's memory there might lurk some revisions that were tried and then discarded. The problem derives from WordPerfect's "undo" feature.*
>
> *By clicking on the "undo" button, the WordPerfect user cancels his latest action, returning the on-screen document to its previous condition. But WordPerfect keeps track of these rejected changes in a history table that—depending upon an option selected by a previous user or by the firm's system manager—can be saved, along with the document itself. When the current user transmits the electronic file for this document to another computer, that history table can go right along with it. A savvy computer expert could open that history and review all of the changes that were ultimately rejected by using the "undo" button. A simple precaution against this problem is to select and delete the unwanted text, rather than using the button. An alternative is to have the firm's systems manager check the status of the "undo" option in WordPerfect.*

> **Ethics Watch**
>
> A law firm has a fiduciary duty to take all reasonable steps to safeguard client confidences. This extends to the use of passwords and other reasonable security measures, possibly including encryption. Most experts recommend changing passwords at least monthly.
>
> A legal assistant must safeguard passwords and faithfully follow other security policies of the law firm. In addition, he should report any perceived security lapses or risks to the person responsible for monitoring security measures in the firm.

E-mail, however, does introduce a new wrinkle: E-mail is stored by the on-line information service (e.g., America Online) or Internet service provider (e.g., Earthlink), as the case might be. When one retrieves e-mail, he is downloading it from the server maintained by that service, but in most cases the message will *not* be erased from that computer. On-line services and ISPs do that at a later time—perhaps a matter of many months. Thus, there is a possibility that the message could be obtained by a hacker.

In one highly publicized case in 1997, an employee of America Online responded to a telephone inquiry from a U.S. Navy paralegal—who did *not* identify himself as such—by providing the identity of a male enlisted sailor who allegedly had posted a profile page indicating an interest in other men. An e-mail message unrelated to that profile page, but sent by the enlisted sailor, had included a reference to the sailor's on-line "handle," which appeared also in the profile page. This led to the navy's inquiry. A federal judge, in granting a preliminary injunction against the sailor's involuntary discharge by the navy, stated that it was "likely" that the navy had violated the federal *Electronic Communications Privacy Act* by obtaining the confidential information without a warrant, subpoena, or court order. The court also commented: "The government knew, or should have known, that by turning over the information without a warrant, AOL was breaking the law." *McVeigh v. Cohen*, 983 F. Supp. 215, 220 (D.D.C. 1998).

Security for Electronic Communications

The *McVeigh* case drew attention to a long-simmering controversy about the privacy of on-line communications—and about the responsibility of on-line information services and ISPs. Some critics even speculated that a corrupt employee of an on-line service might someday be *bribed* to reveal the identity of particular subscribers, or possibly the contents of confidential e-mail. These continue to be unresolved issues.

Another concern is that passwords might not be as secure as people generally believe, making e-mail vulnerable to hackers or other electronic intruders. One well-regarded expert on Internet security, Bryan Pfaffenberger, a University of Virginia professor of technology and culture, has written:

> As your Internet data makes its way from server to server, it passes through many computers. On a less-than-secure system, a computer criminal can set up a program called a *sniffer*, which examines the incoming data for passwords. Since most Internet service providers require you to send your user name and password as plain text, there's little you can do to protect yourself from this form of attack, except to change your password regularly.[7]
> [Emphasis in the original.]

Professor Pfaffenberger also warns that automated programs can run through entire English-language dictionaries, trying each entry as a possible password. That is one reason that experts recommend that passwords contain numerals to interrupt the formation of complete words that might appear in a dictionary (e.g., "ma3xim7um" rather than "maximum3" or "maxim3um"). Although running a "sniffer" (an automated dictionary program) is a major undertaking, it is not beyond the sort of industrial espionage that large corporations sometimes undertake when a great deal of money, power, or prestige is on the line. No one really knows how common e-mail interception is. Because it is a crime, only the most reckless of interceptors are likely to advertise their feats.

Obviously, a key issue regarding e-mail is the attorney's obligation to protect client confidences—including (but not limited to) all communications that should be protected by the attorney-client privilege. Attorneys are not regarded as being negligent if some unauthorized person opens a letter that is sent through the U.S. Mail. (Improperly addressed letters, facsimiles, and e-mails are another matter, of course.) But, does the fact that an electronic "copy" of an e-mail continues to exist after it has been received by its addressee—and then is "stolen" by an unauthorized party—create a new liability for the attorney? This is a question that is yet to be definitively answered by case law.

> **Ethics Watch**
>
> As discussed in Chapter 3, under some circumstances an attorney or paralegal can unintentionally—and without client authorization—waive the privilege of attorney-client communications. In the electronic age, that might occur by transmitting a document, intended for the client, to a third party, instead. All that is required is to enter the wrong telephone number for a facsimile or the wrong address for an e-mail message.
>
> Most law firms have taken one precaution to protect the privilege, even if a document is misdirected. This protection is a "legal statement" incorporated in the cover sheet for facsimile transmissions and used as a header for all e-mail messages. The gist of the statement is that the message is a confidential and privileged one, and that anyone receiving it by error must not read or distribute it. The various jurisdictions differ about the legal adequacy of such a statement to protect the privilege.
>
> A paralegal receiving a communication by error—one which clearly was intended for another party (outside of his law firm)—has an ethical duty not to read the message content. He should notify his supervisor, as well as the person or office that transmitted the message by error.

The Ownership of E-Mail

The ownership of "personal" e-mail received at, or transmitted from, the workplace has been a subject of some controversy. Some people regard it as an egregious violation of privacy for an employer to monitor the e-mail of its employees. Although controversy continues, the underlying law appears to be rather clear.

If an employee is using company-owned equipment (the computer), software, and utilities (electricity and telephone service) to send or receive messages, the employer has a legitimate financial interest in minimizing the personal use of those assets at company expense. Perhaps more important, the employer has potential liability for any improper use of those facilities to harm others (e.g., to harass, libel, or slander another) or to commit a crime (e.g., to make threats or engage in a criminal conspiracy). In a law firm, the employer has a responsibility to protect client confidences from unauthorized disclosure, as well.

In most jurisdictions, the legal presumption is that the employer "owns" all e-mail transmitted through its facilities. The law might require that the employer put employees on notice that they cannot have a reasonable expectation of privacy, and that the e-mail might be monitored. But an employer could simply forbid any personal e-mail on company facilities, which would eliminate any possible expectation of privacy.

In the following "Case in Point," the employer allegedly assured its employees that the company e-mail was confidential and would not be used against them for disciplinary purposes. But it later terminated the plaintiff for inappropriate and unprofessional e-mail messages. Although the messages were sent to the plaintiff's supervisor, the court's opinion gives no hint as to the nature of those messages. And the plaintiff's complaint alleges that his termination resulted from a later "interception" of the messages by other persons. In this case, the defendant-employer has moved for dismissal of the lawsuit for failure to state a valid cause of action. A key issue is the employee's expectation that e-mail communications are entitled to privacy.

A CASE IN POINT

Smyth v. Pillsbury Company

914 F. Supp. 97 (E.D. Penn. 1996)

WEINER, District Judge.

In this diversity action, plaintiff, an at-will employee, claims he was wrongfully discharged from his position as a regional operations manager by the defendant. Presently before the court is the motion of the defendant to dismiss....

A claim may be dismissed under Fed.R.Civ.P. 12(b)(6) only if the plaintiff can prove no set of facts in support of the claim that would entitle him to relief. [Citations omitted.] The reviewing court must consider only those facts alleged in the Complaint and accept all of the allegations as true. [Citation omitted.] Applying this standard, we find that plaintiff has failed to state a claim upon which relief can be granted.

Defendant maintained an electronic mail communication system ("e-mail") in order to promote internal corporate communications between its employees. Complaint at ¶ 8. Defendant repeatedly assured its employees, including plaintiff, that all e-mail communications would remain confidential and privileged. Complaint at ¶ 9. Defendant further assured its employees, including plaintiff, that e-mail communications could not be intercepted and used by defendant against its employees as grounds for termination or reprimand. Complaint at ¶ 10.

In October 1994, plaintiff received certain e-mail communications from his supervisor over defendant's e-mail system on his computer at home. Complaint at ¶ 11. In reliance on defendant's assurances regarding defendant's e-mail system, plaintiff responded and exchanged e-mails with his supervisor. Id. At some later date, contrary to the assurances of confidentiality made by defendant, defendant, acting through its agents, servants and employees, intercepted plaintiff's private e-mail messages made in October 1994. Complaint at ¶ 12. On January 17, 1995, defendant notified plaintiff that it was terminating his employment effective February 1, 1995, for transmitting what it deemed to be inappropriate and unprofessional comments over defendant's e-mail system in October, 1994. Complaint at ¶¶ 13, 14.

* * * *

Plaintiff claims that his termination was in violation of "public policy which precludes an employer from terminating an employee in violation of the employee's right to privacy as embodied in Pennsylvania's common law." Complaint at ¶ 15.

* * * *

... [W]e find that plaintiff has failed to state a claim upon which relief can be granted. In the first instance, unlike urinalysis and personal property searches, we do not find a reasonable expectation of privacy in e-mail communications voluntarily made by an employee to his supervisor over the company e-mail system notwithstanding any assurances that such communications would not be intercepted by management. Once plaintiff communicated the alleged unprofessional comments to a second person (his supervisor) over an e-mail system which was apparently utilized by the entire company, any reasonable expectation of privacy was lost. Significantly, the defendant did not require plaintiff, as in the case of an urinalysis or personal property search to disclose any personal information about himself. Rather, plaintiff voluntarily communicated the alleged unprofessional comments over the company e-mail system. We find no privacy interests in such communication.

In the second instance, even if we found that an employee had a reasonable expectation of privacy in the contents of his e-mail communications over the company e-mail system, we do not find that a reasonable person would consider the defendant's interception of these communications to be a substantial and highly offensive invasion of his privacy.... Moreover, the company's interest in preventing inappropriate and unprofessional comments or even illegal activity over its e-mail system outweighs any privacy interests the employee may have in those comments.

In sum, we find that the defendant's actions did not tortiously invade the plaintiff's privacy and, therefore, did not violate public policy. As a result, the motion to dismiss is granted.

Digital Signatures

With the advent of so-called electronic commerce came the need to verify the authenticity of the sender's identity. How is one to be sure that the person originating the message is who he claims to be? How can contract offers and acceptances be binding, if one can claim that they are easily concocted electronic forgeries?

A **digital signature** resolves these uncertainties. It also allows the receiver to know if anyone has *altered* the electronic message between its point of transmission and its point of reception. It is the digital signature that makes possible the secure electronic transfer of millions of dollars between banks.

Digital signatures are created using encryption techniques that rely upon information in the body of the message, together with the sender's "private key." The complex technology of this process need not be explained here. Suffice it to say that the recipient of the message must have another, "public" key in order to open the encrypted message. The public key will not successfully open the message if the sender's secret private key was not embedded in it. Consequently, if the public key works successfully, the recipient knows that the originator's identity is valid. Also, any alteration of the message en route will invalidate the embedded private key, and the message will not open. As long as the private key is kept secret, forgery of a digital signature is all but impossible.

> A **digital signature** is a computer-encrypted code that combines elements of a private key (held by the originator) and the message content. The message can be opened only by a recipient with the public key, which will not work if the digital signature is invalid.

THE POWER OF WORD PROCESSING SOFTWARE

A computer with word processing software is vastly more powerful than an "old-fashioned" electronic typewriter. It can do simple things, like telling the printer to use *italics*, **bold**, or underlining. And it can select different fonts, such as `Courier`, Arial, or Universe. In a single document, it can mix all of these typefaces and more, as seen here. But, although these capabilities are useful, they barely reflect the real power of word processing software.

The most basic and invaluable feature of a word processor is its editing capability. After preparing a draft of a memorandum, the author can go back and delete a word or a paragraph, insert new text, move an entire section to a different location in the memorandum, and make a multitude of other changes without having to retype the whole document. This basic editing capability is offered by even the cheapest and least sophisticated of word processors. But as important as that editing capability is, it is the dazzling "power features" of advanced word processors that have contributed so much to the efficient preparation of pleadings, contracts, wills, memoranda, and correspondence.

With word processing software, the legal assistant can create a form letter that he types just once. Then he can create a special "merge file" of several hundred names and addresses. That done, he can instruct the computer to print hundreds of letters, automatically inserting a different name and address in each, and including "Dear Jeffrey:" in the salutation of the letter addressed to that particular individual. Using this same procedure, the word processor can also insert unique words or numbers in the text of each letter: for example, reminding Jeffrey of the amount he still owes on his latest fee statement from the firm.

After typing a fifty-page document, the legal assistant might want to find the precise point where she mentioned the *Americans with Disabilities Act.* She can instruct the computer to search the document for "disabilities act," and it will bring that page instantly to the monitor's screen. The time required to type the instruction and complete the search will be measured in a few seconds, at most.

If she is preparing a court brief using an advanced word processor, the legal assistant can produce a **table of authorities** listing every statute and court case cited in the brief. The authorities can be grouped together as "Decisions," "Statutes," and "Other Authorities." "Decisions" could be subdivided into sections for "U.S. Supreme Court" and other jurisdictions. The table is produced by invisibly "marking" each authority as it is typed in the brief; when the document is ready to print in final form, an instruction to the word processing program causes it to produce the table of authorities. It is done within a matter of seconds. An example of a table of authorities appears in *Figure 9.2.*

> A **table of authorities** lists every statute, court case, and other authority cited in a legal document.

Redlining for Document Revisions

Revisions of any document can be printed in **redlining**, which shows any *new* language highlighted and any *deleted* language in ~~strikeout type~~. The redlining feature is especially useful in contract negotiations, because it allows the attorneys to see at a glance the deletions and additions made in each revision of the document. For example, here is the first draft for a single sentence in the opening paragraph of a contract between American and Japanese companies. As is common in many legal documents, the opening paragraph will define a "short" name for each party to the contract. This sentence was drafted by the Chicago attorney for Jillson Manufacturing:

> **Redlining** is the use of highlighting and ~~strikeout type~~ to indicate new and deleted language, respectively, in the draft version of a document.

> This agreement is made by and between Jillson Manufacturing Corporation, an Illinois corporation ("Jillson"), and Nippon Daiwa Kaisha, a Japanese corporation ("Nippon"), hereafter collectively referred to as the "Parties."

After the Japanese company has reviewed this draft, and their Osaka attorneys have conferred with the attorney for Jillson, the following revision has been prepared using redlining. Remember that the shaded text indicates new language and strikeout text indicates deletions.

> This ~~a~~ A greement is made by and between Jillson Manufacturing Corporation, an Illinois corporation ("Jillson"), and Nippon Daiwa Kaisha, a Japanese corporation ("Nippon Daiwa "), ~~hereafter~~ collectively, ~~referred to as~~ the "Parties."

In this revision, "agreement" has been capitalized and some punctuation has been changed. The shortened name for the Japanese corporation has been expanded, because the single Japanese word "Nippon" (used by Jillson's attorney in the first draft) means "Japan" and is part of the corporate name for many thousands of Japanese companies; "Kaisha" cannot be substituted for "Nippon," be-

FIGURE 9.2 Sample Table of Authorities

TABLE OF AUTHORITIES

PAGE

CASES

Blaeholder v. Guthrie, 17 Cal. App. 297 (1911) 4
Hendrixson v. Cardwell, 68 Tenn. 389 (1876) 5
Lloyd v. First National Trust and Savings Bank, 101 Cal. App. 2d 579 (1951) 3
McLane v. Gilbert, 30 Ala. App. 261 (1941) 4
Miller v. County of Kern, 137 Cal. 516 (1902) 2
Nunes Turfgrass, Inc. v. County of Kern, 111 Cal. App. 3d 855 (1927) 3

CONSTITUTIONAL PROVISIONS

Art. XIII, Sec. 1, Calif. Constitution 2

SECONDARY SOURCES

42 Cal. Jur. 3d, Landlord and Tenant § 270, p. 307 2
Witkin, *Summary of California Law,* 9th Ed., Real Property § 247 2
141 A.L.R. 1240, 1248 3

cause "Kaisha" simply means "company" in Japanese. Several extraneous words have been deleted from the last line.

If the changes shown are acceptable to all parties, the final version of the sentence can then be printed by giving a single instruction to the word processing software. The software prints the document without the highlighting and strikeout type; all deleted language disappears, and all added language remains:

> This Agreement is made by and between Jillson Manufacturing Corporation, an Illinois corporation ("Jillson"), and Nippon Daiwa Kaisha, a Japanese corporation ("Nippon Daiwa"), collectively, the "Parties."

Voice-Recognition Software for Word Processing

For years, it was a fantasy of software developers: to develop a program that could transcribe the spoken word into a printed document. In the 1990s, however, that ambition was realized, and there are now several competing programs that promise "hands-off" word processing power. When voice-recognition software eventually lives up to its full potential, it will be a blessing for the writer who prefers to dictate—while sorting through her notes and other supporting materials—and for writers whose physical or neurological disabilities interfere with keyboarding. And for the rest of us—how many attorneys and legal assistants can type between 140 and 160 words per minute? For that is the claimed capability of several voice-recognition programs already on the market.

Voice-recognition software contains a very large lexicon of English words that are most likely to occur in dictated text. Depending upon the program, the lexicons range from about 150,000 words to as many as 250,000. The voice-recognition technology is based upon the meaningful sounds (phonemes) that are used in spoken English.

The person using the software must first provide a voice sample by reading a prescribed text, which permits the software to create a personalized "vocabulary" of the user's spoken phonemes—not of actual words. By later recognizing those

---

Practice Tip

Every experienced computer user knows that every five or ten minutes he should "save" any document he is creating or revising, so that minimal work will be lost if the computer crashes or the keyboard locks up. Unfortunately, that is a working rule too often "honored by its breach." But everyone who breaches that rule eventually comes to rue his carelessness when he loses an hour's worth of effort. Of similar importance is the practice of "backing up" a computer's hard drive. Many law firms have software that creates an automatic nightly backup on tape or other media. Lacking such a system, or a systems manager in the firm, it becomes the individual user's responsibility.

personalized sounds, the software is then able to match them to the standard English phonemes in the software—and thus to the words in its English lexicon. This process accommodates regional accents, dialects, and individual speech habits. If more than one person will use the software program, each must "train" the program to recognize his or her speech.

The voice-recognition and transcription process is complicated by homophones: "heir" and "air"; "there," "their," and "they're"; and so on. The software attempts to resolve these ambiguities by analyzing the context in which the word is used, and some of these problems can be solved by a grammar check function. But, in an experiment conducted by the editors of *PC Magazine*, the editors found that the software often made incorrect substitutions, such as "this series speech" for "this year's speech," and "holds ahead" for "pulls ahead."[8]

PC magazine tested five competing voice-recognition programs, including IBM's ViaVoice Pro Millennium and Dragon Systems' Dragon Naturally Speaking, Preferred Edition. They found the accuracy rates to hover around 95% for the latter programs, which sounds quite impressive. However, that rate means an average of one incorrect word for every twenty words dictated. When the magazine's testers went back to correct the transcriptions, their combined dictation/editing process produced 100% accuracy at a rate of between 19 and 39 words per minute—dramatically reduced by the time required to correct transcription errors. This is a rate well below that which skilled word processing professionals have, but it might be comparable at the higher end with the typing rates of many attorneys and paralegals. It is important to remember that the text finally produced with 100% accuracy, in these tests, was exactly what they had dictated—not an edited or revised final draft.

At this writing, voice-recognition software is still somewhat limited by the technical challenges that it must meet and by the demands it places upon the processing power of current desktop computers.[9] As software development continues and the processing power of computers improves, voice-recognition software will become much more effective. And progress appears to be happening rapidly on both fronts. The most popular program among legal professionals has been Dragon Naturally Speaking, which is bundled by Corel with its office suite tailored for law firms, WordPerfect Law Office 2000.

USING DATABASE SYSTEMS FOR INFORMATION MANAGEMENT

Next to word processing software and billing systems, **database managers** (also known as "database management systems," or DBMS) are the software programs most often used in law firms. Database management software allows the user to create a database, which is an organized memory structure containing various types of information. For example, a law firm might have a simple database containing client information, such as the following:

- client name
- address
- phone number
- facsimile number
- responsible attorney
- legal matters pending
- legal matters closed
- outstanding fees
- miscellaneous information

To understand the structure of the database, imagine a grid composed of columns and rows. Each column (known as a "**field**") is reserved for a specific type of information to be stored, such as the client's name or phone number.

A **database manager** is a program used to organize information, which then can be sorted or searched.

A **field** in a database is a column dedicated to a particular category of data (e.g., client name).

Other fields are set aside for the client's address, responsible attorney, and so on. An entire row of these fields (known as a "**record**") is dedicated to each client. The records can be identified by a client number or by the client's name. Each field is identified by the type of information stored, such as "address." *Figure 9.3* is an example of a database table.

> A **record** in a database is a row dedicated to a particular entity (e.g., a lawsuit) about which information is stored in various fields.

The client database permits one to quickly search the computer memory for all clients having outstanding fee balances, for example, or for all clients of a particular attorney in the firm. The database can be searched by any combination of criteria: all clients involved in litigation, *with* outstanding balances, *and* for whom Ms. Esquire is the responsible attorney, for example. The resulting list of clients can then be printed out, or those database records can be "tagged" by the computer for future reference. Computers are marvels at locating instantly all records that have been electronically "marked" with a distinctive tag.

Some fields in the database might contain numerical data, and the database program can perform mathematical calculations on that data. But spreadsheet programs are far more powerful in their ability to manipulate numerical data.

USING SPREADSHEETS FOR NUMERICAL DATA

A **spreadsheet** is similar to a database, in that it is a memory structure composed of columns and rows (again, usually referred to as "fields" and "records"). The memory "box" at the intersection of a column and a row is called a "cell." Unlike a database, the primary purpose of a spreadsheet is to manipulate numerical data in complex ways. Although a database can handle simple calculations, a spreadsheet can store and use mathematical formulae for very complex calculations. A key feature of a spreadsheet is its ability to instantly update itself, including every single cell that is affected by a numerical change in another part of the spreadsheet. For example, if a mathematical calculation changes the data in a particular cell of the spreadsheet, that change might also affect the data in dozens (or even hundreds) of other cells in the same spreadsheet. The spreadsheet program is designed to automatically calculate those changes and instantly update all affected cells.

> A **spreadsheet** is an accounting worksheet (or ledger page). A *spreadsheet program* permits the immediate, automatic recalculation of all values affected by a change in the value of any single item (e.g., an interest rate) in the spreadsheet.

An ultrasimple use for a spreadsheet would be to examine the interaction of three variables (interest rate, sales price, and down payment) and their effect upon the monthly payment required to amortize a mortgage in thirty years. If the purchaser's income limits the monthly payment to $1,000, for example, a higher interest rate might require a larger down payment in order to hold the monthly payment below $1,000. Whenever one of the variables is changed, the spreadsheet automatically calculates the new down payment (or monthly payments) necessary to pay off the mortgage in thirty years. Of course, spreadsheet software is designed to accommodate mathematical relationships far more complex than this example. Spreadsheets are particularly useful for analyzing mathematical "what if . . . " situations. *Figure 9.4* shows one page in a simple spreadsheet.

In this simple example, a spreadsheet field (i.e., a column) would be designated for each of the following:

- monthly payment
- principal amount paid each month
- interest amount paid each month
- new balance each month

A spreadsheet record (i.e., a row) would be set aside for each month of the year, for as many years as the duration of the loan. The three variables (interest rate, sales price, and down payment) would be expressed in a separate mathematical formula. A change in any one of the variables will change the data in almost every cell in the spreadsheet. Because there are 360 monthly payments in thirty years, there would be 360 records in this hypothetical spreadsheet. The "new balance" in the final record (i.e., row 360) would be zero, indicating that the mortgage has been fully paid.

FIGURE 9.3 Example of a Database Table

Last Name	First Name	Address	City	State	Zip	Work Phone	Home Phone	Case Number
Allen	Alice	P.O. Box 2342	San Diego	CA	95336	619-998-2589	619-465-4434	91-5234
Appell	Mariam	2341 Huntoon	La Jolla	CA	92039	619-234-5345	619-764-3424	91-2342
Barney	Larry	23492 12th SE	Ocean Spray	CA	95334	619-293-2435	619-243-3332	90-2342
Davis	Karl	2941 Lane	La Jolla	CA	92039	619-443-9944	619-234-3455	90-3424
Johnson	Donald	32455 Coastal	Miami	FL	65773	673-256-2355	673-552-5489	91-2343
Kitchen	Jennifer	2342 45th St. NW	San Diego	CA	95334	619-887-4566	619-342-7521	91-2342
Robert	Den	23332 Westside Road	Marina Bay	CA	93442	615-933-5355	615-933-6500	90-3423
Winslow	Harriet	89404 Humboldt	Las Vegas	NV	78524	204-345-8624	204-346-9908	91-3424

Fields

One record

One file

CHAPTER 9　　Computers in the Law Office　　**357**

FIGURE 9.4　Example of a Spreadsheet

CERTIFICATED SALARIES
in the
COAST AND RANCHO SANTIAGO
COMMUNITY COLLEGE DISTRICTS

(ACTUAL EXPENDITURES in millions)

	1993-94		1994-95		1995-96		1996-97	
	COAST	RSCCD	COAST	RSCCD	COAST	RSCCD	COAST	RSCCD
Certificated Salaries	47.633	27.717	48.573	27.911	49.092	30.107	49.380	32.321
Percent of TOTAL	39%	43%	40%	43%	38%	41%	38%	41%
TOTAL	120.769	64.005	122.461	65.098	128.635	73.977	130.762	78.718
(Object Codes 1000-6000)								

Indicates budget amounts.

Indicates June 1996 estimate for fiscal year 1995-96.

3.25% of $130.762 million = $4.250 million

(Source: RSCCD Tentative Budget, 1996-97.)

> **Practice Tip**
>
> Less experienced computer users often believe that deleting a file—for example, a word processing document, spreadsheet, or database—means that it is irretrievably gone. However, that is not the case. In fact, sophisticated software programs are sold that allow one to recover all, or part, of a "deleted" file. PC Tools and Norton's Utilities are among the better known of these products. The success of these products is based upon the fact that the discarded data is not automatically erased from the hard drive—it is simply hidden from the user. Their success depends also upon prompt recovery efforts before the data has been overwritten by new files. The larger the hard drive and the greater the unused portion of that hard drive, the greater the chances of recovering deleted data.
>
> But this capability for recovery of "deleted" data means that unauthorized intruders could also recover files that the user believes have been deleted. When one deletes a file, that space on the hard drive simply becomes available to store newly created files. If no new files are created, the entire "deleted" file remains available for recovery—by the user, by the firm's systems manager, or by an intruder.

An **office suite** is integrated software containing a word processor, database manager, spreadsheet, and software utilities.

More-complex spreadsheets function in the same way. Their complexity results from having more variables, and from the more-complex mathematical relationships among the types of data. Spreadsheets are used in planning and negotiating business transactions, in tax planning, and in other financial matters.

> **Ethics Watch**
>
> Is it ever ethical—and legal—to totally erase files on a hard drive? The answer is a *qualified* "yes." If it is part of an established, written business practice, it is entirely proper to archive all completed, final documents on a separate drive—or on a tape backup—and wipe clean the drive that is used to prepare and revise drafts. All hard copies of draft documents should be treated in an identical manner.
>
> It is *not* proper to selectively destroy data—whether in file cabinets or on hard drives—just because the data might be potentially embarrassing or damaging. Again, if it is part of a formal business policy and practice, it is acceptable to destroy all files—paper and electronic—that exceed a clearly established age (say, three or five years). The key is that any destruction must be done in the ordinary course of business. That is why a written policy, rigorously and consistently followed, is so important.

OFFICE SUITES: INTEGRATED SOFTWARE PACKAGES

Integrated software (often known as an **office suite**) contains a word processor, database manager, spreadsheet, and usually some software utilities (e.g., a scheduler/calendar), in a single "package." Examples of office suites are Microsoft Office, Lotus's SmartSuite, and Corel's WordPerfect Suite. The advantages of these packages are their all-in-one price, built-in compatibility between suite applications and the relative ease of exchanging information between their bundled applications. However, these integrated applications sometimes include "lite" versions of their separate "full-strength" versions. Certainly, no law firm would want to sacrifice the full features of a dedicated word processor for a less expensive—but less powerful—version in an office suite.

SOFTWARE DESIGNED FOR THE PRACTICE OF LAW

Corel offers WordPerfect Suite in a "legal edition"—most recently, WordPerfect Law Office 2000—that has been customized for the practice of law, simplifying the more common tasks like setting up pages in a pleading format. And there is a wide variety of other specialized application programs designed for the practice of law. They include "form generators," which allow the user to respond to on-screen prompts for information and then print out a "filled-in" blank form (e.g. tax forms and court documents). Other programs help the attorney to draft wills and trusts based upon the attorney's responses to on-screen queries. Such specialized software is available for probate, bankruptcy, personal injury, family law, real estate, and worker compensation law, to name just a few fields.

Legal software is widely advertised in legal newspapers, such as the *National Law Journal*, and in bar association journals, *Legal Assistant Today* magazine, *The Lawyer's PC* magazine, *Perfect Lawyer* magazine, and *Law Office Computing* magazine. Some of these publications evaluate competing software products. In the discussion that follows, the reader will be introduced to some of the software most heavily used in law firms as listed below:

- document management
- case management
- litigation support
- docketing and calendaring

Using Document Management Systems

Law offices seem to generate (and take in) an extraordinary number of documents, and keeping track of all that paper has always presented a challenge. One of the blessings of the computer age has been software programs that make that challenge manageable. **Document management systems (DMS)** are essentially database programs that identify, index, and locate documents of all kinds.

Integrated with the office computer system, a DMS can "capture" each document as it is created, and it can add the document's essential identifying features to the database. It is able to track different versions of the same document as it undergoes revisions. And it can perform a full-text search for keywords to locate all documents in the system that relate to a given topic. Documents received on paper from outside sources can be added to the DMS by scanning them into the system. Popular document management programs include WORLDOX, iManage, and DOCS Open.

The document management system also provides security features that permit individual access under several standards (e.g., "read only"), and can log each entry by the user's name, the date, and the time. This feature can also identify when and by whom changes are made to the document. Documents generated outside of the office can be protected from any alterations by word processing, database management, or spreadsheet programs.

> A **document management system (DMS)** is software that catalogs a document's identifying features for later search and retrieval. The system is capable of a full-text search of all catalogued documents.

Using Case Management Systems

Case management systems have some similarities to document management systems, and the two systems can work well together. While the DMS manages documents for all client matters in the law firm, the **case management system (CMS)** manages a specific client matter, such as a lawsuit. The CMS integrates a calendar and tickler system, contacts diary, task assignment and management record, and case history. Although each client matter is managed as a discrete project, the case management system permits links between different client matters that have some common relationship (e.g., the client, an opposing party, or responsible attorney). Widely used case management systems include Amicus Attorney, Time Matters, and AbacusLaw. Generally speaking, CMS programs do not have the archiving, full-text searching, and access control features that a document management system offers. Consequently, a law firm needs either to install both types of systems or to install an integrated system that offers the features of both.

> A **case management system (CMS)** is software that integrates a calendar, contacts diary, task assignments, and case history in a given client matter.

A sophisticated use for a database is the management of complex litigation. With numerous plaintiffs and defendants, multiple factual and legal issues, scores of witnesses, and thousands of documents, a single case can present an overwhelming management problem. A computer database can store and cross-reference all of the relevant information: names, addresses, dates, events, documents (indexed by subject, author, addressee, date, and content), deposition summaries, and so on.

As computers appear more frequently on the counsel's table in courtrooms, paralegals also will appear more often, sitting at the attorney's side and using the computer to locate critical information during trial. At the very minimum, the computer can instantly search the database index, so that the paralegal can quickly locate the hard copy of a document in the boxes she has lugged into the courtroom that day.

The potential of database managers in the practice of law has not been lost on software publishers, and a number of automated litigation-support programs are available. Medium- and small-sized law firms have been slow to use advanced litigation software, but falling prices and the advantages of this software will soon cause those few firms without it to join the trend to a greater use of this technology.

Law firms generally use a relational database management system (DBMS). The software is called "relational" because it can manage multiple database files (sometimes called "tables") that are related to each other by certain common fields of data. For example, the client name and identifying client matter number might appear in several databases: client list, case list, conflict list, and tickler system. Using the relational DBMS, the paralegal can call up specified information for each matter on today's tickler list, drawing portions of that information from each of the related databases. In other words, a relational DBMS allows related databases to share any information needed. They also allow that information to be edited without opening each database as a separate file. *Figure 9.5* presents a simplified example of multiple relational databases.

Relational databases offer several other advantages. There is no need to make duplicate entries of the same information (e.g., the client's address and telephone number) in multiple databases; that information can be retrieved by the DBMS from the particular database where it is stored whenever that information is needed. Also, it is not necessary to build a single, enormous database table that must be searched in its entirety for every single piece of information that is needed. Relational databases must each have, however, at least one identical field (e.g., client name) that allows them to be linked together and to share their other data.

Full-Text and Imaging Software

A second component of the automated litigation support system is full-text search and retrieval software. Whereas the database would contain key identifying data for each document, and possibly a summary, the full-text software works with the complete documents in their original form: deposition transcripts, memoranda and letters, pleadings, discovery requests and responses,

FIGURE 9.5 Multiple Relational Databases

CLIENT ACCOUNTS	CLIENT MASTER RECORD
Client name	Client name
Client number	Client number
Past due	Client address
Period past due	Client phone
Current billing	Attorney
Total due	Matter 1
	Matter 2
	Matter 3
	Matter 4

CLIENT MATTER 1	CLIENT MATTER 2
Client name	Client name
Client number	Client number
Issue	Issue
Opposing party	Opposing party
Opposing counsel	Opposing counsel
Status of matter	Status of matter

CLIENT MATTER 3	CLIENT MATTER 4
Client name	Client name
Client number	Client number
Issue	Issue
Opposing party	Opposing party
Opposing counsel	Opposing counsel
Status of matter	Status of matter

and the like. Those documents that originated in the law firm can be accessed on the computer or server where they are stored. Other documents can be scanned into the computer, using optical character recognition (OCR) software. Transcripts of testimony can often be obtained from the court reporter on a diskette or CD-ROM. The full-text software makes it possible to do the following:

- to prepare topical indexes of all documents, or of any category of documents, without keying the topical data for each document into the database
- to compare testimony by the same or different witnesses on any given topic
- to locate every reference to a particular person, entity, or issue

Documents that include handwriting, sketches, and diagrams can be stored on a computer by using imaging software. Imaging is a familiar process for anyone who uses facsimile machines. It is just as easy to "fax" a signature as a typewritten sentence. In effect, the software snaps a "picture" of the document and stores that picture in the computer. Because it is not stored as characters—even if printed characters do appear in the document—the resulting image file cannot be searched by the full-text software described above. But the computer can recall and print graphic copies of that document with ease. If the computer has a fax-modem, the document can be transmitted directly from that computer to a facsimile machine. Finally, storing the document on the computer saves an extraordinary amount of file cabinet space. This has led to the rise of commercial services that use both OCR and imaging technology to copy vast quantities of documents and deliver them to the law firm on CD-ROM.

Integrated Automated Litigation-Support Programs

There are two ways to set up an automated litigation-support system. The firm can use currently owned software—for example, case management and document management programs—and purchase full-text, OCR, and (possibly) imaging software from one or more vendors. If well-chosen, these programs might function very well. But the interface between such piecemeal systems is not always smooth.

The other solution is to purchase an off-the-shelf integrated system designed for litigation. There are several advantages to this second approach:

- The interface between integrated components is usually superior.
- Technical support can be obtained from a single vendor, with no one pointing the finger of responsibility for problems toward "that other" company's product.
- The systems include additional features for litigation purposes, which will not be found in generic software produced for the business world at large.

Examples of such integrated products include Summation Blaze, Gravity Verdict and Discovery/Magic.

SECTION 2. COMPUTER-ASSISTED LEGAL RESEARCH

Only two decades ago, **computer-assisted legal research (CALR)** was just beginning to gain wide acceptance among law firms. Since then, the legal profession has undertaken a profound transition from print-based research to computer-based

Computer-assisted legal research (CALR) uses CD-ROMs, on-line services such as Westlaw and LEXIS-NEXIS, or the Internet to locate legal materials.

research. It is a transition still in progress, to be sure, but there is no doubt that CALR will become the predominant mode for legal research in the future. In its early stages, CALR was dominated by LEXIS-NEXIS and Westlaw, with attorneys and paralegals using computers and telephone lines to research those gigantic databases of cases and statutory law.

Initially, the magic of CALR was the ability to use a computer to search cases and other legal materials for the presence of key terms, such as "fiduciary duty" and "breach." But as additional materials and new features were added by those on-line services, legal professionals came to appreciate the easy access to an exhaustive list of legal materials that could not all be maintained in the firm's own library and the immediate ability to download and print the materials that were found. Another advantage was the access to *Shepard's Citations*, not only for the convenience, but because the researcher had greater assurance that the on-line data was current. LEXIS-NEXIS and Westlaw were expensive—but their cost was offset by their time efficiency and their effectiveness as research tools.

The next breakthrough in CALR was the publication of case reporters, statutes, and other legal materials on CD-ROMs. The CD-ROMs were searchable, in the same way as the databases of Westlaw and LEXIS-NEXIS. They were far cheaper to produce than books, and they required far less space in the law office.

THE INTERNET AND THE WORLD WIDE WEB

Then came the Internet. Although not as rapidly accepted by law firms as were Westlaw, LEXIS-NEXIS, and CD-ROMs, it came with the aura of a frontier with unknown possibilities. For the technically savvy and adventurous individual, it offered the opportunity for freewheeling exploration of a new electronic world without boundaries. Although intriguing and entertaining, research on the Internet was not very productive at first. Sources of free legal materials were scarce and hard to find.

The event that was to transform the Internet into the valuable tool it is today was the development of the World Wide Web with a system for linking Web sites. This made possible the development of directories like Yahoo! and search engines like Alta Vista. The advent of the World Wide Web permitted the researcher to follow easily activated links that moved him from one Web site to another, until the sought-after grail was uncovered. Universities and law schools recognized the possibilities offered by the Web and began to establish on-line repositories of published materials, including statutes and recent court opinions. Government agencies, including many courts, established their own Web sites and began to make public documents and records available on-line. The Internet became an irresistible and unavoidable source for legal research. The Internet's role in legal research is discussed in Section 3 of this chapter.

ON-LINE LEGAL RESEARCH WITH WESTLAW AND LEXIS-NEXIS

West Group's Westlaw and Reed Elsevier Inc.'s LEXIS-NEXIS are virtually complete law libraries just waiting for a call from one's computer. In a matter of seconds, they can display the complete text of almost any American court case or statute one might care to see. Even foreign legal authorities are available. Westlaw and LEXIS-NEXIS can be reached via their own dedicated land-lines, or they can be reached on the Internet through ISPs. Access via the Internet is discussed briefly in Section 3 of this chapter.

Both services provide primary authorities for all fifty states, the District of Columbia, and—of course—all federal statutes and court decisions. Administrative regulations are included for the federal government and most states. IRS rulings, administrative law decisions for many federal agencies, and opinions by the attorneys general of the larger state jurisdictions are available. Among the secondary authorities offered by both Westlaw and LEXIS-NEXIS are the following:

- Law reviews, bar journals, and legal periodicals
- Treatises and legal periodicals
- *Restatements of the Law*
- *American Law Reports*
- *American Jurisprudence*

Although the databases offered by both Westlaw and LEXIS-NEXIS are extraordinarily comprehensive, a paralegal might need to go to the firm library or the county law library to find special treatises, particularly those that treat the law of a specific state jurisdiction. But the great bulk of legal research can be done on-line with these legal databases. Both services continue to add new legal sources to their databases, so that the need for a traditional "hard-copy" law library is growing progressively smaller each year. This is an enormous advantage for small firms that cannot afford a large law library, especially those firms distant from a law school or county law library.

In addition to using Westlaw and LEXIS-NEXIS to search legal issues, one can use them also to discover other types of information. For example, it is possible to search only the case names to locate all cases in which a company was a plaintiff or defendant. One can also use key terms to search for cases with similar factual situations, such as defective cylinders on light aircraft engines. Both services provide extensive access to news media in the fields of business, finance, and law.

A paralegal student cannot predict which on-line service—LEXIS-NEXIS or Westlaw—her future employer will be using. It is not practical for most paralegal students to become proficient in both, and law firms normally expect new paralegals to go through a learning period before they are competent in computer-assisted research. Although it is an advantage to be proficient in one of these on-line services, it rarely is a requirement for entry-level paralegal positions.

Making On-Line Research Cost-Effective

Law firms can subscribe to Westlaw and LEXIS-NEXIS in two basic ways. Firms can obtain a license for 24-hour access and unlimited searches. Or, they can subscribe to plans that permit an allotted number of on-line hours per month, with additional on-line time being charged by the minute. The latter, flat-rate plans might include an allotted number of searches, with any additional searches charged separately. Additional charges might also apply when material is downloaded to the firm's computer.

Very large law firms find it more economical to pay the fixed fee for unlimited access, but that is prohibitively expensive for the great majority of law firms, which do not use LEXIS-NEXIS or Westlaw enough to make unlimited access economical. Sole practitioners or very small partnerships who do not use the service frequently can set up a credit card account that is charged only for the searches actually conducted and the documents actually downloaded. The following discussion assumes that the law firm is a monthly subscriber without 24-hour unlimited access.

It is important to plan each on-line search, so that it can be completed as efficiently as possible. Both Westlaw and LEXIS-NEXIS have attorneys available by telephone to assist in preparing a search request. Westlaw attorneys will even test several possible queries to determine which is most effective. There is no charge for these support services.

The attorney and legal assistant have an ethical duty to provide the client with good value for the fees and costs charged to that client. That duty includes an obligation to conduct legal research in a reasonably efficient manner. In some situations, old-fashioned, hands-on library research might be more economical; in other situations, computer-assisted research promises greater cost-efficiency. The legal assistant must keep in mind that the client usually pays for on-line charges, as well as paralegal time, when the research is done on-line. Of course, it is not always possible to know with certainty, in advance, which method of research will be the most efficient.

When on-line research appears more promising, the law firm must still minimize those on-line charges that the client must pay. For that reason, some law firms routinely require attorney authorization before a legal assistant conducts on-line research.

For the newcomer to on-line research, both Westlaw and LEXIS-NEXIS offer free training to the employees of subscribing law firms. Both services also provide self-teaching tutorials with their software and manuals. In addition, they offer free on-line use of *practice* databases, without any charge for the on-line time or the practice searches; the law firm pays only the telephone connect charges. *However, the practice databases are not kept current, so that they cannot be relied upon for actual research purposes.*

> **Practice Tip**
>
> *Time on-line can pass with amazing speed, piling up fees much larger than anticipated. Consequently, it is important to drop off-line when a search request proves ineffective. Attempting to modify the request on-line, under pressure of mounting fees, is not conducive to cool analysis. It is better to hang up and work out a new request off-line. That also provides an opportunity to consult with the attorney or other paralegals before trying the new search request on-line.*

Locating Information in Westlaw or LEXIS-NEXIS

Once the legal assistant has logged on, the next task is to begin the research. Just as a clear focus is important in hands-on library research, it has even greater importance when conducting computer-assisted legal research. Key terms (e.g., malpractice, attorney general, airplane, negligence, or fraud) are doubly important on-line, because both Westlaw and LEXIS-NEXIS use them to search their databases for the information needed. The reader must not confuse key terms with West's Key Number service, which is a distinct search tool for Westlaw and the print publications by West.

Both Westlaw and LEXIS-NEXIS contain hundreds of databases, so that it helps to know which database should be searched. If one is looking for a U.S. Supreme Court case, it would be foolish to use a key term search in the database for all courts, state and federal, even though Supreme Court cases are included. Most likely, the query would turn up cases from other courts, in addition to those of the Supreme Court. Instead, the researcher would select the database that contains Supreme Court decisions only. If she is researching a question of state law, but wants to find *federal* cases applying *state law* to that issue, it makes sense to choose the database that is limited to the federal appellate circuit that serves her state. Some issues are more effectively searched by using a database dedicated to a particular field of law, such as federal tax law, family law, or bankruptcy law.

Finding Primary Authority in Westlaw

This chapter provides an introduction to the potential of on-line legal databases—no more. The paralegal student will need hands-on training before she can use LEXIS-NEXIS or Westlaw effectively. A complete description of the search protocol (i.e., the rules governing the syntax and format for search queries) for these on-line services would take several chapters for each. Even then, it would have no

FIGURE 9.6 Welcome to Westlaw Screen

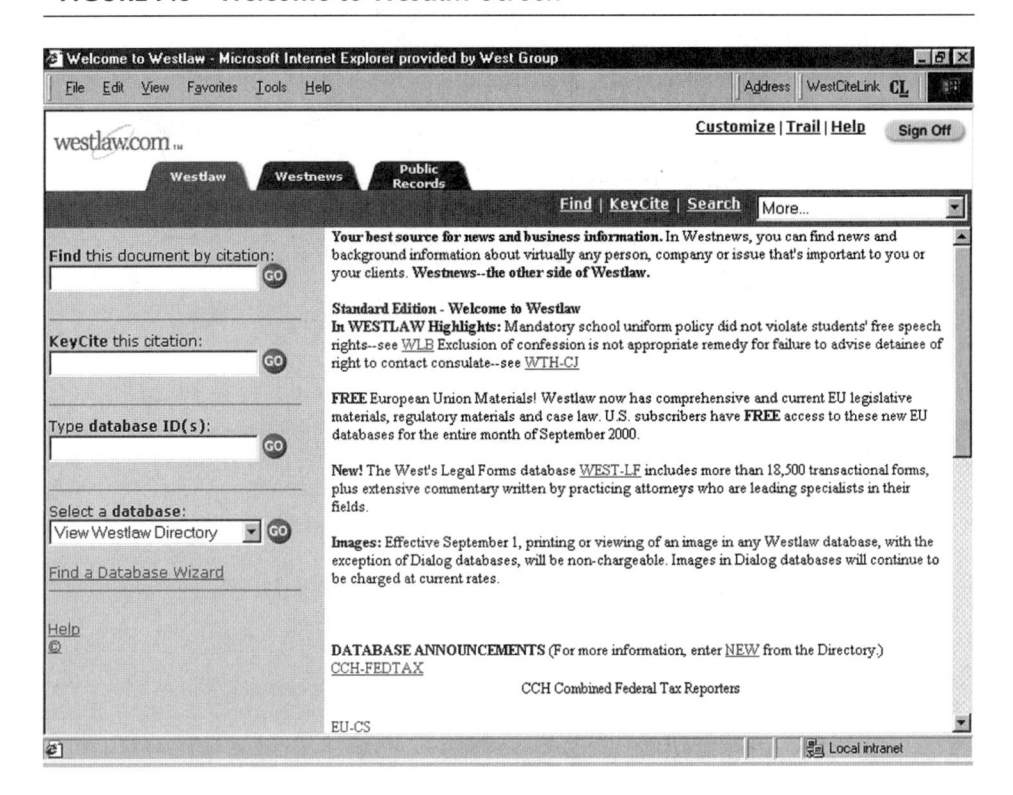

westlaw.com, Copyright by West Group. Reprinted by permission.

practical value unless the student were able to practice on a computer. This chapter provides a general introduction to search capabilities and concepts for the major legal databases. Although this textbook will use Westlaw as an exemplar for an on-line legal database service, the procedures and protocols for LEXIS-NEXIS are somewhat similar. *Figure 9.6* illustrates the opening screen when the user logs onto Westlaw.

Using a Citation to Find Case Law or a Statute

If the paralegal has a citation, it is a simple matter to retrieve a statute or court opinion in Westlaw. This is done using the Find feature. On the toolbar at the top of the Westlaw screen, there is a tab labeled "Find." Clicking on that tab brings up the Find a Document dialog box, seen in *Figure 9.7*. By typing the citation in the space provided in that box, and then clicking the GO button, the paralegal can retrieve the full text of that statute or case, which will appear on the monitor screen.

For example, either

67 sct 1604
or
332 us 301

will retrieve *United States v. Standard Oil Co. of California, et al.,* 332 U.S. 301, 67 S. Ct. 1604 (1947). The reader will recognize that *67 sct 1604* is the citation for the unofficial *Supreme Court Reports* and that *332 us 301* is the citation to the official *United States Reports*.

A statute is retrieved in similar fashion. To review the text of *Kentucky Revised Statutes*, § 403.044, for example, one enters:

ky st s 403.044

FIGURE 9.7 Finding a Document

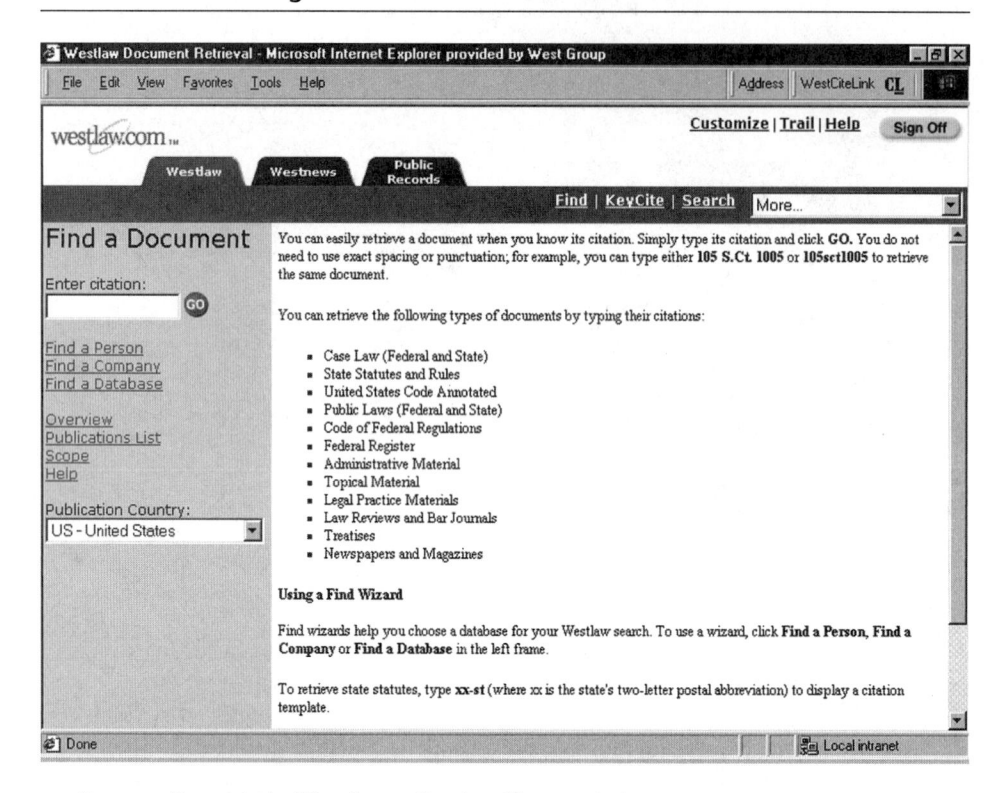

westlaw.com, Copyright by West Group. Reprinted by permission.

In this example, the postal service abbreviation for Kentucky is followed by "st" (for statutes) and "s" (for section), and then the section number. Once the document is on the screen, the paralegal can tell Westlaw to download that document to her printer or hard disk. The Kentucky statute mentioned above appears in *Figure 9.8* exactly as Westlaw has downloaded it to the printer.

Using Westlaw Databases

The court opinion in *United States v. Standard Oil of California, supra,* is stored in several Westlaw databases, including one devoted to Supreme Court Cases alone. The Kentucky statutes also have a database of their own. The hundreds of databases are organized with a substantial amount of overlap, so that the same court opinion might be located in several different databases. For example, a single U.S. Bankruptcy Court case that decided an issue related to insurance law can be located in the databases for bankruptcy law, insurance law, and opinions of all federal courts. For some types of research, one must identify a database before Westlaw can conduct a search.

Choosing the appropriate database can be very important to the success and economy of the search. But the two on-line research services make allowances by having a variety of narrowly focused databases, plus several broad databases. Most searches are composed of key terms that are likely to appear in a discussion of the legal topic the legal assistant is researching. By selecting a broad database, he reduces the chances of missing the information for which he is looking. The disadvantage of using the broad database is that his search might turn up a large number of cases from other jurisdictions—which would be only persuasive authority. There are ways to write a search request to prevent the latter problem, but the general principle is still valid.

FIGURE 9.8 Kentucky Revised Statues, § 403.044

KY ST s 403.044 Page 1
KRS § 403.044

BALDWIN'S KENTUCKY REVISED STATUTES ANNOTATED
TITLE XXXV. DOMESTIC RELATIONS
CHAPTER 403. DISSOLUTION OF MARRIAGE; CHILD CUSTODY
GENERAL PROVISIONS

Copr. © West Group 1998. All rights reserved.

Current through End of 1997 1st Ex. Sess.

403.044 TESTIMONY IN CERTAIN CASES NOT TAKEN FOR SIXTY DAYS AFTER COMPLAINT FILED

In divorce actions in which there are minor children who are the issue of the marriage no testimony other than on temporary motions shall be taken or heard before sixty (60) days have elapsed from the date of service of summons, the appointment of a warning order attorney or the filing of an entry of appearance or a responsive pleading by the defendant, whichever occurs first.

CREDIT(S)

HISTORY: 1980 c 45, § 1, eff. 7-15-80
1972 c 253, § 1; 1968 c 43, § 2

< General Materials (GM) - References, Annotations, or Tables >

PRACTICE AND STUDY AIDS

Bardenwerper, West's Kentucky Practice, Methods of Practice 72.14, n 1
Graham & Keller, West's Kentucky Practice, Domestic Relations Law § 8.9 (1997)

LIBRARY REFERENCES

Evidence, generally. 24 Am Jur 2d, Divorce and Separation § 357 et seq.

KRS § 403.044

KY ST § 403.044

END OF DOCUMENT

westlaw.com, Copyright by West Group. Reprinted by permission.

The most frequently used databases in Westlaw are those for federal and state court cases. The database identifiers that are most frequently used for federal court cases are as follows:

Courts Included	Westlaw Database Name
Combined Federal Cases	ALLFEDS
Supreme Court	
courts of appeal	
district courts	
bankruptcy courts	
tax court	
most other federal courts	
U.S. Supreme Court	SCT
U.S. Courts of Appeals	CTA
U.S. District Court	DCT
U.S. Tax Court	FTX-TCT

Databases for state cases and statutes are identified by the two-letter U.S. Postal Service abbreviation. The identifier for a database containing state court cases adds the letters CS, following the state abbreviation. Thus, Kentucky cases are found in the database identified as KY-CS, and Louisiana cases in LA-CS. It is not necessary to use the shift key to capitalize the database identifiers—the Westlaw software automatically enters them in capitalized form on the screen.

Using Key Terms for Full-Text Searches

A powerful tool in computer-assisted research is the "terms and connectors" query. By specifying key terms related to a legal principle or a factual situation, the legal assistant can instruct Westlaw to conduct a full-text search of many thousands of cases, selecting only those cases that meet the specified criteria. This type of search can be completed in a matter of seconds. *Figure 9.9* is the screen in which one enters the key terms for Westlaw to search.

Designing full-text searches can be quite challenging, and actually it is something of an art. It requires the researcher to anticipate the words that courts are likely to use in their decisions. And he often has to think of alternative approaches: "undue influence" might be too restrictive; perhaps he should try it together with "duress" and "coercion" as alternatives. Searches are much easier to design when legal terms of art are involved; "constructive fraud," "wrongful termination," "due process," and "contempt of court" are good examples.

Cases can be located by searching for key material facts, as well. If the client's case involves engine failure in a small aircraft, the paralegal can search for phrases such as "defective cylinder," "fuel starvation," or "metal fatigue." If the legal or factual issues involve attorneys, Westlaw could be instructed to search for all cases including these words:

attorney lawyer

A **query** is a search request used to locate information in an on-line database.

This is known as a **query**. The query protocol in Westlaw treats the above request as though it stated, "find all cases in which *either* 'attorney' or 'lawyer' ap-

FIGURE 9.9 Searching with Terms and Connectors

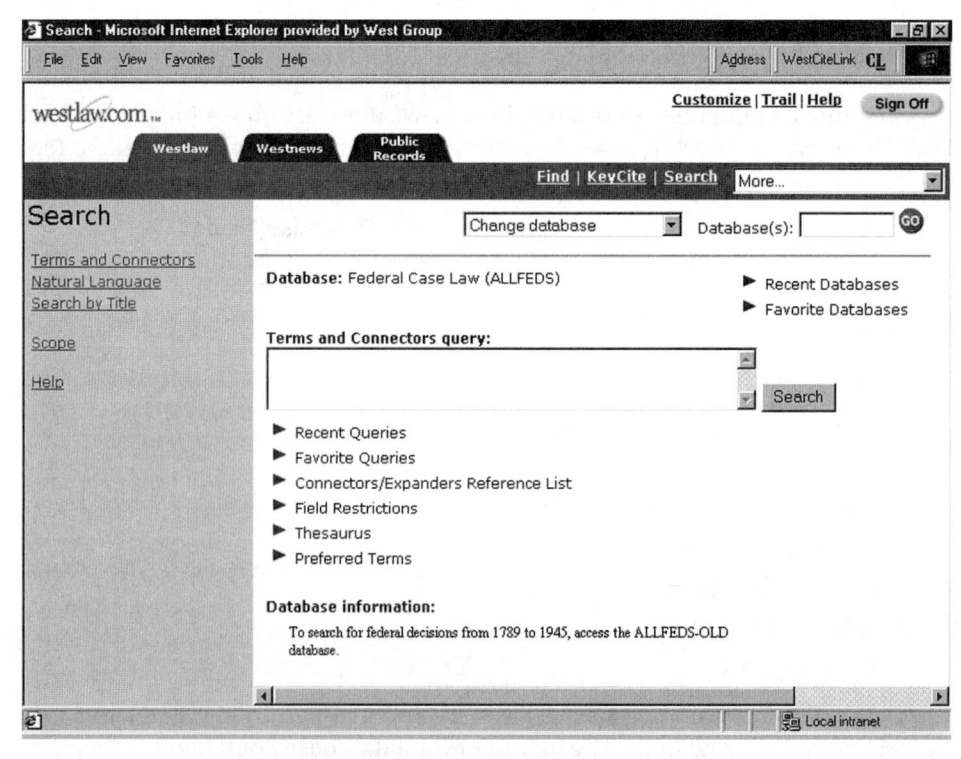

westlaw.com, Copyright by West Group. Reprinted by permission.

pears in the court's decision." In effect, Westlaw treats the blank space between two words as a substitute for the instruction "*or.*"

Westlaw will automatically search for the plural and possessive forms of these words, as well. Obviously, an overwhelming number of cases would be identified by that query, and the search results would therefore be useless. This illustrates an important point in using key terms in computer-assisted research. To avoid retrieving hundreds or even thousands of cases, the query must be designed to restrict the search to a number of cases that the researcher can efficiently review.

In the prior example, some other legal or factual issue must be added, to the query to narrow the results to a manageable number of cases. If the client's case involves malpractice, that term could be added, as shown below:

attorney lawyer & malpractice

That modification would help somewhat, because the ampersand (&) stands for "*and.*" Westlaw now understands that it is to find *one document* with the word "malpractice" together with either "attorney" or "lawyer." But this amended query would still retrieve far too many cases for the legal assistant to review. In some situations, it can be very difficult to identify sufficiently restrictive key terms, and a computer search might not be practical.

Suppose another client has been the victim of constructive fraud by a real estate agent. One could instruct Westlaw to retrieve all cases that include the words "constructive fraud" and "real estate agent." Depending upon the legal issues in question, he might choose to search for "fiduciary duty" in addition to "constructive fraud," and "real estate broker" in addition to "real estate agent." In any event, each of these key terms is a multiword phrase. Phrases must be placed in quotation marks, or Westlaw will think each word is an alternative term that might appear independently anywhere in the court opinion. If he uses the following query,

constructive fraud

Westlaw will retrieve not only cases in which the phrase "constructive fraud" appears, but also those in which the words "constructive" and "fraud" appear *independently of each other* (perhaps pages apart). Just as "attorney lawyer" stood for "attorney *or* lawyer," Westlaw will read this query to mean "constructive *or* fraud." So, the query phrase must be placed in quotation marks, as follows:

"constructive fraud"

And, to limit the search to a reasonable number of cases, the researcher can add the other phrases, as shown below:

"constructive fraud" & "real estate agent" & "fiduciary duty"

This query requires that all three phrases appear in any case retrieved by Westlaw.

Using Connectors and Limiters in Full-Text Searches

Connectors and limiters establish some relationship between two or more search terms. The connector & in Westlaw (or, "*and*" in LEXIS-NEXIS) requires two terms to appear in the same court opinion. In LEXIS-NEXIS, "*or*" identifies two terms as alternatives, only one of which is required to be in any case retrieved. In Westlaw, a blank space between two terms has the same effect. There are other connectors that require a given term to appear either before or after another term. A list of Westlaw connectors and limiters appears in *Figure 9.10*.

A limiter requires two or more terms to appear within a defined proximity. Limiters are used because closely related terms usually appear within the same

FIGURE 9.10 Westlaw Connectors and Limiters

▶ FORMATTING A TERMS AND CONNECTORS QUERY

Searching for Compound Words
A compound word may appear as one word, as a hyphenated word or as two separate words. If your search term is a compound word, use its hyphenated form to retrieve all variations. For example:

Type:	To retrieve:
Whistle-blow	*whistleblow*
	whistle-blow
	whistle blow

Searching for Acronyms
Acronyms may appear with or without periods or spaces. To retrieve the various forms of an acronym, enter it with periods and without spaces. For example:

Type:	To retrieve:
h.i.v.	*h.i.v.*
	h. i. v.
	hiv
	h i v

Using the Root Expander

Type:	To retrieve:
Contribut!	*contributed*
	contributor
	contributing
	contribution
	contributory

Note: Plurals and possessive forms are automatically retrieved without a root expander.

Using the Universal Character

Type:	To retrieve:
gr*w	*grew*
	grow

Using Connectors

Type:	To search for:
& (and)	Terms in the same document
or (space)	One search term or the other
/s	Terms in the same sentence
/p	Terms in the same paragraph
/n	Terms within "n" terms of each other (where "n" is a number from 1 to 250)
+n	The first term preceding the second by "n" terms (where "n" is a number from 1 to 250)
+s	The first term preceding the second within the same sentence
" "	Terms appearing in the same order as in the quotation marks

Type:	To exclude documents with:
% (but not)	Search terms following the % symbol

Using WESTMATE, Copyright by West Group. Reprinted by permission.

sentence or paragraph. For example, the words "attorney" and "malpractice" might appear in cases that do not involve legal malpractice. But if those terms appear within the same paragraph, it is more likely that *legal* malpractice will be the topic. In Westlaw, /p requires the terms to appear within the same paragraph, and /s requires them to appear within the same sentence, as shown below.

attorney lawyer /s malpractice

This query would require that either "attorney" or "lawyer" appear in the same sentence with "malpractice."

Using West's Key Number System in Westlaw

The on-line version of the Topic and Key Number System found in West's digests is known as the Key Number service. Because almost every point of law has its own Key Number, the legal assistant can search for that particular point without limiting her search to particular terms that might not always occur in cases addressing that legal issue. This allows the legal assistant to locate cases that a term-based search might miss. She can activate the Key Number service by clicking on the key icon on the toolbar at the top of the Westlaw screen.

Westlaw then displays an alphabetical list of major topics in the Key Number system. If the researcher clicks on Key Number "35 ARREST," the screen offers two subtopics:

I. IN CIVIL ACTIONS, k1-k57
II. ON CRIMINAL CHARGES, k56-k73

Clicking on the second subtopic produces sixteen subtopics related to criminal charges. If the researcher selected "k64 Private persons, arrest without warrant," Westlaw would prompt her to identify the jurisdiction to be searched. If the researcher were to select California, the result would be as it appears in *Figure 9.11*.

"Natural-Language" Searching

In 1992, Westlaw introduced a new search protocol, called "WIN" ("Westlaw is Natural"). Instead of using multiple alternative terms and a formulaic search request

FIGURE 9.11 Result of Key Number Search

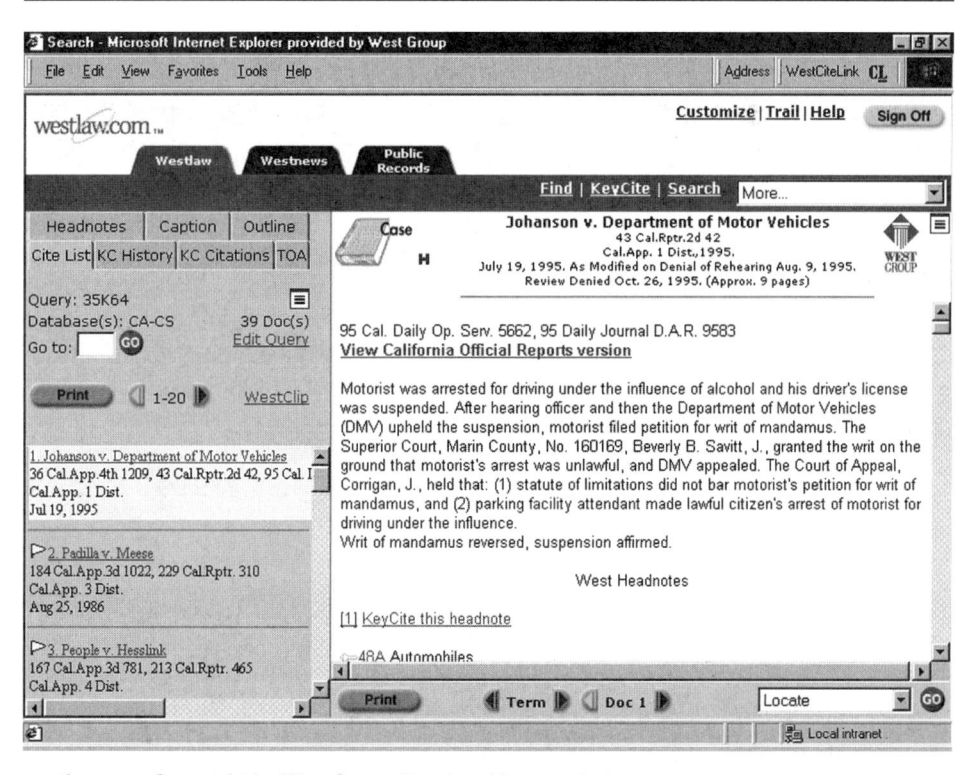

westlaw.com, Copyright by West Group. Reprinted by permission.

with connectors and limiters, the Westlaw user can now enter a search in plain English. The obvious advantage is that a paralegal or attorney can come up to speed with WIN far more quickly, because he does not need to learn a formal search protocol. As one advertisement for Westlaw's WIN suggested, instead of typing:

manufacturer company /s disclos! warn! notice notif! /s side effect /s drug pharmaceutical

the researcher could type instead:

must a manufacturer disclose the side effects of a drug?

The appeal of the plain-language protocol is obvious. This natural language query appears in *Figure 9.12*.

The software for plain-language searching uses a mathematical algorithm that transforms the plain language into a formal protocol search. Westlaw's WIN evaluates the words in the plain-language request and ranks them according to their presumed importance. Important terms of art, such as "conversion" and "disclosure," are assigned greater weight than other words, such as "manufacturer." Phrases such as "products liability" are also heavily weighted, because they are seldom used outside of the field of law.

Cases in the Westlaw database are then searched, and the twenty cases that most closely match the search are retrieved. Those cases are also ranked according to how closely they match the terms that were assigned the greater importance. This process is invisible to the user.

A graduate student of library science found a case on point with the following WIN test query:

Does a defendant have a second opportunity to respond on the merits after making a motion to dismiss an action brought as a motion for summary judgment in lieu of complaint pursuant to NY Civil Rule of Procedure 3213? (abbreviated in NY as: CPLR Section 3213).

FIGURE 9.12   Searching with Natural Language

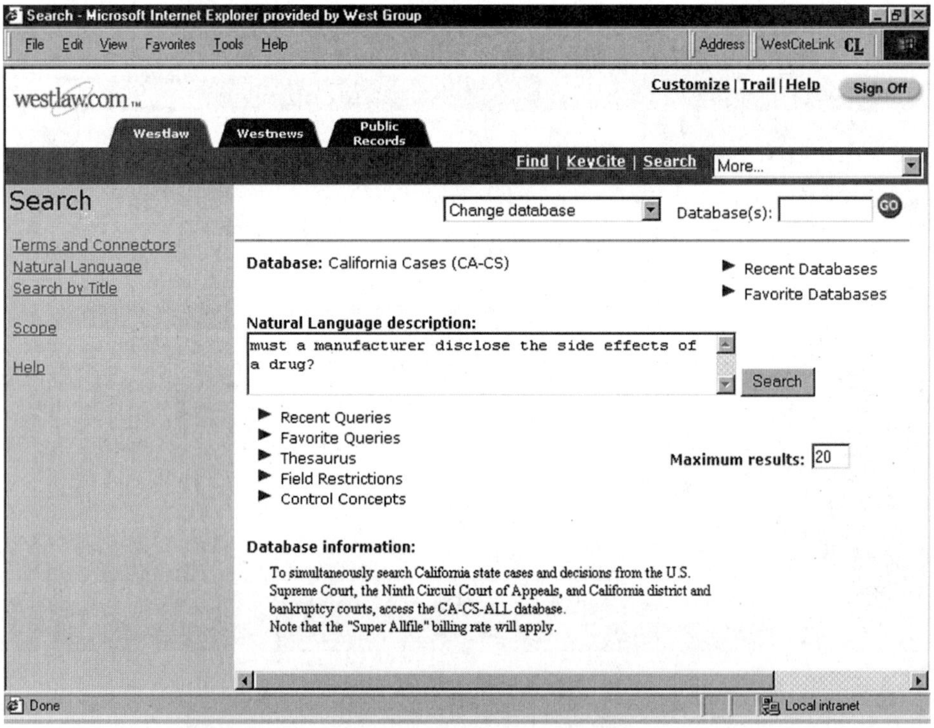

westlaw.com, Copyright by West Group. Reprinted by permission.

Remarkably, the first case retrieved was the relevant case. The same author reports that she tried a great number of strategies with queries written in formal protocol, but without results.[10] Plain-language searches are not always this successful, of course.

It is important to understand that a plain-language search will not retrieve the identical cases that a user-defined query would retrieve. That is because the WIN software creates queries that a user is unlikely to duplicate exactly. Consequently, the legal assistant might wish to try both natural-language and protocol searches and compare the results.

KEYCITE: WESTLAW'S CITATOR SERVICE

Shepard's Citation Service is no longer available through Westlaw. Instead, Westlaw offers its own, extraordinarily useful citator: KeyCite. **KeyCite** is an excellent tool for determining whether a given case is still good law, and it is equally effective for finding other cases that address the same legal issues. It is now possible to validate case law authority with unprecedented thoroughness. There are no paper versions of KeyCite, which is available only on-line, through Westlaw.

KeyCite provides the following information:

- *Citations for any prior or subsequent decisions in the case.* For example, using KeyCite to obtain the history of a case decided by the U.S. Supreme Court would provide the citations for that same case in the trial court and at each appellate level.

- *Negative indirect history.* If other cases appear to reduce the precedential value of a case—for example, by criticizing its holding (even though not reversing the case)—citations for those other cases will be provided.

- *Related cases.* If other cases involve the same parties and facts, but determine different legal issues, citations for those cases will be provided. Because different issues are determined, a related case will not impact the precedential value of the case in question.

- *Citations to the case.* All other published cases (and some not published) that have cited the case will be identified, with their citations. Citations to the case found in secondary sources in Westlaw, including *Corpus Juris Secundum*, will be given.

- *Key Numbers.* Key Numbers are identified for the issues in all headnotes to the case.

> **KeyCite** is Westlaw's on-line citator service.

To use KeyCite for *United States v. Standard Oil of California*, 332 U.S. 301, 67 S. Ct. 1604, 91 L. Ed. 2067 (1947), the researcher clicks on the KeyCite tab on the Westlaw toolbar. A dialogue box opens, in which the case citation must be entered. The official citation, *332 us 301*, or either of the unofficial citations, *67 sct 1604* or *91 led 2067*, may be entered. KeyCite then displays a citation direct history for that case—that is, all cases in which the courts have acted on that case. (See *Figure 9.13*.) The direct history will reveal whether that case has been affirmed, reversed, overruled, remanded for further action, and so on.

Because the source citation used here is to a U.S. Supreme Court opinion, there is no higher court that could reverse that case. But if the Supreme Court had later overruled its own opinion in *United States v. Standard Oil of California*, that would appear in the direct history shown in *Figure 9.13*.

KeyCite automatically displays any negative indirect history: cases in which other courts have commented negatively about the holding in the case in question, without reversing or otherwise directly affecting the validity of that case. The importance of these nonbinding negative comments is that they reveal possible grounds for any court to decline in the future to follow that holding on the

FIGURE 9.13 KeyCite history for 332 U.S. 301

```
KeyCite                                                                    Page 1
                                                        Date of Printing: APR 20,2000

                                   KEYCITE

CITATION:  ℘ U.S. v. Standard Oil Co. of Cal., 332 U.S. 301, 67 S.Ct. 1604, 91 L.Ed. 2067
(U.S.Cal., Jun 23, 1947) (NO. 235)
                                    History
                                 Direct History

          1  U.S. v. Standard Oil Co. of Cal., 60 F.Supp. 807 (S.D.Cal. May 18, 1945) (NO. CIV. 4204-Y)
             (Additional Negative History)
           Judgment Reversed by
          2  Standard Oil Co. of Cal. v. U.S., 153 F.2d 958 (C.C.A.9 (Cal.) Feb 14, 1946) (NO. 11114)
             (Additional Negative History)
           Certiorari Granted by
          3  U.S. v. Standard Oil Company of California, 329 U.S. 696, 67 S.Ct. 67, 91 L.Ed. 608
             (U.S.Cal. Oct 14, 1946) (NO. 235)
           AND Judgment Affirmed by
  =>      4  U.S. v. Standard Oil Co. of Cal., 332 U.S. 301, 67 S.Ct. 1604, 91 L.Ed. 2067
             (U.S.Cal. Jun 23, 1947) (NO. 235)

                             Negative Indirect History
Superseded by Statute as Stated in
          5  U.S. v. Trammel, 899 F.2d 1483 (6th Cir.(Ky.) Apr 03, 1990) (NO. 88-6241), rehearing denied
             (Jun 12, 1990) (Additional History) ***
          6  Piquette v. Stevens, 128 Md.App. 590, 739 A.2d 905 (Md.App. Oct 28, 1999)
             (NO. 5066 SEPT.TERM 1998) (Additional History) **
Declined to Extend by
          7  State of Texas v. American Tobacco Co., 14 F.Supp.2d 956, 1998-1 Trade Cases P 72,205
             (E.D.Tex. Sep 08, 1997) (NO. 5:96CV91) (Additional History) ***
Distinguished by
          8  In re Agent Orange Product Liability Litigation, 635 F.2d 987 (2nd Cir.(N.Y.) Nov 24, 1980)
             (NO. 80-7079, 1069) (Additional History) ***
```

Copyright by West Group. Reprinted by permission.

same legal issue. In *Figure 9.13*, KeyCite notes that the Supreme Court's holding has been superseded by a congressional statute. That statute does not invalidate the earlier Supreme Court decision in *Standard Oil*, but it means that future court decisions will be bound by the statute, not by the holding in *Standard Oil*.

Using KeyCite for Research

In *Figure 9.14*, the history is shown for *Grimshaw v. Ford Motor Company*, 119 Cal. App. 3d 757, 174 Cal. Rptr. 348 (1981). *Grimshaw* was the case, excerpted in Chapter 6, that has eighty-five headnotes. Because the history does not include any further appellate court opinions, the researcher knows that *Grimshaw* has not been reversed or overruled. To see all cases that have cited *Grimshaw*, the researcher clicks on "Citations," which appears on a vertical sidebar to the left of the screen. KeyCite then displays the full citations to *Grimshaw v. Ford Motor Company*, with the negative cases listed first.

The citations are grouped to indicate the depth of treatment the citing case has given to Grimshaw. The greater the number of stars (printed here as asterisks), the more thoroughly the citing case has discussed the holding in *Grimshaw*:

> **** *Examined.* The citing case includes an extended discussion of the holding, usually more than a page.

> *** *Discussed.* The citing case includes a less extensive discussion, generally more than a paragraph, but less than a page.

FIGURE 9.14 Citations to *Grimshaw v. Ford Motor Company*

KeyCite   Page 3

                                                                          Date of Printing: APR 23, 2000

                                                    KEYCITE

CITATION: ⌕ **Grimshaw v. Ford Motor Co., 119 Cal.App.3d 757, 174 Cal.Rptr. 348
(Cal.App. 4 Dist., May 29, 1981) (NO. CIV. 20095)**
                                                    Citations
                                                 Negative Cases

Disagreed With by
      1 MGW, Inc. v. Fredricks Development Corp., 6 Cal.Rptr.2d 888, 897+, 5 Cal.App.4th 92, 260+
          (Cal.App. 4 Dist. Apr 02, 1992) (NO. G006654)   ***   **HN: 56,65,72**

Declined to Follow by
      2 Craigo v. Circus-Circus Enterprises, Inc., 786 P.2d 22, 25+, 106 Nev. 1, 6+ (Nev. Jan 23, 1990)
          (NO. 18515) ""   ****   **HN: 49,51,59**

Distinguished by
      3 General Motors Corp. v. Sanchez, 997 S.W.2d 584, 597+, Prod.Liab.Rep. (CCH) P 15,620+,
          42 Tex. Sup. Ct. J. 969+ (Tex. Jul 01, 1999) (NO. 98-0442)   **   **HN: 52,57**

                                                 Positive Cases
                                           ****   Examined
      4 Roberts v. Ford Aerospace & Communications Corp., 274 Cal.Rptr. 139, 145+,
          224 Cal.App.3d 793, 802+, 54 Fair Empl.Prac.Cas. (BNA) 519+, 5 IER Cases 1649+
          (Cal.App. 2 Dist. Oct 16, 1990) (NO. CIV B040875) ""   **HN: 51,59,66**

Copyright by West Group. Reprinted by permission.

> ** *Cited.* There is some discussion of the holding, usually less than a paragraph.
>
> * *Mentioned.* There is no more than a brief reference to the cited case.

Following each citation, the headnotes in *Grimshaw* are listed for the issue(s) that the citing case has addressed with reference to *Grimshaw*.

If one is interested in particular issues in *Grimshaw*, clicking on "Limit" in the left sidebar causes KeyCite to display all of the headnote numbers. The researcher can then place check marks in front of those headnotes that are of interest, and KeyCite will then display citations for *only* those cases that cited *Grimshaw v. Ford Motor Company* on those selected issues. *Figure 9.15* shows the cases that cited *Grimshaw* on the issue in Headnote 19. This selective display of citations is very helpful to the researcher.

KeyCite's Flags for Cases with Negative History

When viewing an opinion in Westlaw, KeyCite displays a red flag near the top of the screen if the case is no longer good law on *any* given issue(s) in that case, or a yellow flag if the case has negative history (although not reversed or overruled). Clicking on the flag displays the negative history in question.

EVALUATING THE AUTHORITIES THAT A CASE RELIES UPON

In addition to KeyCite, Westlaw offers a Table of Authorities service that examines the case authorities relied upon in a court's opinion and alerts the researcher to any significant negative history in those cases. The concern here is that a case that has not itself been reversed or overruled might have relied for its holding upon earlier cases that have come into question.

FIGURE 9.15 Citations to Headnote 19 in *Grimshaw v. Ford Motor Company*

KeyCite   Page 2

                                                      Date of Printing: APR 23, 2000

KEYCITE

CITATION: ₽ Grimshaw v. Ford Motor Co., 119 Cal.App.3d 757, 174 Cal.Rptr. 348
(Cal.App. 4 Dist., May 29, 1981) (NO. CIV. 20095)
         Citations: limited to Headnotes = 19, Cases, ALR, Law Reviews, Others
                              *** Discussed
 1 Genrich v. State of California, 248 Cal.Rptr. 303, 308+, 202 Cal.App.3d 221, 229+
       (Cal.App. 4 Dist. Jun 16, 1988) (NO. G003793) "" HN: 19,20,21

                              ** Cited
 2 Continental Airlines, Inc. v. McDonnell Douglas Corp., 264 Cal.Rptr. 779, 793+,
       216 Cal.App.3d 388, 414+ (Cal.App. 2 Dist. Dec 07, 1989) (NO. B020292) HN: 19
 3 Aguayo v. Crompton & Knowles Corp., 228 Cal.Rptr. 768, 774, 183 Cal.App.3d 1032, 1041,
       Prod.Liab.Rep. (CCH) P 11,111 (Cal.App. 2 Dist. Jul 29, 1986) (NO. B008513) ""
       HN: 19

                              * Mentioned
 4 Korsak v. Atlas Hotels, Inc., 3 Cal.Rptr.2d 833, 838, 2 Cal.App.4th 1516, 1525
       (Cal.App. 4 Dist. Jan 28, 1992) (NO. D011734) HN: 19,22
 5 People v. Gamez, 286 Cal.Rptr. 894, 900, 235 Cal.App.3d 957, 969
       (Cal.App. 4 Dist. Oct 30, 1991) (NO. G009572) HN: 19
 6 In re Nathaniel C., 279 Cal.Rptr. 236, 245, 228 Cal.App.3d 990, 1004
       (Cal.App. 1 Dist. Mar 22, 1991) (NO. A049524) HN: 19
 7 Mosesian v. Pennwalt Corp., 236 Cal.Rptr. 778, 785+, 191 Cal.App.3d 851, 864+
       (Cal.App. 5 Dist. May 04, 1987) (NO. F003781) HN: 14,19

                          Secondary Sources
 8 EXPERTS AS HEARSAY CONDUITS: CONFRONTATION ABUSES IN OPINION
       TESTIMONY, 76 Minn. L. Rev. 859, 875+ (1992) HN: 19,20

Copyright by West Group. Reprinted by permission.

In *Figure 9.16*, fourteen of the 158 cases cited by *Grimshaw* are listed in alphabetical order in Westlaw's Table of Authorities. Four of those cases have been marked with red flags, indicating that they are no longer good law on one or more of their holdings. Eight other cases are marked with yellow flags, indicating some negative history. The two right-hand columns in *Figure 9.16* identify the page in *Grimshaw* where each case is mentioned and the depth of treatment given that case by *Grimshaw*. Before placing great reliance upon *Grimshaw*, the cautious researcher would review that opinion to determine if its key holding(s) might be questionable. It might turn out, of course, that a bad or questionable case is only one among several other good cases that *Grimshaw* cited for its holding.

USING *SHEPARD'S CITATION SERVICE* ON-LINE

Shepard's Citation Service continues to be available on-line through LEXIS-NEXIS. The on-line version, however, is dramatically different from—and improved over—the print version of *Shepard's*. Although *Shepard's* and KeyCite are competing on-line citators, both offer extraordinary power and flexibility to the researcher. And both services continue to be improved in response to user needs—and in an effort to remain competitive.

The Web site for LEXIS-NEXIS is:

   http://www.lexis.com

On the opening screen, LEXIS-NEXIS offers two "Quick Access" choices: "Shepardize" and "Get a Case." When a citation is typed in the box below "Shepardize," LEXIS-NEXIS prompts the researcher to enter a LEXIS-NEXIS I.D. and Password.

FIGURE 9.16 Westlaw's *Table of Authorities* for *Grimshaw v. Ford Motor Company*

Table of Authorities   Page

                                                                Date of Printing: APR 23,20

                                   Table of Authorities

CITATION: **119 Cal.App.3d 757**
  ▶Grimshaw v. Ford Motor Co., 119 Cal.App.3d 757, 174 Cal.Rptr. 348 (Cal.App. 4 Dist., May 29, 1981) (NO. CIV. 20095)
  158 Cases Cited in Grimshaw v. Ford Motor Co.   depth

  1 ▶Aceves v. Regal Pale Brewing Co., 595 P.2d 619 (Cal. 1979) .... 359+   **
  2 ▶Addington v. Texas, 99 S.Ct. 1804 (U.S.Tex. 1979) 387   **
  3 ▶Adkins v. Brett, 193 P. 251 (Cal. 1920) 369   *
  4 ▶Alter v. Michael, 413 P.2d 153 (Cal. 1966) 396   *
  5 Atchison, Topeka, and Santa Fe Railway Company v. Horn, 85 S.Ct. 892 (U.S.Cal. 1965)... 370   **
  6 ▶Bailey v. Kreutzmann, 75 P. 104 (Cal. 1904) 369   *
  7 ▶Ballard v. U.S., 152 F.2d 941 (C.C.A.9 (Cal.) 1945) 375   *
  8 ▶People v. Bandhauer, 426 P.2d 900 (Cal. 1967) "" 375   **
  9 ▶Bardessono v. Michels, 478 P.2d 480 (Cal. 1970)............................. 366+   **
  10 ▶Barker v. Lull Engineering Co., 573 P.2d 443 (Cal. 1978).................... 376+   ****
  11 ▶Barth v. B. F. Goodrich Tire Co., 71 Cal.Rptr. 306 (Cal.App. 1 Dist. 1968) .. 381   *
  12 Beagle v. Vasold, 417 P.2d 673 (Cal. 1966) "" 375   **
  13 ▶People v. Beivelman, 447 P.2d 913 (Cal. 1968) "".......................... 375   **
  14 ▶Bertero v. National General Corp., 529 P.2d 608 (Cal. 1974)................. 368+   ***

Copyright by West Group. Reprinted by permission.

That done, LEXIS-NEXIS displays the *Shepard's Citations* for the citation that has been entered. *Figure 9.17* shows the first page for citations to *United States v. Standard Oil of California*, 332 U.S. 301, 67 S. Ct. 1604, 91 L. Ed. 2067 (1947).

Near the top of the screen, a red "stop sign" symbol alerts the researcher to the fact that later cases have treated the *Standard Oil* opinion negatively. This negative history could include anything from being reversed or overruled, to being criticized or "distinguished" in later cases. Before listing citations in later cases, *Shepard's* displays the "prior history" of the Standard Oil case. In *Figure 9.17*, one can see that the decision of the trial court (60 F.Supp. 807) was reversed by the 9th Circuit Court of Appeals (153 F. 2d 958). The Supreme Court then affirmed that judgment in the Court of Appeals (332 U.S. 301). Following the prior history, *Shepard's* displays all 348 citing decisions, organized by jurisdiction.

The preceding paragraph describes the "FULL" display option in *Shepard's*. The service also offers a "KWIC" display, which is intended to validate that *Standard Oil* is still good law. The KWIC display omits the prior history and displays subsequent appellate history for that case, together with all citing cases that analyze one or more legal issues in *Standard Oil*. In that format—and as of this writing—only sixty-nine citing decisions are displayed by *Shepard's*. Whether in FULL or KWIC mode, all of the on-line features and tools of *Shepard's* are available.

Shepard's displays a horizontal report menu (beginning with "FOCUS Search") just above the red "stop sign" in *Figure 9.17*. This menu permits the researcher to have *Shepard's* display *all* citing cases ("Unrestricted"), or to limit the displayed citations to one of the following:

- All Neg   All cases with negative comments about the holding(s) in *Standard Oil*.

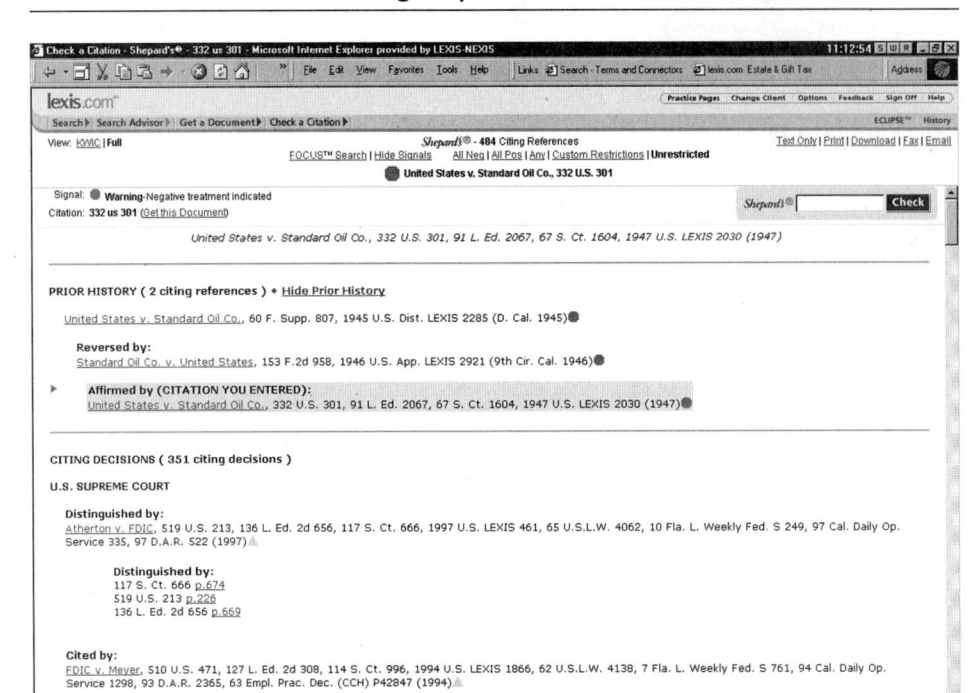

FIGURE 9.17 Screen Showing *Shepards's Citations* for 332 U.S. 301

[Screenshot of Shepard's Citations page on lexis.com showing citations for United States v. Standard Oil Co., 332 U.S. 301, including Prior History, Reversed by, Affirmed by, and Citing Decisions sections.]

Reprinted with the permission of LEXIS-NEXIS, a division of Reed Elsevier Inc. LEXIS and *Shepard's* are registered trademarks.

- All Pos — All cases with positive comments about the holding(s) in *Standard Oil*.
- Any — All cases that include discussions of the holding(s) in *Standard Oil*.
- Custom — Cases meeting criteria that must be identified by the researcher (e.g., jurisdiction, negative or positive analysis, and specified headnote issues).

The difference between "Unrestricted" and "Any" is that the former will display cases with "string citations"—which include *Standard Oil* along with other cases—even though those cases do not discuss the holdings in *Standard Oil*. The "Any" option omits cases with string citations. These options make on-line Shepardization far more efficient than using the print version.

The first option in the report menu ("FOCUS Search") provides a very powerful tool unique to *Shepard's Citation Service*. Selecting this option presents the screen in *Figure 9.18*. The researcher can then enter a terms-and-connectors query that causes *Shepard's* to do a full-text search of all of the cases citing *Standard Oil*. This allows one to screen the citing cases for facts and/or legal issues that would make them relevant to the client's case. *Figure 9.19* displays the first page of citations to *Standard Oil* that were found by a FOCUS Search for the following query:

soldier or sailor w/s injuries

This query resulted in fifty-four citing cases that include the word "soldier" or "sailor" in the same sentence with "injuries." (The LEXIS-NEXIS limiter "w/s" is equivalent to the Westlaw limiter "/s"—meaning, within the same sentence.) The FOCUS Search option is available in both FULL and KWIC modes.

FIGURE 9.18 Screen Showing FOCUS Frame in *Shepard's Citation Service*

Reprinted with the permission of LEXIS-NEXIS, a division of Reed Elsevier Inc. LEXIS and *Shepard's* are registered trademarks. FOCUS is a trademark of Reed Elsevier Properties Inc., Used with the permission of LEXIS-NEXIS.

FIGURE 9.19 Screen Showing Result of Query in FOCUS Search

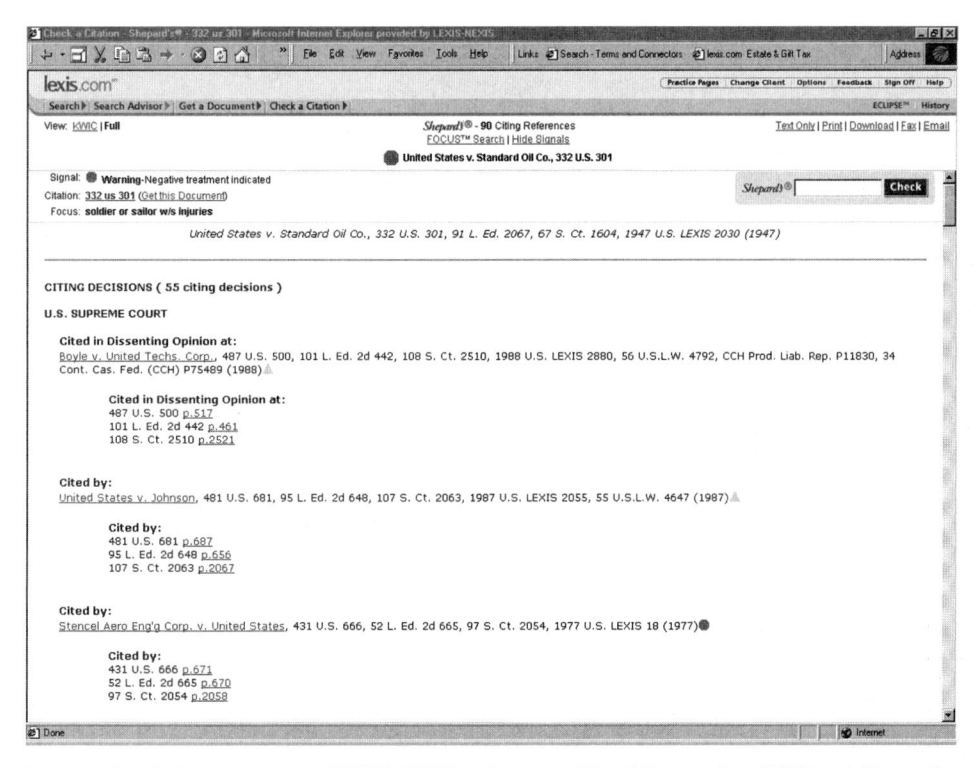

Reprinted with the permission of LEXIS-NEXIS, a division of Reed Elsevier Inc. LEXIS and *Shepard's* are registered trademarks. FOCUS is a trademark of Reed Elsevier Properties Inc., Used with the permission of LEXIS-NEXIS.

USING CD-ROMS FOR LEGAL RESEARCH

When CD-ROM materials first became available for legal research, some paralegals feared that they might reduce the need for their services, because attorneys can do more of their own research without leaving their desks. Instead, it appears that the opposite has occurred: attorneys saw that this new tool for legal research increased the paralegal's efficiency and research skills. Consequently, some attorneys actually became more willing to rely upon paralegals for legal research.

The quantity of legal materials available on compact disk is expanding very rapidly, and eventually entire law libraries will be available in that format. At the present time, West Group offers on compact disks the annotated codes and case reporters for the larger state jurisdictions and for federal law. LawDesk offers the full text of the *American Law Reports* (3rd, 4th and 5th *ALR* series) on compact disk.

Typically, a law firm subscribes to the publisher's compact disk service, which provides updated disks on a regular basis. The computer's CD-ROM drive allows the paralegal to call up a statute (with its annotations) or a court case in a matter of seconds. The statute or case can be read on the computer screen or it can be printed. One advantage of the compact disk is that there is no on-line charge for the research time.

The CD-ROM service includes software that facilitates searching the contents of a compact disk in order to locate a particular statute or court case. The search techniques are similar to those used with the Westlaw or LEXIS-NEXIS on-line services, which are discussed above. Basically, the user enters either a citation or a "search request" using certain key terms. The software then causes the CD-ROM drive to scan the compact disk until that citation or key term is found. The computer screen then displays the statute, court case, or other source found.

SECTION 3. THE INTERNET AS A RESEARCH TOOL

The incredible scope and explosive popularity of the Internet has alerted the American public to the power of on-line computer communications. But long before "Internet" became a household word, many people were already heavy users of "commercial" on-line information services such as Prodigy, CompuServe, Microsoft Network, and America Online. These four enterprises are examples of on-line information services designed for the general public and the worlds of business, science, and education. Less familiar to the general public are the specialized on-line services, such as Delphi, Dow Jones News/Retrieval, DIALOG, Westlaw, and LEXIS-NEXIS.

Each of these services maintains large mainframe computers that store enormous databases full of text material. Each provides dedicated phone lines for users to access those databases via modems. Subscription is required, and the user pays a flat monthly fee for unlimited use, or for a specified number of hours each month. Until the 1990s, the subscriber was limited to the contents of the service's own databases—it was not possible to use the service to reach other database systems around the country or the world (in other words, the Internet). All of that changed with the mushrooming popularity of the Internet, and the development of the World Wide Web (WWW). Each of these on-line services now includes Internet access.

THE INTERNET: NOT A SINGLE ENTITY

In contrast to Westlaw, LEXIS-NEXIS, CompuServe, America Online, et al., the Internet is not any one service or business enterprise. Instead, it is a worldwide network of very large computers that communicate with each other under established protocols (both technical and social). Most of the key computers linking the Internet are located at universities, government agencies, and large corporations. Everyone else gains access to the Internet from office or home computers via telephone and dedicated optical fiber connections to those large computers. Theoretically, anyone could hook in to the Internet and explore it on his own. The problem is, it takes a great deal of technical expertise to do so. Hence, came a new kind of enterprise: the Internet service provider.

USING INTERNET SERVICE PROVIDERS

The **Internet service provider (ISP)** is a commercial or nonprofit service that provides the technical protocols required to connect with, and use, the Internet. It maintains many connection sites (known as "points of presence") around the country, so that the subscriber can reach the ISP—and thus the Internet—without incurring long-distance phone charges. The ISP also provides a user-friendly interface on the computer screen so that maneuvering around the Internet is fairly intuitive, and an e-mail address and password so that the subscriber can send and receive e-mail. Unlike Microsoft Network, CompuServe, America Online, Prodigy, and the like, most ISPs do not maintain their own proprietary database of information and publications. But CompuServe, Prodigy, America Online, et al., now offer access to the Internet through their own services—in other words, these on-line information services have become ISPs, as well.

An **Internet service provider (ISP)** is a company that provides access to the Internet, and software that makes that access convenient to use.

THE WORLD WIDE WEB: ONLY ONE PART OF THE INTERNET

Because one of the subscribing law firm's primary interests is research—"legal" research as well as other types of research—most of what is needed from the Internet will be found on the **World Wide Web** (often just called the "Web"). For some purposes—to exchange information with attorneys and paralegals about defective brakes on a particular model of automobile, for example—one might want to wander from the Web and participate in on-line discussion groups called "newsgroups." But, for most research purposes, law offices probably will stick with the World Wide Web. In fact, the Web is so convenient for sleuthing after information (and entertainment!) it is the fastest-growing part of the Internet.

The Web is composed of the servers—which are high-capacity computers that contain and deliver the information one is seeking—and the content on those servers. The content is in the form of hypertext documents that contain links to other documents. Suppose, for a moment, that a user was reading this paragraph on the World Wide Web right now. Assuming he has a color monitor, the word "hypertext" in the preceding sentence would appear in blue (or some other distinctive color), as well as being underlined. The color and underlining are there to designate that word as a "link" to another document. If he clicked his mouse on that word, this current paragraph would disappear from the screen and he would find the other, linked document on the screen—presumably a document about hypertext.

Consider the application of hypertext to legal research. If someone were reading a law review article on the Web, all of the case citations in the article could be marked for hypertext (color and underlining, remember). By clicking on the citation of any case, *voila*—in moments, the actual text of that court opinion could

The **World Wide Web** is an enormous collection of Web sites (and their documents) that are linked together and stored on servers around the world.

appear on the monitor screen. When the researcher is finished with that case, there is a simple way to go directly back to the law review article where he left off. On the other hand, he might find links in that court opinion to other cases he wants to read—and so, click and go! The famous "paper chase" becomes a "hyperlink chase." No more wandering from stack to stack in the library, only to find the essential volume isn't there. That's because he, and a thousand other people, could be reading the identical law review article or court case on the Web, simultaneously. Westlaw provides internal hypertext links to the documents cited in Westlaw materials, but not to unaffiliated Web sites.

This hypothetical example—which suggests the potential of hypertext for legal research—assumes that the full text of almost all court opinions is *freely* available on the Web, which they are not, *yet*. At the present time, one must subscribe to a service such as Westlaw or LEXIS-NEXIS—or pay them for each search and each document downloaded—in order to have on-line access to the vast body of case law. But it is likely that state and federal government Web sites will offer much of that body of case law in the future. Most states already operate "free" Web sites where the full text of their statutes and regulations can be read, downloaded, or printed. But the states are not likely to put the past 200 years of case law on their sites within the foreseeable future—if ever. However, university libraries might do that, eventually. Westlaw and LEXIS-NEXIS will continue to offer the richest collections of legal materials, and also powerful research tools that are unavailable elsewhere on the Internet.

SCENARIO

Small-Firm Paralegal Becomes the In-house Expert for On-line Research

Roger Wolinsky has been a legal assistant for seven years, the past three years in a small firm with only nine attorneys and two legal assistants. His first four years as a legal assistant were in a large, national law firm with hundreds of attorneys. "Hundreds, *and hundreds*," is Roger's expression. "I just really wanted something more personal, less institutional. This [current] firm is perfect for me."

Because Roger has a master's degree in library science, his first firm had him fill in when there was a three-month vacancy in the firm librarian position. "I really enjoyed that, because it gave me a chance to become proficient in Westlaw. At home, I had been doing a lot of stuff on the Internet, but I didn't have much experience with the sort of highly structured research environment that you have in LEXIS-NEXIS and Westlaw. While I was the acting librarian, attorneys would give me research assignments for Westlaw. It was great—I loved it."

When Roger moved to his current, smaller firm, he found that his computer experience in general—and his Westlaw expertise in particular—were highly valued. "The firm had been slow to integrate computers into its practice of law. It used them for billing purposes, and such, but not much else. The firm thought it was too small to afford a consultant who could come in and set up a software system and provide the training it needed. So, it didn't. When the firm hired me, it made it clear that its hope was that I could make some of those things happen without too much expense.

"The real problem was, the firm didn't have a single attorney, paralegal, or staff person with any real, solid experience in computers. But I had minored in computer applications when I got my M.S. in library science. So, the firm thought I was some kind of expert. The truth is, I'm pretty good at using software, and I know how to ask the right questions. But I'm no expert."

Expert or not, the firm gave Roger the opportunity to put together a plan to "computerize" the firm. He did a lot of research, got involved in some on-line discussion groups, and "picked the brains of anyone who would let me." In effect, he got some free consulting services from his connections on Internet discussion groups. He developed a gradual, phased-in plan to take full advantage of the firm's existing computers. "We weren't using anywhere near the full computing power of those PCs. We retained a freelance systems manager, who set up a local area network. We started with on-line research, using Westlaw and various Internet sources. Next, we plan to implement a document management system. If we add more attorneys, we might buy a case management system, but the senior partner is skeptical about allowing a software package to tell him 'how to practice law,' as he says. We'll see."

All of the attorneys and legal assistants have taken the orientation classes with Westlaw. But Roger is the acknowledged "firm expert" on the Internet and on-line research. "This has been a really challenging, satisfying job for me. I think I'll stay where I am, as long as I'm enjoying it this much." ■

Using Web Browsers

So, how does one make her way to the right server among the thousands that exist in the world? The first part of the answer is that she must have a **Web browser**. A browser is a software program designed for exploring the Web. There are a number of browsers available, including Mosaic (the very first), Lynx, and Opera, but the most feature-rich are Netscape's Navigator and Microsoft's Internet Explorer.

If the user knows exactly where she wants to go on the Web, a browser will take her there. She simply types in an address (e.g., http://www.westlaw.com) and hits the *enter* key. In a few moments, she will have that **Web site** on her screen. Once she is at the site she wants, she usually has many choices, because the site's **home page** (the first screen one encounters at that site) is usually loaded with hypertext links to other pages at that site. She just clicks a link with her mouse, and the chosen page will appear. Web browsers always have "back" and "forward" buttons that let the user navigate easily between the pages and sites she has visited. The buttons are very intuitive to use.

A browser can maintain a convenient, personalized list of a user's favorite Web sites. This is a list that the user controls by adding Web sites to the list, from time to time. One need only click on a listed site and the browser brings that Web page to the screen. This is especially convenient when the desired page has a very long **Uniform Resource Locator (URL)**, which can be awkward to type accurately. Also, many URLs are not intuitive, and therefore, they are difficult to remember. When the user instructs the browser to add a site to his bookmark (or favorite place) list, some Web sites prompt the browser to enter an intuitive name, rather than the actual URL.

In this discussion, there have been several references to the *speed* with which things happen between one's computer and the Internet. But whether an event occurs in moments—or an hour—depends upon a number of factors, including the following:

- the speed of the central processing unit (CPU) in the computer
- the speed of the modem in the computer
- the maximum speed supported by the telephone line to the ISP
- the maximum modem speed supported by one's ISP
- the efficiency of one's browser software

A **Web browser** is software used for roaming the World Wide Web.

A **Web site** is a particular location on the World Wide Web at which some entity (e.g., university, club, individual, or corporation) maintains hypertext documents.

A **home page** is the first document one sees when entering a Web site.

The **Uniform Resource Locator (URL)** is the technical address for an Internet site.

Practice Tip

Occasionally, documents found on Web pages can be so long that they are difficult to review. One can waste a good deal of time only to discover that the particular document is of no help. There is a keyboard command that helps one to sort through long documents on the Web. Simultaneously pressing CTRL + F (i.e., both the CTRL key and the F key) causes the browser to activate a search feature. Typing in a key word or phrase allows one to jump to that word or phrase in the document. If the word or phrase is not found, that might indicate that the document does not address the topic of interest.

- the efficiency of the software on the Web site one is using
- the level of traffic being served at the moment by the ISP
- the level of traffic being handled by the server housing the Web site one is using

Using a Search Engine

Browsers provide links to several search engines. The user can reach others by typing in their URLs. **Search engines** contain highly detailed indexes to the content within many thousands of other Web sites. Because of the way in which search engines work, they need to construct the largest possible index to the hundreds of thousands of Web sites. Because Web sites are constantly being created, and frequently change their content, it would be impossible for the search engine index to be constructed by humans. Instead, computer programs constantly scan the World Wide Web and automatically construct the index.

In addition to the index, the search engine also has a powerful software program that will accept key terms that one types in and then match those terms to its index. It returns a list of potential "hits"—Web sites that appear to match the search query—with brief descriptions of their content. For each, there is a hypertext link (underlined and in color, usually) that one can click—and in *almost* no time she will have that Web site's home page on her screen. Using key terms in a search engine query is very similar to their use in Westlaw or LEXIS-NEXIS, except that no special connectors or limiters are used.

The browser does not limit the user to just one search engine. If one search engine doesn't produce the desired result, it sometimes pays to try the same (or a similar) search request on other search engines, as well. The engines charge nothing for their use, because they are supported by brief ads (e.g., corporate logos) that appear on their screens, and by companies that pay them to thoroughly index their corporate Web sites. So, the browser has nothing to lose by giving access to the search engines. The best-known general-purpose search engines include, Alta Vista, Lycos, Excite, Hotbot, and Northern Light.

> A **search engine** is a specialized Web site that contains a highly detailed index of the content of many thousands of other Web sites, and it has the capability of rapidly searching that index to lead the user to documents and sites of interest.

Internet Access

Alta Vista	http://www.altavista.com
Lycos	http://www.lycos.com
Excite	http://www.excite.com
Hotbot	http://hotbot.lycos.com
Northern Light	http://www.northernlight.com

It is possible to simultaneously submit a single query to more than one search engine. This is done by using a meta search engine. Dogpile and MetaCrawler are effective meta search engines.

Internet Access

Dogpile	http://www.dogpile.com
MetaCrawler	http://www.metacrawler.com

For legal research, useful search engines include the WWW Virtual Library, FindLaw, and LawCrawler. Two other search engines (GSULaw and LawGuru) provide links to a wide variety of *specialized* search engines for law-oriented Web sites. Many of the Web sites found in this manner are maintained by law firms that specialize in that field of law. Because the law firm maintaining a site has the expertise, and its reputation could be damaged by inaccurate information, such sites are usually very reliable sources.

Internet Access

FindLaw	http://www.findlaw.com
GSULaw	http://www.paraleague.com/metaindex.html
LawGuru	http://www.lawguru.com/search/lawsearch.html

Using On-line Directories

In addition to search engines, there are a number of directory services on the World Wide Web. A directory is the on-line equivalent of a table of contents for all of the major Web sites on the Internet. Directories are assembled by human beings, so that someone's judgment is at work in their design and content. The best known of all directories, Yahoo!, is assembled by qualified librarians.

When a researcher first opens a directory, he will find a list of very broad categories, such as Arts & Entertainment, Computers & Internet, Government, Science, and so forth. When he clicks on a category, it opens a list of subcategories. Under Government, for example, one might find Federal Government, State Government, Local Government, and so on. Each time the researcher selects a subcategory, the directory offers a list of increasingly narrow topics. Ultimately, the directory leads one to actual hypertext URLs for Web sites. Clicking on a URL will then take one to that Web site. Among the better-known directories are Yahoo!, Magellan, and Looksmart. A less well-known, but excellent directory is Argus Clearinghouse. The National Federation of Paralegal Associations (NFPA) maintains a directory of legal resources, with links to many sites.

Internet Access

Yahoo!	http://www.yahoo.com
Magellan	http://magellan.excite.com
Looksmart	http://www.looksmart.com
Argus Clearinghouse	http://www.clearinghouse.net
NFPA	http://paralegals.org/LegalResources/home.html

The law firm of Ballard Spahr Andrews & Ingersoll, LLP, sponsors a unique site known as VirtualChase. Although organized as an annotated directory to legal information on the Internet, VirtualChase offers much more. It provides "Teaching Webs" that are essentially course outlines with supporting materials that have been used in classes on Internet research for attorneys. There are materials also for self-instruction and guides for evaluating the quality and reliability of information on Web sites.

Practice Tip

There is one problem with research on the Internet: One must consider the source. There are no rules or qualifications to meet when publishing on the Internet. That is not to suggest that nothing is trustworthy. The vast majority of the information one will find using the URLs in this chapter will be highly reliable.

But there is no way that a university library or government agency can devote the resources available to Westlaw and LEXIS-NEXIS to ensure the accuracy of its Web site's content. The prudent course of action is to verify with another reliable source whatever one has found on the Internet. Perhaps one can do most of the legwork on the Internet—thereby saving a considerable amount of fees. But when the critical case, statute, or other document has been identified, one can obtain a reliable copy from a print library, LEXIS-NEXIS, or Westlaw.

Internet Access

VirtualChase   http://www.virtualchase.com

USING WESTLAW AND LEXIS-NEXIS ON THE INTERNET

If the law office is a subscriber to Westlaw or LEXIS-NEXIS, the attorneys and paralegals can access those services via an ISP. But there seem to be few advantages to this, unless there is no local phone connection for direct access to those services. A possible downside is that data might move more slowly through the Internet than over dedicated land-lines for Westlaw and LEXIS-NEXIS.

Internet Access

Westlaw   http://www.westlaw.com
LEXIS-NEXIS   http://www.lexis.com

> **Practice Tip**
>
> Many Web sites—especially government sites—contain documents in portable document format (PDF). These documents must be downloaded and printed using a software program called Adobe Acrobat Reader. Often, the Web site alerts the viewer to download a free copy of that software if it is not already installed on the viewer's computer. Adobe Acrobat Reader can be downloaded at no charge from the Adobe Web site.
>
> The great advantage of PDF files is that they can duplicate the exact appearance of their originals. For example, IRS tax forms printed with Adobe Acrobat Reader look exactly like the forms one might pick up at the local library or post office.

For some limited legal research purposes, however, it can be less expensive to use the Internet. The federal government and many state governments have put all of their statutes and regulations on their Web sites. Access to government sites is almost always free, as is downloading to a hard disk or printer. Gradually, state and federal court decisions are being added to those Web sites. At the present time, however, these official Web sites provide only a tiny fraction of the official government materials that are available on Westlaw and LEXIS-NEXIS. And none of the government Web sites have the great wealth of secondary source materials offered by Westlaw and LEXIS-NEXIS. Nor do they have citators, such as KeyCite or *Shepard's*.

Internet Access

Adobe Systems   http://www.adobe.com

UNCLE SAM'S WEB SITE FOR PRIMARY SOURCE LEGAL AUTHORITY

The U.S. Government Services Agency (GSA) maintains the FEDLAW Web site that can lead one to almost any primary source legal authority (state as well as federal) that is available on the Internet. It is well-organized and intuitive to use. Originally established for the use of federal employees, it is available to the public free of charge. However, it might sometimes lead one to on-line sites that require a subscription or fee-per-use, especially for the text of court opinions.

Internet Access

FEDLAW   http://www.legal.gsa.gov/

Essentially, FEDLAW is organized as a directory, with major topic headings on the main page of the site. Clicking on a major topic transfers the user to a subpage with more detail. As the user works down that hierarchy, she soon reaches a page with links to other Web sites maintained by various government agencies and universities. The agency and university sites contain the actual text of the primary source materials, which often can be searched by key terms, as well as by citations. State law materials are reached in the same manner. On the main page of FEDLAW, "State Law" is one of the choices offered in a sidebar. That heading takes the user to a page where the individual states are listed. From there, the researcher works her way to the sites containing the text of state primary source authority, in the same manner as for federal law.

INTERNET SITES FOR FEDERAL COURT OPINIONS

Since 1990, the U.S. Supreme Court has provided its opinions on-line through a university library. Originally, Case Western Reserve University maintained the on-line library of opinions, but in recent years Cornell University has assumed that role, and it has acquired the Case Western repository of Supreme Court opinions. The opinions are available in PDF, and they can be downloaded with Adobe Acrobat Reader. Note that this site is not on the World Wide Web, hence the absence of "www" in the address.

Internet Access
Supreme Court Collection   http://supct.law.cornell.edu/supct

In April 2000, the United States Supreme Court debuted its own Web site. At this writing, no opinions earlier than 1999 are available on the site. However, the site provides substantial information about the Supreme Court's operations. Particularly useful is an explanation of the various steps in publishing an opinion of the Court: bench opinions, slip opinions, preliminary prints, and finally hardbound publication in the United States reports. Sources for obtaining an opinion at each of these stages are provided. Court rules, guidelines for handling cases, the Court's docket, and other information is available as well.

Internet Access
U.S. Supreme Court   http://supremecourtus.gov

Washburn University School of Law hosts another useful site for federal court opinions. The Washburn University site provides links to sites with the opinions of the federal circuit courts of appeals, and also Supreme Court opinions and federal court rules.

Internet Access
Washburn University School of Law   http://www.washlaw.edu

The Federal Courts' PACER System

The Public Access to Court Electronic Records (PACER) is an electronic service that permits users to obtain case and docket information from the federal court system. It is operated by the Administrative Office of the United States Courts. At the time of this writing, many of the federal courts do not have their PACER

> **Practice Tip**
>
> Legal research on the Internet has created a new problem for the researcher: how to cite Internet sources in court documents and other publications. The sixteenth edition of The Blue Book discourages citations to the Internet because of their "transient nature" (i.e., "they might not be there tomorrow").
>
> This is a complicated issue, because some Internet sources are never available in print form, and others are available electronically well before they appear in print. The American Bar Association favors a "vendor neutral" citation format that would not give commercial publishers control of the accessibility of the documents, nor of the form of their citation.
>
> In the meantime, The Blue Book's general recommendation is that the citation include the following:
>
> - author
> - title
> - Uniform Resource Locator (URL)
> - date
>
> The citation format for court opinions remains unresolved, but one vendor-neutral format would include the following:
>
> - name of the court
> - year of the opinion
> - sequence number of that opinion, among all opinions by that court in that year

components on the Internet, and these courts must be dialed directly using a modem and communication software. Each court maintains its own databases with case information. To gain access to PACER, one must register with the service center. There is no charge to register, but there are nominal fees for on-line time and for each page downloaded.

Internet Access

PACER   http://www.pacer.psc.uscourts.gov

The information available through PACER includes the following:

- all parties, attorneys, judges, and trustees in a given case
- the causes of action and the damages demanded
- all new cases filed in the bankruptcy courts
- judgments or case status
- appellate court opinions

There is also a national locator index for PACER systems in the district, bankruptcy, and appellate courts. The index can be searched by party name to determine where the case has been filed, the filing date, and the case number.

INTERNET SOURCES FOR STATISTICAL INFORMATION

Not so long ago, a legal assistant's favorite source for rapid access to statistical information might have been the latest edition of a paperback almanac. Another favorite source was the reference desk of a local public or university library. To obtain the most recent and accurate data, the legal assistant had to telephone the office of the government agency that gathered that information—and hope that the agency would be cooperative. Other useful data were collected by universities, but often a legal assistant had no way of knowing about that source.

Today, the Internet is rapidly becoming a prime source for statistical information. The largest single generator of statistical information is the U.S. government. State governments are also important sources for statistical data, as are universities and various nonprofit foundations and think tanks. Most of this data can be found on the Internet. Of course, commercial sites that charge for access can be excellent sources, as well. Useful commercial sites include Westlaw, Dialog, Dow Jones Interactive, and Dun & Bradstreet.

Internet Access

Interagency Council on Statistical Policy	http:/www.fedstats.gov
Census Bureau	http://www.census.gov
Statistical Abstracts of the U.S.	http://www.census.gov/statab/www
Economic Statistics Briefing Room	http://www.whitehouse.gov/fsbr/esbr.html
Westlaw	http://www.westlaw.com
Dialog	http://www.dialogweb.com
Dow Jones Interactive	http://djinteractive.com
Dun & Bradstreet	http://www.dnbcorp.com

ON-LINE DISCUSSION GROUPS

When many Internet users have a common interest, they might establish an on-line **discussion group**. (Although the technical term is "newsgroup," this text will use the popular and more accurately descriptive term, "discussion group.") In a sense, discussion groups are the Internet version of networking. Individuals are generally free to come and go, ask questions and offer answers, share hot tips, and sometimes establish ongoing professional (or social) relationships. Some discussion groups are moderated, which tends to establish more order and continuity. Other groups are completely unmoderated, with peer pressure among the group's users as the only brake upon poor manners (or worse). Discussion groups tend to develop their own subcultures, and participants stay or move on depending upon their interest and comfort level.

An on-line **discussion group** is a forum for exchanging views and news about a topic of common interest.

Web-based discussion groups are hosted by a Web site, and they are usually moderated. A significant advantage of a moderated group is that participation *can* be limited to "members only"—usually those who demonstrate some prior knowledge or expertise in the group's topic. Some groups require prospective participants to submit a statement of qualifications and interest. In some cases, the "members only" restriction is literal: Membership in the group's sponsoring organization (e.g., a bar association) is prerequisite to participation. Some groups permit nonmembers to read the group's dialogue, but not to post messages (sometimes termed "articles").

The American Bar Association (ABA) sponsors on-line "forums" for ABA members. It also permits nonmember guests to "read only" the contents of several discussion groups. A guest must first register a user profile with the ABA. The National Federation of Paralegal Associations (NFPA) has weekly scheduled, live "chat rooms." Some are "private"—that is, open to NFPA members only—but some are open to all paralegals and paralegal students. The National Association of Legal Assistants (NALA) maintains an on-line "conference" center that guests may read, but one must be a member of NALA to post messages there.

Internet Access

American Bar Association	http://www.abanet.org/discussions
National Federation of Paralegal Associations	http://www.paralegals.org
National Association of Legal Assistants	http://www.nala.org

Links to law-related discussion groups and live chat rooms may be found at the Web site maintained by the Washburn University School of Law. This site also provides links to other directories for discussion groups. For discussion groups of *all* types, deja.com provides both a directory and a search service.

Internet Access

Washburn University School of Law	http://www.washlaw.edu/listserv.html
Deja.com	http://groups.google.com

INTERNET SOURCES FOR LEGAL ETHICS

The ABA's Web site provides access to ethical materials. It is possible to download formal opinions of the ABA's Standing Committee on Ethics and Professional Responsibility. The ABA also offers a remarkable service known as ETHICSearch. ABA staff lawyers will respond to ethical questions submitted by e-mail. An e-mail inquiry made in the course of writing this textbook prompted a *very* thorough and helpful response within twenty-four hours! The *ABA/BNA Lawyers' Manual on Professional Conduct* includes chapters entitled "Electronic Communications" and "Internet," respectively. The *Lawyers' Manual* is available on Westlaw in the ABA-BNA Database.

The NFPA maintains a list of its "informal ethics and disciplinary opinions" on its Web site.

Internet Access

ABA Ethics	http://www.abanet.org/legresource/ethics.html
NFPA	http://www.paralegals.org/Development/home.html

There are some sites that specialize in ethical issues related to the Internet. For example, Internet Legal Services maintains a Web site with emphasis on Internet issues. The site offers many full-text articles on ethical issues and also links to other sites with related materials. If a state's code of professional conduct for attorneys is available on-line, a link will take one directly to that Web site. This site also includes an on-line discussion group. Another helpful site regarding on-line ethical issues is provided by the State Bar of Georgia.

Internet Access

Internet Legal Services	http://www.legalethics.com
Georgia State Bar NetEthics	http://www.computerbar.org/netethics

A QUESTION OF ETHICS

David Whittier is a partner in a small law firm where you work as a paralegal. Something of a computer expert, David has assumed responsibility for selecting, purchasing, and managing the firm's computer hardware and software. Among the firm's fifteen attorneys, five paralegals, and support staff, there are a total of twenty-six PCs in the office. Rather than purchase multistation licenses for software, David has purchased a single copy of several application programs the firm uses and has loaded them on the server that the entire firm shares. Heavily used word processing and timekeeping programs have been loaded on all twenty-six computers.

David maintains that this is a legitimate practice, based upon court decisions that have found it legal for consumers to videotape movies and television programs at home for later viewing. He believes the underlying principles are the same. You have often read—in periodicals for paralegals and in other sources—that David's practice is a violation of the licensing agreements for the software that publishers sell to the public. It is your understanding that the firm should be buying a more expensive "site license" for the software programs it is using. What—if anything—should you do about your concerns?

CHAPTER SUMMARY

- The primary uses for computers in law firms are e-mail, word processing, accounting, and billing clients.
- Other uses that are rapidly growing in importance are legal research, and document and case management.
- The increased use of computers at the counsel table will result in increased use of paralegals to assist in the courtroom.
- New paralegals are expected to use word processing software (usually WordPerfect or Word) and to be able to learn the use of other application software.
- The single most important feature of word processing software is its capacity for editing a document without retyping the whole thing.
- A database manager permits the user to organize and manipulate information.
- A spreadsheet permits the user to manipulate numerical data, and the spreadsheet updates itself each time a piece of data is changed.
- Integrated software office suites combine a word processor, spreadsheet, and database in one package.
- Software programs are available that can recover "deleted" files, if those files have not already been overwritten by other, newer data.
- Computer users should have a regular system for backing up data on tape or other media, in order to prevent losing data because of mechanical failures or viruses.
- Computers can be used to research legal authorities on CD-ROM and in large databases maintained by the on-line information services.
- Almost all primary authorities are available in the on-line databases maintained by Westlaw and LEXIS-NEXIS.
- Westlaw and LEXIS-NEXIS also offer a wealth of secondary authorities, as well as many nonlegal databases.
- The Westlaw and LEXIS-NEXIS databases can be searched by key terms, or by "natural-language" queries.
- Westlaw and LEXIS-NEXIS offer KeyCite and *Shepard's*, respectively—each a powerful online citator.
- The most easily used portion of the Internet is the World Wide Web.
- Web browsers, search engines, and directories aid one in finding useful Web sites.
- The "free" law-related Web sites have only a small fraction of the research material available on Westlaw or LEXIS-NEXIS, but many sites offer helpful research guidance.

KEY TERMS

application program	**database manager**	**encryption software**
application software	**digital signature**	**field**
case management system (CMS)	**discussion group**	**home page**
computer-assisted legal research (CALR)	**document management system (DMS)**	**icon**
		integrated software

Internet service provider (ISP)
KeyCite
office suite
optical character recognition (OCR)
query
record
redlining
search engine
spreadsheet
systems manager
table of authorities
Uniform Resource Locator (URL)
Web browser
Web site
World Wide Web

ACTIVITIES AND ASSIGNMENTS

1. Review the advertisements for paralegal positions in a legal newspaper or a major newspaper of general circulation. Review sufficient back issues to obtain a sample of at least thirty different advertised positions. You might also use job announcements posted or circulated by your school. Prepare a tally for each of the following categories:

   - no mention of computer skills
   - mention of computer skills (either general or specific types)
   - general reference to computer skills or "literacy" only
   - mention of Macintosh computers
   - mention of word processing, without specifying a program
   - mention of WordPerfect
   - mention of Word
   - mention of Westlaw, LEXIS-NEXIS, or computer-assisted research
   - mention of Windows
   - mention of other software programs (database, spreadsheet, etc.)

2. If a large library (such as a university library) is available nearby, scan the ads for computer software in periodicals intended for the legal profession (e.g., bar association journals, *Perfect Lawyer, Law Office Computing, The Lawyer's PC,* and *Legal Assistant Today*). Determine the types of software (e.g., database, word processing, spreadsheet, and specialized legal) most frequently advertised. If *Legal Assistant Today* and/or *The Lawyer's PC* is available, check back issues for the past year (i.e., six issues, because they are bimonthly publications) for articles on computer software. What types of software are written about most frequently?

3. If you are a user of some on-line service (e.g., Prodigy, CompuServe, America Online, or an ISP), prepare a report on the type of information available on-line for each of the following topics:

   - paralegal careers and job opportunities
   - on-line legal advice provided by attorneys
   - on-line legal advice offered by non-attorneys
   - materials available on-line for legal research

   You might have to obtain assistance from other on-line users to locate the information available.

4. Visit a public library and use the *Reader's Guide to Periodical Literature* to locate recent articles on computer viruses. Prepare a brief report on the viruses that appear to pose the greatest threat to computer users today and the efforts of the computer industry to combat the virus threat.

5. Draft an e-mail policy that might be appropriate for a small or mid-sized law firm. The policy should address the following issues:

   - responding to e-mail
   - personal e-mail
   - monitoring (i.e., surveillance) of e-mail messages
   - security for client confidences

   Make sure the policy establishes procedures, as well as goals and objectives.

6. If you have access to the Internet, go on-line and compare the features, functions, and value of the following Web sites:

   http://www.findlaw.com
   http://www.lawcrawler.com

   Prepare a report of your findings.

7. Prepare a report on the features, content, functions (i.e., tools), and value of the following Web site:

   http://www.virtualchase.com

8. Prepare a report comparing the features, functions, and value of the following Web sites:

   http://www.gsulaw.gsu.edu/metaindex
   http://www.lawguru.com/search/lawsearch.html

ENDNOTES

[1] Catherine J. Lanctot, "Attorney-client Relationships in Cyberspace: the Peril and the Promise," *Duke Law Journal* (October 1999), p. 164.

[2] Rosemary Shiels, "Technology in Large Firms: the Revolution Is Upon Us," *The American Lawyer,* Vol. XVII, No. 2 (March 1995).

[3] Dianne Molvig, "The 1998 Law Firm Technology Survey," *Wisconsin Lawyer* (February 1999), p. 14.

[4] Frank Andrews, "Computer-Integrated Courtrooms: Enhancing Advocacy," 28 *Trial* 37, 38 (September 1993).

[5] American Bar Association Standing Committee on Ethics and Professional Responsibility, Formal Opinion 99-143, "Protecting the Confidentiality of Unencrypted E-Mail" (March 10, 1999).

[6] Id.

[7] Bryan Pfaffenberger, *Protect Your Privacy on the Internet,* John Wiley & Sons, Inc. (1997), pp. 23–24.

[8] "Editor's Choice: Speech Recognition," *PC Magazine* (November 12, 1999).

[9] Joseph L. Kashi and Thomas Boedeker, "Higher Learning," *Law Office Computing* (December/January 2000), p. 42.

[10] Sheilla E. Désert, "Westlaw Is Natural v. Boolean Searching: A Performance Study," 85 *Law Library Journal* 713, 733 (1993).

CHAPTER 10

Interviews and Investigation

> The ideal interviewer has a photographic memory, total recall, and knowledge of English and other languages, the law, politics, science, business, and the trades; is meticulous, highly trustworthy, empathetic and a superb actor; could sell doormats to Robinson Crusoe, and is attractive with a commanding but comfortable personality and an appreciative sense of humor and radiates great dignity.
>
> Few of us meet that ideal, but all of us can be effective.
>
> *NALA Manual for Legal Assistants, Second Edition (St. Paul: West Publishing Company, 1992) p. 135. Reprinted by permission.*

Information is the life blood of the practice of law. In litigation, much of that information is gathered through the use of discovery, but the power of discovery applies only to other parties in a lawsuit. Chapter 10 describes how paralegals gather information from government records, nonparty witnesses, and other sources. Section 1 portrays the overall process of investigation, from an initial plan to a final report. Discussion of the use of computers and the Internet—begun in Chapter 9—continues in Section 2, with emphasis upon searching public and private databases for relevant information. Section 3 explains the most complex investigation tool that paralegals are called upon to use—the interview. The "difficult" interview is covered in Section 4, with practical suggestions for overcoming reluctance or deception.

Upon finishing this chapter, the student should be able to answer these questions:

- What types of investigation do legal assistants do?
- What types of information can be found in on-line computer databases?
- How is an investigation planned and carried out?
- What services do commercial search companies provide?
- How is evidence handled and preserved?
- What is the role of investigation in jury selection?
- Why do most witnesses cooperate with paralegal investigators?

- How should interviews be planned and conducted?
- How should interview questions be framed?
- How should the legal assistant handle uncooperative witnesses?
- How can the paralegal verify information offered by a witness?
- How can the paralegal recognize deception?
- How should the legal assistant handle an interview of the client?

SCENARIO

Striking Gold

From the client's file, I pulled a newspaper clipping out of the folder labeled, "Wilson, Wesley B." The headline read, "Video Store Franchise Scheme Under Investigation." There was a hand notation of a date on the top margin: "2-17-83." The aging newsprint was beginning to deteriorate. *Better make a couple photocopies and put the original in an acid-free envelope,* I thought.

On my way to the copy room, I studied the photograph in the clipping. A middle-aged man with longish hair stared at the camera, an expression of annoyance clearly on his face. He wore a shirt open halfway down his chest, framing what appeared to be a small medallion suspended on a chain. *Did "wheelers and dealers" still dress that way in the '80's?* I couldn't remember. The man's right hand was raised, as though to brush his hair back, revealing large rings on the two middle fingers. The photo caption read, "Wesley Wilson, reputed investment scam artist, leaves the County Office Building after being questioned by District Attorney Jan Pierce."

The article described the investigation of an alleged scam—known as a "Ponzi scheme"—in which part of the money to be "invested" for the most recently recruited victims was instead diverted to pay phony "profits" to the earlier investors. Of course, the con artist skimmed off a healthy share of all new money he took in, and no funds were actually invested for anyone. There was nothing in the file to reveal what resulted from the district attorney's investigation. *How in the world did our client get mixed up with this guy? Hmm . . . I wonder if our client is squeaky clean, himself?*

Four hours earlier, the firm's new associate, María Morales, had briefed me on the case and asked me to get some background on Wesley B. Wilson. María said that our client, Abraham Mellon, was a wealthy retiree who entertained himself by "getting in on the ground floor" of highly speculative investments. I had to laugh quietly to myself: *"Speculative" is right!* Five years ago, she continued, the client had formed a partnership with this Wilson person and two world-famous golf pros to develop a business that would sell golf course franchises. A fourth partner was one of the best course designers in the business. Our client was to bankroll the deal until sufficient franchises had been sold to put the partnership in the black. Wilson was the deal maker, the franchise salesman, and the general manager. *That looks like three bad decisions, if you ask me.* But I didn't share that thought with María.

Since that briefing, I had reviewed the slender case file and spent some time on the computer. From the civil plaintiff/defendant index for Travis County, the computer identified three lawsuits in which Wilson had been a defendant, and one in which he was a plaintiff. But the county's criminal index didn't have anything listed for a Wesley Wilson. *Of course, that article doesn't identify the county—or even the state. Could that clipping have come from an out-of-state paper? I'll have to ask Mellon where he got it. Well, let's see what else I can get off the old computer.* There were a bunch of real estate transactions and some DBAs, but nothing really exciting.

I told María what I had found so far. It turns out that our client had already told her that Wilson was never charged in that 1983 scam, so that there wouldn't be anything in the criminal court files. I suggested that I go to the county courthouse and check the files on those civil lawsuits, and María thought it was a good plan. As I left her office, I mentally blocked out my plan for the following day: *Better get to the court clerk's office first thing, before the crowd hits. Otherwise, I'll be lucky to find a seat in the file room—not to mention having to wait an hour just to get a file brought up from storage.*

* * * *

Since 8:15 I had been reviewing four thick volumes from just one case—hundreds of pages, most of which were totally irrelevant to my search. This case looked promising, however, because it was a lawsuit brought against Wilson and his partners by about thirty investors in that video store scheme. Just as I was thinking, *I've got to take a break*, I found the sworn affidavit near the end of the fourth volume. By now, it was about 10:30.

The affidavit was by a certified public accountant. He had reviewed the books of Wilson's video franchise partnership and compared them to partnership tax returns and to records subpoenaed from several banks. His conclusion was that the books matched the figures in the tax returns, but that the bank records revealed that the partnership was taking in far more money than its own books or tax returns reflected. It appeared that one of the bank accounts had been used by Wilson to funnel partnership funds into his own coffers. The CPA's affidavit detailed how Wilson managed to siphon funds out of the partnership while covering most of his tracks. As I marked the declaration to be photocopied, I felt a sense of anticipation rising: *Wait until María sees this!*

SECTION 1. THE PARALEGAL ROLE IN INVESTIGATION

Investigation is nothing more than a systematic effort to accumulate useful information. Formal pretrial discovery, which has been covered in Chapter 6, is one form of investigation. Legal research—another form of investigation—is discussed in Chapter 8. This chapter treats the other forms of investigation that law firms commonly use to gather information. Although the word "investigation" might bring to mind a trench-coated "private eye," most legal investigation is much more mundane. In fact, some forms of investigation are little different from the library research that each of us did in high school—except that, increasingly, "library research" is done with computers and on-line databases.

Because the great majority of legal assistants practice in civil litigation, this discussion will emphasize the types of case investigation necessary in litigation. But legal assistants in virtually all specialties are required to use investigative techniques in their work. For example, probate and bankruptcy paralegals often have to search for assets and determine who has legal title to those assets. Family law paralegals often do the same, but they also have to track down missing parents and children.

INVESTIGATIONS THAT PARALEGALS OFTEN PERFORM

The two most common paralegal investigations are done without leaving the law firm: telephone inquiries and database searches. An extraordinary amount of information is available over the telephone. Many government agencies accept telephone inquiries and will provide discrete items of information over the phone if the request is very specific. Private citizens and businesses will often answer phone inquiries that do not appear to violate anyone's privacy or to solicit information that could be used for fraudulent purposes. Title insurance companies routinely accept telephone requests for **property profiles**, which show the current ownership, existing liens and easements, and tax and zoning status of a particular piece of real property.

A **property profile** is an informal report by a title insurance company on the ownership of a piece of real property, and any recorded liens against that property.

On-line Database Searches

In some parts of the country, government records are increasingly available on-line, and Westlaw and LEXIS-NEXIS offer access to many of these. Using a computer terminal in the law firm, a paralegal can now retrieve many government records, including the following:

- plaintiff and defendant indexes (both criminal and civil)
- real property transactions
- voter registrations
- status of bills in Congress or the state legislatures
- motor vehicle registrations
- corporation filings with state governments
- Securities and Exchange Commission filings

And that is only a very tiny sampling of the official records available from on-line databases.

The Internet also contains an enormous amount of information about individuals, companies, and organizations. For example, computers can search telephone listings for virtually the entire United States. For any particular name, a paralegal can print out the addresses and phone numbers listed under that name in various communities across the nation. If the law firm subscribes to a credit reporting agency, such as Equifax, Experían, or Trans Union, the computer can print out the credit history of an individual or a business. In addition to government filings, other on-line databases contain all manner of financial and industrial information. On-line sources for investigation are discussed in Section 2 of this chapter.

Field Investigations by Paralegals

Of course, paralegals sometimes investigate in ways that go beyond the typical tasks mentioned above. For example, assume that a client's business has been accused of violating zoning and noise restrictions. A paralegal might spend several days at city hall listening to tape recordings of meetings of the city planning commission and later interview residents in the neighborhood near the client's business.

Once the paralegal steps outside the law firm, other types of investigation become possible. The most common are the following:

- reviewing public records not available on a computer database
- interviewing potential witnesses and others with possible leads
- collecting information by observing and/or photographing the site of some event

These activities will be discussed in detail later in this chapter.

Forensic medicine is the science of medical knowledge as it applies to the law.

Potentially, a paralegal could conduct almost any form of inquiry, but often that is not an efficient use of resources. Also, some investigations require advanced skills or knowledge that most paralegals would not have: accounting, engineering, **forensic medicine**, fluency in a particular language, and so on. For those investigations, it often is more efficient and productive to employ an expert. Although there are legal assistants who have those very types of expertise, the point is that no single legal assistant is likely to have them all. And some investigations must be conducted in a distant location, where it is more economical to employ an investigator based in that locality.

Commercial companies can perform some types of investigation and research. Their services range from searching government archives to doing a credit and asset search on a business entity. Of course, on-line computer databases are expanding exponentially, and some commercial services might become irrelevant as paralegals gain direct access while seated at a computer terminal in the law firm office.

A **private investigator** is a specialist in gathering information, locating persons, and determining how certain events occurred. In some states, private investigators must be licensed.

Finally, there continues to be a role for the experienced **private investigator** who has the special contacts and techniques needed to ferret out difficult-to-find information and persons. But it is an unusual case that requires the services of a private investigator. Most outside investigations within a reasonable distance can be conducted by legal assistants, once they have developed some basic skills and techniques, and a sense for imaginative inquiry.

THE OBJECTIVES OF A LEGAL INVESTIGATION

Legal investigations can have a variety of purposes. In the early stages of a litigation case, before a complaint has even been filed, the law firm might need to determine whether either party has the basis for a viable legal claim against the other. Sometimes, it seems rather certain that the client does have a claim, but the attorney might be uncertain about the cause of action. The following are examples of some questions an attorney might have about the cause of action:

- Is it a case of fraud or negligent misrepresentation?
- Is the defective drainage system a private or public nuisance?
- Is it better to proceed under a cause of action for strict products liability or for breach of implied warranty?
- Does the potential defendant have affirmative defenses that can defeat the plaintiff's case?

Whether the client is the plaintiff or defendant, everything mentioned here is vitally important to the attorney. This is the exploratory stage of investigation.

Once the cause of action has been determined, the attorney needs to marshal the facts to support that cause of action and the evidence to establish those facts. This stage of investigation is well-focused, because the attorney and the legal assistant know what they are trying to find.

Finally, the investigation might focus upon damages: If the plaintiff was harmed, in what way and at what cost? What would be required to make the plaintiff "whole"? Are there consequential damages? Are punitive damages possible? The paralegal might spend a substantial period of time collecting the information needed to establish possible damages. If the client is the plaintiff, the paralegal will work closely with that client to gather admissible evidence of actual and consequential damages.

Once the investigation has resolved questions about causes of action and damages, it might influence decisions about a possible out-of-court settlement of the case. If the parties are fortunate, it will not be necessary to go through the expense of depositions and other formal discovery. Their respective investigations might give them enough information to enter into settlement negotiations.

PLANNING THE INVESTIGATION

First, one must have an objective, then a plan. The most important feature of effective investigation is a clear sense of purpose. Assume that a legal assistant has been assigned to prepare a plan, and that at least some portions of the investigation are to be conducted by one or more paralegals within the firm. The starting point, therefore, should be a thorough briefing by the attorney. Following that briefing, the paralegal should address the following questions:

- What are the factual and legal issues in the case?
- What essential facts must be established?
- What evidence is needed to establish those facts?
- What are likely sources for the information needed?
- What methods of investigation will be most productive?
- How soon must each major phase of the investigation be completed?
- What is the budget in staff time and expenses?
- Should any phase of the investigation be farmed out to consultants, private investigators, or commercial search firms?
- Who, within the law firm, should supervise and coordinate the investigation?
- Who, within the law firm, should conduct each phase of the investigation?

A memorandum to the attorney proposing answers to these questions can serve as a first draft for the plan of investigation. The legal assistant and the attorney can then go over that draft to ensure that it is properly focused, within time and budget constraints, and otherwise suitable. Even after approval by the attorney, this initial plan must allow for some flexibility, because unforeseen events and information are almost certain to require changes.

At this point, it is very important to identify the legal assistant who will coordinate the investigation, keeping the attorney informed of progress and any problems. Equally important is the latitude that that legal assistant will be permitted, in using her own judgment. Must every expenditure over $20—or $100— have the attorney's prior approval? To what extent may the supervising paralegal exercise her own judgment and depart from the plan of investigation when circumstances call for modification? In other words, how short a tether does the attorney want to keep on the supervising paralegal?

If the budget and available staffing permit, it is a great advantage to have at least two legal assistants participate in the investigation, for the following reasons:

- The investigation can be completed more quickly.
- The investigation is less likely to be interrupted when one of the legal assistants must work on other client matters.
- Two investigators can exchange ideas, theories, and leads (two heads often being better than one).
- Each legal assistant can apply his or her unique talents to tasks that require those talents.

Of course, many successful investigations are conducted by one legal assistant working alone.

EIGHT STAGES OF AN INVESTIGATION

Once the plan has been approved and the paralegal's responsibility and authority are clear, the typical investigation often proceeds along these lines, or stages:

1. gathering background information
2. reviewing or obtaining documents
3. visiting the site of significant events
4. gathering and preserving evidence
5. interviewing nonwitnesses who can provide leads
6. interviewing prospective witnesses
7. preparing a tentative report for the attorney
8. conducting follow-up inquiries, as directed by the attorney

Gathering Background Information

Although the attorney has briefed the paralegal on the factual and legal issues of the case, the paralegal will need to arm herself with the information already available in the case file. This has two purposes: to improve the paralegal's efficiency and to avoid the unnecessary duplication of what has already been done. That case file should include a summary of the client intake interview, and possibly subsequent conversations between the attorney and the client. In some firms, the paralegal will participate in the client intake interview, a great advantage. After studying those notes, the paralegal should review the rest of the file: correspondence, contracts, invoices—whatever might yield useful information. As the legal assistant reviews the file, she will take notes of possible leads to evidence (and also witnesses to interview), questions to be pursued, and so on.

Depending upon the type of case, the legal assistant might be able to gather additional background information from on-line data bases. (See Section 2, in this chapter.) Some documents can be downloaded to the law firm's computer and copies printed right there in the office. Finally, the telephone can be used to make inquiries that do not require a trip out of the office.

Reviewing Documents Outside of the Firm

Although state and federal agency archives are increasingly available on computer databases, many local government records are not. Real property records at the county recorder's office and local court files are two common examples. A trip to the county recorder's office can reveal the history of a particular parcel of land, including all changes in ownership, the attaching and lifting of liens and other encumbrances, and records of subdivision. Photocopies can be obtained of any recorded document. If they are to be introduced as evidence, they must be certified copies.

Reviewing Court Records

Court records can yield useful information in a variety of ways. For example, it is not unusual for a businessperson involved in one lawsuit to have been previously involved in others. Criminal defendants might have been defendants in other criminal cases and in civil actions. A divorcing spouse might have been a party to a prior divorce action. By locating the court records of that prior litigation, a surprising amount of information may be obtained. A particularly valuable document can be a declaration attached to a pleading or to an application for a search warrant, for example. Declarations and sworn affidavits sometimes contain a narrative of events that provides a broader context for understanding the current lawsuit. Individuals named in a declaration or affidavit might be good prospects for future interviews.

Exhibits attached to pleadings can be another source of valuable information. Lists of assets and liabilities can turn up in almost any litigation, but especially in divorce cases and in the files of the U.S. Bankruptcy Court. Other useful exhibits can be copies of contracts, correspondence, deeds to real property, and prospectuses for potential investors. Of course, the legal assistant might have to wade through a thousand pages to find the hidden gem, and sometimes nothing of value turns up.

Using Attorney Services to Obtain Documents

Documents in remote locations can be requested by mail from the custodian of records. If the documents cannot be identified in advance, the law firm will have to weigh the probable value of receiving the documents against the expense of having someone screen the agency files in the city where they are kept.

An attorney service can be retained to obtain copies of particular documents. An attorney service is a business that caters to the needs of law firms by providing courier services, filing documents with the courts or other agencies, serving court papers, and obtaining copies of documents. But, if an attorney service is to obtain copies, the documents to be copied must be identified with great precision—which can be impossible, at times. It might be necessary for the paralegal to go to the agency where the archives are kept and review a great quantity of documents to identify the ones that are useful. The public agency can then provide a photocopy and can certify the document as being a true copy from the agency's files.

Commercial search companies have "document specialists" with expert knowledge of the files of a particular agency (e.g., the Federal Communications Commission or the local courts). Document specialists are often former paralegals, or they are former employees of the agency whose files they search. For a fee, document specialists will go to that agency and locate the documents that are needed. Obviously, a careful briefing by telephone is necessary—lest they search irrelevant records or overlook the very records that are needed—and the document specialists might need confidential information in order to understand the types of documents needed.

Ethics Watch

The responsible attorney's approval must be obtained before releasing any client documents or confidential information. This rule applies to any but the most routine information about a client matter. Remember: If it is not already a matter of public record that the law firm represents a particular client in a given legal matter, even that fact is confidential. Although most commercial services that cater to the needs of attorneys understand the requirements of confidentiality, there can be some risk of compromising that confidentiality. Law firms generally have policies and procedures for obtaining authorization from the responsible attorney in each client matter.

Commercial search companies are becoming more efficient, because in most locations their document specialist can carry a cellular phone into the agency and discuss those files with the legal assistant in the law firm. That permits the legal assistant in a distant city to participate in selecting the documents to be copied.

The Freedom of Information Act and State Public Records Acts

Occasionally, federal or state agencies might be less than cooperative in releasing documents from their files. In that event, it might be necessary to make a formal written request under the federal *Freedom of Information Act* (FOIA) or that state's "public records" statute to obtain those documents. The FOIA, and its exceptions to the general rule of public access, are discussed in Chapter 5. A very thorough and helpful guide to obtaining information under the FOIA appears on the First Amendment Project Web site.

Internet Access

First Amendment Project   http://www.well.com/user/fap/foia.htm

---

The records of private businesses, fraternal organizations, churches, and other associations present a different set of problems. By law, certain records of publicly traded corporations are available to the public, or at least to their shareholders. Corporate filings with state and federal agencies are available (often on-line) because by law they are public records. But closely held corporations whose stock is not publicly traded may withhold their internal records from public scrutiny. The same right of privacy generally applies to partnerships, fraternal organizations, and so forth.

Sometimes, the custodian of records in a business organization will permit an investigator to review specifically identified records, provided that custodian is persuaded of the legitimate reason they are wanted. A letter from the attorney might obtain that degree of cooperation. However, it is a rare business that would permit a paralegal to go on a "fishing expedition" in corporate records, such as anyone can routinely do in the records of public agencies. When business records are not available to the public, it might be possible to obtain them by serving the custodian of records with a subpoena *duces tecum*.

Visiting the "Scene of the Crime"

This form of investigation most often concerns criminal matters, or a personal injury or wrongful death action. Most often, it is an automobile accident—understandably so, because auto accidents account for the greater number of civil lawsuits. But other events also call for a site observation: crimes, flood damage, construction defect cases, and so on.

There is a major difference between the site visit that is intended to obtain information solely for the education of the attorney working on the case and the site visit that is intended to produce evidence that may be admitted at trial. It usually is not necessary to convince the attorney that the paralegal actually went to the correct site, observed it objectively, and reported it accurately. But any evidence to be submitted to the court—measurements, sketches, photographs, verbal descriptions, and so forth—is subject to strict standards for admissibility.

Gathering and Preserving Evidence

Physical evidence (or **real evidence**) is a tangible object that is material to an investigation or legal controversy.

In some investigations, the paralegal might acquire custody of **physical evidence** (also known as **real evidence**): a defective tool, a cash register receipt, correspondence, an insurance policy, and the like. Typically, the client or witness is the owner of those items—not someone who acquired them from another witness or created them for the purpose of litigation. Usually, the witness came into their possession in the ordinary course of events. This fact makes it possible for that person to identify those items as being the actual items involved in the litigation: the actual receipt from the purchase of the defective tool, for example. This type of testimony is another form of laying foundation for the introduction of evidence.

If the paralegal takes possession of potential evidence, someone might later challenge the legitimacy of that evidence: How can the court know that it is the *actual* tool purchased by the plaintiff? Has the evidence been *altered* in any way? Unless the paralegal takes precautions, opposing counsel might be able to make that evidence appear to be "suspect" in the eyes of a jury. In handling real evidence, there are three major issues: (1) foundation for admissibility, (2) identification, and (3) custody and control.

In part, foundation for admissibility requires facts that establish that the physical evidence is the actual thing that was involved in the event in controversy: for example, the actual tool that caused the injury to the plaintiff. Therefore, positive identification of the article is essential for its admission into evidence. Before taking custody of the evidence, the legal assistant must obtain from the original owner the facts that will make it possible for him to later positively identify that article in court.

Using the defective tool as an example, the legal assistant would have the witness orally identify the article to be the tool in question. Then, a series of questions would establish the following:

- when and how the article came into the owner's possession
- that the owner had no other similar article during all relevant times
- that the owner recognizes the article as being the one in question
- that the article caused the injury
- that the owner had retained continuous possession and control of the article from the time of the event until the time it is delivered to the legal assistant

The legal assistant should ask for any additional evidence that establishes that the article in question is the one that caused the injury: a serial number recorded on an accident report; other witnesses to the purchase and/or accident, and so on. All of the foregoing information would be recorded in notes or on tape by the legal assistant.

Before taking actual possession, the paralegal should have the owner mark the article in a manner that will not interfere with its use as evidence. For example, the owner's initials and the date can be inscribed onto the tool (in an area not in controversy, of course) and written on the back of the purchase receipt. Photographs might be useful: the owner holding the tool, close-ups of the entire tool from various angles, a close-up of the receipt; and so forth. If a Polaroid® camera is used, the owner can initial and date the back of each snapshot.

After taking possession, the paralegal must ensure that an unbroken chain of custody and control is maintained. This is done by immediately placing the evidence in locked storage and ensuring that a strictly limited number of persons have access to the key or combination. A record must be kept of any person's access to the evidence. This record should include the following information:

- name
- date and time of access
- purpose of the access
- the date and time that the evidence is returned to secure storage

It must be provable in court—by testimony and by the records of storage and access—that the evidence was in the **continuous custody and control** of the law

Continuous custody and control is the uninterrupted possession of evidence so that it cannot be stolen, damaged, or tampered with.

firm, so that no one could tamper with the evidence. If it is necessary to transfer possession of the evidence to someone outside of the law firm—an expert witness, for example—a written receipt must be obtained showing date, time, names of the transferee and transferor, and the like. All of the foregoing records will be more persuasive if each entry carries the signature of a third person as witness.

Preparing Demonstrative Evidence for Trial

In some cases, the paralegal will be called upon to prepare **demonstrative evidence**—for example, sketches, diagrams, or photographs of an accident scene. If demonstrative evidence is to be used in trial, it must be shown that the evidence fairly represents what it purports to show. That, also, is known as "laying foundation." In the case of the photograph of an accident scene, say, the paralegal-photographer must establish the following by his testimony:

- that he took the photograph in question
- that the scene in the photograph is of the place where the accident occurred
- the point from which the photo was taken
- the date and time of the photograph
- the focal length of the camera lens
- any other technical factors that would establish the photograph as a fair representation of the accident scene

> **Demonstrative evidence** is a real object, as opposed to the testimony about that object.

Interviewing Nonwitnesses for Leads

Before prospective witnesses are interviewed, the paralegal should have as much information as possible. That information aids in planning the interview phase of the investigation (e.g., in which order the witnesses should be interviewed). Information also helps one to frame the questions, and to recognize evasion or deception during the interview. Although much of the background information has been gathered during the earlier phases of the investigation, it can be helpful to take one additional step: to interview persons with no direct, personal knowledge of the event in controversy, but who nonetheless possess information that can lead the investigator to relevant evidence.

SCENARIO

Memorable Interviews: A City Hall Gadfly and Airborne Paramedics

Liz Baker works in a small law firm that specializes in business law and civil litigation. In one case involving a dispute over zoning changes, Liz once interviewed a "city hall gadfly"—a gentleman who attended every meeting of the city council and the city planning commission and took every opportunity to address and upbraid those officials during their public meetings. That individual would not have testified in any trial in that case—he had no role in the dispute and had no direct personal knowledge of relevant evidence. He did, however, have a treasure trove of history about the city and its politics, the businesses involved in the zoning dispute, and the personalities involved. The interview was most enlightening, and it provided Liz with the names of several potential witnesses.

"It was a bit of a relief that Frank wouldn't need to testify, because he probably would have made a terrible witness. I can just imagine the opposing counsel chewing him up and spitting him out. Poor thing—he probably would have come across as some kind of fool. But when you talked with him privately, one on one, you realized that he was a really decent person. And pretty smart, too. He just had this obsession about public officials being held accountable.

"Another interesting case involved a small aircraft accident, in which the pilot was killed and his passenger badly burned. I interviewed two paramedics who treated the fatally injured pilot during a helicopter airlift from the remote crash site. The paramedics told me that they *did not* administer cocaine, or any cocaine derivative, to the injured pilot—a crucial piece of information, because the pilot died shortly thereafter and the metabolites of cocaine were subsequently found in his body. Sometimes, the whole purpose of the interview is to determine that something *did not* occur." ■

There are many examples where nonwitnesses can provide leads. If someone is thought to be hiding assets from creditors, a neighborhood gossip might alert the investigator to the fact that the debtor owns a second home in the mountains (under a different name, of course). In a construction defect case, a handyman might know of prior problems with other homes built by the same contractor. The waitress in a coffee shop frequented by a prospective witness or opposing party might have a surprising amount of information about that person.

> ### Ethics Watch
> When interviewing nonwitnesses, the question of **covert inquiry** might arise. A covert inquiry is one done under false pretense, or at least without being forthright about one's purpose. If one is asking for information that the subject would freely disclose to anyone, there probably is no ethical problem. In that situation, the purpose of the covert inquiry might simply be to avoid publicizing the fact that an investigation is in progress. But if the paralegal must use false pretense to overcome the interviewee's normal reluctance to disclose the information, an ethical question does arise. Before embarking upon covert inquiries, the paralegal should discuss the ethical issue with the responsible attorney.

A **covert inquiry** is one done under false pretense so as to conceal the inquirer's true intent.

Interviewing Prospective Witnesses

A particularly challenging part of investigation is the witness interview. Most witnesses will be **percipient witnesses**—persons who can testify to events they perceived directly and personally with their five senses. The classic example of a percipient witness is an "eyewitness" to some event. By definition, a percipient witness does not offer hearsay evidence—that is, things someone else told him about an event that the witness did not perceive with his own senses.

Another type of witness is the **expert witness**—someone qualified by her training, education, or experience to explain, within her area of expertise, the *significance* of evidence, and to offer opinions about such evidence. Although a percipient witness is not generally qualified to offer opinions, the expert is considered to be uniquely qualified to do so. Although some experts are retained to testify as witnesses, additional experts in the same field might be retained as consultants to the attorney. The testifying expert might be deposed by the other parties in a lawsuit; however, under the work product rule, the *non*testifying expert cannot be deposed. As part of an investigation, the legal assistant may interview both types of experts, but only those who are retained on behalf of the firm's client.

A **percipient witness** is one who can testify to events he experienced or observed with his own five senses.

An **expert witness** is a person qualified by training, education, or experience to explain, within her area of expertise, the significance of evidence, and to offer opinions about such evidence.

Preparing the Tentative Investigation Report

As the investigation progresses, the legal assistant should provide a report on each interview of a prospective witness. Other reports regarding nontestimonial evidence (e.g. documents) should be provided, as appropriate. But even though the legal assistant has kept the attorney informed throughout the investigation, the attorney usually needs a detailed summary before she can determine that the investigation is finally concluded. The report should be considered "tentative" for the very reason that it might provoke new questions and different avenues of investigation. In framing that report, the legal assistant should keep in mind the first three questions that were used to develop the plan of investigation.

1. What are the factual and legal issues in the case?
2. What essential facts must be established?
3. What evidence is needed to establish those facts?

In particular, the attorney will want to know what evidence has been developed to establish each fact necessary to prevail in the client's case.

In the tentative report, all of the information and evidence accumulated should be organized around the legal and factual issues of the case. This can be done issue by issue in narrative form, or by creating a chart with separate sections for each issue. Relevant testimony, documents, and other evidence must be identified for each issue. Because any given witness might be able to testify on a variety of those issues, references to the comments of a single witness might appear in various portions of the tentative report. Copies of the interview summaries and any other interim reports should accompany the tentative report. Finally, the paralegal should add a "comments" section in which he identifies any outstanding issues and possible new avenues for further investigation.

After the attorney has reviewed the tentative report, the legal assistant and attorney can discuss the investigation and determine whether further inquiries are needed. If not, the tentative report will become the final report of the investigation.

THE PARALEGAL'S NOTES AS ATTORNEY WORK PRODUCT

The notes taken by the paralegal during the course of her investigation usually are protected by the attorney work product rule—even if she is an independent paralegal retained by the attorney solely for that investigation. The same protection applies to any photographs, sketches, or other demonstrative evidence she prepares, and to any report she prepares for the attorney. However, if the demonstrative evidence is introduced into evidence at the trial, it is possible that the paralegal who created that evidence will be called to lay foundation for its introduction. In that event, the paralegal will be open to cross-examination about every aspect of her preparation of the demonstrative evidence, including all sources and notes that she used.

The normal work product protection might be overcome, however, if an opposing party can show the following:

- It has a substantial need for the paralegal's notes.
- The equivalent information cannot otherwise be obtained.
- The demanding party's case will be prejudiced if the notes are withheld.

The following "Case in Point" actually concerns notes taken by an investigator retained by an attorney. However, the legal principles should apply equally to the work product of any attorney-supervised paralegal. This case was brought before the Vermont Supreme Court by an attorney who objected to delivering to that state's Professional Conduct Board notes taken by her investigator.

It is interesting to note that the objecting bar counsel was the party who originally brought the complaint alleging an attorney's misconduct before the board—and that her complaint was sustained when the board admonished that attorney for misconduct. It was *after* that board's disciplinary action that the Vermont Supreme Court heard this case. The Supreme Court could have rejected her petition as moot, and therefore untimely—but it did not.

A Case in Point

In re PCB FILE NO. 92.27

167 Vt. 379, 708 A.2d 568 (1998)

Bar counsel appeals from an order of the chair of a Professional Conduct Board (PCB) hearing panel requiring her to provide respondent with a redacted version of notes and summaries of witness statements prepared by her investigator. Although bar counsel has turned the materials over to respondent, she requests that the Court declare the notes of witness interviews prepared by her investigator to be privileged documents under A.O. 9, Rule 10B(1) that are not discoverable absent a showing of good cause. We rule that such documents fall within the attorney-work-product privilege and are not discoverable absent a showing of substantial need and undue hardship, and a finding of good cause.

* * * *

The main issue in this case is whether witness statements and notes taken by bar counsel's investigator of witness interviews are privileged documents. . . .

* * * *

Bar counsel argues that the witness statements and investigator notes are privileged documents under the attorney-work-product rule announced in Hickman v. Taylor, 329 U.S. 495, 67 S.Ct. 385, 91 L.Ed. 451 (1947). In Hickman, the United States Supreme Court held that oral and written statements of witnesses obtained by or prepared by an adverse party's counsel in the course of preparation for possible litigation are not discoverable without a showing of necessity. Id. at 510, 67 S.Ct. at 393. The attorney-work-product rule in Hickman established a qualified privilege for witness statements prepared at the request of the attorney and an almost absolute privilege for attorney notes taken during a witness interview. See Martin v. Office of Special Counsel, 819 F.2d 1181, 1187 (D.C. Cir. 1987). Moreover, the mental impressions, conclusions, opinions and legal theories of an attorney are absolutely protected from discovery regardless of any showing of need. Killington, Ltd. v. Lash, 153 Vt. 628, 647, 572 A.2d 1368, 1379–80 (1990).

* * * *

. . . V.R.C.P. 26(b)(3) provides that documents prepared in anticipation of litigation by the other party's attorney or agent are discoverable "only upon a showing that the party seeking discovery has substantial need of the materials in the preparation of the party's case and that the party is unable without undue hardship to obtain the substantial equivalent of the materials by other means." . . . The rule extends the attorney-work-product privilege declared in Hickman to protect materials "not only when prepared for trial by an attorney but when prepared by the party" or the party's "representative." Reporter's Notes to V.C.R.P. 26(b)(3). After Killington, it is clear that the Vermont common-law, work-product privilege protects notes and summaries of witness interviews taken by bar counsel's investigator, and we so hold....

* * * *

Written or oral statements of witnesses obtained by bar counsel or her investigator are not discoverable absent a showing by respondent of substantial need and undue hardship, and a finding of good cause by the Professional Conduct Board.

In the adjoining "Case in Point," the Vermont Supreme Court—relying upon a U.S. Supreme Court holding—balances the attorney work product protection against the opposing party's need for relevant evidence. This is a classic example of there being "no *absolute* right." It is particularly interesting that Vermont views the attorney-retained investigator's function as being a virtual extension of the attorney's efforts—and, therefore, worthy of protection.

If a paralegal has reviewed other notes in preparation for her own testimony, she can be examined on the content of those notes, as well, and they will no longer be protected under the work product rule. The reason for this exception to the rule is that the paralegal's testimony has placed the content of those notes in controversy. The assumption is that, *but for* having reviewed those notes, the paralegal's testimony might be different. The issue then becomes whether the paralegal has testified in any way that is inconsistent with her own notes. If she has, then her notes may be used to impeach her testimony. In addition, the opposing counsel might find other useful information in those same notes.

> **Practice Tip**
>
> To prevent a waiver of the work product rule, the paralegal should avoid reviewing any protected materials prior to her testimony. She can review the demonstrative evidence itself, of course, because it automatically loses that protection when it is offered as evidence. Alternatively, the paralegal can prepare the demonstrative evidence and then promptly destroy the notes used to prepare it. That, of course, deprives her of anything to review prior to testifying, but it also eliminates any opportunity for the opposing counsel to use the notes for impeachment.

> **Ethics Watch**
>
> In most jurisdictions, it is a criminal offense to destroy material evidence. Although the paralegal's own notes of an interview would not be considered as evidence, a recording of the interview would be evidence—as would a signed statement by a witness. Notes by the paralegal that are relied upon while preparing demonstrative evidence would not themselves be material evidence—they are work product. However, notes made by a percipient witness (even one who is not called to testify) might be evidence, and using them to prepare demonstrative evidence does not transform those notes into attorney work product.

LEARNING ABOUT POTENTIAL JURORS

Because the typical jury of twelve persons is selected from a "pool" of 100 or more people, attorneys are always anxious to know something about the backgrounds of those prospective jurors. It is both legal and ethical to do discreet research on prospective jurors, so long as no direct or indirect contact is made with the prospective juror, her family, employer, or acquaintances. If such contacts occurred, they might contaminate the jury pool. Even if they did not have that effect, the potential for contamination could be the basis for attorney discipline by the court and/or the state bar association.

Customarily, attorneys in a case are given a list of prospective jurors and their addresses. In some jurisdictions, the jurors' occupation, gender, and age will be provided, as well. The name and address, alone, permit an investigator to learn something about the neighborhoods in which the jurors live and to check their voter registration. Voter registration rolls are often available on a microfiche or a computer diskette—and sometimes on-line. If not, they are available for inspection in the county clerk's office. Voter records generally yield political affiliation and age. They might also include occupation, place of birth, and whether that person voted in recent elections. Thus, a number of additional leads can be found for further investigation.

Depending upon state law, it might be possible to obtain motor vehicle records, including moving violations and accidents, for each juror. Plaintiff and defendant indexes can be checked to see if they have been parties to any litigation. A remarkable amount of information about most jurors can be gathered from public sources, although concern for public safety is gradually limiting public access.

Once all of this data has been gathered, the attorney might develop priority categories for prospective jurors: desirable, neutral, undesirable, and unacceptable. For the latter category, the attorney would expect to exercise peremptory challenges to ensure that those individuals do not become members of the final trial jury. Peremptory challenges are exercised only after any challenges for cause have been exercised and twelve otherwise qualified jurors are in the jury box. In any event, the information obtained will be used to frame questions designed to uncover the jurors' biases. During *voir dire,* additional information might cause the attorney to place a juror in a different category.

SECTION 2. OBTAINING INFORMATION ON-LINE

The Internet offers a staggering amount of information about individuals, companies, and organizations. The challenge is to effectively and efficiently locate that information, and then to verify its reliability. General search engines, discussed in Chapter 9, can be helpful. This section will identify some specialized search engines that might be more effective and efficient. Because Web sites come and go, specialized directories are helpful aids to on-line investigation. They tend to update themselves as old Web sites disappear and new ones come on-line.

LOCATING INDIVIDUALS

First, a caveat: There are very few names that are truly unique. Almost everyone has a thousand or more namesakes scattered around the United States. Unless one has some other specific information, it can be a waste of time to simply query large databases for a name. When looking for addresses and phone numbers, the individual's name and city of residence is pretty much the minimum one needs to get started. On the other hand, if the city is unknown—but the year of birth is known—then the search can begin in other types of databases: motor vehicle licenses, for example.

There are a number of ways to locate individuals on the Internet. One of the simplest is to use an on-line telephone directory. Two popular directories are Switchboard and Bigfoot. Other search engines check phone directories, but they also use a broader range of databases where individual information can be found.

Internet Access

Switchboard	http://www.switchboard.com
Bigfoot	http://www.bigfoot.com
Lycos Network	http://www.whowhere.lycos.com
InfoSpace	http://www.infospace.com
Yahoo!	http://people.yahoo.com

Westlaw maintains a variety of databases for locating individuals, including the following:

Name Tracker	PEOPLE-NAME
Credit Bureau Person Tracker	PEOPLE-CBFIND
People Finder—Skip Tracer	PEOPLE-TRACK
People Finder—Telephone Tracker	PEOPLE-PHONE

LEXIS-NEXIS maintains the following databases:

Person locator	P-TRAK
White pages phone directory	P-FIND
Military personnel	M-FIND

There are search engines that specialize in locating e-mail addresses. Who Where? and Yahoo! People Search (Web sites listed above, as telephone directories) will provide e-mail addresses when possible. Another useful search engine is Usenet Addresses. Many people now maintain personal Web pages. Network Solutions' WHOIS search engine provides alternative keyword search formats: name, on-line "handle," company name, and so on. When the Web site is identified, the name and address of the registered holder is displayed.

Internet Access

Usenet Addresses	http://usenet-addresses.mit.edu
Network Solutions WHOIS	http://networksolutions.com/cgi-bin/whois/whois

---

Further Information about Individuals

For a fee, many companies will provide background information to prospective employers or to others with a legitimate need to know. Some will do a complete check of all relevant records for a flat fee per individual. Some charge a discreet amount (generally between $5.00 and $30.00) for each type of information requested: motor vehicle record, civil plaintiff/defendant, criminal record, credit record, and the like. The advantage of using such a service is efficiency and response time.

Internet Access

InterQuest	http://www.interqst.com
Informus	http://www.informus.com
ChoicePoint Online	http://www.choicepointonline.com
Tracers	http://www.tracersinfo.com

SEARCHING PUBLIC RECORDS

Law firms might choose not to use one of the above companies for several reasons. Sometimes it is just as easy and inexpensive for a legal assistant to search a public record on-line. In some cases, the attorneys might not want anyone outside of the firm to know that the inquiries are being made. It might be the client's preference that the firm do the checking directly.

The easiest way to screen many public records from the office computer is by using databases in either Westlaw or LEXIS-NEXIS. Some of the databases in Westlaw are listed below:

Real Property Assessor's Records	RPA-ALL
Motor Vehicle Records	DMV-ALL
Bankruptcy Records	BKR-ALL
Lawsuit Records	LS-ALL
Professional Licenses	LICENSE-ALL

Some of these Westlaw databases can be accessed by state. That is done by using the state's two-letter postal abbreviation. For example, bankruptcy records in New York can be found in the NY-BKR database.

Useful databases in LEXIS-NEXIS include the following:

Assets	ASSETS
Personal property	P-PROP
Bankruptcy	INSOLV
Licenses	LICNSE

Vital records—birth, marriage, divorce, and death—for many states are available on state and/or county government Web sites. On-line directories are convenient ways to find links to those sites. Vital Records Information maintains a Web site with links to such directories. In addition to state government Web sites, Vital Records provides a link to information about U.S. State Department records of U.S. citizens' births, marriages, and deaths overseas.

Internet Access

Vital Records Links   http://www.vitalrec.com/links1.html

INFORMATION ABOUT BUSINESSES

Some of the Westlaw and LEXIS-NEXIS databases (e.g., for real property ownership or bankruptcy filings) listed above contain information about business entities as well as individuals. But each of these on-line services has databases dedicated to information about corporations and other business entities. Westlaw maintains the following databases:

Company profiles	CO-PROFILE
Corporate and limited partnership records	CORP-ALL
Dun & Bradstreet records	DUNBR
"Doing business as" records	ALL-DBA

LEXIS-NEXIS maintains the following databases:

Dun & Bradstreet materials	D&B
State and local corporate filings	INCORP
Secretary of state filings	ALLSOS
"Doing business as" filings	ALLDBA

Of course, Dun & Bradstreet's materials and services can be obtained directly from that company. Dow Jones Interactive is another valuable source of corporate and industry information. The Securities and Exchange Commission offers the EDGAR search engine on its Web site. This makes available a vast pool of corporate financial and securities-related filings. CDB Infotek has long been a popular source for business information, corporate profiles, and searching public records. It operates ChoicePoint Online, which makes these services available via the Internet. Tracers Information Service provides similar services.

Internet Access

Dun & Bradstreet	http://www.dnb.com
Dow Jones Interactive	http://www.djinteractive.com
Securities & Exchange Commission	http://www.sec.gov
ChoicePoint Online	http://choicepointonline.com
Tracers	http://www.tracersinfo.com

Publicly traded companies are relatively easy to research on the Internet. Much more difficult can be privately held companies, because they are required to submit far less information to government agencies. And, because they don't need to worry about tomorrow's stock price, they sometimes share much less information with the news media. The sources discussed below are generally useful for both public and private companies.

The Argus Clearinghouse evaluates on-line research guides that can lead one to excellent sources of information. A useful starting point for business research is Company Information on the Web, which is found at the Virtual Chase. Vault Reports is an on-line service for job seekers. It provides very thorough corporate profiles. Its reports may be purchased on-line. Full-text searches of news media and other sources can yield a great deal of otherwise hard-to-find information. On-line sources that provide full-text searches can be found at Bibliodata's Web site.

Internet Access

Argus Clearinghouse	http://www.clearinghouse.net/index.html
Virtual Chase	http://www.virtualchase.com/coinfo/index.htm
Vault Reports	http://www.vaultreports.com
Bibliodata	http://www.bibliodata.com

EVALUATING ON-LINE INFORMATION

Whenever possible, the on-line investigator should verify, verify, verify. Consider information as basic as an address or birthdate, for example. As with everything else in a computer, "garbage in, garbage out." Whether through human error or technical problems, data can be erroneous or simply corrupted. And then there is the passage of time. Although a birth date should *never* change (the *actual* one, that is), addresses can often be outdated.

One difficulty in verifying data can be simply finding it anywhere else. Another difficulty can result from two or more on-line sources that derived their data from a single inaccurate source. In the age of computers, inaccurate data can replicate like a virus—both biological and electronic. So, the fact that the same address appears in listings from both BigFoot and Switchboard doesn't guarantee anything. When possible, verify by using sources that are unlikely to duplicate each other's inaccuracies: a telephone book listing and a DMV record, for example.

SECTION 3. CONDUCTING INTERVIEWS

One of the most challenging assignments for a paralegal can be the nonclient interview. Whether the subject is a prospective witness or simply someone with information of possible value, a successful interview often taxes one's intellect, tact, and powers of gentle persuasion. It requires great skill to obtain the most value from an interview, and the less skilled interviewer is often unaware of how much more she could have learned if she had been more effective. Understanding the psychology and the dynamics of the interview process is essential to one's success.

THE PSYCHOLOGY OF THE WITNESS

Each witness brings to the interview a unique mixture of motives and attitudes. Although it is impossible for the paralegal to read the subject's mind, it sometimes is possible to read the behavior of the witness, finding clues to possible motives and attitudes. Although each witness has her unique mix, all witnesses share certain instinctive and cultural imperatives (e.g, self-protection and the desire to be believed, respectively). So, a starting point in witness psychology is to observe carefully the influence of ordinary human needs on a particular witness. One's approach to the witness can then be modified so that his or her human needs cause less interference with the interview process.

The Cooperative Witness

At times, the paralegal will interview individuals who have been directed by their employer, their attorney, or some other authority figure to cooperate. But in most instances, the interviewer must depend upon the voluntary cooperation of the witness. In the *NALA Manual for Legal Assistants*, prepared by the National Association of Legal Assistants, seven distinct reasons are given for the voluntary cooperation of witnesses:[1]

1. ego satisfaction: feeling important, and being recognized by others
2. the desire to be liked: *a.k.a.* the desire to please
3. altruism: idealism, wishing to see justice reign
4. novelty and excitement: intrigue with the legal drama
5. catharsis: a need to vent emotions and tell a story
6. loyalty and friendship: wanting to help a friend or relative
7. extrinsic reward: seeking to gain some personal advantage

The *Manual* suggests that the altruist is among the most trustworthy of witnesses, whereas the statements by loyalist and self-serving (i.e., "extrinsic reward") witnesses are to be viewed skeptically. Another caution mentioned is to avoid leading questions—especially when interviewing a witness who wants to be liked, because he might tell the paralegal whatever answer the question suggests.

> **Practice Tip**
>
> *There is an important caveat regarding any efforts to "read" a stranger's attitudes and motivations: the legal assistant can be misled by his initial impressions. He is better advised to make a mental note of those impressions, but to keep his mind open to revising them. Otherwise, he runs the risk of misconstruing much of what the witness says.*

If at all possible, the paralegal should be matched to the anticipated characteristics of the interview subject and his or her testimony. Subject matter expertise is the most obvious criterion. If the person is expected to be uncooperative, then experience in difficult interviews would be another criterion.

SEVEN STEPS FOR SUCCESSFUL INTERVIEWS

Interviews will be productive if they are properly planned and the person being interviewed is comfortable with the process. Special concerns arise when it is the client who is to be interviewed, and those concerns will be discussed later. The following guidelines generally apply to all interviews.

Anyone who is represented by legal counsel for the matter in controversy must not be interviewed without the presence or consent of her attorney. It is a serious violation of professional ethics for an attorney or his agents (that includes legal assistants) to even *contact* the client of another attorney who is retained for that matter. That is true whether that person is a party to the case, or not. The reason is that it defeats entirely the purpose of legal representation if other attorneys can simply ignore that representation and deal directly with the client. Again, however, this restriction applies only if the attorney is retained for the matter in controversy or a clearly related matter. Thus, if there is the possibility of a lawsuit over an auto accident, the witness who has not retained counsel for that matter can be interviewed even though he happens to have an attorney that he uses strictly for estate planning purposes.

> **Ethics Watch**
>
> If, in the course of an interview, the legal assistant discovers that the witness is represented by counsel for that legal matter, or for any clearly related matter, the legal assistant must immediately stop the interview and inform his supervising attorney of that fact.
>
> Similarly, if during the interview the witness indicates a desire to seek legal counsel for that matter, the legal assistant should discontinue the interview. It would be skating on thin ethical ice to ask that person: "Because you do not have an attorney yet, do you mind if we just continue the interview?"

What would be considered a "clearly related" matter? If the interview subject is a driver who has retained an attorney to represent him against criminal charges growing out of the auto accident, that would be clearly related to a possible civil suit arising from the same accident. Anyone in bankruptcy who has retained counsel for those matters should be considered to have legal representation for any matter that could involve civil litigation against the bankrupt person. Similarly, a business person represented by counsel for a broad range of business matters should be presumed to have legal counsel for any matter arising from her business operations.

Minors must not be interviewed without the presence or consent of their parents or guardians, or of an attorney retained on the minor's behalf by the parent or guardian. Although in some states, teachers and school administrators stand *in loco parentis* (i.e., with the responsibilities and powers of the parent) with regard to the students in their charge, that authority is generally limited to the educational process. It would be extremely risky—and probably unethical—to interview a minor in the presence of a teacher or school administrator, in lieu of obtaining parental consent, even if the legal matter arose at school or out of the minor's status as a student.

The Scheduling and the Setting

Because the subject's comfort level is critical to a productive interview, the time and setting should be decided with that in mind. So far as possible, accommodate the subject's schedule, even though that requires conducting the interview in the evening or on a weekend. Be realistic about the amount of time required for the interview. Unless the subject is the client or some other person with a strong interest in the case, never schedule an interview to last longer than one hour. If the first interview session is handled properly, the subject will usually agree to complete the interview in a second session.

The interview subject might be more comfortable if the interview occurs in his home or office. There are several disadvantages in that setting, however. It might be more difficult to prevent interruptions, and it might be more difficult for the paralegal to take charge of the interview. The latter is especially important with uncooperative witnesses.

Ideally, the subject will agree to come to the law firm for the interview. That allows the paralegal to prevent interruptions and places the subject in the paralegal's territory. It also makes it easier to maintain privacy and quiet, and photocopies of any documents the subject brings can be made immediately, on the spot.

In the office, it is better to conduct the interview without the barrier of a table between the legal assistant and the interviewee. Sitting in easy chairs, either facing each other or side by side, is a good arrangement, although it might require a clipboard for note taking. If a table must be used, the legal assistant and the subject can sit together on the same side of the table, which eliminates the table as a psychological barrier and also makes it easy to review any documents that the subject has brought along.

> **Practice Tip**
>
> In some situations, a subject will not want to come to the law firm and will prefer to meet in a neutral location where it will not be obvious that the subject is being interviewed. For those situations, coffee shops often provide reasonable privacy between 9:00 and 11:00 in the morning and between 2:00 and 4:00 in the afternoon. A word to the waiter can ensure that no one will be seated at an adjacent table.

Telephone Interviews

If at all possible, telephone interviews should not be used. They deprive both persons of an opportunity to make eye contact, and to observe facial expressions and body language. Rapport can be much more difficult to establish without face-to-face contact. An obvious exception is the situation where the distance is too great for the legal assistant and interviewee to meet. Another reasonable exception is for brief conversations that follow up on prior in-person interview sessions. In that circumstance, the legal assistant and the subject will probably have some rapport, and both will be comfortable with using the telephone to continue their conversations.

Communication Problems

Occasionally, a subject is not fluent in English or has some disability that interferes with oral communication. For those situations, an interpreter should be employed. In addition, there are services that permit telephone interviews with the hearing impaired. The service provides a telephone "operator" who communicates with the disabled person by teletype machine and with the hearing person by voice. As with any interpretation process, the dialogue requires additional time.

Establishing Rapport

Every interview subject is a human being, and finds himself or herself in the position of being asked to disclose information to a relative stranger. It is natural to be suspicious of the interviewer's motivation and integrity. There might be a fear of being misquoted or of having innocent statements twisted and turned against them at a later time. There can be a reluctance to get involved in other people's problems—especially if it might mean having to testify in court.

Consequently, it is vitally important that the legal assistant conducting the interview help the subject to feel comfortable: with the purpose of the interview, with the interview process, and with the interviewer. How that is done must vary, depending upon the situation and the individual being interviewed. But the interviewer can usually help that process by doing the following:

- expressing appreciation for the subject's time and being inconvenienced
- being down-to-earth and unpretentious
- avoiding any hint of condescension toward the subject
- being forthright and honest about the purpose of the interview
- being respectful and attentive
- beginning the interview with casual conversation, to permit the subject to become comfortable with the interviewer
- avoiding cross-examination or badgering of the witness
- being nonjudgmental

Avoiding Jargon

Although some jargon serves as useful "verbal shorthand" for colleagues in the same occupation, it can be totally confusing to the outsider. Paralegals should avoid the use of legal jargon—or any other jargon—when conducting interviews. The exception might be when the legal assistant and the interview subject share the same jargon. If the paralegal is truly fluent—and also current—in the jargon of medicine, engineering, or skateboarding, say, there is no problem with using that jargon when it is the subject's vocabulary as well.

Occasionally, the interviewer might encounter an interview subject who uses jargon he cannot understand:

> We were VFR when we should've been IFR, and Approach Control was screaming their heads off for our position. I told them to hold their water and squawked "77." Of course, I really shouldn't have done that. Then they go, "What's your emergency alpha five zero victor?," so I just said the rime was building faster than the boots could shake it off and we were losing airspeed. I thought by the time we got on the ground they would never know the difference.

Although an unusual example, the preceding statement certainly makes the point. In that situation, if the paralegal is not conversant with aviation jargon, he must stop the witness and get clarification. In some professions, however—engineering and medicine come immediately to mind—jargon is so embedded in the thought processes that it might be necessary to have a paralegal or outside expert *who is conversant in that terminology* conduct the interview.

Establishing Control

Interviewing is similar to the negotiating process: Whoever gains control of the process has the advantage. If the subject is in control of the interview, she might slant her statements or withhold certain information entirely. If the legal assistant is in control, it is more likely that the witness will respond to the interviewer's need for reliable information.

Control is a fundamental concept of salesmanship. But a salesperson wants the customer to believe that *he* made all of the decisions, when in fact those decisions were orchestrated by the salesperson. If a legal assistant takes "control" of an interview to that extent, the interview will be a failure. The reason is that the legal assistant wants the subject to reveal his true thoughts—not to adopt some suggestion by the interviewer. Unlike a sale, the interviewer wants the subject to be open, forthright, and honest—she does not want to control his responses to her questions.

What, exactly, does "control" mean? Essentially, it means the following:

- setting the agenda and the tone of the encounter
- commanding the respect of the other person
- recognition by the subject that he cannot easily deceive or manipulate the person in control
- inducing in the subject a desire to cooperate

How is control established? Mostly, it is established by the interviewer's appearance and behavior, and it may be partly due to the subject's uncertainty about the situation. It is a matter of psychology. Control results from the perceptions of the other person. If he sees the interviewer as intelligent and knowledgeable, self-confident and assertive, organized and perceptive, he might yield control of the situation—that is, of the interview. It helps also to appear to be righteous—on the side of justice and fairness. Theoretically, it does not matter if these perceptions are inaccurate. Even if the interviewer were ill-informed, insecure, disorganized, and on the side of evil—the interviewee will still defer to the strong and righteous person whom he perceives. In reality, of course, one cannot retain control for long based upon an initial appearance of intelligence, knowledge, self-confidence, assertiveness, organization, and awareness if those qualities do not truly exist.

One result of "control" is that the subject "buys into" the purpose and process of the interview. She does not resist the interview; she helps it to succeed. And if the subject buys into the purpose of the interview, she also tends to identify with that purpose and with the interviewer.

Ethics Watch

Genuine "control" of any relationship—even one as brief as an hour-long interview—can be very seductive for the person in control. It might seem to be a small additional step to suggest a second interview, even if a second session is not really needed. Needless to say, the legal assistant must keep the relationship strictly professional, and he must not exploit any relationship he might have established with the interviewee.

Using an Interview Checklist

Many interview guides include checklists to be followed during the interview. The purpose of the checklist is to ensure consistency and thoroughness. It can also give the inexperienced paralegal a bit more confidence if he conducts the interview under a framework that has already been established by someone more experienced. The disadvantage of checklists is that they can interfere with the spontaneity of the interview process. They also must, by their nature, be generic lists created to cover a broad range of circumstances.

Checklists can be useful in two ways: to help in planning the interview and as a final check at the end of the interview. In preparation, the paralegal can select those items or questions from the checklist that seem appropriate to the case at hand. The paralegal can then create his own checklist, which includes the selected items/questions. The content of the items and questions can be tailored to fit the case at hand. Then, the paralegal adds to the list other questions suggested by what he already knows about the case—questions that would not have been suggested by the checklist. After some fine-tuning, the paralegal should have a reasonably good plan for the interview.

During the interview, the paralegal must not confine himself rigidly to the prepared plan. As unexpected topics or nuances arise, he must be prepared to depart from his plan in order to accommodate those topics and nuances. Near the end of the interview, the paralegal can quickly review his interview plan to ensure that he has not forgotten anything of importance.

During the course of the interview, the legal assistant should assess the interview subject for his potential as a witness under examination in court. She can do so by asking herself questions about the interviewee, such as the following:

- Is he articulate?
- Does he answer directly, without evasion?
- Is he brief and to the point in his answers?
- Does he appear to be honest and sincere?
- Is he untroubled by probing questions?
- Does he have a pleasing manner?
- Will he admit to being ignorant or uncertain on a specific point, or will he attempt to bluff an answer?

The legal assistant should never ask a prospective witness if he is willing to testify in court, unless the attorney has given that assignment to the legal assistant.

USING QUESTIONS EFFECTIVELY

The purpose of the interview is to obtain *the subject's* information and beliefs. Consequently, the rule is this: Let the subject tell her narrative with minimal interruption. After the subject completes the narrative, clarifying and follow-up questions can be used.

The paralegal should avoid using questions that suggest the answer—in other words, leading questions. Leading questions are generally those that can be answered by simply saying "Yes" or "No." If a subject wants to be helpful or wants to be liked, she might answer "Yes" in the belief that it is the answer the interviewer desires—even if the better answer would be "No," or "It didn't happen quite that way."

The better question is one that invites the subject to answer with a brief narrative statement. The following dialogue offers good examples of better ways to phrase questions:

Q: What did you do after the collision?

A: I parked at the curb and ran back to the accident scene.

Q: Can you describe the accident scene for me?

A: There were a bunch of cars, all smashed together. The eerie thing was that there was dead silence.

Q: How many cars had collided?

A: I'm not sure. Maybe five or six.

Q: What happened next?

A: You know, I didn't hear anything and I didn't even think about victims—I mean I was in such a state of shock. I ran back to my car and drove until I found a pay phone to call the police.

If the interviewer had used a leading question instead, the following exchange might have occurred:

Q: After the collision, did you go to the aid of the injured victims?
A: Why . . . Yes. Of course.

Why would the subject respond untruthfully to that leading question? Perhaps the question raised in her mind a moral obligation to assist the injured—an obligation she now fears that she violated. Because she has been asked point-blank whether she went to their aid, she is forced into an instant decision to say yes or no.

In addition to inviting the subject to tell her version of events, it is clear that the interviewer should avoid questions that imply moral judgments on his part or that are likely to cause the subject to feel embarrassed or threatened. The paralegal must always protect the ego of the subject, so that she does not become defensive. If the paralegal needs to elicit an admission of some sort, it is best that she do so in a face-saving manner:

Q: The accident scene must have been horrible.
A: It was awful.
Q: Had you ever seen anything like that before?
A: Nothing like that. All that crumpled metal. Steam from the radiators. The smell of gasoline running in the street. I was scared to death it was going to explode any second.
Q: I don't see how you kept your senses enough to go for help. I would have been hysterical or in total shock. I don't think I could have done anything.
A: At first, I was almost numb. But then. . .
Q: Yes?
A: I don't know how to say this. I saw what looked like a blanket piled up on the side of the road. Then it moved . . . And I knew it was a child.
Q: Oh, no!
A: Earlier, I said it was dead silent. That isn't true. I could hear people moaning. And someone trying to shout, but his voice was so weak . . . The same words over and over, in some foreign language. I felt so helpless.
Q: How awful for you! It must have been overwhelming. Is that when you left to call the police?
A: I didn't leave to call the police. I was just running away. I couldn't stand the sounds of the injured people . . . or the sight of that child. All I thought about was getting away. I should have helped. But I couldn't.
Q: Of course, of course. I understand. But you did say earlier that you called the police, didn't you?
A: Actually, I probably drove for five minutes. I must have passed several pay phones. Finally, I got hold of myself. That's when I turned back to a pay phone I had seen. I called the police, and then I returned to the accident.

It is easy to imagine how a different line of questioning would have reinforced the witness' need to keep her troublesome secret, thereby preventing her admission from ever coming out during that interview.

When the legal assistant believes he has the complete story from the witness, he should review her statements by asking a series of confirming questions:

"Then, after you called the police, you went directly back to the scene of the accident, right?"

The final portion of every interview should be a request for additional names and other leads to potential witnesses.

When Leading Questions Might Be Useful

Although the general rule rejects the use of leading questions, there are situations in which they can be helpful. During trial, an attorney is permitted to ask leading questions during cross-examination under the theory that the witness called by an opposing party is likely to be less forthcoming and is primarily interested in protecting the credibility of his earlier testimony on direct examination. The leading question places the witness in the position of having to agree or disagree, and it is difficult to avoid giving an answer.

Similarly, during an interview with an *uncooperative* witness, the leading question might elicit a "Yes" or "No," whereas the same witness would refuse to provide a narrative response to a general question. In addition, by answering "Yes" to a leading question, the uncooperative witness has effectively accepted a narrative suggested by the interviewer. In subsequent questioning he can be challenged if he tries to back away from that version of events. If necessary, the paralegal could later testify during trial as an impeachment witness if the interview subject tries to tell a version different from the one he agreed with during the interview.

As has been seen with the interview of the auto accident witness, above, leading questions can be used following a narrative to confirm the content of that statement.

HANDLING AN UNFRIENDLY OR A HOSTILE WITNESS

Of course, the most desirable approach is one that defuses the apprehension or hostility of the witness. An introduction from a trusted third party known to the witness might accomplish that. But, usually, the interviewer must overcome the resistance by demonstrating to the witness that she is professional, cordial, and trustworthy. That process can require a substantial amount of time, during which the interview might not be very productive. In some situations, overcoming the resistance might be the entire purpose of the initial interview, and a second session might be needed to obtain any substantive information. Getting the witness to agree to a second session can be a victory in itself, because he is likely to be less resistant during the second meeting.

The interval between interview sessions can permit the witness to mull over his impressions of the interviewer. Of course, the witness can refuse to meet a second time, or he might agree to meet and then not show up. But that same witness could have refused to meet in the first place. Thus, the decision about proposing a second session is very much a judgment call on the interviewer's part.

Sometimes it is impossible to overcome the hostility or apprehension of a witness. In that situation, the interviewer must use her understanding of human nature and every social and verbal skill she can muster to obtain information from an uncooperative person. Even so, it could be worse—as already mentioned, the witness could refuse to be interviewed at all.

Generally, a hostile witness who agrees to speak to the interviewer will answer questions that do not reach the basis for his hostility. For this reason, it often is best to begin with nonthreatening questions about the witness or the situation—what might be called "background" questions. If the witness is not personally involved in the matter under investigation, then questions about name, employment, and education are likely to elicit answers. *The key to success is inducing the witness to begin talking, and to continue talking.* If the witness observed an automobile accident but does not want to become involved in a trial, questions about his other activities on the day of the accident might get him started. Later, questions about what he observed will have to be asked, but by then he might have lost some of his initial reluctance.

In their excellent guide, *The Gentle Art of Interviewing and Interrogation*, Royal and Schutt recommend that the interviewer appeal to the witness' sense of civic duty and fair play. If a witness shows any indication of refusing to answer further questions, the interviewer should return to "safer" topics and then later use a different line of questioning to approach the topic that is so sensitive for the witness.[2]

VERIFYING INFORMATION FROM AN INTERVIEW

Inevitably, interviews will yield information that is directly contrary to other evidence, possibly contrary to statements made by others who were in a position to have the same knowledge. Although that could indicate dishonesty, it is common for sincere individuals to have very different perceptions of the same events. A significant part of investigation is the process of resolving conflicts between the information obtained from different sources.

When the investigator is able to find only one source of information about a particular fact, it is tempting to accept the accuracy of that source—and its reliability might not even be brought into question, because there is no conflicting information. But any single-source information is by definition uncorroborated, and therefore it is susceptible to a greater risk of being inaccurate. Erroneous information might be worse than useless—it can harm the client's case by misleading the attorney about the facts. An attorney who is unsure of the facts is in a safer position than one who has been misled about the facts, because uncertainty encourages caution. There are a variety of ways to verify information provided during an interview, but the verification process should begin during the interview itself. Verification is accomplished by careful observation, evaluation of the witness and his statements, and follow-up questions that explore the accuracy of those statements.

Demeanor of the Subject

An experienced interviewer does more than listen to the words of his subject. He observes the behavior of the interviewee. Does the subject become ill at ease when particular topics are discussed? Does he avoid eye contact? Does he become ambiguous after giving earlier responses that were clear and specific? The intentional lie will be considered later in this section.

The Subject's Sources

Where did the subject get his information? Is the information first- or secondhand? If it is secondhand, does the subject know how his own source came by that information? Would the subject's informant have any reason to mislead the subject? What circumstance made it possible for the subject to gain his information?

Ill-Founded Opinions

Is the witness making statements of facts, or is he giving his opinion (assumptions?, guesses?) about the facts? If the witness says that someone was in a "jealous rage," that is a statement of opinion—which might be well-founded, or not. The legal assistant must question the witness' basis for reaching that conclusion.

How did the jealousy manifest itself? Could the apparent rage have a cause other than jealousy? Could the "rage" have been a pretense?

If the witness states that the blue Chevrolet sedan ran the red light, was the witness actually able to observe that fact? What were the lighting conditions at that time? Where was the witness in relation to the traffic signal facing the blue Chevrolet? Does the witness have any vision problems? Was the witness wearing eyeglasses at that moment? Casual observers are especially unreliable in their estimates of distance, speed, and the elapse of time.

Dealing with Inconsistencies

Honest persons sometimes make inconsistent statements when describing some past event. That is because their observations were not carefully made—or perhaps were clouded by surprise, fear, excitement, or some other emotion—and because they have not examined their own memories to test for inconsistency. This phenomenon has been demonstrated in countless psychology classrooms when the instructor has arranged for a sudden interruption—several people entering the room and shouting accusations at the instructor or a student, for example. When the students subsequently attempt to reconstruct from memory what occurred, their descriptions of the intruders' appearance often vary wildly, even reporting that a clean-shaven intruder had a beard, or describing an intruder as having a nonexistent foreign accent. Typically, their memories of all significant details—number of intruders, descriptions, statements made, and so on—display similar inconsistencies.

The paralegal must be very alert for significant inconsistencies in the statements of witnesses. The reason is that dishonest persons are rarely able to construct a false tale without embedding serious inconsistencies in their statements. So, the challenge of inconsistencies is to distinguish those that reveal dishonesty from those that reflect inadequate observation or a faulty memory. Unfortunately, the evaluation of inconsistencies can be terribly difficult. Some inconsistencies might not be significant. But, if they do appear significant, the legal assistant must consider such questions as the following:

- Does the interviewee's demeanor give cause for suspicion?
- Does the witness have any motive to be dishonest about this topic (guilt, bias, hostility, etc.)?
- Does the witness claim to have a complete and accurate memory of the events in question?

Cross-Examination of an Interviewee

Cross-examination has several characteristics. The person using the techniques of cross-examination assumes that the witness is not voluntarily forthcoming with the desired information. He might even suspect that the witness is being less than honest. Cross-examination is used to test the accuracy of the statements and the truthfulness of the witness. Cross-examination adopts the tone of an interrogation. Most people do not like to be interrogated. A witness who is cross-examined by the investigating paralegal might not be a friendly witness for the attorney during trial.

Therefore, cross-examination should be a fallback strategy, to be used only when a less confrontational approach is unsuccessful in obtaining the needed information or when the legal assistant is highly suspicious of the statements by the witness. It is best to remember that, in almost every situation, the interviewee is free to walk away and refuse to talk further with the legal assistant. Cross-examination will be productive only if the legal assistant is firmly in control of the interview and if the subject feels either unable to resist the cross-examination or some obligation to continue the interview.

WITNESSES WHO FABRICATE INFORMATION

Witnesses who fabricate fall into three broad categories:

1. the unintentional fabricator
2. the intentional fabricator of "white lies"
3. the premeditating deceiver

Chronic, habitual liars might fall into either the first or the last category, depending upon whether their dishonesty is consciously contemplated or not. Compulsive liars can weave such a complicated web of lies that they lose track of what was true and what has been fabricated; the result is that they sometimes believe that their earlier statements—now long-forgotten lies—are their genuine memories of true events.

Unintentional Fabricators

In addition to the compulsive liar with a confused memory, normally honest people unconsciously invent explanations that help them to "understand" important events and enable them to have a coherent story for themselves and others. Oftentimes, important events develop so rapidly that a person is unable to observe every cause-and-effect event or influence. At other times, a person does not recognize the importance of what is unfolding and fails to pay close attention. Under both circumstances, his memory is left with gaps. To make sense of those events, people often *deduce* what "probably happened" during their memory gaps, providing thereby a reasonable explanation of those events. Through repetitive telling of a story—whether to themselves or to others—"probably happened" can become "did happen" in their minds, and like the compulsive liar they find themselves unable to recognize their own inventions.

The Intentional Fabricators of "White Lies"

Tellers of white lies are often motivated by the same need as some unintentional fabricators: the need to make sense out of confusing situations—not for themselves, however, but for the benefit of their listeners. This can also be related to a need to be believed: The witness might fear that unexplained gaps in his story will undermine the credibility of what he honestly does remember. Or, he might be thinking that his true story might seem incredible unless he lies about some details: *They'll never believe that I looked in her window by chance when I saw that burglar.*

Other tellers of white lies simply want to make their story a bit more "juicy"—but with no harm intended. The egoist can easily fall prey to this, because he will want to make his information—and if he was personally involved in the event, then his own role as well—more important than the true facts would justify. Because egoists are characteristically insecure people who are defending themselves against fears of inadequacy, the temptation to embellish can be very strong.

Premeditating Deceivers

The needs of egoists are not always satisfied with exaggerations—they might intentionally concoct stories that go far beyond "white lies," falsifying the very substance of what occurred. Unless this is done to fend off some real or imagined threat to the egoist's status (e.g., a competitor for a job promotion), it usually is done without any ill intent toward other people. Unfortunately, egoists can develop into compulsive liars out of their constant need to make themselves appear—to themselves, as well as to others—more nearly perfect and admirable than they are. Most egoists cannot conceal their inner insecurity, which often is revealed by an outward display of arrogance, obvious exaggerations of their importance, and condescension toward others. Indications of an underlying insecurity should be a red flag to the paralegal conducting the interview.

Of course, nonegotistical individuals also lie, usually for ordinary reasons such as personal animosity, to hide their own complicity in wrongdoing, or in hopes of being rewarded by someone who might benefit from their lies. Unless this type of witness is exceptionally proficient—usually from years of practice—his lies can be uncovered by careful questioning and comparison to other reliable information.

A special difficulty is presented by the compulsive liar. Because her behavior is compulsive, she simply cannot help herself—she will lie with regularity. Inevitably, some lies become apparent by their inconsistency with objective facts or even her own prior statements. But this type of deception is not easily overcome, because one more lie can always be invented to explain a discrepancy. (Chronic liars learn to think quickly.) In an ongoing relationship such as marriage or long-term employment, people eventually catch on, and the liar loses all credibility. But if the liar is exceptionally bright, her deception can continue undetected for an extraordinarily long time. For the paralegal interviewer, the only protection against the compulsive liar is careful listening, careful observation, careful questioning, and a frequent comparison of her statements to those of other reliable sources.

Handling a Deceptive Witness

Of course, the above topic heading presumes that the legal assistant has discovered the deception. If so, that discovery raises a very difficult problem. Although that witness' story might be disregarded entirely—which ultimately might be the only choice—it could be very helpful if the witness can be persuaded to tell the truth or admit the deception. Therein lie several problems.

The original motive for deception is probably still present. To persuade the witness to change her story, the legal assistant will have to remove the original motive or else overcome it with a new motive. Suppose the original motive for deception was the witness' own embarrassment about what occurred. If the legal assistant can assure the witness that her privacy will be protected and that she will not have to testify, the witness might be willing to speak truthfully.

Unfortunately, eliminating the motive for deception is seldom so easy. The alternative, then, is to overcome the original motive with a stronger one. The legal assistant might be able to appeal to the witness' conscience or sense of justice, as in the following example question:

> "You wouldn't want that injured driver to lose the whole case because of your testimony, would you?"

(Note that the legal assistant tactfully did *not* say "your false testimony.") Or, the legal assistant can argue that the deception will end up being discovered, in any case, as in the following question:

"There are three other witnesses who will testify that your friend was staggering and slurring his speech when he got out of his car—are you *positive* that he was completely sober?"

> **Ethics Watch**
>
> When obvious deception is encountered, it can be very tempting to exaggerate the contrary testimony that others might give, in order to persuade the dishonest witness to tell the truth. This would be unethical, however.
>
> If the legal assistant's own deception is discovered later, it will destroy his credibility and could also cause embarrassment for the law firm.

Asking the witness to sign a written statement might cause him to change his story. However, he also could simply refuse to sign and walk away. The interviewer's goal should be to keep the witness talking, so that it might be risky to present a statement for the witness' signature.

The interviewer could challenge the witness, either by asking him to "prove" the truth of his statements, or even by accusing him of being "less than honest." Obviously, either tactic increases the risk that the witness will become, at best, argumentative, or at worst, combative. Before acting rashly, the paralegal should carefully consider all other options, such as asking the witness for a second session. At the later appointment, the paralegal might be able to present the witness with evidence that demonstrates his deception, and then request an explanation. Outright confrontation of the deception is unlikely to succeed unless the legal assistant is firmly in control of the interview.

RECORDING INTERVIEWS

An audio tape or videotape of an interview can be a very valuable record. Two benefits are that it eliminates the need to take notes (other than reminders for future questions or inquiries) and that there will be no quarrel later about what the witness did or did not say. In fact, it can be used later to impeach the testimony of a witness if he contradicts in court what he has said on tape.

However, many witnesses feel less comfortable and will be less forthcoming if the interview is taped. Some will even insist that the entire interview be "off the record." Audio recordings are less inhibiting than video recordings—assuming the witness is willing to go "on the record"—because the audio equipment can be less obtrusive and no camera operator or lights are needed.

Any recorded witness interview is subject to discovery by the other parties. Therefore, no interview should be recorded unless the attorney is willing to expose it to discovery.

> **Ethics Watch**
>
> Should a legal assistant ever surreptitiously tape an interview? In addition to being an ethical issue, this can be a question of criminal law, because some states make it a criminal offense to secretly tape-record a conversation in which the participants have a reasonable expectation of privacy.
>
> Strictly in ethical terms, the paralegal who tapes secretly is asking the witness to be forthright and honest at the very moment that she herself is being deceptive—because every witness would have a reasonable expectation to be notified if the interview is to be taped. Clearly, the purpose of surreptitious taping is to get on tape statements that the interviewer believes the subject would not voluntarily put on the record.

Recording Guidelines for Interviews

Having first obtained the subject's consent, the tape-recorded interview should begin with a recitation of basic facts about the interview, such as the following:

- date and time
- name of the legal assistant and his law firm
- name of the interviewee
- subject of the interview
- a statement by the interviewee that she consents to a tape recording of the interview

One problem is to account for any time lapses in the recorded conversation. This is best done by announcing any interruption and giving the time of interruption. When the taping resumes, the date, time, and the names of the interviewer and interviewee should be given again, with a statement that the interview is resuming.

SIGNED WITNESS STATEMENTS

Second only to tape recordings, written statements are very valuable records of an interview. Once again, however, many subjects will be reluctant to sign a statement, because they are uncertain about any consequences of doing so. If the paralegal anticipates the need for further pretrial cooperation from the witness, it might be best to delay any written statement until the paralegal has obtained all information that the witness can provide.

If the statement is a declaration—that is, a written statement signed under penalty of perjury—or a sworn affidavit, it can be attached as supporting testimony to a pleading or motion. Otherwise, its primary value would be for possible impeachment. Impeachment is rarely needed for friendly witnesses, and unfriendly witnesses are more often reluctant to sign a statement. Even without a declaration by the witness, the legal assistant could testify in court to earlier contrary statements by the witness.

INTERVIEWING THE CLIENT

In the client's mind, his legal matter might be a critical passage of life—something like going through puberty—although the client is far more frightened now, because during this passage he actually understands how badly things might turn out. It is not at all unusual for a client to be totally obsessed by his legal situation. He might be angry, outraged by the injustice of life, frustrated by the snail's pace of the legal system, apprehensive of the outcome, and generally suspicious of lawyers. The client might have picked the attorney out of the yellow pages or might have obtained her name from the local bar association. He might have brought a breach-of-contract case to the attorney, simply because a friend of a friend said that she had handled his divorce case well. The client might be deathly afraid of losing the case or—in the alternative—of being driven into bankruptcy by the legal fees necessary to prevent the plaintiff from winning. For the client, this might not be a happy period. Now, the legal assistant gets to interview the client.

In some law firms, after the attorney has met with the client and learned enough about the case to make her decision to accept it, the client is turned over to a legal assistant who is to interview the client. While the client is still in the office, the attorney should introduce the client to the legal assistant who will conduct the interview. If the client is no longer in the office, the legal assistant should call the client in advance to arrange the interview. In that conversation, it must be made clear that the legal assistant is not an attorney, but that the attorney has asked him to conduct the interview. In that same call, the legal assistant should also identify any documents that the client should bring to the interview. At the conclusion of the conversation, it is absolutely essential that the client understands that he will be meeting with a non-attorney. That fact should be reinforced again when the client arrives for the interview.

The Client Intake Interview

This **intake interview** is used to obtain detailed information about the client and the case. The client will have signed a retainer letter, but there might be other documents for the client to sign—for example, authorization for the IRS to release tax information to the law firm; authorization for doctors to release medical records, or the like. The paralegal will be expected to explain the purpose of these forms and to obtain the client's signature.

The **intake interview** of a client is used to obtain detailed information about the client and the case, so that the law firm might represent him effectively.

It is best to start the interview with some nonthreatening topics: the client's occupation, family, and so on (assuming those are not issues in the legal matter at hand). In this stage of the interview, the objective is to allow the client to become comfortable with the situation. As the client responds, the paralegal should take notes of all information needed for the file: addresses, phone numbers, employment, person to notify in an emergency, social security number, and the like.

Once the client is comfortable and the personal data have been obtained, it is time to get to the issue of the case. Typically, clients have an enormous pent-up reservoir of information, misinformation, assumptions, and emotions. They often need to vent, and it is best to let them do so. In any event, they should be encouraged to tell their narrative about the case with minimal interruption. In this stage, questions should be limited to audible cues: "Yes"; "I see"; "What happened next?"

Although some paralegals and attorneys advise that the paralegal take detailed notes during the client's narrative, others disagree. Instead, they would note only the topics discussed and concentrate their attention on the narrative. (It is difficult to listen well if one is taking detailed notes.) Asking the client to stop while the paralegal catches up on his note taking interrupts the flow of the narrative. One advantage of using a legal assistant for the intake interview is that the legal assistant can more easily afford the time, and the client can more easily afford the fees.

After the client has finished his narrative, the paralegal can go back over the topics covered and ask the questions she has prepared in advance, as well as those triggered by the client's narrative. At this point, the purpose is to flesh out the narrative, filling the gaps and clarifying the information. The narrative having ended, the paralegal can now take detailed notes. In response to any given question, however, the client might take off on another narrative, and it is a judgment call for the paralegal to decide whether to rein him in so that he focuses on a particular issue, or to listen quietly until the new narrative has run its course.

Gradually, the legal assistant will accumulate detailed notes of the client's comments. It is important to include in those notes the apparently false perceptions, misunderstandings of the law, unfounded assumptions, and so forth, that might distort the client's view of the situation. Eventually, the attorney will need to deal with those perceptions, misunderstandings, and assumptions.

When the interview is approaching an end, it is best to review the notes with the client, so that he will confirm that the paralegal has correctly understood his information and viewpoint. This invites the client to correct anything he believes the paralegal has misunderstood or noted inaccurately.

> **Ethics Watch**
>
> During the interview, the client might wish to discuss the strength of his case, the damages he might be able to collect, and so on. Once again, the legal assistant must emphasize that he is not an attorney: "Mr. Erickson, you will have to discuss those issues with the attorney."

At the conclusion of the intake interview, the legal assistant should go over any tasks for the client: provide names and addresses of witnesses, locate additional documents, and the like. He should assure the client that the attorney will be in touch, and should invite him to call if he has any questions or suggestions to offer. Depending upon the policy of the firm, the legal assistant might offer himself as the client's primary contact for case information and other routine communications.

A QUESTION OF ETHICS

Jeff Mirandini is a paralegal in a Dallas litigation firm. For the past five months, he has been working on a big wrongful death case that is now in trial. His firm is representing the defendant. Now that the trial has started, Jeff is in court every day assisting the two attorneys from his firm who are trying the case. Part of his assignment on this case was an investigation of the fatal accident that led to the lawsuit. In the course of that investigation, he interviewed seven witnesses to the accident, including a truck driver who is now testifying.

The truck driver was called as a defense witness, but now is undergoing cross-examination by the opposing counsel. At one point, the plaintiff's counsel asks an unexpected question of the witness. At first, the witness seems unsure of how to answer, but then he gives an answer that is helpful to the defense. But Jeff realizes that the truck driver's answer contradicts what he had said when Jeff interviewed him three months ago. Jeff immediately scribbles a note to that effect to the attorney sitting beside him. What should the attorney do about the witness' testimony that is helpful to the client but contradicts his earlier statement?

CHAPTER SUMMARY

- Investigation is a systematic effort to accumulate useful information.
- Paralegals can perform most types of legal investigations, but some inquiries require expertise that few paralegals would have.
- Most paralegal investigation is done by telephone and computer, without leaving the office.
- Legal investigations can have a variety of purposes, but in litigation the purpose is usually to find the facts that will win or defeat a lawsuit.
- A legal assistant should prepare a well-considered plan before beginning an investigation.
- Persons represented by counsel must not be interviewed without the consent of their attorney.

- The interview schedule should accommodate the needs of the interview subject.
- The interview will be more successful if the paralegal controls the dynamics of the interview.
- Interview checklists can be helpful in preparing an interview plan, but use of them should not be allowed to dominate the process.
- Generally, witnesses should be encouraged to tell a narrative, after which the legal assistant can ask specific questions.
- Leading questions should be avoided, except in dealing with a hostile or an uncooperative witness.
- The key to success is to get the witness to talk, and to continue talking.
- Compulsive deceivers can be very difficult to recognize.
- Clients should be interviewed with understanding for the emotional stress they are experiencing.

KEY TERMS

attorney service
continuous custody and control
covert inquiry
demonstrative evidence
expert witness

forensic
forensic medicine
intake interview
investigation
percipient witness

physical evidence
private investigator
property profiles
real evidence

ACTIVITIES AND ASSIGNMENTS

1. Interview a classmate about a critical event in his or her life. Let the classmate choose the event. Begin the interview by obtaining background information about the interviewee: name, age, occupation, education, and so on. Then proceed to the event that the subject has chosen. Listen first to the subject's complete narrative, noting only topics to pursue in follow-up questions. After the narrative is over, ask clarifying questions. Then, reconstruct the event by asking confirming questions (which will be leading questions) about the entire event. Have the interviewee confirm or correct each one.

   Write an interview report, summarizing the information obtained.

   The student who was interviewed is then to write a *constructive critique* of the interview, suggesting ways to improve the process.

2. In the public library, find an old newspaper article about an interesting lawsuit in your local court system that required a week or more for the trial. (Be sure that the trial concluded at least three months ago.) Go to the local courthouse and use the plaintiff or defendant index in the court clerk's office to obtain the correct case number for that lawsuit. Then, fill out a request form to review the case file. Go through the file, checking pleadings (e.g., the complaint, answer, motions, and oppositions to motions) for exhibits and/or declarations (or affidavits) that provide information about persons (i.e., individuals, corporations, etc.) involved in that case. Obtain a photocopy of the most informative document found. Write a report summarizing the case.

3. Assume that you are investigating a pool of prospective jurors. Go to the local official who maintains voter registration records (usually the county clerk or registrar of voters) and look up the record for yourself or a member of your immediate family. Obtain a photocopy, or make notes of all the information provided. Using that information, prepare a plan for using that data to obtain additional information about the voter. Include things as simple as driving through the neighborhood, and as sophisticated as using the data to locate other public records about the voter.

4. This exercise is a sophisticated one for the student who likes a challenge. In a recent newspaper, find a lengthy article about a specific

situation likely to result in litigation. It might be an auto accident, a dispute over sexual harassment, or an officer-involved shooting, for example. Using the information in the article, identify at least one *legal issue* that might be prominent in a resulting lawsuit. Then, identify as many factual issues as possible that might determine the outcome of that legal issue.

Now, develop a draft plan for an investigation of that incident, using the questions posed in this chapter. For some questions (e.g., deadlines and budget), you will have to make arbitrary decisions. But try to be as realistic as you can in developing your draft plan.

5. Find a fairly detailed article about a traffic accident that has occurred on surface streets in your community. Go to the scene of the accident and make thorough observations of the physical setting in which the accident occurred. Make a sketch of the street(s) and surrounding area. If possible, mark the location of the accident. (If it is very recent, there might be marks or stains in the roadway.) Using the news article as your source, indicate on the sketch the path of each vehicle up to the point of collision.

Go to the police agency that investigated the accident and request a copy of the police report (if available). Compare the police report with the information in the news article and from your own observations. Prepare a report on the accident, identifying any discrepancies or questions that require further investigation.

6. If you have Internet access, use some of the Web sites identified in Section 2 of this chapter to collect information about yourself. Begin your search with no more than your name, address and Social Security number.

Prepare a chronological log of your search and results, identifying each Web site you have used. Try to use directories (e.g., Yahoo!) to identify additional Web sites that are not mentioned in this chapter.

7. Pair up with another student. Role-play the interview of an uncooperative witness, with one student acting as the investigator and another student acting as the witness. Then, switch roles. The instructor might decide to have two students perform the role play in front of the class, followed by constructive criticism of the interview techniques used.

8. Role-play the intake interview of a new client. The student portraying the client should demonstrate the effects of the client's emotional distress over the situation.

The instructor might suggest different situations (breach of contract, personal injury, slander, etc.) for each pair of students.

END NOTES

[1] ____, NALA *Manual for Legal Assistants* (St. Paul: West Publishing Company 1992), pp. 145–146.

[2] Robert F. Royal and Steven R. Schutt, *The Gentle Art of Interviewing and Interrogating* (Prentice-Hall, Inc. 1976).

CHAPTER 11

Law Office Management and Procedures

"Children and family are very important to the firm," says co-managing shareholder Laura B. Wallenstein. The firm's billable-hour requirement is purposely kept low, at 1,750 hours per year, so that lawyers can lead lives outside the law.

"Job Share Lets Moms Litigate," The National Law Journal, *October 12, 1998 (Reporting about job-sharing in the twenty-two-lawyer New Jersey firm of Flaster Greenberg Wallenstein Roderick Spirgel Zuckerman Skinner and Kirchner)*

Chapter 11 introduces the reader to the working environments of paralegals in law firms, public agencies, and corporations. The structure and organization of various law offices are described, as well as the procedures that they follow in serving their clients. The paralegal's status as an entry-level employee is explained. The paralegal's role as part of a professional legal team is considered. Billing practices are described for paralegals working in law firms.

After reading this chapter, the student should be prepared to answer these questions:

- What defines a *successful* law practice?
- What are the four keys to an effective law practice?
- How does the *Fair Labor Standards Act* affect working hours for legal professionals?
- How does a law practice establish and maintain a sound attorney-client relationship?
- What is the role of a managing partner in a law firm?
- What are the functions of management committees in larger practices?
- Why are some law practices organized as professional corporations or limited liability firms?
- How are client conflict checks performed?
- How do law offices use docket control and tickler systems?
- How are client files organized and maintained?
- How are legal fees and expenses recorded and billed to clients?

- Why are client trust accounts maintained?
- What support staff positions are found in law offices?

SCENARIO

The Firm Policy Is Zero Tolerance

It couldn't have been more clear. It was *crystal* clear. On page 17 of the Wilson, Mark, Chen and Adan policy manual, it was right there in black and white:

> This firm exists to serve the interests of our clients. If we are to do that ethically and professionally, we cannot permit any mistake that has a material, damaging effect upon the legitimate interests of a client. If an inadvertent action or omission might have such a material effect upon the interests of a client, the employee responsible for that action or omission shall immediately inform the managing partner. Failure to do so shall be cause for appropriate discipline, up to and including termination.

Now, I suppose some clever lawyer could say:

> But what, *exactly,* is a "mistake"? That's not defined. And what constitutes a "material, damaging effect upon the interests of a client"? That's not defined, either. So, how can you expect an employee—who is *not* an attorney, after all—to understand the legal implications of your firm's policy? And the implications *are* pretty darn legal when it costs them their job, right?

A clever lawyer might say that. But I'm no clever lawyer. Like our *hypothetical* clever lawyer might say, I'm not even a lawyer of *any* kind, dumb or otherwise. I'm just Bill Manes, the file clerk.

The whole thing started when the Old Man told me to get the Holsteen file. Now, Holsteen's this really rich guy who is constantly in marital difficulties, if you understand what I mean. Last time I looked, his file contained some pretty racy stuff. Especially the report by that PI the firm hired. Good thing that PI report is protected as work product—there'd be hell to pay if Holsteen's current wife saw it.

Anyway, I knew that the Old Man was just leaving for lunch with the e-MarketPlace board chairman, so I figured that I could take my break and catch up on this most amazing client's latest doings. I mean, this is intriguing stuff! The small conference room was empty, so I ducked in there and sat in one of those *incredible* dark leather and rosewood chairs—that chair was worth more than *my* annual salary, I figured.

So, first I scanned the PI's report again. Just to provide a refreshened context for the new stuff, you understand. Then I flipped to the pleadings section and discovered why the Old Man needed the file. The current wife has filed a petition for dissolution. How about that? I was reading her declaration in support of the petition when Sherry stuck her head in the door and said there's a phone call for me. Just when I was getting to the good parts! So, I leave the file there while I go take the call. Big deal: my dentist's office—time for my cleaning. *Great.*

On the way back to the conference room, I get my lunch out of the freezer and run it through the micro for a few minutes. That's my *big mistake.* When I get back to the conference room, here's this expert witness in the ABX shareholder case, standing right there leaning over the table and looking at the open file. With the pleadings folded back so that Mrs. Holsteen's declaration is right there on top, no less. Just the way I left it. I could tell by the amazement in his expression that he was reading the good parts, too. I'm about to say something and retrieve the file from this snoop, when Mr. Fillips comes in. One glance at the file and at the expert and Fillips starts getting red in the face.

"*Who's working with this file?*", he roared. I almost shouted, Marine-recruit style, "*I don't know, sir!*" But there it was: *my* jacket draped over the back of the chair. So, I did the right thing and said, "Mr. Jesson asked me to get it, sir. I was just checking to make sure everything was filed properly when I was interrupted for an incoming call." Fillips' eyes told me what he thought of *that* explanation.

The scariest thing was meeting with Fillips and the Old Man. It was like the Old Man was reading me my Miranda rights. They gave me a copy of the firm policy—which I already had, anyway—and asked me about any "mitigating circumstances." What could I say? I got a phone call and then stopped to fix my lunch? Are those mitigating circumstances?

Besides, the policy talks about "inadvertent" actions or omissions. I don't think what I did was all that inadvertent. I mean, I was reading that file *on purpose,* wasn't I? So, I figure Fillips and the Old Man don't have a case. What do you think? ■

In this opening scenario, the file clerk appears to be in deep trouble at Wilson, Mark, Chen and Adan. Obviously, he doesn't fully appreciate the importance of client confidences and the responsibility of law firm employees to protect those confidences. But, how should the law firm handle this situation? The reader will have an opportunity to address this question in the Activities and Assignments section at the end of this chapter.

SECTION 1. THE SUCCESSFUL LAW PRACTICE

A successful law practice does the following:

- It serves its clients effectively and efficiently.
- It upholds ethical standards and brings credit to the legal profession.
- It provides professional satisfaction and a reasonable economic reward for its owners, managers, and employees.

Client needs and ethical standards should be the first priorities, of course, although the reality of economic pressures sometimes limits what a law office is able to do for the client. Like physicians, attorneys must sometimes balance the ideal goals of their professional practice against the reality of limited resources.

SUCCESS IN A PRIVATE PRACTICE

As explained in earlier chapters, most attorneys and paralegals work in law firms that represent a variety of outside clients. Law firms range from sole practitioners to a small number of very large partnerships or professional corporations employing hundreds of attorneys. In addition to meeting the three criteria for a successful practice listed above, a law firm usually seeks professional prestige in the legal community. A stellar rating by professional peers in the *Martindale-Hubbell Law Directory* is a prized achievement for an attorney or a law firm.

Finally, the socially responsible law firm will divert some portion of its profits into *pro bono* legal services for the community and the less fortunate.

SUCCESS IN CORPORATE AND PUBLIC AGENCY LEGAL DEPARTMENTS

Because the employing corporation is the sole client, a corporate legal department might appear to be immune from the financial pressures of private practice. However, corporate legal departments must justify their continuing existence. They often do this by demonstrating reductions in outside legal costs and—if the corporation is a frequent target of liability lawsuits—by reductions in the damage awards won by plaintiffs who have sued the company. By providing sound, in-house legal guidance, the legal department can encourage ethical and responsible business practices, and it can also reduce the corporation's liability exposure. Some corporation legal departments even take on *pro bono* cases from time to time.

Similar to a corporation, the public agency legal department usually has a single client, the employing government agency. So it, too, will focus primarily upon the three essential criteria for effective law practice. However, it also has a broader responsibility because it is supported by tax revenues and ultimately should serve the well-being of the public at large, not simply the parochial interests of the particular agency in which it exists.

Agencies such as the state attorney general, county counsel, and city attorney are in a different situation, because they often represent other public agencies as their clients. Attorneys who work in a public defender's office are also in a unique situation. They meet their responsibilities to that agency and to society by providing the best possible defense for individuals charged with crimes. Legally and ethically, their client is *not* the agency or the public at large, but that single individual they are charged with defending. In that sense, they are no different from attorneys in a private criminal defense practice. By definition, all public agency legal activities should be *pro bono publico* in nature—that is, for the public good—even though their individual attorneys are compensated for their services.

KEYS TO AN EFFECTIVE LAW PRACTICE

Regardless of the context in which law is being practiced—in a law firm, corporation, or public agency—success almost always rests upon the following key factors:

- dedicated and qualified professionals
- effective law office organization
- sound attorney-client relationships
- efficient law office procedures

Obviously, some of these factors might have very different implications, depending upon the context. For example, attorney-client relations can present very different issues and problems in the context of private law firms and public agencies.

DEDICATED AND QUALIFIED PROFESSIONALS

Qualified, hardworking individuals who perform their tasks in a professional manner are the most important single factor in the successful practice of law. In fact, they make the second and third factors possible. Without qualified professionals, client relations suffer, office procedures are ignored or inadequately implemented, financial controls break down, and marketing serves little purpose, because new clients soon leave. The personal qualities, education, and skills that are expected of legal assistants are discussed in Chapters 1 and 2.

If a firm or legal department has a nucleus of outstanding employees and also enjoys a strong reputation in the legal community, qualified applicants will usually appear—even when there is no current vacancy. Because word-of-mouth is such a large factor in paralegal employment, in particular, well-networked candidates will know where the desirable jobs are. And they often come with the recommendation of a trusted current employee in that office. The fact that a firm has high professional standards and high expectations is not a deterrent to the better candidates—that is exactly the kind of work environment they are seeking.

The Paralegal's Employment Status

A newly hired legal assistant should understand the conditions for his continued employment with that firm. Usually, new employees are considered to be **at-will employees**. This means that they may leave that employment at their pleasure, and the employers may terminate employees at their pleasure. *Either party* can terminate the employment relationship without offering any reason or explanation. There are four circumstances, however, when employment might *not* be at-will:

1. when a statute prohibits some form of discriminatory dismissal
2. when public policy does not permit an arbitrary dismissal
3. when the employer and employee have agreed upon an indefinite period of employment, with termination to be "for cause" only
4. when the employer and employee have agreed upon a fixed period of employment, with termination to be "for cause" only

Both state and federal statutes forbid private employers (usually those employing more than a minimum number of employees) from discharging employees for discriminatory reasons (e.g., race, national origin, gender, disability, and religious belief). These statutes modify the general rule of at-will employment. In the absence of statutory protection, a state's common law public policy might not permit an employer to discharge an employee for certain reasons. For example, public policy might protect an employee who reported the employer's illegal conduct to authorities (the "whistle-blower" protection). To permit that type of dismissal would frustrate the purpose of laws prohibiting the illegal conduct that has been reported. Similarly, public policy might protect an employee reporting sexual harassment by a superior, even if such harassment is not a crime.

Although highly unusual for entry-level paralegal positions, one might be able to negotiate an employment contract that prohibits termination except for **just cause**. The contract might specify what constitutes "just cause," in which case those stated criteria will apply. Otherwise, there is a well established body of case law defining "just cause" for termination. But, entry-level paralegals, in particular, are usually hired as probationary employees (discussed below).

Finally, the employer and employee might have created an oral or written contract that specifies a fixed term of employment and prohibits discharge during that tenure except for specified causes. For that employee who is under a fixed-term contract, the "at-will" employment rule does not apply. But when a fixed-term contract expires, the employment relationship ends. If the employer and employee wish to extend the employment period, they must make a new

At-will employment is a relationship that either the employee or the employer may terminate at any time without offer of any justification for doing so.

In employment law, **just cause** is a principle requiring an honest and reasonable basis for the discipline or dismissal of an employee, the use of fair and reasonable procedures by the employer, and penalties proportionate to the employee's misconduct.

contract. This can be done in words (oral or written), or it can occur silently when the conduct of the parties demonstrates a mutual understanding—for example, the employee continues working and the employer continues paying her salary. All terms of the prior contract are then presumed to continue in effect, unless the parties change them by their mutual agreement or conduct.

Probationary Employees

Many firms require all new employees to complete a probationary period before becoming regular employees. The vast majority of legal assistants are hired in probationary status, the exceptions usually being for those whose previous work for other employers is well known. The legal assistant who is actively recruited to leave her former employer is an example of the latter exception. The intent of a probationary period is for the employer to evaluate the "fit" of the new employee with the position and the firm. Because the probationary employee has no guarantee of being retained, it is easier for the employer to give an opportunity to a candidate who might not be hired if he were to immediately gain regular employee status.

During the probationary period, one is a true "at-will" employee. But the clear implication of that fact is that once the probationary period is completed, one is no longer an at-will employee. In other words, by establishing a probationary (i.e., at-will) status for new employees, the employer has created by implication a *different* status for all regular employees who are no longer on probation. In that circumstance, a court would probably hold that the employer must have good cause to dismiss a regular employee.

Employment Policies and Benefits

When a legal assistant accepts a new position, she should be informed of the employment policies of that office and the employee benefits for her position. Some of this, undoubtedly, will be discussed in the final interview process before she accepts the position. A well-managed firm will have a personnel manual that governs the working conditions and employment relationship. A typical manual will address topics such as the following:

- Working conditions
  - hours
  - holidays
  - overtime
  - compensatory time
  - absence procedures
- Benefits
  - sick leave
  - health insurance
  - vacation
  - retirement and 401(k) plans
- Employee conduct
  - confidentiality
  - security procedures
  - dress and grooming
  - evaluation procedures
  - nondiscrimination

The manual might also include sections on the implementation of the *Family and Medical Leave Act*, the *Americans with Disabilities Act*, state worker compensation laws, and other statutory protections for employees.

Working Schedules and Overtime

Increasingly, law offices are offering greater flexibility for the working schedules of their employees. Early- and late-start schedules are increasingly common, to accommodate the employee's child-care arrangements. A ten-hour day, four-day per-week working schedule has been very successful as an option, particularly because some law firms find there is far less client and courtroom activity on Fridays. Telecommuting is no longer a rarity. The degree to which a legal assistant can avail himself of these options often depends upon the nature of his assignments. The more sophisticated, self-directed, and self-paced they are, the better suited those assignments are to flexible scheduling. Of course, it tends to be the more senior legal assistants who receive such assignments.

As mentioned in Chapter 2, a continuing issue in the paralegal profession is the matter of overtime pay. Salaried attorneys, office administrators—and sometimes paralegals—are considered to be "exempt" employees under the federal *Fair Labor Standards Act* (FLSA). Exempt status means an employee is not eligible for overtime pay. But under the FLSA, an exempt employee is permitted to make *reasonable* adjustments in his working schedule to perform his duties more effectively and conveniently. Because the exempt employee cannot claim overtime pay for working a twelve-hour day or a fifty-hour week, the law does not permit his pay to be docked if he goes out in the middle of the day for a medical appointment—or to meet an old college buddy for a three-hour lunch.

Ethics Watch

Of course, professional employees would not abuse their privileges under the *Fair Labor Standards Act* and would ensure that the needs of clients and the employer are met. In fact, failure to do so could be grounds for dismissal. Exempt employees have the identical obligation to provide timely and professional services as do nonexempt employees—they just have greater discretion about when and where the work is done.

Professional Liability Insurance

Every firm should carry professional liability insurance, also known as an **errors and omissions policy**. Most errors and omissions policies cover all employees of the attorney, and they often cover nonemployees who work under the direction and supervision of the attorney (e.g., investigators, freelance paralegals, and process servers). Legal assistants should confirm that the firm's policy will provide a defense and pay any judgments against them.

The basic purpose of professional liability insurance is to protect the attorney from claims for legal malpractice. The policy also covers some other types of claims arising in the practice of law, such as the following:

- negligence in performing *pro bono* services
- libel or slander
- malicious prosecution
- invasion of privacy
- destruction of evidence
- civil conspiracy

An **errors and omissions policy** (also known as "professional liability insurance") protects the attorney—and usually his employees—against malpractice claims and other professional liability.

- breach of contract
- fraud

The policy should cover third-party claims, as well as claims by clients. For example, beneficiaries of a will or trust might sue an attorney for negligent preparation of the document or for misappropriation of the proceeds of a will or trust.

Most professional liability policies cover only those actions or omissions that occurred during the effective period of the policy, *and* for which claims are made during the policy period. In other words, *both the event and the claim* must occur within the policy period. Unless an insurance company will provide a special rider (e.g., to cover prior events, or to cover late claims made after the policy expires), the attorney might need to maintain his insurance with the same company for the remainder of his career. Otherwise, the insured could not be certain that all potential future claims would be covered.

EFFECTIVE LAW OFFICE ORGANIZATION

The way a law office is organized and managed has a major impact upon its ability to provide the highest quality of professional services to the client. Effective organization and management also have a major impact on the financial success of the law practice. Even those law offices that operate as part of a corporation or government agency must operate within the funds allocated, so that effective organization and management are equally important to them. This discussion will emphasize the management roles of attorneys in law offices of various sizes, and in various settings. Non-attorney managers will be discussed later in this section.

In the past, small law offices were generally legal "general stores" where the client could hire an attorney to file a lawsuit, draw up a will, apply for a copyright, draft a contract, or advise on a tax problem. In recent decades, however, sole practitioners and small partnerships have gravitated toward a "boutique" style of law firm—one that specializes in a single area of law, such as litigation, estate planning, intellectual property, business transactions, or taxation, for example. Although this forces some clients to retain multiple law firms to handle multiple, unrelated legal matters, most small firm clients have only one legal problem—at least, only one at a time. The advantage of the boutique firm, of course, is the opportunity to develop unusual expertise in a single field of law and to standardize boilerplate language, office forms, and procedures.

Office Structure for a Sole Practitioner or Proprietor

A sole practitioner is usually thought of as one attorney who practices law independently, owns the law practice, and does not share profits or losses with others—in other words, a sole proprietor. In many cases, such an attorney truly practices alone and must pay the entire cost of the office and support staff—and is the sole "boss" of the office. But some attorneys who are sole proprietors share office facilities and support staff with several other attorneys, each paying a proportionate share of the rent, salaries for shared staff, and other overhead costs. Being sole proprietors, they don't share profits or liabilities, just the overhead costs. Of necessity, however, they must share the decision making about office facilities, staff employment, and the like. For some attorneys, this arrangement works better if each employs his or her own legal secretary and/or legal assistant, but shares the jointly employed receptionist, word processor, file clerk, and so on.

A further refinement of that office arrangement occurs when one or two attorneys (the "landlord") establish a legal "suite" of offices. In this arrangement, other attorneys become tenants, and their monthly rent includes all of the overhead costs of shared staff, equipment, and so forth. Shared staff members are the employees of the landlords, and shared equipment is their sole property. In a legal suite, tenant attorneys do not share in the decision-making process concerning the offices and staff. Understandably, tenant attorneys are inclined to negotiate lease agreements that protect them from unexpected and unfavorable decisions by the attorney landlords about office staffing and equipment.

In this legal suite arrangement, the paralegal is usually employed by the attorney-landlord, although she will be performing legal services under the direction and supervision of all attorneys in the suite. This situation can provide an opportunity for the sort of varied assignments she might experience in a small partnership with several associate attorneys.

Some sole practitioners lease office space in an established multipartner law firm. In this arrangement, they have full access to the firm's law library and staff members. Of course, they will be responsible for their own separate financial accounts and must bill their own clients. As in the legal suite arrangement, their monthly rent compensates the law firm for all of the shared facilities and staff. This is an excellent arrangement for law firms that anticipate hiring additional attorneys in the future, but currently have extra office space. It is equally advantageous for the sole practitioner who cannot presently afford to set up her own law office. So, this often is a temporary arrangement for both the sole practitioner and the law firm.

The Sole Proprietorship Law Office

Another variation on the legal sole proprietorship involves the employment of additional attorneys as associates. In this structure, the practice is owned by an attorney as sole proprietor, but clearly he is not a sole practitioner. The attorney-proprietor must pay all overhead costs, as well as the salaries of the associate attorneys. And he keeps all profits and suffers all losses incurred by the practice. This arrangement is suited to an attorney who wants total control and ownership of the law practice, but who does not want to practice alone. Of course, if the associates aspire to share in the ownership of a practice in the future, there might be a high turnover rate as they leave to join firms that offer the opportunity to become a partner.

Office Structure for a Small Partnership

A law partnership can exist with as few as two or three partners, of course. And, in such very small partnerships, the primary differences from a sole proprietorship are the collegial nature of the decision-making process and the sharing of profits and liabilities. Partners receive a share of the firm profits, and nonpartners do not. The former are sometimes called **equity partners**, because their ownership interest is what brings them a share of the profits. This text has referred to other attorneys in the firm as "associates"—and that is the term most commonly used. But these latter attorneys sometimes are referred to as "junior partners"—a confusing and apparently contradictory term at best, because they have no ownership interest, profit-sharing, or liability in the partnership. As if that were not confusing enough, some firms designate a relatively new equity partner to be a junior partner, whereas his seniors in the firm are designated as "senior partners." Some firms have a hybrid status known as a **contract partner**. A contract partner receives a salary plus a percentage of all client fees that he generates.

As mentioned in Chapter 2, the partnership interests need not be equal: it is possible to have three partners in a 40\40\20 equity arrangement—or in any

An **equity partner** has an ownership interest in the law partnership, usually by virtue of being one of the founding partners or by making a capital investment in the firm.

A **contract partner** is an attorney who receives a salary and a percentage of all client fees he generates for the firm.

FIGURE 11.1 Management Structure in a Small Partnership

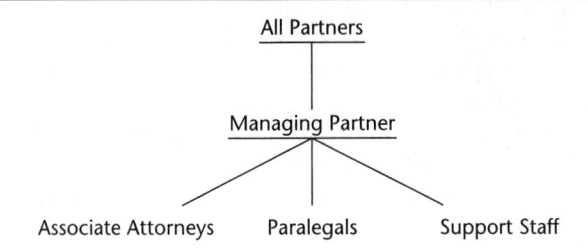

```
                    All Partners
                         |
                  Managing Partner
            _____|_____
           |             |             |
    Associate Attorneys  Paralegals  Support Staff
```

other combination adding up to 100%. The difference in equity shares is established in their partnership agreement, and it might be due to differing amounts of capital investment each has made, differences in seniority with the firm, differences in clients and fees each has brought to the firm, or any combination of factors the partners have agreed upon.

Partnerships with as many as a dozen or so partners might operate much like a very small law partnership, with an informal and collegial decision-making process. However, most partnerships with about six or more partners choose to designate one of them as the managing partner of the firm. Most often, the managing partner will be a senior partner of the firm—perhaps one of the founding partners—who has "paid her dues" over the years by attracting large numbers of clients and generating a substantial amount in client fees. Most likely, she is one with the temperament and skills needed to manage the office and also provide leadership in terms of developing new lines of client business and planning for future expansion. *Figure 11.1* illustrates a small partnership with a designated managing partner

Although a firm of six partners and six associates might require an average of just a few hours per day of the managing partner's time, in some larger firms it will be a full-time responsibility. Even in the smaller partnerships, the managing partner usually is responsible for the following:

- recruiting, supervising, and evaluating the office support staff
- assigning legal assistants and legal secretaries to partners and associates
- resolving personnel issues that arise among support staff
- monitoring the firm budget and authorizing all nonroutine operating expenditures
- supervising firm accounts, including client trust accounts
- selecting vendors to provide ongoing services to the firm
- managing relations with vendors and the firm's landlord

Office Structure for Medium and Large Firms

In a firm of twenty to fifty attorneys, the managing partner might have some responsibility for managing the *law practice* of the firm. His duties might include the following:

- recruiting associate attorneys
- assigning new associate attorneys for supervision by designated partners
- developing new clients
- assigning new client matters to junior partners and associates
- resolving personnel issues that arise among partners and/or associates

Firms with twenty or more partners usually establish management committees that are intended to reduce the workload of the managing partner, but

FIGURE 11.2 Management Committees in a Medium-Size Law Firm

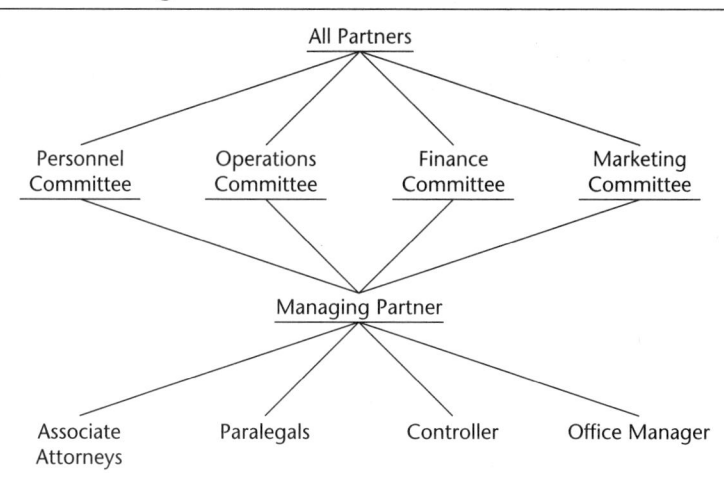

```
                           All Partners
              ┌───────┬────────┼────────┬───────┐
          Personnel  Operations  Finance  Marketing
          Committee  Committee Committee Committee
              └───────┴────────┼────────┴───────┘
                         Managing Partner
              ┌────────┬────────┬────────┐
           Associate  Paralegals Controller Office Manager
           Attorneys
```

which also ensure greater participation and satisfaction with the management of the firm among the other partners. Those committees commonly function (and often make policy) in these areas:

- office operations
- personnel
- finance
- marketing

Figure 11.2 illustrates the position of management committees in a medium-size firm.

Management by Executive Committee

Larger law firms often establish an executive committee of partners to oversee management of the firm. The executive committee operates somewhat as a corporate board of directors, while the managing partner acts as the chief executive officer (CEO), implementing policies and strategies established by the executive committee, and directing daily operations of the office. Executive committees are particularly useful in very large firms, where the complexity of firm operations and the disparate views of the committees for operations, personnel, finance, and marketing sometimes present a managing partner with a management "can of worms." In those situations, the executive committee can resolve policy and strategy conflicts and take some of the "heat" off the managing partner.

Office Structure for Professional Law Corporations

A professional law corporation could be described as an attorney "sole proprietorship," or a law "partnership," organized in corporate form, with attorneys as stockholders instead of as sole proprietors or partners. Thus, a sole practitioner can organize as a professional corporation, as can groups of two or more attorneys. A professional corporation often can be recognized by the "PC" designation appended to the firm name: "Jesson, Arands, Warron and Fillips, PC". As mentioned in Chapter 2, a professional corporation can have individual attorneys, attorney partnerships, and smaller professional law corporations among its stockholders. This is illustrated in *Figure 11.3*.

In prior decades, some law firms chose to organize as a professional corporation for tax advantages, although changes in tax law have since minimized

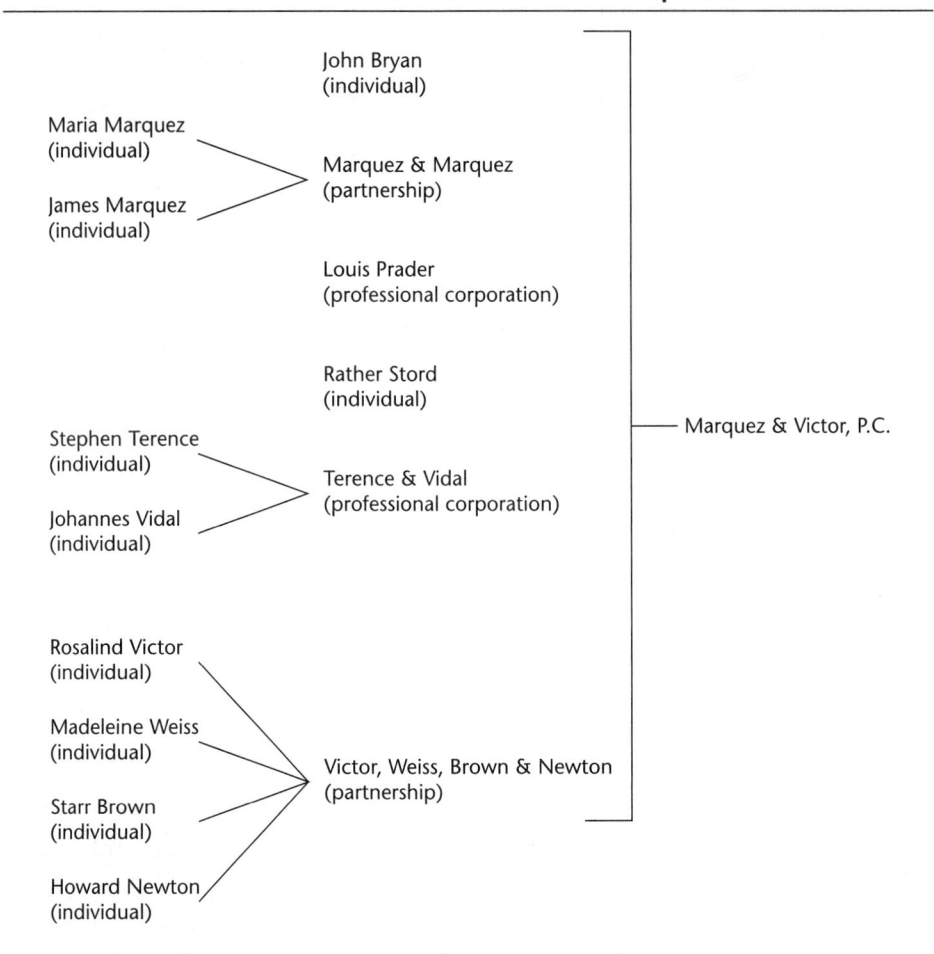

FIGURE 11.3 Stockholders in a Professional Law Corporation

```
Maria Marquez      John Bryan
(individual)       (individual)
                   Marquez & Marquez
James Marquez      (partnership)
(individual)

                   Louis Prader
                   (professional corporation)

                   Rather Stord
                   (individual)                    ─── Marquez & Victor, P.C.
Stephen Terence
(individual)       Terence & Vidal
                   (professional corporation)
Johannes Vidal
(individual)

Rosalind Victor
(individual)

Madeleine Weiss
(individual)       Victor, Weiss, Brown & Newton
                   (partnership)
Starr Brown
(individual)

Howard Newton
(individual)
```

those advantages. Today, the primary advantage of the professional corporation is to limit the personal liability of its attorney stockholders for the debts of the corporation. Because each partner in a partnership is *individually and separately* responsible for the entire debts of the partnership, that potential individual liability can be enormous. The larger the partnership and its financial liabilities, the greater the individual liability exposure. As a stockholder in a professional corporation, however, the individual attorney has no personal liability for the debts of the corporation. A creditor can only claim assets of the corporation, not of its individual attorney-stockholders.

"Limited Liability" Law Firms

Limited liability partnerships (LLPs) and limited liability companies (LLCs) combine the tax advantages of partnerships with the limited liability of a corporation.

Recent alternatives to the legal PCs are the **limited liability partnership (LLP)** and the **limited liability company (LLC)**. These two business organizations—authorized by some states, but not by all—combine the tax advantages of partnerships with the liability limitations of corporations. Unlike normal corporations, the profits of an LLP or LLC are not taxed. Instead, those untaxed profits are passed on to the partners or shareholders, respectively, and taxed only as personal income. This feature eliminates the "double taxation" of both corporate profits and corporate dividends. Both new forms of organization preserve some degree of limitation on the personal liability of the partners (LLP) or shareholders (LLC), but those limitations vary depending upon state law.

Therefore, the professional corporation, the LLP, and the LLC differ from legal sole proprietorships and partnerships only in their legal identity and the financial liability of the attorneys who own them. The way the law offices are organized in a functional sense will depend primarily upon the number of attorneys and other employees, not upon the nature of the corporate limited liability identity. A sole practitioner organized as a professional corporation will function as other sole practitioners who are *not* incorporated; and, a *multi*attorney professional corporation will function as other nonincorporated, multiattorney law firms of a similar size. Therefore, the preceding discussions about sole proprietorships and partnerships apply equally to their equivalent corporate forms.

Legal Consulting Firms

The legal management consulting firm is a relatively new enterprise in the field of law. Staffed by attorneys experienced in private practice, and by experts in fields like accounting, computers, and marketing, such firms are equipped to conduct a thorough analysis of the operations of a law firm of almost any size. They then develop strategies, structures, and procedures that should enable a law firm to become more effective, efficient, and profitable. Their services are likely to be of particular value to a firm that has grown rapidly, but has had difficulty in adjusting the firm's management system to cope with operations on a much larger scale.

> **Practice Tip**
>
> A paralegal with law firm management experience (or an M.B.A. degree) could provide a useful perspective within a legal consulting firm. Inevitably, paralegals see their role and utilization from a perspective that is somewhat different from that of an attorney. As part of a consulting team, the paralegal could provide an objective evaluation of the paralegal role in the client's law office. It would be an opportunity to encourage a fresh evaluation by the managing partner or executive committee of that firm.

Office Structure for Corporate Legal Departments

A corporate legal department is completely different from the professional legal corporation discussed above. A corporate legal department is simply one of many departments in a *non*legal corporation—but it has the responsibility of providing legal services to the corporation. The parent corporation can be in any business under the sun: manufacturing, real estate, banking, transportation, entertainment production, accounting, fast-food eateries, publishing, securities, and so on. These, and many other kinds of enterprises, often find it economical to maintain their own internal legal department, even if they also rely on outside counsel for some (or most) legal services. Another attractive feature of the corporate legal department is management's direct control over its legal affairs, including priorities.

Several types of enterprises are especially likely to maintain their own corporate legal departments: those frequently sued, and those that require a substantial amount of legal services in the ordinary course of business. Manufacturers of medical products are good examples of the former, and investment bankers are good examples of the latter. Corporations frequently involved in litigation generally retain outside legal counsel to represent them in the courtroom. However, they often use their corporate legal departments for the following litigation purposes:

- responding to discovery requests
- coordinating litigation matters with outside counsel
- reviewing (and questioning) bills presented by the corporation's outside counsel
- advising management on ways to avoid future lawsuits

An attorney from the corporate legal department might also sit second chair during the trial.

Corporations generally designate a particular attorney as the corporate **general counsel**, serving as the primary source of legal advice to management. The general counsel is usually the head of the corporate legal department, but she can be an outside attorney on retainer for that purpose. An in-house general counsel typically holds the rank of vice president of the corporation.

A corporation's **general counsel** is the attorney serving as the company's primary legal advisor and who generally manages the legal affairs of the corporation.

Internal Organization of a Corporate Legal Department

The organization of a corporate legal department is similar to that of other departments in a corporation. The attorney in charge of the department holds decision-making authority over all others within the department, but might need ratification by her superiors for some types of decisions (e.g., whether to initiate or settle a particular litigation matter). For enterprises frequently involved in litigation, the control of litigation costs has become a major function of the corporate legal department. Finally, corporate legal departments are often responsible for monitoring developments in legislation and government rule making, and they often coordinate efforts with the corporation's lobbyist or industry lobbyists to influence those developments.

Legal assistants assume a wide variety of responsibilities in corporate legal departments. A key role is the corporate law paralegal who prepares and maintains the official documents and records of the corporation, including the following:

- corporate bylaws
- minutes of directors' meetings
- resolutions adopted by the board of directors
- stock registration statements
- shareholder records
- notices of shareholder meetings
- proxy statements
- stock option plans

Another legal assistant in the same corporate department might have totally different responsibilities, such as coordinating with outside litigation counsel and responding to discovery requests. Very often, the hands-on work of monitoring legislation and rule making, and of coordinating with lobbyists who are on retainer, is done by a legal assistant in the office.

Office Structure for Public Agency Legal Departments

For this discussion, "public agency" will mean some kind of government entity—federal, state, or local. "Legal department" will refer to a legal office within a larger public agency whose primary purpose is not the practice of law—which omits the U.S. Department of Justice, the state attorney general's office, county counsel's office, city attorney's office, state and local prosecutors' offices, and public defenders' offices. These public agencies are essentially government law firms.

The following discussion *does* address such offices as the legal departments found in the U.S. Department of Agriculture, the state motor vehicle department, the county department of education, and so on. Public agency legal departments serve purposes for those agencies that are very similar to the purposes of corporate legal departments—litigation and routine legal services being the primary purposes. The authority of the attorney in charge is similar to that of the head of a corporate legal department. Technically, public agencies do not engage in lobbying the way private entities do; in practice, however, they are heavily involved in communication and coordination with legislators and rule makers and thereby influence those processes. Their legal departments often take an active role in these "nonlobbying" activities by public agencies.

Public agencies, particularly small ones, sometimes retain outside law firms to serve as their primary legal counsel, the equivalent of a corporation's general counsel. But agencies large enough to fund a full-time legal office typically rely upon the chief attorney in that internal department to serve as **chief counsel** for the agency. Just as do corporations, they typically retain outside law firms to represent them in large-scale litigation, unless that representation can be provided by the U.S. Department of Justice or the state attorney general's office, as appropriate.

Public agency legal assistants serve in a multitude of capacities, from litigation paralegal to government contract compliance officer. Just a few of the other specialties found in public agencies are listed below:

- administrative law
- bankruptcy law
- communications law
- employee benefits law
- environmental law
- intellectual property law
- tax law
- worker compensation law

Public agency legal assistants have no billable quotas, of course; however, they don't generally receive annual bonuses, either. As is true in corporations, public agency legal assistants sometimes make lateral transfers out of the legal department into some other position in which their legal background is an asset.

> The **chief counsel** of a public agency is the primary legal advisor to the agency and generally manages its legal affairs.

MEMBERS OF THE LEGAL TEAM

In most law offices, attorneys, paralegals, and legal secretaries are the professional team that provides legal services for clients. In larger offices, the legal team might include **law clerks**, legal librarians, and paralegal managers, as well. Each applies the expertise and skills of her profession to the client matters that the office handles. For a client to be well served, these professionals must work as a well-coordinated team, so that each aspect of the client's matter is handled properly, and nothing "falls through the cracks."

> A **law clerk** is a law school graduate who has not yet passed the bar exam and is employed to assist one or more attorneys in their practice.

The ultimate responsibility for coordinating the team effort rests with the attorney responsible for that client matter. However, some of that responsibility might be delegated to other team members. For example, if the office has a paralegal manager, she might receive the attorney's requests for paralegal services and assign those to individual legal assistants. Or a senior paralegal in the office—although not a manager—might assume that role. The larger and more complex the case, the more delegation is likely to occur.

In large-scale litigation, for example, a firm partner might serve as the attorney of record and supervise one or more associates, and a number of paralegals and legal secretaries who work on that case. The responsible partner might coordinate only with the associate attorneys, who then directly supervise the other team members. Regardless of how this coordination is organized, each member of the legal team must apply diligence and skill to his assignments in that legal matter. If one member fails to follow through, the effectiveness of the team will be jeopardized.

The role of legal secretaries on the professional team varies from office to office. As explained in Chapters 1 and 2, the line between the role and responsibilities of legal secretaries and paralegals is not always a clear one. When legal secretaries begin to influence the *content* of the documents they prepare—for example, by doing legal research—they unquestionably become members of the legal team.

The Law Librarian

The role of law librarians has been growing with the development of on-line research. As a result, they are becoming increasingly important members of the professional legal team. Important as ever for selecting appropriate print resources, librarians are rapidly becoming indispensable guides to the intricacies of the Internet. Often, the firm librarian has been the on-site expert in using Westlaw or LEXIS-NEXIS, and also for using CD-ROM resources. But, now that Internet research is gaining such a prominent role, librarians often are among the few who have developed real expertise in using the search engines and directories that lead one to the appropriate Web site. Nearly 5,000 law librarians belong to the American Association of Law Libraries.

Law Office Administrators and Managers

The preceding discussion has emphasized the management roles of attorneys in the law office. But, as an office grows larger and management duties consume more time, it becomes practical to employ professional, non-attorney managers to assume much of the load. Essentially, there are three basic types of non-attorney managers: (1) those specializing in the management of legal services; (2) those who manage general office-support services; and (3) those who manage both legal and general office-support services.

The office manager is a non-attorney who recruits, hires, and supervises most of the office support staff, including the receptionist, word processors, file clerks, and billing clerks. In some firms, the office manager will also supervise the legal secretaries. It is more common, however, for the legal secretaries and paralegals to be supervised by the attorneys with whom they work. Office managers without specialized training in legal administration are usually found in small and medium-sized firms. The office manager usually reports to the firm's managing partner. If a law firm has a controller, legal assistant manager, and/or librarian, those persons usually report to the managing partner or the legal administrator, not to the office manager. (See *Figure 11.4*.)

FIGURE 11.4 Sample Organization Chart for Large Firm with a Legal Administrator

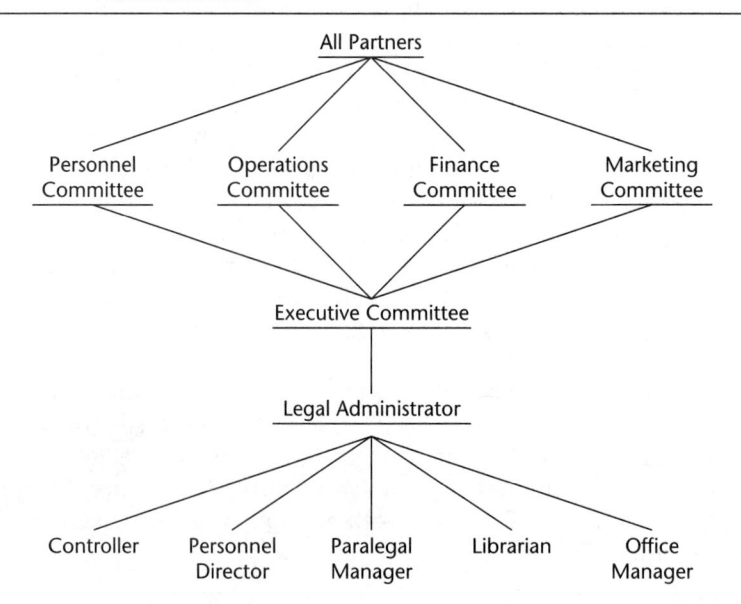

```
                          All Partners
          ┌──────────────────┼──────────────────┐
    Personnel          Operations         Finance          Marketing
    Committee          Committee         Committee         Committee
          └──────────────────┼──────────────────┘
                     Executive Committee
                              │
                      Legal Administrator
        ┌─────────┬───────────┼───────────┬─────────┐
    Controller  Personnel   Paralegal   Librarian   Office
                Director    Manager                 Manager
```

The legal assistant manager is a senior legal assistant who coordinates the work of all legal assistants in the office. She often has responsibility for assigning legal assistants to major cases. Often, she is responsible for hiring, training, and evaluating legal assistants. The legal assistant manager usually reports to the firm's managing partner.

In the larger firms (those with a hundred or more attorneys), the firm often employs a professional legal administrator. A **legal administrator** assumes many of the responsibilities that a managing partner otherwise has in large firms. In effect, her role makes it possible for the managing partner to continue an active practice in law. She is the senior non-attorney manager in the firm, supervising the controller, legal assistant manager, and office manager. She usually reports to the managing partner or to an executive committee of firm partners. Legal administrators generally have specialized education and training in law firm management.

> The **legal administrator** has many of the responsibilities that a managing partner in a large law office would have and is the senior non-attorney in the office.

Internet Access
American Legal Administrators Association   http:\\www.alanet.org

SCENARIO

From Legal Assistant to . . . Legal Administrator?

Bruni Burke is the new legal assistant manager at a mid-sized law firm in Atlanta, Georgia. She started with the firm seven years ago, as an entry-level legal assistant "fresh" out of the University of Southern Mississippi. "I went to Southern Mississippi because I wanted to have a bachelor degree, and I wanted to be ready to move right into a paralegal position when I graduated. The paralegal studies program is part of the political science department at USM, which was also a big attraction, because of my interests. I graduated with a double major in paralegal studies and political science."

Bruni began her paralegal practice in business litigation, but has since worked extensively in real estate transactions, bankruptcy, and intellectual property law. "At first, I loved the excitement of litigation and didn't think that I would want to do anything else. But as time passed, I discovered that each specialty has its own appeal. Litigation is often a 'win-lose' type of thing, but real estate can more frequently be a 'win-win' situation. Bankruptcy and intellectual property are completely different from litigation and transactional law. I find that I now appreciate the variety of assignments and the professional growth from becoming proficient in four specialties."

Because of the firm's growth in recent years—eleven new associates and four additional legal assistants—the firm's executive committee decided to establish a new position for a legal assistant manager. Although the firm usually relies upon word of mouth to fill any paralegal positions, it widely advertised the new manager position. Marisa Pavatto, the firm's managing partner, reports that there was a lot of interest. "After the paper screening, we still had about thirteen serious contenders—including Bruni. After the first round of interviews, we still had *five* who seemed perfect for the job. The caliber of the candidates was awesome!"

Bruni isn't quite sure why she was the firm's final choice. "Of course, there's some safety in going with a 'known' quantity, rather than taking a chance on someone new. But, then, the firm also knew about all of my shortcomings! Needless to say, I'm really pleased." Ms. Pavatto identified several factors that were strongly in Bruni's favor. "She has an exceptionally good relationship with everyone in the firm, from the part-time file clerks to each of the senior partners. Equally important, she has been greatly respected and well-liked by every legal assistant who has worked in this firm over the past seven years. She's a marvelous organizer and also has natural leadership abilities."

Bruni doesn't know how long she wants to continue as a legal assistant manager. "I am really enjoying this new role—especially training three paralegals who recently joined the firm. I'm almost finished with my M.B.A. degree. After that, I'm thinking of getting a certificate in information systems management. Who knows? Maybe someday I'll become a legal administrator." ■

Law Office Support Staff

It is common for an *attorney sole practitioner* to operate his practice with a support staff of one person: the *receptionist + legal secretary + billing clerk + file clerk* type of person. She might also function as a part-time paralegal, depending upon her qualifications and the attorney's preference. Her most essential skills are usually those of a legal secretary. Her most important personal characteristics are resourcefulness, flexibility, and resilience. It is a demanding job.

Staffing Patterns for Law Offices

The Jack or Jane "of all trades" in a sole practitioner's office is not a situation most paralegals will encounter. Most legal assistants work in offices with at least three attorneys and one legal secretary. The great majority of paralegals work in offices even larger. In those larger offices, the staffing patterns will vary. For example, law firms with ten attorneys and four paralegals can probably function well with about ten or twelve support staff members, such as the following:

- receptionist
- word processor
- file clerk
- billing clerk
- office manager
- controller
- five legal secretaries

The actual number of support staff needed will depend upon how the workload is distributed, the type of law being practiced, the availability of computers for each employee, the degree to which tasks have been automated, and many other factors. For example, if the attorneys and paralegals have computers at their desks and do a large portion of their own word processing, there might be less need for legal secretaries and word processing staff.

In the list below, support staff positions appear in the roughly approximate order in which they would be *added* to the staff, when a law firm grows in the number of client matters, attorneys, and paralegals. Receptionists do not appear on this list of possible new positions, because typically even the smallest firms has an employee who takes incoming calls and greets visiting clients. Of course, in a small firm, the receptionist might perform several of the other functions listed—serving as the file clerk and billing clerk, for example. As one goes down the list, the positions toward the end will be common only in the larger law firms with many attorneys. As firms grow, some of the positions higher on the list will be occupied by more than one individual—five file clerks, for example.

- file clerk
- billing clerk

CHAPTER 11 — Law Office Management and Procedures

- word processor
- office manager
- controller
- mail clerk
- systems manager
- legal assistant manager
- librarian
- legal administrator
- investigator

ESTABLISHING A SOUND ATTORNEY-CLIENT RELATIONSHIP

Earlier chapters have discussed the attorney-client relationship as it relates to privileged communications, the attorney's ethical obligations to the client, and the client's right to legal counsel. This discussion, however, considers the attorney-client relationship primarily in a professional and business sense. Certainly ethical obligations are part of that professional relationship, but this chapter will not repeat here the details of those earlier discussions.

Let us assume that the client and the attorney each understand that the client has asked for advice or representation and that the attorney has agreed to provide that service. The client thinks of the attorney as "my lawyer," and the attorney believes that an attorney-client relationship exists in a legal and ethical sense.

Effective communication and mutual trust are at the heart of a sound attorney-client relationship. The attorney must understand clearly what the client needs and expects of him; and, the client must understand clearly what the attorney can and cannot do for her. Mutual trust is essential so that their two-way communication will be open and forthright. And the client must have confidence in the attorney's integrity and ability, so that she can comfortably place her legal matters in his hands and rely upon his advice and representation. Consequently, the initial client interview has enormous importance in getting the attorney-client relationship off to a sound beginning. The paralegal's possible role in the client intake interview is discussed in Chapter 10. And subsequent contacts between the paralegal and the client continue to have great importance.

> **Practice Tip**
>
> It is vital that the client appreciate the paralegal's participation as an effective and economical part of her representation by the attorney. If the client were to get the impression that she simply has been "passed off" to the paralegal because the attorney is uninterested in her case, she is likely to lose confidence in his representation. This places a very real responsibility on the paralegal to be very professional and to demonstrate competence and appropriate self-confidence during all client communications.

Retainer Agreements

When a client hires (i.e., "retains") the attorney, it is customary for her to sign a retainer agreement that identifies the legal matters for which the attorney is retained and sets forth the fees and expenses that the client agrees to pay for that representation. The agreement is an important part of the communication between the attorney and client, so that later disagreements do not arise over the nature of the legal matters to be undertaken or the fees to be paid. In some states, a written retainer agreement is required by law. A sample retainer agreement appears in *Figure 11.5.*

How Legal Fees Are Determined

Some law firms work on a **contingency fee** basis. Under a contingency fee arrangement the law firm will not be paid until it has recovered money for the client. If the client's case is lost, the client owes nothing, and the law firm receives nothing. Contingency fee arrangements are very common in personal injury and wrongful death cases. The contingency fee usually is a percentage of any monetary award won in court (or negotiated out of court) for

A **contingency fee** for legal services is based upon the actual recovery of money for the client. Usually, the fee is a percentage of the amount recovered.

FIGURE 11.5 Sample Retainer Agreement

Adamson, Teshima, Alvarez & Gaum
Attorneys at Law
1723 Embarcadero Boulevard, Suite 1200
San Diego, California 92104
(619) 445-3000

June 23, 2000

Marc Neufeld
3265 Marjoram Avenue
San Diego, California 92104

Re: Agreement for legal representation

Dear Mr. Neufeld:

You have asked this firm to represent you in the prosecution of certain claims, including wrongful termination and unpaid wages, which you have against your former employer, MeritAll, Inc. ("MeritAll). This firm agrees to represent you in this matter subject to the terms and conditions set forth in this letter.

This firm will contact MeritAll and attempt to negotiate a settlement agreeable to you. If that proves impossible, we will file suit on your behalf in the Superior Court seeking damages in an amount to be proved in court.

Upon signing this letter of agreement, you will pay this firm a retainer of two thousand dollars ($2,000.00) as an advance against expenses, such as postage, photocopies, telephone tolls, messenger fees, etc. You agree to pay all reasonable out-of-pocket expenses incurred by this firm in your representation. Photocopies will be charged at the rate of ten cents per page. All other expenses shall be the actual amounts charged to this firm.

In lieu of hourly fees for the services of attorneys and legal assistants, you agree that this firm shall retain thirty percent (30%) of any monies recovered by us on your behalf, whether through settlement of court judgment. You agree to give all reasonable cooperation in our efforts on your behalf. In the event you withdraw your authorization for us to proceed in this matter before completion of settlement negotiations and/or trial in court, you agree to pay our hourly fees for the time actually expended on your behalf. Our attorneys charge between $200 and $350 per hour, and the services of legal assistants are billed at rates between $80 and $120 per hour.

We look forward to a successful representation of your interests.

ADAMSON, TESHIMA ÁLVAREZ & GAUM   AGREED:

BY: _____   _____
      Theodore Gaum, Esq.   Marc Neufeld

the client. Even under a contingency fee arrangement, the client usually pays for all "out-of-pocket" expenses incurred: filing fees, postage and photocopying, witness fees, medical exams, and the like.

Although some firms charge their clients on a fixed fee-for-service basis (much like doctors who charge a "usual and customary" fee for an appendectomy), the great majority of law firms bill the client for the hours actually spent by attorneys and paralegals on that client matter. Under the latter system, attorneys and paralegals must keep accurate records of the time they spend on each legal matter. The client is then billed (usually monthly) for the hours spent by each professional. Naturally, attorneys bill at higher hourly rates than do legal assistants, and senior partners bill at much higher rates than do new associates. Hourly rates for *entry*-level paralegals in the late 1990s were generally in the range of $30 to $60 per hour. Well-qualified, *experienced* paralegals billed at rates generally in the range of $75 to $100 per hour, with a small number billing at rates in excess of $100. There are significant regional differences, however, and billing rates in small communities tend to be significantly lower than rates in metropolitan areas.

BILLABLE HOURS AND QUOTAS

Some law firms have annual quotas for billable hours. These quotas are generally in the range of 1,400 to 1,800 hours per year for paralegals, but there appears to be an upward trend in these expectations. Some firms offer bonuses based upon the hours billed *in excess* of the quota. Even firms without quotas might base bonuses on the annual total of hours billed, and a firm might use hours billed as a tool to evaluate their utilization of paralegals. Quotas, and any bonuses based upon them, present a potential problem for legal assistants.

Unlike attorneys, legal assistants cannot become "**rainmakers**," soliciting clients and bringing in new business. Instead, legal assistants are dependent upon attorneys for their assignments. If there are not enough assignments, and if the paralegal is reasonably efficient, it could be difficult to meet the quota. In that circumstance, there is a *dis*incentive for the paralegal to work efficiently. Most law firms preclude this problem by keeping their paralegal staff at or near the bare minimum for the firm's usual workload. Some firms prefer to be understaffed, requiring overtime work or temporary help to keep up with the overload. Of course, understaffing can lead to other problems: stress, involuntary overtime, disruption of family life, and exhaustion.

> An attorney who attracts new clients to the firm is known as a **rainmaker**.

Ethics Watch
Quotas can place legal assistants under a great deal of pressure, because it might be difficult to meet that quota. A legal assistant might be tempted to resolve this problem by "padding" his time sheets. But padding a time sheet is fraught with danger. If it goes undetected—initially, at least—the client will be defrauded of the additional fees he must pay, and the attorney's fiduciary duty to that client will have been breached. Of course, falsifying time sheets in any manner is grounds for dismissal.

Even if there is no quota for billable hours, some new paralegals are intimidated by the requirement to keep time sheets and accumulate billable hours. They should not be. Time sheets are not difficult to keep if the paralegal conscientiously records his time at the conclusion of each and every task. The time sheet also provides a useful record of events—a professional diary, so to speak. For example, old time sheets can hold the answer to questions about prior events in the management of a client's case. Time sheets can also verify that the legal assistant has complied with instructions, met deadlines, and so on. *Figure 11.6* illustrates a sample time sheet.

Billing with Timekeeping Units

Most law firms keep time records in *increments* of six minutes (often called "units"). That means that a minimum of six minutes will be billed, no matter how brief the task performed. Thus, a client will be billed for six minutes (one "unit" of billable time) for a single phone call—even if that call lasts only 30 seconds. In some firms, the client will be billed for the *closest* unit. For example, a firm using 6-minute billing units might charge a client for only 2 *units* (i.e., 12 minutes) for a task that actually required 14 minutes, and 3 units (18 minutes) for a 17-minute task. Other firms always "round up"—*never* down. With a large number of attorneys and paralegals in a firm, the accumulated difference from consistently rounding up can equal a great deal of money.

> ### *Practice Tip*
> If slack periods should occur in the office, a two-sentence "work needed" memo to all attorneys often generates new assignments. It certainly makes a stronger impression than pretending to be busy when one is not. If a paralegal produces good work, the request for more assignments is not likely to make the firm partners think that she is expendable.
>
> Another solution in slow periods is to have a long-range project that will benefit the firm: reorganizing the law library, customizing a computer software program, updating training materials, and the like.

FIGURE 11.6 Sample Time Sheet

Adamson, Teshima, Álvarez & Gaum

DAILY TIME SHEET   DATE: _9-21-00_   LEGAL ASSISTANT: _Westfeldt_

Page _1_ of _1_ pages for this date

CLIENT NAME	BILLING NO.	TASK DESCRIPTION	START	STOP	TIME BILLED
Sakawa	4278	Tel. from T. Narako re procedure	8:17	8:25	
		for transfer of SDG&E bonds			
	✓	Tel. to Transfer Agent re same	9:20	9:23	
	✓	Tel. from Transfer Agent requesting	11:42	11:50	
		bond registration numbers			
South Bank	2381	Prep. for trial:	8:25	9:15	
		- Compile trial notebook	9:25	11:42	
		- Notify client and witnesses of	12:45	2:07	
		trial division and schedule			
		- highlight depo summaries			
Quiñonez	1102	Research trustee's liability for	2:10	3:47	
		self-dealing with closely held	4:00	5:43	
		corporation; draft memo of law			
		re same			
Firm	7	Review resumes for BK paralegal	5:45	6:35	

Some firms use 10 minutes as their minimum billable unit of time, and a few very prestigious firms even bill in 15-minute units. In the latter firms, it is far easier to meet annual quotas, because only four 1-minute phone calls on four separate client matters would generate a full "hour" of billable time. Of course, it is possible that these firms establish higher quotas for attorneys and paralegals.

When a legal assistant works for 60 minutes without interruption on a legal matter for one client (e.g., a pending lawsuit), she might lump all of the work for that client (say, six phone calls and 40 minutes of legal research) within a single billable period of one hour. Under that practice, each phone call is not billed separately. Instead, all of the phone calls *and* the legal research are accounted for on her time sheet as though they were parts of a single, uninterrupted process—much the way the gardener charges for mowing the lawn, trimming the hedges, and so forth. The client actually receives a full sixty minutes of paralegal work—part of it legal research and part phone calls—for one hour of billable time. To most legal professionals, that probably seems the reasonable and fair way to charge the client for their services.

The alternative timekeeping system would have the paralegal account for each of the 6 phone calls separately—billing the client for 6 minutes on each call even though all six calls required a total of only 20 minutes to complete. That would produce 36 minutes of billable time for the phone calls alone (6 calls at the standard "unit" of 6 minutes), and the legal research time would be entered separately as an additional 40 minutes of paralegal work. This latter system *never* allows the client to receive 60 minutes of paralegal work for each hour billed, unless a single task (whether one phone call or an uninterrupted period of legal research, for example) actually consumes 60 minutes. Obviously, this lat-

FIGURE 11.7 Billing Multiple Matters for Same Client

Adamson, Teshima, Álvarez & Gaum

DAILY TIME SHEET DATE: _9-22-00_   LEGAL ASSISTANT: _Westfeldt_

Page _1_ of _4_ pages for this date

CLIENT NAME	BILLING NO.	TASK DESCRIPTION	START	STOP	TIME BILLED
Sakawa	4278	Tel. call to client re preparation for meeting with Sanchez & Bros.	8:40	8:55	
	✓	Brief attorney Mitchell re status of client preparations; plan division of responsibilities for completion of same	9:00	9:25	
Sakawa	4280	Research directors' liability for inadequate due diligence prior to rejecting hostile buy-out offer	9:30	11:50	
	✓	Review client's errors and omissions policy re coverage for negligent due diligence	1:20	1:40	

ter system tends to inflate the billable hours—and, consequently, the client's bill—raising significant ethical questions.

Billing Multiple Client Matters

A related problem involves interruptions in the work flow. If the same legal assistant were working on the same client matter, but was interrupted several times regarding other clients' legal matters, how should her work be recorded for billing purposes? The usual practice is to bill the standard time unit (e.g., 6 minutes) for each activity that interrupts the flow of her work. Of course, that time is billed to those clients whose legal matters have caused the interruptions.

The rationale for this system maintains that each interruption disrupts one's train of thought, and clients should bear the cost of the inefficiency that results—an inefficiency that the law firm cannot prevent. Another justification is that several minutes are consumed in making memoranda of each conversation and recording the activities on the paralegal's time sheet. Some would argue, however, that the inefficiency and record keeping are unavoidable costs of doing business—much like rent and the cost of bar association memberships—and should be absorbed by the law firm as an overhead expense. *Figure 11.7* illustrates timekeeping for multiple client matters.

MEETING BILLABLE QUOTAS

Where quotas are difficult to meet, part of the problem is that occasional minutes, here and there, constantly—and inevitably—fall between the cracks. Often it is impossible to efficiently stop one activity for one client and immediately begin the next activity for another client, without the loss of a

> **Practice Tip**
>
> Before accepting a position, the applicant should inquire about the firm's billing policies. He should find out also whether the firm has an annual quota for hours billed by legal assistants. If the firm's expectation for billable hours seems unrealistic, he might want to speak informally with a paralegal in the firm to discover how that expectation is met.

few minutes. A related problem is that many firms expect paralegals to perform work that cannot be billed to clients: updating materials in the law library, helping the support staff to prepare materials for a mailing, researching material for a firm publication, or reviewing applications for paralegal positions.

Some clients, particularly corporations, have become increasingly critical of the billing systems used by law firms. They often require detailed bills that are reviewed for questionable charges, and it is common for corporate clients to negotiate reductions in their bills. Because of the intense competition for clients, a minor trend has developed toward a system of fixed fee-for-service billing. In this system, clients would be charged a fixed amount based upon the difficulty and value of the service provided—not based upon the specific time required.

TIMEKEEPING AND BILLING

Whether kept "the old-fashioned way" on paper time sheets, or entered in the computer as the legal assistant completes each discrete task on client matters, the units of time and the corresponding task descriptions are fed into the firm's computerized billing system. As timekeeping becomes increasingly computerized, that task can be accomplished in large part by software, with the billing clerk "cleaning up" any cryptic or unclear entries that have been made.

Most firms bill each client monthly for all work done and expenses incurred during the preceding month. After the close of the month, it usually takes a week or two to prepare a statement for mailing to the client. The statement preparation includes the following stages:

- With or without computer assistance, a billing clerk consolidates all billed time for each client.
- A tentative itemization of billed time is prepared.
- The responsible attorney reviews and corrects the itemization.
- A final itemization is prepared with a summary statement of all fees and costs.

A critical part of this process is the attorney's review of the tentative itemization of billed time. The attorney might revise the activity description so that it is more understandable to the client, and to reflect the professional nature of the task performed. The latter purpose is important, because a client might wonder—justifiably—why he is being billed $75 per hour for a legal assistant to "prepare copies of documents for response to discovery." The client will be more receptive if he understands that the legal assistant actually "review[ed] client files and select[ed] documents for response to discovery."

Another purpose of the attorney's review is to occasionally delete ("write off") or reduce ("write down") some of the time billed by attorneys and/or paralegals. Any time written off either will not appear on the client's statement or will appear with a "no-charge" notation. Attorneys write time off (or down) for a variety of reasons. Some of these reasons are:

- to cultivate the client's goodwill (typically with the "no-charge" notation)
- to reduce the fees charged for work that was not efficiently performed
- to eliminate fees for work (e.g., legal research) that unexpectedly yielded no benefit to the client
- to eliminate fees for work that was on the borderline between professional and clerical functions

---

Practice Tip

Unless a firm policy prohibits it, the legal assistant can keep a photocopy of each day's time sheet for her own records. It simplifies locating vital information at a later time, and it also provides a record of the client matters she has worked on. If she later changes law firms, that information might be needed to eliminate potential conflicts of interest. Conflicts of interest are discussed in Chapter 3.

FIGURE 11.8 Monthly Client Statement

Adamson, Teshima, Álvarez & Gaum
Attorneys at Law
1723 Embarcadero Boulevard, Suite 1200
San Diego, California 92104
(619) 445-3000

Marc Neufeld
3265 Marjoram Avenue
San Diego, California 92104

Re: Neufeld v. MeritAll

STATEMENT

Period ending July 15, 2000
Reference No. 4-2436

	TIME	CHARGES
Previous balance		0.00
Initial meeting with client; set-up client file	1.5 hrs	0.00
Review client documents: employment agreement with MeritAll, pay records, employee evaluations	2.3	506.00
Call MeritAll to learn name of their counsel; call MeritAll attorney to explain client's allegations	0.6	132.00
Meet with MeritAll personnel dir and MeritAll attorney	1.0	220.00
Prepare demand letter to MeritAll	0.4	88.00
TOTAL CONTINGENT FEES		**946.00**

(Please refer to your retainer agreement)

MISCELLANEOUS

photocopies	1.40
postage	.55
TOTAL MISC.	1.95

DUE NOW: 0.00

See enclosed accounting for balance in your Retainer Account.

While the itemized list of professional services and fees charged is being reviewed, the billing clerk will consolidate all of the firm expenses that are chargeable to the client. These typically include the following:

- long-distance telephone charges
- Westlaw or LEXIS-NEXIS on-line fees
- postage and messenger fees
- court filing fees and recording fees
- photocopies
- mileage and parking fees

Some firms also charge a flat fee for facsimile transmissions (e.g., two dollars) plus a charge for any pages in excess of some standard quantity (e.g., fifty cents for each page in excess of ten pages).

The responsible attorney will then review and approve the list of expenses to be charged. After the attorney has approved the itemized professional services and the summary of expenses, the statement will be prepared in final form to be mailed to the client. Most firms request payment upon receipt, or within thirty days. Accounts that fall more than a specified period in arrears (e.g., 90 days) are sometimes assessed a small percentage each month on the outstanding balance (e.g., 1% per month). Payment and interest policies should be part of the retainer agreement. An example of a monthly billing statement appears in *Figure 11.8*.

CLIENT TRUST ACCOUNTS

From time to time an attorney will receive funds on behalf of clients that are then temporarily held for the clients' benefit. These funds might be in the form of litigation settlements, insurance settlements, escrow funds in real estate or other transactions, the corpus (i.e., principal amount) of a trust, and so forth. The attorney's fiduciary duty to the client places her in the role of a trustee for these client funds. Consequently, the bank account in which they are kept is termed a **client trust account**. If the law firm has an in-house controller, he will be responsible for maintaining the trust account and ensuring that client funds are deposited in it. However, the attorney continues to bear the fiduciary responsibility for the trust account, even if the controller and an independent auditor monitor that account.

> Client funds held by an attorney are deposited in separate **client trust accounts** so that they will not be commingled or misused.

As explained in Chapter 3, it is unethical and illegal to commingle the client funds with law firm funds. Some law firms maintain the trust account and the firm account at different banks, so that inadvertent commingling is less likely to occur. The attorney is forbidden to use trust account funds for any purpose other than the clients' direct benefit. Thus, no salaries or other firm expenses can be paid out of the trust account. Trust account funds may not be "borrowed" to ease temporary cash-flow problems in the law firm's account—that would be embezzlement. And, of course, they may not be used for the attorney's personal expenses. Generally, a client's funds held in trust cannot be withdrawn to cover legal bills that that client has not paid. An attorney who violates these rules is subject to discipline, including possible disbarment. Penalties for trust account violations are among the most severe given for any attorney misconduct. Under some circumstances, criminal penalties can apply for the misuse of clients' funds.

The controller usually prepares periodic reports on the trust account, summarizing trust account activity and the beginning and ending balances for that period of each client's funds in that account. An independent auditor reviews the trust account activity as part of his annual audit of the firm. For obvious reasons, if the trust account balance is included among the assets in the law firm's annual balance sheet, it must be shown in the identical amount as a liability, as well.

In the following "Case in Point," the District of Columbia Court of Appeals ordered the disbarment of an attorney who commingled and then recklessly misappropriated client funds. The commingling occurred when the attorney was temporarily without a trust account for clients—for reasons not explained in the opinion—and deposited client funds into his operating account, instead. The misappropriation occurred when the attorney inadvertently caused the account to become overdrawn by writing numerous checks for business and personal expenses. Two checks written for bona fide client expenses bounced, because of insufficient funds in the account.

A CASE IN POINT

In re Micheel

610 A.2d 231 (D.C. 1992)

[All footnotes omitted.]

[All bracketed words shown as in the original opinion.]

TERRY, Associate Judge:

Bar Counsel charged respondent Richard A. Micheel with commingling funds, misappropriating client funds, and dishonesty. A hearing committee found, after a hearing, that Micheel was guilty of commingling and misappropriation, but not dishonesty. Concluding that the misappropriation was the result of "simple negligence but not more," the hearing committee recommended that Micheel be suspended for two months.

The Board on Professional Responsibility accepted the hearing committee's conclusion that Micheel had commingled and misappropriated funds, but did not engage in dishonest conduct. The Board concluded, however, that Micheel's misappropriation in this case was the result of recklessness rather than simple negligence. Relying on this court's holding that disbarment is the appropriate sanction in "virtually all" cases of misappropriation involving more than simple negligence, In re Addams, 579 A.2d 190, 191 (D.C. 1990) (en banc), the Board recommended that Micheel be disbarred. We adopt the Board's recommendation.

The pertinent facts are undisputed. Mr. Micheel was retained by Roger Gregory, an acquaintance and fellow attorney, to represent him in connection with the purchase of a house in Silver Springs, Maryland. Micheel collected a total of $144,200.00 from various sources for disbursal at the settlement. These funds included checks for $127,700.00 from the mortgage lender, $9,000.00 from Mr. Gregory, and $7,500.00 from the seller as an adjustment in the price. Because he did not have a client trust account at that time, Micheel deposited all of these checks in his regular office checking account.

* * * *

Micheel candidly admitted before the hearing committee that he was guilty of commingling and technically guilty of misappropriation, and the hearing committee and the Board found that he had committed those violations. He testified, however, that the shortages in his bank account were merely the result of his own poor accounting practices, not of any intent on his part to misappropriate client funds. The hearing committee credited this testimony and concluded that Micheel did not intentionally misappropriate the funds.

* * * *

The hearing committee and the Board found that Micheel had engaged in commingling and misappropriation, both violations of DR 9-103(a). Micheel does not challenge these findings, nor could he, for it is clear that his conduct constituted both commingling and misappropriation. Depositing client funds into an attorney's operating account constitutes commingling; misappropriation occurs when the balance in that account falls below the amount due to the client. See, e.g., In re Hessler, 549 A.2d 700 (D.C. 1988). Misappropriation in such situations is essentially a per se offense; proof of improper intent is not required. In re Harrison, 461 A.2d 1034, 1036 (D.C. 1983).

* * * *

We made clear in Addams that the need to maintain "public confidence in the bar" justified our stricter treatment of misappropriation cases. Addams, supra, 579 A.2d at 197 (citation omitted). We cited with approval an opinion noting that "modest discipline [in cases of misappropriation] threatens public respect for the legal profession and will impair public confidence in the court's regulation of the bar. . . ." Id. at 198, citing In re Deragon, 398 Mass. 127, 133–134, 495 N.E.2d 831, 834 (1986) (dissenting opinion). We concluded that because the relationship between attorney and client is and must be founded on complete trust, a breach of that trust by a lawyer who misappropriates client funds "is so reprehensible, striking at the core of the attorney-client relationship, that the respondent must carry a very heavy burden [to rebut the presumption of disbarment]." In re Addams, supra, 579 A.2d at 198–199. Thus we hold that "[a] clear rational basis for [the] conclusion that attorneys who knowingly misappropriate client funds stand in a different position than attorneys who commit other acts involving dishonesty." In re Dulansey, supra, at 190. Accordingly, we reject Micheel's constitutional argument and adopt the Board's recommended sanction of disbarment.

It is, therefore ORDERED that respondent, Richard A. Micheel, shall be disbarred from the practice of law in the District of Columbia, effective thirty days from the date of this opinion.

> **Practice Tip**
>
> In the third from final paragraph of the opinion, above, Micheel provides an example of an appellate court's adopting the language of a dissenting opinion in an earlier case. The Micheel court has here quoted from its own opinion in In re Addams, 579 A.2d 190 (D.C. 1990) (en banc), in which the Addams court cited the dissenting opinion from In re Deragon, 398 Mass. 127, 495 N.E.2d 834 (1986). In Addams, the court had adopted that dissenting view in a Massachusetts case to be the correct statement of the common law for the District of Columbia. Although a paralegal could not cite the dissenting opinion in In re Deragon as legal authority of any kind, she could cite its adoption by Addams as primary authority for the District of Columbia.

The *Micheel* case is a classic illustration of the reasons for requiring client trust accounts and forbidding any commingling of client funds. Clearly, trust accounts will not protect client funds if an attorney is determined to steal or embezzle them. But they can protect client funds from the sort of inadvertent misappropriation that occurred in *Micheel*. If the attorney had simply opened a new trust account and deposited the funds in it, the misappropriation would not have occurred, and he would not have lost his license to practice law.

WHEN A CLIENT'S ATTORNEY LEAVES THE FIRM

The client, the law firm, and the departing attorney are presented with a dilemma when an attorney decides to leave the firm to strike out on his own, or to join a different firm. And this circumstance is becoming more frequent as many firms, for economic reasons, eliminate the opportunity to make partner status in that firm.

The answer to the dilemma boils down to three questions:

1. Is it the firm's client, or the attorney's client?
2. Does an attorney breach his fiduciary duty to his former firm if he takes clients with him?
3. What are the rights of the client?

As one might guess, the last question turns out to be the most important of the three. The short answers to all three questions are as follows:

- The client doesn't "belong" to the attorney or to the firm—he has the absolute right to choose his own legal counsel.
- Although the departing attorney might have fiduciary duties to his former law firm, those duties cannot override the client's right to choose his attorney.
- "The customer is king" (or queen, as the case might be).

To reach a different conclusion, the ethical standards for the practice of law would have to place the self-interest and mutual obligations of attorneys above the rights of their clients—an indefensible standard.

Consequently, the client has three choices:

1. stay with the law firm
2. go with the departing attorney
3. find a new attorney

If the client decides to stay with the old firm, he will choose a new attorney from within that firm. If he goes with the departing attorney, the old firm must forward all of his client files to the departing attorney's new office. If he finds a new attorney, the old firm must forward all of his client files to the new attorney.

SECTION 2. EFFECTIVE LAW OFFICE PROCEDURES

One indicator of good law office management is the use of sound office procedures. Effective law office procedures will serve the following purposes:

- the efficient and economical delivery of client legal services
- compliance with all statutes of limitations and court deadlines
- the protection of client confidences
- positive working relationships with persons outside of the office
- an atmosphere of order and structure in the workplace
- smooth working relationships within the office

As stated above, it is the use of sound procedures that makes these things possible. It does no good for procedures to be proclaimed, if they are not practiced. This fact suggests two things, as follows:

1. Each office professional has an obligation to follow the procedures that have been established.
2. Managers must develop office procedures in a fashion that gives all employees a reason to believe that they are appropriate and necessary.

A well-managed office will have an office "policies and procedures" manual that governs the day-to-day practice of law and the related support operations. The policies and procedures manual might include the following topics:

- client conflict check
- docket control and tickler system
- case management by the responsible attorney
- assignment of paralegal and staff support to major legal matters
- authorization to disclose client and/or case information to outside parties
- security procedures for facsimile and e-mail transmissions
- security for client files
- archiving and destroying files
- timekeeping and billing

THE CLIENT CONFLICT CHECK

Before accepting a new client, a law firm must ensure that there is no conflict of interest for the firm to represent that client. If the firm has ever before represented another client with an adverse interest to the new client, a conflict does exist, even if the prior matter was closed years before. The conflict check is a system used to reveal such conflicts of interest.

In the past, the conflict check involved a laborious review of an alphabetized card filing system, in which each former client (and adversary party) was entered on a separate card. For some clients with alternative names (e.g., maiden and married, or corporations that later merged with other corporations), it was necessary to have multiple cards. Today, conflict systems usually are computerized and conflict checks easily completed.

When a conflict of interest is discovered, the firm must either decline to accept the new client, or it must obtain the consent of both the old and the new client to waive the conflict. The consent of the former client is required because the firm has confidential information about that client that might, conceivably, come out in the course of the new client's matter. The new client's consent is required because he might be concerned that the law firm has some loyalty to the former client that could discourage vigorous representation of his interests.

Practice Tip

There is one caveat about relying upon a computer for conflict checks: The computer will not find a match for names with slightly different spelling—"Clark" and "Clarke," for example—unless it contains a miniprogram similar to a spell checker that offers alternative spellings. Without such a miniprogram, human error could cause the client's name to be entered without the final "e", and the computer would not find a match.

A similar problem can exist with business names. The firm should have a consistent policy about entering the names of business entities. If one entry is "AME" while another is "American Management Enterprises," the computer cannot make a match, unless both names are tried.

Ethics Watch

Conducting the conflict check is not usually a paralegal's duty, but paralegals must be concerned about it when they change law firms. Depending upon the laws and professional code of ethics in each state, a law firm could be barred from representing a client because one of its paralegals had previously worked for another law firm that represented a client adverse to the present firm's new client. It is entirely possible that a legal assistant might be queried by his employer about legal matters worked on during his employment with another law firm.

Computers are particularly effective for conflict-of-interest checks, because a conflict database can be reviewed in a minute or two whenever the firm considers taking on a new client matter. If one contrasts the convenience of a computer-based conflict system with the task of manually creating and searching a paper filing system that requires a separate index card for each client and opposing party, one can appreciate the simplicity and speed of the database. Malpractice insurance carriers generally favor a computer system for checking conflicts, because such systems are more likely to be used consistently and accurately.

DOCKET CONTROL AND TICKLER SYSTEM

"Docket" is the term for a court's calendar of scheduled hearings, trials, and other proceedings. In a law office, the **docket** is the firm's calendar of deadlines and important events. Of greatest concern are the deadlines established by statute, court rules, and court orders. The most critical statutory deadlines are in the statute of limitations, which requires that litigation (or other formal claim) be initiated before a set period of time has passed. Generally, missing the statute of limitations forever bars any further claim against the other party in that matter. Statutes, court rules, or court orders also establish procedural deadlines for each phase of a court proceeding, and failure to meet those deadlines can result in court-imposed sanctions, and in extreme cases can result in a judgment for the opposing party.

Other important deadlines and events are identified by the law firm or by other parties, for example:

- opinion letter to be prepared at client's request
- opposing counsel's answer to the client's complaint

A law office **docket** is a calendar of deadlines, hearings, meetings, and other important events.

CHAPTER 11 ⚖ Law Office Management and Procedures 461

- opposing counsel's answer to a request for discovery
- acceptance or counteroffer due in contract negotiations
- deposition of expert witness
- annual report to insurer due for renewal of professional liability insurance
- firm response due in audit by Internal Revenue Service
- pretrial conference with client and testifying expert witness
- revised firm partnership statement to be recorded with county and state bar
- close of escrow on client's real estate purchase

Failure to anticipate some of the preceding deadlines might not carry the very dire consequences for the client that can result from missing a statute of limitations or a court filing deadline, but nonetheless can result in malpractice suits, bar discipline, lost clients, and a damaged reputation for the firm.

Law offices use a tickler system to do the following:

- to monitor critical dates
- to identify the attorney and paralegal who are responsible for meeting the deadline
- to provide early reminders so that essential tasks can be completed without undue haste
- to provide final warnings shortly before the deadline expires
- to alert the responsible attorney and paralegal when the due date has arrived

The docket (calendar) and tickler system (alert procedures) are usually maintained by a calendar clerk who has a strong knowledge of statutes of limitations and court rules. *Figure 11.9* provides a sample law firm docket for one day.

Some small firms might still use a manual tickler system in which reminder slips are prepared in advance and filed in a chronological card file system. There is an index card for each date of the month, and reminder slips for that date are placed immediately behind that card. Each morning, the calendar clerk delivers the slips for that day to the responsible attorney and/or paralegal.

Most law firms now use computer software for docket control and the tickler system. If the computers are connected on an intraoffice network, each legal assistant and attorney can call up the day's reminders on his desktop computer. When the task has been completed, the attorney or legal assistant can change the status in the computer from "pending" or "due" to "completed." As a backup, the calendar clerk can check each morning to ensure that the "due" items have been changed to completed status.

Docketing Software for Deadlines and Calendar Matters

A docketing program is used to track deadlines, court appearance dates, appointments, and other calendar matters. As mentioned earlier, one of its principle functions in a law firm is to "tickle" paralegals and attorneys in advance of important due dates. Docketing software is very similar to the calendar software that businesses use, but it has been designed for the particular needs of the legal profession. In a law firm, one staff member is usually designated to maintain the docketing program, although others can view it and enter information.

All computers have an internal clock that keeps track of the current date and time. It operates with an internal program that accounts for leap years, so that it always has the correct date. Docketing software uses the computer's internal

> **Practice Tip**
>
> The software program used for docket control can provide a daily printout for each legal professional of deadlines, meetings scheduled, incoming discovery responses due, and so on. Most docket control software programs allow the paralegal to enter each afternoon (or Friday) any specific tasks she plans to complete the next day (or week), and her daily or weekly printout can include such self-scheduled items as well. If all attorneys and paralegals routinely enter court appearances, depositions, client meetings, appointments, and the like, the calendar database can be used to identify those dates and times when they can be available for a meeting.

FIGURE 11.9   Docket Calendar

Adamson, Teshima, Álvarez & Gaum

DAILY CALENDAR

Thursday, February 25, 1999

FILINGS & SERVICE		ATTY/PARALEGAL
Complaint	Neuheld v. MeritAll	Gaum/Kryder
Resp to Interrogs	South Bank v. Bart Meckle	Álvarez/Drake
Notice to Creditors	In re MBC	Álvarez/Drake
Petition - Chap 7	In re Mary Welles	Teshima/Kryder
Complaint & Summons	Neuheld v. MeritAll	Gaum/Kryder

APPTS & MTGS

8:00	Partners' mtg	Conf Room B
9:15	Mtg with Sakawa MetroMod buy-out offer Teshima and Gaum	Conf Room C
11:30	Mtg with South Bank/Wilson misc. debt collect Gaum	South Bank main office
12:00	Lunch with South Bank/Wilson Gaum	South Bank dining room
1:30	Hearing--Motion to Compel South Bank v. Bart Meckle Álvarez	Law & Motion - Dept 21
1:30	Deposition of Wilson South Bank v. eMart Inc Gaum	Meld Winkel & Sorter
2:00	Interviews for paralegal psn Teshima	Office

clock as a reference point, and it adds many more sophisticated features, including the day of the week and the ability to calculate future dates. So, if the paralegal instructs the program to identify the exact date 60 days (or 1,017 days) hence, it can do so. In fact, docketing programs generally accommodate two entries, a reference date and a period of days (e.g., April 10, and 90 days) and automatically calendar a future event based on that information.

An extremely valuable feature is the automatic conflict alert, in case one enters two events that are to occur at the same time. A sophisticated docketing program might allow the user to reserve a period of hours and days, so that conflicts will be identified if any other event overlaps that reserved period. All docketing programs provide advance reminders, based upon the date or number of days that the user specifies. The reminders then appear on the daily printout, along with that day's appointments and events. This, of course, is the heart of the tickler system. In addition to daily printouts, the software will print weekly or monthly calendars of events and deadlines. In lieu of printouts (or in addition to them), the software can cause the reminder to appear in the on-screen calendar of the responsible paralegal's computer. The software also allows one to enter additional information when an event is calendared. This could range from a list of documents to an outline of the procedures to be followed in a business transaction, for example.

LAW OFFICE FILES

Law offices typically maintain at least six types of files:

1. client (or corporate) legal matters
2. client billing records
3. office financial records
4. office personnel records
5. correspondence unrelated to specific client matters
6. other office records

Although the legal assistant might provide input to several of these, her day-to-day responsibilities usually involve working with the client matter files. So, this discussion will focus on the filing system used for client matters.

A file is opened for each new client. And if that same client later brings a separate legal matter to the firm, another file will be opened for that particular matter. Consequently, if the office is working on seven legal matters for a single client, the office will have seven files for that client. Most offices have a form (sometimes called a "New File Memorandum") on which the attorney or legal assistant enters the information needed to open a file. Using that information, a secretary or file clerk will then set up a new file. *Figure 11.10* shows a typical New File Memorandum.

A client file is usually contained in a partitioned folder—similar to a manila folder, but of heavier-weight paper pressboard—with several pressboard "pages," or dividers, which conveniently separate the file into basic categories, such as the following:

- client information and retainer agreement
- correspondence (incoming and outgoing)
- attorney and paralegal notes
- legal research
- pleadings and court documents
- discovery requests and responses

In other words, all of the documents in a given category are grouped together within a single partition of the file. The documents are normally two-hole punched at the top and are secured in the file by bending down two soft metal prongs that pass through the punched holes.

If the legal matter does not involve court proceedings, the latter two categories are not needed. Instead, their space in the file will be devoted to other documents, according to the nature of the legal matter. These might include such things as the following:

- contract proposals and counterproposals
- financial data
- creditors' claims

FIGURE 11.10 New File Memorandum

Adamson, Teshima, Alvarez & Gaum

NEW FILE INFORMATION

DATE:	6-23-00
CLIENT NUMBER:	4-2436
NAME:	Neufeld, Marc
RESIDENCE:	3265 Marjoram Ave San Diego 92104
HOME PHONE:	619-524-4957
BUSINESS:	unemployed
BUS PHONE:	none
MATTER:	Neufeld v. MeritAll
NATURE;	wrongful termination and unpaid wages
ATTORNEY:	Gaum
OTHER PARTY:	MeritAll, Inc. 4 Embarcadero San Diego 92105
COUNSEL:	unknown
FEES:	contingent
RETAINER:	$2,000

- former and current wills and codicils
- patent or trademark applications

Documents that lend themselves to a chronological order (correspondence, pleadings, discovery requests and responses, contract proposals and counterproposals, etc.) are usually placed in the file chronologically, with the most recent document for that category on top. This makes it easy to locate the most recent pleading or letter, but it also makes it awkward to read a series of correspondence chronologically, from the beginning to the most current. In practice, however, it isn't that often that an attorney or paralegal needs to do that kind of chronological review, unless he or she is coming into a case some time after its initiation.

A small lawsuit or other legal matter usually can be contained in a single partitioned folder. A larger case might require several "volumes" of folders. In that event, each volume can be devoted to a single category, such as correspondence, or proposals and counterproposals. In litigation, it is not unusual to have multiple volumes devoted to discovery, and other volumes devoted to nothing but pleadings. When an entire volume is devoted to a single category, unpartitioned folders are normally used. *Figure 11.11* illustrates a partitioned file for a small lawsuit.

FIGURE 11.11   A Client File

Ethics Watch

All client files must be treated as confidential. That means much more than simply locking them up each night. Client files must be protected from inadvertent disclosure while they are being used in the office or elsewhere. One of the most common oversights is to leave a client file lying open on the desk when meeting with someone else from outside of the office—another client, an expert witness, and so on.

Filing Systems for Client Matters

There are two basic systems for organizing client files: alphabetical and numerical. The alphabetical system is well-suited to a sole practitioner and other small law offices. But many larger firms have found it more useful to assign a unique number to each client matter and to maintain the files in numerical order. In an alphabetical system, a particular client matter could be filed under several alternative names when it involves a corporate client. For example, West Publishing is a division of the West Group and International Thomson Publishing (ITP), but paralegal textbooks carrying the West name are produced by a division of Thomson Learning, Delmar. A law firm representing Delmar Publishers in a matter involving infringement on the copyright of a West Legal Studies textbook might file that matter under "West," "International Thomson Publishing," "ITP," "Thomson," or "Delmar." Of course, an index containing cross-references to all alternative names would permit the file to be located in an alphabetical system—or in a numerical system, for that matter.

The real advantage of the numerical system is that it can be set up to reveal additional information about the case. For example, numbers 001 to 099 could be reserved for large clients, 100 to 199 for wills and estate planning, 200 to 349 for real estate transactions, and so on. The year the file is opened could be indicated by a leading two-digit number—96.101 for a large client matter opened in 1996, for example. If it is desired to group together all of the cases opened in a given year, this numbering system makes that automatic. Otherwise, it would be necessary to ignore the preceding number (96) and file everything under the following number (101). Incidentally, it is common for courts to assign case numbers that begin with the year in which the case is first filed. But, of course, the court's case number and the law firm's client matter filing number have nothing to do with each other and serve different purposes.

An alternative numerical system uses the first two digits (01, 02, 03, etc.) to identify the responsible attorney, the second two digits the client, and the third two digits the particular client matter. Very large firms could use the same system by increasing each range to three digits (e.g., 003 to identify a particular attorney). This type of numerical system is easier to work with if the ranges are separated by periods: 003.217.012, for example. One advantage of this system is that it places in the same filing cabinet(s) all of the files for which a given attorney is responsible. This system, however, has one disadvantage: Because the files for a given client are grouped together (assuming the same attorney is responsible for all of them), it could be easy to carelessly misfile a document (e.g., a letter from the client regarding a real estate purchase) in the file for another legal matter of that same client (e.g., a patent application).

In large offices, keeping track of the many thousands of files can be a critical but difficult task. Some firms place a physical placeholder in the drawer whenever a file is removed. But computers offer a more elegant alternative. The file location and status (e.g., active or closed) can be maintained in a computer database (explained in Chapter 9), so that anyone in the office can check on the location of any file without even leaving his desk. The same computer database would serve as the index, so that a file could be identified by searching for a related name (ITP, Delmar, or West, for example). Bar coding technology increases even more the efficiency of a computerized document management system.

AUTHORIZATION TO RELEASE DOCUMENTS OR INFORMATION

The improper disclosure of documents or information to outside parties can have horrendous consequences. Confidential client information could be compromised. The attorney-client privilege could be jeopardized. And adverse parties might gain documents or information that could damage the client's interests. For all of these reasons, a well-managed firm should have a procedure to prevent improper disclosure. The procedure might give a legal assistant or legal secretary standing authority to disclose certain types of nonsensitive documents or information, but require an attorney's authorization for any other disclosures. For example, any pleading filed with the court without **judicial seal** is a public document; discovery requests and responses, however, would not be unless they were also lodged with the court.

> A court places certain sensitive documents under **judicial seal**, which means that they cannot be examined without first obtaining permission of the court.

ARCHIVING INACTIVE CLIENT FILES

Eventually, most client files will become inactive. It makes no sense to consume large amounts of office space with file cabinets or boxes full of inactive files. The solution is to close any file that has been *inactive* for a defined period of time (e.g., 180 days) and is not expected to become active again within the next year. Although most offices have such standards, it is usually left to the discretion of the responsible attorney for that matter to leave a file open or to close it. Occasionally, for example, an inactive file might contain documents or information relevant to another ongoing legal matter for the same client. If the attorney anticipates a need to occasionally refer to the inactive file, it might be better to leave it open and conveniently available.

Closed files are generally stored in a different location where they are secure and protected by an automatic sprinkler system. How long should the office retain closed files? That is a difficult question to answer, because a number of variables can affect the decision. Some of these are listed below:

- any requirement under statute or bar association rules to keep closed files for a specified minimum period
- the statute of limitations on any action the client might bring, or might have brought against her by some other party, related to the matters in the file
- the statute of limitation on any malpractice action the client might bring against the law firm, related to the legal services provided in that matter

There is a possibility that the client wants the files to be preserved indefinitely. To be on the safe side, the firm might offer to deliver the closed file into the client's custody after the required minimum storage period has elapsed. There are some files that probably should be retained for at least ninety-nine years: child adoption documents and estate planning documents, for example.

For firms with very large quantities of closed files, one option is to transfer them to photographic microform. Microform reduces the space required for storage to a tiny fraction of the space needed to store the original paper documents. As technology improves and becomes less expensive, firms might begin scanning most documents into a computer for electromagnetic storage on disk. (This technology is discussed in Chapter 9.)

Eventually, a file might become so "stale" (i.e., completely inactive for many years) and have so little discernible relevance to current or future activities of the client that the firm contemplates its destruction. In most states, however, the client has an overriding ownership interest in his own legal files. Depending upon state statutes and ethical rules, the law firm might offer the client the choice of taking custody of the file or authorizing its destruction.

When the time comes to destroy closed files, they must be shredded. It is very important that the person shredding the files certifies their destruction in a signed and dated document. That certificate of destruction becomes a permanent record of the office in order to demonstrate that the confidentiality of the client files was preserved. There are commercial companies that provide confidential, certified destruction of files. These companies then provide the required certification for the law office to keep.

LAW OFFICE COMMUNICATIONS

When legal assistants use any mode of external communication—telephone, e-mail, facsimile transmission, or U.S. mail—three considerations must be kept in mind:

1. confidentiality and security
2. clarity of the message
3. professional tone of the message

The first consideration must always be the protection of client confidences and other sensitive information. Clarity is essential so that the message will be understood. A professional tone causes the recipient to give the message his serious attention.

Earlier chapters have discussed the risks of transmitting e-mail and facsimiles to the wrong addresses or phone numbers. It is an error easily made, but also one easily avoided. Attention to detail and a few simple precautionary procedures (e.g., separate lists for the addresses and numbers of "friendly" parties and the "opposition") are all that are required.

> ### *Practice Tip*
> *As already mentioned, many law firms require an attorney's authorization before any file documents may be transmitted outside of the office. In the absence of such a policy, the legal assistant must use sound judgment and exercise caution. It is especially important to treat telephone requests for documents with great caution, because it can be difficult to verify the requester's true identity. It is a good practice to ask for written confirmation of any telephone request by mail or facsimile transmission. Following receipt of that written confirmation, the legal assistant can call the requesting office if further verification seems appropriate.*

Using the Telephone and Voice Mail

When telephoning another office, one should identify herself and the office in which she is employed. In some situations, the nature of the communication requires that she also identify the client matter she is calling about. For example, one cannot request an extension of time to respond to discovery without identifying the client matter. This is an "implied-consent-by-client" exception to the general rule against revealing a client's identity. The rationale is that, by retaining the attorney for representation, the client consents to all reasonably necessary disclosures.

Brevity and clarity are just as important in telephone conversations as they are in written correspondence. People tend to be busy and appreciate a brief, professional conversation. This is especially important when leaving voice mail messages. Even so, one of the common problems with voice mail is the *omission* of essential information. One should always include the following:

- one's name
- name of the office
- telephone number
- date of the call
- reason for the call
- any further message (e.g., information or request for call back)

If the caller might be unfamiliar to the person being called, it is a good idea to spell the last name.

> **Practice Tip**
>
> *People who work in law firms often forget that the firm's name might be difficult to understand when stated rapidly. Unless the other party is already familiar with the firm name, it is best to state the name with very brief pauses between words:* "Jefferson, Farrell, Almond *and* Marks," *rather than* "jefurson-fairalalmonanmarks." *The same courtesy should be extended when giving one's telephone number: state it slowly, and then repeat it once for confirmation. These courtesies are doubly important when leaving voice mail messages. There is no excuse for compelling the other party to replay a message while trying to decipher the firm name or phone number.*

A QUESTION OF ETHICS

The law firm in which paralegal Victoria Kettler works has a demanding quota for billable hours: 1,900 hours per year. Victoria and the other paralegals in the office find it very difficult to bill sufficient hours each working day to reach the annual quota.

The firm practice is to bill in 6-minute increments, or units. Victoria has been working on a very large case that often occupies a major part of each working day. Normally, when Victoria has worked for an extended period on a given client matter, she has grouped a number of discrete activities (e.g., phone calls, memos, and research) together in one continuing time period, instead of recording each activity separately—although recording them separately would increase her total billable hours on the daily time sheet.

With the year coming to an end in only three months, Victoria recognizes that her hours might fall short of the annual quota. Currently, there isn't enough work available to reach her quota by simply working longer days. Victoria is considering recording each activity separately on the major case now underway, so that she can reach her quota. The firm has not expressed any policy on this recording practice, either orally or in writing. What should Victoria do?

CHAPTER SUMMARY

- A successful law practice delivers a high quality of legal services and maintains high ethical standards.
- In addition to achieving an effective practice, a private law firm attempts to generate profits and gain professional prestige.

CHAPTER 11 — Law Office Management and Procedures

- There are four keys to success in the practice of law: (1) professional employees, (2) effective law office organization, (3) sound attorney-client relationships, and (4) efficient office procedures.
- The office personnel manual establishes working conditions and governs the employment relationship.
- Both the employee and the employer have the right to terminate an at-will employment relationship, at any time and for any otherwise lawful reason.
- Sound attorney-client relationships depend upon effective communication and mutual trust.
- The retainer agreement is a contract between the client and the attorney.
- Many law firms designate a managing partner who oversees firm operations.
- Larger law firms establish management committees to oversee firm operations, personnel, finance, and marketing.
- Professional law corporations limit the liability of the attorneys who own them.
- Limited liability partnerships and limited liability corporations combine the tax advantages of partnerships and the limited liability of corporations.
- Corporate and public agency legal departments are similar in their organization.
- A corporation usually designates an attorney to serve as general counsel.
- An office policies and procedures manual governs the manner in which the office practices law.
- The client conflict check must be completed before a law office takes on a new client.
- The law office docket is a calendar of deadlines, hearings, meetings, and other important events.
- Each law office maintains a tickler system to alert paralegals and attorneys to approaching deadlines.
- Maintaining the confidentiality of client files is a major responsibility of the law office.
- Inactive client files are archived and retained until no necessity or obligation requires their further retention.
- Billing statements for clients are based upon the time and expense records kept by legal professionals and support staff in the office.
- The responsible attorney reviews and approves billing statements before they go to the client.
- Client trust accounts must be completely separate from the firm's own accounts, and no client funds may be commingled with firm funds.

KEY TERMS

at-will employment
chief counsel
client trust account
contingency fee
contract partner
docket
equity partner
errors and omissions insurance
errors and omissions policy
executive committee
general counsel
judicial seal

just cause
law clerk
legal administrator
limited liability corporation (LLC)
limited liability partnership (LLP)
probationary employee
rainmaker
retainer agreement

ACTIVITIES AND ASSIGNMENTS

1. This chapter lists subjects that might be addressed in a law office personnel manual. Draft a section on *one* of the following topics for possible inclusion in a personnel manual for a law office with twenty-five employees:
   - overtime and compensatory time off
   - evaluation procedures
   - dress and grooming standards
   - antidiscrimination policy

   Of course, a "draft" is never expected to be a final product. But be prepared to explain the rationale behind the provisions you have drafted.

2. Using the opening scenario for this chapter as your basis, answer the following questions: What is the appropriate discipline for the file clerk's careless handling of the Holsteen file? What do you think of William's conclusion that the senior partners "don't have a case"? Then, prepare a written analysis of Bill Manes' situation in light of the firm's policy statement.

3. Review the opening scenario at the beginning of this chapter. What is the firm's duty to its client, Mr. Holsteen, now that this breach of confidentiality has occurred?

4. Find out whether a classmate has worked as the only support staff in a sole practitioner's office. Interview the classmate to learn the following:
   - the range of duties required
   - the difficulties of being the only support staff
   - the satisfactions that came from being a Jack or Jane "of all trades"

   Make an oral or written report of your interview.

5. For this activity, use the blank time sheet in *Figure 11.12*. (Your instructor might provide a blank form that she prefers.) A sample of a completed time sheet appears in *Figure 11.13*. You will use the blank time sheet to simulate what paralegals do to keep track of their billable time.

   Using the blank form, record all class activities for an entire class period. In the column labeled "Client," enter instead a single word (e.g., "discussion" or "quiz") that identifies the general class activity in progress. Under "Work Description," describe more specifically the activity in progress ("receive corrected homework;" "complete vocabulary quiz;" "class discussion on alternative careers," etc.). In the "Start" and "Stop" columns, enter the *exact time* that each activity begins and ends. For the time being, leave the "Time Billed" column blank.

   Remember that every discrete class activity must be entered, with starting and stopping times. If you miss an entry, your "law firm" will not be able to bill the client for that time. As you begin this exercise, the instructor might remind you to make entries, but do not count on it. Stay alert!

   At the end of the class period, calculate the *units* of billable time for each activity, using an increment of 6 minutes as 1 unit. Then, recalculate the units using an increment of 10 minutes for 1 billing unit.

FIGURE 11.12 Blank Time Sheet

Adamson, Teshima, Álvarez & Gaum

DAILY TIME SHEET DATE: _____ LEGAL ASSISTANT: _____

Page ____ of ____ pages for this date

CLIENT NAME	BILLING NO.	TASK DESCRIPTION	START	STOP	TIME BILLED

FIGURE 11.13 Completed Time Sheet

Adamson, Teshima, Álvarez & Gaum

DAILY TIME SHEET DATE: _6-3-00_ LEGAL ASSISTANT: _John Erickson_

Page _1_ of _1_ pages for this date

CLIENT NAME	BILLING NO.	TASK DESCRIPTION	START	STOP	TIME BILLED
Homework		Received graded homework from instructor; explanation by instructor re comments on papers	7:03	7:12	2
Discussion		Q and A re chapter 4 contents	7:14	7:25	2
Lecture		Lecture re conflict of interests and how to deal with them	7:25	7:55	5
Break			7:55	8:10	3
Review		Review of legal terms for quiz	8:11	8:23	2
Quiz		Quiz on vocabulary from Chap. 4	8:25	8:40	3
Panel		Panel discussion about confidentiality breaches	8:45	9:15	5
Assignment		Instructor explained essay assignment due next week	9:15	9:30	3

APPENDIX A

Sample Deposition Excerpts and Summaries

Excerpt from the Deposition of Elizah Walsh:

1 Q WHERE WERE YOU WHEN THE FIRE ALARM SOUNDED?
2 A GEE—I'M NOT SURE. IT ALL—IT HAPPENED SO FAST. FIRST
3 THERE WAS THE ALARM—I THINK I WAS IN THE STORA . . . NO, IT
4 WASN'T THERE—I WASN'T THERE. MAYBE I WAS IN THE HALLWAY OUT-
5 SIDE THE STORAGE ROOM. ANYWAYS, THE ALARM GOES OFF AND SOME-
6 ONE YELLS "SMOKE" AND EVERYBODY STARTS SCREAMING. GUYS
7 WERE RUNNING EVERY WHICH WAY. IT WAS CHAOTIC. COURSE, I WAS
8 PRETTY CALM, 'CAUSE I SERVED ON SHIP IN THE NAVY, AND ALL. NOT IN
9 ACTUAL COMBAT, YOU UNDERSTAND, BUT WE HAD A FEW FIRES AND—
10 MS. WACHS: ARE YOU SURE THE WORD WAS "SMOKE," MR. WALSH?
11 WITNESS: YEAH, I THINK SO. COURSE IT COULD HAVE BEEN "SPOKE," HE'S
12 THE FIRE MARSHALL. NO, IT WAS "SMOKE."
13 BY MR. MORAN:
14 Q WHAT TIME WAS IT WHEN THE ALARM WENT OFF?
15 A MAYBE NINE-THIRTY, NINE-FORTY.
16 Q HOW MANY EMPLOYEES WERE ON DUTY THEN?
17 A GEEZ, HOW SHOULD I KNOW? I WASN'T THE FOREMAN OR ANY-
18 THING, YOU KNOW. I JUST TRIED TO DO MY JOB.
19 Q WHO WAS THE FOREMAN THAT NIGHT?
20 A IT WAS THAT S.O.B., FRIXETT. HE ALWAYS WORKED THE NIGHT
21 SHIFTS.
22 Q WAS MR. FRIXETT IN THE BUILDING WHEN THE ALARM
23 SOUNDED?
24 A I DON'T KNOW. HE WAS USUALLY AROUND. YOU NEVER
25 KNEW WHEN HE WOULD POP UP AT YOUR SHOULDER, CHECKING UP
26 ON YOU. HE WAS A REAL JERK. HE WAS ALWAYS GETTING GUYS IN
27 TROUBLE.

APPENDIX A Sample Deposition Excerpts and Summaries

1 Q DO YOU HAVE ANY MEMORY AT ALL ABOUT WHETHER HE
2 WAS—WHETHER MR. FRIXETT WAS IN THE BUILDING?
3 A NAW, NOT REALLY. HE MAY HAVE BEEN UP IN ACCOUNTING WITH
4 BLAZE, FOR ALL I KNOW.
5 Q WHO'S BLAZE—IS HE THE CONTROLLER?
6 A THAT'S A JOKE. NO, BLAZE IS JILL DAVIDOVICH. WE CALL HER
7 "BLAZE" 'CAUSE SHE HAS THE SAME LAST NAME AS THAT ACTRESS
8 THAT PLAYED THE STRIPPER IN THAT PAUL NEWMAN MOVIE. SHE EVEN
9 KINDA LOOKS LIKE HER.
10 ANYWAY, BLAZE—I MEAN JILL—JILL AND FRIXETT HAVE A LITTLE
11 SOMETHING GOING ON THE SIDE, AND THEY'D SNEAK UP TO AC-
12 COUNTING AT NIGHT 'CAUSE NO ONE WOULD BE THERE—IF YOU KNOW
13 WHAT I MEAN.
14 Q DO YOU KNOW IF THEY WERE UP IN ACCOUNTING ON THE
15 NIGHT OF THE FIRE?
16 A I DON'T KNOW. SOMETIMES, THOUGH, WHEN NO ONE COULD
17 FIND FRIXETT AND BLAZE, WE'D PHONE UP TO ACCOUNTING. NO ONE
18 WOULD ANSWER, BUT FRIXETT ALWAYS SHOWED UP IN A COUPLE OF
19 MINUTES. IT WAS KIND OF AN INSIDE JOKE WITH THE CREW.
20 Q MR. WALSH, DID YOU RECOGNIZE ANY STRANGERS IN THE
21 BUILDING THAT EVENING—ANY ONE YOU DIDN'T KNOW?
22 BY MS. WACHS: HOW CAN HE "RECOGNIZE" A STRANGER, COUNSELOR?
23 BY MR. MORAN: I'LL REPHRASE, COUNSELOR.
24 Q DID YOU OBSERVE ANY STRANGERS IN THE BUILDING THAT NIGHT?
25 A NO, SIR. NEVER SAW ANY STRANGERS.
26 Q DO YOU MEAN "NEVER THAT NIGHT," OR "NEVER AT ALL?"
27 A NEVER THAT NIGHT.
28 Q YOU TESTIFIED EARLIER THAT YOU HAD NO IDEA HOW MANY
29 PEOPLE WERE IN THE BUILDING THAT NIGHT. IS IT POSSIBLE THAT SOME
30 UNAUTHORIZED PERSON ENTERED THE BUILDING UNSEEN?
31 BY MS. WACHS: ANYTHING'S POSSIBLE, COUNSELOR.
32 BY MR. MORAN:
33 Q DID YOU SEE ANY UNAUTHORIZED PERSONS IN THE BUILDING
34 THAT NIGHT?
35 BY MS. WACHS: OBJECTION—ASKED AND ANSWERED.
36 BY MR. MORAN: I BEG TO DIFFER, COUNSELOR. THE WITNESS HAS
37 TESTIFIED THAT HE DIDN'T OBSERVE ANY STRANGERS. I'M ASKING IF HE
38 SAW ANY UNAUTHORIZED PERSONS, POSSIBLY INCLUDING SOMEONE
39 WHO WAS NOT A STRANGER. YOU MAY ANSWER, MR. WALSH.
40 A NO UNAUTHORIZED PERSONS, NO.
41 Q WERE YOU THE ONLY SECURITY GUARD ON DUTY THAT NIGHT?

1   A   IN THAT BUILDING? YEAH.
2   Q   HOW MANY OTHER SECURITY GUARDS WERE ON DUTY IN
3   OTHER BUILDINGS AT THE COMPANY?
4   A   THERE SHOULD HAVE BEEN THREE OTHERS, BUT I DON'T KNOW.
5   Q   WHY DON'T YOU KNOW?
6   A   SOMETIMES A GUARD CALLS IN SICK, AND THEY DON'T GET A
7   REPLACEMENT. THEN ONE OF THE REST OF US HAS TO MAKE ROUNDS
8   AT THE OTHER BUILDING A FEW TIMES.
9   Q   YOU MEAN, ONE OF THE GUARDS PRESENT ON SITE HAS TO
10   LEAVE THEIR USUAL POST AND GO TO THE UNGUARDED BUILDING?
11   A   YEAH, THAT'S RIGHT.
12   Q   ON THE NIGHT OF THE FIRE, DID YOU HAVE TO MAKE ROUNDS
13   AT ANY OTHER BUILDING?
14   A   NO SIR, NOT THAT NIGHT.
15   Q   DID YOU LEAVE THE BUILDING DURING YOUR SHIFT FOR ANY
16   OTHER REASONS?
17   A   I'M NOT SURE.
18   Q   YOU'RE NOT SURE? WOULDN'T YOU REMEMBER IF YOU HAD
19   DONE THAT?
20   Q   WELL, THAT WAS A COUPLE OF MONTHS AGO. IT'S HARD TO RE-
21   MEMBER WHAT EXACTLY HAPPENED WHEN.
22   Q   SO ON SOME OCCASIONS YOU DID HAVE TO COVER ANOTHER
23   BUILDING DURING YOUR REGULAR SHIFT?
24   A   YEAH. IT'S HAPPENED A FEW TIMES.
25   Q   HOW MANY TIMES?
26   A   I'M NOT SURE. A FEW TIMES.
27   Q   IS IT POSSIBLE YOU LEFT THE BUILDING ON THE NIGHT OF THE FIRE?
28   A   SURE. EVERYBODY LEFT THE BUILDING.
29   Q   I MEAN BEFORE THE FIRE.
30   A   IT'S POSSIBLE. LIKE MY ATTORNEY SAYS, ANYTHING'S POSSIBLE.
31   Q   BUT DID YOU LEAVE THE BUILDING THAT NIGHT, BEFORE THE FIRE
32   BY MS. WACHS: OBJECTION—ASKED AND ANSWERED.
33   BY MR. MORAN: BUT HE DIDN'T ANSWER. HE SAID HE'S NOT SURE—
34   IT'S POSSIBLE.
35   BY MS. WACHS: THAT'S AN ANSWER, AND IT'S ALL THE ANSWER
36   YOU'RE GOING TO GET.
37   BY MR. MORAN:
38   Q   MR. WALSH, DID YOU BRING ANY FLAMMABLE LIQUIDS WITH
39   YOU WHEN YOU REPORTED FOR WORK THE NIGHT OF THE FIRE?
40   BY MS. WACHS: MR. WALSH, I'M INSTRUCTING YOU NOT TO ANSWER
41   THAT QUESTION.

Sample summary
for the deposition of Elizah Walsh

472   Witness isn't sure where he was when fire alarm sounded—possibly in storage room or hallway outside of storage room.

Someone yelled "smoke"—or, it could have been "Spoke," the name of the fire marshall. Everyone began screaming and running around. Witness says he remained pretty calm, due to Navy experience.

The alarm went off about 9:30 or 9:35.

He doesn't know how many employees were on duty.

The foreman on duty was Mr. Frixett. He always worked the night shifts. Not sure whether Frixett was in the building when alarm sounded [comments by witness reflect dislike for the foreman].

473   Has no memory of whether Frixett was in building. He may have been in accounting office with female employee, Jill "Blaze" Davidovich, but witness doesn't know.

Witness saw no strangers in the building that night. He saw no unauthorized persons in the building [strangers or not].

473-4   Witness was only security guard on duty in that building the night of the fire. There should have been three other security guards in other buildings, but he doesn't know if all three were.

474   If a guard calls in sick, another security guard may have to cover an additional building. On that night, he did not have to cover another building.

Witness is not sure whether he left the building for other reason(s).

It has been several months. "It's hard to remember what exactly happened when."

On some occasions he has had to cover other buildings. He's not sure how many times.

It's possible that he left the building that night, before the fire.

[Question: "Mr. Walsh, did you bring any flammable liquids with you when you reported for work the night of the fire?" Ms. Wachs directs witness not to answer that question.]

Excerpt from deposition of Matilda Bollen:
(To be used for deposition summary assignment)

1   Q   MS. BOLLEN, PLEASE TELL US SOMETHING ABOUT YOUR PRO-
2 FESSIONAL BACKGROUND.
3   A   I WAS GRADUATED FROM THE UNIVERSITY OF MICHIGAN WITH A
4 DEGREE IN MICROBIOLOGY. I THEN COMPLETED MEDICAL SCHOOL AT
5 U.S.C. IN 1973 AFTER FINISHING MY RESIDENCY AND PASSING MY
6 BOARDS, I PRACTICED WITH AN HMO FOR SEVERAL YEARS. I AM A
7 DIPLOMATE OF THE AMERICAN BOARD OF FAMILY PRACTICE AND THE
8 AMERICAN BOARD OF INTERNAL MEDICINE. FROM 1981 UNTIL 1987 I

SPECIALIZED IN PATHOLOGY AND INTERNAL MEDICINE AT THE COUNTY-U.S.C. MEDICAL CENTER, IN LOS ANGELES.

I HAVE WRITTEN TWO MEDICAL TEXTBOOKS ON PATHOLOGY AND ONE ON PATHOPHYSIOLOGY. I HAVE PUBLISHED EXTENSIVELY IN MEDICAL JOURNALS. A LIST OF MY ARTICLES IS ATTACHED TO THE RESUME WHICH YOU HAVE. SINCE 1985 I HAVE SERVED AS A CONSULTANT PATHOLOGIST AT THE U.C.L.A. MEDICAL CENTER.

Q NO PROBLEMS WITH CROSS-TOWN RIVALRY, I TAKE IT.

A NO. I'M NOT MUCH INTERESTED IN COLLEGE SPORTS.

Q I UNDERSTAND THAT YOU ARE PROFESSIONALLY AMBIDEXTROUS, SO TO SPEAK. COULD YOU TELL US SOMETHING OF YOUR BACKGROUND IN LAW.

A I HAVE ALWAYS BEEN INTERESTED IN MEDICAL ETHICS AND LEGAL ISSUES IN MEDICINE. IN 1987 I ENTERED LAW SCHOOL AT U.S.C. AND RECEIVED MY J.D. IN 1991. I WAS ASSISTANT EDITOR OF THE LAW REVIEW AND GRADUATED WITH HONORS.

Q DID YOU TAKE THE BAR EXAM?

A YES, TWICE—THAT IS, ONCE EACH IN TWO STATES. I WAS ADMITTED TO THE CALIFORNIA BAR IN 1992, AND THE NEW YORK BAR IN 1994.

Q HAVE YOU PRACTICED LAW IN EITHER CALIFORNIA OR NEW YORK?

A YES, IN CALIFORNIA—SINCE 1992.

Q BUT, NOT IN NEW YORK?

A NOT IN NEW YORK. BUT I OFTEN CONSULT WITH CALIFORNIA COUNSEL CONCERNING MEDICAL MALPRACTICE ISSUES UNDER NEW YORK LAW.

Q ARE YOU PRACTICING LAW TODAY, MS. BOLLEN?

A YES. I REPRESENT MEDICAL DOCTORS IN MALPRACTICE LITIGATION. I ALSO CONSULT IN THAT FIELD.

Q AND IN THIS LITIGATION, ARE YOU SERVING AS AN EXPERT WITNESS FOR THE PLAINTIFF?

A YES, THAT'S CORRECT.

Q HOW OFTEN HAVE YOU SERVED AS AN EXPERT WITNESS IN MALPRACTICE LITIGATION?

A SEVEN TIMES.

Q HAVE ALL OF THOSE CASES BEEN ON BEHALF OF PLAINTIFFS?

A YES, I HAVE—THEY HAVE.

Q MS. BOLLEN—OR SHOULD I SAY DR. BOLLEN? OR COUNSELOR?

A AS YOU WISH.

Q DR. BOLLEN, DO YOU CONTINUE TO PRACTICE MEDICINE?

1   A   I DON'T TREAT PATIENTS, NO. HOWEVER, I TEACH PART-TIME IN
2   THE MEDICAL SCHOOL AT U.S.C.
3   Q   WHAT COURSES DO YOU TEACH, DOCTOR?
4   A   I USUALLY TEACH ONE CLASS IN PATHOPHYSIOLOGY EVERY
5   SEMESTER. OCCASIONALLY, I PRESENT SEMINARS ON MEDICAL ETHICS
6   OR LEGAL ISSUES IN MEDICINE.
7   Q   WHAT IS "PATHOPHYSIOLOGY"?
8   A   IT IS THE PHYSIOLOGY OF DISEASED ORGANS AND THE
9   CHANGES WHICH ACCOMPANY THE DEVELOPMENT OF DISEASE.
10   Q   WE'LL GET BACK TO THAT LATER, BUT RIGHT NOW, THIS LITI-
11   GATION CONCERNS AN ALLEGED MISDIAGNOSIS—THAT IS, A FAILURE
12   TO CORRECTLY DIAGNOSE LYMPHATIC CANCER. ARE YOU AN ONCOLO-
13   GIST, DOCTOR?
14   A   NO, I'M NOT.
15   Q   WHAT QUALIFIES YOU, THEN, TO EVALUATE THE DIAGNOSIS
16   MADE BY A BOARD-CERTIFIED ONCOLOGIST OF MANY YEARS' EXPERI-
17   ENCE? A DOCTOR WHO ALSO IS RECOGNIZED FOR HIS CANCER RE-
18   SEARCH?
19   A   FIRST OF ALL, I WOULD NEVER QUESTION THE CREDENTIALS OF
20   DR. EXACTO. HE IS, INDISPUTABLY, A LEADER IN CANCER RESEARCH
21   AND IS HIGHLY QUALIFIED TO DIAGNOSE LYMPHATIC CANCER. THE IS-
22   SUE IN THIS CASE IS NOT HIS QUALIFICATIONS, BUT WHETHER HE WAS
23   NEGLIGENT IN HIS DIAGNOSTIC PROCEDURES IN A PARTICULAR IN-
24   STANCE. I BELIEVE THAT HE WAS—INEXCUSABLY SO.
25   BY MS. RYDER: OBJECTION—NON-RESPONSIVE.
26   BY MR. WOOD: JOIN.
27   BY MS. TYMES:
28   Q   PLEASE ANSWER MY QUESTION, DOCTOR. WHAT ARE YOUR
29   OWN QUALIFICATIONS TO EVALUATE THE DIAGNOSIS BY DR. EXACTO.
30   A   I HAVE SPECIAL QUALIFICATIONS IN PATHOLOGY. I HAVE PRAC-
31   TICED BOTH AS A TREATING PHYSICIAN AND A PATHOLOGIST. I TEACH
32   IN THE FIELD OF PATHOLOGY. I HAVE CORRECTLY DIAGNOSED LYM-
33   PHATIC CANCER A NUMBER OF TIMES.
34   Q   HOW MANY TIMES, DOCTOR?
35   A   OFF THE TOP OF MY HEAD, I CAN'T SAY EXACTLY. BUT AT LEAST
36   A DOZEN TIMES.
37   Q   WHEN WAS THE LAST YEAR IN WHICH YOU PRACTICED AS A
38   PATHOLOGIST?
39   A   I LAST PRACTICED ON A FULL-TIME BASIS IN 1987. HOWEVER, AF-
40   TER PASSING THE CALIFORNIA BAR IN 1992 I RESUMED A PART-TIME
41   PRACTICE AS A CONSULTANT AT U.C.L.A. MEDICAL CENTER. MEDICAL

CONSULTING IN PATHOLOGY IS NOW ABOUT TWENTY PERCENT OF MY CAREER. TEACHING AT U.S.C. IS ABOUT TWENTY PERCENT. I KEEP MY HAND IN.

Q HAVE YOU TREATED ANY PATIENTS SINCE 1986?

A NO, I HAVE NOT.

Q PERHAPS YOU COULD ENLIGHTEN ME AND THE FIVE OTHER ATTORNEYS PRESENT TODAY. ACCORDING TO YOUR ANALYSIS, IN WHAT WAY WAS DR. EXACTO NEGLIGENT IN HIS DIAGNOSTIC PROCEDURES?

A DR. EXACTO RAN THE USUAL TESTS FOR DIAGNOSIS OF THE PRESENTING SYMPTOMS. AND HE FOUND NO PATHOLOGY. BUT HE DID NOT RECOGNIZE THAT THOSE SYMPTOMS—ALTHOUGH ATYPICAL FOR LYMPHATIC CANCER—COULD INDICATE THE PRESENCE OF A LYMPHOMA. IN OTHER WORDS, DR. EXACTO LOOKED AT THE USUAL CAUSES FOR THE PRESENTING SYMPTOMS, BUT DIDN'T QUESTION THOSE PRESUMED CAUSES AND PURSUE THE POSSIBILITY OF LYMPHATIC CANCER WHEN NO PATHOLOGY WAS IDENTIFIED THROUGH HIS INITIAL ROUTINE TESTS. THAT ERROR WAS NEGLIGENT.

BY MR. WOOD: OBJECTION—THE WITNESS IS OFFERING A LEGAL CONCLUSION.

BY MS. LOPEZ: BUT THE WITNESS IS AN ATTORNEY, AS WELL AS A DOCTOR. SHE IS EMINENTLY QUALIFIED TO REACH A LEGAL CONCLUSION REGARDING THESE FACTS.

BY MR. WYATT: WHO CARES? THE OBJECTION HAS BEEN MADE. IF IT COMES UP AT TRIAL, THE COURT CAN RULE ON THE OBJECTION.

BY MS. TYMES: SO IT CAN—AND IT WILL. BUT LET'S GET ON WITH THIS.

Q DOCTOR, HOW WOULD YOU HAVE DIFFERED IN EVALUATING THE PLAINTIFF'S PRESENTING SYMPTOMS? IN OTHER WORDS, WHAT SHOULD DR. EXACTO HAVE DONE WHICH HE DID NOT DO?

A IF DR. EXACTO HAD ORDERED A LYMPHANGIOGRAM, THE PRESENCE OF THE LYMPHOMA WOULD HAVE BEEN APPARENT. ALTHOUGH THAT MIGHT NOT BE THE FIRST ADDITIONAL TEST TO COME TO MIND, IF HE HAD PROCEEDED BEYOND THE ROUTINE TESTS WHICH HE ORDERED—AND WHICH WERE UNPRODUCTIVE—EVENTUALLY HE WOULD HAVE ORDERED THE LYMPHANGIOGRAM. BUT HE NEVER WENT BEYOND THE OBVIOUS—AND THE OBVIOUS TESTS SHOWED NOTHING ABNORMAL. THE LACK OF FURTHER TESTING WAS FATAL TO THE PATIENT. THAT'S ABOUT AS SERIOUS AS YOU CAN GET.

APPENDIX B

Sample Brief of Court Opinion

MEMORANDUM

TO: George Teshima
FROM: Marge Boynton
RE: Brief of *Morris v. Berman,* 159 Cal. App. 2d 770 (1958)
Statute of Limitations/Laches, and
Actions for Undue Influence
DATE: March 15, 2000

I. Factual Background

This case was an action to establish a constructive trust in real and personal property, and for an accounting.

Leo, a divorced father of two daughters, married a widow, Anne. Anne was the mother of one son by her previous marriage. Leo and Anne were married in 1939.

The trial court made numerous findings of fact. Beginning immediately after the marriage of Anne and Leo, Anne set in motion a plan to alienate Leo's daughters from their father. She induced Leo to transfer ownership of Leo's separate real property into joint tenancy with herself. Her conduct continued for some years and involved participation by an attorney and a tax advisor, the former a friend and accomplice of Anne's, and the latter a relative and accomplice of Anne's.

Through a complicated series of transactions, Anne's plan progressed successfully from the time of her marriage to Leo in 1939 through the date of Leo's death in 1952. Leo's daughters commenced this action several months after Leo's death.

II. Procedural History

The defendants (Anne and her accomplices) demurred generally on the grounds that the action was barred by laches and by the statute of limitations. The demurrer was sustained with leave to amend.

The plaintiff then filed an amended complaint alleging fraud and undue influence. The defendants again demurred generally and on the grounds of laches and the statute of limitations. The trial court rejected the second demurrer to all but one cause of action. In the defendants' answer, they did not plead defenses to the effect that the causes of action were barred by laches and the statute of limitations. After the trial but before the findings and judgment had been signed, the defendants moved to amend their answer by alleging that the causes of action were barred by laches and the statute of limitations. Their motion to amend was denied.

III. Trial Court Holding

The trial court found that Anne and her son had gained control of Leo's properties by exercising undue influence upon him, and that they continued to hold the properties as trustees for Leo and his heirs. The confidential relationship and undue influence having continued, and the property having then been held by them as trustees, ". . . it appears that the causes of action were not barred by the statute of limitations or by laches."

IV. Holding by Court of Appeal

The Court of Appeal affirmed.
Key holding (at pp. 794–795):

> As a general rule, the statute of limitations does not run where the parties occupy a fiduciary relationship toward each other and the relationship has not been repudiated or terminated by the parties. This rule is applicable to resulting trusts. . . . (31 Cal.Jur.2d 451 sec. 22; See also *Estate of Clary,* 203 C. 335, 341, 264 P. 242.)

(Supreme Court hearing denied.)

V. Comments

Although not explicit in the record, from the extensive detail about the defendants' misconduct, it appears virtually certain that the daughters had been aware of the undue influence over a period of many years. There is no indication whether they expressed objections prior to their father's death.

The undue influence prior to the father's death appears to have created the basis for holding the property in trust, that trust then continuing after death, and for tolling the statute of limitations for transactions in the earlier years of the marriage.

APPENDIX C

Sample Memorandum of Law

NOTE: The legal issues in the following memorandum are more difficult than those that new paralegals normally would research. However, the memorandum illustrates well the integration of material from a variety of primary and secondary sources. To fully understand the memorandum, the student should first review the following terms in the Glossary:

emblements	lessor	remainderman
leasehold	personal representative	tenancy at will
lessee		

An ordinary dictionary can be consulted to clarify the difference between *annual* and *perennial* plants.

Memorandum of Law

TO: George Teshima
FROM: Marge Boynton
RE: Definition of "Growing Crops," and the Lessee's Right to Harvests Following Termination of Lease
DATE: February 17, 2000

Questions Presented:

1. What is the definition of "growing crop" as used in a lease agreement, where that term is not defined?
2. What are the rights of a lessee to the subsequent multiple harvests of a perennial crop following the termination of a lease of uncertain term, or of a tenancy at will?

I. Brief Answers

1. Although not defined by statute, California courts have considered the meaning of "growing crops" in the context of property taxation. The courts

generally have regarded a "growing crop" to be an annual plant already sown, but not yet ready for harvest. In some cases, the fruit of trees has been regarded as a growing crop, if the fruit is mature or has set.

2. Unless otherwise provided by the terms of the lease, under the *doctrine of emblements* a former lessee has the right to enter the property following termination of the lease period for the purpose of maintaining and harvesting a crop, *provided that* the following conditions are met:

   a. It was a tenancy at will or a lease of uncertain duration;
   b. The crop was planted before the notice of termination; and,
   c. The exercise of the lessee's right to enter and harvest occurs within a reasonable time after the tenancy has ended.

In the case of perennial crops or fruit trees, secondary authorities suggest that the right of emblements is limited to the harvest of a *single* crop.

II. Statement of Facts

In January 1996, the client entered into a ten-year lease under which more than 240 acres of his land were leased to a farmer for agricultural purposes. Paragraph Fifteen of the lease agreement provides that the lessor may terminate the lease at any time after three years, by giving 90 days' notice in writing. Another paragraph states, "In the event this lease is terminated by the lessor, prior to the termination date provided in this Lease Agreement, lessor shall permit lessee to harvest any growing crop on said land."

On September 1, 1999 the client/lessor notified the lessee in writing that the lease would be terminated effective January 1, 2000. Between 1996 and 1999, the lessee had planted alfalfa on various portions of the land under lease. By the fall of 1999, 197 acres were planted in alfalfa. The lessee now claims the right to harvest subsequent annual crops of alfalfa for a period of four years, or in the alternative to be compensated for the market value of those crops.

III. Analysis

Because the term "growing crop" is not defined in the lease, nor by statute, we must rely upon case law and secondary authorities. In *Miller v. County of Kern*, 137 Cal. 516 (1902), the California Supreme Court considered the question of whether alfalfa is a "growing crop" in the context of property taxation law. (Section 1 of Article XIII of the California State Constitution exempts "growing crops" from taxation.) At pages 524–525, the Supreme Court stated:

> Alfalfa is not a grass indigenous to the land of California; it is a perennial plant, which, when properly cared for, like fruit-trees, produces annual crops of hay or pasturage, for an indefinite number of years. As a hay crop, it is unlike wheat or barley, sown for hay, which produces but a single annual crop and no more.

The Supreme Court further compared alfalfa to berry vines, asparagus, celery and other plants, "which, when planted, are more or less permanent in the soil and produce annual crops from year to year without replanting, as does the alfalfa root . . ." (At p. 525.) The *Miller* court held, therefore, that alfalfa is not a "growing crop" as that term is used in Article XIII of the California State Constitution.

Although our client's situation does not raise a question of taxation law, the Supreme Court's distinction between annual and perennial crops may be helpful. (See also, *Nunes Turfgrass, Inc. v. County of Kern*, 111 Cal. App. 3d 855, 168 Cal.

Rptr. 842 [citing *Miller*, and holding that turf grass is not a "growing crop" for tax purposes even though it is harvested as sod and must be replanted annually].)

In the case of a tenancy at will, or of a leasehold of uncertain duration, the tenant's right of emblements is well established. "Emblements are profits rightfully arising from the rightful labor of the tenant. The term includes *annual* crops to which the tenant has contributed his labor, as well as fruit grown on trees, at least where the fruit is *mature and ready to pick when the estate terminates,* although the trees themselves are not included." [Emphasis added. Footnotes omitted.] *42 Cal. Jur. 3d,* Landlord and Tenant § 270, p. 307. (See also, 141 A.L.R. 1240.)

Witkin has stated:

> The emblements doctrine at common law did not apply to the product of perennials, such as fruit and nut trees or vines requiring only one planting and thereafter in theory bearing crops naturally (fructus naturales) rather than by regular labor (fructus industriales). There is some modern authority recognizing the necessity of regular cultivation and care of orchard crops and applying the emblements doctrine thereto. However, if the fruit has not even set at the time of termination, the right to emblements may be denied. [Citations.] Witkin, *Summary of California Law,* 9th Ed., Real Property § 247.

In *Lloyd v. First National Trust and Savings Bank,* 101 Cal. App. 2d 579 (1951), 225 P.2d 962, the appellate court considered the case in which a personal representative claimed ownership of a crop of oranges which was harvested after the death of the life tenant. Although the court based its holding upon the terms of the instrument creating the life estate, it discussed (in *dictum?*) the doctrine of emblements:

> It is plaintiff's position that the common-law rule has been modified pertaining to fruit grown on trees because, for income tax purposes, where citrus groves are sold with fruit on the trees, a portion of the sales price must be allocated to the fruit and the balance to the land and trees. . .
> (Page 583.)

It is noteworthy that the *Lloyd* court did not comment on this attempt to draw an analogy to case law on "growing crops" in tax situations. Addressing the plaintiff's theory, the court stated:

> If the doctrine of emblements were applied to fruit on trees, under all conditions, a life tenant's estate would have a claim from the moment the fruit is set, even though the fruit did not mature and was not picked until fourteen or fifteen months after the death of the life tenant and even though all labor [subsequent to the life tenancy] had been performed by the remainderman.
> (Page 584.)

The *Lloyd* court continued:

> According to some authorities, intention has been declared the criterion in deciding whether fruit of trees and perennial roots should be included within the doctrine of emblements, and it has been held that if the trees, bushes or vines require only one planting and will bear successive annual crops, the produce goes to the betterment of the land and will be classed with *fructus naturales*, and the right of emblements will not attach [citations].
> (Page 584.)

Noting that case law had not drawn "an exact line of demarcation as to where the doctrine [of emblements] will apply" to fruit grown on trees, the *Lloyd* court cited *Blaeholder v. Guthrie*, 17 Cal. App. 297, 119 P. 524 (1911), which held that if the fruit is mature at the termination of the estate the doctrine should be applied. In *Blaeholder*, orange and walnut crops grown during the lifetime of a life tenant were held to be governed by the doctrine of emblements. But in that case, all work had been done upon the crop for that year, and the fruit had matured and was ready to pick at the time of the death of the life tenant.

No California case has been found which determined the rights to multiple annual harvests subsequent to the termination of a lease or tenancy at will. However, a Tennessee court has held that the right of emblements does not include more than one crop from the same stubble. *Hendrixson v. Cardwell*, 68 Tenn. 389 (1876).

The doctrine of emblements carries with it a right of entry upon the property to maintain the crop and harvest it. *Lloyd, supra*, 101 Cal. App. at 582 (quoting *31 C.J.S. 47,* § 40). But that right is limited by necessity and time. "The right of a tenant to take and carry away unharvested crops upon the termination of his tenancy, when such right exists, must be exercised within a reasonable time after the tenancy has ended. [Citations.]" 141 A.L.R. 1240, 1248. The determination of what constitutes a "reasonable time" may present a difficulty. An Alabama court has held that the time allowed depends upon the facts of each particular case, such as the weather, reasonable opportunity for removal, etc., to be determined by the trier of fact. *McLane v. Gilbert*, 30 Ala. App. 261, 4 So. 2d 203 (1941).

IV. Conclusion

Under California case law, the term "growing crops" has been defined in the context of taxation law under the California Constitution. However, the distinction made by the courts between annual and perennial crops in the context of taxation law may be useful in defining the limits of the doctrine of emblements.

In discussing the doctrine of emblements, the secondary sources cited above postulate a theory which effectively limits the displaced tenant to a single post-tenancy harvest, whether it be of an annual crop or the fruit of perennial trees. Since, in the case of alfalfa, new growth rises each year from the stubble left by harvest, the holding by the *Hendrixson* court in that regard seems eminently reasonable. Otherwise, it would appear that a former tenant has all rights to subsequent harvests for the entire lifetime of a newly planted perennial field crop, and thereby could deny the former lessor of the fruits of ownership for an indefinite period into the future.

APPENDIX D

Code of Ethics and Professional Responsibility of the National Association of Legal Assistants, Inc.

PREAMBLE. A legal assistant must adhere strictly to the accepted standards of legal ethics and to the general principles of proper conduct. The performance of the duties of the legal assistant shall be governed by specific canons as defined herein so that justice will be served and goals of the profession attained. (See Model Standards and Guidelines for Utilization of Legal Assistants, Section II).

The canons of ethics set forth hereafter are adopted by the National Association of Legal Assistants, Inc. as a general guide intended to aid legal assistants and attorneys. The enumeration of these rules does not mean there are not others of equal importance although not specifically mentioned. Court rules, agency rules and statutes must be taken into consideration when interpreting the canons.

DEFINITION. Legal assistants, also known as paralegals, are a distinguishable group of persons who assist attorneys in the delivery of legal services. Through formal education, training and experience, legal assistants have knowledge and expertise regarding the legal system and substantive and procedural law which qualify them to do work of a legal nature under the supervision of an attorney.

Canon 1. A legal assistant must not perform any of the duties that attorneys only may perform nor take any actions that attorneys may not take.

Canon 2. A legal assistant may perform any task which is properly delegated and supervised by an attorney, as long as the attorney is ultimately responsible to the client, maintains a direct relationship with the client, and assumes professional responsibility for the work product. (See NALA Model Standards and Guidelines, Section IV, Guideline 5.)

(Reproduced with permission of the National Association of Legal Assistants, Tulsa, OK. www.nala.org).

Canon 3. A legal assistant must not: (See NALA Model Standards and Guidelines, Section IV, Guideline 2.)

a. engage in, encourage, or contribute to any act which could constitute the unauthorized practice of law; and

b. establish attorney-client relationships, set fees, give legal opinions or advice, or represent a client before a court or agency unless so authorized by that court or agency; and

c. engage in conduct or take any action which would assist or involve the attorney in a violation of professional ethics or give the appearance of professional impropriety.

Canon 4. A legal assistant must use discretion and professional judgment commensurate with knowledge and experience but must not render independent legal judgment in place of an attorney. The services of an attorney are essential in the public interest whenever such legal judgment is required. (See NALA Model Standards and Guidelines, Section IV, Guideline 3.)

Canon 5. A legal assistant must disclose his or her status as a legal assistant at the outset of any professional relationship with a client, attorney, a court or administrative agency or personnel thereof, or a member of the general public. A legal assistant must act prudently in determining the extent to which a client may be assisted without the presence of an attorney. (See NALA Model Standards and Guidelines, Section IV, Guideline 1.)

Canon 6. A legal assistant must strive to maintain integrity and a high degree of competency through education and training with respect to professional responsibility, local rules, and practice, and through continuing education in substantive areas of law to better assist the legal profession in fulfilling its duty to provide legal service.

Canon 7. A legal assistant must protect the confidences of a client and must not violate any rule or statute now in effect or hereafter enacted controlling the doctrine of privileged communications between a client and an attorney. (See NALA Model Standards and Guidelines, Section IV, Guideline 1.)

Canon 8. A legal assistant must do all other things incidental, necessary, or expedient for the attainment of the ethics and responsibilities as defined by statute or rule of court.

Canon 9. A legal assistant's conduct is guided by bar associations' codes of professional responsibility and rules of professional conduct.

National Association of Legal Assistants, Inc.   Adopted: May 1, 1975

1516 S. Boston • Suite 200 • Tulsa, OK 74119-4464   Revised, 1979, 1988 and 1995

APPENDIX E

National Federation of Paralegal Associations, Inc.

**MODEL CODE
OF ETHICS AND PROFESSIONAL RESPONSIBILITY
AND GUIDELINES FOR ENFORCEMENT**

PREAMBLE

The National Federation of Paralegal Associations, Inc. ("NFPA") is a professional organization comprised of paralegal associations and individual paralegals throughout the United States and Canada. Members of NFPA have varying backgrounds, experiences, education and job responsibilities that reflect the diversity of the paralegal profession. NFPA promotes the growth, development and recognition of the paralegal profession as an integral partner in the delivery of legal services.

In May 1993 NFPA adopted its Model Code of Ethics and Professional Responsibility ("Model Code") to delineate the principles of ethics and conduct to which every paralegal should aspire.

Many paralegal associations throughout the United States have endorsed the concept and content of NFPA's Model Code through the adoption of their own ethical codes. In doing so, paralegals have confirmed the profession's commitment to increase the quality and efficiency of legal services, as well as recognized its responsibilities to the public, the legal community, and colleagues.

Paralegals have recognized, and will continue to recognize, that the profession must continue to evolve to enhance their roles in the delivery of legal services. With increased levels of responsibility comes the need to define and enforce mandatory rules of professional conduct. Enforcement of codes of paralegal conduct is a logical and necessary step to enhance and ensure the confidence of the legal community and the public in the integrity and professional responsibility of paralegals.

In April 1997 NFPA adopted the Model Disciplinary Rules ("Model Rules") to make possible the enforcement of the Canons and Ethical Considerations contained in the NFPA Model Code. A concurrent determination was made that the Model Code of Ethics and Professional Responsibility, formerly aspirational in nature, should be recognized as setting forth the enforceable obligations of all paralegals.

The Model Code and Model Rules offer a framework for professional discipline, either voluntarily or through formal regulatory programs.

Reproduced with permission of the National Federation of Paralegal Associations, Inc.

§ 1. NFPA Model Disciplinary Rules and Ethical Considerations

1.1 A PARALEGAL SHALL ACHIEVE AND MAINTAIN A HIGH LEVEL OF COMPETENCE.

Ethical Considerations

EC-1.1(a) A paralegal shall achieve competency through education, training, and work experience.

EC-1.1(b) A paralegal shall participate in continuing education in order to keep informed of current legal, technical and general developments.

EC-1.1(c) A paralegal shall perform all assignments promptly and efficiently.

1.2 A PARALEGAL SHALL MAINTAIN A HIGH LEVEL OF PERSONAL AND PROFESSIONAL INTEGRITY.

Ethical Considerations

EC-1.2(a) A paralegal shall not engage in any ex parte communications involving the courts or any other adjudicatory body in an attempt to exert undue influence or to obtain advantage or the benefit of only one party.

EC-1.2(b) A paralegal shall not communicate, or cause another to communicate, with a party the paralegal knows to be represented by a lawyer in a pending matter without the prior consent of the lawyer representing such other party.

EC-1.2(c) A paralegal shall ensure that all timekeeping and billing records prepared by the paralegal are thorough, accurate, honest, and complete.

EC-1.2(d) A paralegal shall not knowingly engage in fraudulent billing practices. Such practices may include, but are not limited to: inflation of hours billed to a client or employer; misrepresentation of the nature of tasks performed; and/or submission of fraudulent expense and distribution documentation.

EC-1.2(e) A paralegal shall be scrupulous, thorough and honest in the identification and maintenance of all funds, securities and other assets of a client and shall provide accurate accounting as appropriate.

EC-1.2(f) A paralegal shall advise the proper authority of non-confidential knowledge of any dishonest or fraudulent acts by any person pertaining to the handling of funds, securities or other assets of a client. The authority to whom the report is made shall depend on the nature and circumstances of the possible misconduct (e.g., ethics committees of law firms, corporations, and/or paralegal associations, local or state bar associations, local prosecutors, administrative agencies, etc.). Failure to report such knowledge is in itself misconduct and shall be treated as such under these rules.

1.3 A PARALEGAL SHALL MAINTAIN A HIGH STANDARD OF PROFESSIONAL CONDUCT.

Ethical Considerations

EC-1.3(a) A paralegal shall refrain from engaging in any conduct that offends the dignity and decorum of proceedings before a court or other adjudicatory body and shall be respectful of all rules and procedures.

EC-1.3(b) A paralegal shall avoid impropriety and the appearance of impropriety and shall not engage in any conduct that would adversely affect his/her fitness to practice. Such conduct may include, but is not limited to: violence, dishonesty, interference with the administration of justice, and/or abuse of a professional position or public office.

EC-1.3(c) Should a paralegal's fitness to practice be compromised by physical or mental illness, causing that paralegal to commit an act that is in direct violation of the Model Code/Model Rules and/or the rules and/or laws governing the jurisdiction in which the paralegal practices, that paralegal may be protected from sanction upon review of the nature and circumstances of that illness.

EC-1.3(d) A paralegal shall advise the proper authority of non-confidential knowledge of any action of another legal professional that clearly demonstrates fraud, deceit, dishonesty, or misrepresentation. The authority to whom the report is made shall depend on the nature and circumstances of the possible misconduct (e.g., ethics committees of law firms, corporations and/or paralegal associations, local or state bar associations, local prosecutors, administrative agencies, etc.). Failure to report such knowledge is in itself misconduct and shall be treated as such under these rules.

EC-1.3(e) A paralegal shall not knowingly assist any individual with the commission of an act that is in direct violation of the Model Code/Model Rules and/or the rules and/or laws governing the jurisdiction in which the paralegal practices.

EC-1.3(f) If a paralegal possesses knowledge of future criminal activity, that knowledge must be reported to the appropriate authority immediately.

1.4 A PARALEGAL SHALL SERVE THE PUBLIC INTEREST BY CONTRIBUTING TO THE IMPROVEMENT OF THE LEGAL SYSTEM AND DELIVERY OF QUALITY LEGAL SERVICES, INCLUDING PRO BONO PUBLICO SERVICES.

Ethical Considerations

EC-1.4(a) A paralegal shall be sensitive to the legal needs of the public and shall promote the development and implementation of programs that address those needs.

EC-1.4(b) A paralegal shall support efforts to improve the legal system and access thereto and shall assist in making changes.

EC-1.4(c) A paralegal shall support and participate in the delivery of Pro Bono Publico services directed toward implementing and improving access to justice, the law, the legal system or the paralegal and legal professions.

EC.1.4(d) A paralegal shall aspire annually to contribute twenty-four (24) hours of Pro Bono Publico services under the supervision of an attorney or as authorized by administrative, statutory or court authority to:

1. persons of limited means; or
2. charitable, religious, civic, community, governmental and educational organizations in matters that are designed primarily to address the legal needs of persons with limited means; or

3. individuals, groups or organizations seeking to secure or protect civil rights, civil liberties or public rights.

1.5 A PARALEGAL SHALL PRESERVE ALL CONFIDENTIAL INFORMATION PROVIDED BY THE CLIENT OR ACQUIRED FROM OTHER SOURCES BEFORE, DURING, AND AFTER THE COURSE OF THE PROFESSIONAL RELATIONSHIP.

Ethical Considerations

EC-1.5(a) A paralegal shall be aware of and abide by all legal authority governing confidential information in the jurisdiction in which the paralegal practices.

EC-1.5(b) A paralegal shall not use confidential information to the disadvantage of the client.

EC-1.5(c) A paralegal shall not use confidential information to the advantage of a paralegal or of a third person.

EC-1.5(d) A paralegal may reveal confidential information only after full disclosure and with the client's written consent; or, when required by law or court order; or, when necessary to prevent the client from committing an act that could result in death or serious bodily injury.

EC-1.5(e) A paralegal shall keep those individuals responsible for the legal representation of a client fully informed of any confidential information the paralegal may have pertaining to that client.

EC-1.5(f) A paralegal shall not engage in any indiscreet communication concerning clients.

1.6 A PARALEGAL SHALL AVOID CONFLICTS OF INTEREST AND SHALL DISCLOSE ANY POSSIBLE CONFLICT TO THE EMPLOYER OR CLIENT, AS WELL AS TO THE PROSPECTIVE EMPLOYERS OR CLIENTS.

Ethical Considerations

EC-1.6(a) A paralegal shall act within the bounds of the law, solely for the benefit of the client, and shall be free of compromising influences and loyalties. Neither the paralegal's personal or business interest, nor those of other clients or third persons, should compromise the paralegal's professional judgment and loyalty to the client.

EC-1.6(b) A paralegal shall avoid conflicts of interest that may arise from previous assignments, whether for a present or past employer or client.

EC-1.6(c) A paralegal shall avoid conflicts of interest that may arise from family relationships and from personal and business interests.

EC-1.6(d) In order to be able to determine whether an actual or potential conflict of interest exists a paralegal shall create and maintain an effective recordkeeping system that identifies clients, matters, and parties with which the paralegal has worked.

EC-1.6(e) A paralegal shall reveal sufficient non-confidential information about a client or former client to reasonably ascertain if an actual or potential conflict of interest exists.

EC-1.6(f) A paralegal shall not participate in or conduct work on any matter where a conflict of interest has been identified.

EC-1.6(g) In matters where a conflict of interest has been identified and the client consents to continued representation, a paralegal shall comply fully with the implementation and maintenance of an Ethical Wall.

1.7 A PARALEGAL'S TITLE SHALL BE FULLY DISCLOSED.

Ethical Considerations

EC-1.7(a) A paralegal's title shall clearly indicate the individual's status and shall be disclosed in all business and professional communications to avoid misunderstandings and misconceptions about the paralegal's role and responsibilities.

EC-1.7(b) A paralegal's title shall be included if the paralegal's name appears on business cards, letterhead, brochures, directories, and advertisements.

EC-1.7(c) A paralegal shall not use letterhead, business cards, or other promotional materials to create a fraudulent impression of his/her status or ability to practice in the jurisdiction in which the paralegal practices.

EC-1.7(d) A paralegal shall not practice under color of any record, diploma, or certificate that has been illegally or fraudulently obtained or issued or which is misrepresentative in any way.

EC-1.7(e) A paralegal shall not participate in the creation, issuance, or dissemination of fraudulent records, diplomas, or certificates.

1.8 A PARALEGAL SHALL NOT ENGAGE IN THE UNAUTHORIZED PRACTICE OF LAW.

Ethical Considerations

EC-1.8(a) A paralegal shall comply with the applicable legal authority governing the unauthorized practice of law in the jurisdiction in which the paralegal practices.

§ 2. NFPA Guidelines for the Enforcement of the Model Code of Ethics and Professional Responsibility

2.1 BASIS FOR DISCIPLINE

2.1(a) Disciplinary investigations and proceedings brought under authority of the Rules shall be conducted in accord with obligations imposed on the paralegal professional by the Model Code of Ethics and Professional Responsibility.

2.2 STRUCTURE OF DISCIPLINARY COMMITTEE

2.2(a) The Disciplinary Committee ("Committee") shall be made up of nine (9) members including the Chair.

2.2(b) Each member of the Committee, including any temporary replacement members, shall have demonstrated working knowledge of ethics/professional responsibility-related issues and activities.

2.2(c) The Committee shall represent a cross-section of practice areas and work experience. The following recommendations are made regarding the members of the Committee.

1. At least one paralegal with one to three years of law-related work experience.
2. At least one paralegal with five to seven years of law related work experience.
3. At least one paralegal with over ten years of law related work experience.
4. One paralegal educator with five to seven years of work experience; preferably in the area of ethics/professional responsibility.
5. One paralegal manager.
6. One lawyer with five to seven years of law-related work experience.
7. One lay member.

2.2(d) The Chair of the Committee shall be appointed within thirty (30) days of its members' induction. The Chair shall have no fewer than ten (10) years of law-related work experience.

2.2(e) The terms of all members of the Committee shall be staggered. Of those members initially appointed, a simple majority plus one shall be appointed to a term of one year, and the remaining members shall be appointed to a term of two years. Thereafter, all members of the Committee shall be appointed to terms of two years.

2.2(f) If for any reason the terms of a majority of the Committee will expire at the same time, members may be appointed to terms of one year to maintain continuity of the Committee.

2.2(g) The Committee shall organize from its members a three-tiered structure to investigate, prosecute and/or adjudicate charges of misconduct. The members shall be rotated among the tiers.

2.3 OPERATION OF COMMITTEE

2.3(a) The Committee shall met on an as-needed basis to discuss, investigate, and/or adjudicate alleged violations of the Model Code/Model Rules.

2.3(b) A majority of the members of the Committee present at a meeting shall constitute a quorum.

2.3(c) A Recording Secretary shall be designated to maintain complete and accurate minutes of all Committee meetings. All such minutes shall be kept confidential until a decision has been made that the matter will be set for hearing as set forth in Section 6.1 below.

2.3(d) If any member of the Committee has a conflict of interest with the Charging Party, the Responding Party, or the allegations of misconduct, that member shall not take part in any hearing or deliberations concerning those allegations. If the absence of that member creates a lack of a quorum for the Committee, then a temporary replacement for the member shall be appointed.

2.3(e) Either the Charging Party or the Responding Party may request that, for good cause shown, any member of the Committee not participate in a hearing or deliberation. All such requests shall be honored. If the absence of a Committee member under those circumstances creates a lack of a quorum for the Committee, then a temporary replacement for that member shall be appointed.

2.3(f) All discussions and correspondence of the Committee shall be kept confidential until a decision has been made that the matter will be set for hearing as set forth in Section 6.1 below.

2.3(g) All correspondence from the Committee to the Responding Party regarding any charge of misconduct and any decisions made regarding the charge shall be mailed certified mail, return receipt requested, to the Responding Party's last known address and shall be clearly marked with a "Confidential" designation.

2.4 PROCEDURE FOR THE REPORTING OF ALLEGED VIOLATIONS OF THE MODEL CODE/DISCIPLINARY RULES

2.4(a) An individual or entity in possession of non-confidential knowledge or information concerning possible instances of misconduct shall make a confidential written report to the Committee within thirty (30) days of obtaining same. This report shall include all details of the alleged misconduct.

2.4(b) The Committee so notified shall inform the Responding Party of the allegations(s) of misconduct no later than ten (10) business days after receiving the confidential written report from the Charging Party.

2.4(c) Notification to the Responding Party shall include the identity of the Charging Party, unless, for good cause shown, the Charging Party requests anonymity.

2.4(d) The Responding Party shall reply to the allegations within ten (10) business days of notification.

2.5 PROCEDURE FOR THE INVESTIGATION OF A CHARGE OF MISCONDUCT

2.5(a) Upon receipt of a Charge of Misconduct ("Charge"), or on its own initiative, the Committee shall initiate an investigation.

2.5(b) If, upon initial or preliminary review, the Committee makes a determination that the charges are either without basis in fact or, if proven, would not constitute professional misconduct, the Committee shall dismiss the allegations of misconduct. If such determination of dismissal cannot be made, a formal investigation shall be initiated.

2.5(c) Upon the decision to conduct a formal investigation, the Committee shall:

1. mail to the Charging and Responding Parties within three (3) business days of that decision notice of the commencement of a formal investigation. That notification shall be in writing and shall contain a complete explanation of all Charge(s), as well as the reasons for a formal investigation and shall cite the applicable codes and rules;

2. allow the Responding Party thirty (30) days to prepare and submit a confidential response to the Committee, which response shall address each charge specifically and shall be in writing; and

3. upon receipt of the response to the notification, have thirty (30) days to investigate the Charge(s). If an extension of time

is deemed necessary, that extension shall not exceed ninety (90) days.

2.5(d) Upon conclusion of the investigation, the Committee may:
1. dismiss the Charge upon the finding that it has no basis in fact;
2. dismiss the Charge upon the finding that, if proven, the Charge would not constitute Misconduct;
3. refer the matter for hearing by the Tribunal; or
4. in the case of criminal activity, refer the Charge(s) and all investigation results to the appropriate authority.

2.6 PROCEDURE FOR A MISCONDUCT HEARING BEFORE A TRIBUNAL

2.6(a) Upon the decision by the Committee that a matter should be heard, all parties shall be notified and a hearing date shall be set. The hearing shall take place no more than thirty (30) days from the conclusion of the formal investigation.

2.6(b) The Responding Party shall have the right to counsel. The parties and the Tribunal shall have the right to call any witnesses and introduce any documentation that they believe will lead to the fair and reasonable resolution of the matter.

2.6(c) Upon completion of the hearing, the Tribunal shall deliberate and present a written decision to the parties in accordance with procedures as set forth by the Tribunal.

2.6(d) Notice of the decision of the Tribunal shall be appropriately published.

2.7 SANCTIONS

2.7(a) Upon a finding of the Tribunal that misconduct has occurred, any of the following sanctions, or others as may be deemed appropriate, may be imposed upon the Responding Party, either singularly or in combination:
1. letter of reprimand to the Responding Party; counseling;
2. attendance at an ethics course approved by the Tribunal; probation;
3. suspension of license/authority to practice; revocation of license/authority to practice;
4. imposition of a fine; assessment of costs; or
5. in the instance of criminal activity, referral to the appropriate authority.

2.7(b) Upon the expiration of any period of probation, suspension, or revocation, the Responding Party may make application for reinstatement. With the application for reinstatement, the Responding Party must show proof of having complied with all aspects of the sanctions imposed by the Tribunal.

2.8 APPELLATE PROCEDURES

2.8(a) The parties shall have the right to appeal the decision of the Tribunal in accordance with the procedure as set forth by the Tribunal.

Definitions

"**Appellate Body**" means a body established to adjudicate an appeal to any decision made by a Tribunal or other decision-making body with respect to formally-heard Charges of Misconduct.

"**Charge of Misconduct**" means a written submission by any individual or entity to an ethics committee, paralegal association, bar association, law enforcement agency, judicial body, government agency, or other appropriate body or entity, that sets forth non-confidential information regarding any instance of alleged misconduct by an individual paralegal or paralegal entity.

"**Charging Party**" means any individual or entity who submits a Charge of Misconduct against an individual paralegal or paralegal entity.

"**Competency**" means the demonstration of: diligence, education, skill, and mental, emotional, and physical fitness reasonably necessary for the performance of paralegal services.

"**Confidential Information**" means information relating to a client, whatever its source, that is not public knowledge nor available to the public. ("**Non-Confidential Information**" would generally include the name of the client and the identity of the matter for which the paralegal provided services.)

"**Disciplinary Hearing**" means the confidential proceeding conducted by a committee or other designated body or entity concerning any instance of alleged misconduct by an individual paralegal or paralegal entity.

"**Disciplinary Committee**" means any committee that has been established by an entity such as a paralegal association, bar association, judicial body, or government agency to: (a) identify, define and investigate general ethical considerations and concerns with respect to paralegal practice; (b) administer and enforce the Model Code and Model Rules and; (c) discipline any individual paralegal or paralegal entity found to be in violation of same.

"**Disclose**" means communication of information reasonably sufficient to permit identification of the significance of the matter in question.

"**Ethical Wall**" means the screening method implemented in order to protect a client from a conflict of interest. An Ethical Wall generally includes, but is not limited to, the following elements: (1) prohibit the paralegal from having any connection with the matter; (2) ban discussions with or the transfer of documents to or from the paralegal; (3) restrict access to files; and (4) educate all members of the firm, corporation, or entity as to the separation of the paralegal (both organizationally and physically) from the pending matter. For more information regarding the Ethical Wall, see the NFPA publication entitled "The Ethical Wall - Its Application to Paralegals."

"**Ex parte**" means actions or communications conducted at the instance and for the benefit of one party only, and without notice to, or contestation by, any person adversely interested.

"**Investigation**" means the investigation of any charge(s) of misconduct filed against an individual paralegal or paralegal entity by a Committee.

"**Letter of Reprimand**" means a written notice of formal censure or severe reproof administered to an individual paralegal or paralegal entity for unethical or improper conduct.

"**Misconduct**" means the knowing or unknowing commission of an act that is in direct violation of those Canons and Ethical Considerations of any and all applicable codes and/or rules of conduct.

"**Paralegal**" is synonymous with "**Legal Assistant**" and is defined as a person qualified through education, training, or work experience to perform substantive legal work that requires knowledge of legal concepts and is customarily, but not exclusively performed by a lawyer. This person may be retained or employed by a lawyer, law office, governmental agency, or other entity or may be authorized by administrative, statutory, or court authority to perform this work.

"**Proper Authority**" means the local paralegal association, the local or state bar association, committee(s) of the local paralegal or bar association(s), local prosecutor, administrative agency, or other tribunal empowered to investigate or act upon an instance of alleged misconduct.

"**Responding Party**" means an individual paralegal or paralegal entity against whom a Charge of Misconduct has been submitted.

"**Revocation**" means the rescission of the license, certificate or other authority to practice of an individual paralegal or paralegal entity found in violation of those Canons and Ethical Considerations of any and all applicable codes and/or rules of conduct.

"**Suspension**" means the suspension of the license, certificate or other authority to practice of an individual paralegal or paralegal entity found in violation of those Canons and Ethical Considerations of any and all applicable codes and/or rules of conduct.

"**Tribunal**" means the body designated to adjudicate allegations of misconduct.

APPENDIX F

ABA Standing Committee on Legal Assistants

MODEL GUIDELINES FOR THE UTILIZATION OF LEGAL ASSISTANT SERVICES

Guideline 1:

A lawyer is responsible for all of the professional actions of a legal assistant performing legal assistant services at the lawyer's direction and should take reasonable measures to ensure that the legal assistant's conduct is consistent with the lawyer's obligations under the ABA Model Rules of Professional Conduct.

Guideline 2:

Provided the lawyer maintains responsibility for the work product, a lawyer may delegate to a legal assistant any task normally performed by the lawyer except those tasks proscribed to one not licensed as a lawyer by statute, court rule, administrative rule or regulation, controlling authority, the ABA Model Rules of Professional Conduct, or these Guidelines.

Guideline 3:

A lawyer may not delegate to a legal assistant:
 a. Responsibility for establishing an attorney-client relationship.
 b. Responsibility for establishing the amount of a fee to be charged for a legal service.
 c. Responsibility for a legal opinion rendered to a client.

Guideline 4:

It is the lawyer's responsibility to take reasonable measures to ensure that clients, courts, and other lawyers are aware that a legal assistant, whose services are utilized by the lawyer in performing legal services, is not licensed to practice law.

Guideline 5:

A lawyer may identify legal assistants by name and title on the lawyer's letterhead and on business cards identifying the lawyer's firm.

(© American Bar Association. All rights reserved. Reprinted with permission of the American Bar Association)

Guideline 6:

It is the responsibility of a lawyer to take reasonable measures to ensure that all client confidences are preserved by a legal assistant.

Guideline 7:

A lawyer should take reasonable measures to prevent conflicts of interest resulting from a legal assistant's other employment or interests insofar as such other employment or interests would present a conflict of interest if it were that of the lawyer.

Guideline 8:

A lawyer may include a charge for the work performed by a legal assistant in setting a charge for legal services.

Guideline 9:

A lawyer may not split legal fees with a legal assistant nor pay a legal assistant for the referral of legal business. A lawyer may compensate a legal assistant based on the quantity and quality of the legal assistant's work and the value of that work to a law practice, but the legal assistant's compensation may not be contingent, by advance agreement, upon the profitability of the lawyer's practice.

Guideline 10:

A lawyer who employs a legal assistant should facilitate the legal assistant's participation in appropriate continuing education and pro bono publico activities.

APPENDIX G

The United States Constitution

[This text of the Constitution follows the engrossed copy signed by George Washington.]

We the People of the United States, in Order to form a more perfect Union, establish Justice, insure domestic Tranquility, provide for the common defence, promote the general Welfare, and secure the Blessings of Liberty to ourselves and our Posterity, do ordain and establish this Constitution for the United States of America.

ARTICLE I.

Section 1.

All legislative Powers herein granted shall be vested in a Congress of the United States, which shall consist of a Senate and House of Representatives.

Section 2.

Clause 1: The House of Representatives shall be composed of Members chosen every second Year by the People of the several States, and the Electors in each State shall have the Qualifications requisite for Electors of the most numerous Branch of the State Legislature.

Clause 2: No Person shall be a Representative who shall not have attained to the Age of twenty five Years, and been seven Years a Citizen of the United States, and who shall not, when elected, be an Inhabitant of that State in which he shall be chosen.

Clause 3: Representatives and direct Taxes shall be apportioned among the several States which may be included within this Union, according to their respective Numbers, which shall be determined by adding to the whole Number of free Persons, including those bound to Service for a Term of Years, and excluding Indians not taxed, three fifths of all other Persons. [The part of this Clause relating to the mode of apportionment of representatives among the several States has been affected by Section 2 of amendment XIV, and as to taxes on incomes without apportionment by amendment XVI.] The actual Enumeration shall be made within three Years after the first Meeting of the Congress of the United States, and within every subsequent Term of ten Years, in such Manner as they shall by Law direct. The Number of Representatives shall not exceed one for every thirty Thousand, but each State shall have at Least one Representative; and until such enumeration shall be made, the State of New Hampshire shall be entitled to chuse three, Massachusetts eight, Rhode-Island and Providence Plantations one, Connecticut five, New-York six, New Jersey four, Pennsylvania eight, Delaware one, Maryland six, Virginia ten, North Carolina five, South Carolina five, and Georgia three.

Clause 4: When vacancies happen in the Representation from any State, the Executive Authority thereof shall issue Writs of Election to fill such Vacancies.

Clause 5: The House of Representatives shall chuse their Speaker and other Officers; and shall have the sole Power of Impeachment.

Section 3.

Clause 1: The Senate of the United States shall be composed of two Senators from each State, chosen by the Legislature thereof, for six Years; and each Senator shall have one Vote. [This Clause has been affected by Clause 1 of amendment XVII.]

Clause 2: Immediately after they shall be assembled in Consequence of the first Election, they shall be divided as equally as may be into three Classes. The Seats of the Senators of the first Class shall be vacated at the Expiration of the second Year, of the second Class at the Expiration of the fourth Year, and of the third Class at the Expiration of the sixth Year, so that one third may be chosen every second Year; and if Vacancies happen by Resignation, or otherwise, during the Recess of the Legislature of any State, the Executive thereof may make temporary Appointments until the next Meeting of the Legislature, which shall then fill such Vacancies. [This Clause has been affected by Clause 2 of amendment XVIII.]

Clause 3: No Person shall be a Senator who shall not have attained to the Age of thirty Years, and been nine Years a Citizen of the United States, and who shall not, when elected, be an Inhabitant of that State for which he shall be chosen.

Clause 4: The Vice President of the United States shall be President of the Senate, but shall have no Vote, unless they be equally divided.

Clause 5: The Senate shall chuse their other Officers, and also a President pro tempore, in the Absence of the Vice President, or when he shall exercise the Office of President of the United States.

Clause 6: The Senate shall have the sole Power to try all Impeachments. When sitting for that Purpose, they shall be on Oath or Affirmation. When the President of the United States is tried, the Chief Justice shall preside: And no Person shall be convicted without the Concurrence of two thirds of the Members present.

Clause 7: Judgment in Cases of Impeachment shall not extend further than to removal from Office, and disqualification to hold and enjoy any Office of honor, Trust or Profit under the United States: but the Party convicted shall nevertheless be liable and subject to Indictment, Trial, Judgment and Punishment, according to Law.

Section 4.

Clause 1: The Times, Places and Manner of holding Elections for Senators and Representatives, shall be prescribed in each State by the Legislature thereof; but the Congress may at any time by Law make or alter such Regulations, except as to the Places of chusing Senators.

Clause 2: The Congress shall assemble at least once in every Year, and such Meeting shall be on the first Monday in December, unless they shall by Law appoint a different Day. [This Clause has been affected by amendment XX.]

Section 5.

Clause 1: Each House shall be the Judge of the Elections, Returns and Qualifications of its own Members, and a Majority of each shall constitute a Quorum to do Business; but a smaller Number may adjourn from day to day, and may be authorized to compel the Attendance of absent Members, in such Manner, and under such Penalties as each House may provide.

Clause 2: Each House may determine the Rules of its Proceedings, punish its Members for disorderly Behaviour, and, with the Concurrence of two thirds, expel a Member.

Clause 3: Each House shall keep a Journal of its Proceedings, and from time to time publish the same, excepting such Parts as may in their Judgment require Secrecy; and the Yeas and Nays of the Members of either House on any question shall, at the Desire of one fifth of those Present, be entered on the Journal.

Clause 4: Neither House, during the Session of Congress, shall, without the Consent of the other, adjourn for more than three days, nor to any other Place than that in which the two Houses shall be sitting.

Section 6.

Clause 1: The Senators and Representatives shall receive a Compensation for their Services, to be ascertained by Law, and paid out of the Treasury of the United States. [This Clause has been affected by amendment XXVII.] They shall in all Cases, except Treason, Felony and Breach of the Peace, be privileged from Arrest during their Attendance at the Session of their respective Houses, and in going to and returning from the same; and for any Speech or Debate in either House, they shall not be questioned in any other Place.

Clause 2: No Senator or Representative shall, during the Time for which he was elected, be appointed to any civil Office under the Authority of the United States, which shall have been created, or the Emoluments whereof shall have been encreased during such time; and no Person holding any Office under the United States, shall be a Member of either House during his Continuance in Office.

Section 7.

Clause 1: All Bills for raising Revenue shall originate in the House of Representatives; but the Senate may propose or concur with Amendments as on other Bills.

Clause 2: Every Bill which shall have passed the House of Representatives and the Senate, shall, before it become a Law, be presented to the President of the United States; If he approve he shall sign it, but if not he shall return it, with his Objections to that House in which it shall have originated, who shall enter the Objections at large on their Journal, and proceed to reconsider it. If after such Reconsideration two thirds of that House shall agree to pass the Bill, it shall be sent, together with the Objections, to the other House, by which it shall likewise be reconsidered, and if approved by two thirds of that House, it shall become a Law. But in all such Cases the Votes of both Houses shall be determined by Yeas and Nays, and the Names of the Persons voting for and against the Bill shall be entered on the Journal of each House respectively. If any Bill shall not be returned by the President within ten Days (Sundays excepted) after it shall have been presented to him, the Same shall be a Law, in like Manner as if he had signed it, unless the Congress by their Adjournment prevent its Return, in which Case it shall not be a Law.

Clause 3: Every Order, Resolution, or Vote to which the Concurrence of the Senate and House of Representatives may be necessary (except on a question of Adjournment) shall be presented to the President of the United States; and before the Same shall take Effect, shall be approved by him, or being disapproved by him, shall be repassed by two thirds of the Senate and House of Representatives, according to the Rules and Limitations prescribed in the Case of a Bill.

Section 8.

Clause 1:: The Congress shall have Power To lay and collect Taxes, Duties, Imposts and Excises, to pay the Debts and provide for the common Defence and general Welfare of the United States; but all Duties, Imposts and Excises shall be uniform throughout the United States;

Clause 2: To borrow Money on the credit of the United States;

Clause 3: To regulate Commerce with foreign Nations, and among the several States, and with the Indian Tribes;

Clause 4: To establish an uniform Rule of Naturalization, and uniform Laws on the subject of Bankruptcies throughout the United States;

Clause 5: To coin Money, regulate the Value thereof, and of foreign Coin, and fix the Standard of Weights and Measures;

Clause 6: To provide for the Punishment of counterfeiting the Securities and current Coin of the United States;

Clause 7: To establish Post Offices and post Roads;

Clause 8: To promote the Progress of Science and useful Arts, by securing for limited Times to Authors and Inventors the exclusive Right to their respective Writings and Discoveries;

Clause 9: To constitute Tribunals inferior to the supreme Court;

Clause 10: To define and punish Piracies and Felonies committed on the high Seas, and Offences against the Law of Nations;

Clause 11: To declare War, grant Letters of Marque and Reprisal, and make Rules concerning Captures on Land and Water;

Clause 12: To raise and support Armies, but no Appropriation of Money to that Use shall be for a longer Term than two Years;

Clause 13: To provide and maintain a Navy;

Clause 14: To make Rules for the Government and Regulation of the land and naval Forces;

Clause 15: To provide for calling forth the Militia to execute the Laws of the Union, suppress Insurrections and repel Invasions;

Clause 16: To provide for organizing, arming, and disciplining, the Militia, and for governing such Part of them as may be employed in the Service of the United States, reserving to the States respectively, the Appointment of the Officers, and the Authority of training the Militia according to the discipline prescribed by Congress;

Clause 17: To exercise exclusive Legislation in all Cases whatsoever, over such District (not exceeding ten Miles square) as may, by Cession of particular States, and the Acceptance of Congress, become the Seat of the Government of the United States, and to exercise like Authority over all Places purchased by the Consent of the Legislature of the State in which the Same shall be, for the Erection of Forts, Magazines, Arsenals, dock-Yards, and other needful Buildings;—And

Clause 18: To make all Laws which shall be necessary and proper for carrying into Execution the foregoing Powers, and all other Powers vested by this Constitution in the Government of the United States, or in any Department or Officer thereof.

Section 9.

Clause 1: The Migration or Importation of such Persons as any of the States now existing shall think proper to admit, shall not be prohibited by the Congress prior to the Year one thousand eight hundred and eight, but a Tax or duty may be imposed on such Importation, not exceeding ten dollars for each Person.

Clause 2: The Privilege of the Writ of Habeas Corpus shall not be suspended, unless when in Cases of Rebellion or Invasion the public Safety may require it.

Clause 3: No Bill of Attainder or ex post facto Law shall be passed.

Clause 4: No Capitation, or other direct, Tax shall be laid, unless in Proportion to the Census or Enumeration herein before directed to be taken. [This Clause has been affected by amendment XVI.]

Clause 5: No Tax or Duty shall be laid on Articles exported from any State.

Clause 6: No Preference shall be given by any Regulation of Commerce or Revenue to the Ports of one State over those of another: nor shall Vessels bound to, or from, one State, be obliged to enter, clear, or pay Duties in another.

Clause 7: No Money shall be drawn from the Treasury, but in Consequence of Appropriations made by Law; and a regular Statement and Account of the Receipts and Expenditures of all public Money shall be published from time to time.

Clause 8: No Title of Nobility shall be granted by the United States: And no Person holding any Office of Profit or Trust under them, shall, without the Consent of the Congress, accept of any present, Emolument, Office, or Title, of any kind whatever, from any King, Prince, or foreign State.

Section 10.

Clause 1: No State shall enter into any Treaty, Alliance, or Confederation; grant Letters of Marque and Reprisal; coin Money; emit Bills of Credit; make any Thing but gold and silver Coin a Tender in Payment of Debts; pass any Bill of Attainder, ex post facto Law, or Law impairing the Obligation of Contracts, or grant any Title of Nobility.

Clause 2: No State shall, without the Consent of the Congress, lay any Imposts or Duties on Imports or Exports, except what may be absolutely necessary for executing it's inspection Laws: and the net Produce of all Duties and Imposts, laid by any State on Imports or Exports, shall be for the Use of the Treasury of the United States; and all such Laws shall be subject to the Revision and Control of the Congress.

Clause 3: No State shall, without the Consent of Congress, lay any Duty of Tonnage, keep Troops, or Ships of War in time of Peace, enter into any Agreement or Compact with another State, or with a foreign Power, or engage in War, unless actually invaded, or in such imminent Danger as will not admit of delay.

ARTICLE II.

Section 1.

Clause 1: The executive Power shall be vested in a President of the United States of America. He shall hold his Office during the Term of four Years, and, together with the Vice President, chosen for the same Term, be elected, as follows

Clause 2: Each State shall appoint, in such Manner as the Legislature thereof may direct, a Number of Electors, equal to the whole Number of Senators and Representatives to which the State may be entitled in the Congress: but no Senator or Representative, or Person holding an Office of Trust or Profit under the United States, shall be appointed an Elector.

Clause 3: The Electors shall meet in their respective States, and vote by Ballot for two Persons, of whom one at least shall not be an Inhabitant of the same State with themselves. And they shall make a List of all the Persons voted for, and of the Number of Votes for each; which List they shall sign and certify, and transmit sealed to the Seat of the Government of the United States, directed to the President of the Senate. The President of the Senate shall, in the Presence of the Senate and House of Representatives, open all the Certificates, and the Votes shall then be counted. The Person having the greatest Number of Votes shall be the President, if such Number be a Majority of the whole Number of Electors appointed; and if there be more than one who have such Majority, and have an equal Number of Votes, then the House of Representatives shall immediately chuse by Ballot one of them for President; and if no Person have a Majority, then from the five highest on the List the said House shall in like Manner chuse the President. But in chusing the President, the Votes shall be taken by States, the Representation from each State having one Vote; A quorum for this Purpose shall consist of a Member or Members from two thirds of the States, and a Majority of all the States shall be necessary to a Choice. In every Case, after the Choice of the President, the Person having the greatest Number of Votes of the Electors shall be the Vice-President. But if there should remain two or more who have equal Votes, the Senate shall chuse from them by Ballot the Vice-President. [This Clause has been superseded by amendment XII.]

Clause 4: The Congress may determine the Time of chusing the Electors, and the Day on which they shall give their Votes; which Day shall be the same throughout the United States.

Clause 5: No Person except a natural born Citizen, or a Citizen of the United States, at the time of the Adoption of this Constitution, shall be eligible to the Office of President; neither shall any Person be eligible to that Office who shall not have attained to the Age of thirty five Years, and been fourteen Years a Resident within the United States.

Clause 6: In Case of the Removal of the President from Office, or of his Death, Resignation, or Inability to discharge the Powers and Duties of the said Office, the Same shall devolve on the Vice-President, and the Congress may by Law provide for the Case of Removal, Death, Resignation or Inability, both of the President and Vice President, declaring what Officer shall then act as President, and such Officer shall act accordingly, until the Disability be removed, or a President shall be elected. [This Clause has been affected by amendment XXV.]

Clause 7: The President shall, at stated Times, receive for his Services, a Compensation, which shall neither be encreased nor diminished during the Period for which he shall have been elected, and he shall not receive within that Period any other Emolument from the United States, or any of them.

Clause 8: Before he enter on the Execution of his Office, he shall take the following Oath or Affirmation:—"I do solemnly swear (or affirm) that I will faithfully execute the Office of President of the United States, and will to the best of my Ability, preserve, protect and defend the Constitution of the United States."

Section 2.

Clause 1: The President shall be Commander in Chief of the Army and Navy of the United States, and of the Militia of the several States, when called into the actual Service of the United States; he may require the Opinion, in writing, of the principal Officer in each of the executive Departments, upon any Subject relating to the Duties of their respective Offices, and he shall have Power to grant Reprieves and Pardons for Offences against the United States, except in Cases of Impeachment.

Clause 2: He shall have Power, by and with the Advice and Consent of the Senate, to make Treaties, provided two thirds of the Senators present concur; and he shall nominate, and by and with the Advice and Consent of the Senate, shall appoint Ambassadors, other public Ministers and Consuls, Judges of the supreme Court, and all other Officers of the United States, whose Appointments are not herein otherwise provided for, and which shall be established by Law: but the Congress may by Law vest the Appointment of such inferior Officers, as they think proper, in the President alone, in the Courts of Law, or in the Heads of Departments.

Clause 3: The President shall have Power to fill up all Vacancies that may happen during the Recess of the Senate, by granting Commissions which shall expire at the End of their next Session.

Section 3.

He shall from time to time give to the Congress Information of the State of the Union, and recommend to their Consideration such Measures as he shall judge necessary and expedient; he may, on extraordinary Occasions, convene both Houses, or either of them, and in Case of Disagreement between them, with Respect to the Time of Adjournment, he may adjourn them to such Time as he shall think proper; he shall receive Ambassadors and other public Ministers; he shall take Care that the Laws be faithfully executed, and shall Commission all the Officers of the United States.

Section 4.

The President, Vice President and all civil Officers of the United States, shall be removed from Office on Impeachment for, and Conviction of, Treason, Bribery, or other high Crimes and Misdemeanors.

ARTICLE III.

Section 1.

The judicial Power of the United States, shall be vested in one supreme Court, and in such inferior Courts as the Congress may from time to time ordain and establish. The Judges, both of the supreme and inferior Courts, shall hold their Offices during good Behaviour, and shall, at stated Times, receive for their Services, a Compensation, which shall not be diminished during their Continuance in Office.

Section 2.

Clause 1: The judicial Power shall extend to all Cases, in Law and Equity, arising under this Constitution, the Laws of the United States, and Treaties made, or which shall be made, under their Authority;—to all Cases affecting Ambassadors, other public Ministers and Consuls;—to all Cases of admiralty and maritime Jurisdiction;—to Controversies to which the United States shall be a Party;—to Controversies between two or more States;—between a State and Citizens of another State;—between Citizens of different States,—between Citizens of the same State claiming Lands under Grants of different States, and between a State, or the Citizens thereof, and foreign States, Citizens or Subjects. [This Clause has been affected by amendment XI.]

Clause 2: In all Cases affecting Ambassadors, other public Ministers and Consuls, and those in which a State shall be Party, the supreme Court shall have original Jurisdiction. In all the other Cases before mentioned, the supreme Court shall have appellate Jurisdiction, both as to Law and Fact, with such Exceptions, and under such Regulations as the Congress shall make.

Clause 3: The Trial of all Crimes, except in Cases of Impeachment, shall be by Jury; and such Trial shall be held in the State where the said Crimes shall have been committed; but when not committed within any State, the Trial shall be at such Place or Places as the Congress may by Law have directed.

Section 3.

Clause 1: Treason against the United States, shall consist only in levying War against them, or in adhering to their Enemies, giving them Aid and Comfort. No

Person shall be convicted of Treason unless on the Testimony of two Witnesses to the same overt Act, or on Confession in open Court.

Clause 2: The Congress shall have Power to declare the Punishment of Treason, but no Attainder of Treason shall work Corruption of Blood, or Forfeiture except during the Life of the Person attainted.

ARTICLE IV.

Section 1.

Full Faith and Credit shall be given in each State to the public Acts, Records, and judicial Proceedings of every other State. And the Congress may by general Laws prescribe the Manner in which such Acts, Records and Proceedings shall be proved, and the Effect thereof.

Section 2.

Clause 1: The Citizens of each State shall be entitled to all Privileges and Immunities of Citizens in the several States.

Clause 2: A Person charged in any State with Treason, Felony, or other Crime, who shall flee from Justice, and be found in another State, shall on Demand of the executive Authority of the State from which he fled, be delivered up, to be removed to the State having Jurisdiction of the Crime.

Clause 3: No Person held to Service or Labour in one State, under the Laws thereof, escaping into another, shall, in Consequence of any Law or Regulation therein, be discharged from such Service or Labour, but shall be delivered up on Claim of the Party to whom such Service or Labour may be due. [This Clause has been affected by amendment XIII.]

Section 3.

Clause 1: New States may be admitted by the Congress into this Union; but no new State shall be formed or erected within the Jurisdiction of any other State; nor any State be formed by the Junction of two or more States, or Parts of States, without the Consent of the Legislatures of the States concerned as well as of the Congress.

Clause 2: The Congress shall have Power to dispose of and make all needful Rules and Regulations respecting the Territory or other Property belonging to the United States; and nothing in this Constitution shall be so construed as to Prejudice any Claims of the United States, or of any particular State.

Section 4.

The United States shall guarantee to every State in this Union a Republican Form of Government, and shall protect each of them against Invasion; and on Application of the Legislature, or of the Executive (when the Legislature cannot be convened) against domestic Violence.

ARTICLE V.

The Congress, whenever two thirds of both Houses shall deem it necessary, shall propose Amendments to this Constitution, or, on the Application of the Legislatures of two thirds of the several States, shall call a Convention for proposing Amendments, which, in either Case, shall be valid to all Intents and Purposes, as Part of this Constitution, when ratified by the Legislatures of three fourths of the several States, or by Conventions in three fourths thereof, as the one or the other Mode of Ratification may be proposed by the Congress; Provided that no Amendment which may be made prior to the Year One thousand eight hundred and eight shall in any Manner affect the first and fourth Clauses in the Ninth Section of the first Article; and that no State, without its Consent, shall be deprived of its equal Suffrage in the Senate.

ARTICLE VI.

Clause 1: All Debts contracted and Engagements entered into, before the Adoption of this Constitution, shall be as valid against the United States under this Constitution, as under the Confederation.

Clause 2: This Constitution, and the Laws of the United States which shall be made in Pursuance thereof; and all Treaties made, or which shall be made, under the Authority of the United States, shall be the supreme Law of the Land; and the Judges in every State shall be bound thereby, any Thing in the Constitution or Laws of any State to the Contrary notwithstanding.

Clause 3: The Senators and Representatives before mentioned, and the Members of the several State Legislatures, and all executive and judicial Officers, both of the United States and of the several States, shall be bound by Oath or Affirmation, to support this Constitution; but no religious Test shall ever be required as a Qualification to any Office or public Trust under the United States.

ARTICLE VII.

The Ratification of the Conventions of nine States, shall be sufficient for the Establishment of this Constitution between the States so ratifying the Same.

ARTICLES IN ADDITION TO, AND AMENDMENTS OF, THE CONSTITUTION OF THE UNITED STATES OF AMERICA, PROPOSED BY CONGRESS, AND RATIFIED BY THE LEGISLATURES OF THE SEVERAL STATES, PURSUANT TO THE FIFTH ARTICLE OF THE ORIGINAL CONSTITUTION

ARTICLE I.

Congress shall make no law respecting an establishment of religion, or prohibiting the free exercise thereof; or abridging the freedom of speech, or of the press; or the right of the people peaceably to assemble, and to petition the government for a redress of grievances.

ARTICLE II.

A well regulated Militia, being necessary to the security of a free State, the right of the people to keep and bear Arms, shall not be infringed.

ARTICLE III.

No Soldier shall, in time of peace be quartered in any house, without the consent of the Owner, nor in time of war, but in a manner to be prescribed by law.

ARTICLE IV.

The right of the people to be secure in their persons, houses, papers, and effects, against unreasonable searches and seizures, shall not be violated, and no Warrants shall issue, but upon probable cause, supported by Oath or affirmation, and particularly describing the place to be searched, and the persons or things to be seized.

ARTICLE V.

No person shall be held to answer for a capital, or otherwise infamous crime, unless on a presentment or indictment of a Grand Jury, except in cases arising in the land or naval forces, or in the Militia, when in actual service in time of War or public danger; nor shall any person be subject for the same offence to be twice put in jeopardy of life or limb; nor shall be compelled in any criminal case to be a witness against himself, nor be deprived of life, liberty, or property, without due process of law; nor shall private property be taken for public use, without just compensation.

ARTICLE VI.

In all criminal prosecutions, the accused shall enjoy the right to a speedy and public trial, by an impartial jury of the State and district wherein the crime shall have been committed, which district shall have been previously ascertained by law, and to be informed of the nature and cause of the accusation; to be confronted with the witnesses against him; to have compulsory process for obtaining witnesses in his favor, and to have the Assistance of Counsel for his defence.

ARTICLE VII.

In Suits at common law, where the value in controversy shall exceed twenty dollars, the right of trial by jury shall be preserved, and no fact tried by a jury, shall be otherwise re-examined in any Court of the United States, than according to the rules of the common law.

ARTICLE VIII.

Excessive bail shall not be required, nor excessive fines imposed, nor cruel and unusual punishments inflicted.

ARTICLE IX.

The enumeration in the Constitution, of certain rights, shall not be construed to deny or disparage others retained by the people.

ARTICLE X.

The powers not delegated to the United States by the Constitution, nor prohibited by it to the States, are reserved to the States respectively, or to the people.

ARTICLE XI.

The Judicial power of the United States shall not be construed to extend to any suit in law or equity, commenced or prosecuted against one of the United States by Citizens of another State, or by Citizens or Subjects of any Foreign State.

ARTICLE XII.

The Electors shall meet in their respective states, and vote by ballot for President and Vice-President, one of whom, at least, shall not be an inhabitant of the same state with themselves; they shall name in their ballots the person voted for as President, and in distinct ballots the person voted for as Vice-President, and they shall make distinct lists of all persons voted for as President, and of all persons voted for as Vice-President, and of the number of votes for each, which lists they shall sign and certify, and transmit sealed to the seat of the government of the United States, directed to the President of the Senate;—The President of the Senate shall, in the presence of the Senate and House of Representatives, open all the certificates and the votes shall then be counted;—The person having the greatest number of votes for President, shall be the President, if such number be a majority of the whole number of Electors appointed; and if no person have such majority, then from the persons having the highest numbers not exceeding three on the list of those voted for as President, the House of Representatives shall choose immediately, by ballot, the President. But in choosing the President, the votes shall be taken by states, the representation from each state having one vote; a quorum for this purpose shall consist of a member or members from two-thirds of the states, and a majority of all the states shall be necessary to a choice. And if the House of Representatives shall not choose a President whenever the right of choice shall devolve upon them, before the fourth day of March next following, then the Vice-President shall act as President, as in the case of the death or other constitutional disability of the President.—The person having the greatest number of votes as Vice-President, shall be the Vice-President, if such number be a majority of the whole number of Electors appointed, and if no person have a majority, then from the two highest numbers on the list, the Senate shall choose the Vice-President; a quorum for the purpose shall consist of two-thirds of the whole number of Senators, and a majority of the whole number shall be necessary to a choice. But no person constitutionally ineligible to the office of President shall be eligible to that of Vice-President of the United States.

ARTICLE XIII.

Section 1.

Neither slavery nor involuntary servitude, except as a punishment for crime whereof the party shall have been duly convicted, shall exist within the United States, or any place subject to their jurisdiction.

Section 2.

Congress shall have power to enforce this article by appropriate legislation.

ARTICLE XIV.

Section 1.

All persons born or naturalized in the United States, and subject to the jurisdiction thereof, are citizens of the United States and of the State wherein they reside. No State shall make or enforce any law which shall abridge the privileges or immunities of citizens of the United States; nor shall any State deprive any person of life, liberty, or property, without due process of law; nor deny to any person within its jurisdiction the equal protection of the laws.

Section 2.

Representatives shall be apportioned among the several States according to their respective numbers, counting the whole number of persons in each State, excluding Indians not taxed. But when the right to vote at any election for the choice of electors for President and Vice President of the United States, Representatives in Congress, the Executive and Judicial officers of a State, or the members of the Legislature thereof, is denied to any of the male inhabitants of such State, being twenty-one years of age, and citizens of the United States, or in any way abridged, except for participation in rebellion, or other crime, the basis of representation therein shall be reduced in the proportion which the number of such male citizens shall bear to the whole number of male citizens twenty-one years of age in such State.

Section 3.

No person shall be a Senator or Representative in Congress, or elector of President and Vice President, or hold any office, civil or military, under the United States, or under any State, who, having previously taken an oath, as a member of Congress, or as an officer of the United States, or as a member of any State legislature, or as an executive or judicial officer of any State, to support the Constitution of the United States, shall have engaged in insurrection or rebellion against the same, or given aid or comfort to the enemies thereof. But Congress may by a vote of two-thirds of each House, remove such disability.

Section 4.

The validity of the public debt of the United States, authorized by law, including debts incurred for payment of pensions and bounties for services in suppressing insurrection or rebellion, shall not be questioned. But neither the United States nor any State shall assume or pay any debt or obligation incurred in aid of insurrection or rebellion against the United States, or any claim for the loss or emancipation of any slave; but all such debts, obligations and claims shall be held illegal and void.

Section 5.

The Congress shall have power to enforce, by appropriate legislation, the provisions of this article.

ARTICLE XV.

Section 1.

The right of citizens of the United States to vote shall not be denied or abridged by the United States or by any State on account of race, color, or previous condition of servitude.

Section 2.

The Congress shall have power to enforce this article by appropriate legislation.

ARTICLE XVI.

The Congress shall have power to lay and collect taxes on incomes, from whatever source derived, without apportionment among the several States, and without regard to any census or enumeration.

ARTICLE XVII.

The Senate of the United States shall be composed of two Senators from each State, elected by the people thereof, for six years; and each Senator shall have one vote. The electors in each State shall have the qualifications requisite for electors of the most numerous branch of the State legislatures.

When vacancies happen in the representation of any State in the Senate, the executive authority of such State shall issue writs of election to fill such vacancies: Provided, That the legislature of any State may empower the executive thereof to make temporary appointments until the people fill the vacancies by election as the legislature may direct.

This amendment shall not be so construed as to affect the election or term of any Senator chosen before it becomes valid as part of the Constitution.

ARTICLE XVIII.

Section 1.

After one year from the ratification of this article the manufacture, sale, or transportation of intoxicating liquors within, the importation thereof into, or the exportation thereof from the United States and all territory subject to the jurisdiction thereof for beverage purposes is hereby prohibited.

Section 2.

The Congress and the several States shall have concurrent power to enforce this article by appropriate legislation.

Section 3.

This article shall be inoperative unless it shall have been ratified as an amendment to the Constitution by the legislatures of the several States, as provided in the Constitution, within seven years from the date of the submission hereof to the States by the Congress.

ARTICLE XIX.

The right of citizens of the United States to vote shall not be denied or abridged by the United States or by any State on account of sex.

Congress shall have power to enforce this article by appropriate legislation.

ARTICLE XX.

Section 1.

The terms of the President and Vice President shall end at noon on the 20th day of January, and the terms of Senators and Representatives at noon on the 3d day of January, of the years in which such terms would have ended if this article had not been ratified; and the terms of their successors shall then begin.

Section 2.

The Congress shall assemble at least once in every year, and such meeting shall begin at noon on the 3d day of January, unless they shall by law appoint a different day.

Section 3.

If, at the time fixed for the beginning of the term of the President, the President elect shall have died, the Vice President elect shall become President. If a President shall not have been chosen before the time fixed for the beginning of his term, or if the President elect shall have failed to qualify, then the Vice President elect shall act as President until a President shall have qualified; and the Congress may by law provide for the case wherein neither a President elect nor a Vice President elect shall have qualified, declaring who shall then act as President, or the manner in which one who is to act shall be selected, and such person shall act accordingly until a President or Vice President shall have qualified.

Section 4.

The Congress may by law provide for the case of the death of any of the persons from whom the House of Representatives may choose a President whenever the right of choice shall have devolved upon them, and for the case of the death of any of the persons from whom the Senate may choose a Vice President whenever the right of choice shall have devolved upon them.

Section 5.

Sections 1 and 2 shall take effect on the 15th day of October following the ratification of this article.

Section 6.

This article shall be inoperative unless it shall have been ratified as an amendment to the Constitution by the legislatures of three-fourths of the several States within seven years from the date of its submission.

ARTICLE XXI.

Section 1.

The eighteenth article of amendment to the Constitution of the United States is hereby repealed.

Section 2.

The transportation or importation into any State, Territory, or possession of the United States for delivery or use therein of intoxicating liquors, in violation of the laws thereof, is hereby prohibited.

Section 3.

This article shall be inoperative unless it shall have been ratified as an amendment to the Constitution by conventions in the several States, as provided in the Constitution, within seven years from the date of the submission hereof to the States by the Congress.

AMENDMENT XXII

Section 1.

No person shall be elected to the office of the President more than twice, and no person who has held the office of President, or acted as President, for more than two years of a term to which some other person was elected President shall be elected to the office of the President more than once. But this article shall not apply to any person holding the office of President when this Article was proposed by the Congress, and shall not prevent any person who may be holding the office of President, or acting as President, during the term within which this article becomes operative from holding the office of President or acting as President during the remainder of such term.

Section 2.

This article shall be inoperative unless it shall have been ratified as an amendment to the Constitution by the legislatures of three-fourths of the several states within seven years from the date of its submission to the states by the Congress.

AMENDMENT XXIII
Section 1.

The District constituting the seat of government of the United States shall appoint in such manner as the Congress may direct:

A number of electors of President and Vice President equal to the whole number of Senators and Representatives in Congress to which the District would be entitled if it were a state, but in no event more than the least populous state; they shall be in addition to those appointed by the states, but they shall be considered, for the purposes of the election of President and Vice President, to be electors appointed by a state; and they shall meet in the District and perform such duties as provided by the twelfth article of amendment.

Section 2.

The Congress shall have power to enforce this article by appropriate legislation.

AMENDMENT XXIV
Section 1.

The right of citizens of the United States to vote in any primary or other election for President or Vice President, for electors for President or Vice President, or for Senator or Representative in Congress, shall not be denied or abridged by the United States or any state by reason of failure to pay any poll tax or other tax.

Section 2.

The Congress shall have power to enforce this article by appropriate legislation.

AMENDMENT XXV
Section 1.

In case of the removal of the President from office or of his death or resignation, the Vice President shall become President.

Section 2.

Whenever there is a vacancy in the office of the Vice President, the President shall nominate a Vice President who shall take office upon confirmation by a majority vote of both Houses of Congress.

Section 3.

Whenever the President transmits to the President pro tempore of the Senate and the Speaker of the House of Representatives his written declaration that he is unable to discharge the powers and duties of his office, and until he transmits to them a written declaration to the contrary, such powers and duties shall be discharged by the Vice President as Acting President.

Section 4.

Whenever the Vice President and a majority of either the principal officers of the executive departments or of such other body as Congress may by law provide, transmit to the President pro tempore of the Senate and the Speaker of the House of Representatives their written declaration that the President is unable to discharge the powers and duties of his office, the Vice President shall immediately assume the powers and duties of the office as Acting President.

Thereafter, when the President transmits to the President pro tempore of the Senate and the Speaker of the House of Representatives his written declaration that no inability exists, he shall resume the powers and duties of his office unless the Vice President and a majority of either the principal officers of the executive department or of such other body as Congress may by law provide, transmit within four days to the President pro tempore of the Senate and the Speaker of the House of Representatives their written declaration that the President is unable to discharge the powers and duties of his office. Thereupon Congress shall decide the issue, assembling within forty-eight hours for that purpose if not in session. If the Congress, within twenty-one days after receipt of the latter written declaration, or, if Congress is not in session, within twenty-one days after Congress is required to assemble, determines by two-thirds vote of both Houses that the President is unable to discharge the powers and duties of his office, the Vice President shall continue to discharge the same as Acting President; otherwise, the President shall resume the powers and duties of his office.

AMENDMENT XXVI

Section 1.

The right of citizens of the United States, who are 18 years of age or older, to vote, shall not be denied or abridged by the United States or any state on account of age.

Section 2.

The Congress shall have the power to enforce this article by appropriate legislation.

AMENDMENT XXVII

No law varying the compensation for the services of the Senators and Representatives shall take effect until an election of Representatives shall have intervened.

GLOSSARY

ABA The American Bar Association.

abstract of judgment A summary of the key elements of a court judgment, sufficient to reveal the legal effects of that judgment.

abuse of discretion Said of any court decision that lacks a reasonable foundation, whether in the evidence or the law, or that exceeds the authority of the court.

accessory after the fact One who knowingly aids a felon in evading apprehension and punishment.

accessory before the fact One who contributes to the planning or execution of a crime without being present during its commission.

accrue To mature; said of a cause of action when the necessary facts exist to sustain it.

acknowledgment The act of verifying one's own signature before a notary public.

act of Congress A statute enacted by the Congress of the United States.

action Any lawsuit or petition to the court for a determination of the rights and obligations of the parties to that proceeding.

adjudicate To make a final judicial determination of a controversy.

administrative law The law as expressed in government rules and regulations.

administrative law judge A person who presides over a quasijudicial, noncriminal hearing in an executive branch agency (e.g., worker compensation judges).

admissible Said of evidence that may be presented to the trier of fact (whether jury or judge), because it is relevant and not excessively prejudicial.

adversary system The legal system which seeks justice by relying upon the opposing parties (and their attorneys) to present all relevant evidence and legal authority.

advisory arbitration A hearing before an impartial party whose proposed resolution of the controversy is not binding upon the parties to that dispute.

affiant A person who makes an affidavit.

affidavit A written statement made under oath before a person authorized to administer such an oath.

affidavit of service An affidavit that some legal paper has been delivered to another person. *See also* **proof of service**.

affirm 1. To declare that a lower court judgment will stand undisturbed, "The court of appeal affirmed the trial court's decision."
2. To declare that a statement is true and made without reservation.

affirmative defense A legal defense that would overcome all allegations by the plaintiff, even if those allegations were true.
"The defendant raised the affirmative defense that the plaintiff committed a material breach of the contract before any of the alleged breaches by the defendant."

affirmative duty The duty to take some action on one's own initiative, without being called upon by another to take such action.
"The board of directors had an affirmative duty to protect the financial interests of the stockholders."

agency The relationship between agent and principal, in which the agent acts on behalf of the principal who is legally bound by the agent's authorized actions.
"The real estate broker and her client were in an agency relationship."

agent A person authorized to act for another (the principal) so that the principal is legally bound by the act of the agent.

allegation A statement (e.g., in a complaint or other pleading) of some fact that the party intends to prove.

alternative dispute resolution (ADR) The submission of a dispute to mediation or arbitration, as opposed to its submission to a court.

American Bar Association The nation's largest organization of attorneys.

amicus curiae "Friend of the court." One who, although not a party to the lawsuit, is interested in the outcome and offers arguments and legal authority to influence the court's ruling on a matter before it.
"The government filed an *amicus curiae* brief in the lawsuit between the Big Three automakers and the United Autoworkers' Union."

analogy The application of a legal principal found in one situation to a different situation, based upon similarities in the facts.

annotated code A publication of codified statutes, with notes about court decisions applying or interpreting those statutes, references to related law review articles, and references to recognized legal treatises or encyclopedias. *See also* **code**.

annotation An explanatory or illustrative note. A collection of commentary on some legal issue. *See also* **annotated code**.

answer The pleading filed by a defendant in a lawsuit, which is responding to the allegations and claims by the plaintiff.

appearance Coming before the court as a party to some dispute. An appearance may be in person or through an attorney. *See also* **general appearance** and **special appearance**.

appearance of impropriety The appearance to others that one is acting unethically or unlawfully, although in reality one's actual conduct might be both ethical and legal.

appellant The dissatisfied party that appeals the decision of a lower court.

appellate brief A memorandum of points and authorities that a party submits to the appellate court, in hopes of influencing its decision.

appellate court A court with the authority to either affirm or reverse a lower court's decisions on questions of law or legal procedure.

appellee The party that responds to an appeal by the dissatisfied party.

application program Computer software that is designed for a particular function (e.g., word processing, computer-aided design, or desktop publishing).

arbitration The resolution of a dispute by submitting it to a neutral third party who hears evidence and argument, and then imposes his decision (the "award"). Arbitration is generally quicker, less expensive, and less formal than adjudication by a court. *Compare to* **mediation**.

arbitrator A neutral third party (other than a court of law), who receives evidence and makes an "award" to resolve a dispute.

arraign To bring the defendant before the court to hear the criminal charges against her, to be informed of her due process rights, and to enter her plea. *See also* **plea**.

arraignment The court proceeding in which a criminal defendant is arraigned.

arrest To detain involuntarily, or to take into physical custody, a person suspected of crime.

arrest warrant A court order authorizing the arrest of a person.

arson The crime of setting property on fire. The property set afire might be that of the arsonist if other persons, their property, or their legal interests are harmed or placed in danger.

assault Any attempt or credible threat to cause physical injury to another individual. Any intentional act which causes genuine fear or apprehension of bodily harm in the person toward whom that act is directed. Any unlawful touching of another person. Assault can be both a tort and a crime.

associate attorney An attorney in a law firm who does not have the status or rights of a partner. *Compare to* **partner**.

asylum A refuge or shelter from criminal prosecution.

at-will employment A relationship in which either the employee or the employer may end that employment at any time, without offering any reason or justification.

attorney-client privilege The privilege of confidentiality that protects communications (written or verbal) between an attorney and his client. The attorney-client privilege belongs to the client, not to the attorney. *See also* **privileged communication**. *Compare to* **work product rule**.

attorney general A state or federal official charged with the enforcement of public laws and with the prosecution of offenses. The attorney general also defends statutes that are challenged in court and may serve as legal counsel to elected officials. "The attorneys general of seven states have joined in filing a suit for fraud against the nation's leading brokerage house."

attorney service A company that specializes in providing services to law firms, including service of process, courier services, off-site photocopying, and so forth.

attorney work product The research, analysis, investigations, theories, impressions, plans, or strategy of an attorney that have been developed in preparation for litigation. The work of the attorney's employees and of retained (but nontestifying) consultants or investigators. The attorney work product belongs to the attorney, not to the client. *See also* **work product rule**.

automatic stay Upon the filing of a petition for bankruptcy, the immediate suspension of all legal proceedings affecting the assets of the bankruptcy estate. The automatic stay is provided by statute. Tenants facing eviction and homeowners facing foreclosure sometimes file bankruptcy petitions simply to obtain the benefits of the automatic stay.

avoid To cancel or nullify an illegal or improper act. "The bankruptcy court avoided the gift—made by the debtor only one month before the bankruptcy petition—of the rare coin collection."

bad faith Acting without honest intent. Acting in violation of a contractual obligation to the other party. Violation of the duties imposed by law upon people who have business dealings with others. "Bad faith" implies conscious disregard for the rights of others, motivated by dishonesty or malice.

bail A pledge to the court, made to guarantee a person's appearance in court at a later date.

bail bond A contract under which a third party (the surety) promises to pay a fixed amount to the court if the defendant fails to appear as promised.

bailiff A peace officer whose duty is to keep order in court, to supervise the conduct of the jury, to maintain custody of criminal defendants, and (in some jurisdictions) to serve and/or execute certain orders of the court.

bar association An association of attorneys, organized to promote ethical standards and excellence in the practice of law.

Bates stamp To number documents consecutively, using a mechanical stamping device that advances one number each time it is used.

bench warrant A court order for the arrest of some person.

beneficiary A person named in a will, a trust, or an insurance policy to receive a benefit.

best evidence rule A rule of evidence that requires that a party offer the original evidence (e.g., rather than some photographic or xerographic copy of the original). If the original is not available, a copy may be introduced, subject to proof of its validity.

beyond a reasonable doubt *See* **proof beyond a reasonable doubt**.

Bill of Rights The first ten amendments to the U.S. Constitution.

billable hour Sixty minutes of legal services that are billed to the client.

billable quota A minimum number of billable hours that an attorney or legal assistant is required to bill to clients in a month, or a year.

binding arbitration A hearing before a neutral third party whose decision is binding upon the parties to that controversy.

blanket immunity *Also,* **transactional immunity**. Immunity granted by a court or by another body authorized by statute (e.g., a committee of the state legislature), under which a person may not be prosecuted for an offense. Blanket immunity usually is offered in exchange for testimony, or for other assistance in the prosecution of others. *Compare to* **use immunity**.

book To make a formal, written entry of criminal charges against the accused. Usually associated with taking a photograph, fingerprints, and the like.

bound over Ordered to appear for trial at a later date, either as a defendant or witness, or to post bond guaranteeing such an appearance.

breach of contract The failure, without a legal excuse, to perform any act promised in a contract.

brief A summary of facts and legal analysis.
  1. A *brief of a court opinion* summarizes the facts and legal analysis in that opinion.
  2. A *memorandum of points and authorities* summarizes the facts and legal arguments (with citation to appropriate legal authority) that support the client's case.

burden of proof The duty of a party to establish by convincing evidence the truth of some material fact. *Compare to* **standard of proof**.

business records exception An exception to the "hearsay rule" (which generally excludes second-hand evidence). "Business records" are those *routine* records of events, transactions and reports that are made without anticipation of litigation.

candor rule The ethical rule that requires an attorney to inform the court of relevant law or facts, even if such law or facts are unfavorable to the attorney's client.

capacity The legal competency to perform some act without review or approval by others (e.g., to enter into an irrevocable contract; to enter into marriage; to make a last will and testament).
The role or status in which a person is acting. "He was sued in his capacity as an individual, and as a corporate officer."

capital crime A crime punishable by death.

care The concern, attention and caution that is required under the law in a given situation.
"The swim coach owed a special duty of care to her athletes."

case at bar The case presently before the court.
"The case at bar differs from the authority you cite, counselor, in that this defendant never executed the written agreement."

case brief A summary of a court opinion, prepared by an attorney or a paralegal.

case citation A notation of the volume and page in a case reporter where the opinion of the court may be found.

case in chief The first portion of the trial, during which the party bearing the burden of proof presents her evidence and then rests her case. *See also* **prima facie**, **burden of proof**, and **directed verdict**.
"When the plaintiff finished her case in chief, the defendant moved for a directed verdict on grounds that she had not met her burden of proof."

case law The principles of law, as reflected in the accumulated decisions of courts over time, that the courts apply when no constitutional or statutory provision controls. Judge-made law. Synonymous with "**common law.**"

case management system (CMS) A software program that organizes and tracks all activities in preparation for trial or for some other client matter.

case of first impression A controversy that presents an entirely novel question of law for the court to decide; a case without any governing precedent.

cause of action The factual basis for a viable lawsuit; the facts that give a plaintiff legal right to a remedy.

cease and desist order An order, issued by a court or administrative law judge, to stop some activity and refrain from resuming it.

censure To formally reproach or reprimand someone for specified misconduct.

certified copy A copy of some document in the records of a government agency, and officially verified to be a true copy of the original.

Certified Legal Assistant® *Also,* **CLA**. A designation awarded by the National Association of Legal Assistants to qualified candidates who pass an examination.

Certified Legal Assistant Specialist® *Also,* **CLAS**. A Certified Legal Assistant® who has passed a subsequent examination in a legal specialty.

certify To attest to the genuineness of some document or other tangible thing.

challenge for cause A request by a party to a jury trial that a prospective juror be excused for good reason, based upon the information obtained during *voir dire*. *Compare to* **peremptory challenge**. *See also voir dire*.

change of venue Removal of a lawsuit from the court in which it was initiated to another court, usually in a different district or county. A change of venue is granted in the interest of justice (e.g., to escape the influence of pretrial publicity) or for the convenience of the parties and witnesses. *See also,* **venue**.

checks and balances The power relationship among the branches of government (legislative, executive and judicial) under which the powers of each branch are effectively limited by the powers of the other two branches. *Compare to* **separation of powers**.

chief counsel The senior legal advisor of a government agency. *Compare to* **general counsel**.

circuit A judicial division of the court system of the United States or some state.

circuit court A U.S. Court of Appeals. An intermediate appellate court or a trial court in some states.

circumstantial evidence Evidence from which inferences can be drawn to establish relevant facts. Sometimes called "indirect evidence." "The defendant's fingerprints on the murder weapon support the theory of the prosecution—that he fired the fatal shot. But they do not prove that he did." *Compare to* **direct evidence**.

citation 1. A written notice (e.g., a traffic ticket) to appear in court.
2. A reference to legal authority (e.g., to a statute or to case law). *See* **case citation**.

citator A reference work that identifies the judicial history of a case and provides citations to other, subsequent court opinions that have mentioned that case. *See* **Shepard's Citations** and **KeyCite**.

cite check 1. To verify the accuracy of case citations in a document.
2. To verify that a case is still good law.

citizen's arrest An arrest made by a private citizen, usually for an offense committed in his presence.

civil damages A monetary judgment awarded in a civil case.

civil law The law controlling private and public rights, obligations, and remedies, other than those arising under criminal law.
"The attorney general has filed a civil lawsuit rather than bringing criminal charges against the companies accused of price-fixing."

civil liberty A fundamental freedom established by the U.S. Constitution (e.g., speech, press, religion, or due process). *Compare to* **civil right**.

civil litigation Court proceedings to establish the rights of opposing parties and to gain remedies under civil law.

civil offense A violation of the law that carries no criminal penalty.

civil right A personal right established by state or federal legislation (e.g., the *Voting Rights Act of 1965*). *Compare to* **civil liberty**.

CLA Certified Legal Assistant.® A designation awarded by the National Association of Legal Assistants to qualified candidates who pass an examination.

class action A litigation procedure that permits someone to sue on behalf of large numbers of persons with a common interest, without joining each person as a named plaintiff. The party filing the "class action" then represents all persons similarly situated and must convince the court that he will do so fairly and effectively. The number of persons in the "class" must be so great as to make it impractical to join each of them in the suit.

clear and convincing evidence A standard of proof requiring greater certainty than the usual standard for civil litigation (**preponderance of evidence**), but not requiring such certainty as the standard for criminal prosecution (**beyond a reasonable doubt**). Evidence establishing a fact to be highly probable.

client trust account A financial or bank account in which client funds are held separate from other funds.

code A compilation of statutes or administrative regulations organized by subject (e.g., the *United States Code,* and *Code of Federal Regulations,* and the penal or motor vehicle codes of the various states).

code of civil procedure A compilation of statutes governing the procedures for civil litigation in a given jurisdiction (e.g., the *Kansas Civil Procedure Code*).

Code of Federal Regulations (CFR) The codification of all federal executive agency regulations in a single, multivolume publication.

collateral estoppel The doctrine that prohibits relitigating between the same parties any issue already determined by a valid court judgment. *See also* ***res judicata.***

color of law The appearance of a legal authority that does not exist; the fraudulent pretense of legal authority.

commingle To mix together funds belonging to different parties.
  "The state bar suspended the attorney from the practice of law for commingling the funds of clients."

common law The accumulation of legal principles found in court opinions over time, which the courts apply when no constitutional or statutory provision controls. Judge-made law. Synonymous with "**case law.**"

compensatory damages Damages that compensate the victim for her actual injuries and no more. Damages that "make the injured party whole."

competency Possessing the characteristics that qualify a person to act in some particular capacity in court (e.g., to give testimony, to serve as a juror, or to defend himself against a criminal charge).

complaint The pleading that initiates a lawsuit, setting forth the allegations that establish a cause of action and seeking a remedy from the court.

computer-assisted legal research Legal research using CD-ROMs, Westlaw, LEXIS-NEXIS, or the Internet.

concurrent jurisdiction The simultaneous authority of two court jurisdictions to hear and determine some controversy.

concurrent powers The simultaneous authority of state and federal government to govern a given matter or activity.

concurring opinion An opinion by a minority of the justices of an appellate court that agrees with the conclusion of the majority opinion but offers different reasoning or analysis. "Two justices joined in a concurring opinion that severely criticized the reasoning of the court majority, but nonetheless reached the same result." *See also* **minority opinion.**

conflict check A review of law firm records to determine whether a prospective new client presents a conflict of interest for that firm.

conflict of interest The existence of competing loyalties. Said to exist when a fiduciary has a personal interest that conflicts with his obligations as fiduciary, or when a public employee has a personal interest that conflicts with her duty to the public. "The attorney declined the new case, because his duty to other clients would create a conflict of interest."

consequential damages Damages that compensate an injured party for indirect losses that are not a clearly predictable result of the wrong done. *Compare to* **compensatory damages**.

conspiracy Mutual participation by two or more persons in planning or designing some crime or unlawful act.

constitutional law The law found in a constitution; in common usage, the law of the United States Constitution.

constructive Something that is true in law, although not in literal fact (e.g., constructive fraud, constructive notice, and constructive eviction).

constructive eviction Depriving the tenant of his rightful use and enjoyment of the premises, without depriving him of physical possession. Constructive eviction occurs when the landlord takes some unreasonable action, thereby making the premises unsuitable for the purpose for which they were rented. "Disconnecting all utilities made the house uninhabitable and constituted a constructive eviction."

constructive fraud Conduct that has all the consequences of fraud, even though fraud may not have been intended. (Constructive fraud requires a breach of some preexisting fiduciary duty to others.)

constructive notice Information that all persons are presumed under the law to have, because of the "notorious" nature of that information or because the information is part of the official records of that jurisdiction.

consummation The realization or fulfillment of an agreement.

contempt of court Disobedience of a court order. Any act that obstructs the operation of the court or that defames the court or lessens its dignity. Although contempt of court is defined by statute in most jurisdictions, common-law contempt of court still exists.

contempt powers The power of a court or legislative body to find someone to be in contempt of that court or body.

contingency fee A fee arrangement by which an attorney agrees to represent a client for a sum (usually a percentage) that will be paid only if the client recovers some amount.

"Because the client's case was lost, the law firm received no contingency fees."

continuous custody and control The uninterrupted safeguarding and preservation of evidence, so that its condition is unchanged.

contract An agreement that is legally binding upon the parties and that creates mutual obligations to do or not do some acts.

contract partner An attorney who receives a salary from the law firm, plus a portion of the client fees she generates.

corporation An artificial legal "person" created under the authority of government, and having an existence separate from that of the persons who create it or own it. Corporations may sue and be sued, enter into binding contracts, and own property.

counsel 1. An attorney at law.
2. A form of address often used for attorneys.
3. Competent legal advice.

counselor Also, **counsel**. A form of address often used for attorneys.
"Counselor, please wait until the court has finished speaking."

court The judge or justices of the court.
"If the court wishes, we can proceed to the next witness before lunch, your honor."

court clerk An officer of the court who receives pleadings, issues summonses, coordinates the court calendar, and performs various ministerial tasks necessary to the efficient operation of the court.
"Woe to the paralegal who alienates the court clerk!"

court-martial A military court established under federal statute, which tries members of the military forces for criminal offenses proscribed by the *Uniform Code of Military Justice*.

court of appeals An appellate court, usually of intermediate jurisdiction (i.e., not the highest court of that jurisdiction), established to hear appeals from the trial courts and to reduce the number of appeals that must be heard by the highest appellate court. As with all appellate courts, its jurisdiction is limited generally to questions of law and legal procedure, and it does not serve as the trier of fact. *See also* **appellate court**. *Compare to* **trier of fact**.

court of equity A court that administers justice according to principles of equity, as opposed to traditional rules of common law. In most states, the courts of equity and common law have been merged.

court of general jurisdiction A trial court with unlimited civil and criminal jurisdiction.

court of last resort The highest court with appellate jurisdiction over the controversy at issue. (Usually the state "supreme court" for actions brought in state courts.)

court of law A court with authority to exercise judicial functions under the common and statutory law of its jurisdiction.

covenant of good faith and fair dealing A promise within a contract that the parties will exercise their rights and fulfill their obligations reasonably and in accord with the intended purposes of the contract, and that neither party will unreasonably interfere with the other party's enjoyment of the benefits of their agreement. In some states, the covenant is implied by law in every contract.

covert inquiry A surreptitious investigation.

crime against persons A criminal offense that injures a person or deprives a person of his right to be left in peace (e.g., murder, assault, or false arrest.)

crime against property A criminal offense that takes or damages property belonging to another.
"Although she burned down her own house, her arson was a 'crime against property' because it defrauded her insurance company."

crime-fraud exception An exception to the attorney-client privilege, which requires an attorney to reveal a client's statement that he intends to commit a serious crime or fraud.

criminal contempt Contempt of court or of a legislative body sufficiently serious to be punished as a criminal offense.

criminal law The law that defines prohibited acts and provides for their punishment by imprisonment, death or fine.

cross-examination The questioning of a witness called by the opposing party.

custodian of records The person responsible for maintaining the routine business records of a company or public agency.

damages Financial compensation recovered in court by a person who has been harmed by the unlawful conduct of another.

database manager Computer software that organizes complex data by categories and manipulates that data to produce reports required by the user.

de facto In fact; in reality.
"The defendant was the *de facto* chief operating officer of the company, even though he held no title."
Compare to **de jure**.

de jure As a matter of law. Authorized by law.
"It is her right *de jure* to withhold her consent."
Compare to **de facto**.

de novo Again; anew; without regard for the first occurrence. "The court will hear the matter *de novo*, as though no prior hearing was held."

declaration A sworn or unsworn statement offered in a court proceeding. A written statement that includes an affirmation that it is made under penalty of perjury. (Certain unsworn declarations—for example, "deathbed declarations"—are admissible as exceptions to the hearsay rule.)

declaratory judgment A judicial determination of the rights of the parties, without any coercive mandate or award of damages.

default Failure to do something that one should do. In some circumstances, a default can result in a waiver of one's rights.

default judgment In litigation, a judgment entered by the clerk or the court after a defendant has failed to answer the complaint.

deficiency judgment A court judgment for the remainder of a debt still owed, after the creditor has exhausted the collateral.

demand letter A letter written by an attorney, on behalf of a client, demanding that another person do, or refrain from doing, some act.

demonstrative evidence Evidence received by the court or jury directly, as opposed to testimonial evidence. "The demonstrative evidence in the case included a bloodstained shirt and a switchblade knife."

demur To file a demurrer.

demurrer A challenge to the sufficiency of a complaint, stating that *even if all facts alleged are true,* the complaint fails to state a viable cause of action. A demurrer is filed in lieu of an answer, because the defendant is alleging that the complaint is worthless. The court either sustains or denies the demurrer. In the latter event, an answer must then be filed. *Compare to* **answer**.

deponent A witness who is deposed.

depose To take testimony by deposition.

deposition Sworn testimony by a witness, taken out of court. A common method of discovery prior to trial.

detain To stop, or to restrain a person's freedom of movement, for a very brief inquiry.

dictum *Pl., dicta.* A statement on some legal issue, made in a court opinion, that goes beyond the facts or issues before the court. A statement that is unnecessary to deciding the issues properly before the court. (Because the statement was unnecessary to the court's decision, there is no assurance that it was based upon careful legal analysis.) *Compare to* **holding**.
"The court's comment on that issue is of no precedential value, because it was dictum."

digest A publication with short paragraphs summarizing court opinions on various topics.

digital signature An electronic "signature" created by combining elements of a private, secure key and the content of the message.
"The e-mail authorization was verified by the client's digital signature."

diligence The attention and effort that an attorney applies to a client matter. *See also* **due diligence**.

diminished capacity Lacking in sufficient mental alertness or awareness; said of a person who committed some act while intoxicated, delirious with fever, or traumatized by a past experience.

direct evidence Evidence that can prove a fact without the necessity of drawing an inference. *Compare to* **circumstantial evidence**.
"The defendant's fingerprints prove that his hand touched the weapon."

direct examination The questioning of a witness by the attorney or party who called that witness.

directed verdict An order by the court requiring the entry of a judgment against the party who had the burden of proof, thereby relieving the jury of its obligation to deliberate upon the evidence. The directed verdict results from the failure to establish a *prima facie* case. *See also* **prima facie** and **burden of proof**.

disbarment Expulsion of an attorney from the state bar. In effect, revocation of an attorney's license to practice law.

disclaimer A disavowal of responsibility or liability for some event or person.

discovery The pretrial process by which litigating parties obtain information from each other.

discovery cutoff date The date by which all pretrial discovery must be completed.

discretionary jurisdiction The legal authority of a court to hear, or not hear, a controversy, at its sole discretion.

discussion group People who exchange information and ideas on a topic of mutual interest by leaving messages at a common Internet site.

disposition The final resolution of a controversy before the court.
"The court will determine the disposition of your motion after the oral argument by counsel."

dissenting opinion An opinion by a minority of the justices of an appellate court that disagrees with the majority opinion both in reasoning and result. *See also* **minority opinion** and **concurring opinion**.

distinguish To declare the holding in a given case to be irrelevant, because the facts or legal issues in that case differ from those in the case before the court.

diversity jurisdiction The jurisdiction of a federal court over an issue brought under state law, based on the fact that the parties are citizens of different states.

diversity of citizenship The fact that parties to a lawsuit are citizens of different states. The basis for federal court jurisdiction over disputes arising under state laws.

docket A calendar of scheduled court proceedings.

document management system (DMS) A software program that places identifying data for documents in a database, to facilitate later identification and retrieval, and that can execute full-text searches of those documents.

double jeopardy Being tried again for the same criminal offense following a *valid* earlier trial on that offense. The double jeopardy rule does not apply if a mistrial occurs in an earlier attempted trial, because a mistrial is, by definition, invalid. Also, the rule does not bar a later trial on other criminal charges arising from the same event.

"After acquittal in state court on charges of excessive force, the police officers were tried again in federal court on charges of civil rights violations."

due care The caution that a reasonable and prudent person would exercise under the circumstances. The degree of care legally required by the circumstances. The absence of negligence. *See also* **duty of care**.

due diligence The cautious examination, investigation, or reflection that a prudent person would conduct, under the existing circumstances, prior to making a particular decision.

due process The fair and reasonable procedures that are "due" any criminal defendant or civil litigant. Often stated as "due process of law." Federal due process is required by the Fifth Amendment, and state due process is required by the Fourteenth Amendment.

duress Unlawful pressure or threat used by one person to induce another to act.

duty A legal obligation to others, arising either out of a contract between the parties, out of a special relationship between the parties, or out of our duty to all other persons as a matter of law.

duty of care The duty of each person to use "due care" in the conduct of his affairs, so that the rights of others are not infringed. Violation of this duty is **negligence**. *See also* **due care**.

element An essential part of a particular crime or cause of action.

"The crime of fraud requires the element of misrepresentation."

emblements Annual crops produced by the labor of a tenant, who has the right to harvest them after her tenancy on the land has expired.

employment at will An employment relationship in which the employer and employee each retains the right to terminate the relationship at any time and for any reason. An employee at will has no vested property interest in that employment and may be discharged without just cause. *See also* **wrongful discharge**.

enabling statute A statute that authorizes some public officer or agency to take some action; the statute that authorizes the promulgation of an executive agency regulation.

en banc An augmented bench of jurists. Said of a hearing held before more than the usual number of jurists.

"Upon motion for a rehearing, the eleven justices heard the appeal *en banc*."

encryption software A computer program that can transcribe a communication into code.

entrapment Any action or statement by a law officer that is intended to encourage the commission of a crime, for which the perpetrator will then be arrested. Entrapment induces a crime that otherwise would not occur.

equitable remedy Nonmonetary relief granted by the court, such as an injunction.

equity 1. The value of real property, in excess of any existing debt against it.

"The owner wants to borrow against the equity in his house."

2. Justice based upon fairness, rather than upon the strict rules of common law.

equity partner A person with an ownership interest in a partnership.

errors and omissions policy A form of professional liability insurance to protect a law firm against damages for legal malpractice and other civil wrongs.

esquire A title accorded to attorneys in written address. (Abbreviated as "Esq.")

"W. Ross Driscoll, Esquire."

estoppel An equitable doctrine under which one cannot press a claim against another if the following facts apply: (a) the plaintiff led the defendant to follow some course of action; (b) the defendant was entitled to rely upon the plaintiff's good faith, and acted accordingly; (c) the defendant's reliance has left him exposed to the claim that the plaintiff now attempts to pursue.

"After assuring the tenant that he would sign a new lease at reduced rent if the tenant constructed a barn, and the tenant having since constructed the barn, the landlord is now barred by estoppel from refusing to sign a new lease and evicting the tenant for failure to pay the higher rent under the old lease."

evasion of arrest The crime of eluding capture by fleeing or hiding from law enforcement officials. *See also* **unlawful flight**.

evidence in rebuttal Evidence presented by the plaintiff at the conclusion of defendant's case and intended to discredit the defendant's witnesses and evidence.

ex parte With the participation of one side only. Said of any proceeding in which the court may act without the participation of all parties.

"The court granted the *ex parte* motion for a temporary restraining order and ordered the parties to appear in ten days for a hearing on the motion for injunction."

ex parte contact Contact by one interested party, without participation by other interested parties.

exclusionary rule A rule that excludes from admissibility any evidence obtained in violation of constitutional protections (e.g., by "rubber-hose" interrogations or unlawful searches).

exculpatory evidence Evidence tending to establish one's innocence.

execute 1. To sign a document (e.g., a contract), thereby giving it validity.
2. To perform the obligations imposed by a contract.
3. To put a condemned person to death.

executive order An order issued by the president, a governor, or mayor, under authority granted to that official by constitution or statute.

exemplar A single sample that serves as a model or example of a larger number of essentially similar things.

"The exemplar tire shown to the jury was the same brand, model, and size as the automobile tire that blew out in the accident."

exemplary damages *Also,* **punitive damages**. Damages in excess of compensatory damages, awarded to punish conduct that was characterized by violence, malice, fraud, oppression, or wanton conduct by the defendant. *Compare* **compensatory damages**.

exempt employee An executive, administrative, or professional employee who is exempt from the overtime pay requirement of the federal *Fair Labor Standards Act*.

exhaustion of remedies The prior, unsuccessful attempt to obtain relief through all available subordinate agencies and procedures prior to presenting the matter to the court. *See also* **futility doctrine**.

expert witness A witness qualified in a particular field by her education, training, and experience to render admissible opinions that may be considered by the judge or jury.

extradition The involuntary transfer of an accused person from one jurisdiction (e.g., nation or state) to another jurisdiction where he will be prosecuted.

Fair Labor Standards Act A federal law setting minimum standards for the working conditions of employees. *See also* **exempt employee**.

false arrest *See* **false imprisonment**.

false imprisonment The unlawful detention of a person, depriving her of liberty without a basis in law. *See also* **arrest**.

federal question A question of law arising under the U.S. Constitution, federal statutes, or treaties of the United States.

federal question jurisdiction The authority of a court to hear and determine a matter arising under federal law.

Federal Register The daily publication by the federal government of new and proposed regulations, requests for comments upon proposed rules, and other legal documents.

felony A criminal offense punishable by death or by imprisonment for one year or more. Any criminal offense defined by statute to be a felony.

felony murder The criminal liability of one felon for a homicide caused by his accomplice in the commission of a felony.

fiduciary A person who manages or controls the property of another and, therefore, who holds a position of great trust. (In this sense, "property" can be a property interest of any kind, including a client's legal claims against others.)

"The attorney's malpractice was a violation of her fiduciary duty to her client." *See also* **fiduciary duty**.

fiduciary duty The special duty of loyalty owed by a fiduciary to the person whose property he manages or controls.

field A category of like information (e.g., phone number, name, or rate of interest) in a database or spreadsheet. *Compare* **record**.

forensic medicine The application of medical science in the resolution of legal controversies.

form book or **form file** A collection of sample pleadings, memoranda, letters, and so on, used as exemplars in the later preparation of similar documents.

forum When jurisdiction is available in more than one court, the court in which a legal proceeding is brought. Said particularly of the plaintiff's choice of forum between state and federal courts, where diversity of citizenship would confer federal jurisdiction. *Compare to* **venue**.

401(k) plan A pension plan sponsored by the employer, to which employees make tax-deferred contributions.

fraud Gaining something of value from another person through intentional deception. The deception can be actively stated, or it can be passively concealed. The victim must reasonably rely upon the falsehood to her actual detriment. *Compare to* **constructive fraud** and **misrepresentation**.

fraudulent transfer The transfer of title to property for the purpose of defrauding or delaying a creditor. Transfers made in contemplation of bankruptcy are often fraudulent, in which case the bankruptcy court will nullify the transfer. *See also* **avoid**.

Freedom of Information Act **(FOIA)** The federal statute governing public access to government documents and records.

freelance paralegal A legal assistant who works as an independent contractor for, and under the supervision of, attorneys in two or more law firms.

fresh pursuit *See* **hot pursuit**.

frivolous appeal An appeal brought without any reasonable grounds for believing it possible to prevail; an appeal that no reasonable attorney would believe has merit.

frivolous claim A claim that lacks any plausible merit.

full faith and credit The constitutional requirement that each state recognize as valid the actions and records of other states.

futility doctrine The principle that one is not obligated to seek relief where there is no possibility of receiving it. *See also* **exhaustion of remedies**.

garnish To attach a portion of a debtor's wages or accounts, so that funds are paid directly to the creditor in satisfaction of the debt, rather than to the debtor.

general appearance Appearance in court by a defendant or respondent (personally or through an attorney), thereby accepting the jurisdiction of the court. *Compare to* **special appearance**.

general counsel A corporation's chief legal advisor (either in-house counsel or outside counsel).

general damages Monetary damages awarded for the immediate and direct consequences of a civil wrong, which are of a general and predictable nature (e.g., loss of a limb); a type of **compensatory damages**.

general denial A defendant's denial of "each and every" allegation in a complaint.

general intent The intent to commit a criminal act, but not necessarily to cause the specific injury which might result from that act.

general police powers The power of state and local governments to regulate conduct and restrict personal freedom for the protection of public health, safety, welfare, and morals.

general verdict A comprehensive, global verdict for the plaintiff, or for the defendant; a verdict without specification of preliminary findings by the jury.

good cause A legally sufficient reason for excusing some obligation or duty; a legal excuse, granted at the discretion of the court.

good faith Honesty and the absence of both malice and any intent to take unconscionable advantage of another. *Compare to* **bad faith**. *See also* **covenant of good faith and fair dealing**.

grand jury A jury whose function is to hear complaints and to determine whether an accused should be held for trial. Grand juries never determine actual guilt or innocence. *Compare to* **petit jury**.

In some jurisdictions, grand juries also investigate the operation of government agencies and make recommendations for greater efficiency and effectiveness.

guardian *ad litem* A person appointed by the court to represent a minor or unborn child in a particular legal proceeding before that court.

habeas corpus A writ commanding that a person (usually a prisoner or child) be brought before the court to determine whether that person should be released from detention. *See also,* **writ of *habeas corpus***.

HALT "Help Arrest Legal Tyranny." A consumer-advocate group dedicated to reducing the legal profession's "monopoly" on legal services and to making those services more widely available and less expensive. **HALT** favors the use of legal technicians or non-attorney providers for less-complex legal services. *See also* **legal technician** and **non-attorney provider**.

harmless error Error in the legal reasoning of a lower court, which nevertheless reached the identical legal conclusion it would have reached if it had used the correct rule of law; an error that did not change the outcome of the case and therefore did no harm to the losing party.

headnote In published court opinions, a brief numbered paragraph that appears before the opinion and that summarizes the court's holdings on a particular legal issue. "Headnote 3 summarizes the court's holding on the issue of punitive damages for legal malpractice."

hearing on appeal Oral arguments before an appellate court, usually to supplement written briefs and to allow the court the opportunity to ask questions of the attorneys. *See also* **appellate court**.

hearsay evidence Testimony or documentary evidence that reports what another person said out of court (and not under oath).

hearsay rule The rule of evidence which precludes the admission of most hearsay evidence.

holding The court's statement of the law on an issue before it. To be the court's "holding," the statement must be necessary for resolution of the legal controversy before the court. *Compare to* **dictum**.

home page The first page (and entry point) of an organized Web site on the Internet.

hot pursuit *Also,* **fresh pursuit**. The authority of a police officer to pursue a felony suspect into a different jurisdiction (e.g., the adjoining state) to make an arrest. The hot pursuit doctrine requires the officer to be in continuous and close pursuit so that the suspect cannot elude the officer, even temporarily. Some states have adopted the *Uniform Extra-territorial Arrest on Fresh Pursuit Act*, but the hot pursuit doctrine has existed in the common law since the days of piracy.

hung jury A deadlocked jury unable to deliver the required number of votes for a verdict. (In a criminal case, a single dissent creates a hung jury.) If the deadlock cannot be overcome by further deliberations, the court will declare a mistrial. *See also* **mistrial** *and* **double jeopardy**.

immunity Exemption from an obligation or from prosecution. Immunity from prosecution is often given to suspects who cooperate with investigators. *See also* **transactional immunity** *and* **use immunity**.

impeach 1. To attack or challenge the credibility of a witness.
"The attorney used the transcript of her deposition to impeach the witness' new version of events."
2. To accuse a public official of a serious offense.
"The federal judge was impeached by the House of Representatives on grounds of bribery, but the Senate acquitted him after a brief trial."

impeachment 1. The use of probing questions to raise doubts about the credibility of a witness.
2. The process used by the House of Representatives (and state legislatures) to accuse public officials of "high crimes and misdemeanors" for which they may be removed from office.

implied Suggested or alluded to, but not stated in words.

implied power A power of government not expressly stated in a constitution, but deduced from those powers which are stated.
"The power to establish an Air Force is implied by the power granted in the Constitution to establish an Army and Navy."

imputed conflict of interest The tainting of an entire law firm with *presumed* conflict of interest, because one of its attorneys has an actual conflict of interest in a particular legal matter.

in camera Done in the judge's chambers, beyond public view.
"The CIA documents were examined by the court *in camera* to determine if they were relevant."

inchoate crime A crime that is begun, but not completed; a crime that, if completed, will result in a further crime (e.g., assault, solicitation or conspiracy).

incompetent A person who is not able to manage her own affairs.

independent contractor A person who is not an employee, but who works on a piecework basis. In contrast to an employee, an independent contractor is not responsible to the employer for the *manner* in which he does his work, but only for the finished product.

independent paralegal 1. A freelance paralegal who works as an independent contractor serving a number of attorneys, but whose work product is assigned, reviewed, and supervised by attorneys.
2. [*Not used in this text*] A non-attorney provider who provides legal services directly to the public, without supervision by an attorney. *See also* **legal technician** *and* **non-attorney provider**.

independent regulatory agency A government agency that is not directly controlled by the chief executive (i.e., president or governor).

indict To accuse someone of a crime by returning a true bill of indictment. *See also* **grand jury** *and* **indictment**.

indictment *Also* **true bill of indictment**. A written and sworn accusation that a suspect has committed a crime, returned by a grand jury upon recommendation of the prosecutor. *See also* **grand jury**. *Compare to* **information**.

indigent A person unable to afford her own attorney. Courts appoint public defenders to represent criminal defendants who are indigent. The courts do not, however, appoint attorneys to represent an indigent in civil litigation.

individual A human being, as opposed to other legal "persons" (partnerships, corporations, associations, etc.). *See also* **person**.

individual capacity One's legal capacity as a human being, as opposed to any other concurrent capacities (as trustee, beneficiary, corporate director, partner, association officer, etc.). In the same litigation, a person can be sued in his individual capacity and in other appropriate capacities.

information A formal, written accusation against a criminal defendant, prepared by the prosecutor (as opposed to a grand jury). *Compare to* **indictment**.

infra Appearing below. Cited below. *Compare to* **supra**.

infraction A minor criminal offense, punishable only by fine, never by imprisonment (e.g., minor traffic offenses).

inherent powers The powers of government that derive from the very nature of government (e.g., to define and punish crimes) and that need not be expressly granted by a constitution.

in-house general counsel An attorney and employee of a corporation, who serves as its chief legal advisor.

injunction A court order to refrain from doing, or to cease doing, some act that is actually or potentially harmful to another party. (Rarely, a "mandatory injunction" orders someone to *do* some particular act.) *Compare to* **temporary restraining order** and **writ**.

in loco parentis Standing in the place of one's parents. Possessing the authority and responsibility of one's parents.

"Under the law of this state, every public school teacher stands *in loco parentis* to every pupil in her charge."

in personam **jurisdiction** A court's jurisdiction over the person of the defendant, as opposed to its jurisdiction over the defendant's property.

in rem **jurisdiction** A court's jurisdiction over property under its control (i.e., within its territory).

Insanity *See* **legal insanity**.

insolvent 1. Unable to pay debts when they are due. 2. Liabilities in excess of all assets.

intake interview The initial interview of a new client to gather all necessary personal data and information about the legal matter presented.

Internet service provider (ISP) A company that provides the subscriber with access to the Internet.

interrogatories A list of written questions delivered to another party in a lawsuit, to which that party must respond in writing and under oath. One form of discovery.

interstate commerce Trade, communication, financial and business transactions, and the transportation of goods, services, or persons among the states.

intraoffice memorandum A memorandum prepared for use within the law office. *Compare to* **memorandum of law**.

jailhouse lawyer A prison inmate who assists other inmates with their legal defense.

judge-made law *See* **common law**.

judgment The decision of the court that, upon entry in the court's records, becomes the final disposition of the matter before it (subject, however, to later review by appellate courts).

judgment creditor One who has received a judgment for damages against another, but has not yet been paid.

judgment debtor A defendant against whom a money judgment has been entered, but not paid.

judgment debtor examination A proceeding in which a judgment debtor appears before the court to be examined under oath concerning his assets.

judgment lien An encumbrance upon the real property of a judgment debtor, recorded in the jurisdiction where the real property is located. A judgment lien must be "satisfied" by payment before the encumbered property can be sold. *See also* **abstract of judgment**.

judgment notwithstanding the verdict *See* **judgment NOV**.

judgment NOV *Also,* **judgment notwithstanding the verdict**. A judgment entered by the court that is contrary to the verdict returned by the jury. *Compare to* **directed verdict**.

judgment on the pleadings A court judgment based upon the complaint, answer and other pleadings already filed with the court.

judgment proof Lacking any assets that a judgment creditor might receive.

judicial immunity The absolute protection against any civil liability for actions that a judge takes in her judicial capacity.

judicial review The power of the courts to review statutes, administrative regulations, and actions of government officials, and to void those that violate a higher legal authority (e.g., the Constitution).

judicial seal The power of the courts to close judicial records from public view.

jurisdiction The authority of the court to determine the legal issues and the rights of the parties before it.

jury instructions Instructions given by the court on the law to be applied during jury deliberations.

jury selection *See voir dire.*

jury tampering 1. Unauthorized contact or communication with a juror. 2. The attempt to influence or corrupt a juror.

just cause 1. The existence of reasonable grounds under the law for taking a particular action. 2. In employment law, the rule that an employee shall not be disciplined or discharged except upon reasonable grounds and that the penalty shall be proportionate to the misconduct.

justice court An inferior trial court of very limited civil and criminal jurisdiction, presided over by a justice of the peace. Because many justices of the peace are not attorneys, most states are eliminating the justice court and merging its functions with the municipal court, presided over by judges who are qualified attorneys.

KeyCite The on-line citator service in Westlaw.

key number In the publications of the West Group, a classification system that identifies various legal issues by topic and number (e.g., Rescission of Contracts 127.7). That same legal issue can then be researched in all West publications (and in Westlaw) by referring to the same key number.

laches Inexcusable delay in bringing a claim, which prejudices the defense of the other party.

larceny *See* **theft**.

law The rules of human conduct and relationships that have been established by legislation or by a judicial recognition of generally accepted principles.

law clerk 1. A law school graduate who has not yet passed the bar and is employed to assist an attorney in the practice of law. (Less often, a nongraduated law school student employed as a "summer associate" in a law firm.)
2. An attorney employed as a research assistant to an appellant court justice—a very prestigious position for a new member of the bar.

lay foundation To establish the admissibility of evidence through credible testimony that identifies that evidence and its relationship to an issue before the court.

leasehold An interest in real property held under a lease from the owner.

legal administrator A law office manager who supervises the non-attorney employees and coordinates their responsibilities and functions; a person qualified to do so through a combination of education, training, and experience in law and management.

legal assistant A paralegal. Someone with legal skills and knowledge who performs legal work under the direction and supervision of an attorney.

legal insanity Mental illness that deprives one of the capacity to form criminal intent; illness that makes one incapable of assisting in her own legal defense.

legal nurse consultant A registered nurse with education or training in the law, with emphasis in forensic medicine, who consults with and assists attorneys in legal matters relating to medicine and medical care.

legal procedures The steps that must be followed to represent a client and protect her legal interests.

legal process Any action of the court (e.g., issuing a summons) claiming jurisdiction over a person or property. *See also* **service of process**.

legal technician A non-attorney who is licensed (or otherwise authorized by law) to provide limited legal services directly to the public, usually for simple legal matters.

legislative intent The purpose for which a legislature has enacted a statute.

lessee The tenet of a **leasehold**.

lessor The landlord of a **leasehold**.

LEXIS-NEXIS The legal database system operated by Reed Elsevier, Inc.

liability An obligation arising under the law.
"The company will be exposed to enormous legal liability if it does not stop dumping hazardous waste."

libel A defamatory statement, damaging to one's reputation or livelihood, published in print, pictures, or signs. *Compare to* **slander**.

license Permission to do something that otherwise would be illegal to do.
"The defendant was convicted of practicing medicine without a license."

licensure The granting by government of licenses to engage in a professional practice, such as law or medicine. Membership in a state bar is the usual method of licensure for attorneys.

limited liability company (LLC) A privately held company that provides the stockholders the limited personal liability of incorporation and the tax advantages of a partnership.

limited liability partnership (LLP) A variation of the **limited liability company**.

litigation A lawsuit. Court proceedings for the purpose of determining the rights and obligations of the parties to a controversy or in order to obtain a remedy for a civil wrong.

local area network (LAN) A small network of interconnected computers, usually within a single office or building.

lodge To deposit something with the court for possible future reference during a judicial proceeding.

long-arm statute A statute that establishes the court's jurisdiction over a person not present in that state or the court's other geographic jurisdiction.

loss of consortium Loss of the benefits of the marital relationship, including affection, companionship, care, and sexual relations.

majority opinion The opinion of the court, reflecting the views of the majority of justices and stating the holding of the court on the issues before it.

malpractice The failure to apply reasonable effort and/or skill in one's professional duties to a client or patient; professional incompetence.

managing partner In a law firm, the partner designated to supervise the daily operations of the firm (especially those of the support staff operations).

mandate An order of the court, written or verbal, that one must obey. *See also* **writ of mandate**.

mandatory appeal An appeal that an appellate court must hear, by law.

mandatory authority The legal authority of a court's own jurisdiction, which it is legally obligated to recognize and enforce; the law of a court's own jurisdiction.

marriage The legal and sexual union of two persons as partners for life, with the mutual obligation to care and provide for each other's needs.

master A person (often a retired judge) appointed by a court to receive evidence and present a recommendation to the court.

material Significant or substantial. Related to the heart of the matter. Influential.
"The evidence offered is material to the issues in this case."

material fact A fact that can affect the outcome of a legal proceeding.

mediation Dispute resolution with the assistance of a neutral party who uses the skills of diplomacy to bring the parties to an agreement. Unlike an arbitrator, a mediator never imposes a judgment or award, but seeks any resolution the parties will accept. *Compare to* **arbitration**.

mediator A neutral third party who uses the skills of diplomacy to bring the parties to an agreement.

memorandum of law An objective written analysis of a legal issue, prepared to inform the attorney and/or client. A memorandum of law is a confidential document, not intended for submission to the court or to opposing parties. In it, legal authorities (favorable and unfavorable) are cited for further research. *Compare to* **memorandum of points and authorities**.

memorandum of points and authorities *Also,* **brief**. A written analysis and persuasive argument submitted to the court on some legal issue. Unlike a memorandum of law, it is a partisan document advocating the client's position before the court. *Compare to* **memorandum of law**.

mens rea A criminal intent.

minimum contacts Sufficient dealings in, or with persons of, another jurisdiction so that its courts may assume personal jurisdiction over the defendant.

ministerial act A routine government action that is performed in accord with established rules and procedures, and that permits the actor little or no discretion.

minority opinion An opinion by a minority of the justices of an appellate court. A minority opinion may either concur in or dissent from the entire majority opinion or it may concur in part and dissent in part. *See also* **concurring opinion** and **dissenting opinion**.

minutes Records of the proceedings of a corporation's board of directors, or of a shareholders' meeting.

Miranda warning The warning that a law enforcement officer must give to a suspect prior to certain interrogations, in order to use any responses as evidence against the suspect. Essentially, the warning informs the suspect of her due process rights (e.g., to remain silent and to have legal counsel). Failure to give the warning never invalidates the arrest itself, but it might bar the admission of any incriminating statements by the suspect.

misdemeanor A criminal offense of intermediate gravity, between an infraction and a felony. Any criminal offense punishable by imprisonment for a maximum of one year or less. Any criminal offense defined by statute to be a misdemeanor. *Compare to* **infraction** and **felony**.

misrepresentation 1. A false and misleading statement of fact.
2. A failure to disclose something one has a duty to disclose, thereby misleading someone entitled to that disclosure.
3. An essential element of the tort of fraud. *Compare to* **fraud**.

mistrial An invalid trial, declared by the court when some misconduct or procedural problem prevents the completion of a valid trial. Mistrials usually result from deadlocked juries or the death or illness of a juror or attorney. *See also* **double jeopardy**.

modify To change or alter the prior decision of a court.

motion *in limine* A motion prior to or during jury trial to exclude prejudicial evidence or issues.

motion to dismiss A request that the court remove a matter from further consideration.

NALA National Association of Legal Assistants.

negligence The failure to use due care. The failure to exercise the caution and care that a reasonable and prudent person should exercise under the circumstances.

NFPA National Federation of Paralegal Associations.

no contest *Also,* **nolo contendere**. A plea to a criminal charge, in which the defendant accepts the punishment provided by law but does not either admit or deny actual guilt. The Latin phrase means, "I will not contest it." The punishment will be imprisonment and/or fine, exactly as though the defendant were to plead guilty. However, the "no contest" plea cannot be used as an admission of liability in later civil litigation. This plea cannot be entered except by permission of the court.

nolo contendere *See* **no contest**.

non-attorney provider An unlicensed person who provides legal services directly to the public, without supervision by an attorney. *Compare to* **legal technician**.

nonsuit Failure to present evidence necessary to sustain a cause of action; failure to present a *prima facie* case. *See also* ***prima facie* case**.

notary public A public official authorized to take an acknowledgment (by the maker) of his signature on a document, to administer oaths, and to certify documents. *See also* **acknowledgment**.

notice Information or knowledge that would cause a prudent person to make inquiry or take other action to protect her interests.
"The defendant was on notice that this would be an issue at trial, because questions regarding it were raised during her deposition."

nuisance Any unreasonable or unlawful activity or thing that deprives another person of the reasonable use and enjoyment of his land (a private nuisance) or that interferes with the rights of the general public (a public nuisance). *See also* **private nuisance** and **public nuisance**.

obstruction of justice Attempting to hinder or delay the judicial process, particularly in criminal law.

of counsel To be employed by a law firm as an advising attorney; an attorney emeritus.

offer of compromise A proposal to settle a dispute without admission of liability by either party.

office suite A software program that integrates a word processor, database manager, spreadsheet, and other commonly used programs.

officer Someone holding a position of authority and trust.
1. A public official.
2. A sworn peace officer (i.e., someone with special powers of arrest).
3. An officer of the court (i.e., attorney, prosecutor, clerk, bailiff, etc.).
4. The president, secretary, or treasurer of a corporation, association or labor union.

officers of the court Judges and attorneys are officers of the court, sworn to uphold the law and seek justice.

official reporter The case reporter designated by statute or court rule to publish the court opinions of that jurisdiction.

"on all fours" Said of an earlier case that is substantially similar in material facts and that presents identical legal issues to the case at bar. Because of the close similarity, the case on all fours has special value as a precedent for deciding the case at bar. *See also* **case at bar**.

on-call letter The written promise by a witness under subpoena to appear in court within a stated period of time after being called.

on its own motion An action by the court on its own initiative, without a request being made by any party.

on point Having relevance to the issues before the court; said of a case that can serve as precedent.

opening statement An attorney's initial statement to the court and/or jury, in which she outlines the evidence to be presented and the logical conclusions to be drawn from that evidence.

opinion letter A letter written by an attorney, at the request of the client, in which the attorney presents a legal conclusion about the circumstance in question.

order to compel response A court order commanding a party to respond to questions or requests presented in discovery. *See also* **discovery**.

order to show cause A court order commanding some person to appear in court and show good reason why the court should not take a particular action.
"The court issued an order to the plaintiff's counsel to show cause why he should not be sanctioned in the amount of $1,000 for failure to appear at the scheduled time."

ordinance A city or county statute.

original jurisdiction The authority to hear a legal proceeding at its inception; trial jurisdiction.

overrule On the part of an appellate court, to make a decision that rejects its own prior holding on the same issue of law, thereby depriving the earlier decision of any future value as precedent.
"After fifty-eight years, the U.S. Supreme Court in *Brown v. Board of Education,* 347 U.S. 483 (1954), overruled its decision in *Plessy v. Ferguson,* 163 U.S. 537 (1896), in which the Supreme Court had held racial segregation to be constitutional under the 'separate-but-equal' doctrine."

own recognizance *Also,* **personal recognizance**. Recognition by the defendant of his obligation to appear in court. The defendant's promise to appear in court. Release without bond upon one's promise to appear in court.
"The defendant was released without bail on his own recognizance."

palimony A financial obligation similar to alimony, arising from a mutual agreement between two unmarried persons who have lived together in a committed relationship.

paralegal Legal assistant. Someone with legal skills and knowledge who performs legal work under the direction and supervision of an attorney.

Paralegal Advanced Competency Exam (PACE) A written examination administered for the National Federation of Paralegal Associations (NFPA) that is used to certify paralegals as possessing advanced competency.

parallel citation A citation to the identical court opinion in a different case reporter.

parole Release from confinement before the full sentence has been served, on condition that the paroled convict comply with specified conditions of parole. *Compare to* **probation**.

partner A co-owner of an enterprise. In law firms, a partner shares in the profits, liabilities, and management of the firm. *See also* **equity partner**. *Compare to* **associate attorney**.

partnership A joint venture in which the co-owners share in both profits and losses, and are individually and jointly responsible for the liabilities of the enterprise.

party 1. A litigant. A plaintiff, defendant, petitioner, or respondent in a court proceeding.
2. A person who has entered into a contract.
See also **real party in interest**.

penal code A collection of statutes defining and punishing crimes (e.g., *California Penal Code*).

pendent jurisdiction Federal jurisdiction over a state law matter based upon its close relationship to another matter already within the jurisdiction of the federal court.

percipient witness A witness who can testify to events observed with her five senses. *Compare* **expert witness**.

per curiam Literally, "by the court." A notation identifying an opinion written by the entire court, rather than by a particular justice.

peremptory challenge A challenge to remove a prospective juror without offering any reason. In civil and criminal trials, attorneys for each party are generally permitted a limited number of peremptory challenges. (Challenges "for cause" are not limited in number, but are granted at the discretion of the court.) *See also,* **voir dire**. *Compare to* **challenge for cause**.

perjury Making a false statement under oath.

person An individual (i.e., a human being), or some other legal entity that can sue or be sued (e.g., a corporation, a partnership, or an association).

personal jurisdiction The authority of the court over the defendant, as opposed to its authority over the property of the defendant. *See also* ***in personam* jurisdiction**.

personal property All property other than real property, including intangibles such as the right to sue in tort.

personal recognizance A criminal defendant's pretrial promise to appear, without the requirement that any property or bond be posted with the court to guarantee that appearance.

personal representative The executor (or administrator) of an estate.

personal service The delivery of legal documents (e.g., a court summons) to the actual person to whom they are directed or (in some jurisdictions) to a person authorized to accept them on her behalf.

persuasive authority Legal authority that a court may consider or reject, at its discretion. *Compare to* **mandatory authority**.

petitioner A person who requests that the court take some action.

petition for review A request that an appellate court accept a case on appeal.

petit jury A trial jury, generally consisting of between six and twelve jurors (as opposed to a "grand" jury, which generally consists of between nineteen and twenty-three jurors.) *Compare to* **grand jury**. *See also* **trier of fact**.

physical evidence Tangible things that tend to prove or disprove some fact.

plaintiff The aggrieved party who initiates a lawsuit by filing a complaint with the court. *See also* **complaint**.

plea The accused person's response to a criminal charge: "guilty," "not guilty," or "no contest." *See also* **no contest**.

plea bargain 1. (*v.*) To negotiate a guilty plea in return for a reduced sentence.
2. (*n.*) An agreement that results from negotiating the plea and sentence.
Defendants agree to plead guilty to avoid the possibility of a harsher sentence, should the case go to trial. Prosecutors plea bargain to ensure a conviction and punishment. The court must approve the plea bargain.

pleading Any paper filed by litigants in which they state their allegations, claims, and defenses. Petitions, complaints, demurrers, answers, and counterclaims are properly called "pleadings," but in popular usage the term sometimes describes all papers filed with the court in a lawsuit.

pocket part A paper supplement inserted in a cardboard pocket inside the back cover of legal publications.

police powers *Also,* **general police powers**. The powers of state and local government to regulate conduct and to restrict freedom to protect the public health, safety, welfare, and morals.

political right *Also,* **civil right**. A personal protection established by statute (e.g., the *Voting Rights Act of 1965*). *Compare to* **civil liberty**.

precedent An earlier court decision that states a legal principle that can be used to resolve a similar case. The closer the similarity of facts and legal issues, the greater value the earlier case has as precedent. *See also* **on point** and **on all fours**.

preempt To assume exclusive authority over some issue. To bar any legislation on that issue by a lower authority. Some issues (e.g., immigration) are of such overriding federal concern under the U.S. Constitution that any state legislation on those issues is preempted by federal authority and is therefore void. State legislatures can preempt all local legislation on matters of state concern (e.g., marriage and divorce), as well, so that counties and cities may not regulate them.

prejudicial Harmful to the interests of justice. Tending to deprive a party of fair justice. Having the tendency to arouse the bias or antagonism of a jury.

prejudicial effect Having the tendency to create unfair prejudice in the minds of the jury.

prejudicial error A mistake in law or procedure, committed by the trial court, that deprives a party of fair justice. Prejudicial error is grounds for reversal by the appellate court. *See also* **harmless error**.

prejudicial evidence Evidence with a tendency to cloud the jurors' minds with bias or passion. In ruling on admissibility, the court must balance any prejudicial effect against the relevance of the evidence offered. *See also* **relevance**.

preliminary hearing A pretrial hearing to determine whether there is "probable cause" that the defendant committed the crime. Upon finding probable cause, the court will order the defendant to stand trial. *See also* **probable cause**.

preponderance of evidence The usual standard of proof in civil litigation. Evidence of greater weight or credibility than the evidence offered in opposition. Evidence that indicates that a fact is more probable than not.

presiding judge The chief judge of a court, with responsibility for assigning cases to all judges in that court.

presumption A rule of law by which the establishment of one fact shall create an assumption of another fact, until that assumption is refuted by evidence. "Under the law, a woman's child is presumed to be the issue of her husband if the child was conceived during their marital cohabitation."

presumption of innocence The legal principle that requires the government to prove an accused to be guilty of the crime.

pretrial conference A conference of the parties or their attorneys, held in the judge's chambers, at which procedural matters related to trial are decided.

pretrial discovery The process in which opposing parties are required to exchange information related to the case.

prima facie "On first impression." Presumably true, upon the evidence first available.
1. Said of a fact tentatively established until proven false by contrary evidence.
2. The showing that the plaintiff must make in order for a case to be submitted to the jury.
"Because the plaintiff failed to establish a *prima facie* case, the court entered a directed verdict for the defendant."
See also **burden of proof**, **case in chief**, and **directed verdict**.

prima facie **case** The presentation of evidence that, if unchallenged, would establish all required elements of the cause of action or the alleged crime.

primary source A statement *of* the law. A constitution, statute, regulation or court opinion. Compare to **secondary source**.

principal 1. The amount of money owed, excluding interest.
2. A person who authorizes and directs an agent to act on her behalf. *See also* **agency**.

private investigator A person retained to gather information about some circumstance.

private nuisance A nuisance depriving one or a few persons of the reasonable enjoyment of their property. *See also,* **nuisance**.

privilege of confidentiality The protection against compelled disclosure that is accorded to certain categories of information, such as communications between husband and wife, doctor and patient, or attorney and client.

privileged Protected. Confidential. Exempt from compelled disclosure.

privileged communication A communication that occurs within a special relationship recognized by law (e.g., spousal, attorney-client, doctor-patient, clergy-penitent), and that courts generally may not compel to be disclosed.

probable cause Facts that suggest to a reasonable mind that a person has more likely than not committed a crime. Probable cause is a crucial factor in legitimizing certain searches and arrests, and it is the basis for returning grand jury indictments or binding a defendant over for trial following a preliminary hearing. *See also* **reasonable suspicion**.

probation Release of a convicted person without any postconviction imprisonment, on condition of good behavior and compliance with other requirements set by the court.

probative value Having the capacity to prove or disprove relevant facts.

pro bono For the public good. Legal services provided without compensation.

procedural due process The procedures required by the Constitution to ensure essential fairness in criminal prosecution and civil litigation. *See also* **due process**. *Compare to* **substantive due process**.

procedural law The law that establishes the procedures that must be used to assert one's rights under substantive law. *Compare to* **substantive law**.

product liability The liability of manufacturers and vendors of a product for injuries that it later causes. *See also* **strict products liability**.

professional corporation A professional practice (e.g., law or medicine) incorporated under state law.

proof beyond a reasonable doubt The standard of proof for criminal trials. Evidence that convinces a reasonable and prudent person to believe, to a moral certainty, that an accused did commit a criminal act. If *any* reasonable doubt exists, the juror must vote for acquittal.

proof of service An affidavit (or written statement under penalty of perjury) that states that certain legal documents were delivered to the person identified in the proof. *See also* **affidavit of service**.

property profile An informal report from a title insurance company, giving a legal description of the property in question, names of the owners of title, existing liens and other encumbrances, and so forth.

proprietary trade secret Information developed and owned by a business that uses it to gain competitive advantage, and that is not information shared with or available to the public or competitors. Courts commonly issue protective orders to limit the use and distribution of trade secret information when it must be disclosed in litigation. *See also* **protective order**.

prosecutor's information A written accusation prepared by a prosecutor and filed with the court to initiate criminal proceedings against the accused. An "information" is generally used in lieu of a grand jury indictment. *Compare to* **indictment**.

protective order An order issued by the court to protect proprietary trade secrets from unauthorized disclosure to competitors. *See also* **proprietary trade secret**.

prudent person One who acts with wisdom, care, and caution, and with due regard for the circumstances and possible consequences.

public defender An attorney paid by the government to represent a criminal defendant who cannot afford to retain an attorney.

public law A statute with general application to the public at large.

public nuisance A nuisance that interferes unreasonably with the public health, safety, or welfare, or that deprives the public of a common right of enjoyment.

"The court declared the illegal gambling hall to be a public nuisance and ordered its immediate closure."

public policy The general principles of conduct and social relationships that are so firmly established in law that no court will enforce contracts or administrative acts that violate those principles.

"Public policy" is not well-defined in specific terms, except when it is invoked by a court in a specific case. The courts appear to derive the rules of public policy from the cumulative body of statutory and case law.

"The Social Welfare Department's regulation denying benefits to single parents who do not undergo sterilization surgery is void as a violation of the public policy of this state."

punitive damages *Also* **exemplary damages**. Damages in excess of compensatory damages, awarded to punish conduct that was characterized by violence, malice, fraud, oppression, or wanton conduct by the defendant. *See also* **damages**. *Compare to* **compensatory damages**.

query An inquiry. In Westlaw or LEXIS-NEXIS, a search instruction composed of key terms, a key number, or a question in natural language.

question of fact A question reserved for the "trier of fact" (the judge or jury of the trial court). A question of truth or falsity concerning past events. *Compare to* **question of law**. *See also* **trier of fact**.

question of law A question regarding the meaning and application of the law, as opposed to a question of fact. A question reserved for determination by the judge of the trial court and subject to review by appellate courts. *Compare to* **question of fact**.

quid pro quo "This for that." An exchange of items or services of value. In sexual harassment, a demand for sexual favors in exchange for something else (e.g., retaining one's job).

quiet title A lawsuit to obtain a judicial determination of ownership rights. In an action for quiet title, an adverse claimant is brought before the court to either prove his claim or be barred thereafter from asserting his claim.

rainmaker An attorney who attracts new clients to the firm.

ratify To validate or approve something already done. A principal may later validate the action of her agent even if it exceeded the authority of the agent when it was done.

real evidence Evidence that the trier of fact perceives with the five senses, rather than through descriptive testimony.

real party in interest The person with a legal right to enforce a claim. In some cases, the "real party in interest" is neither named nor joined as a litigant, but is recognized as such by the court.

"In *United Aircraft Workers Local 721 v. Johnson Air Maintenance,* the real party in interest was the grievant, employee Hector Marshall."

real property All property other than personal property. Land, buildings, plants and trees, and anything else permanently attached to the land.

reasonable Having a basis in reason or logic, as opposed to being arbitrary or capricious. Appropriate to the circumstances, as viewed by a person of normal intelligence, honesty, temperance, and fairness.

reasonable doubt A doubt based in reason (as opposed to imagination or invention) and arising from the circumstances. Doubt that would cause a prudent person to act cautiously if the matter were important to herself. *See also* **proof beyond a reasonable doubt**.

reasonable person A person of normal intelligence, motivated by reason and fairness (as opposed to caprice or malice), and one who acts with due regard for both the circumstances and possible consequences to self and others.

reasonable suspicion Suspicion based upon articulable facts that are sufficient to support a detention or search under the Fourth Amendment. Reasonable suspicion may not be based upon an officer's "hunch" or intuition—it must be based upon facts which would cause another officer of comparable experience to suspect criminal conduct.

record 1. (*v.*) To have a document entered into the official records of that jurisdiction.
"The deed was recorded with the county clerk."
2. (*n.*) A portion of a computer file (particularly in a database or spreadsheet) that includes a series of "fields" or "cells" containing discrete data organized by category.

redline 1. A feature of word processing software that highlights new language in a document and shows deleted language in strikeout type.
2. To set insurance premiums based upon the geographical community in which an insured resides, rather than upon other objective criteria of risk.

Registered Paralegal *Also* **R. P.** A designation awarded by the National Federation of Paralegal Association (NFPA) to qualified paralegals who have successfully completed the **Paralegal Advanced Competency Exam**.

regulation An agency-created rule that implements policies and procedures established by a higher government authority.

rehearing A second hearing before a court to argue and determine the same issue. A rehearing is granted at the discretion of the court when it is claimed that some error or oversight occurred in the first hearing.

relevance Relationship to an issue before the court. The tendency to prove or disprove a material fact. *See also* **material**.

relevant evidence Evidence tending to prove or disprove a material fact.

remainderman Under a will, the person who is to receive all that remains after all specific bequests have been distributed.

remand To return a matter from an appellate court to the trial court for further action, often with instructions from the appellate court on the law or procedure to be applied.

remove To transfer a case from one court to another, most often from state court to federal court based upon diversity jurisdiction.

reporter A collection of volumes containing court opinions.

request for admissions A discovery device in which one party asks the other to admit certain facts so that they need not be contested at trial.
"ADMIT: that you are an officer of Xzyzzx Corporation."

request for production of documents A discovery device in which one party asks the other to permit the examination and copying of relevant documents. (Sometimes termed a "demand for inspection of documents.")

res judicata A matter already determined by a court of competent jurisdiction and, therefore, not subject to relitigation between the same parties.

respondent A person responding to or opposing the petition under consideration by the court.

rest its case To conclude the introduction of evidence at trial.
"The defense rests."

Restatements A series of volumes describing (i.e., "restating") the law on various topics. The Restatements of Law are written by scholars of the American Law Institute and are highly influential.

restraining order *Also* **temporary restraining order** or **TRO**. An order, similar to an injunction, forbidding the defendant to commit a threatened or anticipated act, pending a hearing on the application for injunction. The purpose of the restraining order is to maintain the status quo and prevent irreparable harm until the merits of the matter are heard by the court. *Compare to* **injunction**. *See also ex parte.*

retainer 1. A contract (**retainer agreement**) between an attorney and her client, identifying the services to be provided and the fees to be paid. A commitment by the attorney to take the case and represent the interests of the client.
2. A sum paid in advance to an attorney as an inducement to take the case and/or a down payment for legal services.

retainer agreement A contract between an attorney and her client for legal services.

reverse To set aside the judgment of a lower court.
"The trial court's decision was reversed on appeal."

ripeness The existence of a genuine, present controversy ready for judicial determination.

rules of evidence Rules established by statute or by the courts governing the admissibility of evidence. *See also* **admissible**.

sanction 1. (*n.*) A penalty imposed by the court on a party and/or an attorney for misconduct in a judicial proceeding. The penalty may be financial, or it may involve the exclusion of evidence otherwise admissible or even the dismissal of a cause of action or counterclaim.
2. (*v.*) To impose a penalty for misconduct. "The court sanctioned the attorney for presenting a frivolous claim."
3. (*v.*) To approve, ratify or legitimize the action of another. "The tournament was sanctioned by the college athletic association."

scope of employment The normal activities and responsibilities of an employee, which the employer can foresee.

seal 1. Closure to public inspection: "The affidavit supporting the search warrant was placed under seal by the court."
2. An authenticating mark or stamp.

search engine A software program that allows the user to search the content of Web sites on the Internet.

second chair The role of an assisting attorney at trial: "John's going to sit second chair to Jennifer in the Mayberry case."

secondary source A statement *about* the law, which courts may consider or ignore. The writing of some commentator without the authority to state the law. Compare to **primary source**.

section A discrete statutory provision to be read and interpreted as a whole. Usually, a numbered subdivision of a statutory code.
"Section 1222 of the *Internal Revenue Code*."

self-incrimination Actions or statements causing the actor or speaker to appear guilty. Constitutional safeguards protect one from *compulsory* self-incrimination, but they do not protect one from the taking of body fluids or tissue samples, nor samples of one's physical appearance, voice, or handwriting.

separation of powers The division of governmental powers (legislative, executive, and judicial) among three separate branches, so that all powers are not concentrated in one branch. Separation of powers is the arrangement that makes the system of **checks and balances** possible.

serve 1. To deliver legal process (e.g., a court summons) to the person named.
"The defendant was served with copies of the complaint and summons."
2. To deliver any legal notice or document (e.g., discovery requests) to a party in a judicial proceeding.

service of process The delivery of a document for legal process. *See also* **legal process**.

settlement agreement An out-of-court agreement between litigating parties (or potential litigants) to resolve their differences.

settlement conference A pretrial conference at which the parties and their counsel meet in chambers with the judge and attempt to reach a settlement of the case.

sexually hostile environment A circumstance in which a reasonable person would be substantially offended by unwelcome and patently sexual actions or innuendo.

Shepard's Citations A case citator published by a division of Reed Elsevier, Inc. A volume (or online service) that identifies court opinions and selected legal publications that mention or cite a given legal authority (e.g., a statute or court opinion).

Shepardize To use *Shepard's Citations* to learn the subsequent history of a case, to check its continued validity as precedent, and to identify other cases that have cited it.

sidebar A conference in court between the judge and all counsel, out of the hearing of the jury, usually to discuss the propriety of questions or the admissibility of evidence.

slander A defamatory oral statement, damaging to one's reputation or livelihood. Slander is ephemeral, without the continuing existence of a libel. *Compare to* **libel**.

SLAPP "Strategic litigation against public participation." A SLAPP suit is usually filed by a business enterprise against individuals or citizen groups who appear before government agencies (e.g., a city council) to oppose an application for a permit. Although most SLAPP lawsuits lack merit, they often intimidate citizens into silence because of the expense and inconvenience required to oppose them.

small claims court A court of very limited civil jurisdiction for the resolution of small lawsuits. Attorneys generally are not permitted to appear in small claims court, and the lay parties represent themselves before the court.

sole practitioner An attorney practicing alone, without partners or associates.

sole proprietorship A business owned by a single individual, who is personally liable for all debts and obligations of that business. *See also* **corporation** and **partnership**.

solicitation 1. The act of an attorney or other person enticing someone to become a client of the attorney.
2. The act of soliciting a crime.

special appearance An appearance by a party before a court for the sole purpose of challenging the court's jurisdiction. By making a "special" appearance, the party does not automatically submit itself to the court's jurisdiction. *Compare to* **general appearance**.

special damages Actual damages that are not the natural and predictable result of the civil wrong, but that result in part from special circumstances; a type of **compensatory damages**. *Compare to* **general damages**.

special verdict A jury verdict responding to a specific question posed by the court (as opposed to a general verdict deciding the entire case). Courts often require special verdicts in complex cases when otherwise it might be difficult for the jury to arrive at a well-reasoned general verdict.

specific intent The intent to commit a criminal act and to cause the harm that results from that act.

spreadsheet A computer application that organizes numerical data and manipulates that data according to complex formulas. *See also* **application program**.

standard of care The degree of care that a reasonable and prudent person would exercise under the circumstances. *See also* **due care** and **duty of care**.

standard of proof The burden of proof that applies to a particular type of case (e.g., civil or criminal). The degree of persuasion that the evidence must achieve. *Compare to* **burden of proof**.

standing The right to bring an action, based upon one's legal interests that are at stake and the relationship she shares with the defendant.
"The plaintiff lacks standing to sue because she was never a partner, nor even a potential partner, in the deal that went sour."

stare decisis The legal principle that precedents should not be overturned, except for strongly persuasive reasons.

status conference A pretrial conference of the judge and the parties' attorneys to evaluate the progress of discovery and to estimate the date and duration for a trial.

statute An act of legislation. Law written by a legislative body or by the voters through the initiative process.
"The applicable statute in this case is the *Americans with Disabilities Act*."

statute of frauds The requirement that certain categories of contracts (e.g., for sale of real property) must be in writing in order to be enforceable.

statute of limitations The statute that establishes the period of time within which a claim must either be brought against the defendant or forever be abandoned.

statutory law The law as stated in legislation.

stay of judgment A delay in the entry of the court's judgment, so that it does not become effective unless entered at a later date.
"The court's judgment will be stayed while the parties seek mediation of their dispute."

stipulate To establish something by mutual agreement and, thus, remove it from controversy.
"The plaintiff will stipulate that the defendant is a sworn peace officer."

stipulation An agreement between opposing parties to resolve an issue without argument before the court.
"Your honor, by stipulation the parties have agreed that the testimony of their respective experts will be admitted into evidence."

strict products liability The doctrine that a manufacturer or seller is liable for any injury caused by a defective product, without requiring proof that the defendant was negligent in design or manufacture.

subject matter jurisdiction The authority of the court to hear cases of the kind before it.
"This court lacks jurisdiction over patent appeals, counselor. Now that the nature of the case is clear, this court has no alternative but to dismiss it."

suborning of perjury The solicitation or encouragement of perjury.

subpoena Also **subpena**. A command to appear and give testimony.

subpoena *duces tecum* A command to appear and bring documents or other evidence.

substantive due process The Constitutional requirement that, in addition to the use of fair procedures, the laws being applied must themselves not be arbitrary and capricious.
"Procedural due process is meaningless if people are executed just for being left-handed—even if they do receive all the trappings of a fair trial."

substantive law The law that establishes each person's rights and responsibilities. *Compare to* **procedural law**.

substituted service Delivery of legal documents to someone other than the person to whom they are directed. Service of process by means other than personal service.

summary The portion *preceding* a court opinion in which the reporter of decisions presents an *unofficial* summary of the case and the holding of the court.

summary judgment A finding that no controversy of fact exists and that one party is entitled to prevail as a matter of law.

summer associates Second- and third-year law students who work as apprentices in a law firm during the summer break.

summons An order commanding a defendant to appear and to answer the complaint in a lawsuit.

supra Appearing above. Cited above. *Compare to* **infra**.

Supremacy Clause Article VI, Section 2 of the Constitution, which states that the Constitution and other federal law shall be "the supreme Law of the Land," and requires the judges of state courts to enforce that law.

Supreme Law of the Land The Constitution of the United States, federal statutes, and treaties.

suspended sentence A criminal sentence imposed by the court, but held in abeyance for a period of time while the convict, during good behavior, complies with specific conditions imposed by the court. Failure of the convict to comply with those conditions can result in the sentence being reinstated.

sustain To approve and uphold.
"The objection is sustained."

sworn affidavit A statement made under oath before a person authorized to administer such an oath. An **affidavit**.

syllabus The unofficial summary and/or headnotes, prepared by the reporter of decisions, that precede(s) the opinion of the court in most case reporters.

systems manager A person expert in computer hardware and software who maintains and troubleshoots a computer system.

table of authorities A list of all legal authorities cited in a **memorandum of points and authorities**.

temporary restraining order (TRO) *See* **restraining order**.

tenancy at will Possession of property by a tenant, but without any fixed term. A tenancy that may be terminated by either the landlord or the tenant upon delivery of reasonable notice to the other.

term of art A word (or combination of words) that carries a meaning peculiar to a particular discipline or profession.
"In the law, 'constructive fraud' is a term of art."

theft *Also* **larceny**. Taking property that belongs to another. Stealing.

three-strikes law A statute that mandates lengthy sentences (e.g., 25 years to life) for persons convicted of a third felony or violent crime.

tickler system A procedure used by law firms to ensure that deadlines are met.
"Tickle me ten days before our response is due."

tort A civil wrong that injures another (e.g., fraud, assault, slander, or negligence).

tort law The law of torts and their remedies.

transactional immunity *See* **blanket immunity**.

transactional law The practice of law concerned with business transactions, including the sale and merger of business concerns.

transferred intent The presumption of specific intent when the victim of a criminal act is other than the actor's intended victim.
"In that jurisdiction, the law treats a drive-by homicide of an innocent bystander as premeditated murder, even though the intended victim was not struck by the gunfire."

trial brief A **memorandum of points and authorities** in which an attorney attempts to persuade the court to rule in the client's favor on legal issues arising during trial.

trial by court A trial in which the judge serves as the trier of fact. A trial without a jury.

trial court The court of original jurisdiction that determines all questions of fact and law. A trial court's decisions on questions of law are subject to review by the appellate courts.

trial notebook A notebook containing all pleadings, witness lists, memoranda of points and authorities, and other documents needed for handy reference during trial.

trier of fact The person(s)—judge or jury—who must determine all questions of fact (as opposed to questions of law). The trier of fact is the sole "judge" of the credibility of witnesses and other evidence. *See also* **question of fact**.

TRO A temporary restraining order. *See also* **restraining order**.

true bill of indictment *Also* **indictment**. A sworn criminal accusation returned by a grand jury to initiate a criminal prosecution. *See also* **grand jury**.

trust account A separate bank account in which an attorney deposits all client funds—and *only* client funds.

trustee A person who holds property in trust for the benefit of another person (the beneficiary). *See also* **fiduciary**.

UCC *See* **Uniform Commercial Code**.

unauthorized practice of law (UPL) The practice of law by a person not licensed to do so.

unconscionable So one-sided and unfair as to offend the conscience. Oppressive and resulting from great disparity in bargaining positions. Said of a contract provision, or of fraudulent or dishonest conduct by one party toward another, that shocks the conscience of the court. Courts refuse to enforce unconscionable terms in a contract. *See also* **public policy**.

unconstitutionally vague Said of a statute that is so ambiguous that a reasonable person cannot know what he may, and may not, do.

Uniform Acts A variety of statutes adopted by most state legislatures, based upon drafts by the National Conference of Commissioners on Uniform State Laws.

Uniform Commercial Code *Also* **UCC.** A uniform statement of commercial law drafted by the National Conference of Commissioners on Uniform State Laws. Every state has enacted the UCC with some modifications, so that companies nationwide are able to conduct business under a fairly uniform set of rules.

Uniform Resource Locator (URL) The Internet address for a Web site or server.

unlawful detainer The unlawful continued possession or occupancy of real property which belongs to another (e.g., after a lease has expired or been terminated). An action for unlawful detainer is a proceeding to evict the tenant.
"The landlord has brought an unlawful detainer action for failure to pay rent."

unlawful flight Leaving a jurisdiction for the purpose of avoiding arrest or prosecution. *See also* **evasion of arrest**.

unofficial reporter A case reporter which has not been designated by statute or court order to be the official reporter for a given court.

URL *See* **Uniform Resource Locator**.

use immunity Immunity granted by a court or by another authorized body (e.g., a congressional committee), under which a witness' testimony cannot be used against him in a court of law. "Use immunity" also bars the prosecutor from identifying and pursuing other evidence against the witness based upon leads in the testimony itself. In any subsequent prosecution, the prosecutor must demonstrate that all evidence was obtained independent of the testimony given under immunity.
"The congressional committee offered use immunity, but it refused to give blanket immunity to the uncooperative witness."
Compare to **blanket immunity**.

venue The locality of the court in which a case is heard. Venue is not a question of jurisdiction, but of the interests of justice.
"To minimize the impact of pretrial publicity, the court granted a change of venue."
Compare to **forum**.

verdict The decision of the jury. *Compare to* **directed verdict** and **judgment**. *See also* **judgment NOV**.

verification A sworn statement that the facts alleged in a pleading or stated in a response to discovery are true.

verify To state under oath that the facts alleged in a pleading or stated in a response to discovery are true.

vicarious criminal liability Legal responsibility for a crime committed by another person, usually as the result of acting as an accomplice or accessory in that crime. *See also* **felony murder**.

void Null. Without legal validity or effect. ("Null and void" is redundant, because the terms are synonymous in their legal sense.)

voidable Capable of becoming void, but not automatically void.
"The contract was voidable, at the option of the minor."

voir dire The process of examining prospective jurors to determine their qualification to serve. The court and attorneys question the jurors to discover bias or any other basis for disqualification. *See also* **challenge for cause** and **peremptory challenge**.

waive To surrender some right.
"The defendant waives her right to a preliminary hearing."

waiver The surrender of some right.
"The failure to make an objection during the deposition constituted a waiver of the right to object to that testimony during trial."

warrant To give assurance of the truth of some fact.
"The seller warrants that it holds valid title to the property."

warrant A court order authorizing a search or arrest.

Web browser Software that facilitates access to the World Wide Web on the Internet.

Web site A server on the World Wide Web that maintains a distinct URL address.

Westlaw The legal database system operated by West Group.

whistle-blower A person who reports a law violation by the organization in which he works.

with prejudice Denying the right or option of trying again.
"Counselor, you may not file an amended complaint, because your original complaint was dismissed *with prejudice*."

without prejudice Allowing the right and option of trying again.
"The complaint is dismissed without prejudice. If you can repair the deficiencies, counselor, you can refile. Just make sure you do it right next time."

work product rule The rule that holds that the impressions, strategy, working documents, analysis, and investigations of an attorney preparing for litigation are not subject to discovery by other parties. It applies to the employees of the attorney, and also to the nontestifying consultants or investigators retained by the attorney. The attorney, not the client, controls the work product, so that the client cannot waive its protection under the rule. *Compare to* **attorney-client privilege**.

World Wide Web A loosely connected, international network on the Internet, devoted to sites that use hypertext links to facilitate moving from one Web site to another.

writ An order by a court compelling some act. *Compare to* **injunction**.

writing A document, tape recording, film, or other media containing information.

writ of attachment A court order which authorizes the pre-judgment seizure of assets belonging to a defendant, usually to ensure that those assets will be available to satisfy any judgment against the defendant.

writ of *certiorari* The order of an appellate court requiring a lower court to deliver up and certify the record of a case for review by the appellate court.

writ of execution A court order implementing an earlier judgment of the court. A writ ordering that a particular piece of property is to be sold at public auction to satisfy a judgment.

writ of *habeas corpus* A court order commanding that the custodian bring a person in custody before the court and show cause why that person should not be released.

writ of mandate *Also* **writ of *mandamus*** A court order commanding that a public official do his duty.

wrongful discharge The involuntary termination of an employee without just cause and in violation of the employee's property interest in retaining the employment. (Wrongful discharge does not apply to employment at will.) *See also* **employment at will**.

INDEX

AAfPE. *See* American Association for Paralegal Education
abuse of discretion, 136
Access, 346
accessibility to clients, 11
accessory after the fact, 234
accessory before the fact, 234
accrues, 175
adjudication, 160, 167
administrative law
   adjudication, 160, 167
   Administrative Procedures Act, 154, 157, 161, 164
   agencies, enacting, 152
   application, 151, 152
   authority, legal, 154, 155
   cease and desist orders, 163
   Chevron USA v. Natural Resources Defense Council, Inc., 165
   Citizens to Preserve Overton Park, Inc. v. Volpe, 165
   Code of Federal Regulations, 154, 157
   due process, 160
   enabling statute, 155
   ex parte contact, limitations on, 161
   executive orders, 153
   Federal Register, 154, 155
   Gibson et al. v. Berryhill et al., 162
   Goldberg v. Kelly, 160–161
   independent regulatory agencies, 152, 153
   Interstate Commerce Commission (ICC), 153
   judicial review, 163–165
   limitations, 156
   Matthews v. Eldridge, 161
   ministerial act, 152
   National Labor Relations Board (NLRB), 153
   order, administrative, 157
   paralegal role, 166
   penalties, 163
   policy implementation, 153
   public hearings, 162
   public law, 162
   public participation, 156
   record keeping, mandatory, 157
   regulations, 154
   Securities and Exchange Commission (SEC), 153
   separation of powers, 156
   subpoena of records, 157
   Youngstown Sheet & Tube Co. v. Sawyer, 154
administrative law judge, 161

Administrative Procedures Act, 154, 157, 161, 164
administrator, legal, 41, 446, 447
Administrators, Association of Legal, 56
admission to the bar, 33
admissions, request for, 192, 193
ADR. *See* Alternative dispute resolution
adversary system, 174
advisory arbitration, 223
affidavit of service, 215
affidavits, sworn, 185
affirmative defense, 183
affirmative duty, 83
affirming actions of lower courts, 163
affordable legal services, challenges to finding, 12
Alden v. Maine, 121
allegations, presentation of, 180
alternative dispute resolution
   advantages, 221
   advisory arbitration, 223
   application, 220
   arbitration, 222–223
   binding arbitration, 223
   contractual clauses, 223–224
   court approval, 222
   Federal Arbitration Act of 1925, The, 224
   mediation, 221, 222
   paralegal role, 225
   procedures, 224
   shuttle diplomacy, 222
   Uniform Arbitration Act, 224
American Association for Paralegal Education, 109
American Bar Association
   Model Rules of Professional Conduct, 76–78
   paralegal education, role in, 108–109
   role, 9
   Standing Committee on Legal Assistants, 497–498
   view of paralegal role, 16–17
analysis. *See* Research, legal
annotated code, use of, 299, 300
answer, filing an, 183, 184
appeal, 136–137
appearance, 131
appellant, 136
appellee, 136
application programs, 346
apprentices, development of, 32
Approach, 346
arbitration, 222–223

arbitrator, 223
archiving client files, 466–467
arraignment, 272
arrest
    definition, 263
    evasion, 268
    notice, 268
associate attorney, 33
associations, paralegal, 25
asylum, 116
asylum state, 133
at-will employees, 435–436
attorney-client privilege
    affirmative duty, role, 83
    application, 82
    assertion, 83–84
    attorney work product rule, 84–85
    crime-fraud exception, 83
    exceptions, 83
    inadvertent breach of confidentiality, 84
Attorney Grievance Commission of Maryland v. Goldberg, 73–74
attorney services, 181, 401
attorney work product rule, 84–85
authorities, table of, 352
authorization for release of information, 466
automatic stay, 210

background information, gathering, 400
bail bond, 268, 269
bail hearing, 268
bankruptcy, 9
bar, admission to the, 33
bar associations, establishment of, 32–33
Barron v. Baltimore, 245
basis for appeal, 136
Bates stamp, 77–78
Batson v. Kentucky, 253
bench warrant, issuance of a, 268
benefits, employee, 436
best evidence rule, 179
Betts v. Brady, 255, 256
billable hours, 42, 79, 451
billing, 450–454
binding arbitration, 223
booking a suspect, 268
bound over for trial, 274
Boyd v. United States, 260
Brady v. State of Maryland, 275
breach of contract, 173
briefs, 197, 199, 332–334, 479–480
Brown v. Board of Education of Topeka, Kansas, 124

calendar matters, 461–462
California v. Ciraolo, 261–262
CALR. *See* Computer-assisted legal research
candor before the court, 89–90
candor rule, 90

capital crimes, 231
career
    attraction, 17
    benefits, 18
    growth, 17
    opportunities, 17
case citation, 128
case in chief, 201
case law, 126, 217, 304–305
case management systems, 359
case of first impression, 288
case reporters, using, 300–304
cause of action, 175, 181
cease and desist orders, 163
censure, 72
certification, paralegal, 101, 103, 104
certified copies, 216
Certified Legal Assistant Examination, 104–105, 108
Certified Legal Assistant Specialist, 105
certiorari, writ of, 142
challenge for cause, 200
characteristics, paralegal, 19–20
Chevron USA v. Natural Resources Defense Council, Inc., 165
chief counsel, 445
Chinese Wall, 86
circuits, 140–141
citations, 240, 336, 365, 366
citator service, 373
citators, using case, 314–315
cite checking, 216–217
citizen's arrest, 264
Citizens to Preserve Overton Park, Inc. v. Volpe, 165
Civil Procedure, Code of, 297
Civil Rights Attorney's Fees Awards Act of 1976, 78
CLA. *See* Certified Legal Assistant
clear and convincing evidence, 205
clerks, law, 445
CMS. *See* Case management systems
Code of Federal Regulations, 154, 157
code sections, locating, 298–299
college education, 24
"color of law," 263
commingling of funds, 89
common law
    application, 126–127
    contemporary view, 127
    law, 116, 120
communication, client, 77
compensation, 22–23
competency, verification of
    certification, 101, 103, 104
    licensure of legal technicians, 102–103
    NALA philosophy, 100, 104–105
    NFPA philosophy, 100
    regulation, 101
    titles, protection of legal, 101–102
competent representation, 76

INDEX

complaint, filing, 180, 182
Complete Job-Search Handbook, The, 65
computer-assisted legal research, 363, 364
    development, 361–362
    Internet, importance of the, 362
    LEXIS-NEXIS, 362–363
    Westlaw, 362–363
computer systems manager, 39–40
computers, 347
    billing functions, 343
    case management systems, 359
    court proceedings, application in, 343–344
    database management, 354–355
    digital signatures, 351
    docket control, 343
    document management, 343
    document management systems, 359
    e-mail, 346–350
    encryption software, 347
    evidence, presentation of, 344
    full-text search and retrieval software, 360–361
    integrated automated litigation-support programs, 361
    integrated software packages, 358
    laptops, efficiency of, 345
    legal research, importance in, 343
    literacy requirements, 345–346
    McVeigh v. Cohen, 348
    optical character recognition software, 361
    privacy, 348, 349
    record keeping, 343
    redlining, 352
    relational database management system, 360
    Smyth v. Pillsbury Company, 350–351
    spreadsheets, 355–357
    tickler system, 343
    transcription, real-time, 344, 345
    video simulations, computer-generated, 345
    voice-recognition software, 346, 353–354
    word processing software, 342, 351–352
concurrent jurisdiction, 139
concurrent powers, 125
concurring opinions, 142, 291
confidentiality, 80
conflict check, 85, 459–460
conflicts of interest
    ABA standards, 85
    changing firms, impact of, 86
    Chinese Wall, 86
    conflict check, 85
    definition, 85
    ethical wall, erection of, 86
    imputed conflict of interest, 86
    screening process, 86
    Smart Industries Corp. v. Superior Court, 87–88
consortium, loss of, 176
conspiracy, 233, 234
Constitution, United States, 499–515
constitutional law, 119, 124
consulting firms, legal, 443
contempt, criminal, 235
contempt of court, 72
contempt powers, 211, 212
contingency fee, 449, 450
continuous custody and control, 403
contract partner, 439
cooperative witness, 413
Corel's WordPerfect Suite, 357
corporate legal departments, 41, 42, 443–444
court of general jurisdiction, 128
court of last resort, 120
courts of equity, 127
covert inquiry, 405
crime-fraud exception, 83, 85
criminal law
    accessory after the fact, 234
    accessory before the fact, 234
    act, criminal, 232
    appeals, 277–278
    application, 231
    arraignment, 272
    arrest, 263, 268
    bail, 268
    bench warrant, issuance of a, 268
    booking a suspect, 268
    bound over for trial, having defendant, 274
    Brady v. State of Maryland, 275
    capital crimes, 231
    characteristics, 231
    citation, 240
    citizen's arrest, 264
    coercion or necessity, 239
    "color of law," 263
    common law crimes, 235
    conspiracy, 233, 234
    contempt, criminal, 235
    detainment, 264
    diminished capacity, 239
    discovery, pretrial, 274
    due process (*See* Due process)
    entrapment, 239
    exculpatory evidence, 274
    false arrest, 263
    Florida v. Royer, 264–267
    general intent, 232
    grand jury, 242, 271
    habitual offender laws, 235
    inchoate crime, 233
    indictment, 242, 270
    infractions, 240
    inquiry, law of, 263
    intent, criminal, 232
    irresistible impulse concept, 239
    Kolender v. Lawson, 236, 237
    liability, criminal, 233
    mens rea, 232

M'Naghten Rule, 239
motions, pretrial, 276
no contest plea, entering a, 272
nolo contendere, pleading, 272
offenses, civil, 241
offenses, criminal, 240
Papachristou v. City of Jacksonville, 236
persons, crimes against, 240
petit jury, 241
plea, 272, 273
preliminary hearing, 242, 274
presumption of innocence, 242, 243
probable cause, existence of, 236
probation, 277
proof beyond a reasonable doubt, 241
property, crimes against, 240
reasonable suspicion, 264
recognizance, release on their own, 268
requirements, 232
rights, 243–244
sentencing, 277
severance, motion for, 276
solicitation, 233
specific intent, 232
statutory crimes, 235
suspended sentence, imposing, 277
three-strikes rule, 235
transferred intent, 233
trial, proceeding to, 276
true bill, presentation of, 242
venue, motion for change of, 276
vicarious criminal liability, 234, 235
warrant, arrest, 268, 269
writ of *habeas corpus,* 278
cross-examination, 180, 202–203, 422–423
"Crown's peace," 235
curtilage, 260
custodian of records, 216
cutoff date, discovery, 197

damages, 143, 176
database management, 354–355
databases, using, 366, 367, 397
DBMS. *See* Relational database management system
de novo, 74
deadlines, managing, 214
deceptive witnesses, 424–425
declarations, 185
delegation of responsibilities, 15–16
demand letters, 328, 329
demonstrative evidence, preparation of, 404
demurrer, filing a, 183
denial, general, 183
Department of Air Force Records v. Rose, 159
deponent, 193
deposition notices, drafting, 215

depositions, 192, 193
sample, 472–478
summarizing, 215
videotaping, 194–195
detainment, 264
development, historical, 8
Dickerson v. United States, 247, 248
dictum, 165
digests, using, 305
digital signatures, 351
diligence in representation, 76
diminished capacity, 239
direct examination, 201, 202
directed verdict, motion for, 203
disbarment, 72
discovery, 186–187, 189, 274
discovery doctrine of limitations, 175
Discovery/Magic, 345, 361
discovery requests, drafting, 214
discretionary jurisdiction, 137
discrimination, 91–92
dismiss, motion to, 183, 185
disposition of the case, 312
dissenting opinions, 142, 291
diversity jurisdiction, 139
division of powers, 119
DMS. *See* Document management
docket control, 343, 460, 461
document management, 343, 359
double jeopardy, 250, 251
Dragon Naturally Speaking, Preferred Edition, 354
due diligence, 330
due process, 252
Barron v. Baltimore, 245
Batson v. Kentucky, 253
Betts v. Brady, 255, 256
Boyd v. United States, 260
California v. Ciraolo, 261–262
in camera proceeding, 253
curtilage, 260
definition, 244, 245
development, 245
Dickerson v. United States, 247, 248
double jeopardy, 250, 251
Estes v. Texas, 252
exclusionary rule, 259, 260
Faretta v. California, 258
Gideon v. Wainwright, 255–257
hot pursuit, searches made in, 262
Illinois v. Perkins, 248–249, 248–250
immunity, granting of, 254
impartial jury, 253
indigence, determination of, 257
legal counsel, right to, 255, 257
Mapp v. Ohio, 260
Miranda v. Arizona, 246, 247

Miranda warning, 246–248, 259
Oliver v. United States, 260
Powell v. Alabama, 255
procedural rights, incorporation of, 245
public trial, right to, 252
sealing of records, 252, 253
self-incrimination, 246–247, 253, 254
self-representation, right to, 258
speedy trial, right to, 252
transactional immunity, 254
United States v. Dickerson, 247
use immunity, 254
witnesses, right to challenge, 254, 255
duties, typical, 7

e-mail, 346–350
employment agencies, role of, 54
en banc, 210
enabling statute, 155
encryption software, 347
English common law, 127
entrapment, 239
equity partners, 439
Erie Railroad Co. v. Tompkins, 127
errors and omissions policy, 437
estate planning, 9
Estes v. Texas, 252
ethical wall, erection of, 86
ethics
　American Bar Association, role of, 72
　attorney's conduct, concern for, 95
　censure, 72
　clients ethics, concerns about, 95
　Code of Ethics and Professional Responsibility, The, 75
　contempt of court, 72
　criminal violations, 72
　disbarment, 72
　disclosure of status, 93–94
　discrimination, 91–92
　fiduciary duty, 71
　guilty clients, representation of, 94
　jury tampering, 75
　master, role of, 74
　Model Code of Ethics and Professional Responsibility, 75
　officers of the court, 71
　paralegal conduct, 73
　professional responsibility, standards of, 71
　reprimands, public, 72
　sanctions, imposing, 72
　sexual harassment, 91–92
　state regulation, 72
　suborning of perjury, 72
　suspension from practice, 72
evidence
　admission, 177, 178
　best evidence rule, 179
　confidentiality, privilege, 178–179
　exclusion, 178
　hearsay, 180
　material fact, 177
　offers of compromise, inadmissibility of, 179
　prejudicial effect, 178
　presentation, computers, 344
　probative value, 178
　relevance, test of, 177
　rules of evidence, 177
ex parte contact, limitations on, 161
Excel, 346
exclusionary rule, 259, 260
exculpatory evidence, 82, 274
execution, writ of, 210
executive committee, 441
executive orders, 120, 153
exemplar, 216
exempt employee, 23
exhaustion of remedies, 164
exhibits, 216, 220
experience, overcoming lack of, 61–63
expert witnesses, 405
extradition, 116, 133

401(k) plan, 23
fabricators, 423–424
Fair Labor Standards Act, 23
false arrest, 263
family law, 9
Faretta v. California, 258
Federal Arbitration Act of 1925, The, 224
federal court system
　admission, 33
　concurrent jurisdiction, 139
　diversity jurisdiction, 139
　diversity of citizenship, 139
　federal question jurisdiction, 138
　geographic jurisdiction, 140
　jurisdiction, 138
　pendent jurisdiction, 139
　personal jurisdiction, 140
　structure, 138
Federal Privacy Act, 159
federal question, 137
federal question jurisdiction, 138
Federal Register, 154, 155, 158
FEDLAW, 386
fees, legal, 14–15, 449
felony trials, 135
fiduciary duty, 20, 71
field investigations, 397
Figler, Howard, 65
file systems, 463–466
firm categorization, 33
firm size, 7–8, 35–36

first position, finding your, 25
flight risk, 270
Florida Prepaid Postsecondary Education Expense Board v. College Savings Bank, 121
Florida v. Royer, 264–267
forensic medicine, 398
form book, 332
form file, 332
forum, 134
fraudulent transfers, 211
Freedom of Information Act, 158, 159, 402
freelance paralegals, 43–45
frivolous appeal, 136
frivolous claims, avoiding, 89
Full Faith and Credit Clause, 128, 129
full-text search and retrieval software, 360–361
funds, safeguarding client, 89
futility doctrine, 164

garnishment of wages, 211–212
general appearance, 131
general counsel, 443
general damages, 176
general intent, 232
general jurisdiction, 131
general police powers, 125
general verdict, 208
geographic jurisdiction, 140
Gibson et al. v. Berryhill et al., 162
Gideon v. Wainwright, 255–257
glass ceilings, avoiding, 36–37
Goldberg v. Kelly, 160–161
good cause, setting aside for, 183
grand jury, 242
grand jury subpoena, 271
GrandView, 345
Gravity Verdict, 361
"gray areas," 6
Grimshaw v. Ford Motor Company, 187–188
growth, career field, 17
guardian *ad litem,* 143

habeas corpus, writ of, 278
habitual offender laws, 235
HALT, Inc., 12
harmless error, 209
headnotes, 310
hearing on appeal, 315
hearsay rule, 180
hidden job market, 52, 53
hierarchy, 119, 123
holding, 310
hostile witness, 420–421
How to Land Your First Paralegal Job, 65
hung jury, 251

Illinois v. Perkins, 248–250
immigration, 9

immunity, 254
impartial jury, 253
impeachment, 194, 203
imputed conflict of interest, 86
in-house general counsel, 330
in limine, motions, 198, 199
in personam jurisdiction, 131
In rem jurisdiction, 131
inactive client files, 466–467
inchoate crime, 233
independent contractor. *See* Freelance paralegals
indictment, 242, 270
indigence, determination of, 257
information, 242
infractions, 240
inherent powers, 125
injunction, 176
inquiry, law of, 263
insolvency, 210
intake interview, 427–428
integrated automated litigation-support programs, 361
integrated software packages, 358
intent, criminal, 232
International Shoe Company v. State of Washington, 132
Internet
    browsers, using web, 383
    directory services, using, 385
    discussion groups, 389
    ethical materials, sources for, 390
    federal court opinions, 387
    FEDLAW, 386
    home page, 383
    hypertext, importance of, 381
    LEXIS-NEXIS (*See* LEXIS-NEXIS)
    PACER System, 387–388
    search engines, using, 384–385
    service providers, 380, 381
    speed factors, 383–384
    statistical information, sources for, 388
    Supreme Court opinions, 387
    uniform resource locator, 383
    Web site, 383
    Westlaw (*See* Westlaw)
    World Wide Web, 381
internship program, 61–62
interrogatories, 189–190
interstate commerce, 130
Interstate Commerce Commission (ICC), 153
interviews. *See also* Investigation
    checklist, using a, 417–418
    client interviews, 426–427
    communication issues, 415
    control, establishing, 416–417
    cooperative witness, 413
    covert inquiry, 405
    cross-examination of interviewee, 422–423
    deceptive witnesses, 424–425
    expert witnesses, 405

fabricators, characteristics of, 423–424
guidelines, 414
hostile witness, 420–421
inconsistencies, 422
intake interview, 427–428
jargon, avoiding use of, 416
leading questions, 420
nonwitnesses, 404–405
percipient witnesses, 405
psychology of the witness, understanding, 413
questions, choosing effective, 418–419
rapport, establishing, 415–416
recording, benefits of, 425–426
scheduling, 415
setting, selecting a, 415
telephone interviews, 415
verification of information, 421–422
written statements, 426
intraoffice memorandum, 334
investigation. *See also* Interviews
  attorney services, using, 401
  background information, gathering, 400
  business entities, 411–412
  continuous custody and control, 403
  court records, reviewing, 400–401
  database searches, 397
  demonstrative evidence, preparation of, 404
  evidence, gathering, 402–404
  field investigations, 397
  forensic medicine, 398
  Freedom of Information Act, 402
  individuals, locating, 409–410
  jurors, potential, 408–409
  objectives, 398
  physical evidence, 402–404
  plan, creating an effective, 399
  private investigator, role of, 398
  property profile, 397
  public records, 402, 410–411
  real evidence, 402–404
  role, paralegals, 396
  search companies, 401
  site investigation, 402
  stages, 400
  telephone inquiries, 397
  tentative investigation report, preparing, 406
  verification of on-line information, 412–413
  work product rule, 406–408
IRAC method, 288
irresistible impulse concept, 239
ISP. *See* Internet

jailhouse lawyer, 97–98
jargon, avoiding use of, 416
job, finding the right
  associations, joining paralegal, 53
  CareerPath.com job postings, 56
  directories, application of attorney, 57
  employment agencies, role of, 54
  evaluation, self, 58–60
  experience, overcoming lack of, 60–61
  hidden job market, 52, 53
  Internet searches, 55–56
  legal press, application of, 53–54
  Martindale-Hubbell Law Directory, 57
  Monster.com job postings, 56
  National Law Journal, 53
  networking, importance of, 53
  open job market, 52
  placement offices, effectiveness of, 54
  postings, Internet, 56
  turnover rates, 52, 53
  West's Legal Directory, 57
Johnson, President Lyndon, 8
Johnson v. Avery, 97–98
judge, administrative law, 161
judgment, declaratory, 177
judgment, default, 183
judgment debtor, 210, 211
judgment lien, 211
judgment notwithstanding verdict, 208
judgment on the pleadings, 185
judgment proof, 210
judicial immunity, 142, 144
judicial independence, 145
judicial notice, 199
judicial review, 122, 123, 163–165
judicial seal, 466
judicial self-restraint, 123
jurisdiction
  appearance, 131
  change of venue, 134
  classification, 131
  concurrent jurisdiction, 139
  discretionary jurisdiction, 137
  diversity jurisdiction, 139
  extradition, 132–133
  federal court system (*See* Federal court system)
  federal question jurisdiction, 138
  forum, 134
  general appearance, 131
  general jurisdiction, 131
  geographic jurisdiction, 140
  long arm jurisdiction, 132
  pendent jurisdiction, 139
  personal jurisdiction, 131, 140
  in personam jurisdiction, 131
  In rem jurisdiction, 131
  special appearance, 132
  state court system (*See* State court systems)
  state law, 128, 129
  subject matter jurisdiction, 131
  Supreme Court, 141
  venue, 134
jurisdiction shopping, 129
jury, 200, 219, 408–409

jury instructions, 206
jury tampering, 74, 75
just cause, 435
justice courts, 135

Kentucky v. Dennison, 133
key number system, West's, 305, 307
KeyCite, 373–375
Kolender v. Lawson, 236, 237

laches, doctrine of, 176
LAMA, 24, 56
LANs. *See* Local area networks
large size firms, 34, 439–440
law school, prelude to, 18–19
laying foundation, 202
leading questions, 420
Legal Aid Society, 62
Legal Assistant Management Association. *See* LAMA
legal assistant manager, 34
Legal Assistant Today, 65
legal assistants. *See* Paralegal
legal counsel, right to, 255, 257
legal nurse consultant, 49
legal press, 53–54
legal technician, 12
legalese, 327
legislative authority, 124
legislative intent, 117, 118
LEXIS-NEXIS. *See also* Westlaw
    freelance paralegals, 44
    Internet access, 386
    Shepard's Citation Service, 376–379
liability insurance, professional, 437–438
librarian, law, 40–41, 446
licensure, 9, 102–103
limited liability company, 442–443
limited liability partnership, 442–443
litigation. *See also* Pretrial procedures *and* trial procedures
    accrues, 175
    adversary system, 174
    affidavit of service, 215
    answer, filing an, 183, 184
    assertion of rights, 173
    breach of contract, 173
    case law, locating, 217
    cause of action, 175
    cite checking, 216–217
    classification of suits, 173
    complaint, filing, 180, 182
    consortium, loss of, 176
    cooperation with opposing counsel, 213, 214
    damages, civil, 176
    deadlines, managing, 214
    definition, 172
    deposition notices, drafting, 215
    depositions, summarizing, 215
    discovery doctrine of limitations, 175
    discovery requests, drafting, 214
    exhibits, 216, 220
    general damages, 176
    injunction, 176
    judgment, declaratory, 177
    jury selection, 219
    laches, doctrine of, 176
    mandamus, writ of, 177
    objections, drafting, 215
    on-call letter, 219
    paralegal responsibilities, 211–212
    parties, 174
    process, 172
    proof of service, 215
    reasons for suit, 173
    records, obtaining, 216
    remedies, equitable, 176
    responses to discovery, drafting, 214
    second chair, 219
    service of process, 181
    special damages, 176
    standing, 174, 175
    statute of limitations, 175
    temporary restraining order, 176, 177
    termination of legal relationships, 173
    tickler system, 214
    torts, 173
    trial, assisting at, 219
    trial notebook, preparation of, 217, 218
    voir dire, 219
    witnesses, coordination of, 218
    wrongful acts, 173
LLC. *See* Limited liability company
LLP. *See* Limited liability partnership
local area networks, 40
lodged, 194
long arm jurisdiction, 132
Lotus 1-2-3, 346

malpractice, 21
management, office
    administrator, legal, 446–447
    archiving client files, 466–467
    at-will employees, 435–436
    authorization for release of information, 466
    benefits, employee, 436
    billing (*See* Billing)
    calendar matters, 461–462
    clerks, law, 445
    clients departure from firm, 458–459
    communications procedures, 467–468
    conflict check, 459–460
    docket control, 460–461
    employees, importance of qualified, 434–435
    errors and omissions policy, 437
    factors, key, 434
    fees, legal (*See* Fees, legal)

file systems, 463–466
inactive client files, 466–467
legal assistant manager, 447
liability insurance, professional, 437–438
librarian, law, 446
office manager, 446
organizational structures, 438–442
overtime pay, issue of, 437
policies, firm, 436, 459
probationary employees, 436
procedures, effective, 459
schedules, working, 437
secretaries, legal, 445
success, approaches to, 434–433
support staff, 448–449
team, legal, 445–448
telephone communication, 468
tickler system, 460–461
timekeeping (*See* Timekeeping)
voice mail communication, 468
management, paralegal, 38–39
managing partner, 33
mandamus, writ of, 177
mandatory appeal, 141
mandatory authority, 286, 287
Mapp v. Ohio, 260
Marbury v. Madison, 122, 123
marketing director, 39–40
marketing plan, developing an effective, 63
Martindale-Hubbell Law Directory, 57
master, 74
material fact, 177
Matthews v. Eldridge, 161
McVeigh v. Cohen, 348
mediation, 221, 222
mediator, 221
medium size firms, 34, 439–440
memoranda of points and authorities, 334–335
memorandum of law, 333–334, 481–484
mens rea, 232
Microsoft Office, 357
Milliken v. Meyer, 128, 129, 132
minimum contacts, 132
ministerial act, 152
Miranda v. Arizona, 246–247
Miranda warning, 246–248, 259
misdemeanor trials, 135
Missouri v. Jenkins, 78–79
mistrial, declaration of, 208
M'Naghten Rule, 239
motions, pretrial, 276
motions *in limine*, 198, 199

NALA
    Certified Legal Assistant Examination, 104–105
    Certified Legal Assistant Specialist, 105
    Code of Ethics and Professional Responsibility, The, 75
    competency, verification of, 100, 104–105

definition of legal assistants, 7
    Ethics and Professional Responsibility, Code of, 485–486
    future, view of professional, 105–106
    job postings, Internet, 56
    licensure, philosophy on, 107
National Association of Legal Assistants. *See* NALA
National Federation of Paralegal Associations. *See* NFPA
National Labor Relations Board (NLRB), 153
National Law Journal, 53
negligence, 297
networking, importance of, 53, 62
NFPA
    college education view, 24
    competency, verification of, 100
    definition of legal assistants, 7
    Education Task Force, development of, 109
    Ethics and Professional Responsibility, Model Code of, 487–494
    freelance paralegals, 44
    future, view of professional, 105–106
    Internet career center, 56
    licensure, philosophy on, 107
    Model Code of Ethics and Professional Responsibility, 75
    Paralegal Advanced Competency Exam, 105
    Suggested Curriculum for Paralegal Studies, adoption of, 109
no contest plea, entering a, 272
nolo contendere, pleading, 272
nonparalegal positions
    administrator, legal, 41
    applications, 46
    attributes, desirable, 47–48
    computer systems manager, 39–40
    development, 46
    librarian, law firm, 40–41
    marketing director, 39–40
    occupations, potential, 47
nonsuit, motion for, 203
notice, giving formal, 181
nuisance, 286

objections, 195, 196, 215
obstruction of justice, 72
OCR. *See* Optical character recognition software
of counsel, 33
offenses, civil, 241
offenses, criminal, 240
office management. *See* Management, office
office manager, 446
officers of the court, 71
official reporter, 300
Oliver v. United States, 260
Olmstead v. United States, 291–294
on all fours, 290
on-call letter, 219
on its own motion, 200

on point cases, 290
on-the-job training, 25
open job market, 52
opinion letter, 330
opinions, understanding legal, 307, 310, 311
optical character recognition software, 361
ordinances, 122
origin of paralegals, 8
overruled, 161
overtime pay, 22–23, 437

PACE. *See* Paralegal Advanced Competency Exam
PACER System. *See* Public Access to Court Electronic Records
Papachristou v. City of Jacksonville, 236
paper chase, 311–312
Paradox, 346
Paralegal Advanced Competency Exam, 105, 108
paralegal coordinator, 34
paralegal programs, 23–24
parallel citation, 320
paraprofessional, 9
parties, 174
partisan politics, role of, 145
partner, 31
partnership, 31, 439–440
PC. *See* Professional corporation
penal code, 297
pendent jurisdiction, 139
percipient witnesses, 405
peremptory challenges, 201
personal jurisdiction, 131, 140
personal service, 131
persuasion, guidelines for effective, 335
persuasive authority, 287
petit jury, 241
petitioners, 129, 136
Pfaffenberger, Bryan, 348
placement offices, effectiveness of, 54
plaintiff, 118
plea, entering a, 272
plea bargaining, 273
pleadings, 285, 331–332
Plessy v. Ferguson, 123
pocket parts, 298
police powers of state government, 125
politics in court decision, role of, 145
Powell v. Alabama, 255
precedent, 120, 123, 124
preempt, 125
prejudice, with, 183
prejudice, without, 18
preliminary hearing, 242, 274
presiding judge, 141
pretrial conference, 197
pretrial procedures
    admissions, request for, 192, 193
    affidavits, sworn, 185

affirmative defense, 183
allegations, presentation of, 180
answer, filing an, 183, 184
attorney service, 181
briefs, 197, 199
cause of action, establishing, 181
complaint, filing of, 180, 182
conference, pretrial, 197
cutoff date, discovery, 197
declarations, 185
defendant options, 181, 183
demurrer, filing a, 183
denial, general, 183
depositions, 192, 193
discovery, 186–187, 189
dismiss, motion to, 183, 185
good cause, setting aside for, 183
Grimshaw v. Ford Motor Company, 187–188
interrogatories, 189–190
judgment, default, 183
judgment on the pleadings, 185
judicial notice, 199
motions *in limine,* 198, 199
notice, giving formal, 181
objections to discovery, 195, 196
production of documents, request for, 192, 194
protective orders, 196
response to interrogatories, 191
service of process, 181
settlement, 197–198
status conference, 197
stipulation, pretrial, 199
stipulation of facts, 186
strike, motion to, 199
subpoena *duces tecum,* 192
summons, delivering a, 181
third parties, subpoenaing evidence from, 195
prima facie case, establishing, 201, 203
primary sources, 286
privacy, 159, 347–349
private investigator, role of, 398
privilege confidentiality, 178–179
pro bono legal service, volunteering for, 62
probable cause, existence of, 236
probate, 9
probation, 277
probationary employees, 436
probative value, 178
process, 172
product liability litigation, 41
production of documents, request for, 192, 194
professional corporation, 32, 441–442
proof of service, 215
property, crimes against, 240
property profile, 397
proprietary trade secret, 196
proprietor, sole, 438–439
protective orders, 196

Public Access to Court Electronic Records, 387–388
public agencies, 42–43, 444–445
public defender, 268
public records, 157–159, 410–411
public trial, right to, 252
Puerto Rico v. Branstad, 133, 134
punitive damages, 188

qualifications, 23–25
questions of fact, 136
quid pro quo, 92
quiet title, 131
quotas, billable, 22–23, 79, 451, 453–454

rainmakers, 451
Rashomon defense, 204
real estate, 9
real evidence, 402–404
reasonable fees, 77
reasonable suspicion, 264
reasons for suit, 173
rebuttal evidence, presentation of, 204
recognizance, release on their own, 268
record, 355
record keeping, 343
redlining, 352
rehearing, 315
relational database management system, 360
relationships, establishing successful firm, 34–35
relevance, test of, 177
remands a case, 208
remedies, equitable, 176
reporters, 300
research, legal
    on all fours, 290
    analogy, reliance on, 290–291
    analysis, 288
    annotated code, use of, 299, 300
    case reporters, using, 300–304
    cases, locating specific, 304–305
    CD-ROM, use of, 380
    citators, using case, 314–315
    citing appropriate sources, 288
    code sections, locating, 298–299
    computer-assisted (*See* Computer-assisted legal research)
    computers, importance of, 296
    concurring opinions, 291
    defining the issues, 286
    digests, using, 305
    dissenting opinions, 291
    focused, remaining, 294
    identification of key terms, 296
    Internet, use of (*See* Internet)
    IRAC method, 288
    key number system, West's, 305, 307
    mandatory authority, 286, 287
    Olmstead v. United States, 291–294

    opinions, understanding legal, 307, 310, 311
    paper chase, 311–312
    parallel citation, 320
    persuasive authority, 287
    pocket parts, 298
    on all fours, 290
    on point cases, 290
    primary sources, 286
    purposes, 285
    secondary sources, 287
    sections, 298
    Shepardizing, 295, 315, 323
    Shepard's Citations, using, 315, 317–322
    starting point, locating, 296
    statutes, application of, 289, 290
    statutory codes, using, 297–298
    stopping, guidelines for, 294
    summary, case, 307
    syllabus, 307
    treatises, using, 314
    understanding the assignment, 285
    verification of authorities, 295
respondent, 136
responses, 191, 214
responsibilities, typical, 7
resumes, mass mailing of, 63
retainer, 77, 449, 450
reversed decision, 143
rights, assertion of, 173
ripeness, 164
Roe v. Wade, 123

sanctions, imposing, 72
satisfaction, career, 10
scope of employment, 73
Scottsboro Boys, 116, 132, 133
screening process, 86
sealing of records, 252, 253, 289
second chair, 219
secondary sources, 287
secretaries, legal, 6, 7, 34–35, 445
Securities and Exchange Commission (SEC), 153
Self-help legal guides, role of, 12–13
self-incrimination, 246–247, 253, 254
self-representation, right to, 258
sentencing, 277
separation of powers, 156
service of process, 131, 181
settlement agreement, 198
settlement conference, 197–198
severance, motion for, 276
sexual harassment, 91–92
Shepardizing, 295, 315, 323
Shepard's Citation Service, 376–379
Shepard's Citations, using, 315, 317–322
shuttle diplomacy, 222
site investigation, 402
small claims court, 10, 135

small firm, qualities of a, 34
Smart Industries Corp. v. Superior Court, 87–88
SmartSuite, 357
Smyth v. Pillsbury Company, 350–351
sole practitioner, 31, 438–439
solicitation, 233
solicitation, client, 91
special appearance, 132
special damages, 176
special verdict, 207
specialties, 37–38
specific intent, 232
speedy trial, right to, 252
spreadsheets, 355–357
St. John v. Wisconsin Employment Relations Board, 129
standard of proof, 205, 206
standing, 164, 174, 175
Standing Committee on Legal Assistants, The, 17, 497–498
stare decisis, doctrine of, 312
state court systems, 134–135
state law
    application, 125–126
    case law, 126
    common law, application of, 126–127
    court of general jurisdiction, 128
    courts of equity, 127
    enforcement, 128
    English common law, 127
    Full Faith and Credit Clause, 128, 129
    interstate commerce, 130
    jurisdiction, 128, 129
    Milliken v. Meyer, 128, 129
    public policy, 128
    residency requirements, role of, 129
    St. John v. Wisconsin Employment Relations Board, 129
    Uniform Acts, 126
statistical information, sources for, 388
status conference, 197
statute of limitations, 175
statutes, 117, 289, 290
statutory codes, using, 297–298
statutory crimes, 235
stipulation, pretrial, 199
stipulation of facts, 186
strike, motion to, 199
Stump v. Sparkman, 142–145
subject matter jurisdiction, 131
suborning of perjury, 72
subpoena, 80, 157
subpoena *duces tecum,* 192
substantive law, 6
substituted service of process, 132
Suggested Curriculum for Paralegal Studies, adoption of, 109
Summation Blaze, 345, 361
summer associate, 18
summons, delivering a, 181

support staff, 448–449
Supremacy Clause, 120
Supreme Court, 141–142
Supreme Law of the Land, 120
suspended sentence, imposing, 277
sustains, 183
sworn affidavit, 242
syllabus, 307
systems manager, 40

teaching opportunities in paralegal education, 39
technician, legal, 12
telephone inquiries, 397
temporary restraining order, 176, 177
tentative investigation report, preparing, 406
term of art, 327
termination of legal relationships, 173
three-strike rule, 235
tickler system, 214, 343, 460, 461
timekeeping, 450–451, 454
Tobacco Papers, The, 81–82
torts, 173
training, 6
transactional immunity, 254
transcription, real-time, 344, 345
transferable skills, 59–60
transferred intent, 233
treatises, using, 314
trial notebook, preparation of, 217, 218
trial procedures
    case in chief, 201
    challenge for cause, 200
    closing statements, 204–205
    cross-examination, 202–203
    defendant's case, presentation of, 203–204
    direct examination, 201, 202
    directed verdict, motion for, 203
    impeachment, 203
    jury selection, 200
    laying foundation, 202
    nonsuit, motion for, 203
    opening statements, 201
    peremptory challenges, 201
    prima facie case, establishing, 201, 203
    Rashomon defense, 204
    rebuttal evidence, presentation of, 204
    resting its case, 203
    voir dire, 200
    witness preparation, 201–202
trier of fact, 136
true bill, presentation of, 242
trust accounts, 89, 456–457
turnover rates, 52, 53

UCC. *See Uniform Commercial Code*
unauthorized practice of law
    casual advice, dangers of, 98–99
    definition, 13

exceptions, 97
jailhouse lawyer, 97–98
Johnson v. Avery, 97–98
teaching the law, 100
Unauthorized Practice of Law Committee v. Parsons Technology, Inc., 14
Uniform Acts, 126
Uniform Arbitration Act, 224
Uniform Child Custody Jurisdiction Act, 126
Uniform Commercial Code, 130
United States v. Dickerson, 247
unlawful detainer, 12
unlawful flight, 133
unofficial reporter, 300
UPL. *See* Unauthorized practice of law
URL. *See* Internet
use immunity, 254

venue, 134, 276
verdicts and judgments
   appellate court, decision to send case to, 208–210
   automatic stay, 210
   clear and convincing evidence, 205
   contempt powers, 211, 212
   en banc, 210
   enforcement, 210–211
   fraudulent transfers, 211
   garnishment of wages, 211, 212
   general verdict, 208
   insolvency, 210
   judgment debtor, 210
   judgment debtor examination, 211
   judgment lien, 211
   judgment notwithstanding verdict, 208
   judgment proof, 210
   jury instructions, 206
   mistrial, declaration of, 208
   preponderance of evidence, 205
   special verdict, 207
   standard of proof, 205, 206
   writ of execution, 210
ViaVoice Pro Millennium, 354
vicarious criminal liability, 234, 235
video simulations, computer-generated, 345
voice mail communication, 468
voice-recognition software, 346, 353–354
voir dire, 200, 219

Wagner, Andrea, 65
"War on Poverty," 8
warrant, arrest, 268, 269

Westlaw
   authorities, 363, 375–376
   citation to find case law, using, 365, 366
   citator service, 373
   connectors, using, 369–370
   cost-effectiveness, 363–364
   databases, using, 366, 367
   Internet access, 386
   key number system, using, 371
   KeyCite, 373–375
   limiters, using, 369
   locating information, 364
   natural-language searching, 371–372
   on-line research, 362–363
   primary authority, locating, 364–365
   query, 368, 369
   terms, using key, 368, 369
West's Legal Directory, 57
whistle-blower, 96
witnesses, coordination of, 218
WordPerfect Law Office 2000, 357
WordPerfect Suite, Corel, 357
work product rule, 406–408
World Wide Web, 381
writ of *certiorari,* issuance of, 142
writ of execution, 210
writ of *habeas corpus,* 278
writ of *mandamos,* 177
writing, legal, 324
   active language, using, 326
   advantages, 324
   briefs, 332–333, 334
   citation, proper, 336
   concise, language, 327
   correspondence, effective, 328
   demand letters, 328, 329
   editing and revision, 328
   form file, 332
   ineffective writing, 324
   legalese, 327
   memoranda of points and authorities, 334–335
   memorandum of law, drafting, 333–334
   opinion letter, 330
   persuasion, guidelines for effective, 335
   pleadings, drafting, 331–332
   sentence length, management of, 326
   term of art, 327
wrongful acts, 173

Youngstown Sheet & Tube Co. v. Sawyer, 154

System Requirements

Windows:
- Intel® Pentium® processor
- Microsoft® Windows® 95 OSR 2.0, Windows 98 SE, Windows Millennium, Windows NT® 4.0 with Service Pack 5, or Windows 2000
- 64 MB of RAM
- 24 MB of available hard-disk space

Macintosh:
- PowerPC® processor
- Mac OS software version 8.6(*), 9.0.4, or 9.1
- 64 MB of RAM
- 24 MB of available hard-disk space